Planning for Post-Disaster Recovery:

A Review of the United States Disaster Assistance Framework

Gavin Smith

Public Entity Risk Institute

Public Entity Risk Institute is a tax exempt nonprofit whose mission is to serve public, private, and nonprofit organizations as a resource to enhance the practice of enterprise risk management. For more information on PERI, visit the organization's website: www.riskinstitute.org

Public Entity Risk Institute
11350 Random Hills Road, Suite 210
Fairfax, VA 22030
(p) 703.351.1846
(f) 703.352.6339
www.riskinstitute.org

ISBN 978-0-9793722-5-4

Volume 1, 2011

Printed in the United States of America

There is a compelling need for an academically rigorous yet practically grounded analysis of recovery. There are few books that provide such analyses. Gavin's book does this by integrating the latest findings from recovery studies and his own first-hand experience in practice. Whilst the book has a USA focus, it sheds light on the key underlying dimensions of recovery. Among other things, it underscores the complex nature of recovery, the imperative for pre-event planning, and the need to develop collaborative partnerships to navigate through this turbulent and often conflict-ridden process. As a result, this book will be of great interest to scholars and practitioners in diverse fields working on the many issues associated with post-disaster recovery efforts in the USA and around the world.

Bruce Glavovic PhD, MNZPI, Professor, EQC Chair in Natural Hazards Planning, Associate Director: Massey-GNS Science Joint Centre for Disaster Research, Resource & Environmental Planning Programme, Massey University

Though critical in every respect, disaster recovery is an under examined aspect of emergency management. Thus *Planning for Post-Disaster Recovery: A Review of the United States Disaster Assistance Framework*, whose author bridges both the academic and practice communities, is a highly welcomed addition to the literature on this often neglected topic. This excellent book achieves its stated purpose of advancing our understanding of disaster recovery and providing the basis for furthering pre-disaster and post-disaster recovery planning and actions. This is done through a comprehensive analysis of prior recovery research, actual recovery experiences following such events as Hurricane Katrina, and the dimensions of the U.S. disaster recovery assistance network, including its various governmental and nongovernmental entities, policies, and practices. The book adds greatly to our scholarly knowledge on disaster recovery. But it does so much more by providing insightful guidance for transforming the U.S. disaster recovery assistance network into a more effective system, one that is more attuned to local needs, is more integrated and coordinated, and is supported by sound legislation. Reflecting the author's varied career background, the book has much to offer both academics and practitioners concerned with disaster recovery issues. It is must reading for those interested in understanding recent disaster recovery experiences in the U.S. and ways to improve future recovery efforts in a society increasingly at risk to large-scale disasters. Insightful sidebar case studies and photos contribute significantly to the readability of this fine book.

William A. Anderson, PhD, National Research Council, National Academy of Sciences

Gavin Smith has written the definitive text and reference book on planning for post-disaster recovery. Smith has a rare ability to lucidly translate contemporary planning theory and research to a critically important topic that will increasingly command the attention of urban land use planning practice in the 21st century.

Phillip R. Berke, PhD, Professor of Land Use and Environmental Planning, Department of City and Regional Planning, University of North Carolina – Chapel Hill

Alas this book has evolved from the brilliant clashing of four minds in one: Gavin the scholar, Gavin the practitioner, Gavin the researcher, and Gavin the stakeholder. This is a timely piece that transcends specific disasters by repositioning the floodlight on the complexities of disaster recovery, institutions, aid networks and related planning principles, coordination frameworks, and negotiation processes. This book was certainly worth the wait for pre-disaster planning and post-disaster recovery professionals and researchers. Congratulations!

Ann-Margaret Esnard, PhD Professor, School of Urban and Regional Planning, Florida Atlantic University

Dedication

To mom, for always being there to listen and teaching me the importance of kindness and compassion for others.

To dad, for sharing with me the wonders of the natural world as reflected in the times we spent together on the water, in the woods, and in the garden.

To Libby for her love, patience, and enduring support. This book would not have been possible without you.

To the people of Mississippi, who exhibited grace and generosity beyond all measure to those that sought to help them following Hurricane Katrina.

To the people of Shoreacres, Texas, as they recover from Hurricane Ike.

Contents

Dedication. vii

Preface xxi

Acknowledgements xxv

Introduction. 1

Chapter 1: The Disaster Recovery Assistance Framework 11

Chapter 2: The Public Sector: Federal, State, and Local Governments 35

Chapter 3: Quasi-governmental and Nongovernmental Organizations . . 77

Chapter 4: Nonprofit Relief Organizations 127

Chapter 5: The Private Sector and For-Profit Organizations 157

Chapter 6: The International Community 195

Chapter 7: Individuals and Emergent Groups 239

Chapter 8: Planning for Disaster Recovery. 265

Chapter 9: Addressing the Challenges of the Disaster Recovery
Assistance Framework: Creating the Disaster Recovery Act 321

Chapter 10: The National Disaster Recovery Framework:
A New Vision for Recovery? 377

Postscript 405

Index 407

About the Author 427

Figures

Figure 1. Mississippi governor Haley Barbour (right) talks with Gavin
Smith, executive director of the Governor's Office of Recovery and Renewal
(left), and Mike Womack, director of Mississippi Emergency Management
Agency (center), following the Governor's Recovery Expo. 2

Figure 2. The Governor's Expo was intended to provide information to
residents and local officials on the Mississippi Gulf Coast about recovery
programs and policies, reconstruction techniques, and providers of
these services. This information was conveyed through training sessions,
demonstrations, informational booths, and the placement of over 20
modular housing units on the Expo grounds. The two day event drew
over 50,000 coastal residents. 4

Figure 1–1. Hurricane Katrina Memorial in Biloxi, Mississippi. The creation
of post-disaster memorials represents what Haas, Kates, and Bowden refer
to as part of the second phase of reconstruction. Below, the white cap on
top of the black wall represents the height of the hurricane-induced storm
surge, while the tile mosaic and walkway serve as a symbolic reminder of
the forces that caused such destruction. The memorial also includes various
personal items enclosed in a glass cabinet that were found in the
community after the storm 21

Figure 2–1. Emergency Support Function-14 (ESF-14) staff works in the
Joint Field Office following the spring 2010 floods in Nashville, Tennessee . . .42

Figure 2–2. Banner displaying the logos of the Rebuild Iowa Office and
ESF-14 following the 2008 floods. Iowa, like many states following a
major disaster, created a state-level organization to address the c
omplexities of disaster recovery 56

Figure 2–3. The reconstruction of a new city hall in Long Beach, Mississippi,
after Hurricane Katrina was funded by the post-Katrina Community
Development Block Grant program. The sign in the foreground notes the
Mississippi Development Authority, the state agency responsible for the
administration of the federal funds, as well as the private sector firm
tasked with construction 59

Figure 2–4. Pictured is a debris management staging area in the
New Orleans neighborhood of Lakeview. 62

Figure 2–5. As housing damages in coastal Mississippi after Hurricane Katrina make apparent, elevating structures is not a foolproof method for eliminating exposure to the damaging effects of flooding. Other possible land use planning solutions include the rezoning of high-hazard areas; the limiting of public reinvestments like roads, water, and sewer in these areas; the clustering of housing developments away from places prone to natural hazards; and the relocation of at-risk housing and infrastructure. Attempts to alter pre-event development policy, however, can be fraught with conflict as development interests and those living in these areas often seek to return to what existed prior to the disaster. 63

Figure 2–6. This home in Belhaven, North Carolina, was elevated using Hazard Mitigation Grant Program funds. The town, funded after Hurricane Fran in 1996, had successfully elevated thirty-two homes prior to Hurricane Floyd, which struck the same area in 1999. The savings, defined as losses avoided from the potential flood damages associated with Hurricane Floyd, measured over $1.3 million (see State of North Carolina, Hazard Mitigation in North Carolina: Measuring Success, 2000, 25) 64

Figure 3–1. Hazard Reduction and Recovery Center students conduct survey of damages following Hurricane Ike 99

Figure 4–1. Kaboom!, a nonprofit focused on the repair and reconstruction of damaged playgrounds following disasters, relies heavily on local volunteers to assist a small permanent staff 129

Figure 4–2. Volunteers help to remove flood-damaged drywall from a home in New Orleans after Hurricane Katrina. This labor-intensive process, often referred to as "gutting" a home, allows for the supporting infrastructure to dry prior to the home's repair. Studs and other woody materials exposed to floodwaters are usually treated with a bleach solution in an attempt to prevent mold from growing behind the walls once they are repaired, but this technique does not always work. The appearance of mold following the reconstruction of flood-damaged homes represents a serious health risk, particularly among children, elderly people, and those with respiratory problems 130

Figure 4–3. Members of the congregation held services in this Pass Christian, Mississippi, church the day after Hurricane Katrina. Faith-based organizations play an important role in recovery and often partner with local churches to assist in the reconstruction of damaged places of worship, help members of the congregation, or provide other types of assistance to the larger community. 139

Figure 4–4. A multistakeholder post-disaster housing construction "build-a-thon" involved Habitat for Humanity, a national nonprofit; Americorps, a federal organization devoted to volunteer service; and Charles Schwab, a private sector investment firm that sponsored the home construction project 143

Figure 4–5. The success of this nonprofit is closely associated with the development of strong horizontal ties in a community. Kaboom! partners with volunteers drawn from local communities and members of the private sector like Home Depot (see the sidebar in Chapter 5 on the role of home improvement retailers in recovery). The home improvement retailer helps to fund the costs of playground construction, provides needed building materials and tools, and encourages employees from neighboring stores to participate in the effort. This type of activity represents the targeted actions that nonprofits often pursue in response to perceived gaps in the delivery of assistance from other members of the disaster recovery assistance network 144

Figure 4–6. Students from the Gulf Coast Community Design Studio and the Moore Community House Women in Construction Program raise the first wall on their joint design-build project. 145

Figure 5–1. Not surprisingly, the sign noting a lot for sale in coastal Mississippi following Hurricane Katrina does not acknowledge that the area sustained a storm surge in excess of twenty feet. Requiring hazard disclosure during real estate transactions is one of many tools that can be used to better inform potential buyers of coastal and other high-risk property. In reality, intensive development along U.S shorelines continues at a rapid pace, including after major disasters. Attempts to limit development in these areas following disasters are often controversial and foster heated debate 159

Figure 5–2. Pictured is the address and insurance provider spray-painted on what remains of a coastal Mississippi home. Homeowners often use this technique to assist claims adjusters find damaged property amidst debris fields, missing street signage, and damaged or destroyed landmarks. Homeowners also use this technique to express their displeasure with their insurance provider as conflicts often arise between policyholder and insurance companies regarding the level of coverage and the timeliness of payment 168

Figure 5–3. The Broadmoor neighborhood used both yard signs and banners as part of a coordinated marketing campaign to let the media and potential providers of assistance know that they were intent on returning and rebuilding their community 171

Figure 5–4. The Louisiana State Police patrol New Orleans after Hurricane Katrina 173

Figure 5–5. The casino industry is a primary economic force along the Mississippi Gulf Coast. Prior to Hurricane Katrina, state law required that casinos could not be located on shore, thereby necessitating the construction of floating barges to house gambling operations (left). When Katrina struck, the barges were torn from their moorings and cast on shore, landing on neighboring communities (right). The state legislature has since rescinded this law, which some believe will foster large-scale casino development along the coast 178

Figure 5–6. Some businesses, like this damaged marina in Biloxi, depend on areas subject to known natural hazards. The speed at which they can resume operations has economic implications for the community, including those that work there and those who depend on the services they provide 179

Figure 6–1. This temporary tent camp was built by local residents in Talca, Chile, after the 2010 earthquake. The residents intend to remain here until their former houses are rebuilt on their existing lots 198

Figure 6–2. Philip Berke, professor at the University of North Carolina at Chapel Hill, talks with local residents on a houseboat in a Thailand coastal village following the Indian Ocean tsunami. 199

Figure 6–3. The village of Shishmaref, located north of the Bering Strait in Alaska, is one of roughly a dozen communities facing an immediate threat from coastal erosion. The structure pictured above was impacted by a severe fall storm that resulted in substantial coastal retreat within a matter of hours. Surviving houses have been moved to less threatened sites on the small barrier island by towing them across the ice in winter. Coastal erosion is significantly exacerbated by the thaw of permafrost that has historically helped to stabilize the island 200

Figure 6–4. The image of Thai housing highlights the importance of recognizing existing economic, social, cultural, and environmental factors that should be considered when developing pre- and post-disaster recovery assistance strategies 203

Figure 6–5. This photo of a coastal fishing village in Thailand (note the fishing nets suspended in the river) exemplifies the proximity of housing to the natural resources upon which those in the community depend. Sound pre- and post-disaster recovery assistance should reflect local conditions, including those associated with development and the often strong social capital that exists among communities in the developing world 208

Figure 6–6. The image of squatter housing in Manila, Philippines, juxtaposed with the downtown skyline shrouded in smog, dramatically shows the extreme social vulnerability of many of the city's residents, whom reside in the shadows of new urban growth. The houses are sited within the confines of a channelized drainage system, whose nearby neighborhoods are protected by a concrete levee. After Typhoon Ondoy, which struck the area in 2009, both squatter settlements and the wealthy neighborhood that the levee was intended to protect were severely flooded 209

Figure 6–7. An official from Medair, in Jacmel, Haiti, after the 2010 earthquake, assesses the traditional construction methods used to build this home and suggests repair and reconstruction techniques to make it more earthquake and hurricane resistant. The discussion also represents a larger effort to pretrain local residents who will be involved in efforts to rebuild the community. Medair is a Switzerland-based nonprofit relief organization that has primarily focused on providing shelter to Haitians displaced by the earthquake 211

Figure 6–8. Temporary housing designed and built by Techo para Chile, a Catholic-supported nongovernmental organization, after the 2010 Chilean earthquake and tsunami. Techo para Chile provides houses that are free to occupants, constructed using volunteer labor, and located on donated sites. The 3x6 meter units, which cost about $400, are typically built in housing settlements of 30 to 40 dwellings. This unit is located in Constitución, Chile. 217

Figure 7–1. A resident returns to the 9th Ward in New Orleans after Hurricane Katrina to find his home destroyed 241

Figure 7–2. The local capacity-building effort led by Manpower Development Corporation (MDC), a Chapel Hill-based nonprofit, and by faculty in the Department of City and Regional Planning at the University of North Carolina at Chapel Hill targets low-income communities along the eastern seaboard and Gulf Coast. The intent of this FEMA-funded community demonstration project is to help communities assess their vulnerability to natural hazards and develop locally grounded strategies that are based on their understanding of pre- and post-disaster conditions. 245

Figure 7–3. The spray-painted notations on the front of this house in Shoreacres, Texas, after Hurricane Ike convey a variety of information, including the type of damage sustained, the homeowner's flood insurance policy, a warning to potential intruders, and a sense of humor as evidenced by renaming the original street address, Shoreacres Circle 250

Figure 7–4. Individuals often return to their communities to begin the recovery process, including the repair or reconstruction of their home. In some cases, this may involve the use of a FEMA-provided temporary housing unit that is placed on the homeowner's lot (as evidenced in this photo) or in what are referred to as group sites. The provision of temporary housing in the afflicted area allows individuals to interact directly with different providers of assistance and cobble together insurance proceeds, loans, grant awards, or nonprofit assistance 250

Figure 7–5. The Broadmoor Improvement Association (see yard sign in front of a home in the New Orleans community) exemplifies the transition from an emergent group to a more formal quasi-governmental organization . . . 260

Figure 8–1. In this meeting conducted by the Mississippi Governor's Office of Recovery and Renewal in Jackson County, Mississippi, following Hurricane Katrina, representatives from federal and state agencies, nonprofits, foundations, and quasi-governmental organizations described their programs and then fielded questions in an effort to link available resources with local needs 272

Figure 8–2. The creation of vision statements was an integral part of the New Hartford, Iowa, disaster recovery planning process. 278

Figure 8–3. A public meeting in Palo, Iowa, focused on the linkage between the community's vision statement and the creation of disaster recovery goals 278

Figure 8–4. The timing of disaster recovery planning, including the use of post-disaster design workshops, may be a necessary means of implementing aspects of a plan developed after a disaster or of refining a plan that was created before an event. This post-disaster community design workshop in Oakville, Iowa, reflects part of a post-disaster recovery planning process that was not established before the 2008 Iowa floods. 281

Figure 8–5. In this Iowa City post-disaster recovery workshop, note the documentation of the process using flipcharts and video 289

Figure 9–1. The Dispute Settlement Center, located in Orange County, North Carolina, is representative of a growing number of nonprofit organizations dedicated to the resolution of multiparty disputes. Specific services include mediation and facilitation training as well as the provision of technical assistance to help individuals and organizations resolve disputes 330

Figure 9–2. ESF-14 staff lead a meeting in rural Greensburg, Kansas, after a tornado nearly destroyed the community in 2007. The resulting recovery plan emphasizes a number of sustainability themes, including public safety, energy efficiency, livability, economic vitality, and green development practices (see the *Long-term Community Recovery Plan: Greensburg and Kiowa County, Kansas* (August 2007) at greensburgks.org/recovery-planning/ long-term-community-recovery-plan/GB_LTCR_PLAN_Final_HiRes.070815. pdf). While the Greensburg plan has helped the community manage the recovery process, it is indicative of the approach currently used by FEMA, which emphasizes the post-disaster delivery of planning assistance rather than playing a dual role that includes pre-event capacity-building initiatives. 337

Figure 9–3. After Hurricane Ike, FEMA's Long-Term Community Recovery Program began providing technical assistance through a process they refer to as community mentoring. Using videoconferencing, ESF-14 staff brought together local officials from Colorado, Florida, Iowa, and Mississippi who were involved in long-term recovery efforts. The purpose of the videoconference was to foster the sharing of information and lessons with officials in hard-hit coastal communities in Texas. Topics discussed included beginning the planning process, identifying reconstruction projects and associated funding, coordinating local planning efforts within a region, building a strong working relationship between cities and counties, and collaborating with the state as it faced challenges associated with the administration of disaster funding 339

Figure 10–1. The White House Long-Term Disaster Recovery Working Group hosted this listening session on the National Disaster Recovery Framework 390

Figure 10–2. This banner highlights the "emerging themes" in the National Disaster Recovery Framework 397

Exhibits

Exhibit 1–1. Resource Rules and Understanding of Local Needs 14

Exhibit 1–2. The Hypothetical Timing of Disaster Assistance: An Example of Federal Government and Nonprofit Stakeholders 17

Exhibit 1–3. Disaster Recovery Timeline 20

Exhibit 1–4. Rocky Mountain Model of Disaster Recovery 22

Exhibit 1–5. Community Types by Degree of Horizontal and Vertical Integration. 25

Exhibit 1–6. Transforming the Disaster Recovery Assistance Framework . . . 27

Exhibit 2–1. National Response Framework, Emergency Support Functions and Coordinators 41

Exhibit 2–2. Local Disaster Recovery Committee 52

Exhibit 3–1. Professional Associations with Disaster-Related Programs or Responsibilities 86

Exhibit 3–2. Proposed Planning for Natural Hazards Division 114

Exhibit 7–1. The Disaster Research Center Typology of Organized Responses 253

Exhibit 8–1. Integrating Planning Tasks with Conflict Resolution Steps . . . 276

Exhibit 8–2. Plan Quality and Alternative Dispute Resolution Principles 277

Exhibit 8–3. Disaster Recovery Planning Hierarchy 290

Exhibit 8–4. Drawbacks of Traditional Dispute Resolution Institutions 294

Exhibit 9–1. Suggested Elements for a Theory of Sustainable Community Recovery 325

Exhibit 9–2. Collaborative Operations in Hazards Management 345

Exhibit 9–3. The National Response Framework Capability Building Cycle 347

Exhibit 9–4. Key Planning Elements Found in Comprehensive Plans, Comprehensive Emergency Management Plans, and Hazard Mitigation Plans 350

Exhibit 9–5. Planning Authorities 351

Exhibit 9–6. The Hazard Mitigation Planning Process 353

Exhibit 9–7. Emergency Management Accreditation Standards 362

Exhibit 9–8. ESF-14 Conceptual Diagram 369

Exhibit 10–1. National Disaster Recovery Framework, Recovery Support Functions, and Coordinators 382

Exhibit 10–2. Summary of Recommendations 400

Sidebars

The Politics of Disaster 39

The State of Florida's Post-Disaster Redevelopment Planning Initiative 44

The Emergency Management Assistance Compact 48

Hillsborough County, Florida, Post-Disaster Redevelopment Plan 53

North Carolina's Disaster Recovery Assistance Programs after Hurricane Floyd 56

Kinston, North Carolina: The Value of Pre-event Planning and the
Speed and Quality of Recovery 65

A Brief History of Regional Planning and Hazards Management in the
United States 82

Two Approaches to Regional Disaster Recovery Planning 84

New Urbanism and the Disaster Recovery Assistance Framework 87

Translating Research to Practice 92

Gulf Coast Community Design Studio. 95

The Transformation of Self-Reliance in High-Hazard Communities 103

Professional Associations in Recovery following Hurricane Katrina 104

Case Study: The Broadmoor Project 116

Case Study Exhibit 1. The Broadmoor "Partner Network". 117

Case Study Exhibit 2. Broadmoor Improvement Association
Community Development Plan 120

National Voluntary Organizations Active in Disasters 128

Council on Foundations' Principles of Good Disaster Management 137

Tulsa Partners: A Sustained Commitment to Floodplain Management
and Hazard Mitigation 146

Boosterism, Disaster Recovery, and a Tale of Two Hurricane-Prone Cities. . 160

FEMA On-Call Contracts Related to Recovery 164

The Role of Home Improvement Retailers in Recovery 170

The Governor's Commission on Recovery, Rebuilding, and Renewal. . . . 182

Project Impact: Strengthening Hazard Mitigation and Community
Preparedness through Public-Private Partnerships. 184

Learning from Disaster Recovery in Developing Countries 197

Two Approaches to International Cooperation: The Dutch Dialogues
and a Pre-Event Memorandum of Agreement 206

Comparing U.S. International and Domestic Assistance Programs 215

Horizontal and Vertical Integration in Monserrat before and after
Hurricane Hugo 223

The Hyogo Framework for Action 226

Lessons from Emergent Multiorganizational Networks and their
Application to Recovery 256

The Charlotte and Mecklenburg County, North Carolina, Floodplain
Mapping Program: The Power of Coalition Building and Participatory
Planning 269

The Plan-Making Hierarchy in the Los Angeles Recovery and
Reconstruction Plan 280

The Use of Geographic Information Systems in Recovery Planning 282

Legislative 294

Bureaucracy 294

Courts 294

The Role of Negotiation in Post-Disaster Resource Allocation Disputes . . . 297

Assessing, Understanding, and Mitigating Vulnerability in the
Post-Disaster Environment: The Role of the Planner as Mediator 302

The Oregon Natural Hazards Workgroup Pre-Disaster Planning for
Post-Disaster Disaster Recovery: The Cannon Beach Pilot Program 335

Preface

Research and knowledge about the disaster recovery process has been viewed as the forgotten step-child of hazard and disaster research for the past 30 years. Particularly in comparison to our understanding of preparedness, response, and mitigation, it has often been observed that recovery has been somewhat ignored. However, spurred by recent catastrophic events and the recognition by disaster and hazard scholars that our knowledge of recovery was inadequate, there have been an impressive number of recovery studies undertaken over the past decades. This growing body of knowledge needs a compendium of research findings and an analytical assessment of where we stand in our ability to recover from disasters.

Planning for Post-Disaster Recovery: A Review of the United States Disaster Assistance Framework provides this assessment. With the publication of this book, we now know more about the existing manner in which the recovery process is conceptualized, organized, managed, and undertaken. We also have a better understanding of the structural problems, policy weaknesses, lack of coordination, and difficulties inherent in establishing recovery from disasters that is resilient, sustainable, and equitable. In addition to dissecting the complex, loosely-coupled network of federal, state, and local components that are involved in the recovery process, this book offers compelling suggestions for improving disaster recovery.

No one is better prepared to write this book than Dr. Gavin Smith. He possesses the scholarly, research, and practical backgrounds that are essential to this effort. Smith received his Ph.D.in Urban and Regional Science from Texas A&M University. As a student, he was a research associate with the Hazard Reduction & Recovery Center in the College of Architecture. Upon graduation he served as a staff member on the North Carolina Division of Emergency Management and was instrumental in the state's recovery effort after Hurricane Floyd and nine other disasters. After a couple of years in the private sector, he was selected to be the Director of the Office of Recovery and Renewal in the Governor's Office of the State of Mississippi. In this capacity he directed the recovery efforts for the state. Currently he serves as Executive Director of the Center for the Study of Natural Hazards and Disasters at the University of North Carolina at Chapel Hill and the Coastal Hazard Center, a Department of Homeland Security Center of Excellence. He has intellectual and hands-on familiarity with the topic.

Gavin Smith has undertaken a detailed, comprehensive, and analytical assessment of the United States Disaster Recovery Assistance Framework (DRAF). It is a significant accomplishment that indicates that the weakness in how communities and regions recover from disaster is a result of structural, policy, and planning failures and contradictions inherent in the DRAF. The analysis focuses upon assessing DRAF based upon three metrics: 1) understanding local needs, 2) the timing of assistance, and 3) the strength of vertical and horizontal integration. After describing the nature of the DRAF in chapter one, Smith discusses the key components in chapters 2 through 7. Chapter two analyzes federal, state and local governments. Quasi-governmental and nongovernmental organizations, such as community development corporations, homeowners associations, special districts, regional planning organizations, professional associations, and colleges and universities are the focus of chapter three. Nonprofit relief organizations, such as the American Red Cross; faith-based, environmental, and social justice groups; community organizations; and foundations are analyzed in chapter four. The private sector and for-profit organizations are considered in chapter five. Chapter six considers the role that the international community plays, or should play, in the United States DRAF. Finally, chapter seven investigates the roles of individual and emergent groups in this complex network.

In examining these components, Smith finds that there are inherent problems with roles, collaborations, shared knowledge, and understanding among the participants. With regard to being able to provide for local needs, there is often a schism between those with the greatest knowledge of local needs and those with the most prescriptive rules and power to influence the recovery process who also happen to have the least knowledge of local needs. Smith notes that the problem with the timing of assistance is not that it is slow and delays the recovery process; it is that it is often unplanned and uncoordinated between the various components. Finally, the DRAF is generally plagued by weak horizontal and vertical integration both with individual components and across the network.

The analysis abounds with insightful observations and some "out of the box" thinking. For example, the discussion of the international community and its relationship to the DRAF insightfully notes that the United States may have given considerable attention to the delivery of assistance to aid other nations in recovery efforts, but has not developed significant policies or programs to receive aid from other nations when we have been struck by disaster. At the time of Katrina, significant aid was offered by many nations, but little was accepted. The discussion of absorptive capacity, conditionality, and disaster diplomacy results in a call for a change in policy that will allow for the United States to receive such aid. Also, it is argued that the United States has much to learn from the recovery of other nations and can benefit from such programs as the United National International Strategy for Disaster Reduction.

Having analytically examined the DRAF and noted its significant problems, Smith offers a number of suggestions for remediating this system in chapters 8 and 9. Although it is not a panacea, pre-disaster recovery planning is espoused throughout the book as a necessary development that must be undertaken at the federal, state, and local levels. Pre-disaster recovery planning can increase local capacity to recovery, improve horizontal and vertical integration, assess local needs, and improve the timing of recovery. In addition, due to the contentious nature of the recovery process, it is strongly argued that this planning must be undertaken through Alternative Dispute Resolution and collaborative planning strategies. Chapter 8 provides a detailed analysis of pre-disaster recovery plans and presents guidelines for their development.

Chapter 9 discusses the nature and creation of a Disaster Recovery Act at the federal level. The United States currently lacks a Disaster Recovery Act that would be akin to the Disaster Mitigation Act of 2000. The Stafford Act of 1988 and the National Response Framework are shown to be counter-productive to such elements as pre-disaster recovery planning and collaboration that are needed to improve the disaster recovery process. Chapter 10 discusses the draft of the National Disaster Recovery Framework (NDRF) which is currently being developed by FEMA. On a very positive note, NDRF is attempting to address many of the weaknesses inherent in the recovery process and network that are addressed by Smith.

This book is a policy and practice juggernaut. Who should read it? It is a vital source of knowledge for policy makers and officials at federal, state, and local levels, for it advances the notion that policy must be based upon sound planning, not incremental programs. It should be read by emergency managers and recovery officials in both public and private sector organization because it clearly shows that the status quo and "recovery business as usual" are not working. It should be required reading in all departments of urban planning in colleges and universities. Planners have a critical role to play in the recovery process, but they have generally not been involved. This book is their call to arms. Finally, hazard and disaster scholars will benefit from the extensive literature review and depth of the analysis. Hopefully, it will stimulate members of the research community to use this as a springboard for the development of a theory of disaster recovery.

Finally, I must insert a "truth in advertising" statement. I chaired Gavin Smith's dissertation at Texas A&M University. Gavin, thank you for this book. I learned so very much from it.

Dennis Wenger, PhD
Program Director
Infrastructure Management and Hazard Response
National Science Foundation

Acknowledgements

The intent of this book is twofold: to advance our understanding of recovery and to apply this knowledge in practice through pre-disaster planning and post-event actions. The attempt to bridge research and practice has grown out of my personal experiences as a practitioner, researcher, and one who has witnessed firsthand what a disaster can do to communities, including my hometown.

I have worked as a practitioner and researcher before and after a number of major disasters and thus have had the unique opportunity to interact with a number of special people from the many organizations described in the following pages. Several individuals deserve special recognition. Following Hurricanes Fran and Floyd, I had the good fortune of working for Eric Tolbert, director of the North Carolina Division of Emergency Management. His steady guidance, patience, and unflappable nature in the face of a crisis was always balanced by a willingness to give me the autonomy to try new ideas during the turbulent times that define a disaster. While I lost a friend and mentor, his untimely death was an even greater loss to the profession of emergency management.

I also had the pleasure of working with two governors following major disasters: James B. Hunt of North Carolina after Hurricane Floyd, and Haley Barbour of Mississippi after Hurricane Katrina. While representative of differing political philosophies, they both exhibited strong leadership, which is a fundamentally important aspect of disaster recovery. In both cases, I drew upon their wisdom, energy, and compassion to help those in need.

Individuals affected by disasters are often mistakenly referred to as "disaster victims." I have found this to be far from the truth and have learned as much or more from them as they have learned from me or others I have worked with over time. The reluctance of those tasked with recovery to effectively incorporate the locally grounded knowledge possessed by individuals into policies and plans continues to limit the effectiveness of recovery efforts.

Disasters are highly personal events. The stories of individuals and communities affected by extreme events, while often filled with anguish, are also representative of amazing tales of personal determination and collective resilience. Yet the academic pursuit of knowledge often fails to effectively capture and convey this reality. For this reason, I have made liberal use of sidebars in order to show how individuals at different times and in different circumstances have faced the many challenges associated with disaster recovery and applied varied tactics to address them.

REVIEW COMMITTEE

I would like to thank a number of highly regarded experts in the field of disaster recovery, whose comments have significantly improved the quality of this book. I owe a particular gratitude to colleagues who reviewed the entire manuscript in its early stages and offered constructive criticism as well as encouragement. My review committee offered professional guidance and helped to identify additional literature and improve the conceptual model. Any limitations are entirely the fault of the author.

Members of my review committee include Dan Alesch, Philip Berke, Tom Birkland, Arietta Chakos, Ann-Margaret Esnard, Bruce Glavovic, Gerry Hoetmer, Shirley Laska, Scott Miles, Jim Schwab, and Bill Siembieda. Special thanks go to Dennis Wenger, my former dissertation committee chair, who has provided sage advice over the years, starting at the Hazard Reduction and Recovery Center at Texas A&M University and continuing to this day.

PUBLIC ENTITY RISK INSTITUTE

Gerry Hoetmer, former executive director of the Public Entity Risk Institute (PERI), initially approached me about writing this book when it was still an emerging idea and helped shepherd the process. Claire Reiss, PERI's interim executive director, assumed Gerry's role when he retired and helped to ensure the book's completion. Jessica Hubbard has directed the many activities required to drive the process, including the coordination of all participants. Lydia Bjornlund and Jane Cotnoir, my editors, provided numerous suggested changes to the manuscript and they merit special recognition. Lydia helped clarify my thoughts while Jane methodically edited a book that has grown increasingly complex over time. Colleen Gratzer of Gratzer Graphics LLC designed the page proofs and the cover.

PHOTOGRAPHER

Finally, I would like to thank Donn Young, a native of New Orleans, who lost most of his life's work, including over 1,250,000 photographic images, in Hurricane Katrina. After the storm he was asked to document the event and his images resulted in the photographic prospectus *40 Days and 40 Nights*. Many of the photographs from his collection have been used throughout this book.

Introduction

The tugboat, dubbed the S.S. Hurricane Camille, came to rest in Gulfport, Mississippi, following the 1969 storm. After Hurricane Katrina, the tug remained in place, but over 50,000 homes were destroyed or severely damaged along the Mississippi Gulf Coast as the result of a storm surge that in some places exceeded 25 feet.

Photo by Gavin Smith.

DISASTER LOSSES CONTINUE TO MOUNT in the United States and around the world. The Indian Ocean tsunami (2004), Hurricanes Katrina (2005) and Ike (2008), the Haiti earthquake (2010), and the threat of climate change–induced hazards provide stark reminders of past and future challenges, including those associated with disaster recovery. The common approach to disaster recovery in the United States is to rely on the administration of narrowly defined federal grant programs rather than the larger assistance network and the many resources it can provide. The result is typically the uncoordinated implementation of varied programs administered by different stakeholders acting in isolation.

The failure to plan for disaster recovery results in a process of rebuilding that often presages the next disaster. It also limits the collective maximization of governmental, nonprofit, and private resources, including those resources that are available at the community level. As individuals, groups, communities, and organizations routinely struggle to recover from disasters, they are beset by a duplication of effort, poor interorganizational coordination, the development and implementation of policies that are not shaped by local needs, and the spreading of misinformation. Yet the perceived value of pre-event planning for post-disaster recovery remains low.

To address these weaknesses, I created the disaster recovery assistance framework, an approach that helps to consolidate what we know about recovery and defines the problems that underlie this largely disjointed process. My impetus for doing so grew out of a belief that inherent in planning principles, alternative dispute resolution (ADR) techniques, and the modification of existing hazards management programs is the potential to transform current practice and improve recovery outcomes, and that addressing the challenges of disaster recovery requires an environment that will facilitate the emergence of collaborative problem solving among a network of stakeholders and assistance providers.

My idea for this book emerged after Hurricane Katrina, when I was asked to lead the Mississippi Governor's Office of Recovery and Renewal. The early conceptual elements of what I refer to as the disaster recovery assistance framework were used to explain the process of disaster recovery to staff, local officials, and members of the governor's office. This framework also served as a means to set forth the primary objectives of the Office of Recovery and Renewal: to identify the types of resources (funding, policy formulation, and technical assistance) available across the network of disaster recovery assistance providers; to advise the governor, his cabinet, and local officials on existing and proposed disaster recovery policies; and to conduct education, training, and outreach efforts aimed at building local capacity (see Figure 1). Since that time, the disaster recovery assistance framework has been further refined on the basis of personal experience derived from practice following Hurricanes Katrina, Floyd, and Fran, and other disasters; the identification and writing of the case studies used in this

Figure 1. Mississippi governor Haley Barbour (right) talks with Gavin Smith, executive director of the Governor's Office of Recovery and Renewal (left), and Mike Womack, director of Mississippi Emergency Management Agency (center), following the Governor's Recovery Expo.

Source: Governor's Office of Recovery and Renewal, State of Mississippi.

book; a review of the literature; and discussions with hazard scholars, practitioners, and those who assumed leadership positions following disasters.

A REACTIVE APPROACH TO RECOVERY

Communities are defined by their physical characteristics and spatial patterns of development, economic interdependencies, social bonds, and sense of place. Disasters disrupt and fracture these constructs. Thus, it is not surprising that the principal impulse after an event is to return to what is familiar—that which defined the community prior to the event—even if pre-event conditions may have been fraught with social injustice, high hazard vulnerability, inadequate housing and public infrastructure, economic fragility, and poor leadership. And so it is that while people and groups are busy trying to seek temporary housing; pick up debris; navigate complex, bureaucratic grant and loan options and insurance settlements; identify those organizations capable of providing gap financing and targeted technical assistance; return people to work; revitalize the economy; and confront a host of other problems, many of which may be unique to a particular area and are not easily addressed through existing programs, decisions are often made that could fundamentally alter the nature of communities (see Figure 2 on page 4).

Such reactive decisions—including whether to adopt more stringent reconstruction standards; how to reconfigure the physical footprint of a community; how to allocate scarce resources; and how to return the community to a sense of normalcy—fail to take advantage of opportunities to enact positive change. These decisions are frequently made with limited information during a time when there is intense pressure to act and show tangible progress. Moreover, the information that *is* available, including the level and type of damages sustained; the eligibility criteria for financial aid; and post-disaster policies adopted by participants across the network, is subject to different interpretations and constant revisions during the recovery process. Thus, members of the community may resist taking the time needed to think through, adopt, and implement a more meaningful process that has the potential to alter pre-event conditions.[1] And in so doing, they may fail to protect against actions that may not be in the community's best interests—actions such as the imposition of technical solutions with limited public involvement; attempts to derive short-term profits through redevelopment practices that result in an inequitable distribution of affordable housing or an increase in overall hazard vulnerability; the widespread use of a largely top-down, highly prescriptive set of disconnected policies; and the equation of success with the speed of recovery rather than with a more deliberative approach that reflects pre- and post-disaster social, economic, and environmental conditions.

Figure 2. The Governor's Expo was intended to provide information to residents and local officials on the Mississippi Gulf Coast about recovery programs and policies, reconstruction techniques, and providers of these services. This information was conveyed through training sessions, demonstrations, informational booths, and the placement of over 20 modular housing units on the Expo grounds. The two day event drew over 50,000 coastal residents.

Photos by Gavin Smith.

Some researchers caution that the window of opportunity to effect change does not stay open very long.[2] Adolf Ciborowski contends that the likelihood a community will capitalize on the opportunities afforded during recovery depends on the type and extent of damages it has sustained.[3] Limited technical and fiscal capabilities; a lack of political will to enact change; entrenched development interests; and the failure to engage in representative, participatory decision making often results in an overreliance on federal grant programs that limit the search for locally driven solutions.[4]

These and other issues add to the challenges facing those who try to develop and implement disaster recovery plans. They also point to the importance of developing plans before a disaster occurs, as planning for recovery requires navigating through a very complex social, political, economic, and interorganizational milieu. In New Orleans after Hurricane Katrina, for example, the first exposure that many residents and community groups had to planners was the early designation of their neighborhoods as areas facing possible elimination and conversion to open space. In Mississippi, technical experts in the design of New Urbanist communities were brought in to contemplate the reconstruction of coastal towns using an intensive weeklong series of architectural design "charrettes" in locales that did not have a strong pre-disaster planning culture (see Chapter 3).

Many of the factors cited above, which are endemic to recovery, lead to high levels of conflict across the assistance network. Yet under the appropriate circumstances, they can also elicit cooperation. Thus, it is imperative that practitioners and scholars provide adequate guidance on the myriad questions that are tied to planning for recovery: Who make up the disaster recovery assistance network and what are their roles in recovery? Who is in charge? How do members of the network interact in the pre- and post-disaster environment? How does the current design of the U.S. approach affect recovery outcomes? What role does pre- and post-disaster planning play in recovery? These research questions, explained in the context of the disaster recovery assistance framework, form the basis of this book and guide the discussion and recommendations that follow.

BLENDING RESEARCH AND PRACTICE

This book blends what we know about disaster recovery from the research literature and an analysis of existing practice to uncover both problems and recommended solutions. It is intended for hazard scholars, practitioners, and others who have not assimilated or acted upon the existing body of knowledge, or who are unexpectedly drawn into the recovery process following a disaster. After a review of the research literature and existing policies, plans, manuals, and guidance documents, an unfortunate reality remains: disaster recovery is the least understood aspect of emergency management among both scholars and practitioners.[5] Perhaps more disturbing is the realization that researchers pointed to this problem at least twenty-five years ago.[6] In addition, the body of knowledge that does exist has not been effectively disseminated to those who engage in disaster recovery activities.

In their study of recovery following Hurricane Andrew, Betty Hearn Morrow and Walter Peacock provide a sobering account of how members of the disaster recovery assistance network—including federal, state, and local government officials; nongovernmental organizations; the private sector; and the insurance industry—failed to coordinate the distribution of assistance and other post-disaster actions.[7] Hurricane Katrina represents another highly publicized breakdown across the network, caused in part by the failure to effectively implement a plan for response and recovery in New Orleans that had actually been created prior to the storm—even though a number of hypothetical scenarios described expected catastrophic losses in the event of a major hurricane.[8] Recovery operations after Katrina exposed a weak economy, ineffective local government, and poor connectivity among federal, state, and local actors.[9] Yet other case studies have documented examples in which members of the assistance network distributed aid equitably,[10] incorporated hazard mitigation into recovery efforts,[11] enacted policy changes,[12] and linked local needs to available programs.[13] In most cases, the ability or inability to achieve these objectives was tied to the act of planning for post-disaster recovery.[14]

THE IMPORTANCE OF PRE- AND POST-EVENT PLANNING

In 2006, Dennis Wenger and I defined disaster recovery as "the differential process of restoring, rebuilding, and reshaping the physical, social, economic, and natural environment through pre-event planning and post-event actions."[15] In other words, recovery is more than the reconstruction of damaged buildings, community facilities, businesses, and infrastructure: the different choices made by members of the assistance network can lead to different outcomes across physical, social, economic, and environmental dimensions. This book expands upon the above definition, arguing that the ability to improve the framework currently used in the United States is predicated on the value of pre- and post-event planning, an approach that has been recognized by a growing number of hazard scholars[16] and practitioners.[17]

It is important to emphasize that pre-event recovery planning is uncommon compared with post-disaster adaptive planning. But the latter, which can result in the development of strategies to confront identified weaknesses in the framework, does not preclude the value of pre-event recovery planning but, rather, highlights its importance. Post-disaster planning is done in an environment that can be hostile to important preconditions of success, such as the meaningful involvement of the members of disaster recovery assistance networks in a sustained, deliberative process. Conversely, pre-event planning allows members of assistance networks to invest the time and resources needed to foster cooperative behavior, assuming that appropriate incentives and sanctions are in place. For disaster recovery planning to succeed, it also requires that communities actively participate in the process. And the ability to facilitate a participatory process aimed at developing a vision for the future is an important function of the practicing planner.[18]

The use of inclusive planning strategies can help to bridge seemingly intractable disputes and identify mutually compatible outcomes.[19] Planners are among a growing number of professionals who have embraced the use of ADR techniques, including policy dialogue, mediation, facilitation, and negotiation, as a means to address multiparty conflict and seek consensus.[20] Planning techniques that assist the disenfranchised—who, in the context of disaster recovery, often include socially vulnerable populations—may require advocating on their behalf, a method first described in the 1960s.[21] ADR is particularly relevant to the post-disaster environment because recovery is often a highly contentious process that involves numerous stakeholders with different needs, priorities, and opinions on the appropriate distribution of assistance and the best way to meet recovery goals.

The viability of a post-disaster opportunity to affect change must be viewed in the context of pre-existing social, cultural, economic, environmental, and institutional conditions,[22] including the pre- and post-disaster "culture of planning." For example, the adoption of new plans or settlement patterns may clash with pre-event cultural ideals. Additional factors hindering the adoption of new ideas include inadequate funding[23] and solutions proposed by nonresidents of the affected community.[24] In some cases, post-disaster conditions are best characterized as "opportunistic," whereby those in positions of power take advantage of the situation to further their own political or economic gains, which may hinder the advancement of legitimate public interests.[25] Walter Peacock and Kathleen Ragsdale, for instance, assert that a market-based disaster recovery process often leads to the restoration of the status quo rather than the incorporation of principles of equity.[26]

ORGANIZATION OF THE BOOK

This book begins with an introduction of the underlying problems associated with disaster recovery in the United States. Chapter 1 describes the disaster recovery assistance framework and how its characteristics influence the delivery of pre- and post-disaster aid. Chapters 2 through 7 provide an in-depth description of stakeholders involved in recovery, including their effect on the timing of assistance, the rules associated with aid delivery, their understanding of local needs, and the level of coordination across the disaster recovery network. Chapter 8 focuses on the role of planning in recovery and includes a discussion of plan quality principles and ADR techniques. Chapter 9 proposes the creation of a disaster recovery act that will set forth a series of steps needed to confront identified problems. The book concludes with a review of the National Disaster Recovery Framework, a new FEMA initiative aimed at improving disaster recovery planning, followed by a reassemblage of the book's recommendations and a summary of their implications.

This book will show that change can occur within the larger assistance framework and that it may be initiated by a number of individual groups or a combination thereof. Varied members of the assistance network can play a leadership role in recovery depending on the nature of the network and the pre- and post-disaster conditions present in different locales. In some cases, state government may prove particularly capable; elsewhere, long-term recovery efforts may be driven by a community-based group or a member of the private sector. Regardless of who takes charge or serves as a central coordinative body, the willingness of the assistance network to engage in planning is an important factor to consider when addressing the complexities of disaster recovery. Planning, therefore, is best understood as a means to facilitate those conditions where cooperation emerges, thrives, and is sustained over time.

Endnotes

1   Robert Geipel, *Disaster and Reconstruction: The Friuli (Italy) Earthquakes of 1976* (London: Allen and Unwin, 1982).

2   Carla S. Prater and Michael K. Lindell, "The Politics of Hazard Mitigation," *Natural Hazards Review* 1, no. 2 (2000): 73–82.

3   Adolf Ciborowski, *Urban Design and Physical Planning as Tools to Make Cities Safer in Earthquake-Prone Areas* (Warsaw: Institute of Urban Design and Physical Development, Warsaw Technical University, 1981).

4   Gavin Smith and Dennis Wenger, "Sustainable Disaster Recovery: Operationalizing an Existing Agenda," in *Handbook of Disaster Research,* ed. Havidan Rodriguez, Enrico L. Quarantelli, and Russell Dynes, 234–257 (New York: Springer, 2006).

5   This view is shared by, among others, Philip R. Berke, Jack Kartez, and Dennis Wenger, "Recovery after Disasters: Achieving Sustainable Development, Mitigation and Equity," *Disasters* 17, no. 2 (1993): 93–109; Daniel J. Alesch, *Complex Urban Systems and Extreme Events: Toward a Theory of Disaster Recovery* (Fairfax, Va.: Public Entity Risk Institute [PERI], 2006), 1–8; and Smith and Wenger, "Sustainable Disaster Recovery."

6   Claire B. Rubin, Martin D. Saperstein, and Daniel G. Barbee, *Community Recovery from a Major Natural Disaster* (Boulder: Institute of Behavioral Science, University of Colorado, 1985).

7   Betty Hearn Morrow and Walter Gillis Peacock, "Disasters and Social Change: Hurricane Andrew and the Reshaping of Miami?" in *Hurricane Andrew: Ethnicity, Gender and the Sociology of Disasters,* ed. Walter Gillis Peacock, Betty Hearn Morrow, and Hugh Gladwin, 226–242 (Miami, Fla.: International Hurricane Center Laboratory for Social and Behavioral Research, 1997).

8   U.S. Government Accounting Office (GAO), *Disaster Recovery: Past Experiences Offer Insights for Recovering from Hurricanes Ike and Gustav and Other Recent Natural Disasters,* Report to the Senate Committee on Homeland Security and Governmental Affairs, GAO-08-1120 (Washington, D.C., September 2008), www.gao.gov/new.items/d081120.pdf; Citizens for Responsibility and Ethics in Washington (CREW), *The Best Laid Plans: The Story of How the Government Ignored Its Own Gulf Coast Hurricane Plan* (Washington, D.C.: CREW, 2007), www.citizensforethics.org/files/Katrina%20 DHS%20Report.pdf (accessed July 9, 2010).

9   Peter Burns and Matthew O. Thomas, "The Failure of the Nonregime: How Katrina Exposed New Orleans as a Regimeless City," *Urban Affairs Review* 41, no. 4. (2006): 517–527.

10 Berke, Kartez, and Wenger, "Recovery after Disasters."

11 Claire B. Rubin and Daniel G. Barbee, "Disaster Recovery and Hazard Mitigation: Bridging the Intergovernmental Gap," *Public Administration Review* 45, special issue (1985): 57–63; Robert Stuart Olson, Robert A. Olson, and Vincent T. Gawronski, "Night and Day: Mitigation Policymaking in Oakland, California, before and after the Loma Prieta Earthquake," *International Journal of Mass Emergencies and Disasters* 16, no. 2 (1998): 145–179.

12 Thomas A. Birkland, *Lessons of Disaster: Policy Change after Catastrophic Events* (Washington, D.C.: Georgetown University Press, 2006).

13 Anthony Oliver-Smith, "Post-Disaster Housing Reconstruction and Social Inequality: A Challenge to Policy and Practice," *Disasters* 14, no. 1 (1990): 7–19.

14 Ibid.; Smith and Wenger, "Sustainable Disaster Recovery"; Philip R. Berke and Timothy Beatley, *After the Hurricane: Linking Recovery to Sustainable Development in the Caribbean* (Baltimore: Johns Hopkins University Press, 1997); Spangle Associates Urban Planning and Research, *Evaluation of Use of the Los Angeles Recovery and Reconstruction Plan after the Northridge Earthquake,* 1997, available at http://spangleassociates.com/; Jim Schwab et al., *Planning for Post-Disaster Recovery and Reconstruction,* Planning Advisory Service (PAS) Report 483/484 (Chicago: American Planning Association, 2003); Christopher L. Dyer, "The Phoenix Effect in Post-Disaster Recovery: An Analysis of the Economic Development Administration's Culture of Response after Hurricane Andrew," in *The Angry Earth: Disaster in Anthropological Perspective,* ed. Anthony Oliver-Smith and Susanna Hoffman,

278–300 (New York: Routledge, 1999); Jie-Ying Wu and Mickael K. Lindell, "Housing Reconstruction after Two Major Earthquakes: The 1994 Northridge Earthquake in the United States and the 1999 Chi-Chi Earthquake in Taiwan," *Disasters* 28, no. 1 (2004): 63–81; Philip R. Berke and Thomas J. Campanella, "Planning for Postdisaster Resiliency," *ANNALS of the American Academy of Political and Social Science* 604, no. 1 (2006): 192–207; Robert B. Olshansky, "Planning after Hurricane Katrina," *Journal of the American Planning Association* 72, no. 2 (2006): 147–153.

15 Smith and Wenger, "Sustainable Disaster Recovery," 237.

16 Ibid.; Olshansky, "Planning after Hurricane Katrina"; Geipel, *Disaster and Reconstruction;* Gilbert F. White, "Human Adjustment to Floods," Research Paper no. 29 (PhD diss., University of Chicago, 1945); Mary Anderson and Peter Woodrow, *Rising from the Ashes: Development Strategies in Times of Disaster* (Boulder, Colo.: Westview Press, 1989); Philip R. Berke and Dennis Wenger, *Linking Hurricane Disaster Recovery to Sustainable Development Strategies: Montserrat, West Indies* (College Station, Tex.: Hazard Reduction and Recovery Center, Texas A&M University, 1991); Raymond J. Burby, ed., *Cooperating with Nature: Confronting Natural Hazards with Land-Use Planning for Sustainable Communities* (Washington, D.C.: Joseph Henry Press, 1998); Dennis Mileti, *Disasters by Design: A Reassessment of Natural Hazards in the United States* (Washington, D.C.: Joseph Henry Press, 1999).

17 Schwab et al., *Planning for Post-Disaster Recovery and Reconstruction;* GAO, *Disaster Recovery;* William Spangle et al., ed., *Pre-Earthquake Planning for Post-Earthquake Rebuilding (PEPPER)* (Los Angeles: Southern California Earthquake Preparedness Project, 1987).

18 Judith Innes, "Planning through Consensus Building: A New View of the Comprehensive Planning Ideal," *Journal of the American Planning Association* 62, no. 4 (1996): 460–472; Edward J. Kaiser and David R. Godschalk, "Twentieth Century Land Use Planning: A Stalwart Family Tree," in *The City Reader,* ed. Richard LeGates and Fredric Stout, 366–386 (New York: Routledge, 2003).

19 Gavin Smith, "Lessons from the United States: Planning for Post-Disaster Recovery and Reconstruction," *Australasian Journal of Disaster and Trauma Studies* 2010-1 (2010), www.massey.ac.nz/~trauma/issues/2010-1/smith.htm (accessed July 9, 2010).

20 Lawrence Susskind and Alan Weinstein, "Toward a Theory of Environmental Dispute Resolution," *Boston College Environmental Affairs Law Review* 9, no. 2 (1981): 311–357; Lawrence Susskind, "Mediating Public Disputes: A Response to the Skeptics," *Negotiation Journal* (April 1985): 117–120; David R. Godschalk, "Negotiating Intergovernmental Development Policy Conflicts: Practice-Based Guidelines," *Journal of the American Planning Association* 58, no. 3 (1992): 368–378.

21 Paul Davidoff, "Advocacy and Pluralism in Planning," *Journal of the American Institute of Planners* 31, no. 4 (1965): 331–338; Sherry Arnstein, "Ladder of Citizen Participation," *Journal of American Institute of Planners* 35, no. 4 (1969): 216–224.

22 Eve Passerini, "Sustainability and Sociology," *American Sociologist* 29, no. 3 (1998): 59–70; Thomas Homer-Dixon, *The Upside of Down: Catastrophe, Creativity, and the Renewal of Civilization* (Washington, D.C.: Island Press, 2006).

23 Cheryl Childers and Brenda Phillips, *Sustainable Development or Transformative Development? Arkadelphia, Arkansas, after the Tornado* (Boulder, Colo.: Natural Hazards Research and Applications Information Center, 2002).

24 Passerini, "Sustainability and Sociology."

25 Lawrence J. Vale and Thomas J. Campanella, *The Resilient City: How Modern Cities Recover from Disasters* (New York: Oxford University Press, 2005); Naomi Klein, *The Shock Doctrine: The Rise of Disaster Capitalism* (New York: Henry Holt and Company, 2007); William R. Freudenberg et al., *Catastrophe in the Making: The Engineering of Katrina and the Disasters of Tomorrow* (Washington, D.C.: Island Press, 2009).

26 Walter Gillis Peacock and A. Kathleen Ragsdale, "Social Systems, Ecological Networks and Disasters: Toward a Socio-Political Ecology of Disasters," in *Hurricane Andrew* (see note 7), 26.

Chapter 1

The Disaster Recovery Assistance Framework

In many ways, the ability of the disaster assistance network to administer existing and emergent programs that meet local needs defines success and represents perhaps the most pressing challenge for those who assume roles in recovery.

Photo by Gavin Smith.

T HE UNDERLYING NATURE OF THE disaster recovery assistance framework is defined by the actions of a fragmented network of different stakeholder groups who provide disaster recovery assistance. Members of this network include public sector organizations (federal, state, and local governments); quasi-governmental and nongovernmental organizations (community development corporations, homeowners associations, special service districts, regional planning organizations, professional associations, and colleges and universities); nonprofit relief organizations (national organizations, community organizations, and foundations); private sector organizations (financial and lending institutions, consultants, developers, construction and engineering firms, insurance companies, businesses and corporations, and the media); international relief organizations and nations; and emergent groups and individuals. The assistance they provide is of three types: financial, policy-based, and technical.

Disaster recovery is often described as the pursuit, distribution, and management of financial resources.[1] Indeed, financial assistance regularly exceeds hundreds of millions of dollars during "routine" presidentially declared disasters and billions of dollars following larger events, such as the Northridge Earthquake (1989), Hurricane Andrew (1992), the Midwest Floods (1993), Hurricane Katrina (2005), and Hurricane Ike (2007). In reality, though, most U.S. disasters are small, localized events that do not meet federal disaster declaration criteria and therefore do not receive federal financial assistance. According to a 1998 survey produced by the National Emergency Management Association and Council of State Governments, 4,783 local disasters required "substantial" state assistance, of which 915, or 19 percent, resulted in a state-declared disaster and forty-nine, or less than 1 percent, received a federal disaster declaration.[2] The aggregated losses associated with smaller events account for more in total damages than those associated with federally declared disasters.[3]

In the case of larger events, research has shown that financial assistance may not reach those communities that need it most.[4] Moreover, those communities that receive financial assistance do not always recover "better" or "faster" than those that do not.[5] This is because the prescriptive nature of federal assistance, which tends to dominate the overall distributional "shape" of the framework, often fails to meet local needs. The overreliance on federal monetary assistance can supersede attempts to implement important federal and state-level policy changes, adopt new outreach and educational programs focused on capacity building, or initiate pre-event programs at the community level that foster cooperation. Numerous hazard scholars have found that the pre- and post-disaster releases of federal assistance funds were most successful when agencies developed partnerships with local community groups, nonprofits, and regional organizations.[6]

A central premise of an improved disaster recovery assistance framework is an increased emphasis on planning for disaster recovery. Evidence shows that pre-event planning can create the impetus to effect policy change and maximize various forms of financial assistance that lead to positive outcomes after a disaster.[7] As Frederick Bates and Walter Peacock have shown, major disasters can spark social and political change, but only if the delivery, timing, and scope of pre- and post-event assistance are considered.[8] In this regard, technical assistance, with its principal goals of building capacity and self-reliance,[9] serves an important coordinative function in the pre- and post-disaster environments, affecting financial and policy-related outcomes. While major disasters require outside assistance to supplement local capabilities, technical assistance—pre-event outreach, education, and training strategies—can strengthen partnerships across the disaster assistance network while providing incentives for the coordination and stretching of available resources.

Unfortunately, the current disaster recovery assistance framework discourages such an approach. Most disaster recovery training and educational programs are conducted on an ad hoc basis, and they focus on the administration of federal programs rather than on a collaboratively designed, locally tailored training agenda that emphasizes a long-term commitment to capacity-building strategies across the broader assistance network. Compounding this problem is the inability of federal, state, and local governments to clearly articulate responsibilities for the management of long-term recovery and reconstruction activities. The provision of assistance, including that which may change the pre-event social, political, or economic milieu, benefits from an ongoing dialogue across the provider network. Ideally, this dialogue is guided by local stakeholders. Robert Kates, summarizing the work of his colleagues, notes that advisory services provided by outside technical experts rarely alter the pre-event growth patterns and post-disaster redevelopment strategies that are advocated by entrenched development interests.[10] Their findings are consistent with the experience of several professional associations that tried to alter development patterns in coastal Mississippi after Hurricane Katrina (see Chapter 3).[11]

DIMENSIONS OF THE DISASTER RECOVERY ASSISTANCE FRAMEWORK

The characteristics that define the disaster recovery assistance framework and provide a basis for targeted pre-event planning and post-event action are the nature of the rules governing assistance and the degree to which they reflect local needs, the timing of program delivery, and the level of horizontal and vertical integration within and across organizations.

Understanding Local Needs

Among the most influential factors shaping recovery outcomes are the policies established to guide the distribution of money and the provision of technical assistance. Regrettably, the rules governing these policies tend to be most prescriptive among those organizations with the least understanding of local needs. Moreover, the rules often change, especially following disasters.[12] The extent to which assistance networks can navigate around and even amend disaster recovery rules depends on a number of factors, including past disaster experience; organizational culture; the ability of assistance recipients to communicate their needs through their involvement in the collection, analysis, and display of pertinent information; the presence of stake-holder advocates; access to political power and influence; and the use of a procedural forum to identify problems, share ideas, and propose solutions.[13] The poor integration of the rules governing the distribution of assistance vis-à-vis an understanding of local needs represents a key theme in the framework, as is evident in Exhibit 1–1, a hypothetical representation of an assistance network.

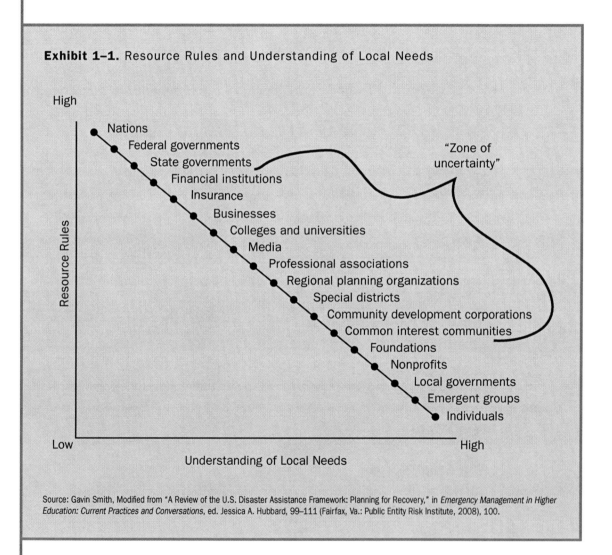

Exhibit 1–1. Resource Rules and Understanding of Local Needs

Source: Gavin Smith, Modified from "A Review of the U.S. Disaster Assistance Framework: Planning for Recovery," in *Emergency Management in Higher Education: Current Practices and Conversations*, ed. Jessica A. Hubbard, 99–111 (Fairfax, Va.: Public Entity Risk Institute, 2008), 100.

The somewhat monolithic characterization of stakeholder nodes represents a simplification of the disaster recovery assistance network as each node is composed of various stakeholders, each with its own set of distinct resources and rules. The stakeholders at the upper and lower ends of the diagonal most accurately reflect the central theme of the graphic: that those with the most prescriptive rules are the ones with the least understanding of local needs, and visa versa. Of course defining a diverse network of stakeholders using two factors (rules and understanding of local needs) has certain limitations as their characteristics are not entirely inversely correlated. For instance, common interest communities (discussed in Chapter 3) may possess a good understanding of local needs yet they tend to adopt strict rules governing the actions of those individuals residing in such locales. Those stakeholders located in the middle are nominally cast in a "zone of uncertainty," which means that practitioners and researchers generally know less about them, including the roles they play in recovery, the policies that influence their resource distribution, and the best ways to integrate their resources into a collaborative recovery effort that meets local needs. (The complexity of these issues is explored in the chapters that follow, which present a more in-depth description of the stakeholders and the roles they play, both independently and as part of the larger network.)

Further hindering coordination is the paternalistic—and inaccurate—assumption that federal and state governments provide most of the resources needed post-disaster, while the locally grounded assets that are critically important in pre-event policy and planning activities, such as those maintained by individuals, nonprofits, small businesses, and emergent groups, are often ignored. Also overlooked in the network may be members of the private sector that finance recovery and reconstruction efforts and rebuild damaged communities. In fact, a growing body of evidence suggests that nonprofit organizations,[14] quasi-governmental organizations, and the private sector, including corporations, small businesses, and consultants,[15] play a more important role in recovery than originally thought.[16] However, they are seldom discussed in the literature, and their contributions are underrecognized in practice. The failure to account for these and other contributions of the network is an unfortunate reality of disaster recovery in the United States.

Particularly troubling is the routine exclusion of those individuals, families, local governments, and other recipients of disaster assistance from the decision-making procedures that directly affect them. This problem, which has been closely studied in the international aid literature,[17] is directly relevant to any analysis of the U.S. approach to recovery. Individuals tend to have limited influence over the allocation of federal assistance or the programmatic rules shaping eligibility, even though those who are directly affected by a disaster tend to have a stronger understanding of local needs.

The failure to provide flexible programs capable of responding to local needs is partly the result of a network in which members lack information about the assistance provided by one another. Without this information, they are unable to consider ways to modify their strategies to reduce duplication; find common ground as they confront seemingly contradictory objectives; or reduce adverse pre-event conditions, such as social vulnerability and inequitable decision-making practices, through post-event actions. On the other hand, communities that develop such information-sharing venues as recovery committees or other participatory forums are more likely to work to change the negative conditions that existed before the event.[18] Anthony Oliver-Smith found that in those communities where proposed activities were clearly linked to local needs, the assistance providers developed strategies more closely approximating existing capabilities.[19] For Philip Berke and Timothy Beatley, an effective recovery planning approach is one that emphasizes the importance of fostering a good fit between the needs of those receiving assistance, the design of programs, and the capacity of organizations responsible for the delivery of assistance.[20]

Increasing our knowledge of the unique contributions of all members of the disaster recovery assistance network and the potential of those members to address the problems described in the disaster recovery assistance framework is a central goal of this book. Rather than maintain a singular focus on the post-disaster delivery of financially based programs, members of the assistance network, particularly the federal government, should engage in a more inclusive collaborative planning process that can help stakeholders gain a better understanding of what resources others can provide and, ultimately, how the provision of these resources can be better coordinated both before and after disasters.

Timing of Assistance

There is no doubt that the post-disaster timing of programs, including grants-in-aid, training, information exchange, and planning, can significantly influence the speed and quality of disaster recovery outcomes.[21] Disaster recovery is often framed by an ongoing tension: how to strike a balance between the speed of recovery and the time required to develop and implement sound recovery policies informed by ongoing deliberation.[22] All too often, communities, states, nations, and other members of the assistance network assume that time-consuming activities like planning and other consensus-building techniques are primarily employed in the wake of a disaster and therefore slow the overall pace of recovery. In practice, many stakeholders have resigned themselves to this reactive approach. But deliberation need not excessively slow recovery, particularly if it is practiced in advance of an event.

To better understand the potential variations in the temporal trajectory of recovery, both across networks and among individual stakeholder groups, we must better understand how and when assistance is provided. Each stakeholder in the network provides assistance at some point or points across the disaster recovery continuum that may include a combination of pre-event planning and post-event actions. The failure to coordinate the timing of assistance after a disaster can result in missed opportunities to meet pressing local needs. Perhaps most important is the effect of limited pre-event expenditures on capacity-building techniques, including plan making, public participation, and facilitated policy dialogue among members of the network. This can further degrade the effective use of recovery funding or the creation of a coherent recovery strategy, both of which can affect the speed, quality, and equitable distribution of recovery assistance after a disaster.[23]

Exhibit 1–2 illustrates a hypothetical scenario of disaster assistance provided by two members of the network—the federal government and nonprofits—across the disaster recovery continuum. The diagram provides a conceptual tool to help describe

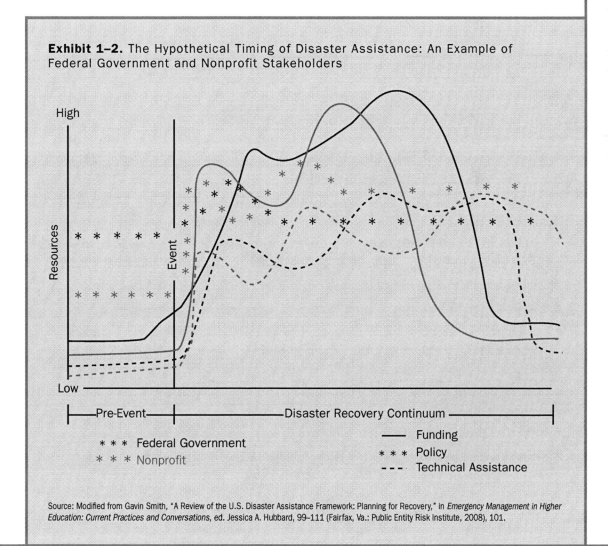

Exhibit 1–2. The Hypothetical Timing of Disaster Assistance: An Example of Federal Government and Nonprofit Stakeholders

Source: Modified from Gavin Smith, "A Review of the U.S. Disaster Assistance Framework: Planning for Recovery," in *Emergency Management in Higher Education: Current Practices and Conversations*, ed. Jessica A. Hubbard, 99–111 (Fairfax, Va.: Public Entity Risk Institute, 2008), 101.

and simplify the timing of assistance among stakeholders, which is highly complex, particularly within the context of the larger network. Thus, the lines of resource distribution over time are not intended to serve as a fine-grained analytical technique; rather, they are one of three dimensions within a larger framework that explains the disaster recovery process as practiced in the United States. For instance, the diagram aggregates the resources that are distributed by organizational type—in this case, the federal government and nonprofits. In reality, however, numerous federal agencies (e.g., the Federal Emergency Management Agency [FEMA], Department of Housing and Urban Development, U.S. Army Corps of Engineers) and nonprofits (faith-based organizations, foundations, and national and community-level associations) exist, each with its own set of resources and rules associated with the timing of disbursement.

A closer examination of the stakeholders in Exhibit 1–2 shows that nonprofit resources (identified in gray) are often provided before federal agencies have fully assessed the situation and begun to deliver their own resources (colored in black). The failure to effectively coordinate the timing of assistance has several negative consequences. For example, nonprofit organizations may help others repair or rebuild their homes in high-hazard areas to their pre-event condition—before more rigorous building codes and ordinances can be adopted, and before federal grant programs can be identified and procured that can offset some or all of the costs associated with these new standards. If the remaining members of the assistance network and the different types of assistance they provide are added to this scenario, it becomes evident just how complicated it is to coordinate the delivery of assistance over time, particularly if a community has not developed a pre-disaster recovery plan or attempts to do so in the aftermath of a disaster.

Exhibit 1–2 also reflects how the pre-event distribution of resources—disaster recovery policies; training, education, and outreach initiatives; and the funding needed to implement them—can play an important but often overlooked role in recovery. For instance, the federal government invests a great deal of time and energy into the pre-event formation of policies associated with the distribution of grant programs, whereas nonprofits are more prone to develop policies rapidly after an event on the basis of an assessment of local needs. Both approaches, which are grounded in organizational culture as well as in existing legal constraints, have important implications for recovery. To work with these conditions and those that are typical of the remaining members of the assistance network, a series of temporally coordinated pre- and post-disaster actions should be instituted. In addition, training in tasks associated with plan implementation—for example, grants administration; the assessment of hazard vulnerability, existing capabilities, and local needs; and disaster recovery exercises—are all best performed in advance of an event. In practice, however, it is also critically important to develop the capacity to deliver training programs post-disaster, given the low levels of pre-event planning for post-disaster recovery.

After disasters, stakeholder groups follow different—and often uncoordinated—resource distribution trajectories, as exemplified by the series of fluctuations shown in Exhibit 1–2. Resource distribution approaches may also be modified after a disaster depending on a number of factors—including, for instance, the reliance on rigid program rules that dictate grant funding cycles (described in Chapter 2), a frustration among nonprofits regarding the speed of public sector assistance, political influences that slow down or speed up the creation or modification of post-disaster policy making, access to donor funding, and the ability to coordinate volunteers. Again, Exhibit 1–2 represents just two organizational types within the larger network and therefore indicates both the complexity and the variability among the different stakeholder groups and how their makeup can influence the temporal nature of recovery.

Several researchers describe the disaster recovery process as an orderly series of post-disaster steps, each of which occurs sequentially over predictable periods of time. Robert Kates and David Pijawka, for example, propose four overlapping periods: Emergency, Restoration, Reconstruction I, and Reconstruction II (Exhibit 1–3 on page 20).[25] They describe assistance-driven activities associated with "capital stock," or the built environment, and "normal activities," or the daily actions of a community, and they use sample indicators to provide evidence of each phase and of the actions that demonstrate the transition between phases. Although a number of hazard scholars have challenged this model as being overly simplistic,[26] it provides a broad conceptual understanding of the post-disaster temporal aspects of recovery. When tested empirically with regard to the 1976 Friuli, Italy, earthquake, the model was found to represent a "typical rhythm."[27]

But while offering a helpful sketch of the general process of post-disaster recovery, this model does not provide the details necessary to critically evaluate the effect of different members of the network and the assistance they can provide. In reality, assistance is not distributed uniformly over time, nor is it easily categorized within the four phases that Kates and Pijawka identify. The recovery process can be more accurately characterized as a complex array of overlapping, often uncoordinated activities—the product of a lack of pre-disaster planning, a differential access to power and resources, pre- and post-disaster disputes, institutional deficiencies, and a reliance on adaptive post-event actions. This observation coincides with the more recent description of the disaster recovery process as "a cascade of seemingly diffused events, many of which may be interrelated."[29]

Exhibit 1–3. Disaster Recovery Timeline

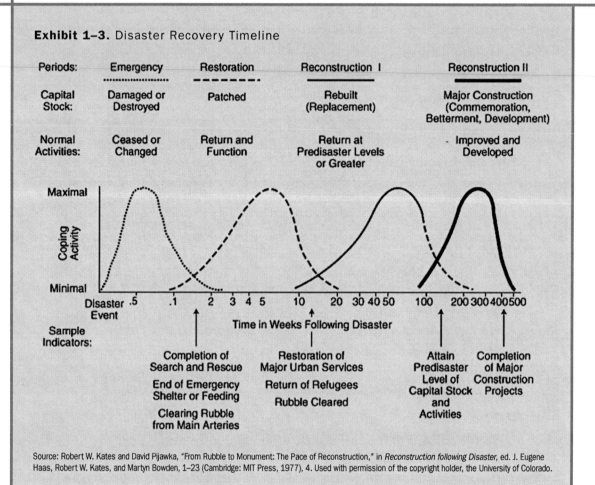

Periods:	Emergency	Restoration	Reconstruction I	Reconstruction II
Capital Stock:	Damaged or Destroyed	Patched	Rebuilt (Replacement)	Major Construction (Commemoration, Betterment, Development)
Normal Activities:	Ceased or Changed	Return and Function	Return at Predisaster Levels or Greater	Improved and Developed

Sample Indicators:

Completion of Search and Rescue

End of Emergency Shelter or Feeding

Clearing Rubble from Main Arteries

Restoration of Major Urban Services

Return of Refugees

Rubble Cleared

Attain Predisaster Level of Capital Stock and Activities

Completion of Major Construction Projects

Source: Robert W. Kates and David Pijawka, "From Rubble to Monument: The Pace of Reconstruction," in *Reconstruction following Disaster*, ed. J. Eugene Haas, Robert W. Kates, and Martyn Bowden, 1–23 (Cambridge: MIT Press, 1977), 4. Used with permission of the copyright holder, the University of Colorado.

The actual recovery process varies with each disaster, both temporally and spatially. For instance, Claire Rubin and colleagues found that reconstruction was occurring in some locations while debris management was under way in others. This reality, which has been corroborated in other studies of recovery, reflects both differing levels and types of damage and the unequal access to resources in the post-disaster environment, all of which can significantly affect the speed of recovery. In fact, recovery may take years or even decades to achieve. Damaged infrastructure, homes, and public buildings may never be repaired or replaced, and some segments of society may never fully recover economically (see Figure 1–1).

In the "Rocky Mountain Model of Disaster Recovery," shown in Exhibit 1–4 (on page 22), Rubin and Roy Popkin see the recovery process as analogous to a mountain range of three peaks, each rising in height as advancements are achieved over time.[32] Progress is obtained through identified "drivers" and "enablers" that facilitate the movement from one peak to the next. Movement from the first peak (minimalist/

Figure 1–1. Hurricane Katrina Memorial in Biloxi, Mississippi. The creation of post-disaster memorials represents what Haas, Kates, and Bowden refer to as part of the second phase of reconstruction. Below, the white cap on top of the black wall represents the height of the hurricane-induced storm surge, while the tile mosaic and walkway serve as a symbolic reminder of the forces that caused such destruction. The memorial also includes various personal items enclosed in a glass cabinet that were found in the community after the storm.

Photo by Gavin Smith.

restoration) to the second peak (foresight/mitigation) is linked to drivers such as a presidential disaster declaration, National Flood Insurance Program requirements, and state laws and regulations affecting recovery. Enabling factors include training courses, exercises, and peer exchanges. Foresight/mitigation involves the adoption of mitigation measures and other activities beyond traditional recovery programs. Movement from this second peak to the third peak (visionary/community betterment) is represented by community-based actions taken to improve residents' overall quality of life relative to that which existed before the disaster—for example, the linking of sustainable development and disaster resilience principles to recovery. Drivers are the same as those linking the movement from the first peak to the second; enablers now include the provision of technical information, specialized training, assistance from peers, and the reliance on consultants and recovery experts. The principal significance of the Rocky Mountain Model relative to the disaster recovery assistance framework is the inclusion of points of intervention by stakeholders that affect the speed and quality of recovery.

Several researchers provide insight into the role of interorganizational networks in recovery, but they have not applied that insight to an in-depth analysis of recovery processes as practiced by all members of the assistance network over time.[33] Rather, their emphasis has been placed on federal and local governments and on nonprofits. The role of state governments in recovery, for instance, remains surprisingly understudied.[34] In addition, the factors that foster change need further exploration. The framework described in the following chapters posits that relationships across the network can change—in part through policy dialogue, negotiation, and the act of plan making. Similarly, positions can become entrenched, hindering the ability to implement coordinated recovery strategies. As Philip Berke, Jack Kartez, and Dennis

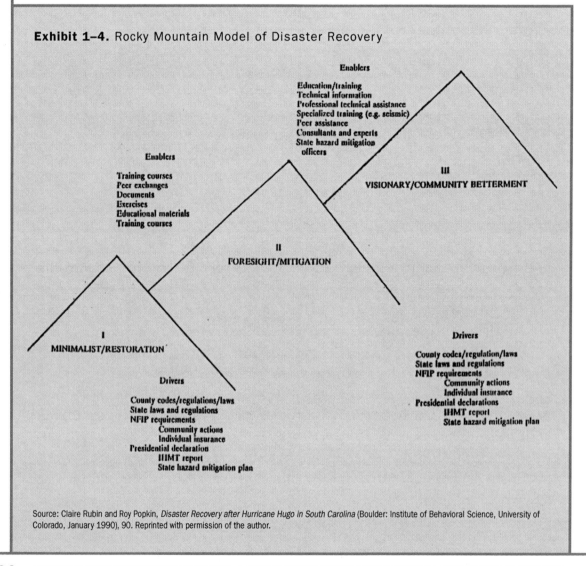

Exhibit 1–4. Rocky Mountain Model of Disaster Recovery

Enablers
Education/training
Technical information
Professional technical assistance
Specialized training (e.g. seismic)
Peer assistance
Consultants and experts
State hazard mitigation
    officers

Enablers
Training courses
Peer exchanges
Documents
Exercises
Educational materials
Training courses

III
VISIONARY/COMMUNITY BETTERMENT

II
FORESIGHT/MITIGATION

I
MINIMALIST/RESTORATION

Drivers
County codes/regulation/laws
State laws and regulations
NFIP requirements
        Community actions
        Individual insurance
Presidential declarations
        HMT report
        State hazard mitigation plan

Drivers
County codes/regulations/laws
State laws and regulations
NFIP requirements
        Community actions
        Individual insurance
Presidential declaration
        HMT report
        State hazard mitigation plan

Source: Claire Rubin and Roy Popkin, *Disaster Recovery after Hurricane Hugo in South Carolina* (Boulder: Institute of Behavioral Science, University of Colorado, January 1990), 90. Reprinted with permission of the author.

Wenger note, "Research is needed on how institutional arrangements act as incentives or barriers to adapting responses that meet local needs, capacities, and opportunities during recovery."[35]

Horizontal and Vertical Integration

The third dimension of the disaster assistance framework is the level of coordination within and across organizations. The typology of horizontal and vertical integration provides a tested means to explain these relationships as well as to demonstrate how improved interorganizational coordination can lead to a better understanding of local needs, the crafting of less prescriptive policies and funding mechanisms, and the improved timing of assistance.

Horizontal integration is measured by the strength of local relationships. It assumes that the involvement of local groups and individuals in the decision-making process is prevalent, strong, and sustained over time. Participants may include local government officials, quasi-governmental organizations, business owners, local financial institutions, the media, community and emergent groups, and area residents. Inclusive planning and policy-making strategies at the community level can strengthen horizontal relationships. For instance, when community members are actively engaged in formulating a disaster recovery strategy that includes a description of how resources (funding, policies, and technical assistance) will be used to achieve community goals and local needs, they are empowered to act rather than play the role of passive "disaster victims" on whom assistance is imposed. This is made evident in Chapter 3 and the case study of the Broadmoor community in New Orleans, which developed strong horizontal relationships, thereby avoiding what they refer to as the "negative cycle" of disaster recovery.

The current disaster recovery assistance framework, which is dominated by the delivery of post-disaster assistance, does not respect local capacities, needs, and the value of pre-event investments in building stronger institutions. The larger assistance network's unwillingness to invest the time needed—ideally, before an event occurs—to assess local needs and capabilities and couple that understanding with external assistance strategies that reflect a community's unique conditions effectively discounts the importance of locally grounded resources and the varied levels of horizontal integration found in communities.

A community with poor horizontal integration lacks the stakeholder involvement needed to develop a collective vision of recovery. Failing to include relevant local stakeholders who possess key resources, including a deep local knowledge base and trusted relationships, can limit the search for creative solutions and the development of enduring agreements and plans, and can lead to further fragmentation and conflict among those who have not been engaged in the decision-making process. Conflict can be particularly acute after a disaster when local government officials and other community-based members of the assistance network have not taken the time beforehand to develop resource-allocation strategies or describe available resources to those who have been directly affected by it. The development of strong pre-event relationships and the sharing of information—through both formal institutional vehicles such as a disaster recovery committee and informal information dissemination channels such as nonprofits, community groups, and faith-based organizations—can help position communities to better confront the substantial challenges of disaster recovery. However, without an equal commitment to building strong vertically integrated networks, communities are unable to mine external resources or effectively argue for changes in policies that are overly prescriptive or that fail to meet local needs.

Vertical integration is defined by strong connections between members of a community and organizations and networks that provide external assistance. Positive linkages to state and national organizations, for instance, can result in an enhanced power base and influence the ability to more effectively bridge the divide between overly prescriptive programs and local needs. The sidebar in Chapter 2 on North Carolina's disaster recovery assistance programs after Hurricane Floyd offers an example of strong vertical linkages between communities, the state's Division of Emergency Management, the governor's office, and FEMA. The strength of these relationships, forged from past disaster experiences, helped with the procurement of congressionally appropriated post-disaster grant funding as well as with the development and modification of federal rules that addressed local needs. The vertical integration between state and local governments also led to the development of twenty-two state programs that targeted needs that were not being met by federal agencies.

Strong vertical ties also apply to other members of the assistance network, including national foundations, corporations, national lending institutions, and insurance companies. Maintaining these vertical ties provides a way to effectively communicate local needs and secure needed resources. After Hurricane Katrina, for instance, the Mississippi Governor's Office of Recovery and Renewal sought to inform external assistance providers about the needs of coastal communities and to link those needs to organizations that were capable of addressing them (see the sidebar in Chapter 5 on the Governor's Commission on Recovery, Rebuilding, and Renewal).

Communities with weak vertical integration have little ability to influence the allocation of externally provided resources. Nor do they possess a good understanding of the many program rules across the network, which exacerbate the problem of external assistance providers dictating how assistance will be provided. Without a strong local advocate that is recognized by those providing externally based assistance, communities are left to struggle with the administration of narrowly defined, sometimes conflicting programs rather than being able to determine what is in their best interest. Compounding this problem is the inability to coordinate the timing of program delivery, which can also hinder the larger aims of a community.

Berke, Kartez, and Wenger use a horizontal and vertical integration typology to describe the level of interorganizational coordination present during the disaster recovery process (Exhibit 1–5).[38] Communities that maintain strong horizontal and vertical integration are referred to as Type 1 communities. These communities are likely to recover more quickly than the other three types and to do so in a way that addresses unique local needs. Type 2 communities have strong horizontal but weak vertical integration—for example, small, tight-knit rural communities that have not maintained relationships with state and federal agencies or with external members of the assistance network. Because of a limited understanding of recovery programs and policies, including their rules and timing of delivery, Type 2 communities depend on state emergency management agencies, private sector consultants, regional planning organizations, professional associations, and others to provide guidance. Type 3 communities are those with weak horizontal and strong vertical integration. They have a good understanding of the state and federal organizations responsible for providing assistance, but because they lack a community vision derived from meaningful public

Exhibit 1–5. Community Types by Degree of Horizontal and Vertical Integration

horizontal \ vertical	strong	weak
strong	type 1	type 2
weak	type 3	type 4

Source: Philip R. Berke, Jack Kartez, and Dennis Wenger, "Recovery after Disasters: Achieving Sustainable Development, Mitigation and Equity," *Disasters* 17, no. 2 (1993): 102. Reprinted with permission from the publisher, John Wiley and Sons.

participation and the identification of local needs, recovery efforts tend to be driven by highly prescriptive federal programs that are often ill-timed relative to the assistance delivered by other members of the network. Finally, Type 4 communities are characterized by weak horizontal and vertical integration and are thus the least equipped to face the challenges associated with disaster recovery. These communities can neither effectively seek outside assistance nor coordinate the internal actions necessary to implement recovery programs and plans.

TRANSFORMING THE DISASTER RECOVERY ASSISTANCE FRAMEWORK

The disaster recovery assistance framework is beset by different sets of program rules and local needs; the uncoordinated timing of assistance; and low levels of horizontal and vertical integration. These characteristics underlie the fundamental problems associated with disaster recovery in the United States. Upon further examination, however, they also indicate strategic actions—grounded in research findings and practice—that can be taken to effectively confront those problems. This book posits that plan making and alternative dispute resolution (ADR) principles provide the means to transform the framework over time. Describing how such a transformation occurs can expand our understanding of the recovery process, including its inherent weaknesses, and thus illuminate specific improvements that can be achieved and institutionalized through both the creation of new programs and policies and the modification of those that already exist.

Transforming the dimensions of the U.S. disaster recovery assistance framework means developing a better collective understanding of local needs and, through targeted collaborative planning techniques, systematically coordinating available resources in order to optimize funding, policies, and technical assistance. It also means developing stronger horizontal and vertical relationships across the assistance network through routine and extended interaction and cooperation among its members. However, given the obstacles that currently exist—limited organizational learning, an unwillingness to share information, and competitive rather than collaborative strategies—such a transformation will require significant modifications to current practice and policy.

The disaster recovery assistance framework and the process of its transformation are shown in Exhibit 1–6. The top graphic in the framework (1a–1c) shows how the various stakeholders in any local network can, through collaborative planning and the application of ADR techniques over time (the time series T1, T2, and T3), gain a greater understanding of local needs, as reflected in the shift of the diagonal line of stakeholders to a vertical position (i.e., T1–T2). This enhanced understanding, described in

Exhibit 1–6. Transforming the Disaster Recovery Assistance Framework

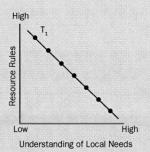

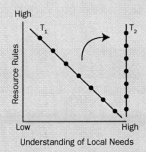

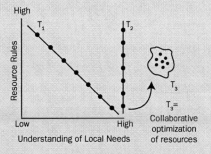

$T_3 =$ Collaborative optimization of resources

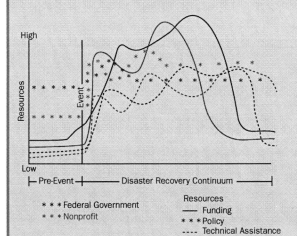

* * * Federal Government
* * * Nonprofit

Resources
—— Funding
* * * Policy
---- Technical Assistance

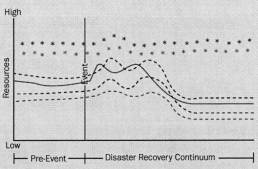

Chapter 8 as part of a recovery plan's procedural nature and codified in its fact base (i.e., local demographic conditions, settlement patterns, vulnerability to hazards, and the array of programs and policies available to confront the challenges associated with disaster recovery), can be used to undergird the plan's proposed actions as they are operationalized in multiparty agreements and policies that reflect the unique needs of the local community. Ideally these actions are undertaken in both the pre- and post-disaster time frame. Further, the plan, including associated agreements and policies, can and should emphasize the importance of acting collectively over time (i.e., T3) and thereby optimizing the use of the scarce resources (funding, policies, and technical assistance) that the network can provide.

As many of the case studies and sidebars in the chapters that follow will demonstrate, planning has the *potential* to positively influence the dimensions of the assistance framework over time—amending overly prescriptive policies, improving the link between pre- and post-event resources and local needs, coordinating the timing of disaster assistance, and increasing the level of horizontal and vertical integration. Unfortunately, since most members of the assistance network do not actively engage in pre-event planning for post-disaster recovery, how can we assume that planning can affect change across a network that has historically relied on a post-disaster, loosely defined adaptive strategy?

A planning-based approach is used to explore the conditions in which the disaster recovery assistance process can function as an interconnected system guided by an operational plan. Consensus building and ADR techniques provide the means for changing the procedural characteristics of the disaster assistance framework while institutionalizing a community's operational and spatial orientation to hazards through the development of disaster recovery plans. Plan making can be used to build an administrative, regulatory, and participatory tool that guides both the selection of policies reflecting local needs and conditions, and the identification of funding sources and technical assistance required for implementation. ADR techniques, such as policy dialogue, negotiated rule making, facilitation, and collaborative planning strategies, emphasize the importance of engaging in repeated interaction, identifying mutually beneficial outcomes, sharing information, and recognizing that the effective development and implementation of plans benefit from the active involvement of stakeholders across organizational networks. These techniques are also instrumental when addressing conflict-laden issues ranging from the equitable distribution of resources to the involvement of existing and emergent stakeholders in decision making and building institutions capable of sustaining action over time.

Astute communities can alter traditional assistance delivery mechanisms, forcing the federal government to provide additional resources or change the rules that govern assistance delivery. This is particularly true, for instance, where states have access to good pre- and post-disaster data as well as to political power. Other advantageous factors include organizations that strive to distribute assistance equitably, state officials who develop policy and program alternatives in response to narrowly defined federal assistance strategies, and community-based groups that emerge to coordinate the many resources that are available after a disaster.

While planning has been shown to play an important role in hazard management, including disaster recovery, much of what we know is derived from case study research, not a quantitatively driven comprehensive analysis of state and local plans and their effects on recovery outcomes. Moreover, existing policies and programs do not provide adequate support for disaster recovery planning. In fact, they create powerful disincentives to develop pre-event recovery plans. For example, the current emphasis on the delivery of post-disaster grant programs and the nonexistent commitment to build the collective capacity of the network to plan for recovery has effectively marginalized the role of planning and the land use planner. Viewing the recovery process as simply the post-disaster quest for financial assistance has resulted in skewed metrics of success and recovery outcomes that are shaped by largely prescriptive grant programs that do not meet local needs, are inappropriately timed, and do not foster horizontal or vertical integration. Also worth noting is that the current disaster recovery assistance delivery system is shaped by access to power and conflicts associated with the distribution of assistance. Politically powerful stakeholders often seek to maintain the status quo or benefit financially from reconstruction strategies that advance their own interests.

The issue of whether to invest in pre-event recovery plans in anticipation of a disaster that may or may not occur or to retain the emphasis on post-disaster assistance delivery reflects the importance of critically analyzing the timing of that assistance across the resource-based dimensions of the framework. The second time series graphics (2a and 2b) in Exhibit 1–6 represent both the traditional approach taken by a hypothetical collection of two members of the assistance network (initially displayed as Exhibit 1–2), and a modified approach emphasizing a greater commitment to funding for pre-event recovery plans, hazard mitigation measures, and other identified needs; the provision of technical assistance in the form of capacity-building initiatives (e.g., training, education, and outreach); and the formulation of policies that reflect the outcomes of a deliberative planning process that strives to better address local needs while taking advantage of the collective capacity of the larger network. In theory, these actions should shorten the post-disaster recovery continuum, reduce the amount of post-disaster resources needed, and enhance the quality of disaster recovery outcomes.

The third set of images in Exhibit 1–6 represents changes in the level of vertical and horizontal integration over time. The movement from a Type 4 community to a Type 1 community represents a linear progression that in reality may or may not follow this simplified expression of transforming the level of vertical and horizontal integration. Some communities may remain at a given level of integration with little change over time. In others, the movement from one type to another may not occur in a sequential manner; rather, a disaster may serve as a precipitating event that causes a multitype transformation. Communities may also regress, transforming from a Type 1 community to a Type 4 community as part of a breakdown in planning or the consolidation of power and post-disaster resources in the hands of a few organizations that do not embrace collaboration across the network. Thus the ability of planning to function effectively must account for the realities of the current system, including the limitations noted in this chapter and throughout the text.

LOOKING AHEAD

Considering the strong interorganizational impediments to planning, the creation of a new disaster recovery act is necessary to systematically address weaknesses in the current disaster recovery assistance framework. The elements of such an act are drawn from the literature and observations described in Chapters 2 through 7 and synthesized in Chapters 8 and 9. Chapter 10 critically analyzes the emerging National Disaster Recovery Framework in terms of its ability to address identified limitations. Emphasis is placed on substantially increasing the investment of resources (funding, policies, and technical assistance) in pre-event planning efforts and capacity-building initiatives that span the larger assistance network so as to better capitalize on the myriad resources, including a number of response-oriented programs found in emergency management that are available but remain untapped, underused, or uncoordinated with those engaged in disaster recovery. The long-term aim of this approach is to establish a national recovery coalition that strives to create an enduring culture of planning for recovery.

Chapters 2 through 7 discuss the members of the disaster assistance network and their roles in recovery through the lens of the three dimensions described in this chapter, beginning with the public sector. Scholars and practitioners continue to debate whether government, nonprofits, or the private sector should lead recovery efforts.[45] These chapters and the remainder of the text argues that the public sector should create the conditions in which collaboration among all members of the disaster assistance network is fostered through planning. The power of planning is most evident when a deliberative process is used to build and nurture relationships, identify outcomes that elicit mutual gains across stakeholder groups, and develop opportunities for collaboration to emerge.

Endnotes

1   Paul Friesema, *Aftermath: Communities after Natural Disasters* (Beverly Hills, Calif.: Sage, 1979); Frederick L. Bates and Walter G. Peacock, "Disasters and Social Change," in *The Sociology of Disasters,* ed. Russell R. Dynes, Bruna De Marchi, and Carlo Pelanda, 291–330 (Milan, Italy: Franco Angeli Press, 1987); Rutherford Platt, *Disasters and Democracy: The Politics of Extreme Natural Events* (Washington, D.C.: Island Press, 1999).

2   National Emergency Management Association (NEMA) and Council of State Governments (CSG), *Report on State Emergency Management Funding and Structures* (Lexington, Ky: NEMA/CSG 1998), 10.

3   Gavin Smith and Dennis Wenger, "Sustainable Disaster Recovery: Operationalizing an Existing Agenda," in *Handbook of Disaster Research,* ed. Havidan Rodriguez, Enrico Quarantelli, and Russell Dynes, 234–257 (New York: Springer, 2006).

4   Raymond Burby et al., *Sharing Environmental Risks: How to Control Government's Losses in Natural Disasters* (Boulder, Colo.: Westview Press, 1991).

5   Dale J. Roenigk, "Federal Disaster Relief and Local Government Financial Condition," *International Journal of Mass Emergencies and Disasters* 11, no. 2 (1993): 207–225.

6   Walter Gillis Peacock, Betty Hearn Morrow, and Hugh Gladwin, eds., *Hurricane Andrew: Ethnicity, Gender and the Sociology of Disasters* (Miami, Fla.: International Hurricane Center Laboratory for Social and Behavioral Research, 2000); Christopher L. Dyer, "The Phoenix Effect in Post-Disaster Recovery: An Analysis of the Economic Development Administration's Culture of Response after Hurricane Andrew," in *The Angry Earth: Disaster in Anthropological Perspective,* ed. Anthony Oliver-Smith and Susanna Hoffman, 278–300 (New York: Routledge, 1999); Dennis Mileti, *Disasters by Design: A Reassessment of Natural Hazards in the United States* (Washington, D.C.: Joseph Henry Press, 1999); Mark G. Welsh and Ann-Margaret Esnard, "Closing Gaps in Local Housing Recovery Planning for Disadvantaged Displaced Households," *Cityscape: A Journal of Policy Development and Research* 11, no. 3 (2009): 195–212.

7   Christine Ohlsen and Claire Rubin, "Planning for Disaster Recovery," *MIS Reports* (ICMA) 25, no. 7 (1993); Nancy Skinner and Bill Becker, *Pattonsburg, Missouri: On Higher Ground* (Washington, D.C.: President's Council on Sustainable Development, 1995); Jim Schwab, "Flood Case Study: Arnold, Missouri," in *Planning for Post-Disaster Recovery and Reconstruction,* Planning Advisory Service (PAS) Report 483/484 (Chicago: American Planning Association, 1998), 217–228.

8   Bates and Peacock, "Disasters and Social Change."

9   Smith and Wenger, "Sustainable Disaster Recovery."

10 Robert W. Kates, "Major Insights: A Summary and Recommendations," in *Reconstruction following Disaster,* ed. J. Eugene Haas, Robert W. Kates, and Martyn Bowden, 261–293 (Cambridge: MIT Press, 1977).

11 Philip R. Berke, Yan Song, and Mark Stevens, "Integrating Hazard Mitigation into New Urban and Conventional Developments," *Journal of Planning Education and Research* 28, no. 4 (2009): 441–455.

12 Gavin Smith, "Holistic Disaster Recovery: Creating a More Sustainable Future" (course developed for the Emergency Management Institute Higher Education Project, Federal Emergency Management Agency, 2004), available at training.fema.gov/EMIWeb/edu/sdr.asp.

13 Gavin Smith, "Lessons from the United States: Planning for Post-Disaster Recovery and Reconstruction," *Australasian Journal of Disaster and Trauma Studies* 2010–1 (2010), www.massey.ac.nz/~trauma/issues/2010-1/smith.htm (accessed July 9, 2010); Smith, "Holistic Disaster Recovery"; Smith and Wenger, "Sustainable Disaster Recovery."

14 Robert G. Paterson, "The Third Sector: Evolving Partnerships in Hazard Mitigation," in *Cooperating with Nature: Confronting Natural Hazards with Land Use Planning for Sustainable Communities,* ed. Raymond Burby, 203–230 (Washington, D.C.: Joseph Henry Press, 1998).

15 Richard T. Sylves, "Federal Emergency Management Comes of Age: 1979–2001," in *Emergency Management: The American Experience, 1900–2005,* ed. Claire Rubin, 111–159 (Fairfax, Va.: Public Entity Risk Institute [PERI], 2007); Naomi Klein, *The Shock Doctrine: The Rise of Disaster Capitalism* (New York: Henry Holt and Company, 2007).

16 William F. Shughart, "Katrinanomics: The Politics and Economics of Disaster Relief," *Public Choice* 127 (April 2006): 31–53.

17 Barbara E. Harrell-Bond, *Imposing Aid: Emergency Assistance to Refugees* (Oxford: Oxford University Press, 1986); Mary B. Anderson and Peter Woodrow, *Rising from the Ashes: Development Strategies in Times of Disaster* (Boulder, Colo.: Westview Press, 1989).

18 Robert Geipel, *Disaster and Reconstruction: The Friuli (Italy) Earthquakes of 1976* (London: Allen and Unwin, 1982).

19 Anthony Oliver-Smith, "Post-Disaster Housing Reconstruction and Social Inequality: A Challenge to Policy and Practice," *Disasters* 14, no. 1 (1990): 7–19.

20 Philip R. Berke and Timothy Beatley, *After the Hurricane: Linking Recovery to Sustainable Development in the Caribbean* (Baltimore: Johns Hopkins University Press, 1997).

21 Claire B. Rubin, "The Community Recovery Process in the United States after a Major Natural Disaster," *International Journal of Mass Emergencies and Disasters* 3, no. 2 (1985): 9–28; Robert B. Olshansky et al., "Planning for the Rebuilding of New Orleans," *Journal of the American Planning Association* 74, no. 3 (2008): 273–287; Robert B. Olshansky and Stephanie Chang, "Planning for Disaster Recovery: Emerging Research Needs and Challenges," in special issue, *Progress in Planning* 72, no. 4 (2009): 200–209.

22 Robert B. Olshansky, "Planning after Hurricane Katrina," *Journal of the American Planning Association* 72, no. 2 (2006): 147–153.

23 Marla Nelson, Renia Ehrenfeucht, and Shirley Laska, "Planning, Plans, and People: Professional Expertise, Local Knowledge, and Governmental Action in Post-Hurricane Katrina New Orleans," *Cityscape: A Journal of Policy Development and Research* 9, no. 3 (2007): 23–52.

24 J. Eugene Haas, Robert W. Kates, and Martyn Bowden, *Reconstruction following Disaster* (Cambridge, Mass.: MIT Press, 1977); Robert W. Kates and David Pijawka, "From Rubble to Monument: The Pace of Reconstruction," in *Reconstruction following Disaster,* 1–23; and Claire B. Rubin and Daniel G. Barbee, "Disaster Recovery and Hazard Mitigation: Bridging the Intergovernmental Gap," special issue, *Public Administration Review* 45 (1985): 57–63.

25 Kates and Pijawka, "From Rubble to Monument."

26 See Enrico L. Quarantelli, *A Review of the Literature in Disaster Recovery Research* (Newark: Disaster Research Center, University of Delaware, 1989); Richard C. Wilson, *The Loma Prieta Earthquake: What One City Learned* (Washington, D.C.: International City Management Association, 1991); Philip R. Berke, Jack Kartez, and Dennis Wenger, "Recovery after Disasters: Achieving Sustainable Development, Mitigation and Equity," *Disasters* 17, no. 2 (1993): 93–109; Mark Sullivan, "Integrated Recovery Management: A New Way of Looking at a Delicate Process," *Australian Journal of Emergency Management* 18, no. 2 (2003) 4–27; Lawrence J. Vale and Thomas J. Campanella, *The Resilient City: How Modern Cities Recover from Disasters* (New York: Oxford University Press, 2005); Smith and Wenger, "Sustainable Disaster Recovery."

27 Robert Geipel, *Long-Term Consequences of Disasters: The Reconstruction of Friuli, Italy, in its International Context, 1976–1988* (New York: Springer-Verlag, 1991), 53.

28 Robert C. Bolin and Patricia A. Bolton, "Recovery in Nicaragua and the USA," *International Journal of Mass Emergencies and Disasters* 1, no. 1 (1983): 125–144; Daniel J. Alesch et al., *Organizations at Risk: What Happens When Small Businesses and Not-for-Profits Encounter Natural Disasters* (Fairfax, Va.: PERI, 2001); Berke, Kartez, and Wenger, "Recovery after Disasters."

29 Daniel J. Alesch, Lucy A. Arendt, and James N. Holly, *Managing for Long-Term Community Recovery in the Aftermath of Disaster* (Fairfax, Va.: PERI, 2009), 20.

30 Claire B. Rubin, Martin D. Saperstein, and Daniel G. Barbee, *Community Recovery from a Major Natural Disaster* (Boulder: Institute of Behavioral Science, University of Colorado, 1985).

31 Oliver-Smith, "Post-Disaster Housing Reconstruction and Social Inequality."

32 Claire Rubin and Roy Popkin, *Disaster Recovery after Hurricane Hugo in South Carolina* (Boulder: Institute of Behavioral Science, University of Colorado, 1990).

33 Rubin, "The Community Recovery Process"; Rubin and Barbee, "Disaster Recovery and Hazard Mitigation"; Berke, Kartez, and Wenger, *"Recovery after Disasters";* and Berke and Beatley, *After the Hurricane.*

34 Gavin Smith and Victor Flatt, "Assessing the Disaster Recovery Planning Capacity of the State of North Carolina" (research brief, Institute for Homeland Security Solutions, Durham, N.C., January 2011), 1–8.

35 Berke, Kartez, and Wenger, "Recovery after Disasters," 98.

36 Peter May and Walter Williams, *Disaster Policy Implementation: Managing Programs under Shared Governance* (New York: Plenum Press, 1986); Berke, Kartez, and Wenger, "Recovery after Disasters."

37 Rebecca Hummel and Douglas Ahlers, *The Broadmoor Guide for Planning and Implementation* (Cambridge: Belfer Center for Science and International Affairs, John F. Kennedy School of Government, Harvard University, 2007) 38.

38 Berke, Kartez, and Wenger, "Recovery after Disasters."

39 Smith and Wenger, "Sustainable Disaster Recovery."

40 Ibid.

41 Michael Neuman, "Images as Institution Builders: Metropolitan Planning in Madrid," *European Planning Studies* 4, no. 3 (1996): 293–312; Smith and Wenger, "Sustainable Disaster Recovery."

42 Steven D. Stehr, "Community Recovery and Reconstruction following Disasters," in *Handbook of Crisis and Emergency Management,* ed. Ali Farazmand, 419–431 (Boca Raton, Fla.: CRC Press, 2001).

43 Smith, "Holistic Disaster Recovery."

44 Philip R. Berke and Dennis Wenger, *Linking Hurricane Disaster Recovery to Sustainable Development Strategies: Montserrat, West Indies* (College Station, Tex.: Hazard Reduction and Recovery Center, Texas A&M University, 1991); Rubin and Barbee, "Disaster Recovery and Hazard Mitigation"; Bates and Peacock, "Disasters and Social Change"; Oliver-Smith, "Post-Disaster Housing Reconstruction and Social Inequality."

45 Governor's Commission on Recovery, Rebuilding, and Renewal, *After Katrina: Building Back Better Than Ever* (Jackson, Miss., 2006), www.mississippirenewal.com/documents/Governors_Commission_Report.pdf; Steven Horowitz, *Making Hurricane Response More Effective: Lessons from the Private Sector and the Coast Guard during Katrina,* Mercatus Policy Series, Policy Comment No. 17 (Fairfax, Va.: George Mason University, March 2008); Paterson, "The Third Sector"; Berke and Beatley, *After the Hurricane;* Nelson, Ehrenfeucht, and Laska, "Planning, Plans, and People"; Shughart, "Katrinanomics."

Chapter 2

The Public Sector: Federal, State, and Local Governments

The effects of wind and water are dramatically evident following Hurricane Katrina in the Ninth Ward of New Orleans.

Photo by Donn Young.

A WIDELY HELD BELIEF AMONG MEMBERS of the disaster recovery assistance network is that responsibility for coordinating disaster recovery efforts falls squarely on the shoulders of federal, state, and local government officials. In practice, however, those who assume leadership roles in recovery are not limited to members of the public sector. Another reality is that the actions of two of the three members of the public sector—namely, state and local governments—are strongly influenced by narrowly defined federal programs that are delivered in the aftermath of an event, remain largely uncoordinated, and frequently fail to account for local needs.[1] Moreover, the often all-consuming effort required by states and localities to administer these programs limits their collaborative activities, including pre- and post-event event planning for recovery.

While the stated intent of the National Response Framework (NRF) is to coordinate the activities of the public sector, the framework itself is more accurately characterized as a list of single-purpose programs. The Post-Katrina Emergency Reform Act of 2006, which was passed in reaction to problems exposed after that hurricane, required the creation of a national disaster recovery strategy to supplement the NRF. That strategy, now referred to as the National Disaster Recovery Framework (NDRF), is intended to better address local needs, clarify roles and responsibilities, and describe disaster-resistant building techniques. Since the NDRF is currently being completed, it will be discussed in Chapter 10 as part of a closing argument for the creation of the proposed Disaster Recovery Act.

Addressing issues germane to recovery requires the active involvement of local officials. These are the individuals who not only have a sound understanding of local needs and an intimate knowledge of the social, economic, environmental, institutional, and political conditions in the area, but also have access to important community-level resources and can influence pre- and post-disaster land use choices through land use planning techniques. But often left unresolved is who at the local level should take responsibility for developing a long-term recovery plan—or, for that matter, managing long-term recovery efforts. Elected officials are often under intense pressure to return things to normal, even if this means circumventing important issues that take time to resolve. Identifying needs after a disaster is often reduced to a daily process of "putting out fires" rather than addressing the root cause of those needs. Local emergency managers have historically focused on response-oriented activities, and land use planners often consider disaster-related issues to be outside their professional expertise or purview. Thus, the development of a pre-event recovery plan that systematically addresses issues associated with housing, economic redevelopment, infrastructure, and land use is often neglected until a disaster actually strikes.

Effective disaster recovery benefits from the use of collaborative planning strategies that span the larger assistance network and are crafted in advance of an event. An in-depth understanding of local needs evolves over time, and the ability to build strong horizontal and vertical integration across the network benefits from the adoption of a time-intensive procedural approach that is difficult to attain after a disaster. However, developing coordinated strategies that confront narrowly defined program rules, local needs, and the timing of funding and technical assistance while also fostering strong horizontal and vertical integration across the disaster assistance network requires a level of pre-event collective action among government officials at all levels that is not prevalent in the current system. When public sector stakeholders are focused on administering program-related tasks, it is unrealistic to expect them to spend the requisite time to forge new relationships across the disaster recovery assistance network.

FEDERAL GOVERNMENT

The NRF describes the delivery of disaster recovery assistance as a bottom-up approach. But while this description may apply to the disaster declaration process described in the accompanying sidebar on page 38, the design of federal programs has unduly influenced state and local pre- and post-disaster recovery activities and has actually resulted in a largely top-down system.

Current Disaster Policy

Federal disaster policy is best characterized as a series of disconnected programs without an integrative policy framework guiding pre- and post-event decision making. Program isolationism exists within and across federal agencies, resulting in duplicative efforts, the uncoordinated timing of assistance, counterproductive funding strategies, and a widespread failure to meet local needs following disasters. Further hindering the effective distribution of assistance is the limited involvement of federal agencies in pre-event planning and capacity-building efforts that span larger assistance networks that differ over time and space.

A related but seldom discussed aspect of federal assistance is how its delivery differs across disasters. As noted in Chapter 1, the placement of a particular stakeholder along the diagonal line shown in Exhibit 1–1 varies, depending on the stakeholder's location, type, and level of disaster experience, and nature of organizational culture and leadership, as well as on the manner in which staff interpret federal policy and program initiatives. In addition, placement of those nodes along the diagonal line can change over time, including before or during the disaster recovery process. Planning, the exchange of information, and the development of such procedural forums as recovery committees are all examples of activities that can influence these node shifts. Thus, depending on the context, stakeholders may assume different roles at different times within the disaster recovery process.

Hazards researchers, practitioners, and the media often discuss the disaster recovery process within a federal context. This has numerous problematic implications. First, research focused on the role of the state in recovery, for example, remains limited; and most community-level recovery research in the United States, which tends to focus on case studies, was conducted in the 1980s and 1990s, although Hurricane Katrina spawned a renewed interest in this topic. Second, the media's widespread

The Politics of Disaster

After an event, local officials conduct a preliminary assessment of physical damages—in essence, a quick visual "windshield survey." The information they gather, which they submit to state officials, is used to deploy state assets and determine whether a state declaration of disaster is warranted. If the state believes that the level of damages exceeds its ability to respond, it may seek a federal (major) disaster declaration, whereby the governor's office submits a request to the president of the United States.

Upon receiving a request for a declaration of disaster, the Federal Emergency Management Agency assesses the damage to determine whether monetary losses to housing and infrastructure meet a predetermined per capita threshold. This measure is typically assessed on a county-by-county basis. If the president deems that federal assistance is needed to help state and local governments, an emergency declaration is made. In some cases, such as a major hurricane whose landfall is imminent, the president may declare several counties part of a disaster area in advance of the storm, thereby allowing for the predeployment of resources and staff to the targeted area.

Federal disaster assistance was originally predicated on the notion of providing supplementary aid once local and state abilities were exceeded. Over time, however, the overall practice of distributing federal assistance after an event has become increasingly discretionary, muddying the initial concept. Examples include President Jimmy Carter's declaration of a major disaster after the identification and cleanup of hazardous waste near Love Canal in 1979; his emergency declaration associated with the Mariel boatlift of Cuban evacuees in 1980;[1] and President George W. Bush's emergency declaration of the states located in the debris field after the space shuttle *Columbia* crashed in 2003. Now the concept of providing federal aid only after local and state resources have been exhausted is referred to by one hazard scholar as the "supplemental myth."[2]

The politicization of the declaration process has resulted in an increased number of federal declarations.[3] Even though a major disaster declaration is predicated on an established threshold of damages per capita, creative assessments have led to a number of questionable disaster designations. Because a disaster declaration brings with it access to federal funding that would otherwise not be available, disasters can mean political patronage to affected states and local communities. If additional money (beyond that available under existing federal programs) is sought through a congressional appropriation, lawmakers are often unwilling to question it as they realize that their own constituents may seek similar assistance at some time in the future.

The declaration process also demonstrates the effect that disasters can have on state

criticism of federal recovery efforts following disasters underscores a general lack of understanding about the recovery process and how assistance is provided. Reporters usually focus on the activities of the Federal Emergency Management Agency (FEMA), the U.S. Army Corps of Engineers, and other federal agencies, without undertaking an equally rigorous analysis of the roles that states and local governments play in both successful and unsuccessful attempts to foster collective action, including pre-event planning for post-disaster recovery.

and federal political systems and elected officials. President George H. W. Bush was blamed for the lack of speed with which assistance was provided following Hurricane Andrew in 1992; in reality, however, the state request was slow to come from the governor of Florida. The apparent unresponsiveness of the federal government, encapsulated by a local official's widely reported refrain of "where's the cavalry?," played a role in the subsequent election of Bill Clinton.[4] When Clinton was governor of Arkansas, he quickly learned the political value of federal assistance, a lesson based in part on his own experience during the Carter administration meeting the challenges associated with housing the Cuban refugees in his state.[5] Thus, upon assuming the office of president, he pursued a more aggressive pre-disaster deployment of federal resources.

The unresponsiveness of the federal government again became an issue during Hurricane Katrina in 2005, ultimately contributing to growing public opposition to the policies of the George W. Bush administration and to the election of Barack Obama in 2008. The federal government took the much of the blame, but Louisiana governor Kathleen Blanco also faced severe criticism for her ineffective leadership during the crisis,[6] and that criticism ultimately factored into her decision not to seek reelection.

Conversely, taking effective and decisive action can help one's political career. The Mississippi River floods in 1927 covered a 27,000-square-mile area from Illinois to the Gulf of Mexico, dislocating almost a million people. As this occurred before the federal declaration process was initiated, President Calvin Coolidge appointed Commerce Secretary Herbert Hoover as chairman of a committee comprising five presidential cabinet secretaries to address the flood response and recovery effort. Hoover aggressively pursued his assignment and purposefully used the media to advance his career. A Stanford-trained engineer, he applied the emerging concept of scientific management to break down tasks into smaller actions, earning the dual monikers of "the Great Humanitarian" and "the Great Engineer."[7] Following glowing reports in the media, Hoover further expanded on his exploits, ultimately using the political machine he created during the flood to run for and win the presidency.

1   Claire B. Rubin, ed., *Emergency Management: The American Experience, 1900–2005* (Fairfax, Va.: Public Entity Risk Institute, 2007).

2   Rutherford Platt, *Disasters and Democracy: The Politics of Extreme Natural Events* (Washington, D.C.: Island Press, 1999), 17–22.

3   Ibid.; Richard Sylves, *Disaster Policy and Politics: Emergency Management and Homeland Security* (Washington, D.C.: CQ Press, 2008), 84.

4   Sylves, *Disaster Policy and Politics*.

5   William Jefferson Clinton, *My Life*, vol. 1, *The Early Years* (New York: Vintage Books, 2005), 360-367.

6   Douglas Brinkley, *The Great Deluge: Hurricane Katrina, New Orleans, and the Mississippi Gulf Coast* (New York: Harper Collins, 2006).

7   John Barry, Rising Tide: *The Great Mississippi Flood of 1927 and How It Changed America* (New York: Simon and Schuster, 1997), 262.

The lack of locally derived and championed principles tied to clearly defined goals and objectives hinders recovery efforts because local governments perceive that they have a limited set of options. The strategies, programs, and policies of federal agencies strongly influence the decisions and choices of other aid providers, particularly those at the state and local government levels, while state and local governments have limited influence over the decisions made by federal agencies (although some communities and states have discovered the power of negotiation, as discussed in the sidebars in Chapter 8 on the Charlotte–Mecklenburg County, North Carolina, Floodplain

Mapping Program and on post-disaster resource allocation disputes after Hurricane Floyd in North Carolina). Rather than seeking ways to maximize the distribution of assistance across the network of providers through pre-event planning, communities often adopt reactionary, adaptive programs and strategies driven by federal criteria.

The limited investment of resources in pre-event capacity-building strategies, including planning and alternative dispute resolution techniques, results in a greater dependence on federal funding when a major disaster occurs. It also means that communities are less prepared for smaller events that do not merit federal assistance given that they have not engaged in a meaningful pre-event planning process and thus lack an understanding of both the local needs that may emerge and the limitations of the disaster assistance framework to meet them. Nor is there an incentive for them to proactively address pre-event planning for post-disaster recovery as the federal government has provided increased levels of assistance following disasters over time, especially in areas subject to repeated events.[9] The Disaster Mitigation Act of 2000, which requires the development of pre-disaster state and local hazard mitigation plans, offers important clues about ways in which pre-event disaster recovery planning can reduce this high level of dependence on post-disaster federal assistance.[10] These conditions are discussed in Chapters 8 and 9.

National Response Framework

The NRF is intended to serve as the federal "plan" for recovery until the NDRF is enacted. Originally termed the National Response Plan, the NRF contains seven primary components:

- The core document, which describes the NRF's guiding principles and the roles and responsibilities of participating organizations and agencies
- Fifteen emergency support functions (ESFs), each of which addresses specific response and recovery activities (see Exhibit 2–1)
- Support annexes, which focus on the administrative requirements of the ESFs and describe processes intended to support planning operations
- Incident annexes, which describe the roles of stakeholders across different event types
- National planning scenarios, which emphasize a more in-depth analysis of needs and identify ways to develop plans addressing high-consequence events
- Strategic guidance, which defines national priorities and existing capabilities that are used to support the creation of scenario-based plans
- Playbooks, which are a series of checklists for use by high-level Department of Homeland Security officials to coordinate the response to identified high-consequence scenarios.

Exhibit 2–1. National Response Framework, Emergency Support Functions and Coordinators

ESF #1: Transportation
ESF Coordinator: Department of Transportation

- Federal and civil transportation support
- Transportation safety
- Restoration and recovery of transportation infrastructure
- Movement restrictions
- Damage and impact assessment

ESF #2: Communications
ESF Coordinator: Department of Homeland Security (DHS) (National Communications System)

- Coordination with telecommunications industry
- Restoration and repair of communications infrastructure
- Protection, restoration, and sustainment of national cyber and information technology resources
- Oversight of communications within the federal incident management and response structures

ESF #3: Public Works and Engineering
ESF Coordinator: Department of Defense (Army Corps of Engineers)

- Infrastructure protection and emergency repair
- Infrastructure restoration
- Engineering services, construction management
- Critical Infrastructure liaison

ESF #4: Firefighting
ESF Coordinator: Department of Agriculture (Forest Service)

- Firefighting activities on Federal lands
- Resource support to rural and urban firefighting operations

ESF #5: Emergency Management
ESF Coordinator: DHS (Federal Emergency Management Agency [FEMA])

- Coordination of incident management and response efforts
- Issuance of mission assignments
- Resources and human capital
- Incident action planning
- Financial management

ESF #6: Mass Care, Emergency Assistance, Housing and Human Services
ESF Coordinator: DHS (FEMA)

- Mass care
- Disaster housing
- Human services

ESF #7: Resource Support
ESF Coordinator: General Services Administration

- Resource support (facility space, office equipment and supplies, contracting services, etc.)

ESF #8: Public Health and Medical Services
ESF Coordinator: Department of Health and Human Services

- Public health
- Medical
- Mental health services
- Mortuary services

ESF #9: Search and Rescue
ESF Coordinator: DHS (FEMA)

- Life-saving assistance
- Search and rescue operations

ESF #10: Oil and Hazardous Materials Response
ESF Coordinator: Environmental Protection Agency

- Oil and hazardous materials (chemical, biological, radiological, etc.) response
- Environmental safety and short- and long-term cleanup

ESF #11: Agriculture and Natural Resources
ESF Coordinator: Department of Agriculture

- Nutrition assistance
- Animal and plant disease and pest response

continued on page 43

The NRF does not substantially improve upon the former National Response Plan, integrate federal disaster policy, or adequately describe the role of FEMA's emerging long-term recovery planning initiative. Its key weakness—namely, its failure to address long-term recovery—is discussed throughout this chapter and further clarified in Chapters 8, 9, and 10 relative to accepted planning principles, the draft NDRF, and the proposed Disaster Recovery Act.

A review of the NRF and its ESFs finds that long-term recovery and reconstruction activities among federal agencies remain ill-defined and largely unassigned. ESF-14, Long-Term Community Recovery, is intended to improve the coordination of federal agency programs and help communities to develop post-disaster recovery plans (see Figure 2–1). But while it represents a first step toward the adoption of recovery planning procedures, it has been troubled by a lack of support within FEMA and by limited standing among federal and state agency staff in the field after a disaster. Moreover, most of the ESF-14 personnel deployed after a major federally declared disaster are private sector contractors, and although many of them are practicing planners, they may have little or no experience in the post-disaster environment. Although this is changing as the ESF-14 cadre continues to gain experience as the program matures. Since the program is triggered by a federal disaster declaration, these personnel are not sent to help states and local governments create pre-event recovery plans. Nevertheless, with the advent of the NDRF, the potential exists to build a network of more experienced practitioners over time that stand ready to deliver assistance both before and after a disaster.

Figure 2–1.
Emergency Support Function-14 (ESF-14) staff works in the Joint Field Office following the spring 2010 floods in Nashville, Tennessee.

Source: Federal Emergency Management Agency.

STATE GOVERNMENT

State emergency management agencies tend to be housed in one of four organizational locations: (1) the governor's office, (2) a division or bureau within a civilian department, (3) a division or bureau under the adjutant general, or (4) a division or bureau under the state police.[13] The location of the agency can shape its organizational culture, the roles assumed by its employees, and its political standing among other state agencies.

The Florida Division of Emergency Management, for example, was once located within the Bureau of Community Affairs, which also houses the economic development, coastal management, and growth management divisions. The physical location of these divisions in the same bureau led to a greater level of program and policy connectivity than is often found in other states. Tangible results included the development of enhanced building codes to account for natural hazard-related forces and the creation of a state reinsurance program. While the Florida Division of Emergency Management is slated to move into the Governor's Office, the more recent development of a state-level disaster recovery planning effort has effectively linked the management of coastal resources and local land use planning (see the sidebar on page 44).

continued from page 41

- Food safety and security
- Natural and cultural resources and historic properties protection
- Safety and well-being of pets

ESF #12: Energy
ESF Coordinator: Department of Energy

- Energy infrastructure assessment, repair, and restoration
- Energy industry coordination
- Energy forecast

ESF #13: Public Safety and Security
ESF Coordinator: Department of Justice

- Facility and resource security
- Security planning and technical resource assistance
- Public safety and security support
- Support to access, traffic and crowd control

ESF #14: Long-Term Community Recovery
ESF Coordinator: DHS (FEMA)

- Social and economic community impact assessment
- Long-term community recovery assistance to States, local governments, and the private sector

ESF #15: External Affairs
ESF Coordinator: DHS

- Emergency public information and protective action guidance
- Media and community relations
- Congressional and international affairs
- Tribal and insular affairs

Source: Federal Emergency Management Agency (FEMA), *National Response Framework* (Washington, D.C.: FEMA, Department of Homeland Security, January 2008), www.fema.gov/pdf/emergency/nrf/nrf-core.pdf.

The organizational structure of state emergency management response teams, the interagency groups responsible for response and recovery activities, tends to mirror that of the federal ESFs. As a result, states face difficulties similar to those experienced by the federal government when attempting to address long-term recovery. And while most state emergency management agencies have assigned staff to support and coordinate with federal ESFs 1–13 and 15, very few have developed a state counterpart to

The State of Florida's Post-Disaster Redevelopment Planning Initiative

Florida statutes require that all 203 coastal counties and municipalities develop a post-disaster redevelopment plan. After the 2004 and 2005 hurricane seasons, which saw five hurricanes strike the Florida coast (Charley, Frances, and Jeanne in 2004; Katrina and Wilma in 2005), the state realized that it needed to develop more explicit disaster recovery planning guidance for coastal counties and municipalities. As a result, the Florida Coastal Management Program, working with the state Department of Community Affairs (DCA), Division of Community Planning, began the Florida Post-Disaster Redevelopment Planning Initiative.

The first phase of the program, which started in 2007, involved the development of draft guidelines. These guidelines were based on a review of the disaster recovery planning literature, an assessment of other local recovery plans, and suggestions from a state focus group comprising federal, state, and local government officials; university faculty; and Florida planning organizations. According to the focus group,

> A Post-Disaster Redevelopment Plan identifies policies, operational strategies, and roles and responsibilities for implementation that will guide decisions that affect long-term recovery and redevelopment of the community after a disaster. The plan emphasizes seizing opportunities for hazard mitigation and community improvement consistent with the goals of the local comprehensive plan and with full participation of the citizens. Recovery topics addressed in the plan should include business resumption and economic redevelopment, housing repair and reconstruction, infrastructure restoration and mitigation, short-term recovery actions that affect long-term redevelopment, sustainable land use, environmental restoration, and financial considerations as well as other long-term recovery issues identified by the community.[1]

In the second phase, which is currently under way, the guidelines are being applied to five counties and one municipality. The DCA chose a sample of coastal and inland jurisdictions as well as a municipality in order to assess the merits of multijurisdictional plans versus plans developed at the municipal level. A working group has also emerged to share information and consider regional coordination measures. Key topics include land use, housing, administration of financial resources, environmental restoration, health and social services, and economic redevelopment. Each participating jurisdiction has been assigned a consultant who will assist in coordinating the process and developing the plan. Stakeholder groups have also been formed to lead the overall planning effort. The pilot communities are intended to serve as models for the rest of the state and possibly the nation.

The third phase assesses the plans that used the guidelines during their development and will utilize the findings to modify the guidance materials. The *Post-Disaster Redevelopment Planning: A Guide for Florida Communities,*[2] which further clarifies recommended planning processes across different types of Florida communities, is used to conduct regional workshops designed to educate communities about the nature of the redevelopment process, describe the planning requirements, and provide information about available funding. The third phase will also recommend whatever changes or new legislation is necessary to codify disaster redevelopment planning requirements.

Source: Florida Department of Community Affairs, Division of Community Planning, at www.dca.state.fl.us/fdcp/DCP/PDRP.

1 Florida Division of Community Planning, "Post-Disaster Redevelopment Planning: Overview," at www.dca.state.fl.us/fdcp/dcp/PDRP/overview.cfm.

2 Florida Department of Community Affairs, Florida Division of Emergency Management, *Post-Disaster Redevelopment Planning: A Guide for Florida Communities* (2010), www.dca.state.fl.us/fdcp/dcp/PDRP/Files/PDRPGuide.pdf.

work with ESF-14 staff and their contractors. Virginia and Mississippi, which are in the process of developing a comparable ESF-14, are two of the few known states to do so; in Mississippi after Hurricane Katrina, the Governor's Office of Recovery and Renewal fulfilled this role. For other states, however, the resultant federal-local interaction on recovery planning activities exemplifies a larger gap in vertical integration among local, state, and federal agencies, leading to increased levels of miscommunication and conflict. In the aftermath of federally declared disasters, state emergency management agencies are often overwhelmed, lacking the resources needed to match FEMA staffing levels. In addition, their recovery capabilities in most cases are limited to grants managers and often do not include people with the planning skills and expertise that is particularly relevant to long-term recovery.

Despite the many important roles that they play, state agencies are the least understood member of the public sector in recovery. State governments formulate state policy; coordinate the delivery of assistance; and provide training, education, and outreach programs following disasters. Yet their involvement in disaster recovery varies widely because of different levels of capability and commitment among emergency management organizations and other state agencies tasked with recovery- and reconstruction-related activities. A state's disaster recovery capabilities can be assessed in numerous ways, including the number of experienced state personnel dedicated to long-term recovery-related activities, the degree to which the state delivers quality training programs, the level of financial support provided by the legislature to fund state recovery initiatives (beyond those funded by the federal government), the political standing of emergency management within the governor's office and other supporting state agencies, and the development of a strong state disaster recovery plan that involves other members of the assistance network.

Disaster-Related Funding

States that face repeated disasters, maintain robust economies, and have strong executive leadership are more likely to develop policies and programs beyond those established by FEMA and other federal government agencies (see the previous sidebar). The degree to which they take on responsibilities beyond those prescribed by the federal government also depends on the level of funding appropriated for this purpose and on the size and technical skills of their staff. Some state legislatures finance post-disaster activities or maintain "rainy day" funds to cover nonfederal cost-share requirements, hire staff, and create programs to address perceived shortfalls in federal programs. Most federal disaster recovery grants include a cost-sharing provision, requiring states, local governments, quasi-governmental organizations, nonprofits, or individual citizens to help finance the program. Because many local governments, particularly small and low-wealth jurisdictions, are unprepared to assume these costs after a disaster, states may take on these obligations. However, state cost sharing sometimes reduces the local government's commitment to invest the time and resources needed to effect a sound recovery, including the adoption of pre-event plans to reduce the likelihood of future losses and coordinate the delivery of post-disaster assistance.

Personnel

The media and the general public often assume that FEMA is solely responsible for response and recovery efforts—in part, because of its ubiquitous presence following large-scale disasters. With greater recognition comes greater scrutiny and blame; after such large-scale disasters as Hurricane Andrew and Katrina, for example, the federal government was roundly criticized. The general public is often unaware that a state emergency management agency even exists. Yet state officials are the ones who typically know the sociopolitical context in which to frame the delivery of information, craft effective policy, and determine the appropriate level of capacity building needed for communities. Unfortunately, their ability to capitalize on this knowledge and translate it into action is severely constrained by inadequate staffing both before and after a disaster.

Beyond financial assets, the resources needed to address disaster recovery-related challenges include an adequate supply of people to manage grants and loans, draft and implement policy, and provide other forms of technical assistance. At the federal level, FEMA maintains full-time "core" employees located in its national office in Washington, D.C., as well as in ten regions across the United States. Regional core employees may be deployed to disaster recovery field offices to serve in management, supervisory, or technical positions. Disaster assistance employees (DAEs), who are drawn from around the country, are on call to address episodic spikes in demand following disasters; these individuals operate on a rotational schedule, traveling back to their permanent place of residence after a given period of time. FEMA can thereby deploy hundreds and, in some cases, thousands of employees to a disaster.

To be effective, the administration of federal assistance programs requires the incorporation of local knowledge and perspectives into those programs and policies where appropriate. This may prompt the federal government to try to hire state and local personnel to supplement its DAE cadre. Local personnel tend to be highly motivated to assist in recovery efforts. They also have an in-depth understanding of local conditions, which can significantly bolster FEMA's ability to craft or modify policies based on local needs. However, this approach can degrade state and local capabilities and erode the federal-state-local working relationship: as former state and local officials leave their positions for those available in the federal government, they often take with them important knowledge of how to administer federal assistance programs.[20] And FEMA staff may be reluctant to accept this information, particularly if it suggests altering normal recovery operations and protocols.

By their very nature, large-scale events severely strain state resources. Because state agencies are incapable of matching federal personnel resources, their ability to effectively administer disaster-related programs triggered by a presidential declaration while carrying out their day-to-day activities is strained. While FEMA officials are under intense pressure to ensure that a number of complex, highly bureaucratic federal programs are being implemented in a timely manner, understaffed state agencies are struggling to ensure that state policy is being understood and effectively conveyed to disaster-stricken communities at public meetings and site visits. They rarely take the time needed to train local officials on pre-event planning for post-disaster recovery, nor do they have the technical resources on hand after an event to help local governments link the community goals articulated in local planning documents to post-disaster aid programs—or, conversely, to help communities rethink public investment strategies in known hazard areas recently struck by disaster. Florida's Post-Disaster Redevelopment Planning Initiative, described in the previous sidebar on page 44, is a unique endeavor that has been developed to address these concerns.

A growing number of states are establishing disaster assistance cadres, particularly in regions that are vulnerable to repeated events. At the state level, these cadres comprise former state or local emergency managers, building inspectors, engineers, public works officials, and others who have a good understanding of local issues. State emergency management agencies have also become increasingly reliant on interstate and local agreements tied to the Emergency Management Assistance Compact (EMAC) (see the sidebar on page 48). EMAC and other mutual aid programs, however, tend to emphasize the shared use of personnel for response-related activities following disasters, with much less focus placed on their potential role in recovery.

One drawback of EMAC is that it is not used very much to provide long-term recovery assistance. Personnel who have been instrumental in this regard have included state National Flood Insurance Program coordinators, hazard mitigation specialists, building code officials, damage assessment experts, and those knowledgeable in post-disaster grants management. Diversifying the cadre of experts to include disaster recovery planners and others who have dealt with long-term recovery issues in previous events would enable EMAC to more systematically address recovery- and reconstruction-related issues.

The Emergency Management Assistance Compact

The Emergency Management Assistance Compact (EMAC), which was approved by Congress in 1996, provides a codified vehicle for requesting assistance from other states and local governments after federally declared disasters. Initially proposed by the Southern Governors' Association, it has become a nationwide effort.

EMAC staff serve to buttress existing personnel or spell state and local employees who may have been working extremely long hours under trying conditions. An important aspect of the compact involves the categorization, or "typing," of resources (including personnel) that are needed to accomplish specific tasks. Having experienced staff trained in clearly defined specialty areas greatly improves the efficacy of the team as a whole and enhances each agency's or individual's ability to assume assigned responsibilities.[1]

The use of EMAC in long-term recovery activities is less prevalent than it is in response efforts,[2] although there is evidence to suggest that this trend is changing. State and local officials have begun using EMAC to deploy grants management specialists, floodplain managers, building officials, and engineers during recovery. However, because clear, institutionalized, nationwide protocols for EMAC and long-term recovery have not yet been developed, access to those individuals, groups, and organizations that possess a number of pertinent skills and resources remain underutilized. For example, if EMAC were to deploy personnel pre-event to build local capacity and assist in recovery plan making, it could help to address the long-standing schism between emergency managers and land use planners, thereby furthering recovery efforts. The failure to link the efforts of EMAC to the National Response Framework or the more recent National Disaster Recovery Framework further limits the ability to foster collaboration, which is critically important during response and recovery efforts.[3]

State and local units of government also maintain pre-event mutual aid agreements, which vary in timing and scope. This type of assistance differs from EMAC largely because it is not necessarily triggered by a federal disaster declaration, which is an important distinction as most events do not merit such a declaration. Further, state and local mutual aid agreements can stipulate the delivery of assistance in the pre- or post-disaster environment. In practice, however, mutual aid agreements have been response oriented and have failed to include the sharing of resources needed to address long-term recovery needs.

Given existing policy and its current limitations, the ability of both EMAC and mutual aid agreements to address disaster recovery needs could be improved through renegotiated agreements between FEMA and state, interstate, and interlocal parties. Important changes might include clarifying the nature of disaster recovery assistance—typing procedures, developing pre-event resource-sharing agreements (and the means to pay for them), and expanding the scope of technical expertise available to include members from across the assistance network.

1 William Waugh, "Mechanisms for Collaboration: EMAC and Katrina," *The Public Manager* 35, no. 4 (Winter 2006–2007): 12–15.
2 Ibid.
3 Ibid.

Another disadvantage to using EMAC (in its current form) as a recovery tool is the time required to develop working relationships with local aid recipients or to gain an in-depth understanding of important local issues. Local government officials regularly cite a lack of continuity in policy interpretation and service levels when DAEs, EMAC representatives, and federal contractors rotate in and out of a community. A broader strategy that builds on state and local capacity could address this problem by using EMAC to strategically supplement the local government's pre-disaster recovery planning activities, promoting a greater level of trust through repeated and sustained interaction over time.

A state's capacity to provide recovery assistance is linked to a series of temporal issues. Major events serve as a forcing mechanism, uncovering weaknesses that include being underprepared to address disaster recovery.[21] After disasters, policies are created and altered with greater regularity and speed than at other times, more training programs are offered, and assistance is provided on a much larger scale and with greater intensity. For example, states may use federal funds to temporarily increase the size of their staffs, hiring individuals to administer grant programs, and may seek other forms of assistance. The experiential learning that takes place under these conditions is significant and condensed into a relatively short period. Staff must make a number of important decisions, often with limited information. These analytical skills, honed over time, are extremely important in a post-disaster environment characterized by uncertainty and a necessity to adapt to changing conditions.

Disasters are not constant, however, so the hiring and training of personnel to carry out disaster-related functions is sporadic. The inability of states to retain individuals who have gained this experience limits the institutionalization of critical knowledge at the state level, including its transfer to community officials,[22] and impedes the state's ability to shape post-disaster federal policy to reflect emergent local needs. Inexperienced state officials often defer to federal program directives rather than trying to modify them to reflect state and local needs. But in other cases, political influence, power, and the media can be used adroitly to exert pressure on program administrators to alter rules. These techniques are most effective when coupled with the wise use of data to forward a well-constructed argument that articulates a specific need and the proposed means to address it.[23]

LOCAL GOVERNMENT

Regardless of the type, quantity, or duration of assistance provided by other members of the disaster recovery assistance network, the local unit of government—city, county, or township—is ultimately held responsible for community-level recovery.[24] Yet local officials routinely struggle to meet the expectations of the public, state and federal agencies, and other members of the network. Nowhere is this more evident than in the challenges associated with the receipt and disbursement of assistance.

Resource Management

The difficulty of keeping up with the confluence of resources following a disaster is referred to as *convergence*.[25] Convergence has been studied extensively during the initial response to an event, and state and local officials have established resource management systems to prepare for this widely recognized eventuality. Much less is understood, however, about the convergence of long-term recovery resources and ways to plan for this similarly inevitable occurrence. Most communities do not have clearly identified venues for managing pre-event donations in support of long-term recovery, although such donations are common during the initial aftermath of an event. Some communities and states develop temporary post-disaster relief organizations capable of accepting donations, but these organizations are less likely to be part of a pre-disaster recovery plan. And as neither EMAC nor most local mutual aid agreements are appropriately designed to address long-term recovery needs, they lack the ability to organize the convergence of disaster recovery resources.

This lack of coordinative venues is due, in part, to the reluctance of local governments to engage in pre-event planning for post-disaster recovery. In fact, the current system offers strong disincentives and few incentives for local governments to undertake such planning.[26] Thus, when a disaster does occur, local officials assume undefined roles and take an adaptive approach to the coordination of assistance.[27]

Land Use Policies and Planning Tools

In truth, local governments have a number of land use policies and planning tools that are directly applicable to disaster recovery.[28] They control investment and finance strategies; the adoption of building codes; the development of zoning and subdivision ordinances; and other planning measures that guide the type, density, and location of development.[29] Planners are trained to analyze issues and identify potential solutions or alternatives, facilitate policy dialogue, and use participatory techniques associated with the distribution of scarce resources[30] and the resolution of conflict.[31] These skills are all uniquely suited to the challenges surrounding the coordination of long-term recovery and reconstruction activities,[32] yet they are infrequently used for this purpose.

The failure of local officials to involve planners in pre- and post-event recovery decision making has several negative consequences.[33] Poor pre-disaster land use decisions can constrict the number of reconstruction options available to local officials after a disaster strikes. Once communities have invested in known hazard areas, their physical alteration, including the possible relocation of housing and the abandonment of supporting infrastructure, may face significant opposition and be difficult to implement.[34] Communities often choose instead to invest in increasingly large public works projects, potentially furthering the problem. The construction of protective infrastructure, for example, such as the levee system surrounding New Orleans or the seawall in Galveston after the 1900 hurricane, encourages additional development in hazard-prone areas. However, the collaborative approaches and plan-making techniques that planners regularly use can generate multiple reconstruction options for consideration, and if these options can be discussed openly and well in advance of a disaster, local officials, the business community, and the public can weigh the merits of different recommendations, each informed by reliable information.

The transition from immediate response to long-term recovery activities is typically initiated by the local emergency manager, who is usually responsible for conducting post-disaster damage assessments. Local emergency managers tend to come from police, fire, or emergency medical service backgrounds, a trend that is slowly changing because of the increase in emergency management degree programs and the growing appeal of this still-emerging profession. Response planning, which has a longer history and is more widespread than recovery planning, is a primary responsibility of emergency managers,[35] who play an important coordinative role, linking the actions of multiple stakeholders during response efforts.

As the response or "emergency and restoration" phase transitions into long-term recovery and reconstruction, new tasks are involved, including grant administration, finance, and construction management. Many of these tasks require the knowledge, skills, and abilities of planners. The degree to which emergency managers remain involved depends on the nature of existing plans and procedures adopted by the local government. Those responsible for recovery and reconstruction activities must also be skilled in consensus building and conflict resolution; the collection, analysis, and display of information; post-event planning; project management; and policy making.[36] Following a disaster, staff from public works, finance, planning, code enforcement, economic development, parks and recreation, human services, public health, and other departments may be drawn into the process with little training or understanding of their roles. Research shows that uncertainty among local officials regarding pre- and post-disaster roles hinders the overall recovery process.[37]

Richard Smith and Robert Deyle contend that the timing of assistance provided by planners is crucial to their successful involvement in recovery and that planners can most effectively use their skills during the pre-event phase.[38] They further maintain that the importance of planners has been discounted because, given the planning community's lack of understanding about response activities and the different phases of recovery, many emergency managers view plans developed prior to a disaster as "irrelevant." An unfamiliarity with emergency management and disaster recovery activities limits a planner's ability to help articulate an informed, goal-oriented set of actions, including the identification of those who should carry such actions out

Exhibit 2–2. Local Disaster Recovery Committee

- Mayor
- City council
- City manager/assistant city manager
- Public information officer
- Public works
- Planning
- Finance
- Public health
- Emergency management
- Police
- Fire
- Building official
- Floodplain administrator
- Community groups
- Nonprofit relief organizations and foundations
- Regional planning organization(s)
- University and college representation
- Business owners and organizations
- State emergency management representative(s)
- Citizen representative(s)
- Utility company representative(s)
- Special service district representative(s)

and of ways they will be funded. This has become evident, for example, when ESF-14 contractors are deployed to disaster locations; although many of these contractors are planners, they may have a limited understanding of emergency management and post-disaster recovery programs. The failure to learn, recognize, and share the resources—particularly knowledge—held by different members of the disaster assistance network significantly constrains opportunities to collaborate. The low level of coordination that Jack Kartez and Charles Faupel found between emergency managers and planners limits the important contributions of both groups and has profound recovery implications.[39]

Mary Anderson and Peter Woodrow argue that it is incumbent on local governments to modify their organizational structure to more effectively capitalize on the types of assistance that are available after a disaster.[40] Viewed in the context of long-term disaster recovery, one option involves the creation of a disaster recovery committee (Exhibit 2–2), which would include those who play traditional roles in recovery as well as other, less recognized members of the assistance network, such as those identified in Chapter 1 as located within the zone of uncertainty. This committee would serve several purposes, including the coordination of stakeholders, the pre- and post-event identification of resources (funding, policies, and technical assistance), and the clarification of participant roles and responsibilities. It would also be involved in creating the disaster recovery plan as its members would ultimately be responsible for ensuring that the plan is implemented, monitored, and revised over time (see accompanying sidebar).

Hillsborough County, Florida, Post-Disaster Redevelopment Plan

The Hillsborough County, Florida, Post-Disaster Redevelopment Plan (PDRP) is one of several pilot plans developed under the aegis of the state's Post-Disaster Redevelopment Planning Initiative described in the sidebar on page 44. The plan, completed in February 2010, "identifies policies, operational strategies, and roles and responsibilities for implementation that will guide decisions that affect long-term recovery and redevelopment of the community after a disaster."[1]

The plan's "implementation conceptual framework" is guided by the following principles:

1. Nurture an ongoing Post-Disaster Redevelopment Stakeholder Structure that interfaces with the Local Mitigation Strategy (LMS) Working Group during pre-disaster implementation and with the Redevelopment Task Force.

2. Provide criteria for considering long-term impacts of disaster response and short-term recovery decisions.

3. Set up processes for transitioning from the Emergency Support Function operational structure to long-term redevelopment processes that are sustainable over a 3- to 5-year period of implementation.

4. Develop inclusive lists of organizations and resources that may be available to assist in pre- and post-disaster plan implementation.

5. Integrate long-range policy initiatives from local plans.

6. Capitalize on disaster mitigation and public assistance funds to improve disaster resiliency through pre-disaster research, training, and project planning.

7. Incrementally prepare the community for a more rapid and higher quality disaster recovery through implementation of priority pre-disaster actions each year.

8. Revisit the assumptions and actions of the PDRP every 5 years to adjust for changes in the community and to continually improve the plan.[2]

Appendices address existing regulations as well as numerous pre- and post-event actions. The description of regulations section focuses on state requirements associated with the authority to develop and implement a redevelopment plan, including emergency powers, and local authorities associated with the comprehensive plan, comprehensive emergency management plan (CEMP), and the Hillsborough County Redevelopment Ordinance. The PDRP serves to integrate the authorized actions in the comprehensive plan, CEMP, redevelopment ordinance, and LMS that are relevant to pre-event planning and post-disaster recovery. For instance, Florida requires that comprehensive plans in coastal counties contain a "coastal element" and that this part of the plan must also include a redevelopment component that has been codified to require the creation of a post-disaster redevelopment plan. The CEMP has a recovery annex, which specifies roles and responsibilities, while the redevelopment ordinance contains the authority to establish a redevelopment task force, the determination of post-disaster damages, the evaluation and potential modification of reconstruction standards, and the ability to authorize a temporary reconstruction moratorium (Appendix C, C-5 to C-23).

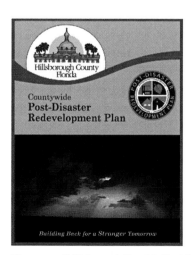

The cover of Hillsborough County's Post-Disaster Redevelopment Plan.

Source: Hillsborough County, Florida.

continued on page 54

continued from page 53

The compendium of pre- and post-disaster actions addresses eight areas: (1) public-private infrastructure and facilities, (2) health and social services, (3) housing recovery, (4) economic redevelopment, (5) land use, (6) environmental restoration, (7) public outreach, and (8) financial administration. The latter two areas serve as support functions that span the remaining six. An assessment of pre-event vulnerability and institutional capacity was conducted across each area; the resultant information serves as the basis for recommended improvements to the plan through the implementation of hazard mitigation measures that reduce potential losses to identified infrastructure, public facilities, and housing; natural systems; and socially vulnerable populations as well as through changes in policy and public investments that enhance the community's institutional capacity where it is deemed insufficient.

The Hillsborough County plan also proactively addresses a number of land use issues in advance of a disaster. Such topics include prioritizing geographical areas where focused rebuilding efforts will occur, establishing clear reconstruction standards, and instituting policies for redeveloping areas that have suffered repeated damages from past events. In each case, the plan describes a strategy that is tied to reducing vulnerability and targeting pre- and post-disaster resources needed to accomplish this aim.

Pre- and post-disaster actions associated with each of eight areas identified above are assigned to members of the Redevelopment Task Force, technical advisory committees, or PDRP staff. Post-disaster actions are

Florida's Post-Disaster Redevelopment Program represents one of the few state-led initiatives of its kind in the country.
Source: Hillsborough County, Florida.

managed by three coordinator positions: the disaster recovery redevelopment coordinator, the economic recovery coordinator, and the hazard mitigation coordinator. The plan suggests that these positions may be subject to modification following a disaster that tests their efficacy. In lieu of an actual event, Hillsborough County has been evaluating its redevelopment ordinance over the past several years through annual exercises. A tabletop exercise was held using a draft of the PDRP plan, and it is recommended that the completed plan be subject to further assessments. The state of Florida is in the process of developing a model exercise for use by pilot PDRPs and future redevelopment plans as they are created.

Source: Hillsborough County, *Hillsborough County Post-Disaster Redevelopment Plan* (Tampa, Fla.: Hazard Mitigation Section, Planning and Growth Management Department, February 2010), www.hillsboroughcounty.org/pgm/hazardmit/.

1   Florida Department of Community Affairs, Division of Community Planning, "Overview," in Post-Disaster Redevelopment Planning (n.d.), http://www.dca.state.fl.us/fdcp/dcp/PDRP/overview.cfm.
2   Hillsborough County, *Hillsborough County Post-Disaster Redevelopment Plan*, 1–3, www.hillsboroughcounty.org/pgm/pdrp/pubs/2010/ introduction.pdf.

DIMENSIONS OF THE DISASTER RECOVERY ASSISTANCE FRAMEWORK

Public sector planning provides a means of addressing existing problems within the disaster recovery assistance framework while fostering the conditions in which collaboration across the network can thrive. The following discussion of the dimensions of the framework across the public sector emphasizes the rules of assistance: an understanding of local needs, the timing of assistance, and the level of horizontal and vertical integration within and across federal, state, and local governments.

Understanding Local Needs

The public sector disaster recovery process is guided by a complex set of rules that influence how money is disbursed, policies are made, and technical assistance is provided following a disaster. Because these rules are highly prescriptive, they limit program flexibility and adaptability to fit local needs, including whatever unique circumstances that arise. Federal rules may change during the recovery process in response to skilled and powerful state and local interests, but most public sector organizations strain to successfully administer programs after an event.

Some states have designed programs to address gaps in federal assistance, increased staff in agencies tasked with recovery activities, and established state recovery committees to oversee the identification of recovery needs and the assignment of state agencies responsible for program implementation (see Figure 2–2 and the sidebar on page 56). States have also provided recovery funding through a disaster contingency fund or a donations-based "governor's fund," in which voluntary donations from individuals, businesses, corporations, and other nations are collected and used to address unmet needs. States often work with nonprofit foundations to help manage the donations process, which may include the identification of needy recipients, the development of distribution protocols, and the monitoring of funding once delivered.

State recovery committees provide a means of identifying financial needs and policy issues, but they are seldom guided by clearly articulated plans that maximize the use of available state resources. As a result, state agencies often overlook the effect that existing programs and pre-event initiatives have on recovery and reconstruction activities. For example, state departments of economic development administer federal Community Development Block Grant (CDBG) funds that are allocated to states on an annual basis. After large-scale disasters, Congress appropriates CDBG-based money to aid in the reconstruction of damaged homes and community infrastructure (see Figure 2–3 on page 59). On a day-to-day basis, CDBG funds may be used to repair or build affordable housing and stimulate economic investment in low-income areas. However, these activities are often undertaken separately from disaster recovery planning

Figure 2-2. Banner displaying the logos of the Rebuild Iowa Office and ESF-14 following the 2008 floods. Iowa, like many states following a major disaster, created a state-level organization to address the complexities of disaster recovery.

Source: Federal Emergency Management Agency.

North Carolina's Disaster Recovery Assistance Programs after Hurricane Floyd

In 1999, after Hurricane Floyd, the North Carolina state legislature appropriated $836 million to address needs that were not met by the federal government. The money was drawn from the state's "rainy day" fund, which was set aside to address unexpected financial shortfalls and budgetary deficits. The broad intent of the Hurricane Floyd Reserve Fund was to help local governments achieve a more sustainable recovery across economic, social, and environmental dimensions than would otherwise have been attainable with just federal assistance programs.

The redevelopment package included twenty-two new state programs administered by ten different agencies. Programs included the remapping of the state's floodplains, the construction of replacement housing, the development of infrastructure for new communities, money to supplement the relocation of low-income residents outside of areas subject to repeated floods, the purchase and relocation of hog farms and junkyards located in the floodplain, and the hiring of redevelopment center staff, including "housing counselors" to walk individuals through the array of state and federal programs.

Hurricane Floyd was a category 2 storm on the Saffir-Simpson scale[1] (i.e., winds ranging from 96 to 110 miles per hour) when it made landfall. The devastation it caused, however, was due not to high winds but rather to the tremendous amount of rain that fell across eastern North Carolina, which was already drenched by rains from Hurricane Dennis two weeks earlier. Saturated soils, the size of the storm, and the amount of rainfall all contributed to the magnitude of flooding.[2]

During the days that followed, approximately 6,600 square miles of eastern North Carolina were under water. In many communities, the flood stage exceeded the 100-year flood event. Fifty-two people lost their lives, and over 1.5 million people lost power. More than 67,000 homes were damaged, thousands of which were inundated by over five feet of water. More than 1,000 roads were closed, including two interstate highways. Twenty-four wastewater treatment plants were flooded or severely damaged. More than 1,400 water rescue missions were conducted. Two hundred twenty-seven shelters were opened, housing approximately 62,000 people; an estimated 41,000 more people took shelter in motels, local fire stations, and churches. The Red Cross, Salvation Army, the Baptist Men, and other relief organizations established over 100 feeding stations, while the North Carolina Emergency Management Division (NCEMD) provided 450,000 MREs (meals ready to eat). And about two-thirds of disaster assistance claims were from those living outside the 100-year floodplain—the area subject to a 1 percent annual chance of flooding.

The flood highlighted the state's outdated flood insurance rate maps (FIRMs), a primary purpose of which is to delineate the 100-year floodplain. Structures located in this mapped area are subject to National Flood Insurance Program regulations. Historically, creating and updating FIRMs has been the responsibility of the Federal Emergency Management Agency (FEMA). However, the federal funds allocated to maintain the maps are insufficient to keep up with changes in flood hazards caused by new development and by physical changes in the hydrology of the nation's floodplains. As a result, the state used $22 million of the Hurricane Floyd Reserve Fund to initiate the North Carolina Floodplain Mapping Program, marking the first attempt by a state to assume responsibility for creating and updating FIRMs.

In addition to recognizing the importance of improving the state's understanding of flood hazard vulnerability, the legislature approved several programs targeting the relocation of flood-prone housing. In eastern North Carolina, many residents owned homes of relatively low value that had been flooded repeatedly. FEMA's Hazard Mitigation Grant Program (HMGP) provides eligible homeowners with pre-disaster fair market value for their homes should they agree to participate in the voluntary program. Recognizing that HMGP funds would be insufficient for many residents to purchase a suitable replacement home in good condition outside the floodplain, North Carolina established the State Acquisition and Relocation Fund to provide up to $75,000 in additional funds per household to enable homeowners to make such a purchase. Individual homeowners who sustained damages but were not eligible for the "buyout program" may have been eligible for the state's Repair and Replacement Program, which made repair grants available to low-income homeowners if the repair costs did not exceed the value of their structures.

The flooding associated with Hurricane Floyd destroyed entire communities. The construction of new communities required new water, sewer, and drainage systems. With this in mind, the state infrastructure program was created to enable the construction of subdivisions outside the floodplain, thereby shifting development to higher ground and reducing the likelihood of future flood-related losses. Also recognizing that a shortage of affordable housing existed in eastern North Carolina before the flood, the state required that at least 50 percent of the eventual owners of homes located within new state-funded developments be individuals and families of low or moderate income affected by Floyd.

In addition to the establishment of communities within the floodplain, the flood exposed other inappropriate land uses, including hog farms and auto junkyards, that had contributed to the environmental degradation of the region. Flooded hog farm operations led to widely disseminated media images of dead hogs and ruptured waste lagoons, while large-scale junkyards added an oily sheen to the floodwater and further contaminated already polluted waterways. In order to reduce future flood-related losses and improve water quality in the rivers across eastern North Carolina, the state's recovery assistance strategy thus included programs to purchase both types of facilities from willing sellers and relocate them. Once these operations were removed, the land where they had once been located was converted into open space in perpetuity.

Although North Carolina's programs are perhaps the most far-reaching of any state's post-disaster efforts to address the shortfalls in federal assistance, the Hurricane Floyd Reserve Fund suffered from some of the same problems that occur at the federal level, including the failure to plan for recovery. Four factors reduced the scope of recovery envisioned by the governor: (1) a state recovery plan was not in place before the event, nor was one developed afterwards; (2) there was no single agency or organization responsible for coordinating the overall effort; (3) there were competing programmatic objectives across federal and state programs; and (4) the program design and administrative procedures did not account for the level of local government capacity to implement federal and state programs simultaneously.

After Hurricane Floyd, the state legislature debated whether to create what was widely dubbed the disaster recovery "Marshall Plan." Initial discussions centered on how the recovery programs could revitalize eastern North Carolina, which was suffering from a declining rural economy, a lack of quality affordable housing, and deteriorating environmental conditions. Although an array of state programs was created, the state failed to create a long-range recovery framework designed to systematically address the breadth of problems facing the region. Two weeks after the hurricane, the NCEMD brought together state agencies, nonprofits, federal agencies, and nationally recognized

continued on page 58

continued from page 57

experts from nearby universities to discuss developing a recovery plan for eastern North Carolina. The initial effort was an outgrowth of the Sustainable Redevelopment Working Group, created after Hurricane Bonnie in 1998 but never put into practice: the group focused on how the existing recovery and mitigation programs could be linked to broader economic, societal, and hazard mitigation goals, but it was told not to address the need for a recovery plan as one would be developed in time. But this never happened.

Instead, the North Carolina Redevelopment Center was created and tasked with managing most state recovery programs. Emphasis was placed on developing programmatic rules rather than on creating a multistakeholder recovery plan that would guide new programs, integrate existing state policies, and involve the larger assistance network in a comprehensive manner. The result was the unrealized potential of what remains perhaps the most significant creation of state programs following a disaster in U.S. history.

After a disaster, local governments, particularly those with a limited capacity to administer basic municipal services, are incapable of implementing large-scale grants without significant assistance. This reality was not effectively incorporated into the Redevelopment Center's activities. The center hired an insufficient number of state-level grant managers to help local governments develop and implement state grant applications and instead hired housing counselors to assist individuals directly. Although these housing

counselors provided an important service, walking disaster victims through a confusing assortment of programs, local governments were overwhelmed with the unprecedented plethora of federal grant and loan programs that followed, and the creation of new state programs further taxed their abilities to administer assistance. Communities relied heavily on the use of consultants, many of whom also became quickly overwhelmed as they tried to assist multiple clients. Moreover, grant deadlines were established for some programs but not for others, thereby hindering the simultaneous implementation of coupled programs, such as the buyout of flood-prone properties and the development of new housing and infrastructure.

North Carolina's programs were designed to complement existing federal programs while taking advantage of a unique window of opportunity to address preexisting chronic problems in the eastern part of the state. While these efforts represent one of the most progressive attempts to incorporate sustainable development principles into recovery, the grand vision initially proposed could have been further realized by the adoption and implementation of a disaster recovery plan.

1 The Saffir-Simpson scale, which is used to measure hurricane intensity as defined by wind speed, does not adequately predict rainfall or storm surge potential, two of the most damaging effects of hurricanes and those that lead to the greatest number of deaths.

2 Jerad D. Bales, Carolyn J. Oblinger, and Asbury H. Sallenger Jr., *Two Months of Flooding in Eastern North Carolina, September–October 1999: Hydrologic, Water-Quality, and Geologic Effects of Hurricanes Dennis, Floyd, and Irene*, U.S. Geological Survey Water-Resources Investigations Report 00-4093 (Raleigh, N.C., 2000), pubs.usgs. gov/wri/wri004093/pdf/report.pdf.

activities so that investments are made in known hazard areas, increasing the vulnerability of low-income segments of the population. Better coordination between a state's economic development and emergency management programs can produce a more integrated policy guiding the wise pre- and post-event expenditure of these funds, thereby reducing social vulnerability and improving affordable and safe housing.

The ability to create recovery strategies targeted to community needs undergirds successful community-level recovery after a disaster.[41] Local government officials have a better understanding of community needs than do federal and state agencies, but an awareness of local needs does not necessarily translate into action. Both disaster-related impacts and the distribution of local government assistance are strongly influenced by pre-event social, economic, and political conditions that shape the adoption of policies before and after a disaster.[42] Long-standing issues of neglect, racial disparity, and economic hardship can be exacerbated by a disaster, as was seen in New Orleans after Hurricane Katrina.[43] Blaming socially vulnerable populations for their plight and seeking their removal from communities; placing a higher priority on assisting residents who are politically connected; and failing to adopt more stringent

Figure 2–3. The reconstruction of a new city hall in Long Beach, Mississippi, after Hurricane Katrina was funded by the post-Katrina Community Development Block Grant program. The sign in the foreground notes the Mississippi Development Authority, the state agency responsible for the administration of the federal funds, as well as the private sector firm tasked with construction.

Source: Governors Office of Recovery and Renewal, State of Mississippi.

building codes because of opposition from strong economic development interests are all policy choices that local officials have made in the wake of disaster. Nonprofits and emergent groups sometimes try to address these issues by bringing them to the attention of the larger assistance network. Although the environmental justice clause of Executive Order 11988 requires federal agencies to enforce the equitable distribution of resources following disasters, federal assistance favors those institutions that are tied to preexisting social networks associated with agency programs.[44] Research has also shown that federal policies, particularly those associated with post-disaster housing assistance, have an inherent bias toward middle-income homeowners as opposed to renters and those living in transitional housing.[45]

Local disaster assistance strategies are also influenced by the perceived lack of importance of pre-event planning and policy making. When forced to prioritize expenditures, local policy makers tend to view planning for post-disaster recovery as less important than economic development or the associated provision of adequate schools, housing, and public infrastructure. Federal and state officials have done a poor job of educating local officials about the economic, social, and environmental benefits of planning for disaster recovery. While a growing number of planners have embraced the concept of sustainable development, including its emphasis on the complementary nature of economic development, the protection of the environment, and the importance of maintaining social equity, these principles are infrequently discussed in the context of hazards and disasters among practicing professionals.[46] The ability to achieve these ends is often compromised by the reluctance of stakeholders to engage in pre-event planning for post-disaster recovery, an underlying element associated with the timing of assistance.

Timing of Assistance

Eugene Haas, Robert Kates, and Martyn Bowden describe disaster recovery as a linear process in which response activities occur before debris removal begins, after which comes the reconstruction of damaged and destroyed infrastructure, housing, and public facilities.[47] This description is overly simplified. It does not account for the fact that the temporal distribution of assistance and the ensuing trajectory of recovery differ across individuals, groups, communities, and regions that send and receive assistance; differences depend on the nature of recovery programs, which are developed in isolation; the abilities and willingness of federal, state, and local officials to administer and coordinate their programs with other members of the assistance network; and varied levels of social vulnerability, administrative capacity, and pre-event planning. All these factors affect the distributional order, speed, and quality of assistance.

Many communities assume a passive role when it comes to recovery, adopting post-event actions based on the programmatic requirements dictated by federal programs. In actuality, the ability to receive and effectively use assistance is an important, yet underemphasized aspect of federal, state, and local recovery policy. That is, there has been little attention paid to policies that emphasize capacity-building initiatives among recipients of assistance or that foster the pre-event deployment of needed training, education, and outreach by those who provide such assistance. This facet of program delivery has been studied mainly by hazard scholars focused on international relief and disaster recovery.[48] In one of the few domestic studies of a recipient's knowledge and capability to use assistance, Christopher Dyer finds that the assistance provided by the federal Economic Development Administration after Hurricane Andrew was largely effective because local communities and disaster victims had achieved a certain degree of recovery and were ready to accept additional assistance.[49] The pre-event assessment of local recovery capabilities and the strengthening of identified weaknesses through plan making and targeted public investments remain less salient, particularly when compared to other local governmental functions, such as disaster response.

The timing of federal recovery programs disproportionately affects the recovery strategies chosen by members of the assistance network, particularly state and local governments. Because federal assistance tends to emphasize the post-event time line through the distribution of assets during the immediate response phase and the disbursement of grants and loans during recovery, the receipt of federal assistance triggers a series of actions associated with program implementation that may be counterproductive to the aims of other stakeholders or the long-term interests of a community. To rectify this situation, there should be more of a focus on pre-event capacity-building strategies. FEMA's post-disaster recovery planning program, for example, should place a greater emphasis on pre-event training in order to grow technical planning capability, demonstrate its value across stakeholder groups, and build a coalition of support to sustain it.[50]

Disaster Relief Programs under the Stafford Act

The problematic timing of assistance is also apparent in federal assistance and congressional appropriations following disasters. The Robert T. Stafford Act of 1988, which improved the codification of federal assistance for presidentially declared disasters, provides a case in point of well-intentioned programs that, because of the uncoordinated timing of their implementation, often result in counterproductive outcomes, wasted federal resources, and an increased likelihood of disaster-induced damages in future events. Three key Stafford Act programs are the Individual Assistance (IA) program, the Hazard Mitigation Grant Program (HMGP), and the Public Assistance (PA) program. IA program funds, which may be available to homeowners within weeks after an event, are used to make temporary housing repairs. HMGP funds, on the other hand, can take months, if not years, to receive. Once temporary repairs are made with IA funds and a sense of normalcy returns, homeowners are less likely to participate in the HMGP, a program that is slow to implement and more disruptive to daily life. In the worst-case scenario, a home repaired with IA funds may subsequently be acquired and demolished under the HMGP, which means that the investment of IA funds has essentially been wasted.

The PA program, which reimburses communities for the repair of damaged public infrastructure and debris management activities, among other eligible expenses, is among the most costly outlays of federal disaster assistance (see Figure 2–4 on page 62). Historically, FEMA PA staff has emphasized a disaster-based cost-containment strategy focused on the speed of recovery rather than a more deliberative approach that would

Figure 2–4. Pictured is a debris management staging area in the New Orleans neighborhood of Lakeview.

Photo by Donn Young.

take a long-term view toward reducing the vulnerability of at-risk infrastructure by incorporating cost-effective mitigation strategies. The PA "406" program, which allows hazard mitigation techniques to be integrated into the repair and reconstruction process, is used on a case-by-case basis. The reluctance to embrace this program is due in part to the resistance of FEMA personnel trained in the cost-containment approach, the limited number of federal and state staff capable of performing the benefit-cost analysis required to demonstrate project eligibility, and resistance of local officials who are unwilling to spend the additional time needed to implement the program.

After a disaster there is intense pressure to get public facilities and infrastructure up and running as soon as possible as both are key triggers in the larger recovery process. For instance, damaged schools as well as police and fire stations must be repaired if children are to return to class and emergency personnel are to provide for the public's safety. Similarly, water, sewer, gas, and electrical systems must get back online before people can move back into their communities and businesses can reopen. This emphasis on the speedy repair and reconstruction of damaged public facilities and infrastructure, especially in high-risk communities, tends to preclude a longer-term view tied to the adoption of post-disaster risk reduction measures that can eliminate the wasteful costs of repeated repairs, reduce losses, and speed recovery after future events (see Figure 2–5).

As noted above, the HMGP is difficult to administer and slow to implement. Moreover, HMGP rules complicate the coordination of the program with other recovery activities. Although it is the principal federal grant program dedicated to the reduction of future natural hazard losses, funds are predicated on a federal disaster declaration. States are eligible to receive funds that equate to 15 percent of federal disaster costs if they have developed a FEMA-approved state hazard mitigation plan. If states have developed an "enhanced" hazard mitigation plan, available funding increases to 20 percent. Local governments can apply for these post-disaster funds if they have developed an approved local hazard mitigation plan that specifies targeted projects. Eligible projects may include the elevation, relocation, or retrofit of hazard-prone housing and critical facilities to better withstand the forces associated with natural hazards; education and outreach programs; and funding to update hazard mitigation plans (see Figure 2–6 on page 64).

Writing a highly technical grant application after a disaster is time-consuming and can be challenging given the array of other pressing needs. In the best-case scenario, a local government has developed its HMGP application in anticipation of a disaster so that the application is ready to submit once a disaster declaration is made. This can

Figure 2–5. As housing damages in coastal Mississippi after Hurricane Katrina make apparent, elevating structures is not a foolproof method for eliminating exposure to the damaging effects of flooding. Other possible land use planning solutions include the rezoning of high-hazard areas; the limiting of public reinvestments like roads, water, and sewer in these areas; the clustering of housing developments away from places prone to natural hazards; and the relocation of at-risk housing and infrastructure. Attempts to alter pre-event development policy, however, can be fraught with conflict as development interests and those living in these areas often seek to return to what existed prior to the disaster.

Photo by Gavin Smith.

Figure 2–6. This home in Belhaven, North Carolina, was elevated using Hazard Mitigation Grant Program funds. The town, funded after Hurricane Fran in 1996, had successfully elevated thirty-two homes prior to Hurricane Floyd, which struck the same area in 1999. The savings, defined as losses avoided from the potential flood damages associated with Hurricane Floyd, measured over $1.3 million (see State of North Carolina, Hazard Mitigation in North Carolina: Measuring Success, 2000, 25).

Source: North Carolina Division of Emergency Management.

significantly speed the implementation of the program (see the accompanying sidebar). The time required to develop and implement HMGP projects may post-date other reconstruction choices available to individuals and communities, including the use of personal savings, loan programs, insurance, and nonprofit assistance. Yet if homeowners or communities have incorporated hazard mitigation measures into the repair and reconstruction of structures targeted for HMGP assistance before an application is submitted and approved, they are no longer eligible for HMGP funding. This rule stifles local initiative and further slows the recovery and reconstruction process. The post-disaster reconstruction investment decisions of the larger assistance network are delayed as developers and local businesses often must wait to see what choices communities make, including the possible relocation of neighborhoods or public infrastructure, both of which shape future development and business recovery in the immediate area.

Disaster Relief Programs under the Disaster Mitigation Act

The Disaster Mitigation Act of 2000 emphasizes the importance of pre-disaster planning and the implementation of hazard mitigation–related projects and policies prior to a disaster. As part of this act, the Pre-Disaster Mitigation (PDM) program is intended to proactively address risk reduction. A further shift toward pre-event hazard mitigation grant administration involves the consolidation of the PDM program with the Flood Mitigation Assistance Program and the Severe Repetitive Loss Program (eligible applicants include homes covered by flood insurance that have suffered repeat flood losses)—now collectively referred to as the Hazard Mitigation Assistance

Kinston, North Carolina: The Value of Pre-event Planning and the Speed and Quality of Recovery

The experience of Kinston, North Carolina, provides dramatic evidence of the value of pre-event hazard mitigation planning and the degree to which it can significantly alter the time frame and the quality of the post-disaster recovery process.

After Hurricane Fran, which struck North Carolina in 1996, it took city and state officials a year to develop an application to acquire and demolish 333 flood-prone residential homes, three mobile home parks, fifty-two apartments, and fifty-two vacant lots.[1] The process required finding participants for the voluntary program, determining whether the properties were cost-effective candidates, identifying heirs for each proposed property, conducting an environmental evaluation of the site, surveying individual parcels, and estimating project costs. Once these tasks were completed, the information had to be packaged and an application written. The application was then submitted to the state for review and forwarded to the Federal Emergency Management Agency (FEMA) for approval. Once it was approved, local officials began the implementation process, which required conducting individual closings, demolishing the properties, hauling off the debris, and clearing the site. Several hundred homeowners initially refused to participate, but when they saw their neighbors move away in large numbers, they changed their minds and asked to be part of the program. However, by then it was too late because the available funds were already committed to other projects.[2]

The city of Kinston chose to develop an HMGP application in anticipation of future funding should another disaster occur in the flood-prone community. Three years later, Hurricane Floyd struck, causing flooding in many of the same areas that had been affected by Fran. This time it took just one week to prepare an application for the acquisition and demolition of several hundred additional homes and submit it to the state for review. The state, which had been working with the city and FEMA to develop the application, obtained federal approval one week later.[3] Their ability to speed the delivery of what is principally defined as a risk reduction program enabled the city and its residents to more effectively incorporate the HMGP into their overall recovery strategy.

After Hurricanes Fran and Floyd, the city of Kinston adopted and updated a post-disaster recovery plan that effectively linked hazard mitigation and disaster recovery initiatives. Specific actions included Call Kinston Home, a redevelopment effort focused on relocating families to existing neighborhoods located outside the floodplain (emphasizing the use of infill lots), thereby avoiding sprawl into the countryside while maintaining the city's tax base and revitalizing established neighborhoods; establishing a community-college led program called Housing and Employment Leading People to Success (HELPS) which sought to assist low income families (primarily renters) involved in the housing relocation program with job training (focused on the reconstruction and repair of flood-damaged housing) and financial counseling in order to assist them become first-time home buyers; developing a green infrastructure plan that guided the use of the large amount of now vacant land adjacent to the Neuse river; and relocating a flood-prone waste water treatment plant (that released raw sewage into the river following Hurricanes Fran and Floyd) as well as several local junkyards thereby improving local water quality.[4]

1   North Carolina Emergency Management Division (NCEMD), Kinston, Lenoir County North Carolina. Urgent Needs Project Summary as of June 9, 1997.
2   NCEMD, *Hazard Mitigation Successes in the State of North Carolina* (Raleigh, 1999), www.p2pays.org/ref/24/23234.pdf.
3   NCEMD, *Hazard Mitigation in North Carolina: Measuring Success* (Raleigh, 2000), www.p2pays.org/ref/14/13619/13619.pdf.
4   NCEMD, *Hazard Mitigation Successes in the State of North Carolina.*

(HMA) program. One drawback of the PDM program—and now of the HMA program, which aims to standardize the application process and thereby ease the burden on applicants—is its competitive nature and the limited availability of funds relative to national demand. Both programs tend to favor wealthier communities that have the technical capacity to write an eligible application or the financial means to hire contractors to develop and administer the grant.

Supplemental Emergency Funding

Following major disasters, Congress appropriates emergency funding in response to shortfalls in the federal assistance available under the Stafford Act. The timing and disbursement of emergency funds usually follow the announcement of federal programs and their associated eligibility requirements. During House and Senate deliberations, decisions are made regarding the amount of funding available, general rules, and the federal agency designated to manage the funds. Appropriations are designed to address perceived needs in infrastructure, agriculture, social services, and housing that are unmet by traditional disaster recovery sources.

Housing needs represent one of the most complex and vital issues in community recovery.[51] The federal agency chosen to administer supplemental housing assistance—either FEMA or the Department of Housing and Urban Development (HUD)—affects the nature of the rules promulgated, the speed of program delivery, the level of coordination with existing disaster recovery programs, and the manner in which the funds are managed.[52] FEMA and HUD represent two very different organizational cultures, and the struggle to effectively integrate their grants management activities after a disaster often limits the efficacy of post-disaster housing recovery.

Except for the HMGP, FEMA has an organizational culture that emphasizes the speed of housing-related program delivery. While it may appear to communities, individuals affected by disasters, and the media that they are agonizingly slow, housing programs, including IA and the temporary housing program, measure success by the speed of payments and the delivery and installation of temporary units. While the HMGP is notoriously slow to implement, particularly when used to acquire, elevate, or retrofit housing, most congressional housing appropriations, including those that are typically administered by HUD, are intended to increase the money available to address needs that exceed available HMGP funds.

A principal mission of HUD is the delivery of safe and decent housing, which is largely performed on a daily basis rather than in response to extreme events. After presidentially declared disasters, HUD manages several programs associated with housing recovery, including the CDBG program, HOME Investment Partnerships Programs, Federal Housing Administration mortgage insurance, the Section 8 Housing Choice Voucher Program, public housing, and rental assistance. The ongoing delivery of housing assistance reflects a more deliberative approach than that used by FEMA. Moreover, HUD's partners at the state and local levels are familiar with annually funded economic development programs and are not used to working with programs that are more episodic in nature or triggered by external events like disasters.

Unlike FEMA, HUD does not have a scalable staff of disaster assistance employees ready to take on more work or responsibility as needed. Its organizational culture reflects a belief that state officials, not federal agency personnel, should provide the bulk of assistance and interact with local officials and grant recipients. This "hands-off" approach can prove beneficial when state and local officials have the capacity to implement housing recovery programs. And if these officials can coordinate with each other and effectively use available data to persuasively state their case, HUD's approach also provides them with an opportunity to shape policy that reflects local needs. In reality, most states rely on contractors, community development corporations, and regional planning organizations to perform the majority of work as HUD targets low-wealth communities that have limited technical, administrative, and fiscal capabilities.

The ability of the managing federal agency to coordinate with other federal housing programs also affects the speed of supplemental housing assistance delivery. Clashes among organizational cultures can hamper the development of complementary program objectives and distributional processes after a disaster, thereby slowing the distribution of aid and leading to further confusion among local officials, homeowners, and renters seeking grant funds. Although FEMA, HUD, and other federal agencies are part of the National Response Framework (NRF), the NRF does not explicitly describe how federal agencies are supposed to coordinate their programs effectively.

After Hurricane Floyd, the state of North Carolina recognized the disconnect among federal agencies and successfully argued that supplemental housing assistance should be administered solely by FEMA. This allowed the state to establish identical program rules for HMGP and what are normally classified as post-disaster CDBG funds, and work with one, rather than two separate federal agencies, thereby simplifying the application and implementation processes.[53] HUD and FEMA, in coordination with the White House, are working to improve the level of coordination across federal agencies and more closely define their respective roles and responsibilities regarding long-term recovery. The creation of the White House Long-Term Disaster Recovery Working Group and the drafting of the NDRF in 2010 are intended to improve federal recovery planning. The success of these efforts will require a sincere commitment not only to coordinate the actions of federal agencies but also to involve the larger assistance network.

State and Local Disaster Assistance

The timing of state recovery assistance is closely associated with the delivery of federal assistance programs. The organizational structure of state emergency management agencies often mirrors that of FEMA, and a large percentage of state staff are responsible for the administration of federal grant programs. States that choose to develop recovery programs usually do so after a major disaster in response to identified gaps in federal assistance. The ability of state agencies to maintain an adequately trained staff of sufficient size to manage grant and loan programs is one of their greatest challenges. Even fewer states maintain personnel trained in disaster recovery planning.

State and local governments, business owners, and individuals are the main recipients of federal and state assistance. The level of pre-event community recovery planning, including the identification of personnel capable of managing post-disaster assistance, affects the speed of program implementation. If state and local governments are unprepared to address the onslaught of demands placed on staff responsible for grants management, it can impede the timely delivery of aid. On the other hand, if they serve as pass-through vehicles without questioning the merits of programs or modifying them to meet identified needs, it can hinder the quality of recovery.

Because of the community's overriding desire to speed recovery, many local officials are reluctant to seek changes in federal or state programs. But sound local policy can actually balance the seemingly conflicting needs of speed versus quality. A post-disaster temporary building moratorium, for example, can provide local officials with the time needed to assess recovery policies and develop or refine the locality's disaster recovery plan. The critical assessment of federal recovery policies and programs, undertaken before a disaster, can yield a better understanding of their delivery time frames and their potential impacts on recovery outcomes. Local governments should use such assessments to identify other resources from across the network that address gaps in federal programs while developing institutional arrangements that pre-position them to access these resources if necessary. Incorporating hazard mitigation measures into recovery also benefits from pre-event planning, as the sidebar on Kinston, North Carolina, suggests. Further, it reduces the likelihood of future disasters and may serve as a linchpin to complementary sustainable development and disaster resilience initiatives.

Also shaping the delivery of assistance from federal agencies and other providers is the timing of actions taken by individual citizens and business owners that prepare them to accept resources, convey local needs, couple the assistance available from external sources with the resources they already possess, and strengthen horizontal and vertical integration across the larger network. Preparedness undertaken prior to an event—for example, individuals and families becoming more self-sufficient by developing an evacuation and re-entry plan; assessing the adequacy of existing insurance coverage and personal savings to cover possible disaster-related damages; learning about recovery grant and loan programs; evaluating and taking steps to reduce the vulnerability of their homes or businesses to hazardous events; and creating a community emergency response team to assist neighbors—can minimize the need for assistance after an event occurs. These factors will be discussed further in Chapter 7.

Horizontal and Vertical Integration

The stated goal of most federal, state, and local recovery plans is to coordinate resources across members of the disaster recovery assistance network. Challenges to the effective coordination of federal, state, and local partners include horizontal fragmentation at the local level as well as vertical fragmentation and fiscal dependency among state and local governments.[54] Improved horizontal and vertical integration can be achieved through investments in such capacity-building activities as planning.[55] The time spent developing a recovery plan helps to foster and solidify relationships by enabling participants to identify common interests, share unique perspectives, and discuss the resources they can offer to address mutually agreed upon goals and objectives. Peter May[56] and, nearly a decade later, Robert Bolin and Lois Stanford[57] found that the degree to which communities are integrated into the existing disaster assistance network affects their ability to access needed resources. A strongly integrated community exhibits an enhanced capacity to solicit assistance, maintain relationships with state and federal stakeholders, and develop pre-event plans.[58]

The pre-event technical assistance that is provided to state and local governments, including training, education, and outreach activities, tends to focus on the means necessary to administer post-disaster grant programs and does not provide adequate support for the creation of strong vertical linkages through planning. This emphasis limits the discussion to a few members of the larger network. The reluctance to engage local officials, nonprofit organizations, and individual citizens in the development or modification of programs before or after disasters reduces the likelihood that existing programs will meet local needs. The assessment of policies, programs, and plans that span the disaster assistance network, which is referred to as a capability assessment (and is discussed in Chapter 8 as part of the overall planning process), provides a way to identify gaps in the means of pre- and post-disaster assistance as well as potentially counterproductive actions. It also provides an opportunity to foster interorganizational cooperation through the agreed-upon modification of programs and sharing of resources. To help develop disaster recovery plans, FEMA relies on contracted professional land use planners, many of whom have the requisite skills to assist in the application of public participation techniques and consensus building. Significant challenges remain, however, as planners brought in after a disaster to participate in ESF-14 often have limited experience in recovery operations, which undermines their credibility in an environment where many FEMA officials question the importance of post-disaster recovery planning.

States and communities often develop task forces or committees to address inter- and intraorganizational coordination[59] (see the sidebars in this chapter on Florida's Post-Disaster Redevelopment Planning Initiative and Hillsborough County's Post-Disaster Redevelopment Plan; in Chapter 5 on the Mississippi's Governor's Commission on Recovery, Rebuilding, and Renewal; and in Chapter 8 on Charlotte–Mecklenburg County's Floodplain Mapping Program, as well as the case study on the Broadmoor Community in Chapter 3). In the post-disaster environment, this represents an adaptive approach to circumstances, whereas pre-event recovery planning is viewed as relatively inconsequential or unimportant. While most states have developed recovery plans, their quality is uncertain.[60] An anecdotal review of state recovery "plans" finds that they do not adhere to widely accepted planning principles, including the identification of processes that enhance good horizontal and vertical integration.[61] State agencies serve as an important liaison between federal agency programs and local needs, and are therefore in a unique position to negotiate with agencies on behalf of communities. They also serve as conduits of information regarding program and policy rules and eligibility, and they provide training programs for local government officials and other stakeholders. Yet states' commitment to planning for recovery, like that of other members of the public sector, remains largely inadequate. The ability to encourage planning for recovery across the assistance network means that the public sector should lead by example and develop the institutional arrangements that facilitate cooperation.

RECOMMENDATIONS

Researchers, the media, and the general public hold the public sector responsible for the success or failure of disaster recovery. At the local level, such success is often measured by the speed of assistance delivered, the amount of funding received from external sources, and the physical reconstruction of affected communities—usually to their pre-event condition. These misguided metrics limit opportunities to incorporate broader goals into the recovery process and to identify complementary objectives. The emphasis on obtaining post-disaster funding undermines pre-event capacity building and community self-reliance. Why plan for recovery when someone else will help to pay for the costs, even if pre-event decisions increase hazard vulnerability? This short-sighted perspective lies at the heart of some of our most pressing challenges. This approach is also anathema to the future orientation of planning principles and techniques.

Three recommendations are made to address these problems.

1. Alter the Culture of State and Local Dependence

Improving recovery outcomes requires modifying the culture of state and local dependence and forging a new sense of empowerment across the larger disaster assistance network. This means moving beyond the current focus on the post-disaster delivery of federal funding and measuring success by the level of pre-event capacity maintained across a more clearly defined, expanded, and interdependent assistance network. An enhanced emphasis should be placed on encouraging state and local governments to attain such capacity while delivering technical assistance strategies that help all members of the network, including FEMA, HUD, and other federal agencies, engage in pre-event planning for recovery. Planning should be used to achieve three key aims: (1) enhance intra- and interorganizational coordination through pre- and post-disaster initiatives, (2) identify local needs and the resources required to meet them, and (3) integrate the concepts of capacity building, self-reliance, and accountability into public sector policies.

2. Increase the Public Sector's Commitment to Engage in Pre-Event Planning for Post-Disaster Recovery

The public sector has a level of recognized authority and a responsibility to plan for disaster recovery. Local governments have both a sound understanding of local needs and an array of planning techniques that can be used to implement recovery planning goals and objectives. State programs and policies play an influential role in shaping local decisions, and federal and state government agencies maintain substantial fiscal resources that can be used to this end.

Federal, state, and local disaster recovery plans should emphasize the coordination of the larger assistance network through the active involvement of planners and the tools they routinely use to address multistakeholder issues. This requires developing plans that are integrated horizontally and vertically, as described in the sidebar on page 44. Since the NRF fails to achieve this important objective, it is the stated aim of the NDRF to improve the coordination of long-term recovery programs. The degree to which it succeeds merits close attention. State and local plans, if they exist, usually fail to comprehensively assess the ability of available financial, policy, and program resources to meet local needs, although North Carolina's post-disaster assistance programs described in the sidebar on pages 53–54 seeks to explicitly address this concern. The reluctance to develop a well-articulated state recovery plan limits the integration of state resources under a common vision, including a coordinated funding strategy;

the development of a clear policy framework that supports local needs and strives to build capacity; and the means necessary to enhance horizontal and vertical integration across the assistance network.

The inadequate application of planning measures during post-disaster recovery and pre-event planning is particularly vexing as local planners use these measures daily to address the timing, location, density, and quality of development. Planners also use participatory techniques to involve diverse stakeholders in collaborative problem-solving processes. These skills, which are sorely needed when addressing important and often contentious issues surrounding pre- and post-disaster recovery, are discussed in Chapter 8.

3. Enhance Local Capacity, Self-Reliance, and Accountability through Planning

Recovery planning objectives should emphasize building local capacity, self-reliance, and accountability. Local capacity-building efforts involve both internal and external activities. Internal capacity building requires the commitment of local officials to direct existing resources (funding, policies, and technical assistance) to pre- and post-disaster recovery needs. Current federal hazards management and disaster recovery policies have created powerful disincentives to engage in this type of behavior. One specific measure to remedy this condition, as suggested in Chapter 9, is to make increased and sustained investments in pre-event aid contingent upon increased accountability of state and local governments for pre- and post-disaster actions that increase their disaster recovery readiness and reduce overall hazard exposure.

Because it is often difficult to sustain support for planning for a disaster that may not occur, a local government should create a local disaster recovery reserve fund or similar revenue source for addressing disaster recovery-related needs in the pre- and post-disaster setting. As part of this effort, it should conduct a departmental audit of existing programs. The program evaluation, or capability assessment, can identify activities that will advance or hinder the disaster recovery goals outlined in the local government's disaster recovery plan.

Capacity building also requires reaching out to other members of the disaster assistance network to maximize their collective resources. Assessing the strengths and weaknesses of programs and assistance strategies allows each member of the network to evaluate its own programs relative to those of other members and enables the network as a whole to identify areas of duplication and gaps in capabilities. Open dialogue and the use of such procedural forums as recovery committees can lead to more formal agreements and plans that will help identify the optimal type, timing, and provider of pre- and post-disaster assistance strategies.

Endnotes

1   Peter May, *Recovering from Catastrophes: Federal Disaster Relief Policy and Politics* (Westport, Conn.: Greenwood Press, 1985); Peter May and Walter Williams, *Disaster Policy Implementation: Managing Programs under Shared Governance* (New York: Plenum Press, 1986); Dennis Mileti, *Disasters by Design: A Reassessment of Natural Hazards in the United States* (Washington, D.C.: Joseph Henry Press, 1999); Gavin Smith and Dennis Wenger, "Sustainable Disaster Recovery: Operationalizing an Existing Agenda," in *Handbook of Disaster Research,* ed. Havidan Rodriguez, Enrico Quarantelli, and Russell Dynes, 234–257 (New York: Springer, 2006).

2   Jim Schwab et al., *Planning for Post-Disaster Recovery and Reconstruction,* Planning Advisory Service (PAS) Report 483/484 (Chicago: American Planning Association [APA], 2003); Smith and Wenger, "Sustainable Disaster Recovery"; Mark G. Welsh and Ann-Margaret Esnard, "Closing Gaps in Local Housing Recovery Planning for Disadvantaged Displaced Households," *Cityscape: A Journal of Policy Development and Research* 11, no. 3 (2009): 195–212.

3   May, *Recovering from Catastrophes;* Mileti, *Disasters by Design.*

4   Ibid.; Thomas A. Birkland, *After Disaster, Agenda Setting, Public Policy, and Focusing Events* (Washington, D.C.: Georgetown University Press, 1997); Thomas A. Birkland, *Lessons of Disaster: Policy Change after Catastrophic Events* (Washington, D.C.: Georgetown University Press, 2006); Federal Emergency Management Agency (FEMA), *National Response Framework* (Washington, D.C.: FEMA, Department of Homeland Security, January 2008), www.fema.gov/pdf/emergency/nrf/nrf-core.pdf.

5   William L. Waugh Jr. and Richard T. Sylves, "The Intergovernmental Relations of Emergency Management," in *Disaster Management in the U.S. and Canada: The Politics, Policymaking, Administration and Analysis of Emergency Management,* 2nd ed., ed. Richard T. Sylves and William L. Waugh Jr., 46–48 (Springfield, Ill.: Charles C. Thomas, 1996); Smith and Wenger, "Sustainable Disaster Recovery."

6   Robert B. Olshansky, "Planning after Hurricane Katrina," *Journal of the American Planning Association* 72, no. 2 (2006): 147–153; Robert W. Kates et al., "Reconstruction of New Orleans after Katrina: A Research Perspective," *Proceedings of the National Academy of Sciences* 103, no. 40 (2006): 14653–14660; Bruce C. Glavovic, "Sustainable Coastal Communities in the Age of Costal Storms: Reconceptualising Coastal Planning as 'New' Naval Architecture," *Journal of Coastal Conservation* 12, no. 3 (2008): 125–134; Robert B. Olshansky and Laurie A. Johnson, *Clear as Mud: Planning for the Rebuilding of New Orleans* (Chicago: APA, 2010).

7   Anthony Oliver-Smith, "Post-Disaster Housing Reconstruction and Social Inequality: A Challenge to Policy and Practice," *Disasters* 14, no. 1 (1990): 7–19; Philip R. Berke and Timothy Beatley, *After the Hurricane: Linking Recovery to Sustainable Development in the Caribbean* (Baltimore: Johns Hopkins University Press, 1997).

8   May and Williams, *Disaster Policy Implementation.*

9   Raymond Burby et al., *Sharing Environmental Risks: How to Control Government's Losses in Natural Disasters* (Boulder, Colo.: Westview Press, 1991); Mileti, *Disasters by Design.*

10 Smith and Wenger, "Sustainable Disaster Recovery."

11 FEMA, *National Response Framework.*

12 Smith and Wenger, "Sustainable Disaster Recovery."

13 Tom Durham and Lacy E. Suiter, "Perspectives and Roles of the State and Federal Governments," in *Emergency Management: Principles and Practice for Local Government,* ed. Thomas E. Drabek and Gerard J. Hoetmer, 101–127 (Washington D.C.: International City Management Association, 1991).

14 Matt Campbell (Long-Term Recovery Branch Chief, FEMA, Broomfield, Colo.), personal communication, July 2008; FEMA, *ESF #14 Long Term Community Recovery National Ops Report* (Washington, D.C.: FEMA, May 5, 2009).

15 Waugh and Sylves, "The Intergovernmental Relations of Emergency Management."

16 Durham and Suiter, "Perspectives and Roles of the State and Federal Governments," 102–103.

17 National Governor's Association (NGA), *Comprehensive Emergency Management: A Governor's Guide* (Washington, D.C.: NGA, 1998).

18 Gavin Smith, "Holistic Disaster Recovery: Creating a More Sustainable Future" (course developed for the Emergency Management Institute Higher Education Project, FEMA, 2004), available at training. fema.gov/EMIWeb/edu/sdr.asp; Smith and Wenger, "Sustainable Disaster Recovery."

19 Smith, "Holistic Disaster Recovery"; Smith and Wenger, "Sustainable Disaster Recovery."

20 Smith, "Holistic Disaster Recovery."

21 Birkland, *Lessons of Disaster;* May and Williams, *Disaster Policy Implementation.*

22 Smith, "Holistic Disaster Recovery."

23 Gavin Smith, "Lessons from the United States: Planning for Post-Disaster Recovery and Reconstruction," *Australasian Journal of Disaster and Trauma Studies* 2010–1 (2010), www.massey. ac.nz/~trauma/issues/2010-1/smith.htm (accessed July 9, 2010); Smith, "Holistic Disaster Recovery."

24 Robert P. Wolensky and Kenneth C. Wolensky, "American Local Government and the Disaster Management Problem," *Local Government Studies* 17, no. 2 (1991): 15–32.

25 Charles E. Fritz and J. H. Mathewson, *Convergence Behavior in Disasters* (Washington, D.C.: National Academy of Sciences/National Research Council, 1957); Jack D. Kartez and Michael K. Lindell, "Planning for Uncertainty: The Case of Local Disaster Planning," *Journal of the American Planning Association* 53, no. 4 (1987): 487–498.

26 Bruce B. Clary, "The Evolution and Structure of Natural Hazard Policies," *Public Administration Review* 45 (1985): 20–28; Peter May and Robert E. Deyle, "Governing Land Use in Hazardous Areas with a Patchwork System," in *Cooperating with Nature: Confronting Natural Hazards with Land-Use Planning for Sustainable Communities,* ed. Raymond J. Burby, 57–84 (Washington, D.C.: Joseph Henry Press, 1998); Claire B. Rubin, ed., *Emergency Management: The American Experience, 1900–2005* (Fairfax, Va.: Public Entity Risk Institute, 2007).

27 Claire B. Rubin, "The Community Recovery Process in the United States after a Major Natural Disaster," *International Journal of Mass Emergencies and Disasters* 3, no. 2 (1985): 9–28.

28 George Mader, *Rebuilding after Earthquakes: Lessons from Planners* (Portola, Calif.: William Spangle and Associates, 1991); William Spangle et al., ed., *Pre-Earthquake Planning for Post-Earthquake Rebuilding (PEPPER)* (Los Angeles: Southern California Earthquake Preparedness Project, 1987); Schwab et al., *Planning for Post-Disaster Recovery and Reconstruction;* Smith and Wenger, "Sustainable Disaster Recovery"; Olshansky, "Planning after Hurricane Katrina."

29 T. J. Kent Jr., *The Urban General Plan,* 2nd ed. (San Francisco: Chandler, 1991); John M. DeGrove, *Land, Growth and Politics* (Chicago: Planners Press, 1984); Edward J. Kaiser, David R. Godschalk, and F. Stuart Chapin Jr., *Urban Land Use Planning,* 4th ed. (Urbana: University of Illinois Press, 1995); Frank S. So and Judith Getzels, eds., *The Practice of Local Government Planning* (Washington, D.C.: International City Management Association, 1988).

30 Edward J. Kaiser and David R. Godschalk, "Twentieth Century Land Use Planning: A Stalwart Family Tree," in *The City Reader,* ed. Richard LeGates and Fredric Stout, 366–386 (New York: Routledge, 2003); Philip R. Berke et al., *Urban Land Use Planning,* 5th ed. (Urbana: Illinois University Press, 2006).

31 Lawrence Susskind and Connie Ozawa, "Mediated Negotiation in the Public Sector: The Planner as Mediator," *Journal of Planning Education and Research* 4, no. 1 (1984): 5–15; David Godschalk, "Volusia County Conflict Resolution Program," in *The Planner as Dispute Resolver,* ed. A. Bruce Dotson, David Godschalk, and Jerome Kaufman (Washington, D.C.: National Institute for Dispute Resolution, 1989).

32 Martha Blair Tyler, Katherine O'Prey and Karen Kristiansson, *Redevelopment after Earthquakes* (Portola Valley, Calif.: Spangle Associates, 2002); Spangle et al., ed., *Pre-Earthquake Planning*

for Post-Earthquake Rebuilding (PEPPER); Schwab et al., *Planning for Post-Disaster Recovery and Reconstruction.*

33 Spangle et al., ed., *Pre-Earthquake Planning for Post-Earthquake Rebuilding (PEPPER).*

34 Lawrence J. Vale and Thomas J. Campanella, *The Resilient City: How Modern Cities Recover from Disasters* (New York: Oxford University Press, 2005).

35 Kathleen Tierney, Michael K. Lindell, and Ronald W. Perry, *Facing the Unexpected: Disaster Preparedness and Response in the United States* (Washington, D.C.: Joseph Henry Press, 2001).

36 Gavin Smith, "The 21st Century Emergency Manager" (Emmitsburg, Md.: Emergency Management Institute Higher Education Project, FEMA, 2002).

37 Robert P. Wolensky and Edward J. Miller, "The Everyday Versus the Disaster Role of Local Officials: Citizen and Official Definitions," *Urban Affairs Quarterly* 16, no. 4 (1981): 483–504.

38 Richard A. Smith and Robert E. Deyle, "Hurricane Case Study: Opal in the Florida Panhandle," in *Planning for Post-Disaster Recovery and Reconstruction,* PAS Report 483/484, by Jim Schwab et al., 235–259 (Chicago: APA, 1998).

39 Jack D. Kartez and Charles Faupel, "Comprehensive Hazard Management and the Role of Cooperation between Local Planning Departments and Emergency Management Offices" (unpublished paper, 1994).

40 Mary B. Anderson and Peter Woodrow, *Rising from the Ashes: Development Strategies in Times of Disaster* (Boulder, Colo.: Westview Press, 1989).

41 Oliver-Smith, "Post-Disaster Housing Reconstruction"; Berke and Beatley, *After the Hurricane.*

42 Betty Hearn Morrow and Walter Gillis Peacock, "Disasters and Social Change: Hurricane Andrew and the Reshaping of Miami?" in *Hurricane Andrew: Ethnicity, Gender and the Sociology of Disasters,* ed. Walter Gillis Peacock, Betty Hearn Morrow, and Hugh Gladwin, 226–242 (Miami, Fla.: International Hurricane Center Laboratory for Social and Behavioral Research, 2000); Susan Cutter, ed., *American Hazardscapes: The Regionalization of Natural Hazards and Disasters* (Washington, D.C.: Joseph Henry Press, 2001).

43 Marla Nelson, Renia Ehrenfeucht, and Shirley Laska, "Planning, Plans, and People: Professional Expertise, Local Knowledge, and Governmental Action in Post-Hurricane Katrina New Orleans," *Cityscape: A Journal of Policy Development and Research* 9, no. 3 (2007): 23–52.

44 Christopher L. Dyer, "The Phoenix Effect in Post-Disaster Recovery: An Analysis of the Economic Development Administration's Culture of Response after Hurricane Andrew," in *The Angry Earth: Disaster in Anthropological Perspective,* ed. Anthony Oliver-Smith and Susanna Hoffman, 278–300 (New York: Routledge, 1999).

45 Mary C. Comerio et al., "Residential Earthquake Recovery: Improving California's Post-Disaster Rebuilding Policies and Programs," *California Policy Seminar Brief* 8, no. 7 (1996).

46 Smith and Wenger, "Sustainable Disaster Recovery."

47 J. Eugene Haas, Robert W. Kates, and Martyn Bowden, eds. *Reconstruction following Disaster* (Cambridge, Mass.: MIT Press, 1977).

48 Barbara E. Harrell-Bond, *Imposing Aid: Emergency Assistance to Refugees* (Oxford: Oxford University Press, 1986); Oliver-Smith, "Post-Disaster Housing Reconstruction"; Berke and Beatley, *After the Hurricane.*

49 Dyer, "The Phoenix Effect in Post-Disaster Recovery."

50 Smith and Wenger, "Sustainable Disaster Recovery."

51 Robert C. Bolin and Patricia A. Bolton, "Recovery in Nicaragua and the USA," *International Journal of Mass Emergencies and Disasters* 1, no. 1 (1983): 125–144; Mary C. Comerio, *Disaster Hits Home: New Policy for Urban Housing Recovery* (Berkeley: University of California Press, 1998); Walter Gillis Peacock, Betty Hearn Morrow, and Hugh Gladwin, eds. *Hurricane Andrew: Ethnicity, Gender and the Sociology of Disasters* (see note 42).

52 Smith, "Holistic Disaster Recovery."

53 North Carolina Emergency Management Division, *Hazard Mitigation in North Carolina: Measuring Success* (Raleigh, 2000), www.p2pays.org/ref/14/13619/13619.pdf.

54 Alvin Mushkatel and Louis Weschler, "Emergency Management and the Intergovernmental System," *Public Administration Review* 45, Special Issue (1985): 49–56.

55 Philip R. Berke, Jack Kartez, and Dennis Wenger, "Recovery after Disasters: Achieving Sustainable Development, Mitigation and Equity," *Disasters* 17, no. 2 (1993): 93–109; Smith and Wenger, "Sustainable Disaster Recovery."

56 Peter May, "Disaster Recovery and Reconstruction," in *Managing Disaster: Strategies and Perspectives,* ed. Louise Comfort, 236–254 (Durham, N.C.: Duke University Press, 1989).

57 Robert C. Bolin and Lois Stanford, "The Northridge Earthquake: Community-based Approaches to Unmet Recovery Needs," *Disasters* 22, no. 1 (1998): 21–38.

58 Bolin and Stanford, "The Northridge Earthquake."

59 Russell R. Dynes, Enrico L. Quarantelli, and Gary Kreps, *A Perspective on Disaster Planning* (Newark: Disaster Research Center, University of Delaware, 1981); David R. Godschalk, David J. Brower, and Timothy Beatley, *Catastrophic Coastal Storms: Hazard Mitigation and Development Management* (Durham, N.C.: Duke University Press, 1989); Smith and Wenger, "Sustainable Disaster Recovery."

60 Smith and Wenger, "Sustainable Disaster Recovery."

61 Gavin Smith and Victor Flatt, "Assessing the Disaster Recovery Planning Capacity of the State of North Carolina" (research brief, Institute for Homeland Security Solutions, Durham, N.C., January 2011), 1–8.

Chapter 3

Quasi-governmental and Nongovernmental Organizations

This new home was designed for Shirley Jackson in East Biloxi by the Gulf Coast Community Design Studio, an organization affiliated with the Mississippi State University College of Architecture, Art + Design (see sidebar on pages 94–98). Note the volunteers walking down the steps.

Photo by Seth Welty.

QUASI-GOVERNMENTAL ORGANIZATIONS ARE SUPPORTED BY the government but managed by the private sector. Nongovernmental organizations (NGOs) are private entities, independent of government and generally nonprofit in nature. By identifying gaps in the delivery of public sector aid and providing specialized assistance, these organizations play an important role in the disaster recovery assistance network.

Specifically, quasi-governmental and nongovernmental organizations address perceived shortfalls in the assistance network, provide targeted governmental services, coordinate the actions of other organizations, serve in an advisory role, research past events, and translate their findings into practice. Some of them make important contributions that are tied to the delivery of technical assistance and knowledge, two elements that are often lacking among public sector stakeholders involved in recovery. These organizations may also provide assistance in managing local government grant programs, writing and implementing plans, conducting training, implementing local capacity-building initiatives, and educating future researchers, policy makers, and emergency management professionals.

The degree to which quasi-governmental and nongovernmental organizations are connected to other actors in the assistance network affects the degree to which their unique skills are maximized. Low levels of horizontal and vertical integration has several negative implications. First, because the assistance they provide often goes unnoticed by other members of the network, their ability to effect change in the mode and timing of assistance provided by others may be constrained. Second, because the type and timing of assistance that they deliver is not well coordinated with government agencies, the private sector, and other entities across the network, the value of that assistance may be limited. To achieve a higher level of integration and thus enhance the ability of quasi-governmental and nongovernmental organizations to provide a "boundary spanning" function across the larger recovery assistance network, as described in the case study of the Broadmoor Project at the end of this chapter, requires the adoption of coordinative strategies.

QUASI-GOVERNMENTAL ORGANIZATIONS

The quasi-governmental organizations involved in recovery assistance include community development corporations (CDCs), homeowners associations (HOAs), special service districts, and regional planning organizations (RPOs).

Community Development Corporations

CDCs were established in the 1960s to help low-income communities manage neighborhood-level planning activities. A number of the economic development and capacity-building services they provide are directly relevant to disaster recovery. Specific actions include developing or repairing affordable housing, creating jobs for low-income individuals, increasing public and private investment in low-income areas, and building local capacity to lead community-based initiatives. CDCs work closely with developers, builders, tradespeople, lenders, and citizens to meet the needs of communities. They often obtain grants that offset costs for real estate developers, thereby providing financial incentives for investment in low-income areas. The three leading national groups that provide technical assistance to CDCs are NeighborWorks, the

Local Initiatives Support Corporation (LISC), and Enterprise Community Partners. NeighborWorks (www.nw.org), a national network of over 220 community development and affordable housing organizations, provides advice on the development of marketing and business plans and the preparation of financial statements. LISC (www.lisc.org) assists CDCs through the delivery of grants and technical assistance. Enterprise Community Partners (www.enterprisecommunity.org) provides capital and expertise for affordable housing and community development.

CDCs are formed by individuals, faith-based organizations, social justice groups, local business owners, or others interested in revitalizing a given area. Prospective CDCs are required to apply for nonprofit status through the U.S. Internal Revenue Service. Their designation as a 501 (c)(3) enables them to seek funding from federal and state agencies, foundations, and members of the private sector. Two federal agencies that regularly assist CDCs are the Department of Housing and Urban Development (HUD) and the U.S. Treasury Department. HUD provides funding toward activities such as grants administration, training, and capacity-building exercises. The Treasury Department provides financial aid through the Community Development Financial Institution Fund (www.cdfifund.gov), which it created to encourage economic revitalization and community development.

Common-Interest Communities and Homeowners Associations

Common-interest communities may include cooperative apartments, condominiums, town house neighborhoods, and master-planned communities. Most common-interest communities are governed by HOAs. HOAs are legal entities, usually established by a developer in order to control the type and quality of homes constructed as well as the management of amenities and public services. The developer often works through the HOA to pass and enforce covenants, conditions, and restrictions that dictate the type, location, and density of land use and with which homeowners must comply. Some communities have detailed restrictions that describe everything from the type of materials that can be used in construction to the paint colors that are allowed, while others have a loosely established set of rules ensuring that homeowners maintain their properties in a manner acceptable to their neighbors.

The HOA is usually responsible for maintaining common areas, including private streets, sidewalks, parks, and other open spaces. Depending on where the development is located and the type and extent of open space within it, responsibilities may include basic lawn care, tree maintenance, snow removal, and sidewalk or street repair. Some HOAs are also responsible for garbage collection, water, sewer, and other public services. HOAs levy assessments to finance these activities and may impose fines on homeowners who do not comply with established rules. When a property is purchased, regulations are placed on the deed and tied to the property in perpetuity. The degree to which these covenants, conditions, and restrictions are aligned with the land use regulations of the larger jurisdiction in which the community is located can be a source of ongoing tension and has direct implications for the management of natural hazards and the manner in which common-interest communities plan for and recover from disasters.

The history of common-interest communities offers insight into their potential role in hazard mitigation and disaster recovery. In 1926, the Supreme Court upheld the constitutionality of zoning, which found that communities have the legal authority to designate parcels of land for different uses. Before the advent of zoning, developers relied on the use of covenants placed on individual lots to regulate land use.[1] In the early 1960s, the Federal Housing Authority (FHA) provided federal home mortgage insurance to owners of condominiums or homes in subdivisions that were part of an HOA. The FHA believed that these areas would maintain their value over time. In reality, this practice played a role in the disinvestment in urban areas and the growth of the suburbs, where HOAs are becoming increasingly ubiquitous.

As part of an effort to protect open space in suburban communities, a growing number of developers are clustering residences, leaving open space to be managed by the association. While this development approach is often used to protect scenic views and recreational opportunities, it can also be a useful tool for mitigating a community's vulnerability to natural hazards. If homes are clustered on a parcel of land away from areas prone to flooding, hurricane-induced storm surges, landslides, and other natural hazards, the community's exposure to the potentially damaging effects of these events can be lessened.

Since the passage of the Clean Water Act of 1977, new developments are required to address storm-water runoff though the identification of detention areas—largely undeveloped areas that are often maintained by HOAs. Like cluster development, the location of storm-water detention areas in open space can reduce the likelihood of flood-related losses. Applying open space principles and cluster development to larger areas has also been used to maintain and preserve rural farmland, scenic views, cultural and historic resources, critical wildlife habitat, and other natural resources.[2] The value of achieving multiple objectives through planning, including the importance of building diverse coalitions that support one another's complementary aims, will be discussed further in Chapter 8.

Special Districts

Special districts provide water, wastewater, and street services to planned developments or to make financial improvements in established areas such as downtowns.[3] In many cases, special districts that address housing and urban development, flood control, soil and water conservation, water and sewer, schools, parks and recreation, airports, cemeteries, and health care facilities extend beyond the boundaries of one jurisdiction. The services and infrastructure they make available may be financed by the issuance of bonds, which are covered by user fees and increased property assessments in the designated area. The ability to derive revenue gives special districts a unique influence over the density and location of development as these funds can be used for the construction and maintenance of infrastructure that plays a central role in guiding growth.

The rapid expansion of these quasi-governmental units makes them increasingly important in shaping pre- and post-disaster settlement patterns, including those tied to public investments that increase or decrease hazard exposure. While special districts typically follow local land use regulations, they function as separate administrative units, reporting to a governing board. This arrangement can be problematic, however, if the district does not adhere to the development policies of the municipal or county jurisdiction in which it is located. In some cases, special districts are required to be part of an RPO in order to resolve conflicting land use choices.[4]

Regional Planning Organizations

Planning tools and processes have long been used in the United States to address regional or multijurisdictional issues, such as urban form,[5] natural resource protection,[6] rural and farmland preservation,[7] protection of green infrastructure,[8] metropolitan and suburban development,[9] growth management,[10] transit-oriented development,[11] and hazards management.[12] Regional planning also has a long-standing tradition of recognizing and attempting to address complementary objectives tied to sustainability (even though at the time such objectives were called something else). As early as the mid-1800s, George Perkins Marsh warned against the indiscriminate clear-cutting of forests in watersheds, which he argued would lead to flood, drought, erosion, landslides, and climate change; he further argued that similar actions of early civilizations along the Mediterranean Sea led to their eventual decline[13] (see the accompanying sidebar on page 82).

The challenges of coordinating multijurisdictional plans, intergovernmental disaster policies, and post-disaster recovery grant programs highlight the importance of a regional approach to emergency management.[14] Emergencies tend to be localized

A Brief History of Regional Planning and Hazards Management in the United States

The roots of regional planning in the United States can be traced back to the creation of the Regional Planning Association of America (RPAA) in 1923 and to the New Deal's emphasis on river basin management, economic development, and flood control in areas prone to natural hazards.[1]

The RPAA brought together leading British and American planners who believed that areawide planning was the best way to direct development. One of its first projects involved the planning and construction of the Appalachian Trail, which regional planner Benton MacKaye believed not only would provide Americans with a valuable means to access nature but also could serve as a buffer against development from eastern cities. By focusing on the importance of topography in determining appropriate human settlement patterns, MacKaye, like Ian McHarg decades later, provided what has become an important tool to reduce the impacts of natural hazards on people and communities. The RPAA was also instrumental in providing the means to share ideas about greenbelts, garden cities, and other innovative regional approaches to community planning. During the 1930s, several greenbelt communities were designed, drawing on the idea of using green space as a buffer around an urban core.

In the 1930s, the unwillingness of local elected officials to develop a regional plan for the Los Angeles river basin led to the misguided expenditure of public funds on roads, ill-planned subdivisions, and flood-control projects that did not recognize the importance of preserving natural areas that were prone to flooding, earthquakes, wildfires, and landslides. With foresight into the future of the basin, Frederick Law Olmsted and Harlan Bartholomew proposed to develop an interconnected series of greenways that linked oceanfront property, floodplains, and steep sloped areas. However, because of strong opposition by the *Los Angeles Times* and development interests, the Los Angeles Regional Planning Commission and local community organizations failed to muster an adequate defense of the plan, and the plan was never implemented.[2]

Recent examples of regional planning organizations (RPOs) that have successfully influenced development and natural hazards management include the San Francisco Bay Conservation and Development Commission, the New Jersey Pinelands Commission, the Lake Tahoe Regional Planning Authority, and the Adirondack Park Agency. The actions of these organizations have highlighted the nexus between protecting natural resources and reducing the vulnerability of communities to the damaging impacts of earthquakes (increased liquefaction in lands created with fill material), wildfires (increased development in the wildland-urban interface), flooding (development in flood-prone areas), and landslides (the removal of vegetation in landslide-prone areas).

The development of plans compliant with the Disaster Mitigation Act of 2000 represents the latest involvement of RPOs in hazard management activities. Several states, including North Carolina, Texas, and Virginia, have encouraged the development of multicounty plans. In many cases, RPOs have coordinated the planning process, the development of the plan, and its implementation over time through the writing and administration of grants that fund preidentified hazard mitigation projects.

1 Peter Hall, *Cities of Tomorrow* (Oxford, England: Basil Blackwell, Ltd., 1988), 148–164.
2 Mike Davis, *Ecology of Fear: Los Angeles and the Imagination of Disaster* (New York: Vintage Books, 1998), 61–68.

events, whereas disasters are often regional in nature, particularly when measured by their physical, environmental, social, and economic impacts. Disaster-related damages are often felt over a wide geographic area, crossing political boundaries and affecting transportation, communication, and social networks that connect jurisdictions to one another. Given the regional nature of most natural hazards and disasters, regional planning provides a viable strategy for addressing land use issues that are beyond the scope of any one jurisdiction.[15]

RPOs, such as regional planning districts, councils of governments (COGs), and metropolitan planning organizations, provide services across multiple counties and municipalities. While they have limited authority over local land use decisions, their strength lies in their ability to facilitate collaborative, multijurisdictional planning. This ability to address regional or metropolitan issues is relevant to the type of aid needed by members of the assistance network before and after a disaster. The fact that the assistance that they give is often guided by accepted planning principles makes RPOs a potentially important player in the recovery process. Moreover, RPOs facilitate vertical linkages with state and federal funding agencies while enhancing horizontal linkages as the designated organization responsible for planning in the area.[16]

Regional planning efforts initiated prior to an event are often based on potential scenarios, including those that may entail significant damages and require large-scale recovery efforts (see sidebar on page 84). The Saint Louis Regional Response System, created in 2003, is but one example of the many regional planning efforts already taking place. Local governments have long been concerned about the risk of a major earthquake along the New Madrid fault, which includes parts of Missouri and Illinois. Following the 9/11 terrorist attacks, concerns about a possible "megadisaster" increased. A team of stakeholders came together to focus on several key objectives, such as developing leadership capabilities, influencing disaster policy, and forging new connections among local governments in the area. Although the group is principally focused on regional preparedness, its multijurisdictional approach could be expanded to address long-term recovery and reconstruction activities, including pre-event planning for post-disaster recovery.

Many regional organizations are a significant source of grants management and planning services before and after disasters. Regional planning agencies often administer Community Development Block Grants (CDBGs), Pre-Disaster Mitigation (PDM) funds, and Hazard Mitigation Grant Program (HMGP) funds. Following major federal disasters, CDBG funds are often appropriated by Congress to aid in the relocation, repair, and reconstruction of damaged housing and in the construction of low- and moderate-income housing; and to address post-disaster economic development. PDM and HMGP funds, on the other hand, are intended to reduce a community's exposure to the damaging effects of natural hazards and disasters. As noted in Chapter 2, HMGP funds are often used in conjunction with CDBG funds to help mitigate future hazard-related losses.

Two Approaches to Regional Disaster Recovery Planning

Regional planning approaches to recovery can take different forms. The Red River Valley Flood Recovery Action Plan emphasized a post-disaster, federally supported approach, while the Association of Bay Area Governments took it upon itself to create a regional plan prior to a disaster.

Post-Disaster: The Red River Valley Flood Recovery Action Plan

In 1997, flooding along the Red River caused the displacement of more than sixty thousand people in Minnesota, North Dakota, and South Dakota. After the event was declared a federal disaster area, President Bill Clinton established a federal interagency task force to help the three states develop a recovery plan. The Federal Action Plan for Recovery emphasized three areas: (1) hazard mitigation, (2) housing, and (3) community sustainability. Federal agency participants included the Federal Emergency Management Agency (FEMA), the Department of Housing and Urban Development, the Department of Energy, the Army Corps of Engineers, the Economic Development Administration, and the Small Business Administration.

In addition to the assistance provided after a disaster under the Stafford Act, FEMA authorized planning and design-based support for the communities that were hardest hit, thereby enabling communities to address new housing construction and the preservation of historic properties and central business districts while providing incentives for business reinvestment. Targeted post-disaster planning assistance served as the precursor to what eventually became Emergency Support Function 14, Long-Term Community Recovery. Emphasis was also placed on the relocation of flood-prone homes, infrastructure, and businesses, amounting to a comprehensive effort to address community hazard vulnerability.

Pre-Disaster: The Association of Bay Area Governments Disaster Recovery Initiative

The Association of Bay Area Governments (ABAG) is a regional planning agency that works with cities and counties in the San Francisco Bay area. ABAG's Disaster Recovery Initiative represents a concerted effort of its regional planning committee to assist communities prepare for an earthquake, which members recognize is inevitable. Using issue papers, presentations, training materials, and lessons observed from previous disasters in California, other states, and abroad, ABAG and its member jurisdictions provide local governments with a wealth of in-depth information on such topical areas as speeding the post-disaster acquisition of federal assistance, protecting and repairing government facilities and services, assisting businesses and local economies to recover from a disaster, implementing long-term housing recovery measures, and repairing damaged lifelines (see quake.abag.ca.gov/recovery). All areas are framed in the larger context of a local disaster recovery plan.[1] In the future, ABAG plans to address four additional areas: infrastructure, education, health care facilities, and land use.

ABAG also surveyed participating local governments to assess their pre-event capacity to address these topical areas and plan for recovery. Based on the results of the survey, ABAG has initiated the development of a best practices document and a toolkit to train local governments in disaster recovery planning. Future training materials will focus on the different needs of large cities, small municipalities, and counties.

1 "Regional Long-Term Disaster Recovery Initiative," Association of Bay Area Governments website at quake.abag.ca.gov/recovery/ (last updated June 10, 2010).

Local governments often turn to regional planning agencies to write and administer these grants. Because RPOs help direct grant programs associated with economic development, natural resource management, housing, hazard mitigation, and disaster recovery, they understand the connectivity between planning and the use of grant funding to achieve stated goals and multiple objectives. The routine involvement of RPOs in contentious environmental, economic development, and social equity–based conflicts also make them well suited to assist communities with post-disaster resource allocation debates.

NONGOVERNMENTAL ORGANIZATIONS

Traditionally, NGOs are further broken down into another class of assistance provider–nonprofit relief organizations (see Chapter 4). For the purpose of this book, however, they are limited to professional associations and colleges and universities.

Professional Associations

Professional associations consist of members with highly specialized technical expertise grounded in practice, whom they can mobilize to address specific issues and garner the attention of policy makers, elected officials, and other members of the assistance network. The resources provided by professional associations are tied to the unique skills of their trades: planning, floodplain management, engineering, building inspection, emergency management, public administration, and the like. Many professional associations advise federal, state, and local policy makers through testimony at legislative hearings and the writing of technical documents, policy briefs, and opinion pieces. They can also influence public opinion by conducting press conferences and other media events. Annual conferences, training, and educational forums provide opportunities for members to exchange ideas, learn the latest information and techniques in their field, discuss internal protocols, and codify how the association proposes to influence policies developed by external agencies and organizations that affect their normal activities and professional responsibilities.

Among the many professional associations that have been involved in disaster recovery–related activities are the Association of State Floodplain Managers (ASFPM), National Emergency Management Association (NEMA), International Association of Emergency Managers (IAEM), American Planning Association (APA), the American Society of Civil Engineers, and the American Institute of Architects (Exhibit 3–1 on page 86). The services that these and other professional associations provide include recovery planning; post-event assessment of damages and analysis of the structural integrity of buildings and infrastructure; grant administration; interlocal and interstate aid coordination; pre- and post-disaster outreach, training, and capacity building; construction management activities; accreditation; policy counsel; and advocacy. Those associations that focus on urban design have played an increasingly important role in recovery, as evidenced by their work in the wake of Hurricane Katrina (see the accompanying sidebar

Exhibit 3–1. Professional Associations with Disaster-Related Programs or Responsibilities

Group	Title
Chief executives	American Society of Public Administrators
	International City/County Management Association
	National Association of County Governments
	National League of Cities
	National Municipal League
	U.S. Conference of Mayors
Line professional	American Institute of Architects
	American Institute of Certified Planners
	American Planning Association
	American Public Health Association
	American Public Works Association
	American Society of Civil Engineers
	American Society of Landscape Architects
	American Society of Professional Engineers
	Government Finance Officers Administration
	International Association of Chiefs of Police
	International Association of Fire Chiefs
	National Emergency Management Association
	National Institute of Municipal Legal Officials
	National Recreation and Parks Association
	National Sheriff's Association

Source: Raymond Burby, ed., *Cooperating with Nature: Confronting Natural Hazards with Land-Use Planning for Sustainable Communities* (Washington, D.C.: Joseph Henry Press, 1998), 222. Reprinted with permission of the publisher.

on page 87). But the levels of financial support they receive to implement their programs fluctuate, demonstrating the need to build an enduring coalition across the larger assistance network that improves the integration of professional associations into pre-event planning activities and more effectively links their expertise into recovery efforts when a disaster occurs.

However, professional associations also muster support for pro-growth interests, which John Logan and Harvey Molotch refer to as the "growth machine."[18] Members of the growth machine include developers, elected officials, local media, and others who stand to gain from continued growth and thus often resist increased regulations. Collectively, these members can shut down more considered approaches to development and successfully oppose stronger building codes, land use measures, hazard notification, post-disaster building moratoria, and other regulations that are part of effective hazard mitigation and recovery strategies. In Saint Louis Missouri, for example, the Home Builders Association, in concert with the city and other

New Urbanism and the Disaster Recovery Assistance Framework

New Urbanism focuses on pedestrian accessibility, a layering of land uses within and across neighborhoods, narrow streets, parks and pathways, and tightly controlled architectural guidelines. In many ways, New Urbanism serves as an alternative to traditional single-use zoning practices prevalent in the United States.[1] The mixed-use approach allows schools, civic buildings, and commercial establishments to be located within walking distance of private homes.

The Mississippi Renewal Forum following Hurricane Katrina

After Hurricane Katrina, attempts were made to incorporate the principles of New Urbanism into the reconstruction of coastal communities. Over one hundred new urbanists came to Biloxi to participate in the Mississippi Renewal Forum, believed to be the largest single planning charrette ever held.[2] (Charrettes are intense, multiday meetings involving professionals and affected stakeholders.)[3] Multidisciplinary teams were assigned to each of the fourteen coastal municipalities to help create "redevelopment plans" that incorporated New Urbanist principles (www.mississippirenewal.com).

One of the areas in which the New Urbanists excel is in the design and construction of improved post-disaster emergency housing. Many forum participants openly questioned

One of a series of Katrina Cottage designs created during the 2005 Mississippi Renewal Forum in Biloxi, Mississippi, Marianne Cusato's 308-square-foot "little yellow cottage" made the transition Katrina Cottage advocates intended, going from a model for temporary emergency housing to a role in a permanent infill neighborhood in Ocean Springs, Mississippi.

Photo by Ben Brown.

why the Federal Emergency Management Agency (FEMA) continued to rely on the use of travel trailers and mobile homes for post-disaster emergency housing. During the charrette process, architects designed several models, including what became known as the "Katrina Cottage" (see figure below). The state of Mississippi later sought congressional funding for the idea and developed a number of alternative housing models (see accompanying figures on page 88) that were built and tested as part of an experimental FEMA program. (It appears unlikely that the concept will replace the traditional use of travel trailers and mobile homes as FEMA has reverted back to past emergency housing practices during subsequent disasters).

However, participants in the forum did not consistently use best practices regarding planning principles and techniques typically used by the professional planning community (described in Chapter 8). For instance, their plans lacked a strong implementation component and so their blending of older neighborhood patterns, which mirrored many of the New Urbanist principles, with newer, post–World War II development, which reflected auto-dependent land uses associated with sprawl, achieved moderate success. Nor did the plans effectively incorporate the principles of hazard mitigation into proposed design parameters.[4]

The discussion of hazard mitigation during the weeklong planning charrette resulted in heated debate among design professionals and state and federal officials who sought to emphasize the importance of linking reconstruction options to the notion of reducing hazard vulnerability. Evidence of this tension was manifested in the open hostility shown by the New Urbanists when they realized that the development of new flood insurance rate maps (FIRMs) would significantly increase the height at which new and reconstructed homes located along the Gulf Coast would need to be elevated. To comply with the amended FIRMs, new construction in areas subject to coastal storm surge, including structures that sustained more that 50 percent damage as a result of Katrina, would need to be elevated approximately three to eight feet higher than those constructed using pre-Katrina

continued on page 88

continued from page 87

standards.[5] In some cases this resulted in homes being elevated more than twenty feet. During the charrette, architects drew caricatures of homes elevated to extreme heights and derisively referred to them as "bird-legged houses." The drawings were intended to highlight what the architects believed to be excessive regulations that would ruin the character of coastal communities.

The extreme vulnerability of Mississippi's coastal communities to the damaging effects of hurricane-induced storm surge and coastal flooding raised the inevitable question regarding the limitation of redevelopment in these areas (see accompanying figure on page 89). In the end, communities did not ban the reconstruction of homes in such areas; however, the fact that land use planning was openly discussed and that attempts were made to reinforce the original urban form of coastal communities that predated the rise of suburban sprawl was a significant accomplishment given that land use planning did not have widespread support across the state prior to Hurricane Katrina. Of those communities that had a land use planner on staff, their involvement in the charrette process was inconsistent as many planners were overwhelmed with other responsibilities. As a result, planning principles and techniques were not always followed, nor was there a sufficient cadre of local officials necessary to ensure that viable ideas were implemented. In the end, results have been mixed. Some communities have adopted new development regulations while others have decided to ignore the work of the New Urbanists altogether.

Deconstructing the Forum

The Mississippi Renewal Forum provides a microcosm of the three principal dimensions of the disaster assistance framework: understanding of local needs, timing of assistance, and horizontal and vertical integration. First, planning for post-disaster recovery should ideally take place before a disaster occurs, particularly in areas that are most vulnerable to the damaging effects of natural hazards. Post-disaster planning for recovery should be undertaken before key reconstruction policies are developed and community-level reinvestment strategies are begun. Stakeholders must also find ample time to discuss alternative plans that reflect the diversity of local needs and the resources available across the larger assistance network. A lack of time for deliberation often results in ill-conceived post-disaster decisions that set in motion reconstruction activities that in turn hinder a sustainable and resilient recovery.

The Mississippi Alternative Housing Program includes images of the Park Model and Mississippi Cottage. The one-bedroom Park Model was built with a permanently attached wheeled undercarriage for exclusive use as a temporary dwelling, whereas the undercarriage of the two- or three-bedroom Mississippi Cottage can be removed and set on a permanent foundation.

Photos by Gavin Smith.

Pictured is an aerial image of Pass Christian, Mississippi following Hurricane Katrina.

Photo by Gavin Smith.

In Mississippi, the renewal forum was held in October, several weeks after Hurricane Katrina made landfall. The timing proved problematic as many citizens and community leaders were struggling to provide basic services. Yet it also provided a unique opportunity to visualize options in communities before they began the large-scale reconstruction of damaged housing, schools, and infrastructure.

The Mississippi Renewal Forum's charrette process also suffered from a lack of horizontal and vertical integration across the larger assistance network; this resulted in several policy conflicts and limited the effectiveness of the overall approach. For example, development interests, which play a critical role in the financing and reconstruction of communities following disasters, were not directly involved in the process. Moreover, architects initially refused to accept reconstruction standards associated with the National Flood Insurance Program. The fact that the documents generated were not plans (as defined in Chapter 8) created additional problems. For example, the spatial configuration of reconstruction scenarios were not tied to local information (i.e., the local fact base), including private property lot lines, existing settlement patterns, and the location of extreme high-hazard areas. Participants suggested the adoption of a New Urbanist "Smartcode" that encourages compact urban form reminiscent of the original development patterns found along the Mississippi coast, but the preexisting settlement patterns limited the applicability of the code to mainly

the waterfront, which is the area most vulnerable to hurricane-induced storm surge. Finally, the visual interpretation of the New Urbanist designs were not always connected to policy recommendations generated through public participation and codified in existing plans adopted by governing bodies.

Over time, after continued dialogue with local officials, members of FEMA's Emergency Support Function 14 (ESF-14), and the Governor's Office of Recovery and Renewal, most of the New Urbanists came to realize that reconstruction options would have to adhere to new building codes and local flood ordinances as well as to revisions of existing local policies. Eventually, five of the lower six coastal counties adopted mandatory building codes (the rest of the state's counties did not), and all coastal communities amended their local flood damage prevention ordinances to reflect new flood elevations determined by a post-disaster reanalysis of flood hazard vulnerability. Several communities also adopted the Smartcode, a design policy that is based on a series of "transects," each of which is characterized by density and urban form parameters. The density is highest in town centers and decreases as development moves outward toward more rural areas.

Lessons and Observations
Several lessons can be derived from the experience of the New Urbanists in Mississippi following Hurricane Katrina, and these can be tied directly to the underlying weaknesses of the disaster recovery assistance framework. First, members of the assistance network, including FEMA's ESF-14, the Emergency Management Assistance Compact (EMAC), professional associations (including the American Planning Association and the American Institute of Architects [AIA]), and hazard scholars, should reach out to the New Urbanists and engage in an open dialogue intended to better coordinate the unique design services they provide to communities with the objectives of the larger disaster recovery assistance network—including, for instance, pre- and post-event recovery planning assistance delivered in coordination with local officials, proposed EMAC teams (see the sidebar in Chapter 2 on EMAC), ESF-14 staff, and others.

continued on page 90

continued from page 89

Second, the effective use of such design professionals as the New Urbanists requires sharing pertinent information about existing recovery programs, particularly those that are intended to mitigate the effects of natural hazards. This information could be used to modify existing New Urbanist strategies in a manner that does not necessarily alter their intent but rather expands upon them to consider the unique conditions associated with natural hazards and disasters. For instance, the transect concept underlying the Smartcode could be broadened to include a new "H Transect" that designates high-hazard areas. Specific design and urban form parameters could be established that limit the exposure of future development in different transects to the damaging effects of varied natural hazards (e.g., hurricane-induced flooding, storm surge, and high winds; earthquake-induced ground motion; wildfire). Examples could include using flood-proofing techniques for businesses that are traditionally located at street level while placing residential development on the second floor, thereby reducing the likelihood of flood-related damages. Considering that a central premise of New Urbanist development is the use of compact urban form, new architectural design plans could limit development in known high-hazard areas while clustering more intensive and, therefore, more walkable development in locations less prone to flooding, landslides, and wildfires. Given the growing number of New Urbanist communities, the adoption of these practices could help to stem the tide of increasing disaster losses.

Third, members of the disaster recovery assistance network should collaborate with New Urbanists on the design and development of improved emergency housing. The Katrina Cottage and the pilot program that it inspired were developed because design professionals at the Mississippi Renewal Forum identified a problem in the provision of recovery assistance and applied their unique perspective and training to solve it. However, there is no guarantee that FEMA will adopt the temporary housing designs they developed as part of its post-disaster emergency housing strategy. The adoption of improved temporary housing standards will likely require the development of a coalition of professional emergency management associations, such as the National Emergency Management Association

and International Association of Emergency Managers, working in tandem with other proponents, including the AIA, university faculty, local officials, and individuals who have lived in different units. Arguments for a change in policy, including compliance with international residential code construction standards, improved energy efficiency, the potential transition of units to permanent housing, and the use of materials that do not emit formaldehyde, should be made to the White House Long-Term Disaster Recovery Working Group, which is tasked with identifying needed changes in federal recovery policy as well as those responsible for the development of the National Disaster Housing Strategy required under the Post-Katrina Emergency Management Reform Act.

Finally, the charrette process should be modified to allow for the more deliberative approaches employed by planners (see Chapter 8), including the application of greater public participation techniques, such as alternative dispute resolution, when appropriate. It should also allow time to gather pertinent information needed for the development of policies that reflect underlying environmental, social, and economic conditions. Understood in the context of disaster recovery planning, this fact base also includes the assessment of hazard vulnerability and the existing legal, regulatory, fiscal, and technical capabilities of the community to act. With these proposed modifications, the charrette process could be added to the tools used by the assistance network before and after disasters to assist in the development and implementation of recovery plans.

1   Jonathan Barnett, Joel Russell, and Ellen Greenburg, *Codifying New Urbanism: How to Reform Municipal Land Development Regulations,* Planning Advisory Service (PAS) Report 526 (Chicago: American Planning Association, 2004).

2   Phone conversation with communications consultant Ben Brown, January 2010.

3   Bill Lennertz and Aarin Lutzenhiser, *The Charrette Handbook: The Essential Guide for Accelerated, Collaborative Community Planning* (Chicago: American Planning Association, 2006).

4   Philip R. Berke, Yan Song, and Mark Stevens, "Integrating Hazard Mitigation into New Urban and Conventional Developments," *Journal of Planning Education and Research* 28, no. 4 (2009): 441–455.

5   Federal Emergency Management Agency (FEMA), "Reconstruction Guidance Using Hurricane Katrina Surge Innundation and Advisory Base Flood Elevation Maps" (November 2005), www.fema.gov/pdf/hazard/flood/recoverydata/katrina/katrina_reconstruction.pdf; FEMA, "Hurricane Katrina Surge Innundation and Advisory Flood Elevation Maps Summary of Methods" (November 15, 2005), www.fema.gov/pdf/hazard/flood/recoverydata/katrina/katrina_ms_methods.pdf.

groups, fought the adoption of more stringent earthquake-resistant building codes.[19] After Hurricane Fran in 1996, the Home Builders Association and the Home Realtor's Association defeated attempts by the North Carolina Disaster Recovery Task Force to require the inclusion of a hazards-disclosure clause as part of coastal property sales.[20]

Colleges and Universities

Researchers at colleges and universities have played an integral role in developing a body of knowledge regarding hazards management. This knowledge includes the physical characteristics of hazards; ways to assess the performance of buildings and infrastructure following disasters; an understanding of how people, groups, and organizations behave prior to, during, and after events; the processes of individual, group, and institutional decision making; and the effects of planning on risk reduction and community recovery outcomes. In 1975, the *Assessment of Research on Natural Hazards* was published, reflecting the collective effort of social science scholars, practitioners, and policy makers.[21] The purpose of the assessment was to identify what was known to date, the questions that remained unanswered, and recommend changes in policy. One problem the study highlighted was the failure of the research community to integrate technological and physical sciences with social, political, and economic realities. Since that time, researchers have made significant strides in gaining a better multidisciplinary understanding of natural hazards and disasters.[22]

Critical funding for hazards research has come from federal agencies and national organizations—notably, Congress, the U.S. Geological Survey, the National Oceanic and Atmospheric Administration, the Department of Homeland Security (DHS) (including the Federal Emergency Management Agency [FEMA] and the DHS Science and Technology Directorate), the Environmental Protection Agency, the National Institute of Standards and Technology, the U.S. Army Corps of Engineers, the Department of Energy, the National Laboratories, and the National Science Foundation (NSF) (see the sidebar on pages 92–93). The private sector has also played a role; utilities, insurance companies, banks, and other financial organizations, and private foundations all fund research programs conducted on university campuses or at think tanks.

Among the most powerful contributions of researchers is the ability to critically assess complex systems and establish cause-and-effect relationships using scientifically verifiable methods. However, researchers tend to focus on the advancement of scientific understanding rather than on the application of their findings in practice. Furthermore, since the researchers' help is infrequently solicited by members of the assistance network, many practitioners are unfamiliar with the existing body of scholarship and thus repeat past mistakes or fail to heed lessons uncovered through research.[23]

Translating Research to Practice

The influence of scientific research on federal and state policies regarding natural hazards mitigation and disaster recovery can be seen in the following two examples.

The National Earthquake Hazard Reduction Program

The National Earthquake Hazards Reduction Program (NEHRP), created by the National Earthquake Hazards Reduction Act in 1977, is a federal initiative that uses engineering and science-based investigation techniques to better understand earthquake hazards and human behavior, and then strives to translate natural hazards and disaster-related research findings into practice, including that associated with disaster recovery. NEHRP also seeks to use this information to improve the adoption of earthquake risk-reduction techniques, which can be accomplished by conducting post-disaster assessments of structural failures and successes, improving the predictive capabilities of earthquake models, and proposing strengthened building codes and land use planning techniques.

The National Earthquake Hazards Reduction Act emerged from the 1964 Alaska Earthquake and the 1971 San Fernando Earthquake.[1] The Alaska earthquake prompted a major study by the National Research Council involving engineers, physical scientists, economists, and sociologists. Their findings, published in 1970, constitute one of the most comprehensive studies of a single earthquake event. Shortly thereafter, an earthquake struck the San Fernando Valley, which spurred California to pass a series of laws addressing the seismic retrofitting of bridges and earthquake-related zoning, and creating the Seismic Safety Commission.[2] Following passage of the NEHRP Reauthorization Act of 2003, NEHRP was moved from within the Federal Emergency Management Agency (FEMA) to the National Institute for Standards and Technology (NIST) even though FEMA was still held accountable for the federal response to, recovery from, and mitigation against earthquake events.[3] The degree to which this will affect the ability of NIST to effectively translate research into practice is unknown.

California's evolving earthquake program reflects the active involvement of elected officials, engineers, and earth scientists[4] and has proven more effective in informing federal and state policy than hurricane-related research.[5] Gaining a better understanding of how earthquake engineers and scientists have influenced policy can help further the connection between research and practice that address other hazards and span other professions, including planning, which has not proven nearly as effective in shaping earthquake policy.[6]

NEHRP has also been influential in the advancement of knowledge associated with disaster recovery.[7] Many of the flaws in disaster recovery (see Chapters 1 and 2), including the idea of recovery as a strictly linear process, the equation of recovery with the physical reconstruction of damaged communities, and the failure to adequately recognize the needs of socially vulnerable groups, have been addressed through NEHRP-funded research. In addition to engineering and social science-related studies, NEHRP has helped develop decision-support tools and applied materials for the practitioner.[8]

The Great Southern California Shakeout

In 2008, the connection between earthquake research and community action was highlighted by the "Great Southern California Shakeout," a preparedness exercise hosted by the U.S. Geological Survey (USGS), the California Emergency Management Agency, State Farm Insurance, FEMA, the American Red Cross, the Southern California Earthquake Center, the California Earthquake Authority, and the Earthquake Country Alliance. The USGS led a group of more than three hundred experts from universities and the public and private sectors to create the "Shakeout Scenario" on which the drill was based.[9] The disaster scenario was used to test outreach and information dissemination efforts and to generate interest in earthquake preparedness.

This consortium of federal and state agencies, university research centers, nonprofit organizations, and the insurance industry developed earthquake drill manuals, advertising and marketing materials, preparedness flyers, and multimedia broadcast messages. This information was tailored for a number of audiences, including individuals, families, neighborhood groups, community emergency response teams, schools, scouting groups, colleges and universities, businesses, nonprofit organizations, faith-based groups, medical centers, and museums.[10]

On November 13, 2008, more than 5.47 million people participated in what is widely recognized as the largest single event of its type in U.S. history.[11] In addition to the earthquake drill, a weeklong series of events, including the convening of disaster preparedness experts and community officials, was conducted to assess the efficacy of the effort so as to improve future exercises. While the Great Southern California Shakeout focuses on preparedness, similar large-scale exercises could be created that focus on preparing not only for the immediate aftermath of disaster, but also for long-term community recovery.

Several mechanisms for linking disaster-related research to practice are already in place. Hazards researchers and practitioners come together at the annual workshop conducted by the University of Colorado's Natural Hazards Research and Applications Information Center (NHRAIC) and at the Emergency Management Institute's annual Higher Education Conference. The National Academy of Sciences (NAS) hosts several roundtable workshops focused on specific disaster-related issues each year; its mission is to enhance the exchange of ideas among scientists, practitioners, and policy makers in order to improve our understanding of natural and human-caused hazards and disasters. But the programs of the NHRAIC, the Higher Education Conference, and the NAS represent missed opportunities. None of these venues systematically engages practitioners to identify the questions that they need answered if they are to do their jobs more effectively, nor do they provide a means for practitioners to identify the issues and priorities that they would like researchers to address.

The effectiveness of hazard centers and university programs can be improved if targeted modifications are adopted. Research centers can engage in collaborative multidisciplinary research and facilitate the exchange of ideas through ongoing face-to-face dialogue among scholars, students, and

1   Thomas A. Birkland, *Lessons of Disaster: Policy Change after Catastrophic Events* (Washington, D.C.: Georgetown University Press, 2006), 134.
2   Ibid., 130–134.
3   Richard Sylves, *Disaster Policy and Politics: Emergency Management and Homeland Security* (Washington, D.C.: CQ Press, 2008), 124.
4   Carl-Henry Geschwind, *California Earthquakes: Science, Risk, and the Politics of Hazard Mitigation* (Baltimore: Johns Hopkins University Press, 2001); Robert Olson, "Legislative Politics and Seismic Safety: California's Early Years and the 'Field Act,' 1925–1933," *Earthquake Spectra* 19, no. 1 (2003): 111–131.
5   Birkland, *Lessons of Disaster*, 126.
6   Ibid.
7   National Research Council, *Facing Hazards and Disasters: Understanding Human Dimensions* (Washington, D.C.: National Academies Press, 2006).
8   Ibid.
9   U.S. Geological Survey (USGS), "USGS and the Great California Shakeout" (October 15, 2009), www.usgs.gov/homepage/science_features/shakeout.asp.
10 The Great California Shakeout website, "Resources," www.shakeout.org/resources/index.html.
11 USGS, "Results Are In: Great Southern California ShakeOut Successful, Sets U.S. Record!" (December 19, 2008), www.usgs.gov/newsroom/article.asp?ID=2098.

Gulf Coast Community Design Studio

The Gulf Coast Community Design Studio (GCCDS), a professional service and outreach program of Mississippi State University's College of Architecture, Art + Design, was created in 2005 in order to provide architectural, planning, and landscape design assistance to coastal communities in Mississippi ravaged by Hurricane Katrina. An underlying goal of the studio is to provide technical assistance that is tied to local community needs. To this end, the GCCDS has three offices, which serve the coastal counties of Hancock, Harrison, and Jackson.

The central office of the Gulf Coast Community Design Studio in Biloxi Mississippi is shared with another community-based organization, Hope Community Development Association.

Photo by Leslie Schwartz.

In its organic evolution, the GCCDS provides an interesting point of comparison with the New Urbanist team that worked on the Mississippi Gulf Coast following Katrina. Like the New Urbanists, the GCCDS participated in the Mississippi Renewal Forum and recognized the value of design professionals in the recovery process. Unlike the New Urbanists, however, the GCCDS maintains a locally grounded, sustained commitment to helping communities rebuild by recognizing the hazards prevalent in the area and working closely with local and elected officials, city and regional planning departments, developers, builders, quasi-governmental organizations, nonprofits, community groups and residents, and others to understand

the resources they all can bring to the table without imposing preconceived ideas on communities.[1] As noted in a GCCDS brochure, "The planning process is a long-term, extended dialogue between many stakeholders and should reflect the range of values and ideas that come from the local community and should build local capacity."[2]

The Mission of the GCCDS
The mission of GCCDS is threefold:

- To provide professional assistance that increases the capacity of local communities and organizations to address issues of housing, public space, and neighborhood development.

- To provide leadership that advances the local, regional, and national dialogue on issues of design, affordable housing, coastal resiliency, and sustainable development.

- To expand design education by providing opportunities for students and interns to explore community-based design, design-build, and sustainability.[3]

Indicative of what its director, David Perkes, calls "working with experience,"[4] this concept contrasts with the overemphasis on expertise, which is best described as

In this aerial image of East Biloxi, Mississippi, a community assisted by the Gulf Coast Community Design Studio, note emergency housing park site in lower right-hand corner of image and individual units scattered throughout the neighborhood.

Photo by Gavin Smith.

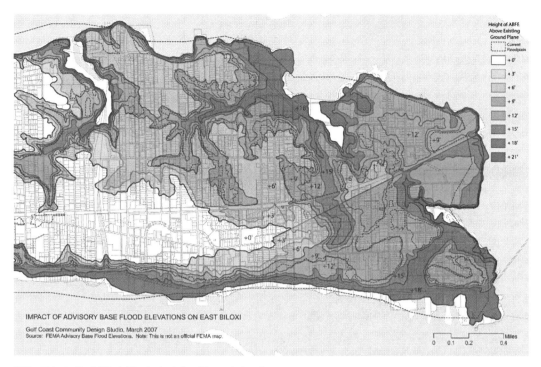

IMPACT OF ADVISORY BASE FLOOD ELEVATIONS ON EAST BILOXI

Gulf Coast Community Design Studio, March 2007
Source: FEMA Advisory Base Flood Elevations. Note: This is not an official FEMA map.

Pictured is an East Biloxi, Mississippi, flood hazard elevation map.

Source: Gulf Coast Community Design Studio.

"uncommon skills or specialized abilities that set one person or group of people apart from others."[5] Within the context of the disaster recovery assistance framework, the provision of education, outreach, and training measures is often framed in this manner—to the detriment of the community and individual. Yet, as will be discussed in Chapters 8 and 9, effective technical experts should be grounded in experience, particularly an ability to learn from those affected by disasters, in order to gain a sound contextual understanding of what makes a community, neighborhood, organization, family, and individual unique. According to Perkes, the concept of experience, which stems from the writings of John Dewey and his seminal book *Experience and Nature,* posits that experience is that set of skills and knowledge that evolves from a common event or series of events that, in turn, shapes collective understanding, mutual learning, and improved practice.[6]

Dissemination of Information

The GCCDS has striven to address the problems endemic to the disaster recovery assistance framework. Much of its work can be tied to the dissemination of information to individual residents, local officials, nonprofits, and the development community. For example, the studio conducts annual assessments of residential properties that enable nonprofits to target recovery assistance while tracking progress over time. This information has been collected in conjunction with a mapping effort that has combined post-Katrina estimated flood elevations associated with the new flood insurance rate maps with land elevations to approximate how high new construction must be elevated (see figure at the top of this page). While the map is not used for regulatory purposes, it allows citizens to more easily understand what has become a confusing exercise and added to the uncertainties of recovery.

In addition, the GCCDS has developed maps that assist in the delivery of coordinated assistance across nonprofit and volunteer groups by creating zones that organizations can use to focus their relief

continued on page 96

continued from page 95

and reconstruction efforts (see figure below). This helps to avoid duplication of time and effort, while allowing aid organizations to centralize their efforts geographically. The idea for the map was generated by a conversation between GCCDS director Perkes and Bill Stallworth, a Biloxi resident and member of the city council, who was at the time using a hand-drawn map to track local needs and assistance delivery. This project also provided a way for residents of East Biloxi to feel engaged in their own recovery; these residents had become frustrated with the charrette process

According to Perkes, the GCCDS "could have elected to produce a version of a plan for East Biloxi. Such work might have been interesting, and it would have represented *our* ideas, but it would not have been useful for the community because it was not what they needed at that time."[8] This quote highlights the underlying principles in the disaster recovery assistance framework. A plan (in essence, a type of technical assistance) that is created without a clear understanding of local needs is less useful than one that is driven by the sustained input of its residents. Moreover, the timing of assistance is critical: whereas the New

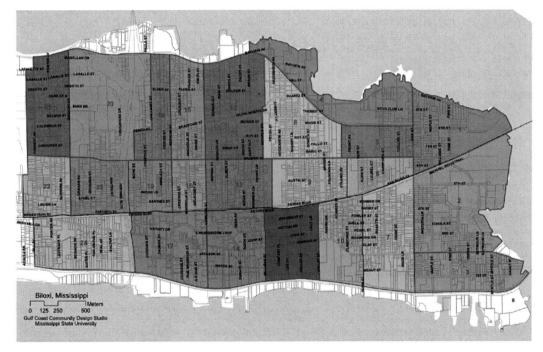

The East Biloxi, Mississippi disaster assistance coordination grids were created by the GCCDS and local nonprofits to help allocate scarce resources and assign disaster recovery organizations to targeted geographical areas.

Source: Gulf Coast Community Design Studio.

being led by the New Urbanists, which they felt limited their direct involvement in community-level decision making.[7] Rather than create a plan that reflected the ideas of technical experts, the GCCDS focused on the needs of local residents and assistance providers, respecting local conditions and working closely with residents and trusted neighborhood-level leaders in the nonprofit and faith-based communities.

Urbanist charrette process was undertaken before there was time to obtain a well-grounded understanding of local needs or identify the resources needed to meet them in a coordinated manner, the GCCDS has recognized that it is critical to invest the time required to build strong horizontal and vertical linkages across both the community and the network of external providers of assistance, including design professionals, foundations, and others.

Three Exemplary Projects
Three projects—the Main Street Neighborhood Study, the *Alternative Construction Research Guide,* and the Renaissance Builder and Developer Guild—provide evidence of how the GCCDS operates.

The Main Street Neighborhood Study
The Main Street Neighborhood Study focused on East Biloxi, an area that suffered the greatest level of damages in the city (see figure on page 94). The study area comprised the historic city center as well as the majority of Biloxi's African-American and Vietnamese residents. Prior to Hurricane Katrina the area was facing significant disinvestment, a preponderance of substandard housing, limited resources, and limited political will to effect change.[9] Following the storm, it faced a number of daunting challenges, including the cost of repairing or rebuilding homes, rising insurance rates, new elevation standards, and the threats associated with large-scale casino development in the community.

The study included background research, market analysis, building-related challenges and opportunities, preliminary proposals, community response, and conclusions. On the basis of an analysis of the area, the study compiled a number of strategies associated with improving the main street corridor, residential and commercial areas, zoning, parking, and streetscapes. In each case, the suggested planning and design elements recognized the community's inherent vulnerability to both storm surge–induced flooding and more routine heavy rains. Examples of such elements include the creation of "no-build zones" adjacent to bayous and of buffer zones that serve as parks and greenways; the construction of multiunit housing in areas requiring elevated construction; a mix of elevation and flood-proofing techniques for commercial structures; the use of permeable surfacing for parking lots; and the use of swales and other landscaping techniques to manage storm-water runoff.[10]

A Gulf Coast Community Design Studio home constructed for Patty Broussard post-Katrina. The home represents a partnership between GCCDS and Design Corps and is a LEED-Accredited building.
Photo by Rick Eades.

In addition to creating a document that assessed damages, local conditions, and strategies for reconstruction, the Main Street Neighborhood Study provided a tool that could be used by foundations, nonprofits, and private investors as they considered how to provide post-disaster assistance. The study, coupled with the coordination grids, has helped to organize and distribute resources drawn from both within the community and external assistance providers, linking resources to identified local needs.

The Alternative Construction Research Guide
In addition to neighborhood-level planning efforts, the GCCDS provides technical guidance on individual housing and lot-scale site design. The creation of the *Alternative Housing Research Guide,* for instance, was intended for "housing providers," including individual property owners, home builders, volunteers, and nonprofits that are involved in rebuilding communities along the Mississippi coast. The effort is also indicative of the dual service and research mission of the studio. Key issues discussed in the guide include installation, performance, and design. For instance, installation-related questions include the number of people and types of skills required to construct different housing types, the overall speed of construction, the means required to deliver materials, the

continued on page 98

continued from page 97

equipment needed to construct or assemble the unit, and any specialized labor required. Performance measures addressed include wind loads, water resistance, fire resistance, energy usage, the life span of the unit, and common failures associated with varied designs. Design elements described include environmental impacts, the versatility of varied products, availability of materials and necessary labor, code compliance, affordability, and the applicability of materials and products to the conditions found on the coast.

To demonstrate the varied construction types to builders, the GCCDS built transportable housing assemblies and use them as part of an outreach and training program for the home-building community. The mock-ups provide a hands-on opportunity to discuss and review varied framing systems and their subcomponents, such as walls, roofing, and flooring assemblies. Additional discussions focus on the design and construction techniques associated with elevated foundations; stacked units; panelized construction; and factory-assembled units, including modular, component, kit, and hybrid homes.[11]

The Renaissance Builder and Developer Guild

In the Governor's Commission on Recovery, Rebuilding, and Renewal report *Building Back Better Than Ever* (see sidebar on pages 182–183), it was suggested that the Renaissance Corporation, a quasi-governmental organization tasked with financing affordable housing construction, should be created.[12] In response, the GCCDS developed the Renaissance Builder and Developer Guild, a partner program focused on fostering public-private partnerships. The guild provides gap financing through the Renaissance Corporation to assist in the construction of low-income housing that meets a series of "renaissance design standards"; created in partnership with local builders, these standards are intended to limit environmental impacts and reflect a design that respects unique site conditions, and developers must meet these standards if they are to receive construction funds provided through the Renaissance Corporation. According to

Perkes, the guidelines were purposefully designed in a way "that wouldn't turn off developers who sought to help with the rebuilding effort along the coast."[13] In order to further increase the likelihood of adopting these construction techniques, the GCCDS works closely with developers, providing advice on individual units and site design through a one-on-one mentoring program as well as frequent workshops and seminars.

Thus, not only have the standards been developed in partnership with builders, but those developers who sought guidance from the GCCDS reported that the help they received resulted in improvements that the builders had not considered, such as a reorientation of the site to consider cluster development that limits environmental impacts while allowing for greater density, a modification of housing plans that improves hazard resilience, and the use of materials that improve energy efficiency.[14] The GCCDS also works directly with homeowners and can provide these services free of charge as the Renaissance Corporation allows for an in-depth consultation with "the client," who would not normally receive this type of assistance without the financial subsidy provided by the quasi-governmental organization.

1   A list of the Gulf Coast Community Design Studio's (GCCDS) partners can be found on the studio's website at www.gccds.org/.

2   GCCDS, brochure (Starkville: College of Architecture, Art + Design, Mississippi State University, 2010).

3   GCCDS website, www.gccds.org/.

4   David Perkes and Christine Gaspar, "Working with Experience," *Cityscape: A Journal of Policy Development and Research* 10, no. 3 (2008): 113–126.

5   Ibid., 113.

6   John Dewey, *Experience and Nature* (Mineola, N.Y.: Dover Publications, 1958).

7   David Perkes, "A Useful Practice," *Journal of Architectural Education* 62, no. 4 (2009): 64–71.

8   Ibid., 65.

9   GCCDS, *Main Street Neighborhood Planning Study: Executive Summary* (Starkville: College of Architecture, Art + Design, Mississippi State University, August 2009), www.gccds.org/planning/mainstreet/main_street_execsummary.pdf.

10   Ibid.

11   GCCDS, *Alternative Construction Research Guide: Methods for Building Communities* (Starkville: College of Architecture, Art + Design, Mississippi State University, n.d.), www.gccds.org/research/altconstruction/intro/intro.pdf.

12   Governor's Commission on Recovery, Rebuilding, and Renewal, *After Katrina: Building Back Better Than Ever* (Jackson, Miss.: Governor's Commission on Recovery, Rebuilding, and Renewal, 2006), www.mississippirenewal.com/documents/Governors_Commission_Report.pdf.

13   David Perkes, personal telephone communication, April 2010.

14   Ibid.

practitioners. They can also provide an administrative means to transfer research findings through technical bulletins, websites, and training programs.

The growing number of college- and university-affiliated hazard centers and emergency management-related certificate and degree programs is encouraging. (A list of college and university programs can be found at the Emergency Management Institute's Higher Education Project's website at training.fema.gov/EMIWeb/edu/collegelist.) Ideally, graduates possess a solid grounding in theoretical models of hazards and disasters, an enhanced analytical proclivity, and some experience in the field that allows them to assess the validity of existing practice and inform potential improvements. While significant progress has been made, however, challenges remain in a university system that rewards basic research while placing limited emphasis on public service, applied research, and the development of materials and educational tools that transfer findings to a wider audience (Figure 3–1).

Figure 3–1. Hazard Reduction and Recovery Center students conduct survey of damages following Hurricane Ike.

Source: Texas A&M University Hazard Reduction and Recovery Center.

Just as the creation of degree programs is helping to educate future scholars and practitioners, the NSF has funded efforts to develop outreach, training, and mentoring programs that encourage more young scholars to engage in hazards-related research.

And a growing number of practitioners are themselves taking advantage of university programs to study hazards and disasters, whether as part of specific coursework, as an area of emphasis within a more general discipline, or in a degree program in hazards or emergency management. This trend represents an important point in the evolution of the profession, indicating that the knowledge generated through research at colleges and universities is increasingly being transferred to those who will apply it in a practice-based setting. The sidebar on pages 94–98 provides an example of how the university can direct its teaching and service mission toward disaster recovery assistance.

DIMENSIONS OF THE DISASTER ASSISTANCE FRAMEWORK

As has been shown, quasi-governmental and nongovernmental organizations' understanding of local needs, the timing of assistance they provide, and the degree to which they facilitate horizontal and vertical integration are important dimensions. However, since very little exists in the literature or within recovery plans that demonstrate how these elements fit into the larger disaster assistance framework, they are often misunderstood and underappreciated by other members of the assistance network. The sidebars and case study in this chapter not only highlight the important role that quasi-governmental and nongovernmental organizations play in recovery, but also show that the type of assistance they provide is greatly enhanced when it is part of a larger effort associated with pre- and post-event planning for disaster recovery.

Understanding of Local Needs

Quasi-governmental and nongovernmental organizations perform numerous activities, often at the bequest of the public sector, that provide insight into the needs of communities and individuals before and after a disaster. RPOs and CDCs, for example, assist local governments, small businesses, and low-income individuals and neighborhoods with the administration of grant programs and capacity-building initiatives such as drafting plans and implementing community development initiatives. Colleges and universities assess the impacts of policies and actions on local governance systems before and after disasters as part of research programs and studies, while professional associations provide a conduit for sharing knowledge and a platform to advocate policy positions. Using knowledge gained through research and practice, the university community and professional associations have joined in a growing effort to advocate for the adoption of pre-event planning efforts.

Regional Planning Organizations

After a disaster, the failure to coordinate across municipal boundaries can stress available resources, hinder the delivery of assistance, and lead to increased levels of multijurisdictional conflict.[24] RPOs are uniquely situated to address some of these issues by forging and enhancing relationships among the organizations within a defined cluster of neighboring counties and municipalities. They often use collaborative problem-solving techniques to identify underlying interests and potential areas of agreement. The creation of regional plans and policies also benefits from the involvement of multiple stakeholders over an extended period of time. Repeated interactions facilitate an in-depth understanding of a community's financial, technical, and administrative capabilities to act before and after disaster strikes.

Community Development Corporations

The concept of sustainable development (see Chapter 6) requires a commitment to the ongoing use of capacity-building techniques in order to achieve greater self-reliance, which is an underemphasized characteristic of sustainable disaster recovery.[25] With a strong understanding of local needs, particularly among socially vulnerable populations, CDCs have long played a role in sustainable development, often focusing on the knowledge and skills that communities need to achieve greater self-reliance. After a disaster, CDCs often provide technical assistance directly to affected individuals in the form of financial counseling and housing repair. Many also serve as "pass-through" organizations, facilitating the flow of money to individuals or providing development assistance to local government agencies.

Homeowners Associations

Like CDCs, HOAs have an in-depth understanding of local needs as its members represent individual property owners in a community or subdivision. Large HOAs are composed of boards, corporate officers, and a number of subcommittees that address a range of topics. In many communities, HOAs provide an organizational vehicle to coordinate action at the neighborhood level through the enforcement of design and development standards, property maintenance, and disaster preparedness initiatives. Neighborhood associations provide a good vehicle for creating community emergency response teams (CERTs), which are made up of individual residents who are trained in a number of preparedness and response activities and stand ready to assist one another after a disaster (CERTs are discussed in more detail in Chapter 9). Understood in the context of the disaster assistance network, HOAs also provide a venue through which homeowners can undertake individual and collective initiatives to plan for disaster recovery.

An HOA's design and development committee may require the adoption of hazard mitigation initiatives, which may include landscaping guidelines that restrict certain plant types and regulate vegetative setback distances from structures, or that establish standards regarding the type of materials used in construction. HOAs may require, for instance, that homeowners remove fire-prone vegetation adjacent to structures or that each home purchase and install hurricane shutters. They may also manage programs that mitigate hazard vulnerability at the neighborhood level, such as through the prescribed burning of underbrush. In addition, HOAs may host seminars that inform residents about public sector and nonprofit recovery programs, or they may create a community website that provides up-to-date information following a disaster about when it is safe to return, what community services are operational, and which reputable contractors are available to perform debris removal, repair, and reconstruction services. Finally, HOAs can serve as a collective voice advocating on behalf of the community, linking the needs of individual homeowners to resources provided by members of the assistance network.

Critics point out that HOAs can limit public participation if they are created by the developer of the neighborhood without meaningful citizen input.[26] Further, the board and subcommittee structure used in HOAs can be highly prescriptive, which can prove problematic. While they often adopt development standards that are more restrictive than those of the local units of government in which they are located, HOAs are often unwilling to pay for design and land use measures that could mitigate the impacts of hazards—even after a major disaster. In fire-prone areas of Southern California, for example, HOAs have resisted paying for the prescribed burning of underbrush, for the widening of narrow streets to better enable fire trucks to reach threatened homes, or for enhancements to water systems that are insufficient to provide adequate water to fight fires.[27] The rapid growth of gated communities that refuse to adopt proven measures to reduce the impacts of wildland-urban interface fires has heightened the risk of large-scale losses (see the accompanying sidebar).[28]

Professional Associations

As the sidebar on page 104 explains, professional associations provide a conduit through which to focus the collective concerns of technical experts, including those tied to recovery needs. Professional associations, particularly those that represent local governments, agencies, and their elected or appointed staff, are acutely aware of local needs, and they establish committees to compile and codify positions that are used to convey the needs of their members and constituents. The testimony of association leaders can influence legislative committees and government agencies that oversee the disbursement of state and federal funding. IAEM and NEMA, for instance, routinely press FEMA and Congress to provide funding for programs that address state and local needs. The Emergency Management Performance Grant, for example, which helps to sustain pre-event capacity by providing funds for the hiring and training of state and local officials, is the subject of regular debate among professional associations, FEMA, and congressional committee members.

The Association of State Floodplain Managers (ASFPM) provides another example of the role that professional associations can play in policy formulation. By subsidizing the cost of flood insurance, the National Flood Insurance Program (NFIP) encourages property owners to build or purchase property in the floodplain.[29] ASFPM is among the leading organizations that have attempted to address this issue. Its No Adverse Impact initiative encourages local governments

The Transformation of Self-Reliance in High-Hazard Communities

The rapid growth of new communities in high-hazard areas and the displacement of more self-reliant, indigenous populations are growing trends.[1] The Los Angeles hills and North Carolina's Outer Banks provide two stark examples of how increased residential development in high-hazard areas is changing the nature of exposure and vulnerability.

Originally, California's "hillsider" population comprised those who sought to escape high-density living in the valley below, namely aging hippies and "back to the land" types.[2] But with the construction of larger homes to replace the smaller cottages that were scattered throughout the area, this "sloping suburbia" has become an enclave of the super rich, many of whom live in gated communities. And as wealth and investments in this area have increased, gated communities have excluded many middle-income residents while deriving the benefits paid for by the larger community.

North Carolina's Outer Banks were originally settled by the English, Irish, and Scotch-Irish. Because many of the residents have a unique speech pattern that blends old English and southern dialects, they are commonly referred to as "hoi toiders" (a term derived from their pronunciation of the phrase "high tide"). The harsh environment and the relative isolation of those living on the Outer Banks initially limited the influence of the mainland and shaped the population's strong sense of self-reliance.[4] The hoi toiders often built their homes on deep lots, moving them back from the coast following storms or in recognition of coastal erosion and the natural migration of barrier islands toward the mainland. Locals also drilled holes in the floors of their homes and other community buildings to allow rising water to enter and exit the structure, thereby reducing the likelihood that it would be moved from its foundation.

Over time, the Outer Banks has become a national destination for vacationers, retirees, and second-home owners, many of whom have moved there from more urban locations, including the Northeast. This has led to the construction of increasingly large rental units; in many areas, the original beach cottages have been replaced with coastal "McMansions." Because these wealthy newcomers have little or no experience dealing with coastal storms and hurricanes, they have reduced the area's level of self-reliance while increasing their communities' exposure to the future impacts of coastal hazards.

1   Mike Davis, *Ecology of Fear: Los Angeles and the Imagination of Disaster* (New York: Vintage Books, 1998).
2   Ibid.
3   Ibid.
4   Rodney Barfield, *Seasoned by Salt: A Historical Album of the Outer Banks* (Chapel Hill: University of North Carolina Press, 1995).

Professional Associations in Recovery following Hurricane Katrina

The ability of external assistance providers to meet local needs can be stymied by the inability of communities and other members of the assistance network to articulate their needs. However, the experience of those who have faced similar conditions can help to bridge this gap. After the hurricanes that struck Florida in 2004, for instance, Florida city managers identified staff who had experience in an array of long-term recovery services and organized them into "recovery strike teams." (The strike team concept comes from the Incident Command System, which refers to a strike team as equipment or a group of individuals that possesses a complementary set of functions or skills.) Four strike teams were set up within Florida's existing emergency response districts; each was assigned a team leader, and an employee of Florida's emergency operations center was tapped to be the state coordinator.

Following Hurricane Katrina, teams were sent to the Mississippi coastal towns of Long Beach and Pass Christian. Their first task was to assess local needs and assign people to address identified problems. Florida aid providers modified the Emergency Management Assistance Compact, which usually focuses on the deployment of first responders, not necessarily those skilled in long-term recovery activities (see the sidebar on page 48). The recovery strike teams then went about assisting with damage assessments and building inspections, addressing the administrative burdens of documenting eligible reimbursable expenses (including payroll), writing grants, and developing a citizens' needs survey.[1]

The International City/County Management Association (ICMA) launched a similar program in Pascagoula, Mississippi, where local officials were consumed by the day-to-day activities related to response and recovery. Code enforcement alone overwhelmed local officials as in the months after Hurricane Katrina, the city issued 7,500 building permits—or about 130–140 per day.[2] To help the community plan for long-term recovery, ICMA worked with Fannie Mae and two nonprofit housing organizations, Neighborworks and Dependable Affordable Sustainable Homes. The team focused on providing staff to back up local officials, who had been so focused on immediate short-term recovery activities that the city was unable to look forward and assess long-term issues. Fannie Mae provided a grant to cover the travel expenses of nine teams that assisted Pascagoula with building inspections, the administration of post-disaster grants, the assessment of redevelopment opportunities, and code enforcement.

1 Christine Shenot, "Local Professionals Team Up on Disaster Recovery," *Public Management (PM)* 89, no. 3 (April 2007): 6–12.
2 Ibid., 11.

to adopt more stringent regulations than are required under the NFIP regarding the type and location of development in and around the floodplain and larger watershed in order to reduce the negative impact of development on adjacent properties and downstream communities.[30]

Colleges and Universities

The organizational culture of colleges and universities shapes the type of research conducted and the degree to which faculty members interact with practitioners, both of which influence researchers' understanding of local needs. The higher education reward structure is typically based on a faculty member's ability to conduct "basic" research that is suitable for publication in peer-reviewed academic journals. Emphasis is placed on advancing knowledge, not necessarily on conducting "applied" research that has direct relevance to practitioners or that meets locally defined needs. Research is informed by gaps in the collective understanding of a topical area, which are identified through the review of existing literature written by other scholars in a relatively narrow band of journals. Researchers then tend to study a limited set of questions that allows them to probe deeply into those specific issues and assess the influence of factors, or "variables," on hypothesized causal relationships. They also tend to focus their work on the topics and areas of study that intrigue them, not necessarily on the needs of communities. Thus, their tendency to employ a disciplinary focus on hazards and disasters-related research, as noted in White and Haas's assessment of hazards research in 1975, continues to limit the advancement of the field.[31]

The advancement of knowledge is also limited by the reluctance of hazards researchers to look to members of the larger disaster assistance network to uncover questions that merit further research. The NAS, the NSF, and other research agencies have undertaken a number of evaluative studies which seek to identify unresolved questions and frame them as a proposed research agenda.[32] In addition, the NAS has a long history of providing recommended policy guidance based on research findings, including work associated with disaster recovery and reconstruction.[33] Unfortunately, these studies are largely devoid of practitioner involvement. Ironically, hazards experts emphasize the importance of community-level recovery policy that reflects the unique nature of local needs before and after disasters.[34] Research conducted at the local level can lead to an extensive understanding of community conditions and needs, particularly if the study is sustained over a long period of time. But except for some anthropological studies, this type of research, often referred to as participant observation, is relatively uncommon in the disaster recovery arena.

The low level of interaction between researchers and practitioners also limits researchers' understanding of field conditions and related contextual variables. Researchers rarely have sufficient time to spend in the field to assess a community's long-term recovery and gain an in-depth understanding of how local needs change over time.[35] To address these and other constraints on how data are collected and research is conducted, several hazards scholars seek to create a multidisciplinary research facility comprising multiple research observatories. One primary aim of the proposed Resiliency and Vulnerability Observation Network (RAVON) would be to conduct longitudinal studies while archiving the data for future comparative analyses.[36]

Finally, the hazards research community's understanding of local needs is limited by its demographic makeup and personal experience. Hazards researchers tend to be older than the general population and are overrepresented by white males. Research "subjects," particularly those who are socially vulnerable, may be reluctant to divulge personal or sensitive information to those who do not look like them or have not faced similar conditions. This can limit the understanding of contextual factors facing individuals affected by disasters, particularly those who are socially vulnerable.

Interestingly, hazards researchers have not effectively demonstrated to the larger social science research community that, as Charles Fritz initially argued, disasters provide a unique opportunity to assess underlying social conditions that are not always readily apparent and are exposed during extreme events.[37] If properly framed, this argument may be a useful means to increase the breadth of scholarly interest among hazards researchers in the social science field.

In response to the "graying" of the hazards research community and the limited number of women and minority scholars, the NSF has funded a program to encourage promising young students and researchers to focus their efforts on hazards-related research. The Enabling Project, led by Dennis Wenger at Texas A&M University, Ray Burby at the University of North Carolina at Chapel Hill, and Tom Birkland at North Carolina State University, has mentored three cohorts of faculty prospects. But while largely considered a success and worthy of continued NSF support, the project has proven difficult to attract a diverse field of applicants, even though the third cohort is the most diverse yet.[38] Viewed in a multigenerational context, this affects the next dimension of the assistance framework—the timing of assistance.

Timing of Assistance

Quasi-governmental and nongovernmental groups conduct a number of pre-event actions associated with planning, policy analysis, research, and coalition building. And as has already been noted, many of their most visible disaster recovery-related actions occur in reaction to a major event: RPOs help collect data or write post-disaster recovery plans; CDCs help low-income residents apply for post-disaster housing assistance; colleges and universities study recovery efforts and document successes and failures; and professional associations provide technical assistance, review policies, and suggest changes. What may be less apparent is that many of these activities can also have profound effects on recovery outcomes. For example, having established pre-event relationships with individual homeowners, neighborhood leaders, and local government officials, HOAs, special service districts, CDCs, and RPOs are in a unique position to assist them in setting up committees and agreements to facilitate pre-event planning as well as post-disaster delivery of assistance. Taking advantage of this situation requires further codifying specific actions and the timing at which they occur.

Following Hurricanes Katrina in 2005 and Ike in 2008, a growing coalition of support has been slowing emerging for the creation of an improved and better coordinated disaster recovery policy.[39] Colleges and universities, for example, continue to play a leading role in this effort, advocating for an increased emphasis on pre-event planning for post-disaster recovery.[40]

Disasters spur new research. The ability to capture "perishable" or time-sensitive information in the immediate aftermath of an event is highly prized by hazard scholars. An individual's recall of an event, including his or her actions and those of assistance providers, is best when the event is still fresh in the mind. The timely recording of high-water marks, debris fields, and physical damages to property provides researchers with critical clues about the physical characteristics of a hazard (such as storm surge inundation, wind speed, and ground motion) and the performance of buildings and infrastructure. Similarly, an evaluation of how institutions functioned immediately after an extreme event offers important information that advances our growing base of knowledge about natural hazards and disasters.

While university and college faculty are often the most vociferous critics of the speed of post-disaster recovery programs, they are perhaps the least prepared or capable of delivering timely, targeted assistance to communities following disasters. It takes too long to initiate, conduct, and publish post-disaster research findings. The journal articles, monographs, conference papers, and books written about a disaster are often completed too late to affect changes in policy or group behavior in the area where the event has occurred. The limited circulation of research findings after the fact further limits their impact. The NSF and the University of Colorado at Boulder's NHRAIC have tried to address this issue by funding post-event "rapid response" research grants that allow hazard scholars to travel to disaster sites to collect, write up, and disseminate information in the immediate aftermath of an event. But challenges remain. The teaching schedules of most hazard scholars limit their ability to commit the extensive blocks of time that are needed to analyze a problem and report findings in a timely manner—particularly given the unpredictable nature of disasters and the need for the research to be conducted immediately following an event. Few hazard scholars can simply drop everything, travel to the location of the event and embark on full-time research.

Professional associations provide a potentially important vehicle for bridging pre- and post-disaster assistance and institutionalizing a culture of planning for post-disaster recovery. These entities not only serve as national-level advocates but also represent thousands of local officials—city managers, floodplain administrators, building officials, finance personnel, city and county attorneys, emergency managers, and land use planners—many of whom will be faced with the challenges of recovery. The ability to harness this collective body of locally grounded knowledge and build a coalition that embraces the importance of pre-event planning for post-disaster recovery can and should play a greater role not only in the debate over the value of being proactive rather than reactive, but also, and more importantly, in the need to act now to inform and train other local officials on specific techniques that they can employ to address existing limitations in the assistance framework.

Horizontal and Vertical Integration

The cooperative strength of quasi-governmental and nongovernmental organizations lies in their ability to effectively harness technical expertise and convey knowledge to other members of the assistance network.

Regional Planning Organizations and Community Development Corporations

RPOs are perhaps the most strategically located within the disaster recovery assistance network; they have the potential to improve horizontal and vertical integration across stakeholder groups and to forge stronger ties with federal, state, and local governments. When RPOs manage federal grant programs for local governments, they interact with the grantor, which may be a state or federal government agency, a private foundation, or a nonprofit organization. CDCs also foster high levels of horizontal integration, particularly among nonprofit organizations, other community groups, and individuals. After disaster strikes, CDCs often work with individuals to address housing needs, social services, and neighborhood-level community development. CDCs may also facilitate relatively high levels of vertical integration with state and federal agencies because they are recipients of state and federal grants intended to assist socially vulnerable communities and individuals. Following Hurricane Katrina, several neighborhood organizations, as well as the Hollygrove and Broadmoor neighborhoods in New Orleans (see the case study on pages 116–122), established CDCs, thereby developing important vertical linkages that complemented existing strong horizontal integration.[41]

Homeowners Associations

HOAs typically have moderate levels of horizontal integration and low levels of vertical integration. The growing prevalence of gated enclaves has increased the spatial and social isolation among neighboring areas. Some gated communities purposefully limit interaction with the broader community through the use of specific design practices and settlement patterns, including perimeter barriers and security, signage, landscaping, and spatial distancing. This limits daily interaction across groups, ultimately hindering the formation of social bonds and the notion of a shared community identity. Thus, residents of gated communities often fail to be full partners in inclusive public participation techniques that address issues that cross neighborhood, subdivision, and municipal boundaries.

Professional Associations

The level of horizontal and vertical integration fostered by professional associations depends on the nature of the organization and the makeup of its membership. Most professional associations take positions on issues that affect their stated mission, goals, and practices and advocate policies that support the work of their members. In the context of disaster recovery, associations may advocate on behalf of the improved integration of hazard mitigation techniques with recovery and reconstruction strategies. ASFPM's "No Adverse Impact" campaign is an example of an advocacy campaign that seeks to reduce the negative effects of existing policy.

The diversity of its membership affects the breadth of a professional association's interactions with other members of the assistance network. ASFPM, for instance, includes federal, state, and local officials; private sector contractors; members of RPOs; university faculty; and those affiliated with nonprofit organizations. Professional associations spend a great deal of time building internal connections among its members and external relationships with others in the disaster assistance network. The formation of committees responsible for external relationships, for example, may include an outreach, education, and training component as well as a group assigned to address policy issues through legislative and congressional engagement.

Colleges and Universities

The horizontal and vertical linkages found between the higher education community and other members of the disaster assistance network are highly variable. In most cases, colleges and universities have a high level of integration across educational institutions of higher learning, largely because of the collegial exchange of ideas and the ongoing publication of highly scrutinized research findings. Yet as the first and second assessment[42] of research on natural hazards suggests, multidisciplinary research, particularly between the physical and social science communities, needs to be improved and the findings more effectively disseminated to practitioners and other members of the assistance network.

The degree of collaboration within the community in which colleges and universities are located varies significantly and is often discussed in the context of the "town-gown" relationship. Sometimes this rapport can be tested. The college or university is often an important (and sometimes the principle) economic engine and public face of the community, which can lead to problems when the interests of the academic institution, public officials, and those residing in the community conflict.

On the other hand, faculty can play an important role in the community by sharing their highly specialized expertise and knowledge with local officials. One means used to improve the level of horizontal integration between communities and universities and colleges emerged as part of Project Impact, a FEMA-created program that focused on the development of local public-private partnerships to advance disaster preparedness and the pre-event adoption of hazard mitigation measures (see Chapter 5). This initiative stimulated the involvement of numerous researchers across the country, particularly those engaged in applied work in the communities in which their universities are located. Specific examples include assessing local vulnerability, studying evacuation patterns associated with past disasters, assisting with the development of hazard mitigation plans, conducting community preparedness surveys, and taking a leadership role in efforts to reduce the vulnerability of colleges and universities through a FEMA-sponsored program titled Disaster-Resistant Universities.[43]

The vertical linkage between colleges and universities and other members of the assistance network can be expressed in two ways: through the generation and transfer of knowledge to practice, and through the training and education of students who represent the future generation of scholars and practitioners. A number of hazard-related centers and institutes have emerged recently. Perhaps the most successful is the University of Colorado's NHRAIC, whose stated mission is to disseminate information and facilitate interaction between researchers and practitioners. A study undertaken by Roy Popkin and Claire Rubin found that the NHRAIC is a critical source of information for both hazards researchers and practitioners.[44] It maintains an impressive library, with more than 28,000 documents; its newsletter, the *Natural Hazards Observer*, has about 15,000 subscribers; and its peer-reviewed series, *Natural Hazards Informer*, provides a condensation of research findings specifically targeting practitioners.

Research that has direct application in practice is often referred to as "applied research" and is a long-standing tradition among land-grant universities. The creation of land-grant universities and colleges was mandated by Congress under the Morrill Acts of 1862 and 1890. In 1914, the passage of the Smith-Lever Act established cooperative extension services in each state.[45] Today's Cooperative State Research, Education, and Extension Service is implemented by extension agents and land-grant university faculty. Operating out of offices located at the state, regional, and county levels, extension agents work directly with the public as well as with university researchers, nonprofit organizations, members of the private sector, and government agencies in such areas as engineering, natural resource management, building construction, agriculture, and public administration, translating research findings and technical materials into viable solutions to address the concerns and priorities of their state. These activities have since been expanded in response to the more recently designated sea- and space-grant universities. Sea-grant universities, for example, are involved in the study and delivery of information related to coastal hazards and what can be done to reduce their impacts.

Perhaps the best example of an organization in the land-grant system explicitly focused on hazards and disasters is the Extension Disaster Education Network (EDEN). EDEN is an emerging multistate effort to link extension specialists from across the United States and from various disciplines "to share education resources to reduce the impact of natural and man-made disasters."[46] This mission is carried out through interdisciplinary and multistate research and educational programs addressing hazard mitigation, preparedness, response, and recovery; linkages with federal, state, and local agencies and organizations; the anticipation of future disaster education needs and actions; and timely and prompt communications. Extension professionals from EDEN serve as delegates of the larger organization while designated points of contact transmit information across the network and to the general public. These delegates work closely with county extension agents through their "eXtension" program, which serves as a portal to disaster experts. Although initially focused on agriculture-related topics, EDEN has expanded to include flooding, children and disasters, disaster-resilient communities, and family preparedness. It has been suggested that the extension service model could be expanded to build pre-event capacity to address disaster recovery-related issues,[47] and perhaps EDEN could play a role in this endeavor.

CONCLUSIONS AND RECOMMENDATIONS

Quasi-governmental and nongovernmental organizations are often the forgotten members of the disaster assistance network even though they provide key resources, have a sound understanding of local needs, and forge horizontal and vertical linkages among members of the assistance network. While RPOs, CDCs, and special service districts perform a range of relevant pre-disaster activities, their resources and expertise in federal, state, and local pre-event recovery planning initiatives are underused. Instead, these organizations are usually tasked with providing disaster recovery assistance largely after the fact. Similarly, the research undertaken by colleges and universities in the aftermath of a particular event may not be directly relevant to those who are struggling to address gaps in the existing disaster recovery assistance framework, or it may be delivered too late in the recovery process or have too limited a distribution to significantly affect change.

The remainder of this chapter proposes specific actions for taking advantage of the unique contributions of quasi-governmental and nongovernmental organizations. The value of these recommendations, as well as of those discussed later in Chapters 8 and 9, is underscored in the Broadmoor case study that concludes this chapter. In many ways, this case study encapsulates the role not only of quasi-governmental actors but also of many organizations found in the larger assistance network. Further, it highlights how an organization can change over time, starting out as an emergent group and transitioning to an established multiorganizational network that is grounded in the community and therefore capable of addressing the principal problems described in the current U.S. disaster recovery assistance framework.

1. Apply the Capabilities of Quasi-Governmental Organizations to Pre-Event Planning

RPOs are well suited to play an expanded role in pre-disaster recovery planning activities, including plan making; community involvement; and education, outreach, and training. Their participation in hazard mitigation and comprehensive planning can provide a unique perspective on the issues that are likely to emerge during disaster recovery. Because RPOs also are routinely tasked with grants management activities, they are well versed in the linkage between pre-event plan making and post-event implementation. Moreover, as their work typically requires the coordination of multiple entities with conflicting opinions and priorities, they have the conflict management and consensus-building skills that are often critical to success in the conflict-laden post-disaster environment as well as in the process-oriented approach associated with plan making.

CDCs also are well suited to assist with pre-disaster recovery initiatives. Most CDCs work with economically disadvantaged neighborhoods, which are disproportionately affected by disasters. Stimulating reinvestment in these areas often require convincing the private sector to embark on projects that may not be their most lucrative options. CDCs typically have strong relationships with developers, particularly those who specialize in the construction of affordable housing, which is important after a disaster as there is often pressure to displace low-income residents or to limit the number of affordable housing units reconstructed in hard-hit areas.[48] One researcher suggests that the recovery process of low-income neighborhoods is analogous to America's history of urban renewal in which low-income, predominantly black communities have been dislocated to remove what is often referred to as urban blight.[49]

In many communities, HOAs provide a means for connecting with populations at the subdivision or neighborhood level. In most states, HOAs have regulatory authority to impose standards, restrictions, and covenants that are transferred to property owners. In this way they can reduce vulnerability and speed individual and family recovery by facilitating the creation of community emergency response teams, adopting hazard mitigation techniques, and disseminating disaster recovery information before and after an event. The costs of these measures can be shared by residents of the community through the creation of a disaster recovery committee and the establishment of binding covenants. Challenges remain, however, as evidenced by the discussion of gated communities that are willing to accept external assistance but refuse to adopt sound mitigation measures. Developing explicit guidance materials through the use of sound subdivision regulations, such as those associated with reducing flood, wildfire, and landslide hazard losses, for example, may be useful.[50] But unless they are widely adopted, such materials alone will do little to minimize losses or improve recovery outcomes.

2. Maximize the Contributions of Nongovernmental Organizations through Existing and Proposed Organizational Venues

The participation of the Congress for the New Urbanism in the Mississippi Renewal Forum after Hurricane Katrina represents one of the boldest experiments in recent history to involve professional associations in post-disaster recovery. Among the most important lessons to be derived from that experience, however, is that relationships between design professionals and other members of the assistance network need to be developed *before* an event. Furthermore, the effort to provide architectural assistance could be enhanced by a better understanding of how existing recovery programs operate and how design options relate to local conditions, including pre-existing hazard vulnerability and settlement patterns.

Planners are often marginalized or brought in to assist after a disaster has occurred, which limits their effectiveness. Thus, an important first step in any proposed venture requires an education and outreach effort that helps to explain the critical role that local planners play in long-term recovery planning. APA has perhaps the greatest potential of any existing member of the assistance network when it comes to training others in planning for disaster recovery. But while APA has begun to offer local planners training in hazard mitigation planning, the training programs in recovery planning are nonexistent. To remedy this situation, APA members have suggested a natural hazards division that would deliver training for local planners in both hazard mitigation and disaster recovery planning[51] (Exhibit 3–2 on page 114).

The ability to conduct meaningful basic and applied research that can inform the actions of the disaster assistance network requires changing the current paradigm of knowledge creation and dissemination. Both researchers and practitioners need to be involved in formulating research questions that advance both knowledge and practice. Richard Sylves notes that the majority of federal agencies and organizations that conduct or fund hazards and disaster research—including predictive modeling and forecasting, engineering, and social science—are not part of the Department of Homeland

Exhibit 3–2. Proposed Planning for Natural Hazards Division

The following goals form the basis for the proposed Natural Hazards Division. A number of suggestions address important limitations in the disaster assistance framework and issues discussed in Chapter 8, "Planning for Disaster Recovery":

- Enhance APA's role in planning for natural hazards and disasters;

- Integrate planning into a broader strategy to better prepare communities for the impact of natural hazards, reduce future losses, and recover from natural hazards and disasters through planning-related research, training, education, and outreach programs;

- Support the development of professional knowledge linking disaster mitigation and recovery planning with comprehensive planning and day-to-day implementation;

- Advocate for a greater role of professional planners in the pre- and post-disaster planning process, to include, but not limited to, seeking organizational and legislative changes at the state and federal level;

- Assist in the development of pre- and post-disaster planning capabilities through the training of local, state, and federal officials; foundations; nonprofits; regional planning organizations; corporations and small businesses; and university students and faculty;

- Develop partnerships with other professional associations, nonprofit organizations, state and federal agencies, local elected officials and personnel, university and college instructors, and others to foster multiobjective planning activities that integrate natural hazards planning into all aspects of planning practice, research, and education;

- Encourage continuing professional development of members through opportunities provided by APA;

- Assist APA with the development of a robust policy agenda targeting identified areas in need of improvement;

- Identify complementary objectives across Divisions; and

- Develop a natural hazards planning research agenda, based on unanswered questions facing practicing planners.

Source: Gavin Smith, Richard Roths, and Michelle Steinberg. American Planning Association Request for the Formation of a Natural Hazards Division, 2007.

Security.[52] Thus, a better effort must be made to make the findings of these research entities an integral part of hazards and disaster policy development at the federal, state, and local levels.

Strengthening the value of applied research also depends on the commitment of researchers to address identified research needs. University workshops and events hosted by such organizations as the NAS and the NSF, conducted in tandem with the growing number of hazards research centers and with such long-standing professional associations as IAEM, NEMA, ASFPM, and the APA, provides a way to address this issue.

One of the drivers of good research is the ability to gain access to verifiable and reliable data sets. This can prove challenging in the area of disaster recovery because access to longitudinal data is difficult to attain yet essential to one's ability to track and evaluate trends over the lengthy process. In 2008, a number of hazard scholars convened to formulate a strategy to address this and other concerns. In the white paper that resulted, they suggested forming research "observatories" that could collect, analyze, and archive data over time in both pre- and post-disaster timeframes.[53]

The formation and ongoing support of the aforementioned RAVON would provide a useful platform for addressing the shortcomings of the research community and the study of long-term recovery. Working together with professional associations, federal and state agencies, and other members of the assistance network, RAVON (or another suitable research organization) could focus on three principal initiatives: (1) establish an evolving repository of research questions, formed by a collective body of researchers and practitioners; (2) improve the degree to which researchers are incorporated into the pre- and post-disaster data collection process; and (3) codify an agreed-upon means for more effectively translating research findings for and disseminating them to a practitioner-based audience. For example, FEMA includes engineering faculty on teams that assess how buildings were damaged by the forces of natural hazards. The teams describe their findings in summary reports and technical documents and offer specific recommendations for design improvements and changes in existing policies or construction standards. This approach could be expanded to include multiple physical and social science domains, including planning.

Another option is to develop a research cadre through the Emergency Management Assistance Compact (EMAC), a nationally recognized resource sharing organization; the National Emergency Management Association (NEMA), a professional association comprised of state emergency management directors, their senior staff, and other practitioners; and private sector contracts with FEMA (in order to work with the ESF-14 cadre or other federal recovery staff) (see Chapters 2 and 5). This could include a coalition of on-call hazard scholars, graduate students, and others who are willing and able to research the questions and issues that a team of practitioners and researchers have identified. Developing credentials, in association with approved institutions like EMAC, NEMA, and FEMA, would reduce the time required to access disaster sites and give the researcher added credibility in states and communities.

The post-disaster environment provides a unique opportunity to introduce students and junior faculty to the issues and complexities associated with recovery. The NSF's mentoring program could include an initiative that takes faculty and their mentors into the field after an event to discuss the prevailing physical, social, economic, and institutional conditions; relate the situation to existing literature; and discuss areas that may merit further research. This experience could be supplemented through the active engagement of professionals in the field and other members of the assistance network in order to ensure that local needs, defined as researchable questions, are adequately addressed.

Building on this approach, the NSF-sponsored Next Generation of Hazard Scholars mentoring initiative could be expanded to include the formulation of the "Next Generation of Hazards Practitioners," led by a coalition of professional associations, the private sector, government officials, and members of the nonprofit community. As in the Next Generation of Hazard Scholars program, promising young practitioners in various fields would be mentored by seasoned members of the disaster recovery assistance network. The program should strive to develop a series of cohorts versed in disaster recovery, who would in turn educate others in their field about their role in disaster recovery, including not only the value of pre-event planning but also the reality that they may be drawn into the process unexpectedly after an event occurs.

Quasi-governmental and nongovernmental organizations, which play critically important roles in recovery, may be excluded from larger government-driven programs or may choose to limit their interaction with the larger network. Yet as the Broadmoor case study so aptly demonstrates, many of these organizations are adept at fostering cooperation. The failure to integrate their unique abilities with those of other members of the assistance network limits the collective potential of all parties.

Case Study: The Broadmoor Project

The Broadmoor project is a neighborhood-level, post-Katrina disaster recovery planning effort in New Orleans that includes neighborhood associations, community development corporations (CDCs), universities, faith-based organizations, foundations, volunteers, students, and the private sector—collectively known as the Broadmoor Partner Network (see Case Study Exhibit 1). The project systematically addresses key limitations in the disaster recovery assistance framework, including those that affect the identification of residents' needs, the type and timing of assistance, and horizontal and vertical integration.

The Planning Process
Broadmoor's planning process used community organizing and empowerment principles to establish a coordinated network of assistance providers and encouraged the active participation of individuals. Rather than a top-down method more typical of the assistance framework, the team took a decentralized approach that focused on

helping individual homeowners and local business owners envision their future. Neighborhood groups were formed to identify the issues and priorities that needed to be addressed and to lead the implementation of the plan. The planning approach was conducted in five phases: impetus for change; community organizing; meeting and consensus; design, draft and release; and funding and implementation. Recognizing that neighborhood residents would recover at different rates, the coalition closely monitored the phases to ensure that all residents were ready before moving from one phase to the next.[1]

Impetus for Change
In the wake of Hurricane Katrina, the community's very existence was threatened by a study suggesting that the Broadmoor neighborhood be converted to open space. To prevent this from happening, it was suggested that the community "prove their viability" through the creation of a redevelopment plan.[2] This served to inspire

Case Study Exhibit 1. The Broadmoor "Partner Network"

Corporate Sponsors
- CH2M Hill
- Digitas (marketing and promotional materials)
- PlanReady (emergency management system, property condition and repopulation)
- Shell (funding of Harvard-related work)
- Deutche Bank (development staff funding)
- Eskew-Dumez-Ripple (visual communication support, design workshop facilitation)
- Travelocity
- Turner Construction
- Xtech (technology)

Foundations and Private Funders
- The Carnegie Corporation
- The RosaMary Foundation
- Anonymous philanthropist (CDC seed and capital grant, Broadmoor Improvement Association planning process grant)
- Digitas (charitable cash donation)
- Surdna Foundation (housing case workers)
- Mercy Corps (capacity-building grants)
- Individual contributions of Broadmoor residents

Universities
- Harvard (consulting: volunteer faculty, staff and students; Community Engagement Project: research, training for community leaders, technical guidance, documenting lessons learned)
- MIT (urban planning and architecture)
- Purdue University
- Xavier (development of Broadmoor adjacent to Xavier, development programs for the educational corridor)
- Bard College (inventory of every property in Broadmoor, resident needs assessment, volunteer network, house and school gutting)

Faith-based
- Free Church of the Annunciation (Annunciation House volunteer house-building army, neighborhood community center, mobile health services, Broadmoor Improvement Association office space and meeting space, teen after-school program, emergency relief services)
- First Presbyterian Church (preschool, community meeting space)
- St. Matthias (educational corridor)
- St. Albans School and the National Cathedral School
- Volunteer church groups from around the country

Community Organizations[1]
- Broadmoor Improvement Association
- Broadmoor Development Corporation

Source: The Broadmoor Project, "Phase 2: Community Organizing," in *Lessons from Katrina: How a Community can Spearhead Successful Disaster Recovery* (Cambridge: John F. Kennedy School of Government, Harvard University, 2007), 24, belfercenter.ksg.harvard.edu/files/uploads/DisasterRecoveryGuide_Phase_2.pdf.
1 Added by the author.

residents to coalesce around a common goal tied to its preservation. The impetus for change phase emphasized the identification of recovery and reconstruction needs as well as an agreed-upon planning process.

One of the first priorities of the Broadmoor Partner Network was to identify returning residents. College students conducted repopulation surveys to ascertain information about people who returned and the condition of their homes. A variety of strategies, including door-to-door surveys, e-mail notifications, flyers, lawn signs, and banners were used to reach out to displaced residents and other members of the larger disaster assistance network.

This information, which was gathered over time to increase the likelihood of an accurate count and the inclusion of those who would ultimately help shape the planning process, was compiled into the *Community Mapping Project: A Guidebook for Neighborhood*

continued on page 118

These images are of various types of housing in the Broadmoor neighborhood. Note in the fourth photo the new home elevated on cinder blocks adjacent to an older home with an aboveground basement. The latter construction technique is typical of the Broadmoor neighborhood.

Photos by Donn Young and Gavin Smith.

continued from page 117

Associations and CDCs to serve as the "fact base" of the plan (see Chapter 8 for further discussion of the value of a fact base in planning).[3] A detailed assessment of all buildings in the Broadmoor neighborhood (see accompanying figures at the top of this page), the guidebook includes information about the physical characteristics of each property and the structure(s) on it, such as type of use, parcel size and shape, number of stories, type of construction, and level and type of damages sustained, as well as data on the status of repair or reconstruction activities across housing, emergency facilities, and commercial structures. These data were incorporated into a geographic information system, enabling the teams to spatially analyze trends and relationships. The information was later used to assess damages, monitor reconstruction progress over time, and identify unmet needs.

Community Organizing
The community organizing phase centered on the creation of a neighborhood association. The Broadmoor Improvement Association (BIA) provided a structure around which residents could organize. It developed community subgroups, each with a moderator, to provide a more intimate meeting environment in which people could formulate ideas that were then brought back to the larger group. The iterative process allowed for the generation of multiple ideas that reflected different needs.

The Broadmoor Partner Network did not mention many of the members of the larger disaster assistance network, such as the Federal Emergency Management Agency, the Louisiana Recovery Authority, and local officials, nor did it discuss the types of assistance they provide. While there is little doubt that the community developed strong horizontal ties across groups, the degree to which vertical integration of government agencies remained unclear.

After Hurricane Katrina, government officials in Louisiana were roundly criticized for their apparent unresponsiveness and incompetence. This, however, should not preclude them from participating in the process as federal and state agencies provide financial and technical assistance to communities in the affected area. Upon on a further review of the planning process, including discussions with the president of the BIA, the association has, in fact, developed vertical relationships with state and federal organizations that are largely focused on gaining access to grant programs to pay for the physical reconstruction of damaged public infrastructure and housing. It is important to note that these relationships are tied to the programs managed by state and federal agencies, many of which did not necessarily meet local needs given their narrowly defined objectives.[4]

Meeting and Consensus
The third phase of the Broadmoor Project—community meetings and consensus building—emphasized the widespread use of collaborative planning and dispute resolution techniques. Meetings were held with subgroups, committees, and the larger community. Subgroup meetings ensured the continued discussion of issues raised during earlier phases. Committees were formed to focus on specific issues in detail, such as crime prevention, economic development, education, emergency preparedness and evacuation, flood hazard mitigation, housing, infrastructure, transportation, and urban planning. Subgroup members were encouraged to participate in meetings of other subgroups in order to exchange ideas and discuss specific elements of the community development plan that may not have been previously addressed.

The issues that emerged from subgroup meetings were compiled and written up in a "consensus document" that was presented and discussed at meetings of the larger community. Only those issues that emerged as part of a consensual agreement among subgroups were presented. Where consensus was not reached, the issues were brought back to the subgroups to resolve before they could be presented to the larger community group. While this approach was intended to drive decision making down to the individual and subgroup level, it might have limited the discussion of issues among all members of the community, placing power in the hands of a few individuals. It is uncertain if this negatively affected decisions about the equitable distribution of assistance to those who might not have been engaged in the process.

The process also used marketing techniques—lawn signs, banners, mailers, t-shirts, bumper stickers, and the use of local and national media outlets—to inform displaced residents and seek external partners and support. The concept of marketing and outreach during recovery, while critical, is rarely discussed in the literature or put into practice. Marketing

continued on page 121

The photo on the top shows the reopening of the Broadmoor neighborhood public library. Note the search and rescue symbols that are still spray painted on the front door. The photo on the bottom shows students using new computers in refurbished library.

Photos by Donn Young.

Case Study Exhibit 2. Broadmoor Improvement Association Community Development Plan

Community Development Plan Draft Outline, 3/23/06

I. EXECUTIVE SUMMARY: three to five page summary of the entire document

II. INTRODUCTION

Purpose: Purpose of the document

Vision: Vision for the community

Scope: What the plan covers and what it does not cover

Goals: Key goals of the plan (e.g., repopulate Broadmoor to pre-Katrina level, create a vibrant and safe community, provide social services for underserved communities, become a model for neighborhood revitalization in New Orleans)

Base Assumptions

History: A brief history of the neighborhood including historic significance

Boundary Map and Urban Context

Administrative Process: Describe how the plan was produced with special attention placed on the key elements of the public process (e.g., public hearings, writing process, amendment process, structure of committees, appointment/election of committees and committee leadership)

III. Existing Conditions

Population/Demography: Race, age, gender, population trajectory

Economic Base: Median income, major employers, types of employment

Environment: Flood risk, natural assets such as trees and bushes, green space

Flood Mitigation

Land Use/Zoning: Residential breakdown (low density, medium density, high density), business, parks, industrial, city zoning maps

Housing: Housing types, owned vs. rented, condition, occupied or vacant, etc.

Urban Design: Lighting, streetscapes, traffic lights, gutters, curbs, signage, communications, historic district, other aesthetics

Community Facilities/Services: Education, library, churches, parks, police

Social Analysis: Quality of life, sense of community, political climate

General Physical Conditions: Road conditions, physical assets, trash, potholes, blight, etc.

Utilities: Water, electric, sewage, gas, and communications

Transportation: Traffic, public transit, pedestrian traffic, bike traffic, etc.

IV. ANALYSIS OF SITUATION

Describe the interrelationships between existing issues

Provide a breakdown of the situation, including the key factors in order of priority

Highlight critical issues

V. DEVELOPMENT PLAN AND RECOMMENDATIONS

Repopulation

Flood Mitigation

Housing

Land Use: Land use, zoning, and historic district

Urban Design

Economic Development: Job creation, new business

Community Development: Library, churches, social programs, quality of life, etc.

General Physical Conditions

Utilities

Transportation

Safety and Security

Emergency Preparedness

Education

VI. IMPLEMENTATION

Strategies

Policies

Specific Actions: Responsibilities, timelines, monitoring, living documents, and updates

Funding

Source: The Broadmoor Project, "Phase 4: Design, Draft & Release of Plan," in *Lessons from Katrina: How a Community Can Spearhead Successful Disaster Recovery* (Cambridge: John F. Kennedy School of Government, Harvard University, 2007), 55, http://belfercenter.ksg.harvard.edu/files/uploads/DisasterRecoveryGuide_Phase_4.pdf.

continued from page 119

efforts targeted assistance providers in order to improve the likelihood of receiving an equitable share of finite resources while garnering additional partners. Emphasis was placed on two contrasting themes: the "virtuous" and "negative" cycles of recovery. The virtuous cycle describes the self-reinforcing benefits of confidence and repopulation, while the negative cycle is associated with a downward spiral of community spirit leading to low confidence among residents, which limits the impetus to rebuild. The marketing campaign sought to enhance the virtuous cycle, which was considered to be critical to enhancing the speed and quality of recovery.

Design, Draft, and Release

The design, draft, and release phase of the plan used a community workshop during which residents presented their ideas to design professionals, who then translated them into a visual representation of the reconstructed community. Committees continued to provide issue-specific input while garnering additional feedback during community meetings. After months of input from committees and public meetings, staff from Harvard University's John F. Kennedy School of Government and Massachusetts Institute of Technology's Department of Urban Studies and Planning worked with Broadmoor residents to develop a plan outline (see Case Study Exhibit 2).

Funding and Implementation

Once the plan was completed, community groups changed their focus from planning to identifying strategies and funding sources needed to implement specific projects. The creation of a community development corporation (CDC) provided the institutional means to lead the implementation effort. The CDC identified funding sources from members of the disaster assistance network, developed additional partnerships, hosted a series of fundraising activities, wrote grants, and solicited financial contributions from philanthropists and others. Once funds were procured, the CDC oversaw project management activities.

The CDC addressed one of the most challenging problems that communities face after a disaster: using the assistance provided by an array of organizations to meet the specific needs of the community. In the post-disaster environment, the CDC served as a boundary-spanning organization, identifying the resources, determining the most effective way to access them, and providing case management services to track the equitable distribution of assistance. Because the CDC emerged from the community-based planning process, it was intimately aware of the goals and objectives stated in the plan. It also provided important institutional capabilities crucial to the successful implementation of the plan. These included the ability to assume debt; provide grants, loans, and venture capital (obtained through second parties like banks, grantees, and fundraising); and develop property.

While the CDC focused on the implementation of projects and policy, the BIA led the creation and oversight of policy formulation and prioritization of the tasks outlined in the plan. It also continued to host subgroup meetings, coordinate communication and outreach efforts, and provide conflict resolution services as warranted.

The Broadmoor Community Model

Designed to provide residents and the larger community with a mechanism to access resources that meet local needs, the Broadmoor Community Model includes both materials intended to be used by others facing recovery and a discussion of how to build the local capacity needed to sustain commitment to the effort over time. Specific materials include guidance on developing community-level groups, such as a neighborhood association and a CDC; community organizing, communication, fundraising and marketing, and community engagement and consensus-building techniques; building public-private partnerships; collecting and analyzing data; and unveiling the plan. They also include grant-writing tips, templates, and funding menus. Supporting documents outline the steps necessary to create and implement a plan that can be easily adapted for use by other communities.

continued on page 122

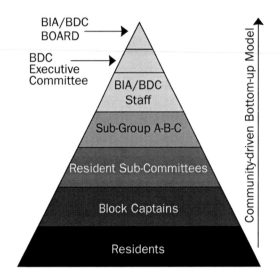

BIA/BDC BOARD

BDC Executive Committee

BIA/BDC Staff

Sub-Group A-B-C

Resident Sub-Committees

Block Captains

Residents

Community-driven Bottom-up Model

The Broadmoor Community Model places residents at the foundation of the community rebuilding efforts. Individual and community needs, and innovative program ideas are advanced through Block Captains, resident subcommittees, and subgroups. Through these avenues, BIA and BDC staff are guided as to what program areas implementation efforts should focus on. With their respective Boards, and in partnerships with each other, the BIA and BDC implement programs, receiving feedback throughout from residents and the various committees on program effectiveness. This feedback loop creates an accountability and quality control mechanism.

Source: The Broadmoor Project, "Phase 5: Funding and Implementation," in Lessons from Katrina: How a Community Can Spearhead Successful Disaster Recovery (Cambridge: John F. Kennedy School of Government, Harvard University, 2007), 64. Used with Permission of Henry Lee, the faculty chair of the Broadmoor Project.

continued from page 121

Applying the Lessons from the Broadmoor Experience

Building local capacity and self-reliance is an important and largely forgotten element of the U.S. disaster recovery assistance framework. The Broadmoor planning effort dramatically illustrates how a community-driven process can be used to successfully navigate this confusing and complex framework. What makes the community unique is the degree to which the planning process it developed addressed the key weaknesses in the current U.S. approach by identifying community needs and resources, developing locally based and appropriately timed solutions, and partnering with

members of the larger disaster assistance network to help achieve desired outcomes.

Specifically, the Broadmoor planning effort developed both technical and leadership skills among residents. It called upon university faculty to provide in-depth training focused on developing the capacity to create and implement a plan of action tailored to the community's unique needs. Training topics included housing finance, land use and zoning, and crime prevention. Community-level capacity-building efforts also strove to ensure that external organizations and individuals, including volunteers, nonprofits, foundations, federal agencies, and international organizations, that wanted to assist Broadmoor's planning and recovery efforts had an opportunity to do so.

In addition, the BIA is seeking to have its neighborhood designated as an improvement district within the larger city of New Orleans in order to secure a sustainable source of revenue for ongoing community-level enhancements. This type of designation, which requires passage of enabling legislation by the Louisiana legislature, will allow the association to collect fees from residents to tackle targeted actions beyond those paid for by the city. The efforts of the BIA are intended to allow them to more effectively self-govern and wean itself from what it recognizes to be reduced levels of charitable giving, in-kind services from nonprofits, and post-disaster recovery funds from the federal government.

Source: This case study was drawn from The Broadmoor Guide for Planning and Implementation, 2007.

1   The Broadmoor Project, Lessons from Katrina: How a Community Can Spearhead Successful Disaster Recovery (Cambridge: John F. Kennedy School of Government, Harvard University, 2007).

2   LaToya Cantrell, President, Broadmoor Improvement Association, personal communication, 2010.

3   Broadmoor Improvement Association, Community Mapping Project: A Guidebook for Neighborhood Associations and CDCs (July 2006), www.broadmoorimprovement.com/resources/community_mapping.pdf.

4   LaToya Cantrell, personal communication, 2010.

Endnotes

1   John R. Nolon and Patricia E. Salkin, *Land Use in a Nutshell* (St. Paul, Minn.: Thompson/West, 2006), 29–30.

2   Nolon and Salkin, *Land Use in a Nutshell*, 214–216.

3   James B. Duncan, "Financing Public Infrastructure," in *Local Planning: Contemporary Principles and Practice,* 332–335 (see note 1).

4   Frank S. So, "Finance and Budgeting," in *The Practice of Local Government Planning,* 435–471 (Washington, D.C.: International City Management Association, 1988).

5   Patrick Geddes, *Cities in Evolution* (London: Williams and Norgate, 1915); Lewis Mumford, *The Culture of Cities* (New York: Harcourt, Brace and Company, 1938); Andres Duany and Emily Talen, "Transect Planning," *Journal of the American Planning Association* 68, no. 3 (2002): 245–266.

6   George Perkins Marsh, *Man and Nature: or, Physical Geography as Modified by Human Action* (New York, 1864; Cambridge, Mass.: Belknap Press, 1965); Ian L. McHarg, *Design with Nature* (New York: Natural History Press, 1969).

7   Benton MacKaye, "The New Exploration: Charting the Industrial Wilderness," *Survey Graphic* 65 (1925): 153–157, 192; Randall Arendt, *Rural by Design: Maintaining Small Town Character* (Chicago: Planners Press, 1994).

8   Mark A. Benedict and Edward T. McMahon, *Green Infrastructure: Linking Landscapes and Communities* (Washington, D.C.: Island Press, 2006).

9   Stephen M. Wheeler, "Planning for Metropolitan Sustainability," *Journal of Planning Education and Research* 20, no. 2 (2001): 133–145; Myron Orfield, *American Metropolitics: The New Suburban Reality* (Washington, D.C.: Brookings Institution Press, 2002).

10 John M. DeGrove, *Land, Growth and Politics* (Chicago: Planners Press, 1984).

11 Peter Calthorpe and William Fulton, *The Regional City* (Washington, D.C.: Island Press, 2001).

12 Raymond J. Burby, Arthur C. Nelson, and Thomas W. Sanchez, "The Problems of Containment and the Promise of Planning," in *Rebuilding Urban Places after Disasters: Lessons from Hurricane Katrina,* ed. Eugenie L. Birch and Susan M. Wachter, 47–65 (Philadelphia: University of Pennsylvania Press, 2006); Jonathan Barnett, "Hazards and Regional Design," in *Smart Growth in a Changing World,* ed. Jonathan Barnett, 95–106 (Chicago: Planners Press, 2007).

13 Roderick Nash, *Wilderness and the American Mind,* 3rd ed. (New Haven, Conn.: Yale University Press, 1982), 104–105.

14 William L. Waugh Jr., "Regionalizing Emergency Management: Counties as State and Local Government," *Public Administration Review* 54, no. 3 (1994): 253–258; Delores N. Kory, "Coordinating Intergovernmental Policies on Emergency Management in a Multi-Centered Metropolis," *International Journal of Mass Emergencies and Disasters* 16, no. 1 (1998): 45–54.

15 William Dodge, *Regional Excellence: Governing Together to Compete Globally and Flourish Locally* (Washington, D.C.: National League of Cities, 1996).

16 Melvin C. Branch, *Comprehensive Planning: Introduction and Explanation* (Washington, D.C.: Planners Press), 1985, 194–195.

17 Eugene L. Lecomte, "Professional Organizations in Hazards Mitigation and Management: How Effective?" (paper presented at the 17th annual Hazards Research and Applications Workshop, Boulder, Colo., July 12–15, 1992).

18 John R. Logan, "Notes on the Growth Machine: Toward a Comparative Political Economy of Growth," *American Journal of Sociology* 82, no. 2 (1976): 349–352; John R. Logan and Harvey L. Molotch, *Urban Fortunes: The Political Economy of Place* (Berkeley: University of California Press, 1987).

19 Thomas E. Drabek, Alvin. H. Mushkatel, and Thomas S. Kilijanek, *Earthquake Mitigation Policy: The Experience of Two States* (Boulder: Institute of Behavioral Science, University of Colorado, 1983).

20   David R. Godschalk, *Coastal Hazards Mitigation: Public Notification, Expenditure Limitations, and Hazard Areas Acquisition* (Chapel Hill: Center for Urban and Regional Studies, University of North Carolina, 1998).

21   Gilbert F. White and J. Eugene Haas, *Assessment of Research on Natural Hazards* (Cambridge: MIT Press, 1975).

22   Dennis Mileti, *Disasters by Design: A Reassessment of Natural Hazards in the United States* (Washington, D.C.: Joseph Henry Press, 1999).

23   Robert K. Yin and Gwendolyn B. Moore, *Utilization of Research: Lessons from the Natural Hazards Field* (Washington, D.C.: Cosmos Corporation, 1985); Alice Fothergill, "Knowledge Transfer between Researchers and Practitioners," *Natural Hazards Review* 1, no. 2 (2000): 91–98; Gavin Smith and Dennis Wenger, "Sustainable Disaster Recovery: Operationalizing an Existing Agenda," in *Handbook of Disaster Research,* ed. Havidan Rodriguez, Enrico Quarantelli, and Russell Dynes, 234–257 (New York: Springer, 2006).

24   Robert A. Stallings, "Conflict in Natural Disasters: A Codification of Consensus and Conflict Theories," *Social Science Quarterly* 69, no. 3 (1988): 569–586; Smith and Wenger, "Sustainable Disaster Recovery."

25   Smith and Wenger, "Sustainable Disaster Recovery."

26   Hugh Mields, *Federally Assisted New Communities: New Dimensions in Urban Development* (Washington, D.C.: Urban Land Institute, 1973).

27   Mike Davis, *Ecology of Fear: Los Angeles and the Imagination of Disaster* (New York: Vintage Books, 1998), 143–147.

28   Stephen J. Pyne, *Fire in America: A Cultural History of Wildland and Rural Fire* (Princeton, N.J.: Princeton University Press, 1982).

29   Raymond J. Burby and Steven P. French, "Coping with Floods: The Land Use Management Paradox," *Journal of the American Planning Association* 47, no. 3 (July 1981): 289–300; Senate Committee on Environment and Public Works, Subcommittee on Transportation and Infrastructure, Doug Plasencia, testimony of the Association of State Floodplain Managers, 104th Cong., 1st sess., February 14, 1995.

30   Larry A. Larson, Michael J. Klitzke, and Diane A. Brown, eds., *No Adverse Impact: A Toolkit for Common Sense Floodplain Management* (Madison, Wis.: Association of State Floodplain Managers, 2003.

31   Mileti, *Disasters by Design.*

32   National Research Council, *Facing Hazards and Disasters: Understanding Human Dimensions* (Washington, D.C.: National Academies Press, 2006); Mileti, *Disasters by Design;* White and Haas, *Assessment of Research on Natural Hazards.*

33   Robert W. Kates et al., "Reconstruction of New Orleans after Katrina: A Research Perspective," *Proceedings of the National Academy of Sciences* 103, no. 40 (2006): 14653–14660.

34   Anthony Oliver-Smith, "Post-Disaster Housing Reconstruction and Social Inequality: A Challenge to Policy and Practice," *Disasters* 14, no. 1 (1990): 7–19; Philip R. Berke and Timothy Beatley, *After the Hurricane: Linking Recovery to Sustainable Development in the Caribbean* (Baltimore: Johns Hopkins University Press, 1997).

35   Gavin Smith, "Recovery from Catastrophic Disasters" (paper presented at the 33rd Annual Hazards Research and Applications Workshop, Broomfield, Colo., July 12–15, 2008).

36   Walter Gillis Peacock et al., *Toward a Resiliency and Vulnerability Observatory Network: RAVON,* Hazard Reduction and Recovery Center (HRRC) report 08-02R (College Station: Texas A&M University, 2008), www.archone.tamu.edu/hrrc/publications/researchreports/RAVON (accessed July 18, 2010).

37   Charles E. Fritz, "Disaster," in *Contemporary Social Problems: An Introduction to the Sociology of Deviant Behavior and Social Disorganization,* ed. Robert K. Merton and Robert A. Nisbet, 651–694 (New York: Harcourt, Brace/World, 1961).

38   Thomas A. Birkland, personal communication with author, 2010.

39   Kenneth C. Topping, "Toward a National Disaster Recovery Act of 2009," *Natural Hazards Observer* 33, no. 3 (January 2009): 1–9; Federal Emergency Management Agency (FEMA), *National Disaster Recovery Framework,* draft (February 5, 2010) disasterrecoveryworkinggroup.gov/ndrf.pdf; Smith and Wenger, "Sustainable Disaster Recovery."

40   Jim Schwab et al., *Planning for Post-Disaster Recovery and Reconstruction,* Planning Advisory Service (PAS) Report 483/484 (Chicago: American Planning Association [APA], 1998); Robert B. Olshansky, "Planning after Hurricane Katrina," *Journal of the American Planning Association* 72, no. 2 (2006): 147–153; Smith and Wenger, "Sustainable Disaster Recovery."

41   Marla Nelson, Renia Ehrenfeucht, and Shirley Laska, "Planning, Plans, and People: Professional Expertise, Local Knowledge, and Governmental Action in Post-Hurricane Katrina New Orleans," *Cityscape: A Journal of Policy Development and Research* 9, no. 3 (2007): 43.

42   Mileti, *Disasters by Design.*

43   FEMA, "Building a Disaster-Resistant University" (August 11, 2010), www.fema.gov/institution/dru.shtm.

44   Roy Popkin and Claire B. Rubin, "Practitioners' Views of the Natural Hazards Center," *Natural Hazards Review* 1, no. 4 (2000): 212–221.

45   George R. McDowell, *Land-Grant Universities and Extension into the 21st Century: Renegotiating or Abandoning a Social Contract* (Ames: Iowa State University Press, 2001).

46   Extension Disaster Education Network (EDEN), "Mission, Vision and Core Functions," at eden.lsu.edu/AboutEDEN/HowEDENWorks/Pages/default.aspx.

47   National Research Council, *Facing Hazards and Disasters;* Smith and Wenger, "Sustainable Disaster Recovery."

48   Walter Gillis Peacock and Chris Girard, "Ethnic and Racial Inequalities in Hurricane Damage and Insurance Settlements," in *Hurricane Andrew: Ethnicity, Gender and the Sociology of Disasters,* ed. Walter Gillis Peacock, Betty Hearn Morrow, and Hugh Gladwin, 171–190 (Miami, Fla.: International Hurricane Center Laboratory for Social and Behavioral Research, 1997); Mark G. Welsh and Ann-Margaret Esnard, "Closing Gaps in Local Housing Recovery Planning for Disadvantaged Displaced Households," *Cityscape: A Journal of Policy Development and Research* 11, no. 3 (2009): 195–212.

49   Thomas J. Campanella, "Urban Resilience and the Recovery of New Orleans," *Journal of the American Planning Association* 72, no. 2 (2006): 141–146.

50   Marya Morris, *Subdivision Design in Flood Hazard Areas,* PAS 473 (Chicago: APA, 1997); Randall Ismay, *Firewise Communities: Where We Live, How We Live* (Quincy, Mass.: Firewise Communities, 2003); Jim Schwab, Lynn Ross, and Lincoln Walther, *Firewise Post-Workshop Assessment: Final Report* (Chicago: American Planning Association for Firewise Communities, 2003); James C. Schwab and Stuart Meck, *Planning for Wildfires,* PAS Report 529/530 (Chicago: APA), 2005; James C. Schwab, Paula L. Gori, and Sanjay Jeer, *Landslide Hazards and Planning,* PAS Report 533/534 (Chicago: APA, 2005); National Fire Protection Association (NFPA), *Safer from the Start: A Guide for Firewise-Friendly Developments* (Quincy, Mass.: NFPA 2009).

51   Gavin Smith, Richard Roths, and Michelle Steinberg. American Planning Association Request for the Formation of a Natural Hazards Division, 2007.

52   Richard Sylves, *Disaster Policy and Politics: Emergency Management and Homeland Security* (Washington, D.C.: CQ Press, 2008).

53   Peacock et al., *Toward a Resiliency and Vulnerability Observatory Network: RAVON.*

Chapter 4

Nonprofit Relief Organizations

A billboard on the Mississippi Gulf Coast expresses thanks for the work of nonprofit relief organizations after Hurricane Katrina.

Photo by Gavin Smith.

N ATIONAL NONGOVERNMENTAL ORGANIZATIONS (NGOS), FAITH-BASED groups, community groups, foundations, and other nonprofit relief organizations have long played a role in recovery assistance in the United States. Often led by a sense of altruism, an emphasis on assisting less powerful groups, and a general mistrust of government, which they may view as overly bureaucratic and unresponsive to local needs following a disaster, these organizations are perhaps best known for providing food, water, clothing, shelter, medical assistance, and crisis intervention in the aftermath of an event. They also assist with housing repair and reconstruction, distribute financial aid through grants and loans, advocate policy change, and undertake recommended actions that address hazard mitigation and disaster recovery-related topics. Owing to, among other things, the financial backing of foundations and the private sector as well as the rising number of demands that are not being met by federal, state, and local governments, the nonprofit community has grown rapidly in the United States.[1]

Nonprofit organizations that provide both immediate and long-term assistance include nationally recognized groups, such as the American Red Cross and the Salvation Army, and faith-based organizations, such as the Baptist Men, Mennonite Disaster Services, and the United Methodist Communities in Relief. These groups are often part of a larger coalition known as National Voluntary Organizations Active in Disasters (NVOAD) (see the accompanying sidebar). Less well recognized are environmental and social justice groups, such as the National Wildlife Federation (NWF) and Oxfam, which are involved in a range of disaster recovery and mitigation-related issues. Other nonprofits include grassroots-based community groups that are drawn into disaster recovery because their constituents are directly affected; examples

---

National Voluntary Organizations Active in Disasters

National Voluntary Organizations Active in Disasters (NVOAD) was formed after Hurricane Camille struck the Mississippi coast in 1969. Made up of a number of faith-based and nondenominational organizations, such as Catholic Charities USA, Feed the Children, Mercy Medical Airlift (Angel Flights), and United Way Worldwide, NVOAD is dedicated to improving the coordinated distribution of disaster relief among nonprofits.[1] To this end, its members are focused on several broad functions, including disseminating information among members and disaster aid recipients; coordinating policy across member organizations; serving as a national voice on issues associated with nonprofit assistance; educating members through training and educational venues; engaging in leadership development; supporting hazard mitigation policies at the federal, state, and local government levels; and conducting outreach efforts to the broader community.

In 2004, NVOAD published its *Long-Term Recovery Manual*.[2] To help communities establish a collaborative venue (a "long-term recovery committee") or a more formal coalition (a "long-term recovery organization"), the manual describes the roles that NVOAD members play in recovery, including donations management, reconstruction, and case management of individuals whose needs are unmet by other programs. Specific tools include mission statements, objectives, bylaws, a proposed organizational structure, job descriptions, and the steps required to form a 501(c)(3) nonprofit.

By expanding coordinative venues like NVOAD and better publicizing their efforts, members of the disaster assistance network could help address key weaknesses in the disaster recovery assistance framework. Compared to government agencies and other members of the network, nonprofit organizations tend to have greater organizational flexibility and less prescriptive rules, so they are often able to provide direct assistance more quickly after a disaster.

1   A complete, up-to-date list of members can be found on the NVOAD website at www.nvoad.org/index.php/member/national-members.html.

2   NVOAD, *Long-Term Recovery Manual*, rev ed. (Arlington, Va.: NVOAD, January 2004), www.disasterrecoveryresources.net/VOAD-LTRecoveryManual.pdf.

include the Rotary Club; the Kiwanas Club; chapters of the Boy and Girl Scouts; and local churches, mosques, or synagogues that may or may not be tied to formalized religious relief networks. And finally there are foundations, which provide direct financial assistance in the form of grants to individuals, communities, and nonprofits; pay for university researchers and members of think tanks to study identified problems and offer solutions; and advocate for changes in recovery policies and programs that fail to address the needs of the principal groups they support.

Nonprofit relief organizations influence the post-disaster distribution of assistance by sharing information (including the open criticism of programs and policies that fail to address identified needs) with other members of the disaster assistance network, leveraging resources, building social support networks, and mobilizing public opinion.[2] They are among the most outspoken organizations to draw attention to the ethical dimensions of assistance in the post-disaster environment, and their ability to work collaboratively with the spectrum of organizations involved in disaster response and recovery—including federal and state agencies, the media, professional associations, and the university community—increases the likelihood of the equitable distribution of assistance.

Nonprofit organizations are characterized by high levels of volunteerism (see Figures 4–1 and 4–2), so they are often able to provide services to disaster victims and communities inexpensively—if not for free. The voluntary nature of their work lends itself not only to large-scale disasters that merit the assistance of federal agencies and large national organizations with deep pockets, but also to smaller, more localized events that rely on nonfederal assistance for those in need. Conversely, however, the level of support they can provide tends to be uneven, influenced by the nature of the event; the degree to which the event generates interest among members, volunteers, donors, and the media; and the priorities of nonprofit leaders who may preselect the type of assistance recipients.[3]

Figure 4–1. Kaboom!, a nonprofit focused on the repair and reconstruction of damaged playgrounds following disasters, relies heavily on local volunteers to assist a small permanent staff.

Source: Kaboom!

Figure 4-2. Volunteers help to remove flood-damaged drywall from a home in New Orleans after Hurricane Katrina. This labor-intensive process, often referred to as "gutting" a home, allows for the supporting infrastructure to dry prior to the home's repair. Studs and other woody materials exposed to floodwaters are usually treated with a bleach solution in an attempt to prevent mold from growing behind the walls once they are repaired, but this technique does not always work. The appearance of mold following the reconstruction of flood-damaged homes represents a serious health risk, particularly among children, elderly people, and those with respiratory problems.

Photo by Donn Young.

Also highly variable is the extent to which the actions of nonprofit organizations are coordinated with those of the public sector and other members of the disaster assistance network during recovery. NVOAD provides a recognized means of coordinating its activities with member groups in the network, yet it is less effective at influencing the actions of the broader system of organizations with regard to long-term recovery and reconstruction. The American Red Cross and the Salvation Army, for example, fill critically important roles in feeding and shelter operations, but they are less recognized for their work in long-term recovery and reconstruction activities.

Nonprofit relief groups also vary greatly in size, complexity, organizational culture, type of assistance provided, and speed with which that assistance is delivered.

NATIONAL ORGANIZATIONS

National nonprofits, such as the Red Cross and the Salvation Army, are formal organizations with a professional administrative staff and supporting volunteers focused on disaster relief. Both the Red Cross and the Salvation Army also have an array of community-based chapters that operate somewhat independently of the central umbrella group. Other national nonprofits, such as faith-based, environmental, and social justice groups, have a similarly diffuse organizational structure.

The American Red Cross

The American Red Cross is unique among nonprofit relief organizations in that it has a congressional mandate to help individuals and communities prepare for disasters and to assist the needy during disaster response and the initial phase of recovery. Its priorities include providing disaster health services (first aid, blood collection and distribution, and the filling of prescription medications), mental health services (counseling and emotional support), mass care (feeding operations and the certification and staffing of shelters), and family assistance (temporary housing and clothing); determining the status of individuals stricken by a disaster; conducting damage assessments; coordinating volunteers; conducting preparedness and outreach; issuing service announcements; maintaining public affairs; and providing logistical support. Over the past two decades, the organization has increasingly emphasized the importance of hazard mitigation as a means of reducing future losses.[4]

Although nonprofits tend to fault the federal government as being too constrained by red tape and narrowly defined and/or interpreted policies to provide timely and effective assistance after a disaster, some nonprofits have come under the same criticism. Following Hurricane Katrina, local emergency managers, state officials, and members of Congress decried the inability of the Red Cross to accurately estimate the number of those who needed shelter, provide for their immediate shelter needs, and account for associated costs.[5] According to Marvin Olasky, the evidence seemed to confirm what Clara Barton, the organization's founder, had feared back in the nineteenth century: "'If the Red Cross becomes too bureaucratic and businesslike, its compassion and effectiveness as a relief organization would diminish.'"[6] Largely in response to the perceived limitations of the Red Cross, faith-based and emergent groups filled the void after the hurricane, providing additional shelter capacity (emergent groups are further described in Chapter 7).

Faith-based Groups

Complementing the work of the Red Cross are the many national (as well as state, regional, and local) faith-based organizations. Along with food, water, clothing, and financial assistance, these organizations often provide spiritual support and mental health counseling. A number of national religious groups have state-based teams of volunteers who travel to disaster sites to assist with debris removal and the repair or reconstruction of damaged housing, places of worship, and small businesses. Many faith-based organizations raise money and collect donated goods through fundraising events, church drives, and regular offerings.

The best-known faith-based relief organization in the United States is the Salvation Army. Originally established in England, it has more than 60,000 employees and thousands of volunteers spread across more than 1,200 community chapters.[7] The principles of the Salvation Army, which include the ability to innovate and to make efficient use of available resources within a framework guided by service and passion,[8] help the organization to excel in providing assistance in crisis situations. After Hurricane Katrina, for instance, the Salvation Army was widely praised for quickly moving into damaged areas and setting up feeding operations. Peter Drucker, the business management scholar, refers to the Salvation Army as "'the most effective organization in the U.S.'"[9]

Environmental Groups

Environmental groups play an important role as policy advocates, local capacity builders, and technical experts across a range of hazards issues, including land use and the role of natural systems in hazard reduction, hazards research and technology transfer, insurance, and the more equitable distribution of post-disaster assistance.[10] For instance, environmental groups have teamed with professional associations, federal and state agencies, and others to seek changes in federal, state, and local laws and policies to discourage development in environmentally sensitive areas prone to natural hazards. In 1999, when Hurricane Floyd caused severe flooding in eastern North Carolina, the North Carolina Chapter of the American Planning Association (led by a number of concerned faculty and students in the University of North Carolina at Chapel Hill's Department of City and Regional Planning), the NWF, the Sierra Club, and the Conservation Fund were among the organizations that called for the establishment of a set of redevelopment principles for post-Hurricane Floyd recovery that emphasized the relocation of flood-damaged neighborhoods out of the floodplain. They argued not only that this would reduce the impact of future hazards, but also that removing farming operations, junkyards, and wastewater treatment plants from riparian areas would reduce point and non-point source pollution and restore the natural and beneficial function of the floodplain.[11] Just a year earlier, the NWF had issued *Higher Ground: A Report on Voluntary Property Buyouts in the Nation's Floodplains*, which represents another example of the role that environmental groups play in the disaster recovery policy dialogue.[12] Further evidence of this nexus is the Land Trust Alliance, which documents land acquisition projects that protect both coastal resources and floodplains.[13]

While environmental experts have long recognized the link between the protection of natural systems and hazard mitigation,[14] the topic received national media attention when the 2004 Sumatra earthquake generated a tsunami that killed more than 283,000 people. Research showed that the removal of mangroves from Indonesia's coast contributed to the devastation of the coastal communities and the staggering loss of life. Similarly, the city of New Orleans was made more vulnerable by the removal of protective wetlands and cypress forests that served to buffer the area from storm surge and provide a spongelike effect during floods. Climate change, sea level rise, and the potential increase in the number and intensity of coastal storms has heightened awareness of the need to develop partnerships that bridge shared concerns among the environmental and natural hazards communities.[15]

Social Justice Groups

Social justice groups strive to inform vulnerable populations about and protect them from threats to their public health, safety, and overall quality of life. Such groups also play a role in disaster recovery, particularly as it relates to the distribution of assistance. Nonprofit relief organizations often join with organizations that have a broader social justice agenda, such as Oxfam, the World Health Organization, and the Church World Service, to address the needs of socially vulnerable populations after a disaster.[16]

An important thread in the social justice movement is the issue of environmental racism. Among the most notorious examples of this unfortunate reality is the disproportionate number of chemical plants, hazardous waste facilities, incinerators, and landfills that are sited near poor, minority neighborhoods.[17] Because residents of such communities have often been excluded from the political process by which land use decisions are made and also possess more tenuous connections to those in power, they may be less likely to fight these decisions or unable to garner the support needed to effectively oppose entrenched political interests. Understood in the context of natural hazards, these same populations are disproportionately vulnerable to the impacts of disasters.[18] Assorted economic, political, and cultural factors tied to race, socioeconomic status, and sex render socially vulnerable populations less able than the general population to recover from disasters.[19]

Given the nonstop media coverage they tend to generate, disasters have a way of dramatically highlighting the plight of those who are poor, elderly, homeless, and illiterate; people with disabilities; single mothers; and non-native speakers. Social justice organizations, many of which know and work with at-risk groups, provide an array of services including feeding, sheltering, and mental health and drug counseling on a daily basis, and the continued delivery of these services becomes critical after a disaster. These groups also serve to bridge the gap between the needs of disenfranchised populations and service providers. They may organize protests, build coalitions with other groups to express their concerns more forcefully, and testify before state and federal committees charged with disaster recovery program oversight.

COMMUNITY ORGANIZATIONS

Community relief groups engage in many of the same tasks as national relief organizations, but they differ in two important ways: (1) they are closely tied to a local jurisdiction or neighborhood and thus are focused almost exclusively on local issues and priorities; and (2) they provide ongoing assistance over time. Community groups are often the primary providers of assistance in smaller, localized tornadoes, wildfires, and floods. Those that focus on social justice, growth and land use, crime, or other local issues may also play an important role in recovery, promoting community-led disaster preparedness and flood-loss reduction initiatives.

In their normal course of activities, community organizations help people find affordable housing, provide financial advice, and engage in a wide range of social services such as child welfare, spousal abuse prevention, drug counseling, and spiritual comfort—assistance that is in even greater need after a disaster, as has been well documented.[20] However, their role in long-term recovery remains less understood. No clear protocols have been established for the involvement of community groups with the disaster recovery assistance network, including the role they may play in pre-event planning for post-disaster recovery (see Chapter 8 for a further discussion of this issue). In a 1987 report to the National Academy of Science outlining the proposed creation of the international decade of hazard reduction, James Mitchell and Abram Bernstein describe the factors that allow sustainable development principles to be integrated into disaster recovery efforts. They note the importance of actively involving individuals and groups with local knowledge and expertise in recovery planning, a process that could lessen dependency on help from outside the community.[21] Further exploration of this issue is needed to more effectively incorporate community groups into recovery and better understand how their involvement can reduce the need for external assistance.

Because they have a good sense of local priorities, community organizations often are better positioned to act promptly after a disaster than are national organizations, private sector agencies, and others from outside the community. Moreover, because they are decentralized, grassroots nonprofits have greater flexibility with which to provide assistance. For these reasons, foundations and other donors often prefer to provide grants and technical assistance to a community organization rather than to a national group.[22] At the same time, however, the ability of local nonprofits to deliver disaster assistance may be constrained by limited resources, and donor organizations sometimes question the long-term viability of community organizations, preferring to fund larger nonprofits instead.

FOUNDATIONS

Foundations are public or private institutions that provide grant funding and technical assistance and may serve as policy advocates across a number of specialized topical areas. They may be established by the state or other groups to serve as a conduit for donations, such as financial and material assistance as well as other goods and services. Public foundations receive resources from multiple donors, including individuals, private foundations, and government agencies, or as part of fees obtained to provide specific services. Private foundations rely primarily on an individual, family, or corporation for resource support. Some foundations provide grants directly to relief organizations, service organizations, and community-level groups that then pass the funds on to other entities focused on regranting activities. Foundations may also work to ensure that assistance is equitably distributed, with particular attention paid to the poor and other socially vulnerable populations.

Local and state-level foundations are often established after disasters to receive and distribute financial assistance and relief supplies, and to help disseminate information. After the massive flooding that occurred in the Midwest in the early 1990s, for instance, the Fargo-Moorhead Area Foundation set up a website to track local needs and identify grant providers.[23] In the early 2000s, the San Diego Foundation created the San Diego Regional Disaster Fund, a supporting organization designed to provide leadership in the philanthropic response to and recovery from regional disasters. The fund played a major role in the San Diego Foundation's relief efforts after the 2003 fires.[24]

The Louisiana Disaster Recovery Foundation (LDRF, www.louisianahelp.org), established by Governor Kathleen Blanco just six days after Hurricane Katrina struck the Gulf Coast, is another example of a private foundation created to help distribute recovery assistance following a disaster. The LDRF's principal mission is to serve as a social justice philanthropy, helping to provide the resources needed to assist in the recovery and reconstruction of coastal Louisiana. Specific areas of emphasis include economic development, housing, land use planning, education, and health care. The largest grant that the foundation has received was $24.4 million from the Bush-Clinton Katrina Fund. Three years after the storm, the LDRF had distributed $33 million to nonprofit organizations for the repair and construction of affordable housing; economic development, including small businesses and microentrepreneurs; civic engagement; and public infrastructure.

Foundations influence policy formulation by acting as advocates on behalf of a group or targeted mission. The LDRF, for example, serves as a staunch advocate for changes in recovery policies that it feels are inequitable.[25] Issue-specific foundations may also have experts on staff who provide testimony at legislative and congressional hearings and other policy-making venues. If experts are not part of their organization, foundations often provide grants to universities, think tanks, professional associations, and other nonprofit organizations to support research, education, and training across a wide range of recovery-related issues, including housing repair or reconstruction, community organizing, and the dissemination of information.

DIMENSIONS OF THE DISASTER RECOVERY ASSISTANCE FRAMEWORK

The Council on Foundations, a nonprofit association comprising over 2,100 grant-making foundations and corporations focused on philanthropy, has developed eight principles of good disaster management (see accompanying sidebar). These principles address many of the key limitations of the disaster recovery assistance framework. The council encourages grant makers to consider developing a plan that includes the pre-event identification of grantees; an exploration of varied organizations through which support is directed (i.e., government agencies, nonprofits, research organizations, multilateral organizations, and the media); the development of internal guidelines; and the establishment of criteria that are streamlined, yet flexible in order to address unanticipated needs.

Understanding of Local Needs

Any organization's understanding of local needs is strongly influenced by its association with the community's residents. Gaining the trust of individuals affected by disaster often evolves through an informal process that is not driven by bureaucratic relationships,[26] whose lines of authority and responsibility do little to establish the interactions and relationships needed to build trust. (See Chapter 9 for a discussion of suggested changes to the existing recovery framework that can facilitate cooperation and trust across the network.) Community organizations tend to have a broad experiential knowledge of local needs, which they have obtained over time and through close association with residents. However, compared to national nonprofits, they tend to have less of an understanding of the larger disaster assistance network and of the rules associated with federal assistance. And in any disaster situation, there is often an inherent tension between the federal agencies that have significant financial resources and the community organizations that are most familiar with local needs. Clearly, recovery efforts are strengthened when community organizations can transfer their knowledge of the community to others within the disaster assistance network.

Community-based Groups

The relationship that community groups have with members of the community, particularly socially vulnerable populations, is a critical asset after a disaster as it helps to foster trust between those providing and those receiving assistance. Individuals often believe that local assistance providers recognize their needs more fully than do

Council on Foundations' Principles of Good Disaster Management

Do no harm. Not all disaster assistance is beneficial. Inappropriate items can overwhelm limited transportation, storage and distribution capacities, thereby delaying the delivery of aid that is desperately needed. Aim to ensure that your grant contributes to the solution and not to the problem.

Stop, look, and listen before taking action. Information is the key to good disaster grantmaking. Every disaster has unique characteristics. Take the time to learn about the specifics of a disaster before deciding how to respond.

Don't act in isolation. Coordination among disaster grantmakers, among NGOs operating on the ground, and between these two groups, can reduce duplication of effort, improve efficient use of resources, and ensure that the highest priority needs are addressed first. Grantmakers can participate in various standing and ad hoc forums—both in person and through electronic means—where needs are discussed, information exchanged, and assistance coordinated.

Think beyond the immediate crisis to the long-term. The emergency phase of a disaster attracts most of the attention and resources. Grantmakers can play a useful role before the crisis by supporting disaster prevention and preparedness activities, and afterward, by filling gaps between emergency relief and long-term development programs.

Bear in mind the expertise of local organizations. Community-based organizations and NGOs with a local presence are the first on the scene when disasters occur. They know best what

assistance is needed and they understand the complex political, social and cultural context of a disaster. However, these organizations are often hampered by lack of resources and organizational capacity. Working with and supporting these organizations allows them to carry out their important role while providing grantmakers with valuable information about the situation on the ground.

Find out how prospective grantees operate. Organizations that work on disasters vary greatly in their approach and overall philosophy. Some specialize only in emergency relief, while others have a long-term development orientation. Some support the work of local organizations, while others do not. It is wise to know what approach you are supporting before making a grant.

Be accountable to those you are trying to help. Grantmakers are accountable, not only to their donors, boards and shareholders but also to the people they seek to assist. Grantmakers need to go beyond merely determining how their grant was spent to engage their grantees in a process that assesses social impact.

Communicate your work widely and use it as an educational tool. Highlighting examples of good disaster grantmaking is an excellent way for grantmakers to educate both internal and external audiences about the disaster process. It is useful to build a knowledge base, record lessons learned, and share your experience with boards, staff, employees, other grantmakers, the media, community groups, public officials, and international organizations.

Source: *Disaster Grantmaking: A Practical Guide for Foundations and Corporations* (Arlington, Va.: Council on Foundations and European Foundation Centre 2007), 9–10.

providers from outside the community, and they suppose that these local groups will work on their behalf. (This perception is not always true; although it is uncommon, community organizations have been known to adopt assistance strategies that reflect long-standing issues of racism and exclusion, focusing their efforts on select individuals and families.)

One of the strengths of community organizations is their extended links to those living in specific neighborhoods. Unlike external assistance providers, the staff and volunteers of community organizations worship in the same churches, synagogues, and mosques; their children attend the same schools; they work in the same companies; and they attend the same community events as do other members of the community. Similarly, when disasters strike, they are just as likely as anyone else in the community to be affected. And at those times, it is the strength of their informal relationships with neighborhood residents that makes them better able to empathize with those they are trying to help and uniquely qualified to target identified needs.

National Organizations

Despite their deep understanding of the needs facing disaster victims and the communities in which they work, grassroots organizations may have less of an understanding of the larger disaster assistance network, including the type and timing of assistance provided by others. National nonprofit relief organizations, like the American Red Cross and Salvation Army, usually have a better understanding of federal assistance, owing in part to their assigned roles providing food and mass care in post-disaster operations and to their participation in NVOAD and the National Response Framework (NRF). Yet the Red Cross was unable to effectively meet local needs following Katrina, a failing that has been partly attributed to the lack of coordination with the Federal Emergency Management Agency (FEMA) and to a reluctance or inability to provide adequate feeding and shelter operations in hard-hit, low-income areas.[27] Moreover, since the Red Cross provides post-disaster services as part of a congressional mandate, federal rules have been developed as part of this agreement that influence their adaptability following disasters. (In contrast, the Salvation Army has a more diffuse and autonomous system that has been driven by improvisation.)[28] Community groups tend to have far more flexibility than large national organizations. The lack of strict rules allows community groups to respond relatively rapidly once a defined mode of assistance is determined.

Faith-based Groups

Spiritual needs are often great following disasters, as people try to make sense of why their communities were struck and to cope with their losses. Churches, synagogues, mosques, and other local faith-based organizations understand these needs in a way that few other organizations do, and so while government and other members of the assistance network remain secular in their approach to recovery assistance and stay away from spiritually based relief strategies, faith-based groups embrace them (see Figure 4–3).[29]

Figure 4–3. Members of the congregation held services in this Pass Christian, Mississippi, church the day after Hurricane Katrina. Faith-based organizations play an important role in recovery and often partner with local churches to assist in the reconstruction of damaged places of worship, help members of the congregation, or provide other types of assistance to the larger community.

Photo by Gavin Smith.

However, the spiritual concept of a disaster as an "act of God," which is particularly prevalent among evangelical denominations, has important negative implications. It suggests, for instance, that disasters are beyond our control when, in fact, many are largely avoidable. Moreover, the notion that God will take care of "believers" regardless of their actions can lead to behavior that does not account for the realities of hazard vulnerability, such as failing to take personal responsibility to reduce future losses through the adoption of preparedness and mitigation measures.

Foundations

A nonprofit organization's ability to draw on external resources is important. The financial resources of nonprofit organizations, particularly those at the community level, are often already stretched thin before a disaster and are likely to be even more depleted by efforts to help those affected by an event once it occurs. Funding provided by foundations allows a nonprofit to address local needs that arise from or are exacerbated by a disaster.

A philanthropic foundation's understanding of local needs is predicated on its access to or relationship with a benefactor or nonprofit grant recipient that is familiar with local conditions. This is particularly true of large, national foundations. Foundation-funded assistance has targeted a number of pertinent recovery issues, including the protection and preservation of art and cultural resources, the adoption of hazard mitigation techniques, the reconstruction of damaged schools and public infrastructure, the purchase of medical supplies, the conduct of disaster preparedness initiatives, and family reunification efforts.[30] Foundations also have a long history of funding research and writing technical reports that assess disaster recovery assistance, including the efficacy of programs, the degree to which programs address local needs, and the comparative analysis of state spending strategies.[31] The RAND Corporation is among the nonprofit organizations that have conducted studies addressing disaster assistance policies and programs, particularly those following Hurricane Katrina.[32]

Timing of Assistance

Nonprofit relief organizations are largely skeptical of public sector bureaucracies and often blame the government's excessive rules for the slow speed of disaster assistance. Generally speaking, nonprofits provide disaster recovery and reconstruction assistance more rapidly than federal and state agencies. Yet there is some evidence to suggest that this is not always the case.[33]

As discussed in Chapter 1, the success of recovery depends not solely on the speed of program delivery. Equally important is the coordinated timing of assistance, which requires an understanding of when and under what conditions assistance is provided by other members of the network, and a coordinated distribution strategy that capitalizes on this understanding. (The failure to coordinate the assistance provided by nonprofits and community groups with that provided by the federal government or the insurance industry is illustrated in the discussion of housing repair on pages 56–58 in Chapter 2.)

The contributions of nonprofits are also used as in-kind services, which helps to leverage the resources of other assistance providers.[34] Through the coordinated distribution of assistance, duplication and counterproductive actions among different members of the assistance network can be avoided, thus allowing for the strategic investment of limited and specialized resources that can stretch large but often narrowly defined grant or loan programs administered by public and private sector stakeholders, such as federal agencies or the insurance industry. Research and practice has shown that being organizationally nimble throughout the disaster recovery process is an important attribute for a nonprofit to thrive in an uncertain environment where program rules change rapidly.[35]

For foundations making grants, it is generally a lengthy process. Staff and board members need to identify concerns or issues they wish to address, solicit interest among potential grantees, review applications, select recipients, and distribute funds. Pre-event planning, in which foundations and other nonprofits identify potential grant recipients, can speed disaster recovery; it also enables organizations to be prequalified so they can develop a spending plan that outlines how the funds will be used. Ideally such grants are provided prior to a disaster so that nonprofit recipients can be more proactive in helping communities and institutions undertake pre-event planning initiatives. The value of pre-event planning is particularly evident in the case of socially vulnerable populations, a frequent target of foundation-provided assistance. Funding can, for instance, be used to address pre-disaster social and economic conditions (i.e., substandard housing, including that which is located in hazard-prone areas; inadequate health care; low educational achievement; and poor job skills) that contribute to a heightened level of vulnerability to disasters.

Research grants can also affect the speed of recovery assistance. Foundation-funded research is often evaluative in nature, assessing the efficacy, speed, and equity of existing programs. The findings can make a difference during the recovery process, particularly if the research into past events has been able to draw lessons that are transferable to other areas and types of disasters. The utility of such research depends largely on the ability of the organization that has conducted it to disseminate the findings to the media and activists who can recommend changes in policy and to appropriate decision makers who can act based on this information.

Like other members of the disaster recovery network, community organizations and foundations benefit from a coordinated assistance delivery strategy. Many nonprofits are run by a board that answers to its members—who sometimes include the benefactors who provide financial support to the organization. Board members are responsible for monitoring and evaluating the impact of grants received or provided. Foundations similarly are guided by a board of directors charged with overseeing their operations. An established system of grantee accountability enhances the likelihood that funds will be used as intended and enables the grant-making organization to measure the impact of the assistance provided. The pre-event development of selection, monitoring, and evaluation systems also allows for the more rapid disbursement of grants, thereby affecting the speed of recovery while improving interorganizational coordination across members of the disaster assistance network.

Horizontal and Vertical Integration

Nonprofit relief organizations are often well situated to help socially vulnerable populations. Taking action apart from the larger assistance network, however, can have unanticipated negative consequences. Efforts to rebuild safer, more resilient communities, for example, can be hampered by well-intentioned attempts to quickly rebuild damaged housing: too often, these efforts fail to incorporate techniques that reflect the latest understanding of risk.[36] The reluctance to coordinate across nonprofit organizations and, more importantly, across the larger disaster assistance network can thus perpetuate or worsen the exposure of the populations that are most vulnerable to the impacts of natural hazards—often the very groups that nonprofits seek to assist on a daily basis.

While nonprofits may best understand local needs (although not always have the best grasp of the means necessary to reduce risk), the generally low level of coordination among them and federal and state agencies, the insurance industry, foundations, the private sector, and others can result in a misinterpretation of gaps in assistance, policies that work at cross purposes, and untimely program delivery, all of which limits their ability to strategically target unmet needs. In a report published in 2006, the U.S. Government Accountability Office (GAO) identified confusion about the roles and responsibilities specified in the NRF as a contributing factor to the lack of coordination between FEMA and the Red Cross after Hurricane Katrina.[37] Both organizations focused on a negotiated set of procedures rather than on their complementary roles as partners in providing mass care, and the lack of clear lines of authority and responsibility hampered working relationships. Additional criticisms included short rotation schedules among staff, the poor transfer of information between shifts, and an inability to effectively track requests for assistance. In another report published two years later, the GAO noted the lack of information sharing among the public sector and participating response organizations after Hurricane Katrina, criticized the public sector for its failure to effectively reimburse faith-based groups and other nonprofit organizations for mass care services, and called for improved coordination between the federal government and NVOAD.[38]

In his review of hazard mitigation partnerships (and in contrast to the previous paragraphs that highlight the limitations of the nonprofit community), Robert Paterson argues that, compared to members of the public and private sectors, nonprofit organizations are better suited to address coordination issues among multiple stakeholders. Public sector stakeholders are increasingly overwhelmed by growing responsibilities, are constrained by restrictive legal rules with which they must comply, have fewer resources with which to accomplish associated tasks, and generate a low level of public confidence. Private sector stakeholders are often mistrusted by the public and may be unlikely to address larger community needs.[39] Yet, when assessed relative to their roles in recovery, nonprofits tend to interact with other nonprofits and foundations more frequently than they do with other types of organizations in the assistance network. Better links among nonprofits and other types of organizations could help to ensure that recovery tasks are assigned to those parties that are best equipped to address them, thereby more effectively coupling resources, minimizing duplication, maximizing program flexibility, and avoiding contradictory actions (see Figure 4–4).

Figure 4–4. A multistakeholder post-disaster housing construction "build-a-thon" involved Habitat for Humanity, a national nonprofit; Americorps, a federal organization devoted to volunteer service; and Charles Schwab, a private sector investment firm that sponsored the home construction project.

Source: Governor's Office of Recovery and Renewal, State of Mississippi.

Further, NVOAD, the most recognized network of nonprofit organizations in emergency management, focuses on sharing information and limiting the duplication of effort during response operations immediately following a disaster, but it is not effectively integrated with long-term recovery planning activities. In the two afore-mentioned reports, the GAO called for improved horizontal integration within the nonprofit community and improved vertical integration between nonprofits and other members of the larger assistance network during long-term recovery.[40]

There is clear evidence of the value that the active involvement of nonprofit orga-nizations in planning can bring (see Figure 4–5). Research assessing recovery efforts in the Caribbean after Hurricanes Gilbert and Hugo, which struck in 1988 and 1989, respectively, highlights the role of nonprofit organizations in the development of post-disaster hazard mitigation plans, which served as a bridge between local groups, government, foundations, and corporations.[41] (The beneficial role of developing pre-event negotiated agreements that better address the limitations inherent in the disaster recovery assistance framework is discussed in Chapters 8 and 9.)

Figure 4–5. The success of this nonprofit is closely associated with the development of strong horizontal ties in a community. Kaboom! partners with volunteers drawn from local communities and members of the private sector like Home Depot (see the sidebar in Chapter 5 on the role of home improvement retailers in recovery). The home improvement retailer helps to fund the costs of playground construction, provides needed building materials and tools, and encourages employees from neighboring stores to participate in the effort. This type of activity represents the targeted actions that nonprofits often pursue in response to perceived gaps in the delivery of assistance from other members of the disaster recovery assistance network.

Source: Kaboom!

Figure 4–6. Students from the Gulf Coast Community Design Studio and the Moore Community House Women in Construction Program raise the first wall on their joint design-build project.

Source: Gulf Coast Community Design Studio.

Numerous benefits are derived from an active involvement with others in the disaster assistance network. For instance, foundations are often ill-equipped to do the work of nonprofits that are on the ground and have a better understanding of local needs. When they act alone, then, their contributions may be underused or may even have unintended negative consequences. The relationship between foundations and nonprofit organizations is largely predicated on the type of grants and assistance provided, which can sometimes make the nonprofit beholden to the foundation.

Similarly, while the interactions of a community group generally stay within the neighborhood, this can change with the advent of a disaster. For example, community church groups may reach out to other denominations for help, or they may receive assistance from national church groups that provide a number of long-term recovery services. Community groups may solicit technical assistance, including information on housing repair, site design, and financial advice, from members of the larger network, as evidenced by the work of the Gulf Coast Community Design Studio (see the sidebar in Chapter 3 and Figure 4–6). Transferring information to others who have greater financial or technical capacity is a particularly important component of horizontal and vertical integration. In other cases, community organizations can serve as a means to address interorganizational coordination across the network, as the sidebar starting on page 146 suggests. And community organizations can bring about needed change if they can identify a receptive, influential audience among policy makers. These are all important facets of bridging local needs and securing resources through improved horizontal and vertical integration across the network.

Tulsa Partners: A Sustained Commitment to Floodplain Management and Hazard Mitigation

Tulsa Partners represents a nonprofit organization that is the evolutionary manifestation of an ongoing community-level effort to reduce the impact of natural hazards. Numerous local programs and policies have emerged over time in response to a large number of disasters. Floods have occurred in the city of Tulsa at an amazing rate, striking in 1908, 1923, 1943, 1957, 1959, 1963, 1968, 1970, 1971, 1973, 1974 (four events), 1976, 1984, and 1986. Tulsa has also experienced tornadoes, ice storms, heat waves, and droughts. In a historical account of how disasters have shaped Tulsa's hazard mitigation and recovery policy, Ann Patton, a dynamic community leader and former newspaper reporter, breaks this process down into five distinct eras: conflict and confrontation (1974–1984), challenge and change (1984–1990), integration (1990–1998), collaboration and expansion (1998–2002), and sustainability (2002–2008).[1]

In 1970, following what was dubbed the "Mother's Day Flood," Tulsa joined the National Flood Insurance Program (NFIP). However, city officials, led by a progrowth, antiregulatory commission, did not adopt the flood insurance rate maps used to regulate floodplain development. After floods in 1971 and 1973, followed by four floods and three tornadoes one year later, citizens began a grassroots effort seeking change. Tulsans for a Better Community formed in 1974 and began an ongoing campaign focused on reducing flood losses. Its platform was tied to four points: (1) stop the construction of new buildings that will flood or make anybody else flood worse; (2) remove the most dangerous of the flood-prone buildings and turn the land into parks; (3) selectively install remedial public works projects, such as channels and detention ponds to convey and hold water, considering their offsite and future impacts on the larger watershed; and (4) involve citizens throughout the process.[2] The community group began to gain support among residents, including a local planning consultant who centered his career around flood loss reduction. For several years, heated debates—referred to locally as the "Great Drainage Wars"—continued among the community group and pro-growth interests and helped hone the message of Tulsans for a Better Community.

In 1976, the Memorial Day flood struck, resulting in three deaths and causing $40 million in damages to 3,000 buildings. Citizens demanded change and got it from a new board of commissioners that was responsive to their concerns. The city adopted a post-disaster temporary building moratorium on floodplain development and passed the first in a series of bond issues tied to flood control. Tulsa voters have since passed several bonds and sales tax increases to continue funding floodplain management initiatives. The city also hired a

Charter members of the city of Tulsa's flood program, 1988.

Source: Ann Patton.

Centennial Park in Downtown Tulsa represents the blending of flood hazard mitigation, enhanced recreational opportunities, and community beautification efforts.

Photos by Ron Flanagan.

hydrologist and reassigned a planner to focus on the development of several new policies, including the creation of a drainage plan.

The 1984 election saw the return of a majority of commissioners who empathized with the plight of flood-prone communities. Shortly thereafter, a second Memorial Day flood occurred, killing fourteen people and causing over $180 million in damages to more than 7,000 homes and businesses. Many of the flooded areas had been inundated several times in the past. The city assessed the damages, identified repetitive flood-loss properties, and imposed a temporary rebuilding moratorium to allow city officials the time needed to develop a proposed strategy to acquire and relocate the most flood-prone properties. The buyout plan was presented to the Federal Emergency Management Agency (FEMA), which was initially reluctant to fund the idea as the project predated the development (in 1988) of the Hazard Mitigation Grant Program. The $17.6 million project was also unique because $11.5 million in local funds were used to implement the buyout. In addition, $1.8 million in federal funds were provided while the remainder was obtained through flood insurance proceeds. Once the necessary financial resources were assembled, 300 homes and 228 mobile home pads were acquired, and the land was converted into open space in perpetuity.

In addition to purchasing flood-prone homes, the city developed a storm-water management department to coordinate the growing number of flood-hazard reduction programs. This department eventually became the steward of a local storm-water utility fund for ongoing planning and program activities. The fund's $2 monthly fee also allowed the city to develop an extensive outreach campaign and construct recreational facilities and parks in the floodplain, thereby diversifying its base of support and limiting future residential and commercial development in the area (see figures at the top of this page). In 1986, another flood occurred following a twenty-four-inch rainfall associated with what was left of a hurricane. Were it not for a breached private levee, which flooded sixty-four structures, the city would have been relatively unscathed.

The storm-water management department was reorganized in the 1990s, reflecting a clear vision of the larger floodplain management program. The head of the new department was a hydrologist who also proved adept at bringing together conflicting stakeholder groups, many of whom eventually became supporters of the enhanced program. By 1992, the city's floodplain management program was ranked one of the best in the country. Tulsa continued the relocation of flood-prone structures out of the floodplain, removing over a thousand buildings during the 1990s, creating additional

continued on page 148

continued from page 147

parks, greenways, water retention areas, and open space (see figure on page 147). The 1990s represented the first decade in over fifty years in which Tulsa avoided a major flood disaster.

In the late 1990s, FEMA designated Tulsa a Project Impact community (see the sidebar on Project Impact in Chapter 5). The federal program provided $500,000 and gave the city broad discretion to develop public-private partnerships focused on risk-reduction and preparedness initiatives. The city decided to name its new program Tulsa Partners and used the funding to address other hazards, including tornadoes and windstorms, lightning, extreme heat, drought,

Dr. Ernst Kiesling, Texas Tech University inventor of the Tulsa Partners–initiated the Oklahoma Safe Room program, checks a surviving shelter after a 2003 tornado in Moore, Oklahoma.

Photo by Ann Patton.

winter storms, hazardous materials, and terrorism. Perhaps most important, the Project Impact designation allowed Tulsa to engage in a number of collaborative ventures with businesses, first responders, and former adversaries, including the local homebuilders association.

New initiatives included the development of a hazard mitigation plan and the creation of the "Safe Room" project (see above figure). The hazard mitigation plan, which addresses all natural hazards prevalent in the area and identifies specific strategies to reduce their impact, became an important community-based decision-making tool (see Chapter 9 for a detailed description of the hazard mitigation planning process). The Safe Room program was initiated because, despite Tulsa's vulnerability to tornadoes and high winds, most homes in the area do not have basements. A safe room is an armored room that provides protection from the impact of tornadic winds. The structure can be built within new or existing homes or located outside, in which case it is often underground. The concept had recently been developed at Texas Tech University. Tulsa Partners began to actively market the safe room, and the initiative, which was begun in close coordination with the local homebuilder's association, has since been used by several other states and has become a national model that was ultimately adopted by FEMA.

Tulsa Partners became a 501(c)(3) nonprofit organization in 2000. This has allowed it to accept donations from the growing number of participating organizations that join it. It has also served as a natural progression of the Project Impact program, whose federal funding ended after three years. The city of Tulsa, members of the private sector and nonprofit community, and individual donors have continued to fund Tulsa Partners, which has expanded to include several new initiatives.

For example, the McReady program, a partnership with McDonald's and the Oklahoma Emergency Management Department, focuses on severe weather awareness and family preparedness. Additional participants include local emergency managers around the state, the National Weather Service, and the Oklahoma Gas and Electric Company. Targeting the spring months when the state is most vulnerable to severe wind events, including tornadoes, the program sets up educational disaster preparedness kiosks in the 170 McDonald's restaurants around the state while tray liners and bags are printed with preparedness information.

The Disaster Resistant Business Council was created in 2007 to lead local business continuity planning efforts. Business continuity (discussed further in Chapter 9), represents a series of actions taken to limit business interruption after a disaster. Adopting the nonprofit Institute for Business and Home Safety's "Open for Business" model program, the council has conducted ongoing education and outreach programs for hospitals, small businesses, and child care providers, among others. Members of the council include representatives from State Farm, the Tulsa Chamber of Commerce, the Association of Contingency Planners, and the Oklahoma Insurance Department.

As part of an increasingly proactive planning effort linking hazards management and environmental issues, the city has adopted plans that address storm-water management, capital improvement and protection, enhanced floodplain management, and hazard mitigation. In each case, actions link the protection or restoration of natural systems—namely, areas in and adjacent to the floodplain— with flood-risk reduction efforts. Tulsa's hazard mitigation plan, adopted in 2002, was one of the first in the country to meet new Disaster Mitigation Act standards. The relocation of flood-prone properties and the acquisition of open space served as the impetus for the development and expansion of a greenway along rivers, creeks, and drainage systems that exceed fifty miles in length. The city also joined the NFIP's Community Rating System (CRS) (discussed in Chapter 9) and developed a comprehensive flood-loss reduction strategy. The associated CRS rating results in a 40 percent reduction in the flood insurance premiums paid by local policyholders.[3] After a major ice storm that destroyed tens of thousands of trees, the "Up with Trees" public-private program was initiated, and thousands of trees were planted in and along the city's extensive floodplains.

The accompanying exhibit offers a series of recommendations, based on Tulsa's evolution toward becoming a less vulnerable, more disaster-resilient community. Many of these recommendations mirror the broader suggestions found throughout this book.

Sidebar Exhibit 1. Recommendations and Lessons from the City of Tulsa

- Develop a shared vision.
- Create a core group of highly committed people, including technical experts and those capable and willing to serve as advocates in a public forum.
- Identify and promote a dedicated champion.
- Create broad goals, specific objectives, and flexible strategies that allow for both a clear set of actions and the ability to adapt as necessary to changing conditions.
- Think holistically as a way to achieve complementary objectives and expand a supportive coalition.
- Frame issues that tend to be viewed in a negative light (i.e. floodplain regulations) and link them to positive outcomes (i.e. creating a greenway and expanded park system).
- Link initiatives to a successful program that has standing in the community.
- Identify complementary objectives and win/win partnerships.
- Identify local needs and strive to meet them.
- Link technical experts with grass-roots community advocates.
- Take advantage of the media to publicize your efforts and translate technical information that can be understood by the general public and used to motivate governmental action.
- Prepare to capitalize on post-disaster opportunities through pre-event planning.
- Invite adversarial groups to the table once you have a clear vision and principles established.
- Celebrate individual and collective success and provide a positive message of mutual learning across the network.
- Identify your coalition's management style and keep it grounded by regularly returning to an established vision and set of principles.

Source: Derived from Ann Patton and Arrietta Chakos, "Community-Based Hazard-Mitigation Case Studies," in Global Warming, Natural Hazards, and Emergency Management, ed. Jane A. Bullock, George D. Haddow, and Kim S. Haddow (Boca Raton, Fla.: CRC Press, 2009), 84–110.

1   Patton and Chakos, "Community-Based Hazard-Mitigation Case Studies."
2   Ibid., 88.
3   Bob Freitag et al., Floodplain Management: A New Approch for a New Era (Washington, D.C.: Island Press, 2009), 182.

CONCLUSIONS AND RECOMMENDATIONS

Nonprofit organizations provide critical services in recovery, including direct assistance to those whose needs otherwise would be unmet. Nonprofits also serve an intermediary or boundary-spanning function, linking the needs of communities and disaster victims with the national or regional organizations that have additional resources to meet these needs. An organizational culture that has fewer rules often has the flexibility that allows for improvisation, an essential characteristic in the turbulent world of disaster recovery.[42] Yet these very attributes sometimes cause nonprofit organizations to clash with more bureaucratic organizations such as government agencies, which may contribute to the latter's reluctance to engage in joint plan making. Recovery plans that are developed without the involvement of nonprofit organizations, particularly those nonprofits that are active in the community, can ultimately and disproportionately have a negative impact on the poor and other socially vulnerable populations.

The following recommendations can help address the limitations of the current approach to recovery planning and maximize the involvement of nonprofit organizations.

1. Create an Interorganizational Culture That Capitalizes on the Strengths of Nonprofit Organizations in the Disaster Recovery Assistance Framework

An underlying strength of the plan-making process is its ability to integrate the resources of multiple parties through collaborative decision making, particularly when stakeholders are aware of one another's talents, resources, and organizational culture. But much of the long-term recovery planning that is undertaken by government agencies is excessively bureaucratic and fails to include nonprofit organizations in a meaningful way. Thus, an explicit aim of federal, state, and local recovery plans should be to recognize the organizational culture of other members of the disaster assistance network and the resources and strengths that they offer. They could then develop strategies that acknowledge and celebrate these differences.

Specifically, nonprofit organizations have knowledge and experience within a community that is a crucial, but often untapped, resource in recovery. They are often nimble organizations that can act quickly and in a targeted fashion, assisting those who may fall through the cracks of poorly designed government programs. In many cases, their principle resource base is tied to volunteerism and goodwill.[43] The ability to harness these strengths requires moving beyond post-disaster platitudes about the great job they do during recovery and more effectively integrating them into pre-event planning for post-disaster recovery activities without stripping them of the very characteristics that make them successful. In this way, the disaster recovery assistance network would be better able to target unmet needs and stretch available resources.

After a disaster, local officials, individuals affected by an event, and the media regularly applaud community nonprofits for their role in individual and community recovery while criticizing federal, state, and local governments for what they perceive to be ineffective programs and management. Yet this widely held perception misses the more important point that the delivery of assistance by one player, assessed independently of the larger network of aid providers, can inadvertently hinder the creation of a more expansive and robust delivery system based on the coupling of resources.

Thus, a key aim of an effective recovery strategy should be to actively involve the nonprofit community in pre-event planning for post-disaster recovery. Nonprofit relief organizations engender trust among communities and assume a range of activities after a disaster. Emphasis should be placed on developing more trusted relationships across the entire disaster assistance network and a greater understanding of mutually compatible resources and recovery objectives. Improved pre-event planning between preexisting coalitions of nonprofit organizations (such as NVOAD) and the public sector allow for mutual learning, one of several underlying principles described in the Council on Foundations report.

2. Apply the Principles of the Council on Foundations to the Disaster Recovery Assistance Framework

The principles of the Council on Foundations, shown in the sidebar on page 137, address many of the major concerns expressed in this book and are represented in several of the recommendations posed in Chapters 3 through 8. These principles should be acknowledged and adopted by other members of the disaster assistance network, including public sector organizations. Their adoption may suggest, for example, that foundations perhaps have a better understanding of the inherent challenges associated with recovery than do other members of the network. Foundations recognize that assistance delivery can overwhelm the capacity of local communities and that distributive strategies should be thus developed and timed accordingly. Moreover, rather than relying on prescriptive grant programs, foundations typically assess post-disaster conditions in consultation with local organizations and then develop grant-making strategies. This enables them to adapt their assistance strategy according to the variability of disaster impacts and the nature of different assistance networks.

The third principle put forth by the Council on Foundations is "Don't act in isolation." Too often, members of the disaster assistance network ignore this critical warning. NVOAD has done a good job of establishing long-standing interorganizational relationships with foundations, other nonprofits, and community organizations; for example, the Salvation Army maintains a memorandum of agreement with the Red Cross in order to avoid duplication of effort and improve coordination.[44] Yet such broad conceptual agreements and principles do not include members of the public sector, private sector, or quasi-governmental organizations, nor are they operationalized in a widely recognized plan and applied to recovery-related issues. (For instance, NVOAD's *Long-Term Recovery Manual* is not widely acknowledged by the larger disaster recovery assistance network.) The ability to effectively incorporate high-level principles into the routine day-to-day actions of members of the assistance network requires linking such ideas to policy delivery vehicles like recovery plans. The need to do this on a national scale is discussed in the critique of the draft National Disaster Recovery Framework (NDRF) in Chapter 10.

3. Improve the Horizontal and Vertical Integration of U.S.-based Nonprofits into the Disaster Assistance Network through Planning

Case studies provide strong evidence of the value of involving nonprofits in planning for disaster recovery.[45] Indeed, the value of nonprofits as boundary-spanning organizations has been recognized in the context of hazard mitigation planning and the adoption of risk avoidance measures.[46] However, coordination between nonprofit organizations and other recovery stakeholders is largely an ad hoc, post-disaster driven approach with the exception of pre-event collaborative venues like NVOAD. While the activities of NVOAD are predominantly focused on the early stages of the disaster recovery process, its *Long-Term Recovery Manual* is a step in the right direction, and further attention should be devoted to making it a part of a larger effort, one that is tied to the NRF and the NDRF.

The level of vertical integration between nonprofit organizations and the public sector during long-term recovery should be improved. Nonprofit organizations play an important role in disseminating information across government institutions,[47] which can help to elicit interorganizational cooperation (see Chapter 8). They also help in the resolution of interorganizational policy disputes.[48] This role is germane to developing and sustaining procedural methods such as plan making and negotiated agreements. However, the ability to coordinate across organizations in the assistance network after a disaster can be hampered by the failure to adequately plan for this eventuality. For instance, in their study of nonprofits and faith-based organizations, Mark Welsh and Ann-Margaret Esnard argue that the largely emergent efforts to help disadvantaged populations identify post-disaster housing solutions could be improved through the more formal pre-event establishment of 501(c)(3) planning organizations dedicated to housing recovery.[49]

The creation of an organization such as Tulsa Partners that is focused on the coordination of pre- and post-disaster assistance across the network enables the development of ongoing efforts such as planning for recovery and initiating training and other capacity-building initiatives. In most cases, states develop this type of an organization after a major disaster in order to solicit donations and other outside funding as it will be less prescriptive than post-disaster government-based programs. But an organization that is intended to coordinate the disaster assistance offered by the many public and private sector organizations should ideally be established before a disaster strikes. It should emphasize building the capacity of the network as a whole and identifying local needs that are not adequately met by existing programs and organizations.

The limited commitment to building local capacity for disaster recovery is a fundamental flaw in the U.S. disaster assistance framework. The reactionary strategy used after a disaster sets the stage for the institutional "disasters" that follow. The broad missions and organizational flexibility of nonprofit organizations enable them to experiment with new ideas and strategies. This is critical in disaster recovery, an environment characterized by great uncertainty. The organizational flexibility of nonprofits makes them strong candidates to take greater ownership of recovery processes.

Endnotes

1   Lester M. Salamon, "The Rise of the Nonprofit Sector," *Foreign Affairs* 73, no. 3 (1994): 109–125.

2   Robert G. Paterson, "The Third Sector: Evolving Partnerships in Hazard Mitigation," in *Cooperating with Nature: Confronting Natural Hazards with Land Use Planning for Sustainable Communities,* ed. Raymond Burby, 203–230 (Washington, D.C.: Joseph Henry Press, 1998).

3   Richard Sylves, *Disaster Policy and Politics: Emergency Management and Homeland Security* (Washington, D.C.: CQ Press, 2008), 158–163.

4   Kenneth Deutsch, *American Red Cross Mitigation Paper* (Washington, D.C.: American Red Cross, 1996).

5   Marvin Olasky, *The Politics of Disaster: Katrina, Big Government, and a New Strategy for Future Crisis* (Nashville, Tenn.: Thomas Nelson, 2006); U.S. Government Accountability Office (GAO), *Hurricanes Katrina and Rita: Coordination between FEMA and the Red Cross Should Be Improved for the 2006 Hurricane Season,* GAO 06-712 (Washington, D.C., June 2006), www.gao.gov/new.items/d06712.pdf.

6   Olasky, *Politics of Disaster,* 68.

7   Robert A. Watson and Ben Brown, *The Most Effective Organization in the U.S.: Leadership Secrets of the Salvation Army* (New York: Crown Business, 2001).

8   Ibid.

9   Ibid., 15.

10 Paterson, "Third Sector."

11 North Carolina chapter of the American Planning Association (NCAPA), "Recommended Principles for Short Term Recovery and Redevelopment," letter by David Godschalk to Gov. James B. Hunt,

November 23, 1999; North Carolina Emergency Management Division, *Hazard Mitigation in North Carolina: Measuring Success* (Raleigh, 2000), 6–7, www.p2pays.org/ref/14/13619/13619.pdf.

12 National Wildlife Federation (NWF), *Higher Ground: A Report on Voluntary Property Buyouts in the Nation's Floodplains* (Reston, Va.: NWF, 1998).

13 Land Trust Alliance, *Directory of Land Trusts Involved in Floodplain or Coastal Protection* (Washington, D.C.: The Alliance, 1995).

14 Stephen O. Bender, "Protected Areas as a Protection against Natural Hazards," in *Expanding Partnerships in Conservation,* ed. Jeffrey A. McNeely, chap. 15 (Washington, D.C.: Island Press, 1995); Raymond J. Burby, ed., *Cooperating with Nature: Confronting Natural Hazards with Land-Use Planning for Sustainable Communities* (Washington, D.C.: Joseph Henry Press, 1998).

15 Gavin Smith, "Disaster-Resilient Communities: A New Hazards Risk Management Framework," in *Natural Hazards Analysis: Reducing the Impact of Disasters*, ed. John Pine, 249–267 (Washington, D.C.: Taylor Francis, 2009); United Nations Development Programme, "A Climate Risk Management Approach to Disaster Reduction and Adaptation to Climate Change," in *Adaptation to Climate Change*, ed E. Lisa F. Schipper and Ian Burton, 229–248 (London: Earthscan, December 2008); Thomas R. Karl, Jerry M. Melillo, and Thomas C. Peterson, eds., Global Climate Change Impacts in the United States (Cambridge: Cambridge University Press, 2009).

16 Dennis Mileti, *Disasters by Design: A Reassessment of Natural Hazards in the United States* (Washington, D.C.: Joseph Henry Press, 1999).

17 Robert D. Bullard, *Dumping in Dixie: Race, Class, and Environmental Quality* (Boulder, Colo.: Westview Press, 1990); Robert D. Bullard, "Environmental Racism," *Environmental Protection* 2 (June 1991): 25–26; Robert D. Bullard, *Confronting Environmental Racism: Voices from the Grassroots* (Boston: South End Press, 1993).

18 Susan Cutter, ed., *American Hazardscapes: The Regionalization of Natural Hazards and Disasters* (Washington, D.C.: Joseph Henry Press, 2001).

19 Kenneth Hewitt, *Interpretations of Calamity: From the Viewpoint of Human Ecology* (London: Allen and Unwin, 1983); Piers Blaikie et al., *At Risk: Natural Hazards, People's Vulnerability and Disasters* (New York: Routledge, 1994); Walter Gillis Peacock, Betty Hearn Morrow, and Hugh Gladwin, eds., *Hurricane Andrew: Ethnicity, Gender and the Sociology of Disasters* (Miami, Fla.: International Hurricane Center Laboratory for Social and Behavioral Research, 2000).

20 Kathleen Tierney, Michael K. Lindell, and Ronald W. Perry, *Facing the Unexpected: Disaster Preparedness and Response in the United States* (Washington, D.C.: Joseph Henry Press, 2001).

21 James Mitchell and Abram Bernstein, eds., Toward a Less Hazardous World: A Proposal to Establish an International Decade of Hazard Reduction, interim report (Washington, D.C.: National Academy of Sciences, 1987).

22 Council on Foundations and European Foundation Centre (EFC), *Disaster Grantmaking: A Practical Guide for Foundations and Corporations* (Alexandria, Va.: Council on Foundations and EFC, 2007).

23 Ibid., 19.

24 San Diego Foundation, *After the Fires Report* (San Diego, Calif., 2003), www.sdfoundation.org.

25 Louisiana Disaster Recovery Foundation, *Policy Papers, 2007,* ed. Linda Usdin, www.louisianahelp.org.

26 Anthony Oliver-Smith, "Post-Disaster Housing Reconstruction and Social Inequality: A Challenge to Policy and Practice," *Disasters* 14, no. 1 (1990): 7–19; Philip R. Berke and Timothy Beatley, *After the Hurricane: Linking Recovery to Sustainable Development in the Caribbean* (Baltimore: Johns Hopkins University Press, 1997).

27 U.S. GAO, *Hurricanes Katrina and Rita.*

28 Watson and Brown, *Most Effective Organization.*

29 Olasky, *Politics of Disaster.*

30 Loren Renz, Jessica Diaz, and Steven Lawrence, *Giving in the Aftermath of the Gulf Coast Hurricanes: Report on the Foundation and Corporate Response* (New York: Foundation Center, 2006),

foundationcenter.org/gainknowledge/research/specialtrends; Council on Foundations, *We Were There: The Role of Philanthropy in National Disasters* (Washington, D.C.: Council on Foundations, 2008).

31 Jennifer Pike, *Spending Federal Disaster Aid: Comparing the Process and Priorities in Louisiana and Mississippi in the Wake of Hurricanes Katrina and Rita* (Albany, N.Y.: Nelson A. Rockefeller Institute of Government, 2007).

32 Mark A. Bernstein et al., *Rebuilding Housing along the Mississippi Coast: Ideas for Ensuring an Adequate Supply of Affordable Housing* (Santa Monica, Calif.: RAND Corporation, 2006).

33 Sylves, *Disaster Policy and Politics*, 162–163.

34 Maurice G. Gurin and Jon Van Til, "Understanding Philanthropy: Fund Raising in Perspective," in *Compendium of Resources for Teaching about the Nonprofit Sector, Voluntarism and Philanthropy* (Washington, D.C.: Independent Sector, 1989).

35 Berke and Beatley, *After the Hurricane*, 30–32; Gavin Smith, "Holistic Disaster Recovery: Creating a More Sustainable Future" (course developed for the Emergency Management Institute Higher Education Project, Federal Emergency Management Agency, 2004), available online at training.fema.gov/EMIWeb/edu/sdr.asp.

36 Burby, ed., *Cooperating with Nature*, 48; Gavin Smith, "A Review of the U.S. Disaster Assistance Framework: Planning for Recovery," in *Emergency Management in Higher Education: Current Practices and Conversations,* ed. Jessica A. Hubbard, 99–111 (Fairfax, Va.: Public Entity Risk Institute, 2008).

37 U.S. GAO, *Hurricanes Katrina and Rita.*

38 U.S. GAO, *National Disaster Response: FEMA Should Take Action to Improve Capacity and Coordination between Government and Voluntary Sectors,* GAO-08-369 (Washington, D.C., February 2008), www.gao.gov/new.items/d08369.pdf.

39 Paterson, "Third Sector," 204.

40 U.S. GAO, *Hurricanes Katrina and Rita;* U.S. GAO, *National Disaster Response.*

41 Berke and Beatley, *After the Hurricane.*

42 James M. Kendra and Tricia Wachtendorf, "Community Innovation and Disasters," in *Handbook of Disaster Research,* ed. Havidan Rodriguez, Enrico L. Quarantelli, and Russell Dynes, 316–334 (New York: Springer, 2006).

43 Jon Van Til, *Mapping the Third Sector: Volunteerism in a Changing Social Economy* (Washington, D.C.: Foundation Center, 1988).

44 Watson and Brown, *Most Effective Organization.*

45 Oliver-Smith, "Post-Disaster Housing Reconstruction and Social Inequality"; Berke and Beatley, *After the Hurricane.*

46 Paterson, "Third Sector."

47 Carnegie Commission, *Facing towards Governments: Nongovernmental Organizations and Scientific and Technical Advice* (New York: Carnegie Corporation, 1993).

48 David Ronfeldt and Cathryn L. Thorup, *North America in the Era of Citizen Networks: State, Society and Security* (Santa Monica, Calif.: RAND Corporation, 1995); Salamon, "Rise of the Nonprofit Sector."

49 Mark G. Welsh and Ann-Margaret Esnard, "Closing Gaps in Local Housing Recovery Planning for Disadvantaged Displaced Households," *Cityscape: A Journal of Policy Development and Research* 11, no. 3 (2009): 195–212.

Chapter 5

The Private Sector and For-Profit Organizations

The return of shrimpers to the Gulf Coast after Hurricane Katrina represents an important indicator of recovery. The 2010 BP oil spill disaster exemplifies another major, perhaps more devastating long-term threat to those who rely on the natural resources of the Gulf Coast.

Photo by Gavin Smith.

T HE ROLE OF PRIVATE SECTOR organizations remains one of the least understood aspects of disaster recovery even though these organizations are among
the most influential members of the assistance network.[1] Following a disaster,
financial institutions provide the monetary resources needed to initiate market-driven
reconstruction projects; insurance companies assess damages and release payouts to
policyholders; and corporations make significant financial donations. Development,
construction, engineering, and architectural firms design, build, and repair housing, public facilities, businesses, and infrastructure; provide the materials needed for
reconstruction; and remove debris. Health care professionals address public health

concerns and provide medical and mental health services for individuals. Consulting firms offer technical assistance to members of the public sector and other stakeholders in such areas as writing and implementing grants, overseeing emergency housing, drafting policies, developing and applying risk assessment models, and assisting communities develop plans.

Most of the nation's critical infrastructure—power lines, utilities, water and sewer facilities, petrochemical operations, ports and harbors, etc.—is owned and operated by private sector organizations. According to the National Strategy for Homeland Security, market forces provide adequate incentives for owners and operators to repair damaged infrastructure as well as protect it from future risk, so government largely leaves this responsibility up to the private sector.[2] But as noted throughout this book, the overreliance on one part of the larger assistance network places an unrealistic burden on that sector's ability to address the complexities of disaster recovery when, in fact, all stakeholders can benefit by adopting coordinated resource-sharing strategies.

The relationship between the private sector and government can be a crucial factor in the recovery and reconstruction of disaster-stricken communities. Government policies, grant and loan programs, and recovery plans shape post-disaster reconstruction options, ultimately affecting how the private sector responds. Just like the regulatory actions of federal, state, and local governments that are instituted prior to a disaster (e.g., building codes, ordinances, and land use plans) can affect development strategies, financial investments, and insurance portfolios, actions that are undertaken in the aftermath of a disaster (e.g., a temporary building moratorium) can affect private sector reconstruction efforts and the decisions of investors. While local officials need to take the time to assess conditions on the ground and then develop or modify recovery plans and reconstruction policies accordingly, private sector investors strive to find some sense of certainty in an often chaotic and changing policy environment. In Florida, for instance, the repeated occurrence of major hurricanes and their associated damages caused several major insurance companies to discontinue providing insurance in the affected areas. As a result, Florida and other hurricane-prone states have developed state-run insurance pools. But the long-term fiscal solvency of this approach is in doubt as many of these pools are undercapitalized considering the building stock at risk.

After a disaster, the choices made by the private sector and for-profit organizations can alter economic trajectories, job opportunities, and the overall viability of a community. Businesses will often seek to profit from the additional demands for goods and services that are needed to support governmental functions as well as recovery and reconstruction activities, or to ensure their position in the competitive marketplace.[3] Preexisting networks that control land use decisions and growth will often strive to maintain their base of power, sometimes at great cost to a community (see Figure 5–1).[4] Local media outlets, which depend on the economic well-being of the area, may champion prodevelopment interests, perhaps limiting an honest evaluation of underlying social problems[5] or inadvertently promoting high levels of pre-event hazard vulnerability. Other parties may criticize reconstruction strategies, federal programs, and private sector investment decisions that advance the pre-event conditions or worsen a community's post-event social, environmental, or economic status (see sidebar starting on page 160).[6] Involving the private sector in early and ongoing discussions about proposed changes in settlement patterns, building codes, and other aspects of recovery that affect their interests can foster cooperation among participants involved in seemingly intractable disputes[7] (see the sidebar in Chapter 8 on the Charlotte–Mecklenburg County Floodplain Mapping Program).

Figure 5–1. Not surprisingly, the sign noting a lot for sale in coastal Mississippi following Hurricane Katrina does not acknowledge that the area sustained a storm surge in excess of twenty feet. Requiring hazard disclosure during real estate transactions is one of many tools that can be used to better inform potential buyers of coastal and other high-risk property. In reality, intensive development along U.S shorelines continues at a rapid pace, including after major disasters. Attempts to limit development in these areas following disasters are often controversial and foster heated debate.

Photo by Gavin Smith.

PRIVATE SECTOR CONTRACTING

Involving the private sector in pre- and post-disaster planning for recovery is also important because the emergency management profession has become increasingly privatized.[8] Federal, state, and local governments rely on several major "on-call" contracts (see sidebar on page 164) for a growing number of services, including pre- and post-disaster training, debris management and removal, policy formulation, the administration of emergency housing programs, the development and application of risk assessment models, grants management, and the writing of hazard mitigation

Boosterism, Disaster Recovery, and a Tale of Two Hurricane-Prone Cities

Media reports after a disaster often provide a nostalgic look back at what was lost, as if previous social, economic, and environmental conditions were idyllic and therefore should be reconstructed as they were before the event. The media's deference to development interests following disasters is representative of the larger notion of economic boosterism. This concept is tied to the competition among towns and cities to generate place-based wealth by attracting outside investment and supporting public infrastructure needed to entice continued growth.[1]

In some cases, the media also play an important role by identifying mistakes that were made before and after a disaster, including low levels of preparedness, risky pre-event settlement patterns, and poor post-disaster reconstruction choices that increase hazard vulnerability, hinder the equitable distribution of assistance, and limit the repair of low-income housing. After Hurricane Andrew, the media uncovered poor code inspection protocols that contributed to shoddy construction and increased disaster losses. Reports after Hurricane Katrina focused on the extreme pre-storm vulnerability facing coastal Mississippi residents and on the effect of chronic poverty in New Orleans on recovery outcomes.

Vincent Gawronski, Richard Olson, and Pedro Carvalho found an inverse correlation between the physical distance of a media outlet and the degree to which it challenged accepted development practices.[2] The media organizations closest to the stricken area were less likely to challenge the dominant growth paradigm whereas those further away were more likely to raise questions about how inappropriate land uses and development practices increased the likelihood of future disasters.

The media often describe a disaster as a window of opportunity to enact positive change, downplaying disaster-related impacts that limit reconstruction and economic reinvestment. The notion of building back better is often equated with unfettered redevelopment as most local newspapers, for example, profit from an expanded readership and thus directly benefit from growth.[3] As John Logan and Harvey Molotch argue in *Urban Fortunes,* "Although newspapers may openly support 'good planning principles' of a certain sort, the acceptable form of 'good planning' does not often extend to limiting growth or authentic conservation in a newspaper's home ground. 'Good planning principles' can easily represent the opposite goals."[4]

The economic development and growth of urban areas has a long history of powerful boosters who advance the notion of the good business climate at all costs.[5] The competing Gulf Coast cities of Galveston and Houston and the strategies they used after economically disastrous events illustrate this point. At the turn of the twentieth century, Galveston's reputation as a thriving port and financial center earned it the moniker "the Wall Street of the South." The city's success was due in large part to its strategic location. Easy access to the Mississippi River and the Gulf of Mexico made it a natural distribution point for cotton that was bought, sold, and shipped to areas along the eastern seaboard.

At this time, Houston was widely viewed as an economic backwater with limited growth potential. All this was about to dramatically change. Congressman Tom Ball of Houston successfully lobbied for a million-dollar congressional appropriation to dredge Buffalo Bayou, transforming a shallow waterway into a navigable canal linking Houston to the Gulf of Mexico. The canal was later transformed into what is now the Houston Ship Channel, currently the third largest port in the United States. In 1901, crews struck oil in east Texas, ushering in the rise of Houston as the nation's oil capital.

In 1900, a Hurricane struck Galveston Island, killing more than 6,000 people and leaving countless others homeless.[6] The extreme damages sustained by the island brought into question the continued support of Galveston as the principal port in Texas.[7] To defend the city from future hurricanes, the city built a seawall (see accompanying figure). The first segment, constructed from 1902 to 1904, was roughly three miles long; today, it is about ten miles long. Millions of cubic yards of sand fill were placed behind the seawall, elevating a 500-block area as much as seventeen feet. More than 2,100 structures were raised, including the 3,000-ton Saint Patrick's Church[8] (see figure, top of page 161).

Pictured at left is an example of a home elevation project undertaken after the 1900 Galveston hurricane. Once the elevation of the home was completed, the area underneath it was replaced with sand as part of a major effort to raise the island on fill material. At right, the construction of the Galveston seawall after the 1900 hurricane.

Courtesy of the Rosenberg Library, Galveston, Texas.

Engineering solutions (commonly referred to as hardening structures) such as seawalls, levees, and dams to reduce the impacts of natural hazards like floods and hurricanes represent major financial investments that have positive and negative effects. In the case of Galveston, the seawall provided a false sense of security as Galvestonians held hurricane parties in hotels located on the waterfront during a hurricane that struck only fifteen years after the 1900 storm.[9] The construction of the seawall also resulted in the loss of the beach because of increased rates of erosion, a predictable consequence of building hardened structures on barrier islands.[10] As a result, the city is engaged in an ongoing process of beach renourishment, a multimillion-dollar program funded by the U.S. Army Corps of Engineers. Such protective measures can also stimulate additional development in known hazard-prone areas.

Following decades of economic decline, Galveston embarked on an economic revitalization campaign, only to be severely tested by Hurricane Ike in 2008. Ike's storm surge and 110-mile-per-hour winds caused more than $24.9 billion in damages, making it the third costliest hurricane in U.S. history, behind Hurricanes Katrina and Andrew. Particularly hard-hit were secondary beach houses on the low-lying areas west and east of the city that were unprotected by the seawall, as well as thousands of homes located on the back of the island. Some of the worst damage occurred in smaller coastal communities on Galveston Bay. For instance, more than 59 percent of the 667 homes in Shoreacres, which is on the northwestern shore of the bay, were destroyed or sustained major damage (see accompanying figure).[11] Evidence suggests, however, that although Ike pounded the seawall with waves and debris for at least twelve hours, damaging pavement and causing sinkholes on the top of the wall, the seawall protected the downtown area from millions of dollars in damage. The city has since engaged in a $10 million project to

Shoreacres, Texas following Hurricane Ike. In the foreground, all that remains of the destroyed home is the slab and a pile of debris. The home in the background was designed to withstand high winds, relying on the use of a steel beam infrastructure. While the house survived, the lower floor was severely damaged by the hurricane's storm surge.

Photo by Gavin Smith.

continued on page 162

continued from page 161

restore the seawall, and another $10 million will be spent on replenishing the beach in front of it, which was washed away during the storm.

Among the most contentious issues facing those tasked with disaster recovery after the storm is the proposed construction of the "Ike dike," a series of levees and retractable storm surge barriers similar to those used in the Netherlands (see the sidebar in Chapter 6 on the evolving flood hazard management approach taken by the Netherlands). The project, which is estimated to cost between $2 billion and $5 billion, has been strongly opposed by environmental groups, which cite the negative impact it will have on the Galveston Bay ecosystem while further incentivizing development in environmentally sensitive areas that currently serve as natural buffers from hurricane-induced storm surge. Suggested alternatives include the acquisition of damaged flood-prone properties and the expansion of existing natural areas.[12] The latter approach is being used on Bolivar Peninsula, a coastal area east of the City of Galveston. Over 700 properties are slated for acquisition in what is perhaps the largest buyout of beachfront properties in the history of the Hazard Mitigation Grant Program. An acquisition project of this type and scale is very rare considering that there are typically few willing sellers of beachfront properties. Once acquired, the land will be converted to open space and maintained as such in perpetuity.[13]

Limited regulations and unchecked growth can have negative environmental impacts that further increase an area's vulnerability to natural hazards. The Galveston Bay area, for instance, has suffered from a long list of environmental maladies tied to the petrochemical

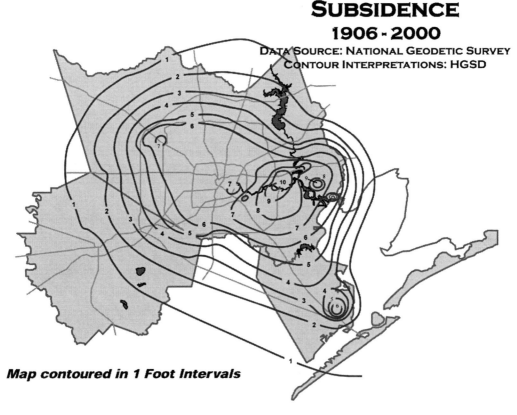

SUBSIDENCE
1906 - 2000
DATA SOURCE: NATIONAL GEODETIC SURVEY
CONTOUR INTERPRETATIONS: HGSD

Map contoured in 1 Foot Intervals

The Harris-Galveston Subsidence District (www.hgsubsidence.org/), which is representative of special service districts discussed in Chapter 3, is a recognized unit of government created by the Texas legislature.

Source: Houston Galveston Subsidence District.

industry, including degraded water quality, toxic Superfund sites, excessive dredging, loss of wildlife habitat, coastal erosion, and subsidence. The past practice of extracting groundwater to supply the surrounding petrochemical facilities, as well as rapid growth, caused the heavy clay soils in the area to compact and the ground elevation to sink—in some cases by over ten feet—leaving large inland and coastal areas subject to repeated flooding and increasingly vulnerable to the impact of hurricane-induced storm surge (see accompanying figure).

The Brownwood subdivision, located on a peninsula that was later annexed by the city of Baytown, Texas, represents one of the more dramatic examples of the effects of subsidence. Construction of the subdivision began in the 1950s. Hurricane Carla, which struck the area in 1961, caused developers to initially halt development activities. Eventually, levees and a pump system were installed in an effort to reduce the likelihood of future flooding, and by the 1970s over 360 homes were complete. However, the withdrawal of groundwater by surrounding petrochemical plants and municipalities caused the neighborhood to sink between ten and fifteen feet, so that high tides and coastal storms caused many homes to be inundated by waters from nearby Galveston Bay. Between 1967 and 1981, the neighborhood reported twenty-six cases of flooding or flood-related evacuations. In 1983, Hurricane Alicia's storm surge destroyed most of the homes in Brownwood. Years later, the city acquired and demolished most of the homes using Hazard Mitigation Grant Program funds. In 1991, the Baytown city council voted to turn the area into a nature preserve.[14]

With the advent of Cold War, the Houston Galveston Bay Area saw a second major boost to the economy. As part of the ensuing "space race," President John F. Kennedy formed the National Aeronautics and Space Administration (NASA). The growing federal agency required a location to monitor future manned spaceflight and train those who would travel to space. During the site-selection process, a powerful group of Texas politicians and businessmen lobbied the selection committee to consider what was then a largely undeveloped former cattle ranch adjacent to Clear Lake City and Galveston Bay. Members of the Texas delegation included Albert Thomas, a local congressman and member of the House Appropriations Subcommittee; Morgan J. Davis, president of Humble Oil; George Brown, part owner of Brown & Root; and Vice President Lyndon Johnson. In 1961, just prior to their site visit, Hurricane Carla struck the upper Texas coast, devastating the area that would ultimately become the Johnson Space Center. Humble Oil donated 1,000 acres to Rice University, which in turn gave the land to the federal government, while Brown & Root was selected to build the facility.[15] Shortly after the announcement of NASA's arrival, Humble Oil, in partnership with Friendswood Development Company, began implementing plans to build Clear Lake City, a 10,500-acre master-planned community that would become home to NASA scientists, engineers, and contractors.

1 Daniel Borstin, *The Americans: The National Experience* (New York: Random House, 1965); John R. Logan and Harvey L. Molotch, *Urban Fortunes: The Political Economy of Place* (Berkeley: University of California Press, 1987).

2 Vincent Gawronski, Richard Stuart Olson, and Pedro Carvalho, "Locally Influenced, Distantly Courageous? Exploring Media Constructions of Katrina's Gulf Coast Impacts," in *Learning from Catastrophe: Quick Response Research in the Wake of Hurricane Katrina*, ed. Natural Hazards Center, 443–456 (Boulder: Institute for Behavioral Science, University of Colorado, 2006).

3 Logan and Molotch, Urban Fortunes, 70–73.

4 Ibid., 73.

5 Borstin, *The Americans*.

6 Erik Larson, *Isaac's Storm: A Man, a Time, and the Deadliest Hurricane in History* (New York: Vintage Books, 1999).

7 Barry J. Kaplan, "Houston: The Golden Buckle of the Sunbelt," in *Sunbelt Cities: Politics and Growth since World War II*, ed. Richard M. Bernard and Bradley R. Rice (Austin: University of Texas Press, 1983).

8 Karri Ward, *Great Disasters: Dramatic True Stories of Nature's Dramatic Powers* (Pleasantville, N.Y.: Readers Digest Association, 1989), 159; John Edward Weems, *A Weekend in September* (College Station: Texas A & M University Press, 1993)

9 Larson, *Isaac's Storm*, 272.

10 Rutherford Platt, "Congress and the Coast," *Environment* 27 (July/August 1985): 12–17, 34–40; Orrin Pilkey and Katherine Dixon, *The Corps and the Shore* (Washington, D.C.: Island Press, 1996).

11 Mike Snyder, "Shoreacres Hardest-Hit by Ike, Study Finds," *Houston Chronicle*, January 14, 2009, www.chron.com/disp/story.mpl/nb/bay/news/6209845.html (accessed December 30, 2010).

12 Eric Berger, "Shielding the Coast: Galveston Oceanographer Says His Proposed Wall and Gate System Could Repel Most Surges," *Houston Chronicle*, April 8, 2009, www.chron.com/disp/story.mpl/hurricane/ike/6363846.html (accessed December 30, 2010).

13 Office of Emergency Management, *Bolivar Blueprint* (Galveston County, Tex., May 2009).

14 Friends of the Baytown Nature Center, "History of Site," www.baytownnaturecenter.org/bnc_information/history_of_site.html (accessed December 30, 2010)

15 Gavin Smith, "Growth Machine Theory: A Qualitative Analysis" (master's thesis, Texas A & M University, 1993).

FEMA On-Call Contracts Related to Recovery

The Federal Emergency Management Agency (FEMA) manages three major on-call contracts used in the pre- and post-disaster environment: the Technical Assistance and Research Contract (TARC), the Technical Assistance Contract (TAC), and the Hazard Mitigation and Technical Assistance Program (HMTAP). These contracts often stipulate that private sector staff must be on-site and ready to begin work within forty-eight hours after a disaster strikes. In most cases, contracts are awarded to multiconsultant teams for five-year terms. While agreements vary in terms of their scope and funding, they often exceed hundreds of millions of dollars. For consultants, these contracts represent highly lucrative opportunities, and the competition for them is fierce.

TARC activities are focused on two broad tasks: (1) conducting architectural and engineering-based studies associated with risk reduction and (2) conducting post-disaster engineering forensic investigations. In-depth risk-reduction studies, which often take more than six months to complete, provide an important tool for building officials, organizations responsible for developing codes and standards, design professionals, and members of the general public who are involved in community reconstruction and recovery. Post-disaster engineering forensic studies require teams of nationally recognized experts from the private sector, academia, and government. For instance, mitigation assessment teams evaluate building performance, identify the causes of observed damages, and recommend how future losses could be reduced or avoided through targeted actions. Findings and recommendations are published in reports intended for design professionals and local officials.

TAC activities are largely intended to assist FEMA with the administration of the Public Assistance (PA) program. Specific PA-related tasks include evaluating damages to infrastructure, engaging in cost repair estimation, monitoring construction, conducting environmental studies, assisting with project development, training potential applicants to implement grants, and reviewing appeals filed by applicants who may question eligibility or cost determinations. The TAC also includes the Nationwide Infrastructure Support Technical Assistance Contract (NISTAC). The NISTAC is used to conduct post-disaster training of local officials, perform damage assessments, undertake housing inspections, and pay for contractors who are assigned to Emergency Support Function-14 and deployed to help communities develop disaster recovery plans after federally declared disasters.

The HMTAP is administered by FEMA's Mitigation Division. HMTAP activities include assessing the performance of the built environment following a disaster; assisting with the evaluation of the Hazard Mitigation and Pre-Disaster Mitigation grant program applications; providing training to states and local governments; and writing guidance materials for states, local governments, and Native American tribes. Post-disaster work typically culminates with a report, bulletin, or manual that describes the findings.

After Hurricane Katrina, the Government Accountability Office found that while the federal government was highly reliant on private sector contracting, three key factors limited the overall effectiveness of contractors: (1) an inadequate level of pre-event planning and a general failure of such contracts to anticipate post-disaster needs; (2) low levels of coordination across federal, state, and local governments, which were hindered by unclear responsibilities and ineffective intergovernmental communications; and (3) an inadequate number of personnel capable of providing adequate contractor oversight.[1] These problems resulted in significant difficulties in providing temporary housing and public buildings, an ongoing tension between an urge to hire national contractors and an emphasis on hiring locally, confusion regarding the federal delivery of ice because of contracting misunderstandings between FEMA and the U.S. Army Corps of Engineers, and challenges associated with the adequate monitoring of the delivery of goods and services as stipulated in contracts.

1   U.S. Senate, Committee on Homeland Security and Governmental Affairs, Subcommittee on Federal Financial Management, Government Information, and International Security, *Hurricane Katrina: Planning for and Management of Federal Disaster Recovery Contracts*, GAO-06-622T (Washington, D.C.: U.S. Government Accountability Office, April 10, 2006), www.gao.gov/new.items/d06622t.pdf.

and disaster recovery plans. Contractors also provide an increased level of post-disaster administrative support to federal agencies, including arranging travel, drafting reports, handling correspondence, and staffing hotlines for the National Flood Insurance Program (NFIP) and the Federal Emergency Management Agency's (FEMA) loss estimation software tool, HAZUS.

Contracting out post-disaster services can be beneficial to community recovery as private sector firms tend to pay higher wages than government agencies and therefore may be able to recruit seasoned experts. Contracts also allow for greater organizational flexibility in that they draw on a large cadre of staff who are trained in specific tasks and can be deployed for a specific period of time to complete identified assignments. Such flexibility is important as recovery processes tend to be reactive and complex rules change over time in response to political pressure, better data, or rotating FEMA staff who have different interpretations of federal programs and policies. In addition, those who have experienced the realities of past disasters while working within the assistance network understand the "rules of the game" and know how to change the rules to better meet the needs of their clients.

However, there are several disadvantages to government outsourcing of disaster recovery services. First, agencies that rely too much on private contractors end up with fewer staff who have the in-depth, hands-on understanding of policy issues necessary to make informed decisions. In the end, federal and state officials may lack the requisite expertise to develop informed policies that reflect local needs or even to effectively manage contractors who are increasingly taking on this role. Ultimately, the public sector loses its base of experiential knowledge from which to assess the efficacy of past actions or develop new, innovative approaches.

Second, relying on private contractors distances federal, state, and local officials from individuals at the community level. Government leaders need to have a deep understanding of local recovery issues so that existing policies can be modified or new policies created that meet community needs, address timing issues, and foster improved coordination across the network. While contractors interact repeatedly with individuals in the community, the information they gain may not be effectively conveyed to government officials and other members of the disaster assistance network.

Third, an overreliance on major contracts favors large firms over smaller businesses. While large organizations have significant resources at their disposal, smaller firms located in stricken areas often have a better understanding of local needs and may be more likely to reinvest the funds they earn in the local economy. Sometimes local firms are brought in as subcontractors. This can be a useful tactic, blending the strengths of each; it can, however, add significant overhead and increase the cost of the contract.

Thus, it is not uncommon for a larger, outside firm to bring in local firms to win the project and then limit their direct involvement. Having numerous subcontracts can also reduce the larger firm's transparency and accountability.[9]

Fourth, large contracts increase the potential for fraud and collusion between contractors and the politicians who appropriate funds to pay for their services. It is common for high-ranking federal officials (including agency personnel and members of Congress) to leave government for the private sector, providing firms with important connections to program information and members of Congress and thereby increasing the likelihood of being selected for future recovery contracts.[10] And finally, even though major firms may possess an array of skilled employees who have a good knowledge of how government contracts function and close relationships with those managing these contracts, the outsourcing of work does not necessarily guarantee access to those individuals as firms routinely win contracts by highlighting the achievements of their top employees only to hand off the work to junior staff once the job is awarded.

FINANCIAL AND LENDING INSTITUTIONS

Evidence suggests that financial and insurance-related businesses are better prepared for recovery than are other types of private sector organizations.[11] Following major disasters, the reconstruction of damaged housing, community infrastructure, public facilities, and businesses require significant financial resources. Practitioners, hazard scholars, individuals who have experienced a disaster, and the media often focus on the financial assistance that is available through federal grant and loan programs, but banks and other lending organizations provide a substantial proportion of the required funding. This is particularly evident in housing and commercial development.[12] Significantly, however, the policies of lending institutions, including the rate, length of repayment, and collateral required, influence the clientele seeking assistance and thus the nature of community recovery across different subgroups. Low-income homeowners, renters, and small businesses, for example, may be unable to afford a loan or fail to meet lender qualifications.

In their study of Hurricane Andrew housing recovery, Walter Peacock and Chris Girard note that a strategy driven by market forces fails to assist the most vulnerable populations.[13] Naomi Klein describes the dangers of unrestrained market forces as "disaster capitalism," in which unchecked economic interests run counter to the larger public good.[14] The limited involvement of the private sector in planning for recovery perpetuates this situation as business decisions are driven by narrowly defined profit motives rather than by the joint search for approaches that provide long-term economic gains while serving the collective needs of the community. For instance, lending institutions react to real and perceived investment risk: the ability to garner an acceptable return on an investment involves calculating the likelihood that financing reconstruction ventures, aggregated across their investment portfolio, will be sufficiently profitable. Financing less profitable projects, such as affordable housing or small-business loans, often require the intervention of governmental, quasi-governmental, or nonprofit organizations. Thus, a challenge for those tasked with planning for recovery includes the search for mutually beneficial outcomes and the adoption of policies that reflect a balance of private sector interests and the public good.

INSURANCE

There is an ongoing tension between the role of insurance and the provision of post-disaster federal assistance.[15] In her book *Disaster Hits Home: New Policy for Urban Housing Recovery*, Mary Comerio argues that financing the costs of reconstruction activities should rest with private insurers and that the primary aim of disaster recovery policy should be to maximize the degree to which this occurs.[16] Insurance proceeds following disasters are one of the largest sources of recovery funding, particularly for homeowners.[17] Yet the number and distribution of hazards-based insurance policies vary widely depending on such factors as the type of hazard and the race and income level of the policyholder.[18] Many individuals do not maintain adequate insurance coverage. They may assume that a standard policy is sufficient or misperceive the level of risk they face. Some policyholders also mistakenly believe that federal grants will cover most of their uninsured losses after a disaster. Studies undertaken in the 1990s to assess participation in the NFIP estimated that just 20–27 percent of homes located in the floodplain maintain flood coverage.[19] The low rate of participation in a program with the most advanced means of approximating risk (relative to other known hazards) speaks to the importance of improving the collective knowledge of hazard vulnerability and reassessing the role of insurance as a principal means to mitigate risk and speed recovery after a disaster occurs. When a disaster does happen, those who are insured often express frustration over the length of time it takes to receive their settlements (Figure 5–2 on page 168).

Howard Kunreuther and Richard Roth contend that for insurance to play a more effective role in stemming the tide of increasingly large federal disaster payouts, policies must be linked to monetary incentives to reduce risky behavior.[20] Similarly, policyholders need to become more aware of the risks they face. This requires estimating potential future losses to determine whether their coverage is adequate. Unfortunately, insurance companies do a poor job of informing clients of natural hazard risk and the role of insurance in post-disaster recovery. For example, insurance agents often rely on

Figure 5–2. Pictured is the address and insurance provider spray-painted on what remains of a coastal Mississippi home. Homeowners often use this technique to assist claims adjusters find damaged property amidst debris fields, missing street signage, and damaged or destroyed landmarks. Homeowners also use this technique to express their displeasure with their insurance provider as conflicts often arise between policyholder and insurance companies regarding the level of coverage and the timeliness of payment.

Photo by Gavin Smith.

designated special flood hazard areas to help clients determine whether they "need" flood insurance. The flood insurance rate maps, which delineate these areas, represent an approximation of risk. In most instances, however, the maps underestimate risk as they are subject to errors and are static representations that do not account for human-induced and natural changes that occur in and around floodplains.

The characteristics of people living in known hazard areas are another factor that influences disaster recovery outcomes. Socially vulnerable populations tend to be underinsured and are less informed about the concept of risk.[21] They also are more likely to live in homes that are less able to withstand a natural hazard's physical forces (winds, ground motion, water, waves, and fire). For instance, the poor disproportionately live in structures that are prone to damages from high winds, such as mobile homes; they are also more likely to live in homes that are inadequately maintained or in substandard rental housing. The reluctance to carry insurance on these structures limits an individual's options should a disaster strike.

Several national nonprofit organizations, including the Institute for Business and Home Safety, the Insurance Institute for Property Loss Reduction, and the Insurance Service Office, have sought to inform consumers, state and local leaders, and business owners about the merits of adequately insuring at-risk property, adopting local and state building codes, and developing incentive programs linking the adoption of higher standards to reduced insurance rates. Kunreuther articulates the need to connect insurance to a comprehensive risk reduction strategy, which would reduce the need for large federal grant and loan programs following disasters.[22] This approach also requires the use of incentives to adopt proven building and land use techniques that reduce the impacts of natural hazards. The Community Rating System, a federal program that offers reduced flood insurance rates for policyholders owning residential properties in communities that adopt more rigorous flood loss reduction strategies, has proven most effective in reducing loses when it is used as part of an overall pre-disaster flood hazard reduction planning process.[23] Given its success, the program could be modified to address a wider range of natural hazards.[24] Hazard scholars have long argued for the need to develop an all-hazards insurance policy that would tie actuarially sound rates to the level of risk faced by the policyholder.[25]

Yet neither insurers nor government officials have adopted the idea of an all-hazards insurance policy. As losses continue to mount, an increasing number of private sector insurance companies have discontinued providing hazard-specific policies in known hazard areas that have repeatedly suffered disasters. In response, states are becoming increasingly reliant on the creation of reinsurance strategies that shift costs to state-run insurance pools. The smaller, geographically defined portfolio of state-level policyholders is subject to significant risk when compared to that held by larger private sector insurance companies.

BUSINESSES AND CORPORATIONS

Paradoxically, local businesses, which have an intimate knowledge of the local economy and are personally invested in its success, are often unprepared for the impacts of disasters. Not only does their lack of preparedness lengthen the time needed for them to reopen, but it also interferes with their ability to provide assistance to their employees and the larger community.[26] Small businesses also lack political muscle to influence the distribution of externally provided recovery assistance.[27]

In an effort to reduce future losses, speed reopening, and deliver goods and services to their customers after a disaster, a growing number of businesses have developed business continuity plans. Business continuity planning emphasizes the minimization or avoidance of a business interruption due to an external peril, such as a downturn in the economy, a power outage, theft, fire, earthquake, or flood. The development of strategies and specific actions that take into account various threat scenarios help businesses resume operations as quickly as possible after a particular threat is realized. A business continuity plan typically includes information about the building(s) in which the business is located; the business's flow of goods and services, daily operations, and employee vulnerabilities; and the suppliers of materials, information, and other resources needed to perform normal business activities. Components of a business continuity plan include a risk assessment, a business impact analysis, and a strategy to

The Role of Home Improvement Retailers in Recovery

Major home improvement retailers have adopted plans designed to increase the preparedness, response, mitigation, and recovery capabilities of their stores, customers, and the broader community following a disaster. The business continuity plans employed by Home Depot and Lowe's, for instance, include the creation of a central emergency operations center and agreements with neighboring stores. This strategy will enable the retailers to assess the impacts of a disaster on communities in which stores are located, identify needs, and deploy resources from other locations to meet the demands of customers both before and after a disaster strikes. Home improvement retailers recognize that consumer needs change over the lifespan of the event. When a hurricane threatens, for instance, coastal residents purchase disaster preparedness kits, plywood to board up their windows, and generators to power their homes in the event of an electrical outage. After the storm, residents need chain saws and other power tools to clear the debris, as well as cleaning supplies, sheetrock, lumber, and other materials to repair damaged homes or businesses.

Many home improvement retailers also provide pre-event training classes on do-it-yourself disaster preparedness and hazard mitigation projects. Programs vary depending on the nature of the hazards prevalent in the area. In hurricane-prone locations, training might include the installation of hurricane shutters and hurricane straps (designed to hold the roof on during a storm) whereas in earthquake-prone areas, training might focus on bolting down bookshelves and strapping water heaters to walls. Recognizing the value of this training and the broader importance of public-private partnerships, the Federal Emergency Management Agency initiated Project Impact (see the sidebar on pages 184–185).

Working in partnership with the architect responsible for creating the post-disaster emergency housing unit dubbed the "Katrina Cottage," Lowe's has developed several housing kits, ranging in size from a 308-square-foot, one-bedroom cottage to a 1,807-square-foot two-story home with five bedrooms and three baths. These units, which are intended to serve as permanent replacement housing, are also being marketed as options for those who are in the market for a new, affordable, and easy-to-build home. All options are international residential code compliant and have many of the architectural characteristics of the pre–World War II housing that remains one of the Gulf Coast's greatest assets.

prioritize needs and implement actions targeting pre-identified threats should an event occur. Specific pre-event tasks may include the identification and development of redundant systems, the safe storage of critical information and supplies, and the identification of a secondary base of operation should the primary business site become inoperable. The home improvement retail industry, for example, has invested in the development of pre- and post-disaster strategies to address critical problems facing stores and the communities in which they are located (see accompanying sidebar).

MEDIA

Disasters are highly newsworthy events, and reports of their impacts have become increasingly ubiquitous, particularly among television and web-based media outlets. Media reports can change the nature of recovery. Research has shown that the media influence the agendas of government organizations, the participation of others in recovery, and the associated disbursement of funding.[28] The media also affect the public's perception of disasters.[29] The visual images of disasters influence many of the decisions undertaken by members of the disaster assistance network, including individual and corporate donations, volunteerism, foundation support, policy making at all levels of government, and legislative action, such as the type and amount of congressional appropriations. In major disasters, national media coverage can perpetuate disaster myths rather than conveying the actual needs of individuals and communities. Conversely, accurate and timely media reports can serve as a critically important resource both before and after disasters. The complexity of disaster recovery policies, programs, and roles make incorporating media organizations into the assistance network imperative, as evidenced by the actions of the Broadmoor community (see Figure 5–3).

Given the immediate nature of the news and the uncertainty that occurs in a disaster, misinformation is commonplace, and its unintentional spread through the media can hinder the coordinated layering of assistance. After Hurricane Katrina, for example, orga-

Figure 5–3. The Broadmoor neighborhood used both yard signs and banners as part of a coordinated marketing campaign to let the media and potential providers of assistance know that they were intent on returning and rebuilding their community.

Photo by Gavin Smith.

nizational failures of the federal government were widely reported while problems across the larger recovery assistance network were generally ignored. Media reports have influenced the focus of numerous congressional investigations into the federal government's role in recovery; however, similar analyses of the role of states and local governments in recovery, which would hold them more accountable for their lack of pre-event planning for recovery, remain virtually nonexistent. On the other hand, the media's glowing reports of the work undertaken by foundations and nonprofit organizations rarely describe the coordinative problems across organizations or some nonprofits' reluctance to incorporate hazard mitigation techniques, such as more stringent post-disaster building code and flood ordinance standards, into housing repair and reconstruction efforts.

The media's impact on the disaster assistance network is tied to their primary function, which is to disseminate information. Newspapers, television, radio, and the Internet all provide avenues for exchange. Messages regarding preparedness and pre-event mitigation have been successful in a number of states and communities (see the sidebar on the National Earthquake Hazard Reduction Program and the Great Southern California Shakeout in Chapter 3 and the sidebar on Tulsa Partners in Chapter 4). During the recovery process, however, stories are often framed in a negative context. News about the slow disbursement of recovery funding, disenfranchised individuals who "fell through the cracks," and the inability of local governments to implement federal recovery programs ignore the bigger picture. Stories about how the recovery process works, including the steps necessary to implement programs and plans, do not make for exciting copy, nor are they typically discussed before an event. Thus, the relationship between the media and those charged with recovery often emerges following a disaster and is dominated by a negative public debate that frequently becomes awkward and at times confrontational.

While the media's role is to report their findings to the public, antagonistic relationships between them and providers of assistance can actually limit their ability to identify tangible evidence of problems in the system, including flawed or uncoordinated policies. Those tasked with recovery often become defensive when confronted by the media, particularly when conversations emphasize negative outcomes rather than positive achievements; this reduces the potential for dialogue, resulting in the withholding of information and the dissemination of misinformation. Uninformed media representatives are less aware of how disaster recovery occurs and their role in it, including the complexities of programs and policies; the role of the public sector and other members of the assistance network; and the importance of pre-event planning for post-disaster recovery. This situation has the unintended effect of hindering recovery.

The media can perpetuate and sometimes even institutionalize disaster myths, including the notion of widespread looting, panic, the abandonment of emergency management roles and responsibilities, and the breakdown of societal norms.[30] As a result, resources may be unnecessarily focused on attempts to prevent looting and other crimes rather than on more pressing needs, such as search and rescue or the restoration of public services (see Figure 5–4). Reports of panic following disasters can also influence the public's perception of disaster-affected communities as helpless rather than self-reliant—an important but underemphasized characteristic of sustainable recovery.[31] Although such helpless behavior has been shown to be overreported, particularly in the response literature,[32] these misperceptions and what the Broadmoor community referred to as the "negative cycle of recovery" can hamper the willingness of people to initiate rebuilding efforts.

In most cases, disaster recovery myths represent a simplification of a more nuanced and complex process while stereotyping organizations in the disaster assistance network. For instance, the fact that the media, and others, frequently ask who's in charge of recovery, belies the fact that in reality there is typically no one assigned this task. Other examples include the stereotyping of nonprofits as "saviors" and no-nonsense organizations that unilaterally cut through the public sector bureaucracy; private sector consultants and developers as unanimously greedy and unconcerned with the welfare of the community;

Figure 5–4. The Louisiana State Police patrol New Orleans after Hurricane Katrina.

Photo by Donn Young.

and government agencies, particularly those at the federal level, as singularly incompetent. Further research is warranted into how the media perpetuate such recovery-related disaster myths.

DIMENSIONS OF THE DISASTER ASSISTANCE FRAMEWORK

While evidence is emerging of the importance of contractors, developers, lending institutions, and others in providing immediate post-disaster assistance, more research is needed to address the private sector's impact on federal, state, and local government decision making and the delivery of long-term recovery programs. This requires refining our understanding of what, when, and how private sector assistance is provided and the degree to which it is incorporated into broader recovery strategies and plans. Like other members of the disaster assistance network, private sector organizations need to assess the merits of coordinating assistance strategies with the larger network before a disaster strikes and be better prepared to implement them during recovery.

Understanding of Local Needs

As government officials relinquish their direct involvement in process-oriented activities like planning and policy making, their understanding of local needs is diminished. To be effective, such activities require an ongoing, in-depth dialogue between government officials, the private sector, and the public. So, too, does the establishment of enduring coalitions needed to support potential changes in existing programs, policies, and plans to confront the weaknesses in the disaster recovery assistance framework.

Corporate Responsibility and Profits

A growing body of research suggests that the private sector has proven more effective than the federal government in meeting local needs following disasters.[33] As Marvin Olasky discusses in *The Politics of Disaster, Katrina, Big Government and a New Strategy for Future Crisis,* businesses are driven by the benefits of exchange.[34] They are adroit at taking informed risks, applying innovative strategies, and developing new products in the marketplace, whereas government agencies take a more deliberative, consensus-seeking approach. Businesses also develop and strive toward specific metrics of success whereas government tends to aim for a series of vague ideas associated with social welfare.[35]

When viewed in the context of disaster assistance, the difference between corporate "rules" and those of government and nonprofit organizations provide important insights into possible recovery strategies. The type of rules developed to disseminate assistance reflects the larger organizational cultures in which members of the assistance network operate. In the case of the private sector, the culture may be one that embraces the concept of corporate responsibility, measured by past levels of charitable giving and other activities supporting post-disaster recovery and the economic well-being of the community. National corporations have access to significant resources following a disaster but may be less familiar with local needs. Large companies, however, may be better able than smaller organizations to continue to pay their employees following a disaster-induced closure. Many corporations also make contributions to local charities, community organizations, and disaster relief agencies; such donations may include money, equipment, staff, logistical assistance, technology, and communications-related support.

The ability of larger, nationally recognized businesses to act is closely associated with the degree to which key decision makers on the ground, who typically manage local stores or facilities, are empowered to allocate resources on relatively short notice. Wal-Mart, for instance, is often able to move quickly in dispersing assistance following a disaster because its corporate executives are willing to decentralize decision making and empower store managers in affected areas.[36] It has been less flexible, however, in long-term recovery initiatives. For example, it refused to adopt changes suggested by the Mississippi Renewal Forum to modify its "big box" store in Pass Christian, Mississippi, by reducing the building's footprint and integrating the store into a proposed new urbanist Wal-Mart "village."[37]

Yet the culture in the private sector is also one that values profit, which sometimes means the ability to obtain short-term economic gains at the expense of the equitable post-disaster distribution of assistance and, ultimately, the public good. A profit is also earned, in part, by meeting the needs of a group of consumers in a larger community. Without a willing buyer of goods and services, members of the private sector must either seek other markets or cease to exist.

Contractors, consultants, and other private sector entities may also be driven by a high degree of professionalism and altruism; even highly competitive and profit-motivated organizations often put aside their own agendas to help individuals and communities after a disaster. But if such ventures undermine a company's ability to turn a profit and remain competitive, the company's altruism will be short-lived. Few companies can provide goods or services at a loss over an indefinite period. The absence of adequate compensation for their contributions ultimately constrains the ability of business and industry to provide disaster assistance.

To address this issue, Olasky suggests that the federal government give tax exemptions to private sector organizations that provide disaster recovery assistance.[38] He also believes that temporary price increases are the best way to stimulate the private sector to bring needed goods and services to affected areas. He argues that allowing market forces to influence this process will result in a more efficient distribution of assistance than the current approach, which relies too much on government agencies.

Many experts believe that adhering to laissez-faire capitalism after a disaster results in significant negative externalities that affect equity, environmental well-being, quality of service, and public safety.[39] Others believe that developing and implementing public sector approaches and projects without involving private sector organizations result in distributional inefficiencies and actions that are uninformed by existing policies. Arguments suggesting that the public or private sector should unilaterally lead recovery efforts fail to acknowledge the importance of developing collaborative strategies that account for and maximize the resources that exist across the assistance network. For instance, the failure of private sector organizations to coordinate the donation of relief supplies with nonprofit organizations, government agencies, and individuals seeking assistance routinely causes logistical problems and results in the widespread receipt of unneeded items. Evidence suggests that businesses benefit from pre-event relationships with disaster relief agencies and that agreements should be in place prior to a disaster in order for corporate donations to effectively target local needs.[40]

Similarly, as government officials relinquish their direct involvement in process-oriented activities like planning, public involvement, and policy making, their understanding of local needs is diminished. An effective planning and policy-making process therefore requires an ongoing, in-depth dialogue among government officials, the private sector, and the public. Contractors, acting on behalf of government agency officials, cannot effectively perform this role by themselves. Nor does this approach lend itself to the establishment of the enduring coalitions needed to support potential changes in existing programs, policies, and plans to confront the weaknesses in the disaster recovery assistance framework.

Striking an appropriate balance between market-driven recovery and reconstruction practices with an inclusive recovery planning strategy coordinated by the public sector remains an ongoing challenge. Several sidebars throughout this book (e.g., Tulsa Partners in Chapter 4, the Charlotte–Mecklenburg, North Carolina, Floodplain Mapping Program in Chapter 8, and the Governor's Commission on Recovery, Rebuilding and Renewal, and Project Impact in this chapter) show that public-private partnerships can be forged, including those that foster private sector consensus-building activities and effective government planning, if parties understand one another's underlying interests.

Information Sharing and Education

The ability to share local needs with the broader assistance network requires improving information-sharing venues. A private sector party that is often underused in this critical role is the media. Improving the media's ability to play a positive role depends on educating national, regional, and local reporters about the realities of long-term recovery. The media should be briefed on the existence of prescriptive programs, the length of time associated with varied aspects of recovery (such as debris cleanup, restoration of public services, and long-term reconstruction activities), the poor connection between program eligibility and local needs, and the low level of horizontal and vertical integration among recovery organizations. They should also be informed about the ways that planning can address limitations in the disaster recovery assistance framework.

Involving the media prior to, during, and after a disaster can improve trust between them and other members of the assistance network, which in turn can increase the likelihood of members working collaboratively to shape policy, allocate funds, and provide technical assistance in a way that meets local needs. Such trust can be achieved without compromising the impartiality of the media, but it requires better information sharing both before and after a disaster. The nuances of disaster recovery cannot be fully understood by reading wire reports or holding brief televised interviews. To gain a more in-depth understanding of local needs, the local media must have ongoing interaction with those affected by an event and those responsible for providing assistance. They can also benefit from exchanges with national organizations that provide a different perspective, including past experience with other disasters.

Harvey Molotch and Marilyn Lester note that disasters can uncover or illuminate larger social and political conditions, as evidenced by Hurricane Katrina and its impact on the people of New Orleans.[41] They believe that these events can empower organizations and inform the media's reporting, thereby influencing government action. However, Eric Klinenberg found in his study of the 1995 Chicago heat wave that community organizations remained largely marginalized and that the media merely framed the story as an interesting "natural disaster" that did not merit great concern.[42] Similar observations have been described following man-made disasters, including oil spills in Great Britain and the United States, where the media's "construction of reality" minimized the apparent impacts.[43]

In the case of the 2010 British Petroleum oil spill, media reports demonstrated that the federal government and private sector failed to develop collaborative pre-event plans. This resulted in a number of problems, including a lack of federal oversight of drilling operations, an unclear delineation of public and private sector roles and responsibilities—both in the immediate aftermath of the event and during long-term recovery, and challenges associated with the determination of appropriate federal relief programs and compensation protocols. The degree to which these problems are addressed in meaningful changes in federal policy and future collaborative planning remains to be seen. Clearly, the media's ability to highlight or distort local needs can play a role in the type, distribution, and timing of assistance.

But as Molotch and Lester suggest, the media can do a lot to dispel myths and provide important information to members of the disaster assistance network. For instance, the *Mississippi Sun Herald* and the *Times Picayune* served as key informational venues following Hurricane Katrina, and both newspapers were awarded a Pulitzer Prize for their efforts. Regular stories of actions undertaken by varied members of the assistance network provided an important context for readers. In addition, specific information concerning policies, meetings, and progress—as well as the lack thereof— did play a role in shaping policy and influencing the delivery of assistance to those whose needs were not being met by federal programs.

Timing of Assistance

After a disaster, insurance companies assess damages and process claims, banks and other financial institutions provide loans, builders and developers reconstruct damaged communities, and a range of businesses sell materials needed to repair damaged housing, community facilities, and infrastructure. Because of its critical role in the design, ownership, and daily operations of public infrastructure systems,[44] the private sector is relied upon to get power, water, and transportation networks up and running as quickly as possible. And the ability of businesses to resume operations has cascading effects on a community's overall economic and physical recovery. The speed with which all these activities can be accomplished, as well as the degree to which they are coordinated with other members of the assistance network, is crucial to understanding the nature of disaster recovery.

Following the Loma Prieta earthquake, which struck the city of Santa Cruz, California, in 1989, local officials developed a post-disaster recovery strategy targeting

Figure 5–5. The casino industry is a primary economic force along the Mississippi Gulf Coast. Prior to Hurricane Katrina, state law required that casinos could not be located on shore, thereby necessitating the construction of floating barges to house gambling operations (left). When Katrina struck, the barges were torn from their moorings and cast on shore, landing on neighboring communities (right). The state legislature has since rescinded this law, which some believe will foster large-scale casino development along the coast.

Photos by Gavin Smith.

the redevelopment of their downtown business district. Business owners complained that the rapidity of recovery resulted in national chain stores and restaurants moving into the area, thereby replacing locally owned shops.[45] In coastal Mississippi following Hurricane Katrina, the broader concept of resources played an important role, as private sector financing and changes in state policies that were favorable to casino owners combined to stimulate reconstruction and the expansion of the industry (Figure 5–5).

More often, however, public sector policies can slow recovery. Owners of homes and businesses must weigh the fiscal costs and benefits of public versus private sector assistance, including the speed at which it is delivered, For instance, should they wait and see if they qualify for a federal grant or should they apply for a loan from a private sector lender? Obtaining the funds needed for repairs allows families to return home, get back to work, and send their children to school. Rapid access to cash allows business owners to reopen more quickly, thereby stemming the loss of revenue and perhaps benefiting from less competition and the increased demand for goods and services that reconstruction brings. Banks and other lending institutions are usually able to provide loans and refinance existing debt faster than most government-based grant programs. In studies of the earthquakes in Anchorage, Alaska (1964), and Managua, Nicaragua (1972), researchers found that business redevelopment decisions were driven by insurance settlements and ready access to capital rather than by government assistance, which came later.[46] The examples cited illustrate the importance of involving the private sector in planning for recovery before and after a disaster strikes (see Figure 5–6).

If the demand for assistance exceeds the perceived capacity of federal, state, and local government, private sector

Figure 5–6. Some businesses, like this damaged marina in Biloxi, depend on areas subject to known natural hazards. The speed at which they can resume operations has economic implications for the community, including those that work there and those who depend on the services they provide.

Photo by Gavin Smith.

businesses will attempt to fill some of this niche market, but not necessarily all of it. For example, builders and developers may be reluctant to pursue contracts in heavily damaged areas where infrastructure has been destroyed, debris must be removed, and redevelopment policies are uncertain. In the case of larger events, demolishing and removing damaged housing and infrastructure and determining reconstruction policy can take months, if not years. Where there has been little pre-event planning, developers and other private sector organizations involved in rebuilding a community may face even greater uncertainty.

Furthermore, an overreliance on the private sector does not ensure that recovery policies equitably address the needs of the poor and other socially vulnerable populations. Where a free market is the driving force, developers, builders, and financial institutions will naturally be drawn to more lucrative middle- and upper-income residential construction projects rather than to less profitable affordable housing. Disaster recovery policies can thus have a gentrifying effect, dislocating the poor, elderly, and working-class populations, particularly in areas that are viewed as desirable places for the affluent to live or build vacation homes. As a result, recovery is slowed even further for a community's most vulnerable populations, whose problems are merely shifted geographically to another neighborhood or jurisdiction. The fact remains that the speed of recovery depends on more than the length of time it takes to physically rebuild a damaged community. It also depends on devising ways to help all residents, including those who are the most in need of assistance.

Finally, the media can affect the timing of resource distribution in several ways. Media reports, for example, can speed delivery by heightening the awareness of politically influential members of the assistance network about gaps in assistance. They can also serve to advance the interests of pro-growth interests by limiting stories that paint a bad picture of the community or that discourage post-disaster reinvestment. At the same time, however, the media can hamper the timing of assistance by disseminating misinformation. And by characterizing success as the speed at which assistance is delivered rather than emphasizing the importance of pre- and post-disaster recovery planning and the adoption of a comprehensive hazard mitigation strategy, the media can undermine the quality of recovery. Similarly, the media's failure to report on the long-term aspects of an event, relying instead on "routinized disaster narratives" that do not capture the reasons for variations in the speed of recovery, can also hinder the development of coordinated assistance strategies.[47] Clearly, building pre-event relationships with members of the private sector offer important ways to highlight endemic problems in the disaster assistance network—including those that involve the business community.

Horizontal and Vertical Integration

Disaster literature regarding the horizontal and vertical integration of assistance has largely focused on the role of government agencies and, to a lesser extent, nonprofit organizations.[48] This may be because governments tend to take on the role of interorganizational coordinator, albeit in a manner that often excludes important members of the assistance network. The limited involvement of the private sector in public sector planning has hindered potentially fruitful public-private collaboration in many ways: it has stifled the widespread adoption of private sector resource distribution methods and decision-making techniques; limited the creation of policies that embrace the linkage between financial incentives, insurance, and wise development; discounted the realities of an increasingly privatized disaster recovery workforce; and largely framed the media as an adversary rather than a partner following disasters. The advantages of having private sector organizations actively engaged in disaster recovery planning are apparent in the accompanying sidebar on the Governor's Commission on Recovery, Rebuilding, and Renewal (sidebar on pages 182–183).

The state recovery planning approach taken in Mississippi merits further research to assess its effectiveness. Important avenues of study include the degree to which a strong private sector emphasis led to the development of a more timely set of actionable recommendations that set the stage for recovery and the efficacy of the Governor's Office of Recovery and Renewal, an organization focused on information dissemination, policy counsel, and the provision of technical assistance, all key resources described in the disaster recovery assistance framework. Mississippi's approach could be contrasted with efforts in Louisiana, which created the Louisiana Recovery Authority, a quasi-governmental organization tasked with administering post-disaster assistance and planning for recovery. In addition to the level of horizontal and vertical integration, comparisons should emphasize the connectivity between network resources and local needs, the timing of assistance, and the degree to which different state organizational structures were able to address identified weaknesses in the disaster recovery assistance framework.

Another example of an important public-private sector partnership is the former Project Impact program (see the sidebar on pages 184–185). FEMA's efforts to actively engage the private sector in pre-event preparedness and hazard mitigation activities provides additional lessons for any future efforts to enhance public-private partnerships in recovery.

The dissemination of accurate and timely information, which is vital both before and after disasters, is necessary for achieving good horizontal and vertical integration. The media play a critical role in this regard, using both formal and informal means to

The Governor's Commission on Recovery, Rebuilding, and Renewal

The Mississippi Governor's Commission on Recovery, Rebuilding, and Renewal, established in the wake of Hurricane Katrina, provides a unique example of how members of the private sector, working in tandem with federal, state, and local officials, nonprofit organizations, foundations, technical experts, and citizens, were able to develop a planning document that would help chart the state's recovery. While the commission was designated a nonprofit, it was privately funded and local business leaders filled key leadership positions on its various committees. Chairman, James Barksdale—a native Mississippian, former chief executive officer and co-founder of Netscape, chief executive officer of AT&T Wireless, and chief information officer of Federal Express—was appointed by the governor shortly after the storm made landfall (see figure below).

James Barksdale, chairman of the Governor's Commission on Recovery, Rebuilding, and Renewal.
Source: Governor's Office of Recovery and Renewal, State of Mississippi.

The commission comprised over 500 volunteers serving on numerous committees (see figure on page 183). Committees and subcommittee chairs included the head of Mississippi Power, the publisher of the *Sun Herald* newspaper, a former oil company executive, bank presidents, a former mayor, and a homebuilder who also ran a prominent kitchen appliance manufacturing company, as well as state agency representatives and nonprofit leaders. In addition, the commission included geographic committees with chairmen appointed from the six most heavily damaged coastal counties as well as representatives from southeast and southwest Mississippi.

The Governor's Commission approach differs from that of most state-level recovery committees, which are typically led by agency officials and financed by state government resources. In fact, it could be argued that this model provided greater horizontal and vertical integration than the traditional state agency-centric approach. For instance, leadership positions were principally filled by individuals who resided in stricken communities. Their in-depth understanding of local conditions and needs grew out of extensive public meetings; the assessment of disaster impacts; and the fact that their homes, businesses, and communities were directly affected by Katrina. The formation of geographic committees provided additional local knowledge and a means to express local needs to other committee chairpersons. And each committee included state agency officials, who provided important information to commission participants regarding existing state and federal programs and who helped to develop policy recommendations that addressed identified gaps in assistance.

The sense of urgency among participants was clear. The commission held the six-day Mississippi Renewal Forum (see Chapter 3) about one month after Katrina. The hosting of such an event so soon after the disaster highlights the tension between being proactive and making decisions when communities are able to effectively engage in decision-making processes that have the potential to reshape their physical, social, and economic condition.

The commission's work as a formal body culminated with the report *After Katrina: Building Back Better Than Ever*. This document, which proposed a broad series of recommendations across the

Infrastructure Committee
- Land Use Subcommittee
- Intermodal Transportation Subcommittee
- Public Services Subcommittee

Housing Committee

Tourism Committee

Small Business Committee

Agriculture, Forestry, and Marine Resources Committee

Defense and Government Contracting Committee

Education Committee

Health and Human Services Committee

Nongovernmental Organization Committee

Financial Committee

Geographic Committees

The organizational structure of the Governor's Commission.

committees' topical areas, was completed by the end of December, just three months after the commission was formed. The speed with which the commission acted, which was due in large part to its organizational structure and the application of private sector procedures, provided the impetus for federal, state, and local action. For instance, the state of Mississippi was more effective, on a per capita basis, than Louisiana in obtaining supplemental appropriations from Congress. Some have argued that this resulted from having a Mississippian as the chair of the Senate Homeland Security Appropriations Committee and a governor who was a former Washington lobbyist and leader of the Republican National Committee.[1] But while critically important, the strong vertical connectivity and understanding of how Washington politics operates account for only part of the reason that Mississippi was able to procure a disproportionate amount of available financial resources. The second factor, which is often discounted, was the commission's ability to link political power with good data in a timely manner. As in the case of North Carolina after Hurricane Floyd, this coupling of good post-disaster information with strong political connections in Washington enabled the governors of these states to forcefully argue their position armed with a clear description of local needs.

Many of the proposed recommendations have been adopted by the state and local communities. Examples include the formation of the Renaissance Corporation, the creation of community-based design studios intended to help residents and communities with building and land use decisions (see the sidebar in Chapter 3 on the Gulf Coast Community Design Studio), and the adoption of flood insurance rate maps that were updated after the storm. Following the issuance of the commission's report, the governor created the Governor's Office of Recovery and Renewal to help communities work through the implications of various policy choices; seek out sources of funding to assist with the implementation of recovery recommendations; and provide technical assistance through education, outreach and training initiatives.

Source: This information was derived from Governor's Commission on Recovery, Rebuilding, and Renewal, *After Katrina: Building Back Better Than Ever* (Jackson, Miss., 2006), www.mississippirenewal.com/documents/Governors_Commission_Report.pdf.

1   Robert B. Olshansky and Laurie A. Johnson, *Clear as Mud: Planning for the Rebuilding of New Orleans* (Chicago: American Planning Association, 2010), 65.

Project Impact: Strengthening Hazard Mitigation and Community Preparedness through Public-Private Partnerships

In 1997, the Federal Emergency Management Agency (FEMA) initiated Project Impact, a program intended to reduce hazard-related losses at the community level through the use of enhanced public-private partnerships.[1] Prior to the 1990s FEMA had placed a limited emphasis on the idea of pre- and post-event hazard mitigation. Under the leadership of James Lee Witt, however, FEMA realized that a comprehensive approach to hazard mitigation required more than the involvement of government agencies. During this time, hazard mitigation was gaining increased recognition and acceptance among practitioners, which represented a shift in the emergency management field from one that had been predominantly focused on response and, to a lesser extent, recovery efforts.[2]

After Hurricane Andrew, the National Academy of Public Administration reported that FEMA had not effectively incorporated hazard mitigation into its operational duties.[3] Shortly thereafter, Witt began to reorganize the agency to account for this oversight. Then, after the 1993 floods that hit the Midwest, Congress amended the Robert T. Stafford Act, placing greater emphasis on the use of post-disaster Hazard Mitigation Grant Program (HMGP) funding to relocate flood-prone properties, business districts, and, in some cases, entire communities to higher ground.[4] Subsequent floods along the Mississippi and Missouri Rivers showed that mitigation was a sound investment of federal dollars as the actions taken spared the human suffering and damage seen in these communities just a few years before (although comprehensive hazard mitigation planning in the larger Mississippi River watershed remains elusive).[5]

Project Impact emphasized an important new focus on pre-event hazard mitigation and disaster preparedness (see figure on page 185). Under this program, FEMA provided seed money to communities across the United States and charged them with developing pre-disaster preparedness and hazard mitigation initiatives that involved the private sector and emphasized the use of information-sharing venues such as conferences, workshops, and media campaigns. This approach represented a significant change from the primary reliance on post-disaster HMGP funds and emergency appropriations from Congress. FEMA provided funding and technical assistance to local governments and gave each state the resources to hire a Project Impact coordinator. By 1999, over 200 Project Impact communities had been designated, including at least one in each state. For example, the city of Tulsa used the federal initiative to launch an ongoing community-led program advancing sustainability and risk-reduction themes (see sidebar on Tulsa Partners in Chapter 4).

Despite its innovative approach, however, Project Impact was highly politicized. For instance, several of the initial Project Impact communities that were strategically chosen by FEMA to receive funding were represented by powerful politicians. Examples include Pascagoula, Mississippi, home of Senator Trent Lott; Charleston, West Virginia, home of Senator Robert Byrd; and New Hanover County, North Carolina, the home state of influential governor James B. Hunt, who had worked with former Arkansas governor Bill Clinton when the latter was governor of Arkansas and who remained a close political ally during Clinton's presidency. (Hunt also developed a strong working relationship with Witt after Hurricane Fran, which struck the state in 1996, and later during recovery from Hurricane Floyd of 1999.)

Project Impact was discontinued under George W. Bush's administration, cited as being ineffective and easily replaced by the Disaster Mitigation Act's Pre-Disaster Mitigation program. In reality, however, few disasters had actually tested the efficacy of Project Impact initiatives.[6] FEMA initially claimed that the Project Impact programs had helped to limit damages from the Nisqually earthquake, which struck Washington, Oregon, and British Columbia in 2001, but a further analysis traced the low level of losses to the fact that the epicenter was several miles below the surface. A more global assessment of Project Impact found that the program contributed to a greater awareness of hazards and to the adoption of mitigation measures by public and private sector organizations within these communities.[7] And a study conducted by the congressionally appointed Multihazard Mitigation Council found that mitigation activities, including Project Impact, were in fact cost-effective.[8]

Ironically, it was the failure to develop meaningful partnerships with key constituent groups that led to significant scrutiny from the Bush administration, the Office of Management and

Budget, state emergency management directors, and some FEMA officials.[9] Critics charged that the program overemphasized the use of funds to implement ill-defined objectives that were difficult to quantitatively assess. Some FEMA employees, particularly those located in the Response and Recovery Directorate, were angered when funds were shifted from their programs to finance Project Impact initiatives. Politics may also have been at play, as Project Impact was uniformly considered to be the brainchild of Witt, who had been

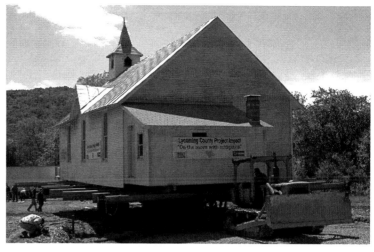

In this relocation of a flood-prone church in Lycoming County, Pennsylvania, note the Project Impact banner advertising the importance of hazard mitigation and public-private partnerships that span the disaster recovery assistance network.

Source: FEMA.

appointed by Clinton. In addition, the manner in which the program was implemented damaged relations between FEMA and state emergency management agencies.[10] At first, the program was driven from Washington rather than through FEMA's regional offices, which maintain closer working relationships with states. Early in the process, FEMA staff from Washington met directly with local officials, bypassing both their own regional office staff and state personnel.

Although Project Impact established effective horizontal integration within participating communities, it selectively fostered strong vertical integration among some federal, state, and local levels of government but not others.[11] Future efforts of the federal government need to be careful not to exclude members of the assistance network, especially members of the very agency in which the program resides, as well as state agency officials, members of Congress, and organizations charged with federal oversight. Any attempt to develop a public-private sector initiative focused on disaster recovery should strive to incorporate this lesson. A well-defined planning process should involve all relevant parties while identifying the tasks best suited for each, respecting the types of assistance each provides, when it is provided, and the degree to which it addresses local needs.

1   Federal Emergency Management Agency (FEMA), *Project Impact: Building Disaster Resistant Communities* (Washington, D.C.: FEMA, 1997).

2   Richard Sylves, *Disaster Policy and Politics: Emergency Management and Homeland Security* (Washington, D.C.: CQ Press, 2008), 21–23.

3   Richard T. Sylves, "Federal Emergency Management Comes of Age: 1979–2001," in *Emergency Management: The American Experience, 1900–2005*, ed. Claire Rubin, 111–159 (Fairfax, Va.: Public Entity Risk Institute, 2007); National Academy of Public Administration (NAPA), *Coping with Catastrophe: Building an Emergency Management System to Meet People's Needs in Natural and Manmade Disasters* (Washington, D.C.: NAPA, 1993).

4   Timothy Beatley, "The Vision of Sustainable Communities," in *Cooperating with Nature: Confronting Natural Hazards with Land-Use Planning for Sustainable Communities*, ed. Raymond J. Burby, 233–262 (Washington, D.C.: Joseph Henry Press, 1998); Sylves, "Federal Emergency Management Comes of Age"; Bob Freitag et al., *Floodplain Management: A New Approch for a New Era* (Washington, D.C.: Island Press, 2009).

5   David R. Godschalk et al., "Missouri after the Midwest Floods of 1993," in *Natural Hazard Mitigation: Recasting Disaster Policy and Planning*, 161–192 (Washington, D.C.: Island Press, 1999); Freitag et al., *Floodplain Management*, 1–8.

6   Thomas A. Birkland, *Lessons of Disaster: Policy Change after Catastrophic Events* (Washington, D.C.: Georgetown University Press, 2006), 113.

7   Tricia Wachtendorf et al., *Disaster Resistant Communities Initiative: Assessment of the Pilot Phase—Year 3*, Final Report no. 39 (Newark: Disaster Research Center, University of Delaware, 2002).

8   Multihazard Mitigation Council, *Natural Hazard Mitigation Saves: An Independent Study to Assess the Future Savings from Mitigation Activities* (Washington, D.C.: National Institute of Building Sciences, 2005).

9   Gavin Smith and Dennis Wenger, "Sustainable Disaster Recovery: Operationalizing an Existing Agenda," *Handbook of Disaster Research*, ed. Havidan Rodriguez, Enrico L. Quarantelli, and Russell Dynes, 252 (New York: Springer, 2006).

10   Ibid., 252.

11   Ibid.; Birkland, *Lessons of Disaster*, 114.

share information, including radio and television broadcasts, newspaper and magazine articles, and Internet news and information services. These avenues of communication are ever widening and have the potential to reach all parts of a community even in the midst of a disaster.[49] Cooperative media networks dramatically increase the speed and breadth of information shared within stricken communities and around the world through twenty-four-hour television news services, blogging, e-mail, text messaging, and Twittering. In addition to serving as a critical source of breaking news, however, the informal nature of newer communication avenues enables the spread of misinformation and rumors. The growing trend toward instant, sensationalized news with limited depth or analysis undermines the transfer and receipt of useful information to members of the assistance network.

Tom Birkland, in *Lessons of Disaster: Policy Change after Catastrophic Events*, reviews newspaper articles and their effect on policy change following disasters.[50] His findings show that the media play an important role in shaping disaster relief through the promotion of policy learning (i.e., the adoption of new or amended policies based on new information and lessons derived from experience) and thus, under the right conditions, can positively influence disaster recovery outcomes. Similarly, in their study of the media and response to disasters, Ronald Perry and Michael Lindell find that interorganizational communications are improved when providers of assistance recognize that the media comprise multiple institutions, each with different approaches to disseminating information,[51] and that using various media channels increases the likelihood of reaching different audiences. Elderly people, for example, tend to get their news from radio, television, and newspaper outlets, whereas younger people rely on the Internet, text messaging, and Twitter to send and receive information. It also stands to reason that the use of various media outlets furthers the sharing of information with providers across the network, helping them gain a better understanding of the nature of the particular disaster and the role of various stakeholders in the community's recovery.

Challenges can arise, however, as the expansion of media channels require people to sift through assorted information sources and reconcile often competing claims. The use of insurance as a recovery tool, for instance, is highly reliant on the access to and sharing of information among the policyholder, insurance provider, and larger network. Yet the role of insurance-related organizations in facilitating integration among members of the disaster assistance network has not been adequately explored.[52] Kunreuther argues that financing and lending institutions, working in concert with the insurance industry, should invest in low-cost loans to finance the incorporation of hazard mitigation measures into the reconstruction of damaged homes, public infrastructure, and development projects.[53] While there is not a great demand for such assistance among homeowners, renters, and developers, low-interest loans for hazard mitigation could help communities reduce future losses. But increasing the supply of and demand for these loans will require the active involvement of federal, state, and local officials.[54] There is also a need to create more accurate models that establish the cost-effectiveness of mitigation alternatives. Reducing the uncertainty of loss avoidance strategies increases the likelihood that insurance companies will adopt such measures; they will be able to price new policies more accurately while purchasers will be able to evaluate the benefits accrued over time and choose whether they want additional protection. Vertically integrated approaches to improve the use of insurance as a recovery tool include the development of complementary federal and state statutes and regulations, and the adoption of land use management actions (plans, ordinances, and codes) at the local level that are recognized by the insurance industry.

CONCLUSIONS AND RECOMMENDATIONS

The private sector will remain a key player in the recovery and reconstruction of disaster-stricken communities regardless of the degree to which the public sector and other members of the assistance network involve it in joint decision making. But failure to include it in pre-event planning for post-disaster recovery has significant implications as the private sector continues to expand its role in the field of hazards management, including disaster recovery. Private investors, insurers, design professionals, and construction companies shape the physical manifestation of post-disaster reconstruction efforts. Investors and financial institutions provide the capital needed to pay for reconstruction and new development. Consultants are involved in virtually all aspects of recovery, including policy formulation, debris management, and disaster recovery planning. Insurance payouts finance a substantial percentage of reconstruction, and the nature of their policies influences the type of redevelopment that occurs.

The following recommendations are based on enhancing public-private partnerships in pre- and post-disaster recovery activities.

1. Involve Developers, Design Professionals, Consultants, and Other Private Sector Stakeholders in Recovery Planning

Relying on market forces to address local needs, without guidance from government officials and other members of the assistance network, can result in the inequitable distribution of goods and services. Letting the market dictate how and when funds are distributed maximizes profits for a select few at the expense of long-term community benefits and the public good. On the other hand, investors routinely cite the uncertainty of the post-disaster policy-making environment as a key reason for their reluctance to initiate new ventures and coordinate their actions with others.

A recovery plan that includes private sector organizations in its development, monitoring, implementation, and modification over time increases certainty about outcomes, particularly as they relate to development and redevelopment opportunities. Engaging in an inclusive planning process can also increase the number of options on the table, including those suggested by members of the private sector. Finally, involving investors, developers, and other private sector firms in planning decisions also can elicit cooperation and consensus during recovery and reconstruction, as evidenced by the sidebars on the Governor's Commission on Recovery, Rebuilding, and Renewal in Mississippi and the City of Tulsa in Chapter 4. Similarly, in Charlotte, North Carolina, an area facing intense development pressure and a strong pro-growth coalition, developers were involved in lengthy deliberations about future growth in the city's floodplains. After engaging in participatory decision-making techniques, the community adopted some of the most stringent floodplain management standards in the United States[55] (see the sidebar on the Charlotte–Mecklenburg County Floodplain Mapping Program in Chapter 8).

Involving developers and design professionals in federal, state, and local pre-event recovery planning activities also enables a community to identify solutions to the difficult issues that invariably emerge in discussions of where and how to rebuild following a disaster—issues such as the appropriateness of various land uses and settlement patterns relative to identified hazard areas (see the sidebar in Chapter 2 on Hillsborough County, Florida's Post-Disaster Redevelopment Plan).[56] This may require the government to limit growth and reconstruction in areas where private sector investors and developers could otherwise derive a profit and where residents would otherwise choose to live. However, the involvement of private sector stakeholders in carefully crafted development alternatives can help forge consensus about the future of the community, thereby averting opposition to strategies identified in the local government's disaster recovery plan.

The timing of private sector involvement in recovery decision making is also critically important. The sidebar on the Congress for the New Urbanism and the Mississippi Renewal Forum in Chapter 3 clearly demonstrates the challenges associated with suggesting major policy changes in the immediate aftermath of a disaster, such as those proposed by the design professionals who participated in the post-Katrina design charrette in coastal Mississippi and by the federal contractors who helped communities develop plans sponsored by Emergency Support Function 14 (ESF-14) (see pages 87–90). The limited involvement of local business owners, investors, and builders in pre-event recovery planning hindered the widespread support and eventual adoption and implementation of post-disaster plans produced by the New Urbanists and FEMA's ESF-14 contractors.

One way to improve pre-event planning for post-disaster recovery is to modify existing federal pre- and post-disaster contracts to include a focus on pre-event recovery initiatives. For instance, federal contracting vehicles distribute millions of dollars annually toward the implementation of numerous disaster recovery and hazard mitigation initiatives. The Hazard Mitigation Technical Assistance Program (HMTAP) funds have been used to train state and local officials in the creation of hazard mitigation plans that are compliant with the Disaster Mitigation Act, while Technical Assistance Contract funds are used to deploy private sector contractors to assist with the development of ESF-14 recovery plans following disasters. These programs should fund comprehensive, *pre-disaster* training in recovery planning, including an ongoing commitment to assist in the development of improved levels of public and private sector capacity to plan for recovery and implement measures identified in plans that are developed collaboratively with members of the larger assistance network.

2. Expand the Role of Media Representatives and Organizations

The involvement of the media in pre-event planning for post-disaster recovery is uncommon. This should not be surprising as pre-event planning itself is still rare. But any pre-event recovery planning process that is undertaken should include the media, using their unique skills more effectively to advance coordination across the disaster assistance network. Building bridges with media representatives and informing news organizations about the activities of the network benefits media organizations, residents of a community struck by a disaster, and the broader public that may experience an extreme event in the future. Such involvement requires informing the media about the nature of recovery programs—including their limitations, some of which are due to statutory regulations. With an enhanced level of understanding, the media may undertake further investigations that reveal deeper underlying problems, such as excessive rules, the challenges of program implementation at the local and state levels, and the implications of a failure to develop pre-disaster disaster recovery plans. By reporting these and other institutional complications, the media could thereby play a role in a larger effort to affect change across the disaster assistance framework.

Media organizations also need to be active partners with government and other members of the assistance network. Although the media are a key provider of information both before and after a disaster, they can fulfill this role successfully only if they coordinate their information gathering and dissemination strategies with those of the assistance network. This requires media organizations to understand the varied roles of stakeholders in recovery, the timing of assistance provided, and the challenges inherent in a system that often limits deliberation and adopts financial solutions to problems without a good understanding of local needs. Like other disaster assistance providers, the media tends to be reactionary, highlighting problems identified post-disaster instead of advocating for more proactive measures like pre-event hazard mitigation planning.[57]

3. Enhance Public-Private Partnerships Focused on Disaster Recovery

Any attempt to develop improved public-private partnerships focused on disaster recovery should draw on lessons from Project Impact—specifically, the need to more fully involve the diverse interests of the assistance network in marketing, policy making, and planning-related initiatives. This is a concept that had not gained widespread attention in government or the private sector. By contrast, the case study of Tulsa in Chapter 4 provides an example of city staff actively using the media to garner support, highlight problems, and celebrate success as part of a larger public-private partnership. In many ways, Project Impact did address the key problems facing the disaster recovery assistance network: by bringing together the public and private sectors and allowing for some degree of program flexibility, communities determined what their needs were and developed a strategy accordingly. Another underlying theme of the program was to develop partnerships and provide resources prior to a disaster. Finally, Project Impact was tied to the creation of an expanded network of stakeholders in a community as well as with state and federal agencies. Future efforts to rekindle Project Impact, or another incarnation of it, must also consider developing a more expansive network of vertically integrated partners.

The ability to garner support from members of the private sector is becoming increasingly important as communities, regions, nations, and multinational coalitions are beginning to confront the implications of heightened levels of hazard vulnerability on an unprecedented scale. A number of factors point to the importance of understanding hazards in a global context. Private sector organizations—including small, locally owned businesses, as well as multinational corporations—are increasingly becoming part of a global economy. For instance, international aid agencies have become more dependent on assistance from private sector consultants.[58]

Disaster research and practical solutions to recovery have a rich cross-cultural history. In the United States, we have much to learn from other nations, yet we often fail to adopt lessons from communities and countries overseas—a shortcoming that is particularly acute when we assess recovery in developing countries. Among the general public, disasters are garnering more attention as an international phenomenon. The media's reach is expanding and able to deliver information around the globe in a moment's notice. Climate change and sea level rise dramatically illustrate the interconnected nature of industry, human actions, and disaster, as well as the need to formulate international cooperative agreements. Thus, it is important to examine the role that international aid organizations and other nations can play in disaster recovery in the United States.

Endnotes

1   Kathleen J. Tierney, "Business and Disasters: Vulnerability, Impacts, and Recovery," in *Handbook of Disaster Research,* ed. Havidan Rodriguez, Enrico L. Quarantelli, and Russell Dynes, 275–296 (New York: Springer, 2006); Mary C. Comerio, *Disaster Hits Home: New Policy for Urban Housing Recovery* (Berkeley: University of California Press, 1998).

2   Stephen Flynn, *The Edge of Disaster: Rebuilding a Resilient Nation* (New York: Random House, 2007), 139–142.

3   J. Eugene Haas et al., "Reconstruction Issues in Perspective," in *Reconstruction following Disaster,* ed. J. Eugene Haas, Robert W. Kates, and Martyn J. Bowden, 25–68 (Cambridge: MIT Press, 1977).

4   William R. Freudenberg et al., *Catastrophe in the Making: The Engineering of Katrina and the Disasters of Tomorrow* (Washington, D.C.: Island Press, 2009).

5   John R. Logan and Harvey L. Molotch, *Urban Fortunes: The Political Economy of Place* (Berkeley: University of California Press, 1987).

6   Vincent Gawronski, Richard Stuart Olson, and Pedro Carvalho, "Locally Influenced, Distantly Courageous? Exploring Media Constructions of Katrina's Gulf Coast Impacts," in *Learning from Catastrophe: Quick Response Research in the Wake of Hurricane Katrina,* ed. Natural Hazards Center, 443–456 (Boulder: Institute for Behavioral Science, University of Colorado, 2006).

7   Gavin Smith, "Holistic Disaster Recovery: Creating a More Sustainable Future" (course developed for the Emergency Management Institute Higher Education Project, Federal Emergency Management Agency, 2004), available online at training.fema.gov/EMIWeb/edu/sdr.asp; Gavin Smith, "Disaster-Resilient Communities: A New Hazards Risk Management Framework," in *Natural Hazards Analysis: Reducing the Impact of Disasters,* ed. John Pine, 249–267 (Washington, D.C.: Taylor Francis, 2009).

8   Naomi Klein, *The Shock Doctrine: The Rise of Disaster Capitalism* (New York: Henry Holt and Company, 2007); Richard Sylves, *Disaster Policy and Politics: Emergency Management and Homeland Security* (Washington, D.C.: CQ Press, 2008), 163–168.

9   Klein, *Shock Doctrine,* 166; Sylves, *Disaster Policy and Politics.*

10   Klein, *Shock Doctrine,* 314–316.

11   James M. Dahlhamer and Melvin J. D'Souza, "Determinants of Business Disaster Preparedness in Two U.S. Metropolitan Areas," *International Journal of Mass Emergencies and Disasters* 15, no. 2 (1997) 265–281.

12   Comerio, *Disaster Hits Home.*

13   Walter Gillis Peacock and Chris Girard, "Ethnic and Racial Inequalities in Hurricane Damage and Insurance Settlements," in *Hurricane Andrew: Ethnicity, Gender and the Sociology of Disasters,* ed. Walter Gillis Peacock, Betty Hearn Morrow, and Hugh Gladwin, 171–190 (Miami, Fla.: International Hurricane Center Laboratory for Social and Behavioral Research, 1997).

14   Klein, *Shock Doctrine.*

15   Howard Kunreuther, "A Program for Reducing Disaster Losses through Insurance," in *Paying the Price: The Status and Role of Insurance against National Disasters in the United States,* ed. Howard Kunreuther and Richard J. Roth Sr., 209–228 (Washington, D.C.: Joseph Henry Press, 1998).

16   Comerio, *Disaster Hits Home.*

17   Robert C. Bolin and Patricia A. Bolton, *Race, Religion, and Ethnicity in Disaster Recovery* (Boulder: Institute of Behavioral Science, University of Colorado, 1986).

18   Peacock and Girard, "Ethnic and Racial Inequalities."

19   Jon Kusler and Larry Larson, "Beyond the Ark: A New Approach to U.S. Floodplain Management," *Environment* 35, no. 5 (1993): 7.

20   Howard Kunreuther and Richard J. Roth Sr., eds., *Paying the Price: The Status and Role of Insurance against National Disasters in the United States* (Washington, D.C.: Joseph Henry Press, 1998).

21   Walter Gillis Peacock, Betty Hearn Morrow, and Hugh Gladwin, eds., *Hurricane Andrew: Ethnicity, Gender and the Sociology of Disasters* (Miami, Fla.: International Hurricane Center Laboratory for Social and Behavioral Research, 1997).

22   Howard Kunreuther, "Has the Time Come for Comprehensive Natural Disaster Insurance?" in *On Risk and Disaster: Lessons from Hurricane Katrina,* ed. Ronald J. Daniels, Donald F. Kettl, and Howard Kunreuther, 175–201 (Philadelphia: University of Philadelphia Press, 2006).

23   Raymond J. Burby, "Policies for Sustainable Land Use," in *Cooperating with Nature: Confronting Natural Hazards with Land-Use Planning for Sustainable Communities,* ed. Raymond J. Burby, 263–291 (Washington, D.C.: Joseph Henry Press, 1998), 282; French Wetmore and Gil Jamieson, "Flood Mitigation Planning: The CRS Approach," *Natural Hazards Informer* 1 (July 1999): 1–9, www.colorado.edu/hazards/publications/informer/infrmr1/infrmr1a.htm; Samuel D. Brody et al., "The Rising Costs of Floods: Examining the Impact of Planning and Development Decisions on Property Damage in Florida," *Journal of the American Planning Association* 73, no. 3 (2007): 330–345; Samuel D. Brody et al., "Identifying the Impact of the Built Environment on Flood Damage in Texas," *Disasters* 32, no. 1 (2008): 1–18.

24   Smith, "Disaster-Resilient Communities," 257–259.

25   Gilbert F. White and J. Eugene Haas, *Assessment of Research on Natural Hazards* (Cambridge: MIT Press, 1975); Kunreuther and Roth, *Paying the Price.*

26   Daniel J. Alesch et al., *Organizations at Risk: What Happens When Small Businesses and Not-for-Profits Encounter Natural Disasters* (Fairfax, Va.: Public Entity Risk Institute, 2001); Daniel J. Alesch et al., *After the Disaster...What Should I Do Now? Information to Help Small Business Owners Make Post-Disaster Decisions* (Green Bay: Center for Organizational Studies, University of Wisconsin, 2002).

27   Daniel J. Alesch and James N. Holly, "How to Survive the Next Natural Disaster: Lessons for Small Business from Northridge Victims and Survivors" (paper presented at the Pan Pacific Hazards Conference, Vancouver, British Columbia, July 29–August 2, 1996).

28   Maxwell E. McCombs and Donald L. Shaw, "The Agenda-Setting Function of Mass Media," *Public Opinion Quarterly* 36, no. 2 (1972): 176–184; Jarol B. Manheim, "A Model of Agenda Dynamics," in *Communication Yearbook* 10, ed. Margaret McMaughlin, 499–516 (Beverly Hills, Calif.: Sage, 1987); Richard Stuart Olson, "Toward a Politics of Disaster: Losses, Values, Agendas, and Blame," *International Journal of Mass Emergencies and Disasters* 18, no. 2 (2000): 265–287; Thomas A. Birkland, *Lessons of Disaster: Policy Change after Catastrophic Events* (Washington, D.C.: Georgetown University Press, 2006).

29   Kathleen Tierney, Christine Bevc, and Erica Kuligowski, "Metaphors Matter: Disaster Myths, Media Frames, and their Consequences in Hurricane Katrina," *Annals of the American Academy of Political Science* 604, no. 1 (2006): 57–81.

30   Dennis E. Wenger et al., "It's a Matter of Myths: An Empirical Examination of Individual Insight into Disaster Response," *Mass Emergencies* 1, no. 1 (1975): 33–46; Dennis E. Wenger and Enrico L. Quarantelli, *Local Mass Media Operations, Problems, and Products in Disasters,* Report Series no. 19 (Newark: Disaster Research Center, University of Delaware, 1989); Henry W. Fischer III, *Response*

to Disaster: Fact versus Fiction and Its Perpetuation: The Sociology of Disaster (New York: University Press of America, 1998).

31 Gavin Smith and Dennis Wenger, "Sustainable Disaster Recovery: Operationalizing an Existing Agenda," in *Handbook of Disaster Research,* 234–257 (see note 1).

32 Kathleen Tierney, Michael K. Lindell, and Ronald W. Perry, *Facing the Unexpected: Disaster Preparedness and Response in the United States* (Washington, D.C.: Joseph Henry Press, 2001), 106–109.

33 William F. Shughart, "Katrinanomics: The Politics and Economics of Disaster Relief," *Public Choice* 127 (April 2006): 31–53; Steven Horowitz, *Making Hurricane Response More Effective: Lessons from the Private Sector and the Coast Guard during Katrina,* Mercatus Policy Series, Policy Comment No. 17 (Fairfax, Va.: George Mason University, March 2008).

34 Marvin Olasky, *The Politics of Disaster: Katrina, Big Government, and a New Strategy for Future Crisis* (Nashville, Tenn.: Thomas Nelson, 2006).

35 Olasky, *Politics of Disaster,* 107.

36 Horowitz, *Making Hurricane Response More Effective.*

37 Mississippi Renewal Forum, *Summary Report* (Gaithersburg, Md.: The Town Paper, November 2005), www.mississippirenewal.com/documents/Rep_SummaryReport.pdf; Sandy Sorlien and Leland R. Speed, "Walking to Wal-Mart: Planning for Mississippi and Beyond," in *Rebuilding Urban Places after Disaster: Lessons from Hurricane Katrina,* ed. Eugenie L. Birch and Susan M. Wachter, 329–341 (Philadelphia: University of Pennsylvania Press, 2006).

38 Olasky, *Politics of Disaster,* 107.

39 Peacock and Girard, "Ethnic and Racial Inequalities"; Klein, *Shock Doctrine;* Sylves, *Disaster Policy and Politics;* Freudenberg et al., *Catastrophe in the Making.*

40 Anisya Thomas and Lynn Fritz, "Disaster Relief, Inc.," *Harvard Business Review* 84, no. 11 (2006).

41 Harvey Molotch and Marilyn Lester, "News as Purposive Behavior: On the Strategic Use of Routine Events, Accidents, and Scandals," *American Sociological Review* 39 (February 1974): 101–112.

42 Eric Klinenberg, *Heat Wave: A Social Autopsy of Disaster in Chicago* (Chicago: University of Chicago Press, 2002).

43 Gregory V. Button, "The Negation of Disaster: The Media Response to Oil Spills in Great Britain," in *The Angry Earth: Disaster in Anthropological Perspective,* ed. Anthony Oliver-Smith and Susanna Hoffman, 113–132 (New York: Routledge, 1999); Gregory V. Button, "Popular Media Reframing of Man-Made Disasters: A Cautionary Tale," in *Catastrophe and Culture: The Anthropology of Disaster,* ed. Susanna Hoffman and Anthony Oliver-Smith, 143–158 (Santa Fe, N.M.: School of American Research Press, 2002).

44 Flynn, *Edge of Disaster.*

45 Charles C. Eadie, "Earthquake Case Study: Loma Prieta in Santa Cruz and Watsonville, California," in *Planning for Post-Disaster Recovery and Reconstruction,* Planning Advisory Service (PAS) Report 483/484, by Jim Schwab et al., 281–310 (Chicago: American Planning Association, 1998).

46 Martyn J. Bowden et al., "Reestablishing Homes and Jobs: Cities," in *Reconstruction Following Disaster,* 69–145 (see note 3).

47 Button, "Negation of Disaster," 129–130.

48 Peter May and Walter Williams, *Disaster Policy Implementation: Managing Programs under Shared Governance* (New York: Plenum Press, 1986); Philip R. Berke, Jack Kartez, and Dennis Wenger, "Recovery after Disasters: Achieving Sustainable Development, Mitigation and Equity," *Disasters* 17, no. 2 (1993): 93–109; Philip R. Berke and Timothy Beatley, *After the Hurricane: Linking Recovery to Sustainable Development in the Caribbean* (Baltimore: Johns Hopkins University Press, 1997).

49 Joseph Scanlon, "Unwelcome Irritant or Useful Ally? The Mass Media in Emergencies," in *Handbook of Disaster Research,* 413–429 (see note 1).

50 Birkland, *Lessons of Disaster.*

51 Ronald W. Perry and Michael K. Lindell, "Communicating Threat Information for Volcano Hazards," in *Bad Tidings: Communication and Catastrophe,* ed. Lynne Masel Walters, Lee Wilkins, and Tim Walters, 47–62 (Hillsdale, N.J.: Erlbaum, 1989).

52 Comerio, *Disaster Hits Home.*

53 Kunreuther, "Program for Reducing Disaster Losses"; Kunreuther "Has the Time Come for Comprehensive Natural Disaster Insurance?"

54 Elliott Mittler, *The Public Policy Response to Hurricane Hugo in South Carolina,* Working Paper # 84 (Boulder: Natural Hazards Research and Applications Information Center, University of Colorado, 1993).

55 Gavin Smith, "Lessons from the United States: Planning for Post-Disaster Recovery and Reconstruction," *Australasian Journal of Disaster and Trauma Studies* 2010–1 (2010), www.massey.ac.nz/~trauma/issues/2010-1/smith.htm (accessed July 9, 2010).

56 Robert G. Paterson, "The Third Sector: Evolving Partnerships in Hazard Mitigation," in *Cooperating with Nature* (see note 23), 220–223.

57 Birkland, *Lessons of Disaster,* 173–174.

58 Krister Anderson and Matthew R. Auer "Incentives for Contractors in Aid- Supported Activities" in *The Samaritan's Dilemma: The Political Economy of Development Aid,* ed. Clark C. Gibson et al., 160–170 (Oxford, UK: Oxford University Press, 2009).

Chapter 6

The International Community

This house in Dichato, Chile, was damaged by the 2010 earthquake-induced tsunami. Note the commercial fishing boat on the next street.

Photo by William Siembieda.

NATURAL HAZARDS AND DISASTERS ARE global problems. The threat is particularly acute in developing nations, where hazard-related impacts account for 90 percent of injuries and deaths, often resulting in humanitarian crises that exceed the capabilities of one country.[1] For communities, vulnerability is further increased by the rapid pace of development in areas prone to hazards—owing, in part, to the effects of globalization.[2] While Hurricane Katrina and the Galveston Hurricane of 1900 stand out as the worst disasters in U.S. history in terms of total damages and loss of life, a number of international disasters provide stark evidence of the routine nature of catastrophic loss. Examples include the 2001 earthquake in Gujarat, India, in which more than 20,000 died; the 2003 earthquake in Bam, Iran, which killed over 31,000 people; the 2004 Indian Ocean tsunami, which killed over 283,000 people in ten countries; and the 2010 earthquake in Haiti, which left more than 230,000 people dead.

Following disasters, developing nations rely extensively on financial assistance provided by international relief organizations and other nations. Historically, such assistance has included a number of programs that provide short-term relief but do little to advance long-term institutional capacity and economic growth. In fact, post-disaster international relief efforts can have direct negative effects on recipient nations, particularly when such efforts fail to account for local needs, existing conditions (including high levels of social vulnerability), or inherent capabilities.[3]

In recent years, international organizations and nations have instituted a range of activities focused on local capacity building and use of the indigenous population's inherent social capital.[4] Developing nations, working with humanitarian and development organizations, have established important institutional arrangements to address what Maureen Fordham refers to as the "desired reconciliation of disaster and development."[5] These efforts can inform the actions of the United States, improving our ability to effectively link development and disaster recovery principles domestically.[6]

International literature on natural hazards and disasters provides a wealth of lessons that are directly applicable to the United States (see the accompanying sidebar). Cross-cultural studies highlight issues related to the timing of recovery;[7] the effects of class inequality and other social, economic, and cultural conditions on recovery outcomes;[8] the problems associated with top-down assistance strategies;[9] and the emerging field of quantifying economic recovery.[10] Of particular interest are studies related to the importance of pre-event planning for disaster recovery.[11] Research conducted by Anthony Oliver-Smith, for example, after a major earthquake struck the north-central coastal and Andean regions of Peru in 1970, found that sustainable development themes, including social equity and hazard mitigation, can be linked to post-disaster recovery if planning strategies reflect local needs, external assistance providers recognize existing capabilities to act, and members of the community understand the nature of the rules associated with disaster recovery programs.[12] Robert Geipel found that Italy's use of an inclusive, participatory approach to rapidly establish recovery strategies after the 1976 Fruili earthquake elicited support from members of the community for new post-disaster initiatives, such as the use of indigenous resources (as demonstrated by survivors of the 2010 Chilean earthquake, shown in Figure 6–1 on page 198).[13]

Learning from Disaster Recovery in Developing Countries

In accounts of disaster recovery in developing countries, the international disaster literature has highlighted a number of important elements that are lacking or inadequate within the U.S. disaster recovery assistance framework. These elements are summarized below as they relate to disaster assistance in four countries: Mexico, Bangladesh, Honduras, and Vietnam.

Timing of assistance and government improvisation. After the Mexico City earthquake in 1985, an 8.1-magnitude quake that killed over 9,500 people and displaced more than 100,000 individuals, the Mexican government rapidly assembled a team of government planners and engineers to lead a massive housing reconstruction effort. The newly formed government agency had a two-year mandate, during which time it constructed 45,000 homes. The agency coupled defined performance goals and a close working relationship with communities. It also hired over 1,200 construction companies, providing jobs for more than 175,000 people.

Timing of assistance and linkage of disasters and development. Bangladesh, which is among the world's most vulnerable nations to the impacts of natural hazards, including typhoons and monsoon-driven rainfall, experienced a flood in 1998 that covered 68 percent of its total land area for ten weeks. The Bangladesh Rural Advancement Committee, a nonprofit focused on development-related activities, shifted personnel to address immediate housing needs and the economic effects of the flood. By emphasizing the expeditious repair of damaged housing and the provision of needed supplies to resume farming operations, the committee hastened recovery and reduced the likelihood of farmers falling further into debt and poverty. The private sector also played an important role as it was able to import much-needed rice (the crop was severely damaged by the flood) more quickly than the national government to feed those directly affected—as well as the country as a whole.

Meeting of local needs through enhanced horizontal and vertical integration. Honduras has been repeatedly struck by hurricanes. The most devastating storm to hit this Central American nation was Hurricane Mitch in 1998, which caused 5,757 deaths and destroyed 35,000 homes. The National Fund for Social Investment (Fondo Hondureño de Inversión Social, or FHIS) focused on hiring local labor—people directly affected by the disaster—to assist in the reconstruction of damaged housing and infrastructure, and it provided those hired with additional training, which reportedly helped to sustain the reconstruction process. Emphasis was also placed on developing strong vertical linkages between the national government and local communities through active recovery planning initiatives. In addition, the FHIS adopted a decentralized approach, sending staff to work directly with communities and giving local officials the autonomy needed to make the decisions they felt were in the best interests of their people. This sped the reconstruction of housing and infrastructure while empowering individuals to help shape their own future.

Hazard mitigation and capacity building. In Vietnam, after a series of major tropical storm-induced floods in 1998 and 1999, the Red Cross sought to help the Vietnamese build more hazard-resistant housing. With an emphasis on recruiting local workers while using indigenous materials, it held a housing design competition that drew the involvement of fifteen local firms. The intent of the program was to foster local empowerment while demonstrating the importance of hazard mitigation and disaster-resilient housing construction techniques to both the private sector and individual homeowners. Ultimately, 7,400 homes were constructed using the winning designs. Following another flood, all but one of the new homes survived. This stimulated a partnership between the Red Cross and the Vietnamese government to build another 2,000 homes using the same design techniques. A nonprofit became involved in the efforts as well, offering training in disaster-resilient building techniques and creating an outreach campaign to promote the importance of adopting these techniques as part of future housing construction projects.

Source: Jeffrey D. Garnett and Melinda Moore, "Enhancing Disaster Recovery: Lessons from Exemplary International Disaster Management Practices," *Journal of Homeland Security and Emergency Management* 7, no. 1 (2010): 1–20.

Figure 6-1. This temporary tent camp was built by local residents in Talca, Chile, after the 2010 earthquake. The residents intend to remain here until their former houses are rebuilt on their existing lots.

Photo by William Siembieda.

FOREIGN ASSISTANCE AND THE UNITED STATES: CONCEPTS AND IMPLICATIONS

While much has been written about the reliance of developing nations on international assistance following a disaster, little research has been done on the role that international aid organizations and foreign nations play in assisting the United States when disaster strikes, or on the challenges that U.S. agencies face in effectively using the resources offered by the international community. What is clear, however, is that although the actions described in the preceding sidebar and throughout much of the international disaster literature have been deemed pertinent to the United States, their adoption by members of the disaster recovery assistance network remains limited. U.S. policies and associated funding strategies have not effectively incorporated what we know about the international community's disaster recovery practices into our own domestic agenda. Nor have U.S.-led international assistance programs, which emphasize the importance of pre-event capacity building and collaborative planning in the developing world, established the procedures necessary to solicit international help in the case of a major disaster here at home. As the experiences of other countries are replete with lessons to be learned (see Figure 6-2), our failure to learn those lessons reflects a limitation in our ability to provide adequate technical assistance, as defined by education, outreach, and training initiatives, to our own citizens and communities.

Absorptive Capacity

The ability of a community or nation to effectively use external assistance in whatever form is referred to as "absorptive capacity."[14] As the situation that unfolded after

Figure 6–2. Philip Berke, professor at the University of North Carolina at Chapel Hill, talks with local residents on a houseboat in a Thailand coastal village following the Indian Ocean tsunami.

Source: Philip Berke.

Hurricane Katrina made evident, members of the U.S. disaster assistance network are not equipped to accept international aid after a disaster or to coordinate its disbursement. Therefore, the recovery assistance framework must develop the means to more effectively *receive* external assistance.[15] Specifically, existing protocols, plans, and institutions, as well as less formal "back-channel" relationships, must be modified, expanded, and more effectively used to facilitate the acceptance of foreign resources; strategies must be developed to coordinate foreign resources with those provided by domestic stakeholders; and the ways to implement plans when a disaster strikes must be improved. The means by which this can achieved is discussed in the section addressing the dimensions of the disaster recovery assistance framework.

Improving this situation will become increasingly important as the effects of climate change are more closely felt and international terrorism continues to spread (see Figure 6–3 on page 200). Both of these threats will necessitate the increased use of multilateral agreements and multinational cooperation. The financial and institutional investments that have been made in preparing for terrorist attacks, as evidenced by the focus of the Department of Homeland Security (DHS) and numerous multinational agreements, as well as lessons from the organizational, diplomatic, and procedural mistakes that were made following 9/11, may provide insights that can be used to expand the breadth of the disaster recovery assistance framework with regard to natural hazards and disasters. Such insights can improve the ability of the U.S. government, nonprofits, foundations, and private sector organizations to receive funding, technical assistance, and policy counsel from foreign governments and international organizations when the need arises.

Figure 6–3. The village of Shishmaref, located north of the Bering Strait in Alaska, is one of roughly a dozen communities facing an immediate threat from coastal erosion. The structure pictured above was impacted by a severe fall storm that resulted in substantial coastal retreat within a matter of hours. Surviving houses have been moved to less threatened sites on the small barrier island by towing them across the ice in winter. Coastal erosion is significantly exacerbated by the thaw of permafrost that has historically helped to stabilize the island.

Photo by Ned Rozell.

Conditionality

Developed nations often mistakenly believe that they are the best suited to determine the needs of developing nations following disasters and may attach specific procedural conditions to humanitarian assistance. Those offering foreign assistance, including foundations that provide the financial backing required to purchase and deliver supplies, may also expect to be granted limited oversight from the receiving country, including a review of plans outlining how the assistance will be distributed.[16] This notion of "conditionality" is often associated with attempts to change a receiving government's behavior,[17] which may partially explain why international relief organizations and nations receiving assistance may view one another with mutual distrust.[18]

With Hurricane Katrina, which spurred an outpouring of international assistance, the concept of conditionality was seen in a new light: under what circumstances would the United States *accept* assistance with real or perceived "strings" attached? In the immediate aftermath of the hurricane, President Bush was lukewarm about taking international assistance, claiming that the nation had sufficient resources.[19] As offers of international assistance grew, Karen Hughes, a long-standing political adviser to Bush, dispatched a cable to U.S. ambassadors across the globe encouraging them to emphasize how foreign assistance was benefiting disaster victims. But the U.S. diplomats were experiencing a very different situation: the United States was actually rejecting the offers of foreign countries and international corporations to send personnel, technical expertise, supplies, and money.

Disaster Diplomacy

In some cases, the United States has turned down assistance because of the political positions of donor nations. Ilan Kelman has studied how disasters facilitate greater international cooperation among those nations that consider themselves "enemies"—defined as "states that are not collaborating diplomatically or politically"—and has coined the term "disaster diplomacy" as a way to describe this relationship.[20] Disaster diplomacy occurs when countries are focused on addressing disaster response and recovery needs, not on diplomacy per se. They do not force the issue; instead, they often work through informal networks apart from more traditional government-based diplomatic channels. It is a multilevel approach that seeks to involve all known stakeholders in a productive dialogue that takes advantage of technical and scientific exchanges and that focuses on matching available resources with local needs. Above all, disaster diplomacy requires the ability to accept assistance when offered. Accepting assistance sends an important symbolic message to those willing to help. While they are unlikely to serve as the principal means of resolving conflict between enemy nations, disasters can provide a catalyst for positive change when conflicting nations have developed pre-event relationships tied to nondisaster-based issues such as a common culture or trade.[21]

Kelman's research adds to the well-documented literature recognizing that disasters can be highly politicized events.[22] Many of the factors that inhibit disaster diplomacy are tied to continuing the status quo. For instance, when a disaster occurs, nations that view one another as enemies may try to take advantage of the situation by using the disaster as a "weapon," which may include the assisting nation emphasizing the other nation's inability to care for itself. In other cases, the disaster may distract from ongoing diplomatic efforts to address root causes of the conflict, or it may excessively raise expectations of future cooperation that may not be achievable. This is particularly true among neighboring nations as they may feel obligated to offer assistance regardless of past relationships.

Hurricane Katrina provided several examples of failed disaster diplomacy. One example in particular occurred when Cuba offered to send 1,600 medics, a number of field hospitals, and other medical supplies. While the State Department said that the assistance was not needed because of the strong response among U.S. medical teams, the White House snubbed Cuba's offer outright. "'When it comes to Cuba,' said [White House spokesman Scott] McClellan, 'we have one message for Fidel Castro: He needs to offer the people of Cuba their freedom.'"[23]

This was not the first time that the United States had let its ideological differences stand in the way of accepting assistance from Cuba. It also rejected the information provided by Cuban meteorologists prior to the hurricane that destroyed Galveston in

1900. In fact, U.S. Weather Bureau officials stationed in Cuba tried to obstruct Cuban weather reports that disagreed with their own analysis of the storm, dismissing the merits of that intelligence as insignificant (at the time, the U.S. War Department was still in Cuba—a result of the Spanish-American War). Bureau officials eventually convinced the War Department to force the Cubans to discontinue sending cables warning of the storm's intensity, even though there is evidence to suggest that the island nation was more advanced than the United States in terms of its ability to predict hurricane behavior.[24]

Another example of diplomacy at issue occurred a few weeks after Katrina, when Iran's Islamic Republic News Agency announced that the Middle East country was prepared to donate 20 million barrels of oil as a gesture of humanitarian assistance. In many ways this was a symbolic offer. Although the oil supply in the Gulf of Mexico was disrupted by Hurricane Katrina, the United States could have purchased oil on the open market or used its own strategic oil reserves. But Iran's offer was conditioned upon the lifting of U.S. economic sanctions against it, and so the United States refused the assistance. Again, the offer of aid can foster disaster diplomacy, but when the offer is explicitly tied to diplomatic negotiations—in essence, when it is used as a weapon—disaster diplomacy will fall apart.[25]

Convergence, Mismatched Assistance, and the Need for Information Sharing

The effective provision of international assistance requires the appropriate scaling of resources so as not to overwhelm the recipient. It also requires an understanding of the social and political conditions in which assistance is provided (see Figure 6–4). In a cross-cultural study of recovery in Nicaragua and the United States, for instance, Robert Bolin and Patricia Bolton found that the delivery of disaster assistance in Nicaragua is guided by kinship ties and an entrenched patronage system, whereas recovery resources in the United States are closely tied to rules-based institutions.[26] To be effective, international organizations must understand the political, cultural, and historical differences that characterize regions, communities, and individuals while delivering resources in a manner that also recognizes the unique distribution systems of the receiving nations.

One major problem is convergence—the sudden influx of people and resources into an affected area following a disaster. Examples frequently cited in the response literature include the assemblage of food, clothing, and other supplies, as well as the arrival of volunteers, media representatives, returning evacuees, and curious onlookers. When inadequate procedures are in place or institutions are unprepared for this eventuality, convergence impedes disaster response operations.[27] As a result,

Figure 6–4. The image of Thai housing highlights the importance of recognizing existing economic, social, cultural, and environmental factors that should be considered when developing pre- and post-disaster recovery assistance strategies.

Photo by Philip Berke.

emergency management organizations and nonprofits have developed domestic donations management systems to address convergence during response and early recovery operations. The development or extension of these services to long-term recovery is much less common, particularly as it relates to the convergence of the international community in the United States.

Rarely has the inadequacy of the systems set up to handle donations been more apparent than in the mismanaged response to offers of international assistance following Katrina. The magnitude of those offers simply overwhelmed the institutions that were designed to send rather than receive foreign resources. Examples abound. The British sent 500,000 meals ready to eat (MREs) only to find that the U.S. Department of Agriculture (USDA) denied their distribution because of fears of mad cow disease. Communications equipment provided by the telecommunications corporation Ericsson sat on a runway in Sweden for eleven days; by the time it arrived in the United States, it was no longer needed. Honduras offered experts on flooding and search and rescue, but the proposal was turned down; Argentina's offer of physicians was similarly rejected. And the Greek government was willing to provide two cruise ships (free of charge) for use as hotels or hospitals, but an agreement between the two countries was dropped once it was determined that the earliest a ship could arrive in New Orleans was October 10, more than a month after the storm made landfall. In the end, the United States paid $249 million to Carnival Cruise Lines to use their ships to house displaced residents.[28]

Given the bureaucratic nature of U.S. federal agencies, their inability to adapt to an emergent challenge in the wake of the hurricane is not surprising. One month after the disaster, President Bush ordered a comprehensive review of the federal response effort, and among the findings was the need to improve the manner in which the federal government accepts assistance from other nations.[29] More specifically, recommendations suggested that DHS and the Department of State improve pre-event planning for this eventuality.

Closely related to international convergence is the mismatch between donated goods and local needs. International providers of assistance do not, generally speaking, maintain close working relationships with U.S. communities (although it could be argued that this is changing as a result of the globalization of economies, the threat of climate change, and the rise of new media platforms); thus, they lack a well-developed understanding of local needs.

The low level of vertical integration between international relief organizations and nations and stakeholders in U.S. disaster recovery assistance networks highlights the importance of developing better information-sharing venues that help to delineate and convey needs, thereby improving the type and timing of assistance provided. Not surprisingly, attempts to develop such systems in the aftermath of a major disaster are hard enough without having to navigate cumbersome international protocols or invest substantial time and resources only to find out that the plans and agreements that can facilitate these efforts do not exist. Moreover, this country's ability to accept specialized assistance requires developing detailed, yet flexible procedures that account for a number of federal rules intended to protect the public. For instance, any donated food or medical supplies must meet Food and Drug Administration (FDA) requirements, and a means must be in place for ensuring that medical staff from other countries have the proper credentials. Because all this takes a long time to accomplish, it should be done in advance of a disaster as part of a coordinated federal recovery plan.

It is important to note, however, that there were successful examples of assistance delivery after Katrina—those that emerged spontaneously in the wake of the storm as well as those that resulted from purposeful pre-event planning. Emergent successes include a Vancouver-based search-and-rescue team that rescued 119 people from rising floodwaters; a feeding operation in San Antonio for evacuees and volunteers that was run by the Mexican military; and a NATO-coordinated series of flights that delivered various types of resources. Examples that stemmed from pre-event agreements and a history of joint training exercises include the coordination of U.S. Navy and Canadian divers charged with removing navigational obstacles and inspecting the levees surrounding New Orleans; a team of experts from the Netherlands that not only helped assess the initial damages to the levee system but also provided guidance in levee repair and construction as well as adaptive land use planning techniques;[30] and a memorandum of agreement between the U.S. Army Corps of Engineers and Dutch public works engineers facilitating the provision of much-needed technical assistance (see the sidebar starting on page 206). These successes point to the importance of developing an overall approach that can accommodate the delivery of varied types of disaster assistance.

As reflected in both the literature and practice, the concept of convergence has been largely applied to response conditions, not long-term recovery. The unplanned arrival of international resources can tax organizations that are already overwhelmed by processing domestic assistance (e.g., grants, loans, and insurance settlements) through more recognized operational channels, including federal agencies, foundations, nonprofits, and insurance companies. Research on international assistance has shown that the delivery of humanitarian relief that is not effectively linked to a sound pre-event recovery plan developed by local recovery networks can have the unintended consequences of increasing vulnerability[31] and impeding the recovery process.[32] The lack of an effective, vertically integrated system that links local needs to potential international resource providers exacerbates convergence writ large.

INTERNATIONAL ASSISTANCE AND SUSTAINABLE DEVELOPMENT

An important principle that can be derived from the international realm involves taking a more holistic view of disaster recovery. As it applies to the U.S. disaster recovery assistance framework, this means taking advantage of available pre-event "resources"—namely, policy lessons and technical assistance strategies from other nations, including the developing world. During a keynote address to the Eighth World Conference on Earthquake Engineering, Dr. Frank Press, then president of the National Academy of Sciences, described the conceptual linkages among disaster relief, development, and disaster resilience. His remarks form the basis of what would eventually become the United Nations' (UN) International Decade for Natural Disaster Reduction. That initiative contained several broad ideas, which were operationalized in the International Strategy for Disaster Risk Reduction to meet several objectives, including new and improved institutional frameworks and strategies based on scientific and engineering knowledge, enhanced public awareness initiatives, and a commitment to gain a greater understanding of natural hazards and their effects.[33]

Development can be described as the ability to foster sustained local capabilities to address issues germane to a community, region, or nation (see Figure 6–5 on page 208). Important factors associated with this concept include stable economic growth, improved public health, equitable food distribution, and quality educational systems. Understood in the context of disaster recovery, development means not only helping a community, region, or nation reconstruct damaged housing and local infrastructure, but also working with members of the stricken area to build the capacity of organizational networks and institutions to engage in long-term development

Two Approaches to International Cooperation: The Dutch Dialogues and a Pre-Event Memorandum of Agreement

The exchange of information between nations through their respective state departments, professional associations, universities, concerned citizens, and other entities provides a way for them to learn from one another. In the field of hazards management, including disaster recovery, these exchanges are often dominated by the United States imparting "lessons" to others while members of U.S. disaster recovery assistance networks rarely translate into practice lessons derived from in-depth explorations of other countries' experiences.

However, one apparently successful example of a cross-national exchange of ideas and potential solutions occurred between the United States and the Netherlands following Hurricane Katrina. The Netherlands faces challenges that are similar to those found in New Orleans: over 50 percent of the country is below sea level, and more than 70 percent of its land area is highly vulnerable to flooding. Not surprisingly, the Dutch have had their share of major floods over time. In 1953, for example, a North Sea storm caused major flooding that killed over 1,900 people and destroyed more than 50,000 structures. Rotterdam, a port city located on a delta, much of which is below sea level, is protected by a levee system, yet it suffered significant losses from the storm, as did much of the surrounding area. Not surprisingly, their history has given the Dutch extensive experience in developing techniques to reduce the impacts of such disasters in low-lying communities.

In the exchange of information between the two nations, two approaches were used: (1) the Dutch Dialogues, a collaborative effort between a group of experts in the Netherlands and design professionals and officials from New Orleans; and (2) a pre-event memorandum of agreement (MOA) between the U.S. Army Corps of Engineers (USACE) and Dutch public works engineers.

New Orleans Mayor Mitch Landrieu, Ambassador Rene Jones-Bos, David Waggonner, and Dale Morris at the Dutch Dialogue III Workshop.

Source: David Waggoner and Associates.

Dutch Dialogues. During the exchanges between local participants and invited experts, both parties picked up lessons to take back to their communities. For example, the engineers, planners, and architects from Rotterdam realized that they needed to do a better job of communicating risk to their citizens, many of whom believed that the government-financed levee system would protect them and thus reduce their need to adopt individual risk-reduction strategies.[1] The Netherlands has already embarked on a major floodplain management initiative in anticipation of rising sea levels. The program incorporates design and land use planning techniques that are intended to protect against the 10,000-year flood, whereas communities in the United States typically plan for the estimated 100-year event.[2] In response to Katrina, a second Delta Commission was formed in the Netherlands to improve flood protection strategies.

According to David Waggonner, a local architect and organizer of the Dutch Dialogues, a more sustainable, water-based landscape approach is also taking root in New Orleans.[3] Owing, in part, to the exchange of information during Dutch Dialogue II, which was held in New Orleans in October 2008, citizens and local officials from New Orleans began to understand the need to reconsider land use and settlement patterns and to recognize water as an asset, while planning for large-scale flood-related disasters that may become more likely with a climate change–induced rise in sea level.[4]

In 2010, the American Planning Association devoted a major part of its annual conference, which was held in New Orleans, to the concept of Delta Urbanism, an outgrowth of the first Dutch Dialogue. With a focus on sharing lessons learned by Dutch and U.S. cities in flood-prone deltaic regions, key topics included disaster recovery planning, the role of land use in hazards management, and the realities of planning for rising sea levels. In conjunction with this conference, Dutch Dialogue III was held; workshops addressed the issue of improved water management design features across various geographic scales (see figure on page 206).

US Army Corps of Engineers Memorandum of Agreement. In May 2004, USACE and the Ministry of Transport, Public Works, and Water Management of the Netherlands, known as the Rijkswaterstaat, signed an MOA to further the mutual provision of technical assistance—the exchange of general information and the sharing of research findings, test results, and policy evaluation methods—associated with flood control, floodplain management, and water resource management. Topical areas of joint interest and expertise include dredging, levee design, coastal erosion, coastal navigation, economic evaluation of policy alternatives, environmental protection and restoration, and coastal zone management.[5]

The exchange program entails annual visits by each party in alternating years. In May 2005, a team of Dutch experts traveled to New Orleans to assess the Mississippi Delta region. Because a relationship had been forged between government agencies through the MOA, diplomatic procedures were in place four months later to quickly reassemble teams to assist in the recovery effort following Hurricane Katrina.[6] At meetings held in the Hague, the Netherlands, New Orleans concentrated on how best to strengthen coastal protective measures, such as levees and storm surge barriers, drawing on relevant lessons from the Dutch flood defense project.[7] Also on the agenda was an evaluation of the Louisiana Coastal Protection and Restoration Project, an emerging plan intended to guide the repair of damaged levees and to counter storm-induced coastal and barrier island erosion and the loss of protective wetlands.

1   Ruth Eckdish Knack, "In the Same Boat," *Planning* (August/September 2008): 40–43.
2   Knack, "In the Same Boat"; Ruth Eckdish Knack, "Celebrate the Water. From the Headwaters to the Delta: The Dutch Return to New Orleans," *Planning* (January 2009): 31–33; American Planning Association (APA), Royal Netherlands Embassy, and Waggonner and Ball Architects, *Dutch Dialogues II* (workshop proceedings, New Orleans, October 10–13, 2008), dutchdialogues.com/LinkedDocuments/DDII/DutchDialoguesII.pdf.
3   Author's conversation with David Waggonner, November 2010.
4   APA, Royal Netherlands Embassy, and Waggonner and Ball Architects, *Dutch Dialogues II*.
5   U.S. Army Corps of Engineers (USACE) and Ministry of Transport, Public Works and Water Management, Directorate General "Rijkswaterstaat" of the Netherlands for Information Exchange and Research, Development, Testing, and Evaluation Projects, Memorandum of Agreement, May 2004, see rwsusace.us/.
6   Anne C. Richard, "Katrina Aid: When the World Wanted to Help America," *New York Times*, August 30, 2006, www.nytimes.com/2006/08/30/opinion/30iht-edrichard.2642650.html (accessed February 7, 2011).
7   USACE and Rijkswaterstaat, *US-Dutch Technical Exchange: Louisiana Coastal Protection and Restoration Project* (LACPR) (The Hague, The Netherlands, October 10–11, 2006), www.rwsusace.us/docs/workshops/2ndTechnicalWorkshop10-11October2006.pdf.

Figure 6–5. This photo of a coastal fishing village in Thailand (note the fishing nets suspended in the river) exemplifies the proximity of housing to the natural resources upon which those in the community depend. Sound pre- and post-disaster recovery assistance should reflect local conditions, including those associated with development and the often strong social capital that exists among communities in the developing world.

Photo by Philip Berke.

initiatives—including adaptive strategies that account for preexisting social capital—well after reconstruction has been completed.[34] As J. M. Albala-Bertrand notes, "disasters are primarily a problem *of* development, but essentially not a problem *for* development."[35] Unsustainable development practices based on poor land use planning, inadequate health care, poor educational systems, a weak economy, and agricultural practices that strip areas of their natural resources result in communities that are more vulnerable to the effects of natural hazards (see Figure 6–6).

A number of international organizations play key roles in disaster response and recovery. These include the UN, nonprofit (i.e., nongovernmental) relief organizations, and international financial institutions. Collectively, these organizations have extensive experience in the financing and delivery of assistance after some of the most destructive events in recorded history. They also routinely seek to integrate sustainable development principles into disaster recovery planning and post-disaster operations. Unfortunately, the U.S. disaster recovery assistance framework has not made effective use of these organizations' capabilities to address disasters in its own country, nor has it been willing to systematically draw lessons from those nations that do.

The United Nations*

The primary mission of the UN's programs and policies is to foster peace. Most UN activities center on issues of development, but several of its programs address disaster recovery-related assistance. Given the number of existing UN-funded projects

---

* The following discussions of the UN, nonprofit relief organizations, financial institutions, and U.S. agencies involved in international relief are derived from George D. Haddow and Jane A. Bullock, "International Disaster Management," in *Introduction to Emergency Management* (Amsterdam: Butterworth Heineman), 165–189.

Figure 6–6. The image of squatter housing in Manila, Philippines, juxtaposed with the downtown skyline shrouded in smog, dramatically shows the extreme social vulnerability of many of the city's residents, whom reside in the shadows of new urban growth. The houses are sited within the confines of a channelized drainage system, whose nearby neighborhoods are protected by a concrete levee. After Typhoon Ondoy, which struck the area in 2009, both squatter settlements and the wealthy neighborhood that the levee was intended to protect were severely flooded.

Photo by Gavin Smith.

in developing countries and their established relationships with host nations, the UN is uniquely positioned to provide such assistance. The UN emergency relief coordinator, working through the Office for the Coordination of Humanitarian Affairs (OCHA) and the Inter-Agency Standing Committee, directs the UN effort in partnership with the United Nations Children's Fund (UNICEF), World Health Organization (WHO), World Food Programme (WFP), and United Nations Development Programme (UNDP).

OCHA, which was established in 1998, focuses on managing UN disaster relief programs and policies, particularly when the demands exceed the capacity of a single agency. Coordination is achieved through the OCHA's Disaster Response System, which helps to assess damages, identify local needs, recommend different types of assistance, and monitor the implementation of the resources that are provided.

UNICEF focuses on helping poverty-stricken children, serving as an advocate on their behalf. The fund is well suited to help children after disasters (who are among the most socially vulnerable populations) as it is embedded in a number of countries on a permanent basis and has committed financial and staff resources to further its mission. Over 190 countries have adopted the Convention on the Rights of the Child, which gives UNICEF additional legitimacy.

WHO, charged with protecting and improving health and sanitation, also plays a lead role in disaster response and recovery. Both before and after a disaster, WHO helps at-risk communities alleviate unsanitary conditions that trigger disease outbreaks;

after an event, it supplies medical teams capable of dealing with the rise in injured and sick populations.

The WFP helps developing countries address food and nutritional needs. Disasters and armed conflicts often trigger the WFP to act, distributing food and nutritional supplements to affected areas. The provision of food to disaster-stricken areas is particularly important in developing countries, as noted in the discussion of Bangladesh in the first sidebar of this chapter.

The UNDP, established during the 1960s and the "UN Decade of Development," focuses on building the institutional capacity needed to capitalize on natural resources and develop an enhanced industrial base. Its policies reflect a growing understanding of the link between sustained economic growth and risk reduction. Two new programs—the Emergency Response Division (ERD) and the Disaster Reduction and Recovery Program (DRRP)—have emerged to address this issue. The ERD seeks to improve the level of organization among the UN, disaster-affected nations receiving assistance, and nonprofit organizations involved in delivering assistance to communities and individuals. The DRRP, which is located within the ERD, incorporates hazard mitigation strategies into development projects, plans, and programs; builds local capacity; improves interinstitutional coordination; and conducts assistance delivery training programs.

Nonprofit Relief Organizations

Numerous international relief organizations, such as the Organization of American States (OAS), the Asian Disaster Preparedness Center (ADPC), the Pacific Disaster Center, and the Pan American Health Organization, focus on regional efforts. These organizations assume many of the disaster recovery roles described in Chapters 3 and 4, such as spanning boundaries across public and private sector organizations, providing targeted local assistance, and serving as advocates for socially vulnerable populations. Yet one area in which these organizations differ from many of the quasi-governmental and nonprofit organizations in the United States is in their widespread use of strategies that link sustainable development principles and disaster recovery. Such strategies include technical assistance (training and capacity building), funding, policy counsel, and advocacy (see Figure 6–7).

The OAS, for instance, working through its Unit for Sustainable Development and Environment, has developed a Natural Hazards Project, whose mission is the construction of hospitals, schools, and transportation infrastructure that are less vulnerable to the damaging effects of natural hazards.[36] ADPC, formed in 1986 in response to a request from the UN Disaster Relief Organization (now OCHA), was located within

Figure 6–7. An official from Medair, in Jacmel, Haiti, after the 2010 earthquake, assesses the traditional construction methods used to build this home and suggests repair and reconstruction techniques to make it more earthquake and hurricane resistant. The discussion also represents a larger effort to pretrain local residents who will be involved in efforts to rebuild the community. Medair is a Switzerland-based nonprofit relief organization that has primarily focused on providing shelter to Haitians displaced by the earthquake.

Photo by Liesel Ritchie.

the Asian Institute of Technology; in 1999, it became an independent organization. ADPC focuses on helping communities and countries in Asia and the Pacific region develop sustainable development and risk-reduction strategies,[37] a goal it achieves through training, education, and outreach techniques designed to enhance institutional capacity and awareness.

Financial Institutions

International financial institutions play a significant role in disaster recovery, most notably by providing loans. This is particularly important to developing countries that may not have ready access to the sizeable infusions of cash needed to fund large-scale recovery and reconstruction efforts. Key players include the World Bank and the International Monetary Fund (IMF).

The World Bank, which emerged after World War II to finance the reconstruction of Europe, is made up of two development institutions owned by 186 member countries: the International Bank for Reconstruction and Development and the International Development Association. Charged with providing loans, technical assistance, and other programs to help developing countries alleviate the effects of poverty, the World Bank is a natural partner in worldwide disaster recovery efforts because the large numbers of people who live in poverty in the developing world are especially vulnerable to natural hazards and disasters. The Bank often conducts damage assessments to determine the economic impacts of such events, including the costs of reconstruction, and then provides loans to fund rebuilding efforts. It may restructure the afflicted country's existing debt, amend pre-event projects to reflect new needs, or provide emergency loans that target specific recovery activities. Its loan programs also can be used to build planning capacity and reduce the impacts of future disasters. As part of the loan process, the Bank conducts a vulnerability assessment to ascertain a loan's merit and evaluate possible hazard mitigation measures that can be incorporated into reconstruction projects or future development plans.

The IMF, established shortly after the World Bank, emphasizes improving international cooperation, stimulating economic development, and stabilizing monetary exchange rates among member nations. Following a disaster, the IMF provides financial assistance through its Emergency Assistance Specific Facility, funding reconstruction projects as well as the stabilization of local, regional, and national economies. It also provides a range of advisory services to help nations and communities regain fiscal solvency and sustained economic stability. Specific areas of advice include taxation and other revenue-generating strategies, the reformation of financial institutions, and the wise use of post-disaster assistance.[38]

U.S. Agencies Involved in International Relief

When a disaster strikes another country, the United States responds primarily through the U.S. Agency for International Development (USAID) and the U.S military. These organizations provide financial and technical assistance not only in the immediate aftermath of an event but also over the long-term process of recovery and reconstruction.

USAID's primary mission is to coordinate the provision of development assistance to other countries. Its Bureau for Humanitarian Response oversees the federal government's humanitarian relief efforts. The Office of Foreign Disaster Assistance (OFDA), located within the bureau, coordinates all disaster assistance other than food, which is handled by the Office of Food for Peace. The OFDA comprises four divisions: Operations Support and Program Support, which provide logistics and accounting expertise and help track the assistance provided to others; Disaster Response, which coordinates the delivery of assistance; and Prevention, Mitigation, Preparedness, and Planning, which helps other nations and organizations build local capacity to prepare for the impacts of hazards and disasters and reduce future losses.

Like many agencies in the international community, USAID has a number of teams that are deployed following disasters to help coordinate interorganizational relief efforts. The provision of assistance to a foreign country is initiated when a U.S. ambassador or the Department of State issues a disaster declaration. At that point, the OFDA may send a disaster assistance response team to ascertain damages, recommend a specific set of actions, and initiate the coordination of resources with other countries, international relief organizations, and the affected country's existing network. The OFDA also provides advice and technical assistance through its Technical Assistance Group, composed of land use planners, public health officials, agricultural specialists, physical scientists, and other experts.

DIMENSIONS OF THE DISASTER RECOVERY ASSISTANCE FRAMEWORK

As U.S. communities face the growing threat of catastrophic disasters associated with climate change and continued development in hazard-prone areas, the need to more effectively coordinate with international organizations, researchers, and other nations by identifying lessons and formulating multinational agreements has become increasingly apparent. Although the role of international organizations and nations in the U.S. disaster recovery assistance framework has not been sufficiently analyzed by hazard scholars, it is clear that policies have not been developed to effectively use their resources before and after major disasters strike the United States. As it describes existing international programs in the context of the defining characteristics of the U.S. disaster recovery assistance framework, this section highlights the need for improved plans, agreements, and protocols if the United States is to more effectively harness the resources of those programs both before and after disasters.

Understanding of Local Needs

The policies, programs, and activities of international relief organizations and their donors are grounded in humanitarian, religious, economic, and, in some cases, military ideals and objectives.[39] Each of these factors can influence who receives assistance, as well as the type, timing, and amount. A study conducted by the Overseas Development Institute found that the international distribution of assistance is infrequently based on a sound assessment of need. Rather, UN agencies, nonprofits (often referred to as nongovernmental organizations, or NGOs), and U.S.-based relief organizations usually seek donations based on what they think donors are willing to support. Donors often are interested in funding a relatively narrow set of activities that do not always align with local needs and priorities. Moreover, there are inadequate mechanisms in place to "triage" critical or time-sensitive needs of countries that are competing for a finite amount of resources.[40] Thus, the ability of international aid organizations and nations that seek to meet local needs in the United States, where such mechanisms are even less developed than those found overseas, remain largely unrealized. In fact, until recently, they were nonexistent.

A number of studies have analyzed the challenges associated with delivering international assistance, such as improving its distribution and creating flexible programs that are responsive to local needs.[41] In the international relief literature, needs are described across humanitarian and developmental dimensions. The ability to save lives in the immediate aftermath of a disaster is a short-term response to a much larger dilemma related to unsustainable development patterns, poverty, and chronic public health problems. Addressing these issues in a systematic manner using international relief and development principles is highly complex and involves challenging moral imperatives as well as ongoing monitoring and evaluation.

Care must be taken, for example, to ensure that communities do not become overly dependent on the episodic delivery of funding at the expense of planning for the future and building local capacity. In the context of hazards management and disaster recovery, this means assessing the impact that development and reconstruction choices will have on a community's vulnerability to hazards and reevaluating post-disaster assistance strategies that encourage reinvestment in vulnerable areas. In 1994, eight of the world's disaster relief organizations developed the Code of Conduct for the International Red Cross and Red Crescent Movement and NGOs in Disaster Relief.[42] The code describes a series of principles based on the humanitarian ideal of saving lives and alleviating human suffering in an equitable manner. The latter part of the code includes elements endorsing capacity building, public participation, and reducing vulnerability to natural hazards through the use of sustainable development practices.

But despite the plethora of research that has addressed the difficulties of delivering international assistance to foreign nations, an insufficient amount of research has been done on the unique challenges associated with other countries delivering assistance to communities in the United States. The U.S. disaster assistance network is not designed to accept contributions—be they monetary, technical, or even advisory—from external organizations. Nor are international relief organizations and nations necessarily cognizant of the unique social, economic, and political conditions found in specific U.S. communities or of the assorted types and idiosyncrasies of assistance networks, given that long-standing relationships between these foreign and domestic stakeholders are rare.

There is, however, one type of assistance that international organizations and foreign nations can provide the United States and from which members of the U.S. assistance network can benefit substantially: the lessons learned through extensive practice-based experiences following major disasters in other countries, including those characterized as developing nations. Looking at the experiences of communities worldwide and studying how other nations and international institutions address local needs can yield unique insights into methods that may apply to vexing issues in the United States, including the growing problem of social vulnerability and unsustainable land use patterns in high-hazard areas. Of particular interest is the linkage between capacity building, disaster assistance, development, and sustainability (see the accompanying sidebar). But the insights that can be derived from such inquiries are not widely disseminated, and while organizations such as USAID routinely apply such knowledge to countries abroad, they have not done so domestically. The reluctance to transfer these findings to receptive audiences in the United States is perplexing.

Among the most important insights that the international assistance literature has brought to light is that there is an overarching need to provide locally grounded technical assistance aimed at increasing local capacity and greater self-reliance based on identified pre- and post-disaster needs.[43] This practice is not always followed as developed nations and some nongovernmental humanitarian organizations, like many members of the U.S.

Comparing U.S. International and Domestic Assistance Programs

The similarities and differences between the U.S. programs of international and domestic assistance are instructive. Similarities include the provision of immediate relief and long-term assistance during recovery; a delivery system that is based on an evaluation of damages and existing capabilities; the politicization of assistance; attempts to coordinate assistance strategies; and assistance that is provided when the capacity of receiving nations, institutions, and communities is exceeded. Differences include variations in policies that link disaster recovery and development, and the impact of territorial sovereignty on assistance delivery.

After a disaster abroad, the U.S. Agency for International Development (USAID) and USAID's Office of Foreign Disaster Assistance (OFDA) provide immediate disaster relief to the stricken countries. They also offer long-term assistance to help with recovery and reconstruction activities. In short, they emphasize pre- and post-disaster assistance that links sustainable development principles to disaster recovery. After a disaster within the United States, however, the U.S. disaster assistance framework mostly emphasizes the delivery of monetary assistance, paying little attention to the linkage between pre-event recovery planning and sustainable development. While USAID promotes pre-event capacity-building initiatives in developing countries, there are very few federal programs among the members of the U.S. disaster recovery framework that pursue such initiatives. For the most part, U.S. organizations that have taken the lead in this regard include nonprofits, foundations, and quasi-governmental organizations.

Regardless of whether the United States is responding to a disaster overseas or within its borders, the delivery of assistance is theoretically based on an assessment of damages and local capabilities. In fact, however, the tools and methods used to assess damages and capabilities may not adequately take into account the different ways in which disasters affect different subgroups (and their associated needs) or appropriately value the actual breadth of a community's capability. U.S. domestic programs rely on an initial assessment by local and state officials of physical damages to housing, public facilities, and infrastructure. If damages meet established per capita thresholds, a Presidential Disaster Declaration is issued. In practice (as discussed in the sidebar in Chapter 2 on "The Politics of Disaster"), the process has become highly politicized, leading to an increased number of declarations and rising public expectations regarding federal disaster

continued on page 216

continued from page 215

assistance programs.[1] Further, the declaration process triggers a series of uncoordinated, highly prescriptive federal programs that often fail to address gaps in local institutional capacity as identified by other members of the assistance network.

Political factors and institutional inertia influence the international system of disaster relief as well. U.S. assistance is filtered not only through USAID and OFDA but also through the Department of State, which helps to determine whether foreign regimes are appropriate recipients of assistance. As a result, the decision to provide assistance includes an additional level of scrutiny emphasizing international relationships rather than the needs of communities and individuals residing in afflicted areas. This has the added effect of hindering disaster diplomacy, as described earlier in this chapter.

The Organisation for Economic Co-operation and Development (OECD) provides the most of the international financing for humanitarian assistance, the bulk of which comes from the United States. An assessment by the British think tank, Overseas Development Institute, in 2000, uncovered significant inequities the OECD's practices, revealing that financial assistance often goes to high-profile events rather than being based on actual need.[2] In the United States, the delivery of assistance is also affected by factors unrelated to the level of damages—notably, the political acumen of leaders in an affected area; the influence of those leaders among federal agency officials, members of Congress, and the media; and the extent to which those leaders have access to and use of post-disaster data to clarify the needs of their communities.[3]

Finally, there is the issue of access to information to ensure the equitable allocation of resources. In the case of developing countries, state sovereignty may interfere with the ability of international organizations to gain access to the information needed to make wise decisions in this regard. Similarly, political leadership, existing membership in international networks and organizations, or armed conflict may dictate the manner in which external organizations can deliver the resources they have allocated. In the United States, on the other hand, allocating resources equitably depends on modifying existing institutions and delivery networks as described throughout this book.

disaster recovery assistance network, tend to underestimate the resources available in communities. As a result, the assistance that is provided may be more than is useable, may not complement indigenous resources, or may not be coupled with a strategy that increases the recipient's ability to accept and use it in a timely and coordinated manner.[44] In a study of recovery housing assistance in Turkey, for example, researchers found that the World Bank did not invest the time needed to gain a good understanding of local capacity or to invite assistance recipients to participate in the formulation of housing recovery plans.[45] The ability to recognize native resources, gained through ongoing dialogue among members of the international community and local assistance networks, allows for a more coordinated response and the delivery of targeted assistance that does not duplicate what the receiving nation already possesses or is able to obtain from others.

International organizations and national governments benefit from both established and emergent relationships with other members of the disaster

1 Rutherford Platt, *Disasters and Democracy: The Politics of Extreme Natural Events* (Washington, D.C.: Island Press, 1999).

2 Jonathan Walter, ed., *World Disasters Report: Focus on Ethics in Aid* (IFRC) (Bloomfield, Conn.: Kumarian Press, 2003), 20–22.

3 Gavin Smith, "Holistic Disaster Recovery: Creating a More Sustainable Future" (course developed for the Emergency Management Institute Higher Education Project, Federal Emergency Management Agency, 2004), available online at http://training.fema.gov/EMIWeb/edu/sdr.asp; Smith 2008).

recovery assistance network. Nonprofit organizations and charitable foundations are themselves often disaster assistance recipients that in turn help local communities and individuals. Assistance provided by or through institutions from within a country, particularly those institutions that have invested the time required to gain a good understanding of social and cultural conditions, is more likely to address local needs both before and after disasters (Figure 6–8).[46] In the same vein, the appropriate and effective delivery of technical assistance depends on creating conditions that foster dual experiential learning between the provider and the receiver. Finally, those receiving assistance should play a preeminent role in determining how resources should be applied to local problems.[47]

Timing of Assistance

Among the most challenging aspects of international assistance is overcoming the "disaster relief-recovery gap."[48] After a disaster, the immediate need is for humanitarian assistance: food, clothing, and shelter. Then, after basic survival needs have been met, attention turns to long-term recovery and reconstruction. Research suggests that the optimal time for the delivery of assistance is *before* an event occurs.[49] Indeed, with the advanced risk assessment tools now available, potential donors can evaluate pre-event vulnerability with increasing precision and provide targeted assistance in the form of direct monetary assistance and risk-transfer programs that are intended to reduce future losses.[50] This is the time when development goals and initiatives should be established. Then, in the post-event realm, the provision of humanitarian, recovery, and reconstruction assistance should complement those larger pre-event development goals and initiatives. After a disaster, as new information becomes available, preestablished and ongoing programs and projects may need to change; similarly, the initiation of any new

Figure 6–8. Temporary housing designed and built by Techo para Chile, a Catholic-supported nongovernmental organization, after the 2010 Chilean earthquake and tsunami. Techo para Chile provides houses that are free to occupants, constructed using volunteer labor, and located on donated sites. The 3x6 meter units, which cost about $400, are typically built in housing settlements of 30 to 40 dwellings. This unit is located in Constitución, Chile.

Photo by William Siembieda.

development programs will need to take into account their potential impact on the community's vulnerability to future hazards and post-disaster recovery operations.

In their book on post-disaster development, Mary B. Anderson and Peter J. Woodrow argue that the overriding factor driving international assistance should not be the speed of the response but rather the timeliness of it.[51] This applies to the delivery of funding and technical assistance (education, outreach, and training initiatives) as well as to policy counsel and the formulation of a broader recovery strategy. Funding can be counterproductive if it is ill-timed or provided to a government or organization that does not have an institutional framework to distribute it equitably. Education and training programs can help build the capacity of communities to become more self-reliant, but this requires that such assistance be delivered when a community is ready to accept it and capable of acting on it. Programs designed to link hazard mitigation techniques with potential development initiatives, or discussions about potential changes in pre-event settlement patterns after a disaster strikes, for example, should be initiated prior to a disaster and sustained as part of an ongoing program. In addition, policies should reflect the importance of timing and coordination across indigenous assistance networks during this process.

In the United States, the receipt of international assistance is hindered by the lack of pre-event plans and other agreements that establish the protocols needed to coordinate the type and timing of proffered resources with members of the U.S. disaster recovery assistance network. Prior to Hurricane Katrina, for example, there were very few mutual aid agreements or other types of resource-sharing protocols between international organizations, foreign countries, and the United States—the U.S. Navy and Canadian divers and the USACE and Dutch public works engineers being notable exceptions.

Developing new agreements or modifying existing ones takes time. Without a system to assess local needs and identify appropriate agencies capable of receiving assistance from foreign organizations, the ability to deliver different types of resources at the appropriate time or to modify requests as changing conditions warrant can be exceedingly difficult, and the receipt of such help may never occur.

Three obstacles stand in the way of streamlining the process whereby foreign assistance can be directed to appropriate recipients after a disaster in the United States. First, given the infrequency of disasters that elicit foreign assistance, the development of U.S. protocols to speed the receipt and delivery of foreign resources is less salient when compared to the oft-cited need to improve the existing federal system. Second, the creation of cooperative agreements with other nations and international organizations requires the involvement of U.S. diplomats, who also may have seemingly more pressing policy issues to address. Finally, establishing new cooperative agreements requires navigating the highly politicized world of international assistance, including the matters of disaster diplomacy and national sovereignty. Each of these challenges speaks to the importance of developing pre-disaster plans and associated agreements.

International organizations play an important role in pre-event capacity building in the developing world.[52] Understood relative to the needs of U.S. communities and the strengths of current assistance providers, select organizations could help educate federal, state, and local officials about the importance of linking sustainable development and disaster assistance, using international cases as examples of where this has been accomplished through planning. The importance of local capacity building, achieved through ongoing development practices (including planning), is certainly applicable to U.S. communities, particularly those with limited resources and high levels of social vulnerability. And good pre-event recovery planning can also be used to initiate agreements that position communities (and other nations) to receive the types of assistance they need in a timely and coordinated manner.

Horizontal and Vertical Integration

The U.S. disaster assistance framework does not sufficiently address coordination among international organizations and other nations involved in providing resources —including funding, technical assistance, or policy counsel—to the United States. Capitalizing on the resources of those external players requires expanding the prevalent definition of vertical integration in this country to include them. It also means modifying and expanding existing international agreements and resource-sharing protocols to address both the pre- and post-disaster environment.

Assistance may include information sharing and the formulation of strategies linking capacity building, sustainable development, and disaster recovery as well as financial and material resources. But for this assistance to be well-timed, equitably and efficiently distributed, and responsive to local needs, international organizations must be connected to U.S. government agencies and nonprofits, particularly those experienced in disaster recovery. In addition, the numerous long-standing informal international relationships and exchange programs that exist between quasi-governmental groups, particularly colleges and universities and professional associations, need to be nurtured and supported. All such existing institutional arrangements should be modified to reflect a new reality that positions the United States as a receiver and provider of assistance.

Establishing pre-event relationships with international relief organizations and developing plans with providers of long-term development aid should be part of a larger strategy to address the primary weakness in the U.S. system—namely, the lack of a pre-event capacity to plan not just for the distribution of assistance after a disaster but also for long-term recovery and reconstruction within the context of sustainable development. For example, appropriate assistance strategies require that those receiving resources participate in determining how those resources are to be applied to local problems.[53] Lacking an in-depth understanding of local needs, international organizations may choose to donate financial assistance—most commonly to nonprofits and foundations, which then distribute the funds to local communities and individuals, along with the flexibility to determine how those funds should be used (within the bounds of eligible activities if, in fact, agreements have been established that stipulate such activities). Without such a safeguard, international donors could make unrealistic demands on how the funds are used (as discussed in Chapter 4 regarding the timing of assistance delivered by foundations). With its expertise in linking sustainable development to disaster recovery, USAID can play an important role in sharing its experiences with the Federal Emergency Management Agency (FEMA), the Department of Housing and Urban Development, and U.S. Economic Development Administration, as well as with state and local government agencies involved in recovery and development programs.

The U.S. disaster assistance framework did not have such institutional arrangements in place prior to Hurricane Katrina.[54] After that event, FEMA and the State Department developed the International Assistance System Concept of Operations (IAS CONOPS). The procedural document establishes standard operating procedures for the request of international assistance, sets guidelines to assess the nature of assistance offered (as well as criteria for acceptance or declination), and describes the logistical measures that must be taken to receive and disburse the resources.[55] The degree to which IAS CONOPS is truly integrated into the larger U.S. assistance framework remains unclear, however, so it may face significant challenges once it is tested in the next major U.S. disaster.

The new approach has been incorporated into the National Response Framework (NRF) through two annexes: the International Coordination Support Annex and the Financial Management Support Annex. In this scenario, the State Department coordinates the distribution of international assistance in accordance with the needs identified by DHS and other federal agencies, while the Financial Management Support Annex follows federal resource tracking and accountability procedures. As developed after Hurricane Katrina, for instance, these processes began with the State Department receiving a donation (cash or otherwise) from another country. Once received, the donation was sent to the Hurricane Katrina Task Force, which is composed of representatives from the State Department, USAID, and OFDA. A National Security Council (NSC)–led working group, created to determine how the funds would be used,[56] decided to distribute the funds through FEMA. FEMA, however, asserted that any funds provided to it must be consistent with the provisions of the Stafford Act, thereby constraining their use. Debate among working group members over the issue of greater program flexibility ultimately delayed the release of the funds. In the meantime, the State Department lacked the statutory authority to allow the U.S. Treasury to credit the funds received by holding them in an interest-earning account. FEMA could have assumed this responsibility had it been provided the funds in the first place.

The Hurricane Katrina Task Force sought to improve horizontal integration across federal agencies and departments, with moderate success. While the interorganizational forum did provide a venue to discuss an adaptive resource distribution strategy, stakeholders, including FEMA, the State Department, and the Department of Defense were constrained by unclear lines of authority, narrow federal enabling legislation, and inadequate statutory authority.[57]

In an effort to improve coordination, USAID and the OFDA created a database to track the receipt and disbursement of foreign assistance. However, the program did not monitor whether the assistance was received at the FEMA distribution centers. The lack of guidance and planning also led to the acceptance of supplies, including food and medicine, that were ultimately denied use because they did not meet the standards of the USDA or the FDA. Finally, it was unclear whether the State Department or FEMA was responsible for accepting military assistance—each assuming the other had done so under its own gifting authorities.[58]

The degree to which the resource distribution process and financial management system are tied vertically to those on the ground following a disaster is also unclear and in need of further clarification, including a delineation of resources (i.e., funding, staffing, and training) needed to effectively implement this new policy in both the pre- and post-disaster environment. As noted in Chapter 3, the NRF does not adequately address recovery needs or provide suitable planning guidance. The most recent additions to the NRF focus on the means that the United States can use to improve receipt of cash donations. Much less attention has been paid to the receipt of other types of resources, including medical supplies, equipment, personnel, policy counsel, and other forms of technical assistance. Given the development of the National Disaster Recovery Framework (NDRF), it is critically important that procedures to improve the delivery and receipt of international assistance be incorporated into the evolving U.S. recovery assistance framework.

Incorporating international relief organizations into the U.S. disaster assistance framework also requires an understanding of those organizations—their unique strengths, their potential contributions, the goals and policies that define them, and the degree to which their resources can address identified domestic weaknesses. The stated goals of the Code of Conduct for the International Red Cross and Red Crescent Movement and NGOs in Disaster Relief[59] and the International Decade for Disaster Reduction[60] provide common themes that can help to shape how vertical and horizontal linkages are forged with U.S.-based partners and sustained over time.

In addition to broad conceptual principles used to frame action, new international agreements should include an increased emphasis on clearly defined assistance strategies that describe the means necessary, following major disasters, to provide wealthy nations with resources beyond what their own assistance networks can supply. In the United States, this could mean expanding the disaster declaration process and the rules associated with post-disaster resource distribution described in Chapter 3. In developed nations, however, protocols for "international disaster declarations" do not exist, nor are the types of assistance needed under different scenarios—or the best way to deliver them—adequately defined. It is imperative that efforts to establish such international agreements move beyond broad statements of intent and encompass specific tasks assigned to appropriate stakeholders in what should be more accurately considered an international disaster recovery assistance network. Such agreements should also provide a means for sharing specific resources, including funding strategies, technical assistance (training, local capacity building, and participatory planning), and policies that integrate disaster recovery and development. Ironically, this is an area in which the United States has engaged for some time through USAID with developing countries but seems reticent to embrace at home.

The development of international mutual aid agreements should draw on existing procedures already established within nations and include the organizations tasked with carrying them out. In the case of the United States, for example, the State Department, the Department of Defense, the Federal Reserve Bank, the NSC, USAID, FEMA, and others should be involved. The Hurricane Katrina Task Force or some other coordinative body should be further revisited and expanded to ensure the integration of U.S. agencies and others within the U.S. disaster recovery assistance network. Fostering the buy-in of the international community, including the International Strategy for Disaster Risk Reduction, the World Bank, the UN, the IMF, and WHO, is also important.

Among the most successful models for such an endeavor at the interstate level in the United States is the Emergency Management Assistance Compact (EMAC). Key elements of EMAC—for example, the development of pre-disaster agreements; the creation of large, geographically dispersed mutual aid networks; and the use of accepted resource typing protocols—could be applied to an international compact. Pre-event international resource typing protocols would allow participants to "speak the same language" regarding the contents of a resource package, the means to request it, and an evaluation of whether the resources meet identified needs. This will take time, however, as it requires the cooperation of nations and international organizations across the globe, working in tandem with their disaster recovery assistance networks.

In the developing world, pre-event relationships established through successful sustainable development projects demonstrate "linkages" between development and disaster recovery goals following disasters.[61] The sidebar on this page provides lessons regarding how horizontal and vertical linkages can be strengthened over time and used to facilitate the nexus between disaster recovery and development.

Incorporating the international community into the U.S. disaster assistance network adds another level of complexity to an already multifaceted system. The recommendations that follow offer specific suggestions as to how international

Horizontal and Vertical Integration in Monserrat before and after Hurricane Hugo

The small island nation of Monserrat, located in the eastern Caribbean, is home to about 12,000 people. Hurricane Hugo, which struck the area in 1989, caused major damages, affecting more than 98 percent of the homes on the island. The pre-event institutional framework, including the existence of pre-event disaster recovery plans, was limited. The National Disaster Plan that was in place at the time was focused almost exclusively on disaster response activities, with little emphasis on long-term recovery. Further hampering recovery efforts was the limited experience of government officials and local residents, with the important exception of the governor, who had experienced multiple storms in the past and played an important role in the early stages of recovery.[1] The relatively weak national plan and limited disaster experience among the other local officials resulted in a high level of dependency on external assistance. Since communities possessed low levels of social capital, they were unable to influence the direction of development efforts. Understood in the context of the horizontal and vertical linkage typology, Monserrat exhibited weak horizontal and strong vertical integration among participating organizations.

After Hurricane Hugo, several organizations joined together to deliver assistance. Led by the Canadian University Students Organization, a regional nonprofit with strong connectivity to foreign donors (namely, the Caribbean Conference of Churches), and a local community group, they formed a partnership to coordinate assistance delivery and develop recovery initiatives. Initially, work focused on housing-related assistance. Over time, an emphasis was placed on the strengthening of the community's organizational capacity to address development-related activities.[2] Specific actions included the initiation of new farming methods, construction of a community center, and improvements to the infrastructure responsible for distributing potable water. In the case of Monserrat, the disaster stimulated external and internal assistance, ultimately resulting in enhanced levels of post-disaster capacity and self-reliance, thereby increasing horizontal and vertical integration.

Source: The findings of this case study were drawn from "Monserrat: Recovery after Devastation," in After the Hurricane: Linking Recovery to Sustainable Development in the Caribbean, by Philip R. Berke and Timothy Beatley (Baltimore: Johns Hopkins University Press, 1997), 82–116.

1   Berke and Beatley, "Monserrat: Recovery after Devastation," 85.

2   Ibid., 93.

relief organizations and nations can be better integrated into the United States disaster recovery assistance framework in anticipation of major disasters like Hurricane Katrina as well as larger global catastrophes.

CONCLUSIONS AND RECOMMENDATIONS

The history of international assistance after a disaster has been dominated by the flow of resources from developed countries to the developing world. Foreign practitioners and scholars have often turned to the United States to learn the latest techniques, institutional frameworks, and policies associated with disaster management. But Hurricane Katrina reflected a breakdown in the U.S. response to and recovery from a major disaster—in part because of this nation's inability to accept needed pre- and post-disaster assistance from foreign governments and international organizations. Since then, foreigners have joined U.S. practitioners and scholars to figure out how a similar breakdown can be avoided in the future. Perhaps Hurricane Katrina and the growing threat of climate change (including the relationship between this global phenomenon and natural hazards) will awaken practitioners to adopt new strategies grounded in the lessons from countries other than the United States as well as to modify existing procedures in order to alter what has been a unidirectional flow of assistance from the United States to other nations.

1. Incorporate Lessons from the International Community

Members of the U.S. disaster recovery assistance network have largely failed to adopt lessons from the international community, including those routinely implemented by USAID, OFDA, and other U.S.-based organizations. Among the most important of these lessons is the need to strengthen links between disaster recovery, community self-reliance, and sustainable development, which can be accomplished through the use of planning and other capacity-building strategies. A comparison of U.S. domestic and international strategies provides insights into ways in which the U.S. disaster recovery assistance framework can be modified to better use external resources. The sharing of cross-cultural lessons becomes ever more essential as the world's economic, environmental, and sociopolitical systems become increasingly interconnected and interdependent, as evidenced by recent financial crises, climate change, and international terrorism.

What other lessons can the United States learn from other nations and international organizations that routinely deal with the provision of international disaster assistance, and how can it use these lessons to develop a more robust system capable of averting, or at least minimizing, the problems that occurred after Hurricane

Katrina? Further, how can these lessons be integrated into the U.S. disaster recovery assistance framework so that international assistance given to the United States meets local needs, is appropriately timed, and is effectively blended with other resources provided by domestic stakeholders?

Climate change–induced rises in sea level and the possibility of more intense hurricanes increase the likelihood that the United States—like other nations—will continue to experience catastrophic disasters requiring international assistance. According to the National Oceanic and Atmospheric Administration, 50 percent of the U.S. population currently lives in coastal counties.[62] The possible relocation of neighborhoods or the hardening of at-risk infrastructure in these areas will require resources of an unprecedented magnitude. Is the massive federal investment in the repair and strengthening of the levees in New Orleans an example of our response in the future? At what point will our adaptive strategies require the relocation of large urban areas, including major cities and their associated infrastructure? These policy choices are extraordinarily expensive and laden with conflict. The failure to adopt an integrative long-term plan that recognizes the important role that other nations can play in reducing the future impacts of disasters in this country will result in repeated episodic disaster-induced payouts of increasingly larger amounts and the inexorable, slow onset catastrophes of tomorrow.

The United States is one of the last developed countries in the world to clearly recognize and address the implications of climate change and the need to reduce greenhouse gas (GHG) emissions. Its unwillingness to sign the Kyoto Protocol and other, more recent international climate change agreements sends a strong message to other countries—a message that could bode poorly for the United States in the future (see the sidebar on page 226). However, recent findings of the International Panel on Climate Change (IPCC) and the 2008 election of Barack Obama may signal a reemergence of political support for science-based policy making. The news media routinely report on climate change studies, and a commitment to fund the scientific study of this phenomenon is growing. In addition, a number of plans and programs addressing climate change and its effects have emerged at the international, national, state, and local levels of government.

2. Institutionalize International Assistance through Recognized Agreements and Treaties

A key purpose of the UN is to facilitate peace and international cooperation through negotiated agreements, treaties, protocols, and other collaborative mechanisms. The development of peace-seeking actions is tied to the management of common resources and manifest in the law of the sea, international commerce, humanitarian assistance,

The Hyogo Framework for Action

In 2005, as part of the World Conference on Disaster Reduction held in Hyogo, Japan, 168 governments adopted the "Framework for Action 2005–2015: Building the Resilience of Nations and Communities to Disasters," commonly referred to as the Hyogo Framework. The agreement was built on the earlier "Yokohama Strategy for a Safer World: Guidelines for Natural Disaster Prevention, Preparedness, and Mitigation." The Hyogo Framework links sustainable development and disaster resilience through improved national and community-level capacity-building efforts. Its strategic goals are to

1. Ensure that disaster risk reduction is a national and a local priority with a strong institutional basis for implementation.

2. Identify, assess, and monitor disaster risks and enhance early warning.

3. Use knowledge, innovation, and education to build a culture of safety and resilience at all levels.

4. Reduce underlying risk factors.

5. Strengthen disaster preparedness for effective response at all levels.[1]

The broad goals stated in the Hyogo Framework are indicative of an underlying challenge—namely, to ensure that international agreements are implemented at the local or community level.

Source: *Hyogo Framework for Action 2005–2015: Building the Resilience of Nations and Communities to Disasters,* World Conference on Disaster Reduction, Kobe, Hyogo, Japan (Geneva: International Strategy for Disaster Reduction, 2005), www.unisdr.org/eng/hfa/docs/Hyogo-framework-for-action-english.pdf.
1   *Hyogo Framework for Action,* 6.

development, and the recent efforts to develop adaptive strategies to climate change. The finite supply of natural resources and their inequitable distribution, population growth in developing countries, and the emergence of new economic powers in Asia all present issues that have important implications for how the international community deals with disasters.

Improving the integration of international assistance in the U.S. disaster recovery assistance framework requires inviting additional strata of vertically integrated governance systems to the table—an outreach that requires pre-event planning and the formulation of international agreements and treaties. Enacting change among members of the international community is more likely to be achieved through recognized venues like the World Conference on Disaster Reduction and the Hyogo Framework. Although the unwillingness of the United States to support the more recent Kyoto Treaty, an international GHG emissions reduction program, has increased the level of distrust among other countries, the active participation of U.S. scientists and policy makers in the IPCC, as well as an increased commitment to this issue, may provide a basis for negotiating good-faith agreements that address the global nature of disasters. Such optimism is tempered, however, by the more recent influx of conservative members of the U.S. Congress, who discount the scientific basis of climate change—an indication of the continued politicization of this issue.

As a result, establishing efficient, effective, and equitable international agreements will require moving beyond the established positions of conflicting parties to identify mutual interests and using these findings to improve the cooperative networks, procedures, and plans that are currently in place in the United States. (The application of dispute resolution techniques to identified weaknesses in the disaster recovery assistance framework will be discussed in Chapter 8.) Cooperative planning at the international level means negotiating agreements tied to the reciprocal sharing of resources, including funding, technical assistance, and policy lessons. It also means developing actionable international plans that delineate roles and responsibilities for nations in both the developed and the developing world, as well as for international relief organizations and financial institutions such as the World Bank and IMF. Members of the U.S. assistance network must recognize that engaging with the global community requires taking a more holistic worldview that includes the active participation of other countries in major U.S. disasters.

In his book *Environmental Diplomacy: Negotiating More Effective Global Agreements*, Lawrence Susskind suggests that three weaknesses in international agreements limit their effectiveness: the North-South conflict, state sovereignty, and a lack of adequate incentives to bring parties to the bargaining table.[63] The North-South conflict has a long history. In the last couple of decades, this issue is perhaps most evident in the increasingly contentious debates over who should bear the costs associated with reducing GHG emissions. The deliberations surrounding global environmental protection, international development, and the delivery of pre- and post-disaster assistance all predate the climate change question and remain tied to two underlying issues, which Susskind refers to as "additionality" and "conditionality."[64]

Understood relative to disaster assistance, additionality refers to the question of whether the needed resources will be added to the development-related assistance that is already being provided to southern (or developing) nations. (While equating the South with developing nations and the North with developed nations does not fully capture the diversity of wealth and the nature of changing global economies, it is used for this purpose in order to match Susskind's terminology.) Conditionality refers to any requirements or stipulations that are tied to the delivery of assistance—typically, that provided by the North and given to the South. Interestingly, as the nexus between climate change and natural hazards grows, the ethical dimensions of this dilemma increase as well, more closely approximating earlier environmental conflicts between developed and developing nations. That is, the developed world is disproportionately responsible for environmental degradation tied to industrialization, yet expects the developing world to reduce pollutants and GHG emissions as part of a global initiative without reaping the economic benefits that have been accrued by the North throughout much of the 20th century when environmental regulations were more lax than they are today. In the case of the United States after Hurricane Katrina, the federal government struggled or simply refused post-disaster assistance if there were real or implied conditions associated with it. This was particularly true in the case of developing countries whose political ties to the United States had been strained before the event.

International agreements must also balance the ability to act collectively with issues of state sovereignty. This balancing act often results in weak monitoring and enforcement procedures.[65] The ability to create an oversight body charged with directing independent nations to act in a coordinated manner can be achieved if, in fact, nations recognize the value and benefits of doing so and are allowed to engage on a voluntary basis. Creating appropriate incentives to bargain is a major challenge in a global system of nations, many of which may not see the value of participating. The ability to incentivize cooperative behavior now, even though the benefits of participation may not accrue in the immediate future, adds additional challenges, particularly among elected officials who must seek reelection on a much shorter time scale.[66]

Perhaps the benefits of developing agreements that link more frequently occurring episodic events like disasters with the relatively slow onset impacts of climate change can provide appropriate incentives for the United States to participate in multinational problem solving. The Hurricane Katrina experience demonstrates that no nation is immune from the need for international disaster assistance. Interestingly, it is *Our Common Future*, the report published by the World Commission on Environment and Development, commonly referred to as the Brundtland Commission in 1987,[67] which is widely credited with capturing the attention of U.S. hazard scholars and practitioners, prompting their embrace of the linkage between natural hazard risk reduction and the larger concept of sustainable development.[68] It is apparent that now is the time to recommit to a meaningful global dialogue that more effectively address the threats associated with climate change, both abroad and on our own shores.

3. Modify U.S. Domestic and International Relief Policies and Programs to Facilitate the Receipt of Foreign Assistance before and after Disasters

Looking back through history, the United States has in fact received assistance from other countries following major disasters. Japan provided assistance after the 1906 San Francisco earthquake, and many other nations provided resources following the Johnstown flood of 1889, the Galveston hurricane of 1900, and several other large-scale events. But the advent of a more robust federal emergency management system fueled a growing confidence that the United States needed no help in dealing with any disaster that occurred on U.S. soil, and the nation's policies have reflected this perception.

When a disaster strikes another nation, the United States often responds with substantial financial and technical assistance. USAID, for instance, may stay in the country for many years, assisting it and its communities with recovery efforts that include not only reconstructing housing and infrastructure but also rebuilding the social capital and economic system needed to strengthen self-sufficiency. In addition to USAID, the UN is especially well positioned to help developing nations build local capacity. The techniques used by these two organizations should be modified to address emerging disaster recovery issues in the United States as well as in other nations and codified through recognized agreements with the international community.

Hurricane Katrina, a watershed event in so many ways, brought home the reality that the United States is not immune to disasters that exceed its capacity and thereby uncovered glaring weaknesses in the U.S. disaster recovery assistance framework. And the nation has recognized the need to address its deficiencies, as evidenced by the formation of the Hurricane Katrina Task Force and the development of the NRF annexes. Yet further review reveals a need for a more extensive overhaul. The prescriptive rules underlying the Stafford Act—legislation that reflects a series of narrowly defined grant programs and policies that are intended to address smaller disasters, not those of the magnitude of Hurricane Katrina—hinder the ability of FEMA and the Katrina task force to target specific local needs that surface following an event, not to mention a number of issues associated with long-term recovery, such as pre-event planning, economic redevelopment, and the reconstitution of social networks.

In the United States, pre-event capacity building programs receive little funding. Post-disaster, there is a limited emphasis placed on linking recovery efforts to sustainable development—other than those attempts by Emergency Support Function 14, which remains severely underfunded and understaffed. The pre-disaster delivery of technical assistance should be more closely aligned with institutionalized yet flexible capacity-building efforts.[69] This may be achieved through training, education, and coalition-building initiatives. Policy makers in USAID and the UN should be tapped to help transfer the lessons from the developing world to the U.S. disaster recovery assistance network and the emerging NRDF (see Chapter 10).

4. Institutionalize Lessons through Cross-Cultural Study and Policy Analysis

Hazard scholars regularly discuss the importance of cross-cultural research, the lessons it provides within and beyond the United States, and the need to pursue this type of inquiry more aggressively.[70] The experiences of those providing disaster assistance in other nations offer a number of insights, many of which go to the heart of the problems underlying the U.S. system.

For instance, relief organizations and others mistakenly believe that the federal government is the principal provider of assistance to communities; in fact, the private sector—through insurance, loans, and private capital—is a far greater source of post-disaster funds. Similarly, most U.S. international assistance in recent years has come from corporations and businesses, foundations, and faith-based organizations rather than from government. According to Henrietta H. Fore, the former administrator of USAID, about 80 percent of the funding provided by the United States to developing countries comes from the private sector, which necessitates developing stronger relationships with these organizations and incorporating them into recovery plans, protocols, and agreements.[71]

Unfortunately, the lessons identified by hazard scholars often fail to be widely disseminated and adopted by practitioners.[72] With the focus on climate change, however, there is some evidence that this is beginning to change. It is important to note that climate change scientists (and some political figures) have led this shift in thinking. As noted in Chapter 4, the research community has played an important role in helping to push the concept of hazard mitigation in the United States, leading to the eventual passage of the Disaster Mitigation Act in 2000. But while disaster and development scholars have made strides in their mutual understanding of and respect for one another's work, there remain significant differences in terminology, theory, and the practical application of knowledge.[73] Similar problems are evident in the hazards management and climate change adaptation community. However, the IPCC and a growing number of scholars continue to underscore the connection between natural hazards management and climate change adaptation.[74]

It is incumbent upon those who are focused on the development of climate change adaptation plans to coordinate their activities with natural hazard scholars and practitioners. Hazards researchers have created an extensive body of knowledge that is directly applicable to this issue. Specific examples include an analysis of the social, economic, institutional, and legal influences on the adoption of land use planning and other risk reduction tools; the underlying conditions that foster the formation of supportive policy coalitions; and the need to communicate risk to various segments of society. Conversely, those involved in developing hazard mitigation and disaster recovery plans also stand to gain by working with those individuals involved in developing climate change adaptation plans as these plans are more apt to rely on planners and members of the environmental community, two groups with important but often untapped connectivity to issues surrounding natural hazards.

The climate change/natural hazards connection provides a unique opportunity to act. Worldwide discussions about the need to formulate coastal adaptation strategies in the face of rising seas merge development and sustainability themes. There is a growing recognition of the need to adopt a long-term focus, including changes in human settlement patterns and the selective abandonment of associated infrastructure. U.S. politicians, hazard scholars, and practitioners need to find ways to link these discussions with the ongoing dialogue associated with planning for more episodically occurring disasters and to proactively take steps to reduce their impacts. The Disaster Mitigation Act and policies that are still emerging, such as the NDRF, need to be implemented in tandem with new national climate change policies, plans, and international agreements.

We also need to transfer what we know about convergence in long-term recovery (much of which has been learned through cross-cultural study) to the development of improved systems in the United States before a catastrophic disaster occurs here that causes the United States to become highly dependent on other nations and international organizations. The very idea of this eventuality is foreign to many as the U.S. governance structure and substantial wealth has provided the luxury of self-determination. The assumption that the United States does not need to consider or plan for a situation in which a disaster exceeds its own means is folly. A massive earthquake in Los Angeles, San Francisco, or along the New Madrid fault near Memphis, Tennessee, would cause unprecedented damages, as would a series of major hurricanes striking Miami or New York City. Slow onset events like sea level rise along U.S. coastlines, a multidecade drought in America's food-producing regions, or significant rise in annual mean temperatures also require a new way of thinking, particularly given existing large-scale investments in public infrastructure and human settlements that reflect current climatic conditions, not necessarily those of tomorrow.

The federal government is developing catastrophic planning scenarios to prepare for and respond to many of these events, but the scenarios do not sufficiently address recovery, especially in light of the unique social, economic, and environmental impacts that will occur.[75] The reluctance to plan for long-term recovery suggests that there is a continued need for strong advocates arguing on behalf of improved disaster recovery planning initiatives. In the case of catastrophic disasters, the effective, efficient, and equitable distribution of assistance will depend on the pre-event development of strategies specifically designed to enable U.S. communities to benefit from the resources offered by other nations and international organizations.

5. Establish a Clear Nexus between Planning and International Assistance

Recognition of the linkage between post-disaster assistance and sustainable development principles remains confined to hazard scholars and a small number of agencies, nonprofits, foundations, professional associations, and progressive communities. At present there is no national strategy that provides the impetus for interorganizational collaboration focused on this goal, let alone the means to achieve it. Attaching annexes to the NRF as a way to improve the receipt of international assistance has serious limitations. In its current form, the NRF does not possess the characteristics of a plan; rather, it more closely represents a series of disjointed grant programs and policies. The NRF also fails to adequately address issues related to long-term recovery, including those identified in the U.S. disaster assistance framework. Thus, any attempt to rely on the NRF as a means to coordinate international assistance must first address these deficiencies. In fact, the creation of international annexes that address recovery issues should instead be incorporated into the NDRF.

While a significant amount of research in disaster recovery has focused on industrialized societies,[76] the work being done in developing countries provides important insights. Cross-cultural studies evaluating pre- and post-disaster recovery planning can help inform U.S. policy. Their findings strongly support the value of developing and implementing recovery plans, involving a broad network of stakeholders in the formulation of these plans, and creating strategies that meet local needs.

Experts have long equated improving the U.S. disaster recovery assistance framework with fixing federal recovery programs. This outdated notion fails to acknowledge the scale of the problem and the roles of other members of the assistance network, including the growing importance of foreign assistance. A primary way to address these shortcomings is to improve the level of pre-event planning that occurs among nations and organizations responsible for the administration of programs, particularly those that embrace the linkage between sustainable development and recovery. Agreements between the U.S. government, other nations, and organizations that distribute international relief should specify how post-disaster assistance is to be provided to federal, state, and local recipients. The gaps and weaknesses that have been identified in the U.S. disaster assistance framework can serve as an initial guide.

At the federal level, the NDRF should be used to improve the linkage between assistance offered by other nations, international organizations, and USAID, building on the work started following Hurricane Katrina. A concerted effort should be made to identify gaps in programs provided by the U.S. disaster recovery assistance network so that federal officials and other stakeholders can inform international donors in advance regarding the types of assistance that are most likely to be needed. The typing of international assistance could help to more clearly define the resources in question that may be available. The proposed expansion of EMAC to include international mutual aid is worthy of further study. After a disaster occurs, international organizations should also be poised to assist with unexpected needs that emerge, assuming that adequate steps have been taken to use approaches other than those that rely excessively on the NRF, Stafford Act, and State Department protocols.

State plans should emphasize the coordination of available resources and help inform the NDRF and USAID about unmet needs. State capability assessments (described further in Chapter 8) should evaluate not only state-level programs but also programs available from international organizations, federal agencies, quasi-governmental organizations, nonprofits, and the private sector. For example, state departments of commerce often interact with other nations during trade missions and industry recruitment efforts. These relationships may be useful when dealing with other countries following a major disaster. Multinational corporations may maintain strong relationships with foreign governments and sometimes with those communities in which they are located. If a disaster strikes a state in which they have offices or plants, they might be willing to leverage their relationships with both groups to provide financial or other assistance in tandem with their national government.

Recovery plans developed at the local level provide the means to clarify needs before and after a disaster. Such clarification enables potential donors, including international relief organizations and other nations, to address those needs that they are uniquely suited to tackle. Central to this effort should be helping communities and other members of the assistance network to develop the capacity to plan for recovery in a broader developmental context. The international community has done some of the best work linking the delivery of assistance to local needs. Its approach recognizes the importance of creating the conditions in which individuals play a role in shaping their future since those living in developing countries often do not have the luxury of relying on a wealthy government. This reality can also play out in the United States, particularly when resources prove inadequate to address the magnitude of local needs following catastrophic events. For instance, it was the concerted efforts of architect David Waggonner that ultimately convinced the Royal Netherlands Embassy in Washington, D.C., and the American Planning Association to assist him in implementing the Dutch Dialogues concept. This important juxtaposition of responsibility (which is unaccounted for in the formal recovery policy milieu) is part of the critically important role that individuals and emergent groups play in the disaster recovery assistance network.

Endnotes

1   George Haddow and Jane Bullock, *Introduction to Emergency Management* (Boston: Butterworth-Heinemann, 2003), 165; National Research Council, *Facing Hazards and Disasters: Understanding Human Dimensions* (Washington, D.C.: National Academies Press, 2006), 216.

2   J. M. Albala-Bertrand, "Globalization and Localization: An Economic Approach," in *Handbook of Disaster Research,* ed. Havidan Rodriguez, Enrico L. Quarantelli, and Russell Dynes, 147–167 (New York: Springer, 2006).

3   Barbara E. Harrell-Bond, *Imposing Aid: Emergency Assistance to Refugees* (Oxford: Oxford University Press, 1986); Anthony Oliver-Smith and Roberta Goldman, "Planning Goals and Urban Realities: Post-Disaster Reconstruction in a Third World City," *City and Society* 2, no. 2 (1988): 67–79.

4   Frederick C. Cuny, *Disasters and Development* (Oxford: Oxford University Press, 1983); Philip R. Berke and Timothy Beatley, *After the Hurricane: Linking Recovery to Sustainable Development in the Caribbean* (Baltimore: Johns Hopkins University Press, 1997); International Federation of Red Cross and Red Crescent Societies (IFRC), *Strategy 2010* (Geneva, Switzerland: IFRC, 2000), available at www.ifrc.org/publicat/s2010/; Iolanda Jaquemet, "Post-Flood Recovery in Viet Nam," in *World Disasters Report 2001: Focus on Recovery,* 102–123 (Geneva, Switzerland: IFRC, 2001); Yuko Nakagawa and Rajib Shaw, "Social Capital: A Missing Link to Disaster Recovery," *International Journal of Mass Emergencies and Disasters* 22, no. 1 (2004): 5–34; Jeffrey D. Garnett and Melinda Moore, "Enhancing Disaster Recovery: Lessons from Exemplary International Disaster Management Practices," *Journal of Homeland Security and Emergency Management* 7, no. 1 (2010): 1–20.

5   Maureen Fordham, "Disaster and Development Research and Practice: A Necessary Eclecticism?" in *Handbook of Disaster Research,* 335–346 (see note 2).

6   Melinda Moore et al., "Learning from Exemplary Practices in International Disaster Management: A Fresh Avenue to Inform U.S. Policy?" *Journal of Homeland Security and Emergency Management* 6, no. 1 (2009).

7   Eugene Haas, Robert W. Kates, and Martyn J. Bowden, *Reconstruction following Disaster* (Cambridge: MIT Press, 1977); Philip Berke, Timothy Beatley, and Clarence Feagin, "Hurricane Gilbert Strikes Jamaica: Linking Disaster Recovery to Development," *Coastal Management* 21, no. 1 (1993): 1–23; Daniel P. Aldrich, "The Crucial Role of Civil Society in Disaster Recovery and Japan's Preparedness for Emergencies," *Japan aktuell* 3 (March 2008): 81–96.

8   Robert Geipel, *Disaster and Reconstruction: The Friuli (Italy) Earthquakes of 1976* (London: Allen and Unwin, 1982); T. Cannon, "Vulnerability Analysis and the Explanation of 'Natural' Disasters," in *Disasters, Development and Environment,* ed. Ann Varley, 13–40 (London: Wiley, 1994); J. M. Albala-Bertrand, *The Political Economy of Large Natural Disasters, with Special Reference to Developing Countries* (New York: Clarendon Press, 1993); Anthony Oliver-Smith and Susanna M. Hoffman, *The Angry Earth: Disaster in Anthropological Perspective* (New York: Routledge, 1999); Virginia Garcia-Acosta, "Disaster Research," in *Catastrophe and Culture: The Anthropology of Disaster,* ed. Susanna Hoffman and Anthony Oliver-Smith, 49–66 (Santa Fe, N.M.: School of American Research Press, 2002).

9   Mary B. Anderson and Peter Woodrow, *Rising from the Ashes: Development Strategies in Times of Disaster* (Boulder, Colo.: Westview Press, 1989).

10 Stephanie E. Chang, "Urban Disaster Recovery: A Measurement Framework and Its Application to the 1995 Kobe Earthquake," *Disasters* 34, no. 2 (2009): 303–327.

11 Geipel, *Disaster and Reconstruction;* Oliver-Smith and Goldman, "Planning Goals and Urban Realities"; Berke and Beatley, *After the Hurricane;* Anthony Oliver-Smith, "Post-Disaster Housing Reconstruction and Social Inequality: A Challenge to Policy and Practice," *Disasters* 14, no. 1 (1990): 7–19; Robert B. Olshansky, Laurie A. Johnson, and Kenneth C. Topping, "Rebuilding Communities following Disaster: Lessons from Kobe and Los Angeles," *Built Environment* 32, no 4 (2006): 354–374.

12 Oliver-Smith, "Post-Disaster Housing Reconstruction."

13 Geipel, *Disaster and Reconstruction.*

14   Harrell-Bond, *Imposing Aid;* Anderson and Woodrow, *Rising from the Ashes.*

15   U.S. Government Accountability Office (GAO), *Hurricane Katrina: Comprehensive Policies and Procedures Are Needed to Ensure Appropriate Use of and Accountability for International Assistance,* GAO-06-460 (Washington, D.C., April 6, 2006), www.gao.gov/new.items/d06460.pdf (accessed February 7, 2011).

16   Jorgen Lissner, *The Politics of Altruism: A Study of the Political Behavior of Development Agencies* (Geneva, Switzerland: Lutheran World Federation, 1977).

17   Clark C. Gibson et al., *The Samaritan's Dilemma: The Political Economy of Development Aid* (Oxford: Oxford University Press, 2009).

18   Ahmed A. Karadawi, "Constraints on Assistance to Refugees: Some Observations from the Sudan," *World Development* 11, no. 6 (1983): 537–547.

19   Anne C. Richard, "Katrina Aid: When the World Wanted to Help America," *New York Times,* August 30, 2006, www.nytimes.com/2006/08/30/opinion/30iht-edrichard.2642650.html (accessed February 7, 2011).

20   Ilan Kelman, "Acting on Disaster Diplomacy," *Journal of International Affairs* 59, no. 2 (2006): 215–240; Ilan Kelman, "Hurricane Katrina Disaster Diplomacy," *Disasters* 31, no. 3 (2007): 288–309.

21   Ilan Kelman, "Disaster Diplomacy: Can Tragedy Help Build Bridges among Countries?" *UCAR Quarterly* (Fall 2007): 6.

22   Rutherford Platt, *Disasters and Democracy: The Politics of Extreme Natural Events* (Washington, D.C.: Island Press, 1999); Thomas A. Birkland, *After Disaster, Agenda Setting, Public Policy, and Focusing Events* (Washington, D.C.: Georgetown University Press, 1997); Thomas A. Birkland, *Lessons of Disaster: Policy Change after Catastrophic Events* (Washington, D.C.: Georgetown University Press, 2006); Naomi Klein, *The Shock Doctrine: The Rise of Disaster Capitalism* (New York: Henry Holt and Company, 2007); Richard Sylves, *Disaster Policy and Politics: Emergency Management and Homeland Security* (Washington, D.C.: CQ Press, 2008); William R. Freudenberg et al., *Catastrophe in the Making: The Engineering of Katrina and the Disasters of Tomorrow* (Washington, D.C.: Island Press, 2009).

23   Mary Murray, "Katrina Aid from Cuba? No Thanks, Says U.S.," *MSNBC.com,* September 14, 2005, http://www.msnbc.com/id/9311876/ (accessed November 11, 2010).

24   Erik Larson, *Isaac's Storm: A Man, a Time, and the Deadliest Hurricane in History* (New York: Vintage Books, 1999), 102–108.

25   Kelman, "Hurricane Katrina Disaster Diplomacy"; Kelman, "Disaster Diplomacy."

26   Robert C. Bolin and Patricia A. Bolton, "Recovery in Nicaragua and the USA," *International Journal of Mass Emergencies and Disasters* 1, no. 1 (1983): 125–144.

27   Charles E. Fritz and J. H. Mathewson, *Convergence Behavior in Disasters* (Washington, D.C.: National Academy of Sciences/National Research Council, 1957); Jack D. Kartez and Michael K. Lindell, "Adaptive Planning for Community Disaster Response," in *Cities and Disaster: North American Studies in Emergency Management,* ed. Richard T. Sylves and William. L. Waugh, 5–31 (Springfield, Ill.: Charles C. Thomas, 1990).

28   Richard, "Katrina Aid"; John Solomon and Spencer S. Hsu, "U.S. Refused Most Offers of Aid for Hurricane Katrina," *New York Sun,* April 30, 2007, http://www.nysun.com/national/us-refused-most-offers-of-aid-for-hurricane/53433/ (accessed October 18, 2010); Citizens for Responsibility and Ethics in Washington (CREW), "CREW Releases Report Detailing International Assistance Offers in Wake of Hurricane Katrina," July 27, 2006, at www.citizensforethics.org/node/29651 (accessed February 7, 2011).

29   Frances F. Townsend, *The Federal Response to Hurricane Katrina: Lessons Learned* (Washington, D.C.: The White House, February 2006).

30   Richard, "Katrina Aid"; CREW, "Report Detailing International Assistance Offers."

31   Oliver-Smith and Goldman, "Planning Goals and Urban Realities."

32 Andrew Maskrey, *Disaster Mitigation: A Community-based Approach* (Oxford, England: Oxfam Professional, 1989).

33 James Mitchell and Abram Bernstein, eds., *Toward a Less Hazardous World: A Proposal to Establish an International Decade of Hazard Reduction,* interim report (Washington, D.C.: National Academy of Sciences, 1987).

34 Berke and Beatley, *After the Hurricane;* Charlotte Benson and John Twigg, *Tools for Mainstreaming Disaster Risk Reduction: Guidance Notes for Development Organisations* (Geneva, Switzerland: Provention Consortium, 2007).

35 Albala-Bertrand, *Political Economy of Large Natural Disasters,* 202.

36 Michael K. Lindell, Carla Prater, and Ronald W. Perry, *Introduction to Emergency Management* (Hoboken, N.J.: John Wiley & Sons, 2007), 422.

37 Asian Disaster Preparedness Center, "ADPC Strategy Plan 2010," www.adpc.net/v2007/About%20Us/STRATEGIC%20PLAN%202010/Default-STRATEGIC.asp (accessed October 18, 2010).

38 International Monetary Fund (IMF), "Factsheet: IMF Emergency Assistance: Supporting Recovery from Natural Disasters and Armed Conflicts" (September 15, 2010), www.imf.org/external/np/exr/facts/conflict.htm (accessed October 18, 2010).

39 Cuny, *Disasters and Development.*

40 Jonathan Walter, ed., *World Disasters Report: Focus on Ethics in Aid* (IFRC) (Bloomfield, Conn.: Kumarian Press, 2003), 22.

41 Cuny, *Disasters and Development;* Harrell-Bond, *Imposing Aid.*

42 IFRC, *Code of Conduct for the International Red Cross and Red Crescent Movement and NGOs in Disaster Relief* (Geneva, Switzerland: IFRC, 1994).

43 Anderson and Woodrow, *Rising from the Ashes;* Gavin Smith and Dennis Wenger, "Sustainable Disaster Recovery: Operationalizing an Existing Agenda," in *Handbook of Disaster Research,* ed. Havidan Rodriguez, Enrico Quarantelli, and Russell Dynes, 234–257 (New York: Springer, 2006).

44 Cuny, *Disasters and Development;* Anderson and Woodrow, *Rising from the Ashes.*

45 N. Emel Ganapati and Sukumar Ganapati, "Enabling Participatory Planning after Disasters: A Case Study of the World Bank's Housing Reconstruction in Turkey," *Journal of the American Planning Association* 75, no. 1 (2009): 41–59.

46 Cuny, *Disasters and Development.*

47 Anderson and Woodrow, *Rising from the Ashes.*

48 Jonathan Walter, ed., *World Disasters Report: Focus on Recovery* (IFRC) (Bloomfield, Conn.: Kumarian Press, 2001), 9–12.

49 Frederick Cuny and Eduardo Perez, *Improvement of Low-Cost Housing in Fiji to Withstand Hurricanes and High Winds* (Washington, D.C.: Office of Foreign Disaster Assistance, U.S. Agency for International Development, 1982); Cuny, *Disasters and Development.*

50 Joanne Linnerooth-Bayer, Reinhard Mechler, and Georg Pflug, "Refocusing Disaster Aid," *Science* 309 (August 2005): 1044–1046.

51 Anderson and Woodrow, *Rising from the Ashes.*

52 Cuny, *Disasters and Development.*

53 Anderson and Woodrow, *Rising from the Ashes.*

54 GAO, *Hurricane Katrina.*

55 Ibid.

56 Ibid.

57 Ibid.

58 Ibid.

59 See "Code of Conduct for NGOs in Disaster Relief" at www.gdrc.org/ngo/codesofconduct/ifrc-codeconduct.html (accessed January 30, 2011).

60 See the website of the International Strategy for Disaster Reduction at www.fire.uni-freiburg.de/programmes/un/idndr/idndr.html (accessed January 30, 2011).

61 Berke and Beatley, *After the Hurricane.*

62 National Oceanic and Atmospheric Administration (NOAA), National Ocean Service, *Population Trends along the Coastal United States: 1980–2008* (Washington, D.C.: NOAA 2005).

63 Lawrence Susskind, *Environmental Diplomacy: Negotiating More Effective Global Agreements* (New York: Oxford University Press, 1994), 18–24.

64 Ibid., 18–19.

65 Ibid., 21.

66 Ibid., 23.

67 World Commission on Environment and Development, *Our Common Future (The Brundtland Report)* (New York: Oxford University Press, 1987).

68 Timothy Beatley, "The Vision of Sustainable Communities," in *Cooperating with Nature: Confronting Natural Hazards with Land-Use Planning for Sustainable Communities,* ed. Raymond J. Burby, 233–262 (Washington, D.C.: Joseph Henry Press, 1998).

69 Ganapati and Ganapati, "Enabling Participatory Planning after Disasters."

70 Dennis Mileti, *Disasters by Design: A Reassessment of Natural Hazards in the United States* (Washington, D.C.: Joseph Henry Press, 1999), 261–263; National Research Council, *Facing Hazards and Disasters: Understanding Human Dimensions* (Washington, D.C.: National Academies Press, 2006), 239–242.

71 Beth McMurtrie, "Universities Look to Obama to Expand Their Role in Development Abroad," *Chronicle of Higher Education,* January 23, 2009, A25.

72 Mileti, *Disasters by Design*, 261–263.

73 Fordham, "Disaster and Development Research and Practice."

74 Jane Bicknell, David Dodman, and David Satterthwaite, *Adapting Cities to Climate Change: Understanding and Addressing the Development Challenges* (London: Earthscan, 2009); E. Lisa F. Schipper and Ian Burton, *The Earthscan Reader on Adaptation to Climate Change* (London: Earthscan, 2009).

75 Gavin Smith, "Lessons from the United States: Planning for Post-Disaster Recovery and Reconstruction," *Australasian Journal of Disaster and Trauma Studies* 2010–1 (2010), www.massey.ac.nz/~trauma/issues/2010-1/smith.htm (accessed July 9, 2010).

76 Alcira Kreimer and Mohan Munasinghe, eds., *Managing Natural Disasters and the Environment* (Washington, D.C.: World Bank, 1991).

Chapter 7

Individuals and Emergent Groups

Five years after Hurricane Katrina, a young girl from the Broadmoor neighborhood of New Orleans poses with her dog. While children often exhibit great resilience following a disaster, they can experience significant psychological trauma manifested in nightmares, anger, an inability to concentrate, and fear of leaving their family.

Photo by Donn Young.

WHEN IT COMES TO IDENTIFYING local needs, individuals and emergent groups are perhaps the most informed members of the assistance network. The resources they possess, particularly when aggregated, amount to a substantial base of locally grounded knowledge that provides a unique perspective on recovery policies and plans both before and after disasters and can thus play an important role in addressing community-level needs. Yet because these resources are not always recognized by others in the network, this wealth of knowledge is not systematically collected through participatory procedures that effectively engage individuals and emergent groups, whose input into disaster response and recovery initiatives is thus often unsolicited or overlooked. Moreover, the degree to which individuals and emergent groups can access other resources in the pre- and post-disaster environment is closely associated with their levels of socially constructed hazard vulnerability.[1] The failure to address this issue before a disaster occurs can limit the reciprocal exchange of information between those who are most vulnerable and those who administer post-disaster grant programs and other forms of assistance. This, in turn, can lead to the imposition of assistance rather than to the crafting of flexible programs that are capable of addressing a diverse set of needs.

Given the knowledge base and abundant resources of individuals and emergent groups, it is critically important that the larger network involve these stakeholders in decisions regarding resource allocation strategies and planning, help them voice their needs and those of the community, and share with them the collective knowledge of the network to help them make more informed decisions. Such two-way communication can be especially beneficial when members of the assistance network are assessing and communicating hazard risk, crafting recovery policies, and engaging in pre-event planning for post-disaster recovery. But any such exchange of ideas requires that all parties be able to understand and articulate local needs, particularly those that are not adequately addressed by established programs, policies, and plans.

REDEFINING INDIVIDUALS: MORE THAN A DISASTER VICTIM

Disasters are often seen as uncontrollable forces and described as "acts of God." But framing disasters in this way—as some in the media, government officials, and other members of the assistance network tend to do—perpetuates the notion of individuals as "victims" imbued with a sense of helplessness and in need of routine external assistance. Apart from the fact that this perspective influences the type and quantity of assistance provided,[2] focusing on victimization effectively discounts the many important ways that people—including those characterized as disenfranchised—undertake adaptive strategies both before and after external resources arrive.[3] In isolated communities and localities in the developing world, for example, where few formal organizations engage in hazards management, individuals and communities work together to reduce their own vulnerability as a necessary part of daily life. Non-disaster-specific examples of this phenomenon include subsistence agriculture, the construction of temporary housing, and the adoption of a nomadic lifestyle. These actions are in some ways indicative of a socially resilient community, albeit one without a supportive system of formal governance strategies.

Individuals are often the first providers of assistance following a disaster.[4] This is particularly true in developing countries where people are more likely to rely on families, neighbors, and volunteers for assistance than on government.[5] In the immediate aftermath of a disaster, it is well known that individuals are primary participants in a number of activities, including search and rescue, sheltering, and feeding operations. In recovery research, the study of individuals and families has focused largely on their ability to obtain disaster assistance to meet their own needs. Less is understood about the role of individuals in the larger disaster recovery assistance network.

Not surprisingly, post-disaster conditions create significant psychological stress for people (see Figure 7–1). In the immediate aftermath of an event, individuals must confront a series of issues in rapid succession, including the need to identify food and appropriate shelter, assess damages to personal property, and determine whether family members and friends have been injured or killed. During the recovery process, individuals must deal with the possible loss of their job, the repair of their home (or the identification of a new one), and an array of confusing programs each with different sets of rules and eligibility criteria.

Further contributing to the stress is that individuals, community officials, and the media are routinely surprised by the length of time it takes to receive assistance and the inability to coordinate the flow of information across programs. However, post-disaster conditions also elicit positive, adaptive responses. In a study of the recovery process from a tornado in Paris, Texas, Robert Bolin and Patricia Bolton found that although individuals became highly impatient with the assistance process, they also enjoyed increased family happiness and strengthened family relationships, as well as a decreased emphasis on the importance on material possessions.[6] Similarly, Susanna Hoffman notes that once the initial shock of a disaster subsides, people often feel a "higher purpose," which moves them to address new problems in a purposeful manner.[7] Robert Bolin and Patricia Trainer note that individuals and households recovering from a disaster rely on a combination of autonomous, kinship, and institutional sources.[8] Autonomous recovery involves the use of existing household resources, including financial, material, and individual skills and abilities. Occupants of a household may use

Figure 7–1. A resident returns to the 9th Ward in New Orleans after Hurricane Katrina to find his home destroyed.

Photo by Donn Young.

personal savings to pay for the repair of their damaged home, or they may have the skills and physical capacity needed to remove disaster-strewn debris and repair or reconstruct their dwelling themselves.

Kinship recovery involves receiving assistance from family, friends, or associates who are willing and able to provide it. Characteristics that influence the amount and type of assistance delivered to others include age, health, knowledge, skills, past disaster experience, and geographic proximity to the disaster. A person's willingness and ability to help a family member, neighbor, or friend are influenced by the damages sustained to his or her own property and the trauma and injuries he or she has received as well as by potential risks during the delivery of these services.

Institutional recovery includes assistance provided by organizations in the disaster assistance network. The ability of individuals to obtain help often requires repeated interaction with providers, particularly government agencies. Nonprofit organizations from within and beyond the community, foundations, insurance companies, banks and other financial institutions, private contractors, emergent groups, and the media also play a role in disaster recovery. Trying to make sense of information transmitted through these organizations can be overwhelming, and past disaster experience may influence a person's ability to decipher the rules, timing, and distributional channels through which such help is provided. While some organizations, including nonprofits and emergent groups, have fewer rules and attempt to address the unmet needs of individuals, the ability to obtain assistance from them is uncertain as the horizontal and vertical linkages between these groups and other members of the assistance network is often tenuous.[9]

EMERGENT GROUPS: STRATEGICALLY ADDRESSING GAPS IN ASSISTANCE

Many of the problems with the largely top-down delivery of assistance by the public sector, private sector, and other members of the assistance network—such as perceived inaction, a lack of coordinated policy making on the part of the network, and the fact that governments are overwhelmed following disasters—are addressed by nonprofits, quasi-governmental organizations, and emergent groups that purposefully form to counter these shortcomings. The formation of emergent groups is even more likely when there is a real or perceived threat of disaster, low levels of pre-event planning, and strong previously established relationships.[10] In the context of the disaster recovery assistance framework, emergent groups can help to bridge the gap between governmental programs and local needs, speed the delivery of assistance, and facilitate horizontally and vertically integrated strategies through post disaster planning. For instance, Hurricane Katrina stimulated the formation of several new neighborhood-level planning efforts.[11] Yet again, the potential of these members of the network can be constrained if they have not developed horizontal and vertical relationships with more formal institutions.[12]

According to Thomas Drabek and David McEntire, emergent groups are defined by therapeutic actions, collective problem solving, altruism, massed response, and harmonious relationships.[13] They tend to be informal, assume tasks that they have not previously undertaken, and engage in specific activities for a limited period of time,[14] such as replanting trees after a tornado or identifying funds to pay for the reconstruction of homes destroyed by a landslide.[15] In New Orleans, one emergent group was formed to repair and resell bicycles after Hurricane Katrina.[16]

The "rules" governing these groups emphasize a sense of purpose and an esprit de corps. The most effective emergent groups also have a good understanding of the disaster recovery process, including the rules governing other actors, which enables them to make informed, strategic choices regarding the assistance they will provide. It seems counterintuitive to expect a group that is formed after an event to plan for recovery, but in fact, emergent groups, like other members of the assistance network, engage in adaptive planning processes that are common following disasters.[17]

Most research on emergent group behavior after a disaster has focused on their activities during the response phase. Research has shown, however, that emergent groups may adopt proactive, adaptive, and collaborative problem-solving approaches during recovery and reconstruction.[18] They may, for example, help to educate underrepresented groups such as non-English speakers about preparedness activities and risk-reduction initiatives, thereby providing some empowerment for the disenfranchised.[19] They have also become involved in efforts to limit future development in flood-prone areas, ensure the equitable distribution of recovery assistance, and oppose undesirable post-disaster housing policies.

As is the case with individuals, more research is needed to better understand the role of emergent groups in long-term recovery and reconstruction,[20] including their place in disaster recovery assistance networks. Nevertheless, there is evidence to suggest that collaborative activities between members of the networks, including emergent groups, can improve the understanding of the type and timing of resource delivery. Research findings suggest that clarifying the roles and responsibilities of government agencies and other organizations involved in recovery, improving communication between these providers and the general public, and empowering individuals to make informed decisions regarding risk reduction measures can help facilitate effective recovery. A key part of this strategy involves developing pre-event hazard mitigation and disaster recovery plans.[21]

INDIVIDUALS AND EMERGENT GROUPS WITHIN THE DISASTER RECOVERY ASSISTANCE FRAMEWORK

In the U.S. disaster recovery assistance framework, policies and funding programs are usually developed with little input from those who will be receiving resources if disaster strikes. This contributes to an overall sense among assistance recipients of losing control once a disaster has occurred. The uncertainties associated with grant and loan eligibility creates additional anxiety. At that point, while they are struggling to address basic needs, those with little or no previous disaster experience or who are ill informed can be overwhelmed by the procedures and complexities inherent in the available options. The problem is even more acute among socially vulnerable populations.[22]

However, as was noted above, disasters need not be framed in terms that suggest that those affected are helpless victims unable to contribute to their own recovery. Rather than being seen as an act of God, a disaster can be more accurately characterized as a human construct tied to the interaction of natural hazards, social systems, and land use choices. This is the characterization that members of the disaster recovery assistance network, including planners, should use to shape their roles in preparing for and mitigating the effects of natural hazards.[23]

And in this context, individuals (defined here as citizens and others living in the United States) who have experienced disasters can bring unique insights to issues of hazard vulnerability, program effectiveness, and the potential impact of financial and other types of assistance. They may become powerful advocates, driving the formation of disaster recovery committees and emergent groups that have more collective power to influence policy following disasters.[24] Effective local planning efforts can engender a sense of empowerment and self-reliance among residents while demonstrating the associative value of citizen participation in decision-making processes (see Figure 7–2). For example, unless they have been engaged in an open discussion of the issues, citizens in known high-hazard areas may not always embrace a "community need" if proposed actions after a disaster suggest altering the pre-event status quo, such as initiating stricter building codes, relocating flood-prone neighborhoods, or choosing not to reinvest public expenditures on infrastructure in selected areas. And repeated studies have shown the merits of developing locally informed recovery strategies to drive policy formulation, technical assistance, and the distribution of financial resources.[25] The resulting policies tend to better reflect local needs and are more likely to be supported by those whom they most directly affect.

Figure 7–2. The local capacity-building effort led by Manpower Development Corporation (MDC), a Chapel Hill-based nonprofit, and by faculty in the Department of City and Regional Planning at the University of North Carolina at Chapel Hill targets low-income communities along the eastern seaboard and Gulf Coast. The intent of this FEMA-funded community demonstration project is to help communities assess their vulnerability to natural hazards and develop locally grounded strategies that are based on their understanding of pre- and post-disaster conditions.

Photo courtesy of Manpower Development Corporation.

Anthony Oliver-Smith contends that successful recovery hinges on the increased use of local capabilities rather than an excessive reliance on external resources.[26] However, developing an adaptive, locally driven plan of action is challenging. Individuals and emergent groups that engage in post-disaster recovery activities often have little background in disaster-related activities and may lack knowledge of the resources available across the network. As a result, they may unintentionally hinder recovery efforts by spreading misinformation or failing to effectively coordinate their strategies with others.

Improved coordination across the network can be achieved by involving individuals and emergent groups in pre- and post-disaster recovery planning activities. Of course, since emergent groups form after a disaster, they obviously cannot be involved in pre-event planning. But such planning *can* include procedures that recognize and account for their formation and active involvement once a disaster does strike. One way to do this is to capitalize on the "civic infrastructure," including the collective wisdom of individuals and community groups (i.e., local knowledge grounded in experience), in order to establish safety nets for socially vulnerable populations in case of disaster and to facilitate trust, both horizontally and vertically, across the disaster assistance network.[27] Plans and policies that develop and evolve as part of an ongoing relationship based on trust and mutual learning provide an important contextual base from which to act should disaster strike.

DIMENSIONS OF THE DISASTER RECOVERY ASSISTANCE FRAMEWORK

Little discussion can be found in the literature concerning the importance of individuals or emergent groups in recovery. There is little doubt that these parties play an important role in recovery, but their actions are often overlooked, their value marginalized, and their inclusion in collective efforts somewhat arbitrary. The reluctance to actively involve individuals and emergent groups in planning for recovery has a number of negative implications, as described next in the context of the recovery assistance framework.

Understanding of Local Needs

Individuals receiving disaster assistance often interpret the nature and value of assistance differently than the organizations or agencies providing it.[28] Rules are infrequently explained in advance of an event, leading to confusion when individuals seek help and mistrust when their needs are not met. Emergent groups and individual recipients of assistance have a better understanding of their own needs than do other members of the disaster assistance network. They also tend to recognize and appreciate community-level needs, including those that are not being met by existing programs.[29]

The makeup of emergent groups varies across socioeconomic, racial, ethnic, and sex-based classifications, which provides for a number of important perspectives during recovery,[30] while the ability of emergent groups to understand how existing programs operate helps to shape the nature of the assistance they provide. The disproportionate vulnerability of women and other populations is often evident before an event occurs in such indicators as homelessness, high unemployment, and unfamiliarity with the English language. The degree to which local and state governments tackle these issues before a disaster strikes varies widely, and to the extent that the issues are not addressed in advance, emergent groups play a significant role in attending to them after the fact. Therefore, emergent groups that possess an understanding of both the local conditions and the complex nature of disaster assistance found in the pre- and post-disaster environment can be a powerful voice for socially vulnerable populations during recovery. (It should be noted that emergent groups, by definition, often begin as a collection of individuals who are inexperienced in disasters and emergency management practice.)

Because emergent groups usually consist of people who have been affected by the event, others in the community tend to view them as more trustworthy, particularly compared to federal, state, and local government officials who may represent organizations that committed perceived injustices in the past. For this reason, emergent groups are better able, through post-event conversations, to gain access to detailed information about those seeking assistance. This information, when added to the in-depth knowledge they gained over time while living together as neighbors, allows them to frame individual and family needs within the context of the actual situation and in a way that predetermined questions of grant eligibility cannot.

Closely related to this issue is that of compartmentalization within the public sector. Grant administrators often do not share what they have learned with other organizations, much less with people in their own agencies. In some cases, this approach may be part of an attempt to protect the confidentiality of those seeking assistance. It may also stem from a desire among grant administrators to demonstrate the merits of their programs relative to others, improve the image of their agencies, or gain public recognition and appreciation for themselves after a disaster. They may also believe that their agencies are the sole proprietors of this responsibility, so there is no need to involve other agencies or organizations.[31] This withholding of information can even occur within the same agency owing to issues of mistrust across departments, a devaluation of another program's worth, and internal competition for power and influence.

In contrast to governmental compartmentalization, emergent groups often assume roles akin to case managers, who purposefully search across programs to determine how to cobble together resources that best meet the needs of constituents. Attempts to decipher the services offered by so many disjointed programs can be extremely frustrating, particularly as the rules often change following a disaster. This can result in a breakdown in communication between emergent groups and other members of the assistance network, which can foster the spread of misinformation. The high level of trust that those seeking help after a disaster have in emergent groups can prove detrimental if such groups disseminate inaccurate information, including that which perpetuates disaster myths—stories describing conditions in the aftermath of an event that are not factually based.

Several disaster myths, including the likelihood of widespread panic and the rise in crime and antisocial behavior after an event, have been widely discredited by researchers. Disasters do, in fact, change behaviors, but not in the ways most people expect: findings include a reduced level of socializing, the increased purchase of luxury items, and a greater degree of social problems.[32] At the same time, individuals demonstrate a higher level of altruistic behavior.[33] Adaptive, improvisational behavior is also prevalent as individuals, organizations, and institutions seek ways to address problems that arise during recovery and reconstruction that may not have been expected or accounted for in pre-event plans and policies.[34]

Some common misperceptions regarding long-term recovery include the notion that, following a federally declared disaster, disaster programs provide sufficient monetary relief to "make individuals whole"; that the federal government has a robust recovery plan in place that coordinates the delivery and timing of assistance; and that the occurrence of a major disaster in the community somehow precludes residents from experiencing a similar event in the foreseeable future. While these perceptions were widely discredited by most researchers after the Midwest floods (which occurred in successive years), Hurricane Katrina, and other events of a smaller magnitude, many people who have not experienced a disaster continue to assume that recovery programs are well coordinated and designed to meet local needs and that, once struck by a major disaster, their communities are somehow immune from the devastating effects of a future event. Those affected by a disaster are also often unprepared for the length of time it takes to receive recovery assistance and for the slow pace of reconstruction.

As was seen in Chapter 3, the Broadmoor community, which was initially represented by an emergent group, addressed the importance of "explaining and rejecting" post-disaster recovery myths early in the process, particularly those myths that run counter to the values expressed by the community.[35] This insightful attention to detail was further strengthened by targeting misinformation, which is rampant during recovery, as both part of the initial phase of their planning process and the ongoing dialogue conducted during the plan's development and implementation.

Timing of Assistance

Emergent groups form in response to what they view as overly bureaucratic and unresponsive relief programs that are poorly timed or slow to implement. Their ability to react on the spot, working with whatever resources and capabilities are directly at hand, enables them to address a major limitation in the larger disaster assistance framework—namely, the lack of post-disaster relief strategies that can apply to the unique conditions in a community.

Problems can occur, however, when emergent groups have only a limited understanding of the different programs and the length of time it takes to administer them. Like nonprofits, emergent groups can grow frustrated with the slow nature of recovery. Well-intentioned actions aimed at recovery can be duplicative or counterproductive, especially when they are not coordinated with those of other members of the assistance network. For instance, emergent groups may view the speedy repair of damaged low-income housing as their primary concern but, in so doing, may overlook the need to incorporate hazard mitigation techniques into their reconstruction. However, when emergent groups are able to coordinate with other members of the network, the result is more likely to reflect broader understanding, mutual learning, targeted strategies, and the appropriate modification of existing policies. After the 1989 Loma Prieta earthquake, for example, Latino residents in Watsonville, California, complained that they were receiving inadequate information about disaster relief programs and that the assistance was being inequitably distributed. In response, the city hired a bilingual emergency manager, brought in a Latino ombudsman, and modified its disaster response plan to reflect a more inclusive approach.[36]

Because government agencies, insurance companies, and other established disaster assistance organizations often fail to recognize the significance of the services that can and are provided by emergent groups, they usually do not modify their programs to more effectively use this type of assistance. This shortcoming is evident in pre-event plans that do not allow emergent groups to flourish in the aftermath of a disaster or solicit their participation in decision-making venues once they form. Of course, pre-event recovery plans cannot specify emergent groups by name (since they do not exist), yet their formation can be anticipated and incorporated into plans that include sufficient flexibility to enable them to actively participate in post-disaster decision-making forums. The development of an inclusive participatory framework allows the disaster assistance network to capture issues, concerns, and needs expressed by individuals affected by a disaster and members of emergent groups, such as the differential speed at which individuals and subgroups recover.

The trajectory of household and individual recovery does not follow a standard pattern. This speaks to the need for a pre-event planning process that recognizes the importance of flexibility and adaptation.[37] As noted by Walter Peacock and Kathleen Ragsdale:

> Household recovery is a dynamic process where households, as interdependent social units, interact with their environments to re-establish their living conditions and patterns of interaction. While cooperation certainly exists, recovery typically entails sets of negotiations that can best be characterized as competitive, potentially conflict-ridden, and stressful. Many of the network's social units occupy similar niches, placing them in competition for scarce resources and services. This is particularly the case with households which, as end consumers, must enter into a complex, competitive ecological network en masse in order to negotiate their own recovery.[38]

Thus, temporally defined choices made by individuals affect their recovery outcomes (see Figure 7–3 on page 250).

Individuals and families recover at different rates, which means that similar types of assistance are needed at different times along the larger disaster recovery continuum. Similarly, programs, grants, loans, and insurance payouts provided by members of the assistance network are available at different times during recovery. The temporal disbursement of assistance also varies according to different eligibility criteria and implementation processes across programs (see Figure 7–4 on page 250). Assistance

Figure 7–3. The spray-painted notations on the front of this house in Shoreacres, Texas, after Hurricane Ike convey a variety of information, including the type of damage sustained, the homeowner's flood insurance policy, a warning to potential intruders, and a sense of humor as evidenced by renaming the original street address, Shoreacres Circle.

Photo by Gavin Smith.

Figure 7–4. Individuals often return to their communities to begin the recovery process, including the repair or reconstruction of their home. In some cases, this may involve the use of a FEMA-provided temporary housing unit that is placed on the homeowner's lot (as evidenced in this photo) or in what are referred to as group sites. The provision of temporary housing in the afflicted area allows individuals to interact directly with different providers of assistance and cobble together insurance proceeds, loans, grant awards, or nonprofit assistance.

Photo by Gavin Smith.

provided by the federal government, insurance companies, banks, foundations, and nonprofits all require specific types of information. Along with a certain level of self-confidence to deal with the inherent bureaucracy, it takes time to fill out the necessary paperwork;[39] a persistence to repeatedly contact service providers in person or over the phone; an awareness of and familiarity with technology such as the Internet, blogs, and other media to research program eligibility; and the sharing of information gleaned from others in the community. Taken together, these factors create an extremely complex milieu that is rarely addressed successfully by the assistance network. Emergent groups can help people navigate the bureaucracy to ensure that they obtain needed assistance in a timely manner.

Horizontal and Vertical Integration

The adroit timing and sustained sharing of information among receivers and providers of assistance improves horizontal and vertical integration across the network. Since emergent groups form because of both their isolation from other assistance providers and the perceived weaknesses in the system, they are sometimes critical of other members of the assistance network. Their criticisms can facilitate cooperation and the integration of recovery programs. For instance, an analysis of Santa Cruz, California, after the Loma Prieta earthquake found that an emergent group known as the Neighborhood Survival Network (NSN) served an important function in disseminating information, developing new partnerships, and enhancing self-reliance and institutional capacity. The NSN also brought to light problems related to FEMA's initial outreach efforts in underserved minority populations in rural areas of the county, leading to a greater commitment among federal officials to provide much needed information. The efforts of the NSN were instrumental in shifting Santa Cruz from a community with strong horizontal but weak vertical integration to one with strong horizontal and vertical integration.[40]

However, emergent groups' criticism of other members of the network can also hinder cooperation as it sometimes puts public sector administrators on the defensive, causing them to become more entrenched in their positions and to withdraw from inclusive discourse. This might be their response even when evidence proves the criticism to be valid—that their policies are *not* meeting the needs of communities, that the timing of assistance they provide *is* uncoordinated, or that their goals conflict with those of other programs. Similarly, criticism coming from members of the public sector and the media—for example, statements to the effect that selfish or criminal behavior is inevitable among individuals, that community groups are incapable of expressing local needs, or that such groups possess limited internal resources to assist others—suggest that individuals and community groups must be "managed" by government authorities, which further degrades potentially collaborative relationships.[41]

Building strong vertical relationships among members of the disaster assistance network is critical to successful recovery. For instance, several researchers have found that strong relationships between community and external organizations can significantly influence household recovery.[42] The extent to which the assistance network is willing to act on issues brought to them by emergent groups, individuals, and other local entities following a disaster is influenced by a number of factors. Media attention, for example, often elicits a response from state and federal officials, including governors, state legislators, and members of Congress, so emergent groups are more likely to affect policy change when their concerns are disseminated through influential media channels. In addition, early and frequent conversations between emergent groups and government program administrators can result in a better understanding of needs and available resources. The ability to engage in such dialogue is important as the provision of disaster recovery assistance is often based on negotiated agreements between adroit stakeholders.[43]

Emergent groups also play an important role in the horizontal integration of local organizations. Relationships between emergent groups and other local organizations tend to evolve organically after a disaster as the groups discover one another, learn each other's capabilities, and identify needs that remain unaddressed. If local officials seem unresponsive, emergent groups may resort to the media to gain recognition for post-disaster issues; they may also team up with foundations, nonprofits, or the private sector. Challenges remain as many organizations are dominated by prescriptive rules and strict program management protocols, which can hinder vertical integration, but rigid rules can conversely stimulate greater horizontal coordination among members of the network seeking to fill perceived gaps in assistance or change existing policies and programs.

After Hurricane Andrew, a group of people—largely women—formed Women Will Rebuild because they felt that the local recovery organization, We Will Rebuild, was paying insufficient attention to the needs of women and children. Women Will Rebuild focused on a number of issues, including legal aid, temporary housing conditions, health and mental health issues, child care, the lack of recreational opportunities for children, and domestic violence. The emergent group ultimately persuaded the We Will Build committee to establish two subcommittees addressing their principal concerns.[44] The grassroots organization that formed in the Broadmoor neighborhood after Hurricane Katrina (and described in Chapter 3) provides an additional example of an emergent group and its role in recovery. Once the Broadmoor Improvement Association was created, it lost the characteristics of an emergent group and more accurately took on the characteristics of the Disaster Research Center (DRC) typology's extending organization (Exhibit 7–1).

Originally developed to describe response organizations, the DRC typology provides a useful framework to characterize disaster recovery organizations. *Established* organizations perform routine tasks through an existing organizational structure. In the context of recovery, for example, FEMA is an established organization: it has standard protocols and highly structured rules dictating its role in recovery, its programs are narrowly defined, and changes are often met by strong resistance from administrators. Past research has found that established response organizations that emphasize self-containment can limit coordination with others.[45] The unwillingness of established organizations involved in recovery to coordinate their activities, share information, and solicit input from those receiving assistance significantly hinder the overall recovery process.[46] In contrast to

Exhibit 7–1. The Disaster Research Center Typology of Organized Responses

		Tasks	
		Routine	Non-Routine
Organizational structure	Old	Established	Extending
	New	Expanding	Emergent

Source: Russell Dynes, *Organized Behavior in Disaster* (Lexington, Mass.: D. C. Heath, 1970). Reprinted with permission of the publisher.

Note: The figure shown above is commonly referred to as the Disaster Research Center (DRC) typology because hazard scholars Russell Dynes and E. L. Quarantelli developed it while working at the DRC, the first social science research center of its kind in the world that is solely devoted to the study of disasters. Founded at the Ohio State University in 1963, the DRC moved to the University of Delaware in 1984.[1]

1   David McEntire, Disaster Response and Recovery: Strategies and Tactics for Resilience (Hoboken, N.J.: John Wiley and Sons, 2007), 54; see also the Disaster Research Center website at http://www.udel.edu/DRC/aboutus/index.html.

established organizations, *expanding* organizations perform tasks they have undertaken in the past but do so within a new, often larger organizational structure. In fact, an expanding organization may increase dramatically in size after a disaster. In some cases, it may perform new activities that are aligned with its organizational mission or that complement its traditional pursuits. A faith-based relief group is representative of an expanding organization as it provides assistance to those in need while maintaining its normal functions as a religious institution. For example, in New Orleans, a city known for its strong pre-event network of community-based organizations, Hurricane Katrina helped to galvanize and reinvigorate many faith-based organizations to take on a number of additional tasks associated with recovery, such as picking up debris, trimming trees on public land, creating public signage, hiring construction companies to perform minor street repairs, and maintaining street median landscaping.[47]

The typology defines *extending* organizations as those that perform nonroutine tasks within their pre-existing organizational structure. Thus, the institution's organizational structure does not change, but the tasks it performs are modified to reflect new conditions. A recognized example of an extending organization in response is a construction firm that may be tasked with clearing debris as part of a search and rescue operation.[48] In recovery, a hybrid organizational type—a cross between an extending and an expanding organization—may arise. For instance, local governments often take on characteristics associated with both extending and expanding organizations as their employees and officials are required to assume new tasks that were not assigned to them prior to the disaster (as most local governments do not have a local recovery plan that delineates post-disaster roles and responsibilities). Because of poor pre-event planning, some local officials rely on the emergency management office (if it exists in the community) to address long-term recovery activities, even though emergency managers are better equipped and trained to deal with response and preparedness initiatives, not with the challenges of recovery identified in this book. Similarly, a local land planner may be thrust into the role of grants administrator rather than leading post-disaster recovery planning efforts. And the failure to plan is not limited to local governments but can be found across the entire network. Thus, many organizations in the network could be justifiably classified as hybrids as they are largely unprepared to address long-term recovery. More research is needed to assess the application of the DRC typology to recovery (including the formation of hybrid organizations) and to develop training approaches and modified policies that help to incorporate the findings into practice.

For example, federal, state, and local recovery plans often outline the roles of established organizations, but they are less likely to account for the full involvement of expanding, extending, or emergent groups. The inclusion of these other types of organizations in recovery plans is necessary but is not, in and of itself, sufficient to ensure a sound recovery. A key role of recovery planning should be to improve horizontal and vertical coordination across all members of the disaster assistance network, including those that emerge or expand their activities following a disaster. Pre-event recovery plans should recognize what makes each organizational type within the network unique and seek to capitalize on each type's special characteristics and potentially complementary differences.

As part of their study of search and rescue activities, Drabek and his colleagues expanded the concept of emergence to include multiorganizational networks that form in the wake of disasters (see the sidebar on pages 256–257).[49] Members of such networks include federal and state agencies, specialized and local search and rescue groups, and amateur radio operators. Emergent multiorganizational networks in recovery may also include nonprofit relief organizations; foundations; university and college researchers; volunteers; private sector corporations and businesses; and federal, state, and local government agencies. Since many members of the loosely affiliated disaster recovery assistance network have neither developed nor adopted mutually recognized pre-event roles or authorities, there is often little coordination among emergent networks following a disaster. Thus, a key role for established organizations and networks should be to develop the procedures necessary to facilitate the involvement of emergent, expanding, and extending organizations in collaborative activities, including planning for post-disaster recovery. Considering the weak and sometimes nonexistent linkages across the disaster recovery assistance network, the application of Drabek's model to recovery is instructive.

The defining characteristics of the DRC typology include the type of tasks performed and the organizational structure in which they are undertaken. Both characteristics have a distinct temporal element that can be tied to the concept of pre- and post-disaster planning. For example, established organizations perform similar tasks in pre- and post-disaster conditions. Yet most established emergency management organizations are not equipped or prepared to address long-term recovery needs. Moreover, in most communities it is unclear what organization(s) will assume the responsibility for long-term recovery. Organizations often assume new tasks through pre-event institutional arrangements, but extending organizations face the extreme challenge of adequately performing these new tasks, often without additional personnel or clear lines of authority. Expanding organizations often grow dramatically after a disaster but sometimes without assuming any new tasks: they simply do more of what they have always done.

The application of the emergent multiorganizational networks concept to recovery raises several important questions. Even the most established organizations struggle to confront the complexities of recovery. For example, how can they better coordinate with groups that emerge following disasters? Emergent groups strive to effect change, often without the recognition or support of the assistance network. Thus, under what conditions can they and the (often disenfranchised) individuals they represent become involved in the assistance network without being co-opted or losing their improvisational nature? The fact that many of these relationships emerge after a disaster highlights two important issues: (1) pre-event planning for post-disaster recovery is still relatively uncommon and (2) improved planning efforts must account for the reality of emergence at both the organizational and multiorganizational levels.

CONCLUSIONS AND RECOMMENDATIONS

The argument for the increased involvement of individuals and emergent groups in recovery is based on observed weaknesses in the disaster recovery assistance framework and the niches that both assume following disasters. Pre-disaster planning for recovery should include the individuals who will be affected by a disaster as well as emergent groups and multiorganizational networks that will be involved in the development and implementation of post-disaster assistance strategies. Emergent groups represent an organizational manifestation that targets unaddressed needs through improvisation and adaptation, both of which are critical during recovery.

Lessons from Emergent Multiorganizational Networks and their Application to Recovery

The experiences of emergent multiorganizational networks (EMONs) in search and rescue operations demonstrate the importance of planning in both the pre and post-disaster environment. Many of the same characteristics that Drabek and colleagues identified in their study of search and rescue networks can be found in the disaster recovery assistance network:

- As their name states, EMONs are multiorganizational and require resources that are beyond the control of a single organization.
- EMONs include organizations that vary in size, location, and the degree to which rules are formalized.
- Within EMONs, improvisation is the norm and produces new linkages, resources, and communication modes.
- EMONs tend to be loosely connected prior to the event.
- The integration of some groups into the broader EMON is sometimes hindered by the existence of strong pre-event core groups.[1]

Case studies have highlighted key differences among EMONs that are equally pertinent to the disaster recovery assistance network. For instance, there is significant variation in the type of planning they undertake. In some networks, pre-event plans are closely followed, particularly in areas that have experienced past disasters. In locations where pre-event planning is less developed, interpersonal relationships often prove more influential than formal interorganizational linkages. In addition, the flow of information and extent of centralized decision making differs greatly from one situation to another. In most cases, once the emergent network is established, it remains stable. Drabek's study found one case in which the stability of the network wavered, and the effectiveness of the operation suffered as a result.

Drabek and colleagues made several broad recommendations based on their findings:

- Communication across organizations should be improved to better manage the flow of information, regardless of the type of response system in place at the time of the event.
- The ambiguity of authority hinders operations and therefore should be reduced through better planning.
- Specialized resources, including those obtained from nontraditional organizations, should be used more effectively.
- Information sharing with the media should be improved.

Drabek and his colleagues go on to describe several policy implications for emergency

One way to look at this issue is to return to the concept of disaster recovery resources (i.e., funding, policy, and technical assistance). Understood in the context of collaborative planning, improved outcomes are tied to the open exchange of resources across the assistance network. Bridging the gap between those members of the disaster assistance network that possess substantial financial resources and those that have a sound understanding of local conditions requires not only regular interaction between groups but also the identification of mutually beneficial outcomes that are more effectively achieved through collaboration. The fact that the reciprocal exchange of resources is not a regular part of the relationship between individuals, emergent groups, and others in the network is a fundamental problem. For instance, the public sector routinely develops policy and delivers assistance without garnering the input—and managers, many of which are applicable to the larger disaster recovery assistance network. They maintain that there is a need to recognize that U.S. response systems are multiorganizational and emergent in nature and that after a disaster, emergent networks will continue to function as loosely connected systems. Further, EMONs are unique, and so their management cannot be based on existing private sector or public sector administrative models. An assessment of EMONs requires recognizing their variability and evaluating their performance under different conditions. Evaluation should focus on the network itself, not on a single agency, and should reflect existing social and political conditions.

Drabek et al.'s findings and recommendations are consistent with those from other studies in the recovery literature. The concept of a loosely coupled system that varies depending on social, political, and institutional conditions is evident in the disaster recovery assistance network. Planning should reflect these conditions and provide a degree of flexibility to accommodate emergent groups and networks. It should also provide a tool to help identify the varied resources that different members of the network can bring to the process and determine how the value of those resources can be optimized through collaboration.

Since Hurricane Katrina, research on EMONs has suggested that actors perform a number of emergent intermediary roles—coordinator, itinerant broker, gatekeeper, representative, and liaison—serving as "brokers" between other actors that would not otherwise coordinate activities and thus helping to shape the type of interactions across groups.[2] The coordinator is a peer among actors and transfers information to individuals within the same subgroup. The itinerant broker belongs to a different group than those sending and receiving information. The gatekeeper is a broker who belongs to the same subgroup as the receiving actor but not as the sender of information. The representative is affiliated with the sending but not receiving actor. In the case of the liaison, each of the three actors is unaffiliated.[3] The nature of these communicative relationships is relevant to the individuals who may seek to facilitate the sharing of information—including, for example, planners or mediators assigned to help with recovery efforts.

Source: The findings discussed in this sidebar were derived from Thomas E. Drabek et al., *Managing Multiorganizational Response: Emergent Search and Rescue Networks in Natural Disaster and Remote Area Settings*, Monograph #33 (Boulder: Institute of Behavioral Science, University of Colorado, 1981), xix–xxi.

1   Drabek et al., *Managing Multiorganizational Emergency Responses*.
2   Benjamin E. Lind et al., "Brokerage Roles in Disaster Response: Organisational Mediation in the Wake of Hurricane Katrina," *International Journal of Emergency Management* 5, nos. 1/2 (2008): 75–99.
3   Ibid., 80–81.

using the resources—of those receiving that assistance. Specific examples of the local resource base include past disaster experience; a locally grounded understanding of needs; and an in-depth awareness of the available technical, fiscal, and administrative capacity of local organizations to effectively accept, manage, and coordinate the assistance provided with the resources held by individuals and community organizations, including emergent groups.

Few case studies have addressed the role of the individual or emergent groups in the larger disaster recovery assistance network, and no known quantitative analyses have been undertaken. While more research needs to be pursued, the recommendations that follow emphasize pre- and post-disaster planning and the importance of involving individuals and emergent groups in pre- and post-disaster decision making.

1. Improve Individual and Family Preparedness for Disaster Recovery*

The literature on individual and household recovery sheds light on a number of key issues, including the mode of recovery (autonomous and institutional)[50] and the disparate access to resources among individuals due to varied levels of social vulnerability.[51] While the disaster-related literature emphasizes the importance of involving individuals in post-disaster community-level recovery planning as a way to address these issues,[52] the findings have not been effectively translated to practice. Similarly, despite a significant amount of research undertaken at the household level regarding recovery, including that which is focused on the institutional, social, and political factors that influence vulnerability,[53] there has been little discussion about the need for individuals and households to assume a greater level of self-reliance by engaging in pre-event *recovery* preparedness.[54]

Disaster researchers do, however, suggest that the current recovery assistance system should place a greater emphasis on incentivizing pre-event behavior that minimizes risk.[55] All individuals and households should consider several important pre-event activities, such as becoming more aware of the hazards in the community and taking proactive measures to reduce their impact. Hazard mitigation actions may include retrofitting one's home, purchasing adequate insurance, moving to a less vulnerable location, and becoming more involved in the development of pre-disaster hazard mitigation plans. These plans, which are strongly encouraged under the Disaster Mitigation Act (and tied to the pre- and post-disaster access to hazard mitigation funding), have resulted in their widespread development.

The same cannot be said for local recovery planning. But if the local government has no disaster recovery plan or other pertinent policies, citizens can lead efforts to develop a plan or push for changes in local policies. Preliminary actions in this regard may include reaching out to neighborhood associations, community nonprofits, and other members of the assistance network to garner their support, as was done in the Broadmoor community of New Orleans after Hurricane Katrina. In addition, the findings—developed, in part, by the residents—should be widely discussed and disseminated throughout the community and the larger assistance network. Pre-event preparedness for post-disaster recovery should also cover ongoing training and educational sessions on the grant and loan programs that are triggered by a federal disaster declaration, as well as on other resources that are available following smaller

---

* The following discussion about the steps that an individual and family should take to prepare for long-term recovery was derived from two columns on the PLAN!TNOW newsletter website: "Preparing for the Aftermath of a Coastal Storm: A Personal History" (November 26, 2009) www.planitnow.org/preparing-for-the-aftermath-of-a-coastal-storm-a-personal-history/ and "Protecting Our Natural Heritage and Our Communities from the Impacts of Hurricanes" (April 9, 2009), www.planitnow.org/protecting-our-natural-heritage/. For more information on the nonprofit organization PLAN!TNOW, see www.planitnow.org.

events. These other resources include not only government programs, insurance, and assistance provided by community groups and nonprofits, but also personal savings that should be set aside to address losses.

In the aftermath of a major disaster, individuals in the affected area should compile the necessary documents to register with FEMA. Going through the registration process is a good idea as many individuals may not be aware that they would be eligible for federal assistance, including temporary housing and low-interest loans or grants. Renters should talk with landlords about what they both will do if a disaster strikes and develop a list of joint steps they will need to take if tenants are required to relocate. Those considering reconstruction should talk with others to get recommendations for reputable builders and seek out those with a proven track record of completing work as promised. Criteria for selecting builders in the post-disaster environment (as in pre-disaster situations) include high quality, timeliness, and affordability—standards that are sometimes ignored in the rush to get back to "normal" as quickly as possible. Individuals in a disaster zone may need to consider carefully whether it is feasible to continue to live in an area prone to hazards.

2. Develop Pre-Disaster Recovery Plans That Integrate Individuals and Emergent Groups into Disaster Recovery Operations

The formation of new groups following disasters creates opportunities for cooperation and conflict.[56] Successfully incorporating individuals and emergent groups into the planning process requires first recognizing the important role they play in recovery. This, in turn, means appreciating their defining characteristics and resources, and creating conditions that encourage their participation in planning and other decision-making processes. Pre-disaster recovery plans need to include citizens in their formulation and provide sufficient flexibility to involve emergent groups after an event. Citizen involvement should not be limited to the creation of local plans; individuals have important roles to play in the design of recovery plans at multiple levels. For example, individuals who have lived through disasters and learned how to navigate the complex system of recovery assistance programs are often able to provide valuable insights and offer unique solutions to problems that span local, state, national, and international boundaries. The Emergency Management Assistance Compact and the strike teams described in Chapters 2 and 3 are examples of existing organizational venues that could be used to advance this important objective.

The degree to which federal, state, and local pre-disaster recovery plans account for emergent groups and the important resources they provide is virtually nonexistent. This serious limitation in the recovery planning process should be addressed through national, state, and local policy initiatives and incorporated into technical assistance strategies. Such policies and training, education, and outreach efforts should be informed through ongoing studies in order to better understand the role of emergent group behavior in planning for recovery.

Indeed, Enrico L. Quarantelli has suggested that the DRC typology may not be well suited to the study of highly contentious events such as civil disturbances,[57] so its application to conflict-laden environments merits closer scrutiny and study. For instance, under what conditions can organizational types change over time during the recovery process? What role do potential change agents such as "boundary-spanning" organizations, emergent groups, and individuals skilled in conflict resolution play in the transformation of organizational types, including the development of emergent multi-organizational networks characterized by high levels of coordination and consensus?

The formation and eventual dissolution of an emergent group is a natural process, which sometimes results in the formation of a more formal organization (see Figure 7–5). The collaborative procedures adopted by the assistance network should account for the limited duration of emergent groups and their potential transformation over time. Participatory planning and dispute resolution techniques, which planners use routinely, can inform emergent group actions, thereby limiting duplication and counterproductive efforts. This requires a recovery plan that has not only regulatory and administrative standing among members of the network, but also sufficient flexibility to constructively engage organizations that form following a disaster only to disappear once their work is done or evolve into another organizational manifestation. Involving

Figure 7–5. The Broadmoor Improvement Association (see yard sign in front of a home in the New Orleans community) exemplifies the transition from an emergent group to a more formal quasi-governmental organization.

Photo by Gavin Smith.

individuals and emergent groups in recovery also requires debunking the widely held myth that those affected by disasters are helpless victims who are incapable of playing an important role in recovery.[58]

Endnotes

1   Gilbert F. White, "Human Adjustment to Floods," Research Paper no. 29 (PhD diss., University of Chicago, 1945); Piers Blaikie et al., *At Risk: Natural Hazards, People's Vulnerability and Disasters* (New York: Routledge, 1994).

2   Deborah A. Stone, "Causal Stories and the Formation of Policy Agendas," *Political Science Quarterly* 104, no. 2 (1989): 281–300.

3   Mary B. Anderson and Peter Woodrow, *Rising from the Ashes: Development Strategies in Times of Disaster* (Boulder, Colo.: Westview Press, 1989); David Dodson, Julie Thomasson and Leah Totten, *Building Community by Design: A Resource Guide for Community Change Leaders* (Chapel Hill, N.C.: MDC, Inc., 2002).

4   Thomas Drabek and William Key, "The Impact of Disaster on Primary Group Linkages," *Mass Emergencies* 1 (1976): 89–105.

5   Robert C. Bolin and Patricia A. Bolton, "Recovery in Nicaragua and the USA," *International Journal of Mass Emergencies and Disasters* 1, no. 1 (1983): 125–144.

6   Robert C. Bolin and Patricia A. Bolton, *Race, Religion, and Ethnicity in Disaster Recovery* (Boulder: Institute of Behavioral Science, University of Colorado, 1986).

7   Susanna Hoffman, "The Worst of Times, the Best of Times: Toward a Model of Cultural Response to Disaster," in *Catastrophe and Culture: The Anthropology of Disaster,* ed. Susanna M. Hoffman and Anthony Oliver-Smith, 134–155 (Santa Fe, N.M.: School of American Research Press, 1999).

8   Robert C. Bolin and Patricia A. Trainer, "Modes of Family Recovery following Disaster: A Cross-National Study," in *Disasters: Theory and Research,* ed. E. L. Quarantelli, 233–247 (Beverly Hills, Calif.: Sage, 1978).

9   Barbara E. Harrell-Bond, *Imposing Aid: Emergency Assistance to Refugees* (Oxford: Oxford University Press, 1986); Anthony Oliver-Smith, "Post-Disaster Housing Reconstruction and Social Inequality: A Challenge to Policy and Practice," *Disasters* 14, no. 1 (1990): 7–19; Philip R. Berke and Timothy Beatley, *After the Hurricane: Linking Recovery to Sustainable Development in the Caribbean* (Baltimore: Johns Hopkins University Press, 1997).

10 E. L. Quarantelli et al., *Emergent Citizen Groups in Disaster Preparedness and Recovery Activities: An Interim Report* (Newark: Disaster Research Center, University of Delaware, 1983); Charlie Scawthorn and Dennis Wenger, *Emergency Response, Planning and Search and Rescue,* HRRC publication 11P (College Station: Hazard Reduction and Recovery Center, Texas A&M University, 1990).

11 Clara Irazábal and Jason Neville, "Neighbourhoods in the Lead: Grassroots Planning for Social Transformation in Post-Katrina New Orleans?" *Planning Practice and Research* 22, no. 2 (2007): 131–153.

12 Bruce C. Glavovic, "Sustainable Coastal Communities in the Age of Costal Storms: Reconceptualising Coastal Planning as 'New' Naval Architecture," *Journal of Coastal Conservation* 12, no. 3 (2008): 125–134; Mark G. Welsh and Ann-Margaret Esnard, "Closing Gaps in Local Housing Recovery Planning for Disadvantaged Displaced Households," *Cityscape: A Journal of Policy Development and Research* 11, no. 3 (2009): 195–212.

13 Thomas E. Drabek and David E. McEntire, "Emergent Phenomena and the Sociology of Disaster: Lessons, Trends and Opportunities from the Research Literature," *Disaster Prevention and Management* 12, no. 2 (2003): 97–112.

14 Russell R. Dynes, *Organized Behavior in Disaster* (Lexington, Mass.: Heath Lexington Books, 1970); Robert A. Stallings and E. L. Quarantelli, "Emergent Citizen Groups and Emergency Management," *Public Administration Review* 45, special issue (January 1985): 93–100.

15 Stallings and Quarantelli, "Emergent Citizen Groups and Emergency Management"; Brenda Phillips, "Cultural Diversity in Disasters: Sheltering, Housing, and Long-Term Recovery," *International Journal of Mass Emergencies and Disasters* 11, no. 1 (1993): 99–110; Elaine Enarson and Betty Hearn Morrow, "Women Will Rebuild Miami: A Case Study of Feminist Response to Disaster," in *The Gendered Terrain of Disaster: Through Women's Eyes,* ed. Elaine Enarson and Betty Hearn Morrow, 171–184 (Miami: Laboratory for Social and Behavioral Research, Florida International University, 1998).

16 Emmanuel David, "Emergent Behavior and Groups in Postdisaster New Orleans: Notes on Practices and Organized Resistance," in *Learning from Catastrophe.: Quick Response Research in the Wake of Hurricane Katrina,* 235–261 (Boulder, Colo.: Institute for Behavioral Science, 2006).

17 Jack D. Kartez and Michael K. Lindell, "Adaptive Planning for Community Disaster Response," in *Cities and Disaster: North American Studies in Emergency Management,* ed. Richard T. Sylves and William. L. Waugh, 5–31 (Springfield, Ill.: Charles C. Thomas, 1990); Jack D. Kartez and Michael K. Lindell, "Planning for Uncertainty: The Case of Local Disaster Planning," *Journal of the American Planning Association* 53, no. 4 (1987): 487–498.

18 Quarantelli et al., *Emergent Citizen Groups in Disaster Preparedness and Recovery Activities.*

19 Michael K. Lindell and Ronald W. Perry, *Behavioral Foundations of Community Emergency Management* (Washington, D.C.: Hemisphere Publishing Corporation, 1992).

20 Drabek and McEntire, "Emergent Phenomena and the Sociology of Disaster"; David, "Emergent Behavior and Groups in Postdisaster New Orleans."

21 Marieke Van Willigen, "A Dialogue: Responding to the Long-Term Recovery Needs of Disaster Victims," in *Facing our Future: Hurricane Floyd and Recovery in the Coastal Plain,* ed. John Maiolo et al., 119–125 (Greenville, N.C.: Coastal Carolina Press, 2001).

22 Gavin Smith and Dennis Wenger, "Sustainable Disaster Recovery: Operationalizing an Existing Agenda," in *Handbook of Disaster Research,* ed. Havidan Rodriguez, Enrico L. Quarantelli, and Russell Dynes, 234–257 (New York: Springer, 2006); Welsh and Esnard, "Closing Gaps in Local Housing Recovery Planning."

23 White, "Human Adjustment to Floods"; Anthony Oliver-Smith and Susanna Hoffman, eds., *The Angry Earth: Disaster in Anthropological Perspective* (New York: Routledge, 1999); Dennis Mileti, *Disasters by Design: A Reassessment of Natural Hazards in the United States* (Washington, D.C.: Joseph Henry Press, 1999).

24 Robert Geipel, *Disaster and Reconstruction: The Friuli (Italy) Earthquakes of 1976* (London: Allen and Unwin, 1982); Oliver-Smith, "Post-Disaster Housing Reconstruction and Social Inequality."

25 Anderson and Woodrow, *Rising from the Ashes;* Oliver-Smith, "Post-Disaster Housing Reconstruction and Social Inequality"; Smith and Wenger, "Sustainable Disaster Recovery."

26 Oliver-Smith, "Post-Disaster Housing Reconstruction and Social Inequality."

27 Monica Schoch-Spana et al., "Community Engagement: Leadership Tools for Catastrophic Health Events," *Biosecurity and Bioterrorism: Biodefense Strategy, Practice, and Science* 5, no. 1 (2007): 8–25.

28 Anthony Oliver-Smith and Susana M. Hoffman, "Why Anthropologists Should Study Disasters," in *Catastrophe and Culture: The Anthropology of Disaster,* ed. Susanna M. Hoffman and Anthony Oliver-Smith, 3–22 (see note 7).

29 Robert Bolin and Lois Stanford, "The Northridge Earthquake: Community-Based Approches to Unmet Recovery Needs," *Disasters* 22, no. 1 (1998): 21–38.

30 Dennis Wenger, *Emergent and Volunteer Behavior during Disaster: Research Findings and Planning Implications,* HHRC publication 27P (College Station: Hazard Reduction and Recovery Center, Texas A&M University, 1992).

31 Gavin Smith, "Holistic Disaster Recovery: Creating a More Sustainable Future" (course developed for the Emergency Management Institute Higher Education Project, Federal Emergency Management Agency, 2004), available online at training.fema.gov/EMIWeb/edu/sdr.asp.

32 Dennis E. Wenger, Charles E. Faupel, and Thomas F. James, *Disaster Beliefs and Emergency Planning* (Newark: Disaster Research Center, University of Delaware, 1980).

33 Allen H. Barton, *Communities in Disaster: A Sociological Analysis of Collective Stress Situations* (Garden City, N.Y.: Doubleday, 1969); Charles E. Fritz, "Disaster," in *Contemporary Social Problems: An Introduction to the Sociology of Deviant Behavior and Social Disorganization,* ed. Robert K. Merton and Robert A. Nisbet, 651–694 (New York: Harcourt, Brace/World, 1961).

34 James M. Kendra and Tricia Wachtendorf, "Community Innovation and Disasters," in *Handbook of Disaster Research,* 316–334 (see note 22).

35 The Broadmoor Project, *Lessons from Katrina: How a Community can Spearhead Successful Disaster Recovery* (Cambridge: John F. Kennedy School of Government, Harvard University, 2007), 8, belfercenter.ksg.harvard.edu/files/uploads/DisasterRecoveryGuide_Phase_1.pdf.

36 Kathleen Tierney, Michael K. Lindell, and Ronald W. Perry, *Facing the Unexpected: Disaster Preparedness and Response in the United States* (Washington, D.C.: Joseph Henry Press, 2001), 118.

37 Walter Gillis Peacock and A. Kathleen Ragsdale, "Social Systems, Ecological Networks and Disasters: Toward a Socio-Political Ecology of Disasters," in *Hurricane Andrew: Ethnicity, Gender and the Sociology of Disasters,* ed. Walter Gillis Peacock, Betty Hearn Morrow, and Hugh Gladwin, 20–35 (Miami, Fla.: International Hurricane Center Laboratory for Social and Behavioral Research, 1997), 25.

38 Ibid.

39 Betty Hearn Morrow, "Stretching the Bonds: The Families of Andrew," in *Hurricane Andrew: Ethnicity, Gender and the Sociology of Disasters,* 141–170 (see note 37).

40 Philip R. Berke, Jack Kartez, and Dennis Wenger, "Recovery after Disasters: Achieving Sustainable Development, Mitigation and Equity," *Disasters* 17, no. 2 (1993): 93–109.

41 Russell R. Dynes, "Community Emergency Planning: False Assumptions and Inappropriate Analogies," *International Journal of Mass Emergencies and Disasters* 12, no. 2 (1994): 141–158.

42 See, for example, Peter May, "Disaster Recovery and Reconstruction," in *Managing Disaster: Strategies and Perspectives,* ed. Louise Comfort, 236–254 (Durham, N.C.: Duke University Press, 1989).

43 Helen Ingram, "Policy Implementation through Bargaining: The Case of Federal Grants-in-Aid," *Public Policy* 25, no. 4 (1977): 499–526; Smith, "Holistic Disaster Recovery."

44 Enarson and Morrow, "Women Will Rebuild Miami"; Brenda Phillips, *Disaster Recovery* (Boca Raton, Fla.: CRC Press. 2009), 43.

45 Howard E. Aldrich, *Organizations and Environments* (1979; repr., Stanford, Calif.: Stanford Business Books, 2008); David F. Gillespie, "Coordinating Community Resources," in *Emergency Management: Principles and Practice for Local Government,* ed. Thomas E. Drabek and Gerard J. Hoetmer, 55–78 (Washington, D.C.: International City Management Association, 1991).

46 Smith and Wenger, "Sustainable Disaster Recovery."

47 Marla Nelson, Renia Ehrenfeucht, and Shirley Laska, "Planning, Plans, and People: Professional Expertise, Local Knowledge, and Governmental Action in Post-Hurricane Katrina New Orleans," *Cityscape: A Journal of Policy Development and Research* 9, no. 3 (2007): 41.

48 Gary R. Webb, *Individual and Organizational Response to Natural Disasters and Other Crisis Events: The Continuing Value of the DRC Typology,* Preliminary Paper #277 (Newark: Disaster Research Center, University of Delaware, 1999), 3.

49 Thomas E. Drabek et al., *Managing Multiorganizational Emergency Responses: Emergent Search and Rescue Networks in Natural Disaster and Remote Area Settings,* Monograph #33(Boulder: Institute of Behavioral Science, University of Colorado, 1981).

50 Bolin and Bolton, *Race, Religion, and Ethnicity in Disaster Recovery;* Bolin and Trainer, "Modes of Family Recovery."

51 Blaikie et al., *At Risk;* Walter Gillis Peacock and Chris Girard, "Ethnic and Racial Inequalities in Hurricane Damage and Insurance Settlements," in *Hurricane Andrew: Ethnicity, Gender and the Sociology of Disasters,* 171–190 (see note 37).

52 Geipel, *Disaster and Reconstruction;* Oliver-Smith, "Post-Disaster Housing Reconstruction and Social Inequality"; Berke and Beatley, *After the Hurricane.*

53 Bolin and Trainer, "Modes of Family Recovery"; Peacock and Girard, "Ethnic and Racial Inequalities"; Robert C. Bolin, "Disaster Impact and Recovery: A Comparison of Black and White Victims," *International Journal of Mass Emergencies and Disasters* 4 (1986): 35–50; Mary C. Comerio, *Disaster Hits Home: New Policy for Urban Housing Recovery* (Berkeley: University of California Press, 1998).

54 Gavin Smith, "Preparing for the Aftermath of a Coastal Storm: A Personal History," *Plan!tNow.org,* November 26, 2009.

55 Comerio, *Disaster Hits Home;* Howard Kunreuther, *Recovery from Natural Disasters: Insurance or Federal Aid?* (Washington, D.C.: American Enterprise Institute, 1973); Howard Kunreuther and Louis Miller, "Insurance versus Disaster Relief: An Analysis of Interactive Modelling for Disaster Policy Planning," *Public Administration Review* 45, special issue (1985): 147–154; Howard Kunreuther, "Has the Time Come for Comprehensive Natural Disaster Insurance?" in *On Risk and Disaster: Lessons from Hurricane Katrina,* ed. Ronald J. Daniels, Donald F. Kettl, and Howard Kunreuther, 175–201 (Philadelphia: University of Philadelphia Press, 2006).

56 E. L. Quarantelli and Russell R. Dynes, "Community Conflict: Its Absence and its Presence in Natural Disasters," *Mass Emergencies* 1 (1976): 139–152; Frederick L. Bates and Walter G. Peacock, "Disasters and Social Change," in *The Sociology of Disasters,* ed. Russell R. Dynes, Bruna De Marchi, and Carlo Pelanda, 291–330 (Milan, Italy: Franco Angeli Press, 1987).

57 E. L. Quarantelli, ed., *What Is a Disaster? Perspectives on the Question* (London: Routledge, 1998).

58 Henry W. Fischer III, Response to Disaster: Fact versus Fiction and Its Perpetuation: The Sociology of Disaster (New York: University Press of America, 1998).

Chapter 8

Planning for Disaster Recovery

One of many challenges facing land use planners and other members of the disaster recovery assistance network is to develop plans that account for hazard risk while considering recovery strategies that allow for redevelopment. Note the elevated new construction in the background.

Photo by Gavin Smith.

I N THE UNITED STATES, THE type and timing of funding, policies, and technical assistance provided by the disaster recovery assistance network limits collaboration, stifles local creativity, and engenders long-term dependence on federal programs that are often ill-equipped to address root problems faced by disaster-stricken communities. Thus far this book has critiqued the various aspects of the U.S. disaster recovery process through the lens of the disaster recovery assistance framework and its various members and stakeholders. We now examine how the application of planning principles and alternative dispute resolution (ADR) techniques can facilitate the coordination of resources across the assistance network and help to address identified limitations in the assistance framework.

The three principal dimensions of the disaster recovery assistance framework—that is, the connection between resources, rules, and understanding of local needs; the timing of assistance; and the level of horizontal and vertical integration—vary geographically and temporally depending on the makeup of and interactions among members of different assistance networks. This has significant implications for planning. Many experts argue that the public sector should lead recovery planning efforts; however, it is the nonprofit relief organizations, quasi-governmental organizations, members of the private sector, and emergent groups that can and usually do assume a leadership role (as evidenced in many of the sidebars throughout this book). Since different members of the network take ownership of recovery in different locales, this provides another, albeit rarely discussed argument for an inclusive and adaptive planning approach that emphasizes pre-event capacity building across the entire network. But for such an approach to succeed nationwide, it is the responsibility of the public sector to strongly encourage and support with adequate resources pre-event capacity-building initiatives, thereby creating the conditions that allow leaders to emerge and collaborative partnerships to thrive.

DISASTER RECOVERY: CONFLICT OR COOPERATION?

Disasters elicit both conflict and cooperation. Immediately after a disaster, acts of altruism and cooperative behavior flourish at the community level.[1] Cooperation is less common in long-term recovery, however, which is fraught with conflict.[2] Competition for scarce resources such as targeted funding, policy determinations that affect stakeholders differently, and inconsistent access to technical assistance all hinder the achievement of goals, such as the adoption of equitable resource distribution strategies and hazard mitigation–based initiatives, that would benefit the larger community.[3]

Conflict also results from a mismatch between the needs of individuals, groups, and institutions and the resources that are available through members of the assistance network. Recipients of disaster assistance often have unrealistic expectations about the amount, type, and timing of available resources after a disaster—in essence, because they do not understand the overall recovery process. Exacerbating the conflict is a sense of entitlement. For instance, communities often fail to acknowledge how their pre-event actions may have contributed to the extent of their post-disaster needs, to the speed at which aid can be distributed, or to the duration and type of assistance that may be required. Many communities, reluctant to embrace the goals of preparedness and greater self-reliance through pre-event hazard mitigation and disaster recovery planning, actually perpetuate their vulnerability and hinder their ability to recover from disasters when they occur.[4]

But conflict is not necessarily a bad thing. It is also a precondition of adaptation and change. While the historical relationship between major disasters and federal policy reveals the reactionary nature of U.S. disaster assistance strategy,[5] it also demonstrates that learning can occur under the appropriate circumstances[6] and that disaster recovery planning can help to achieve this goal.

Guided by the use of ADR principles, the pre-event development of disaster recovery plans can be instrumental in preventing conflicts from becoming intractable dilemmas. For instance, it can enable a community to proactively confront a number of predictable conflicts tied to post-event development pressures, including the impulse to return to the conditions that made the community vulnerable to natural hazards in the first place. Using planning techniques agreed upon in advance makes sense as the reconstruction of a community involves a complex set of issues tied to the identification of what is appropriate regarding the type, density, and location of post-disaster human settlements.[7] In addition, a cooperatively derived planning process can help to address long-standing issues that predate a disaster, such as race- or class-based conflicts while increasing the level of trust between participants and local officials.[8]

The strength of participatory planning derives from the active involvement of members of disaster assistance networks in identifying issues and formulating solutions, and from an ongoing exchange of ideas that allows participants' unique abilities to emerge (see sidebar starting on page 269). For example, inclusive planning processes can help to capitalize on the high levels of trust engendered by nonprofit organizations among community residents, as well as on these organizations' inherent flexibility. Moreover, because nonprofits can also serve as invaluable agents of local empowerment,[9] the failure to involve them in pre-event planning can have serious consequences—as when efforts to quickly repair or reconstruct damaged housing to pre-event conditions run counter to the community's intended goal of incorporating hazard mitigation measures into its recovery.

Private sector stakeholders are often at the center of disaster recovery conflicts. In the aftermath of a disaster, private businesses may be blamed for price gouging, non-competitive contractor awards, reconstruction that displaces low-income residents, and insurance payouts that are perceived as inadequate or slow to arrive. Owing, in part, to this biased and restrictive view of their role in recovery, their involvement in pre- and post-event recovery planning activities is often limited. At the same time, however, the private sector is responsible for the design and physical reconstruction of communities, the writing of pre- and post-disaster recovery plans, the administration of grant programs, the payment of insurance claims, the removal of debris, and the sale of white goods and construction materials, all of which are important aspects of recovery. Moreover, the ability of local businesses to resume operations is crucial to a community's economic recovery. Clearly, engaging them in planning for recovery has important consequences, as the accompanying sidebar demonstrates.

Conflict during recovery has a clear institutional basis extending well beyond public-private sector disputes. Among the most contentious issues are those tied to regulatory and planning programs and the organizations that manage them. The post-disaster environment provides fertile ground for attempts to alter existing policies and programs as well as for organized resistance to new proposals. The National Response Framework (NRF), which was developed in 2008 to improve inter- and intra-agency coordination during long-term recovery, is really a compendium of federal programs carried out independently of one another without an overarching policy or set of coordinating guidelines. In 1999, Dennis Mileti had made the same observation after analyzing the hazard mitigation policy milieu prior to the adoption of the Disaster Mitigation Act of 2000.[10] Unfortunately, the disaster recovery assistance framework remains uncoordinated even after Hurricane Katrina.[11] Moreover, the 2010 draft for the National Disaster Recovery Framework (NDRF), discussed in Chapter 10, fails to clarify the means of effectively coordinating federal recovery programs under an overarching vision.

The reluctance of state and local governments to develop pre-event plans for post-disaster recovery perpetuates an overreliance on federal solutions. But given that federal programs are uncoordinated, narrow in scope, inflexible, difficult to administer, ill timed, and ineffectively linked to the resources available across the assistance network, a limited understanding of the federal system and of ways to obtain assistance from other sources can hinder disaster recovery. The inability of the recovery framework to meet local needs then leads to confusion, mistrust, and anger among members of the network—particularly among those that work closely with communities. What is needed is a locally driven, collaborative approach that accounts for the range of stakeholders in different recovery assistance networks, including those stakeholders that emerge over time (see Figure 8–1 on page 272).

DEFINING THE PROBLEM: THE LACK OF AN INTEGRATIVE POLICY FRAMEWORK

Planning as currently practiced in the United States does not effectively support disaster recovery. The contributing factors to this problem include (1) the lack of a robust federal government recovery strategy grounded in pre-event planning, (2) limited capacity among public sector stakeholders to help create conditions that are

The Charlotte and Mecklenburg County, North Carolina, Floodplain Mapping Program: The Power of Coalition Building and Participatory Planning

In 1995, Tropical Storm Jerry caused significant flooding in the city of Charlotte and Mecklenburg County, North Carolina. Two years later, the remnants of Hurricane Danny dropped more than thirteen inches of rain in the area. Neither flood resulted in a presidential disaster declaration, however. The lack of federal assistance prompted the city and county to investigate local measures to reduce flood losses, improve water quality, and preserve the natural functions of the floodplain—all without unnecessarily limiting growth. One public official saw the process as a way to avoid what he termed the "hydo-illogic" cycle—a process in which a post-event storm-water planning study recommends an expensive mitigation solution upon which the local government does not act, leaving the city vulnerable to future flooding.[1]

First, Mecklenburg County sought to create a vision that reflected the desired future of the area. Charlotte is a major southern city that welcomes growth. It is also prone to significant, repetitive flooding. A broad-based collection of interests, including developers, environmentalists, community organizations, planners, engineers, city elected officials, county commissioners, and city and county staff, came together to craft an acceptable solution. But first, rather than prematurely discussing possible solutions, they spent more than two months identifying and clearly defining the problem. Although many grew impatient, coalition members admitted in hindsight that the work done up front helped stakeholders identify shared interests and set the stage for success.

Once the problems were clearly defined, the group considered a number of alternatives. Participants focused on resolving identified problems (reducing flood losses and improving water quality) rather than dwelling on symptoms, perceptions, or emotions. For instance, developers noted that they did not want to build homes that would flood in the future, nor did they want to be blamed for the construction of flood-prone homes that had been built in the 1960s. Honest and open dialogue provided room for the exchange of ideas, continuing discussion,

and negotiation. Efforts were made to stay focused rather than becoming sidetracked by potential "deal killers."[2]

The result was a city/county guidance document that identified six primary strategies for incorporating flood mitigation into community recovery efforts: (1) the establishment of new floodplain development standards, (2) the adoption of an enhanced flood warning system, (3) the creation of a drainage system maintenance plan, (4) the design of a public information campaign, (5) the formation of an interagency steering committee, and (6) the development and implementation of watershed-based hazard mitigation plans. Each strategy was tied to specific action-oriented tasks with time lines and parties responsible for their implementation. An overriding theme of the document was the use of verifiable data to ground specific policy choices in a sound fact base.

The new policies were based on the creation of new flood insurance rate maps (FIRMs) (see figure on next page). Rather than develop maps that were static depictions of current conditions, like those historically created by the Federal Emergency Management Agency, the city and county used geographic information systems (GIS) to design maps that reflected the flood hazard conditions of the future, when all allowable development had occurred in the floodplain. The maps included information derived from existing zoning maps and estimates of future settlement patterns and land uses. The GIS-based maps allowed for better analysis, including the ability to project estimated future impacts—an important benefit given that new development, with its concomitant increase in impervious surfaces and placement of fill material in the floodplain, can cause changes in flood elevations. (See the sidebar later in this chapter for a more detailed description of GIS.)

Charlotte/Mecklenburg Stormwater Services, which was tasked with providing technical information to the larger assemblage of participants, created a number of scenarios that demonstrate the relationship between

continued on page 270

continued from page 269

This flood insurance rate map depicts both current and projected future flood hazard conditions in Charlotte, North Carolina, based on an expected build out of the floodplain.

Courtesy of Mecklenburg County Stormwater Services.

Water quality features and a greenway trail in an area once occupied by flood-prone homes.

Courtesy of Mecklenburg County Stormwater Services.

development and future flood risk. It showed how flood elevations changed when different floodplain build-out scenarios were applied to the model. The "future conditions" mapping effort increased flood elevations by as much as eleven feet and expanded the floodway, the area within the floodplain where development is severely restricted. This approach also enabled the group to quantify expected flood losses under a number of different hypothetical conditions and assumptions, many of which were requested

by developers. Tying proposed actions to real dollar figures helped developers, local government officials, and other key stakeholders better understand the problem and the implications of different scenarios. Although the group acknowledged that the ability to map future flood hazards could lead to the passage of more stringent regulations, they agreed to support the program.

Prior to Hurricane Danny, Mecklenburg County had sought to improve water quality through the Surface Water Improvement and Management Panel. County commissioners wanted to attain a level of water quality that would allow for "prolonged human contact."[3] To achieve this aim, a coalition of environmentalists, citizens, developers, and local officials created a stream buffer plan that identified buffer widths according to the acreage drained by each creek or stream in a series of watersheds. The larger the drainage area, the larger the buffer required. If the buffer area exceeded the mapped floodplain, new development was not allowed within the larger boundary. The plan improved water quality while also mitigating the impact of flooding. With the area along the creek kept free of development, the existing vegetation was able to filter pollutants while the open space provided for additional water storage (see accompanying figure).

The use of information that developers recognized as valid allowed county and city officials to negotiate an agreed-upon regulatory framework and expand support for additional mitigation initiatives. For instance, the new maps served as the basis for the flood hazard analysis component of the city and county's watershed-based hazard mitigation plans. The resulting hazard mitigation strategy emphasized the relocation of flood-prone homes and a number of other complementary objectives. And the development of a robust risk assessment, including the collection of detailed information about individual structures in the floodplain, paid off handsomely for the city and county. In 1999, after communities affected by Hurricane Floyd had applied for and received Hazard Mitigation Grant Program (HMGP) funds for eligible mitigation projects, the state had surplus federal dollars. The city and county were notified of the excess money and told that unless the funds were obligated quickly, they would revert back to the federal government. County officials were able to assemble the necessary information in a matter of days and developed an application that typically takes months to construct. Shortly thereafter, Mecklenburg County received approximately $10 million in HMGP funds to acquire 116 flood-prone homes. With that money, plus an additional $2.2 million derived from local storm-water management fees, it purchased and demolished the homes and reverted the land to open space (see figure above). The open space extended an existing greenway and the stream buffer system (see accompanying figure), thereby reducing flood risk, enhancing local recreational opportunities, and improving water quality—all of which were key objectives identified in the early stages of the consensus-building process.

This apartment complex was demolished in 2009 following the acquisition of property using a combination of FEMA's Pre-Disaster Mitigation grant program and local storm-water management funds.

Courtesy of Mecklenburg County Stormwater Services.

1 Author's personal communication with Dave Canaan, director, Mecklenburg County Water and Land Resources, 2001.
2 Ibid.
3 Ibid.

This aerial photo shows a neighborhood where the City of Charlotte and Mecklenburg County acquired about fifty homes and created open space, water quality ponds, and greenways.

Courtesy of Mecklenburg County Stormwater Services.

Figure 8–1. In this meeting conducted by the Mississippi Governor's Office of Recovery and Renewal in Jackson County, Mississippi, following Hurricane Katrina, representatives from federal and state agencies, nonprofits, foundations, and quasi-governmental organizations described their programs and then fielded questions in an effort to link available resources with local needs.

Courtesy of Governor's Office of Recovery and Renewal, State of Mississippi.

conducive to developing sound recovery plans, and (3) the lack of resources committed to pre-event planning across the assistance network. Government organizations tasked with disaster recovery have yet to fully understand the value of pre-event planning for post-disaster recovery, relying instead on a post-disaster approach spelled out by the Stafford Act and the NRF—two policies that create powerful disincentives to plan in that they both emphasize post-disaster monetary assistance with little or no effort to balance this approach with comparable pre-event capacity-building initiatives.[12] In addition, these policies do not hold states and communities accountable for actions—or inactions—that place people and property in harm's way or limit people's ability to effectively recover from disasters that occur.

The Post-Katrina Emergency Management Reform Act (PKEMRA) of 2006 requires the development of a national disaster recovery strategy. Like the Stafford Act, the PKEMRA was precipitated by a major disaster that publicly highlighted significant problems. According to federal legislation, the NDRF will define federal responsibilities (as the NRF purports to do), describe cost-effective programs intended to meet local needs (an important element of the disaster recovery assistance framework), and promote the use of disaster-resistant building materials. It will not, however, explicitly emphasize the steps needed to undertake effective pre-event recovery planning efforts (including providing for adequate levels of resource support). Although the creation of Emergency Support Function 14 (ESF-14) and the passage of both the Disaster Mitigation Act and the PKEMRA provide some evidence that planning for recovery is gaining acceptance, the strategies and programs they have created remain disconnected. As stand-alone policies devoid of an integrative framework, they lack the capacity to effect the change needed across disaster recovery assistance networks. The degree to which the NDRF will provide this framework remains to be seen, as is further discussed in Chapter 10.

The federal government has invested a modest amount of resources in the post-disaster development of local recovery plans following federally declared events. But there are no federal education or training programs for pre-event recovery planning, nor is there a federal effort to build a coalition of support to advance the value of such planning. The reactive, piecemeal approach that currently exists has led to the creation of a small number of local plans after major disasters rather than to a systematic effort to train a cadre of stakeholders that are capable of developing robust recovery plans nationwide. And the limited involvement of state officials in the development of post-disaster local recovery plans sponsored by the Federal Emergency Management Agency (FEMA) has further hindered the degree of vertical integration between local, state, and federal agencies. The extent of integration across the public sector will likely remain low until either the federal government provides the financial and technical resources needed to hire and train state staff focused on planning for disaster recovery, or states take greater ownership of the idea and use existing staff or create new positions focused on this issue.

At the state level, recovery is often led by emergency management agencies and defined largely as the administration of post-disaster federal programs. Historically, state emergency management departments had hired a limited number of employees with a background in planning. The emergence of hazard mitigation in the late 1980s and the passage of the Disaster Mitigation Act of 2000, which requires the development of state and local plans, have addressed this problem to some extent. A small but growing number of states are currently engaged in local recovery planning initiatives, some of which are tied to legislative mandates while others represent experimental pilot programs. Promising pre-disaster initiatives include those under development in Florida and Oregon. Florida's experimental recovery planning program (see the sidebar on page 44) requires local recovery plans, developed by participating counties and cities, to link disaster recovery initiatives with existing land use plans. In Oregon, plans are being developed voluntarily with technical assistance provided by the Oregon Natural Hazards Workgroup at the University of Oregon's Community Service Center (see the sidebar on page 335).

Unfortunately, the larger professional planning community has yet to embrace its role in pre-event planning for post-disaster recovery.[13] Many planners who have become recovery planning advocates either became directly involved in recovery activities after a disaster or studied the implications of failing to do so before a disaster occurs. For instance, following the Oakland Hills, California, wildfires in 1991, which destroyed over 2,800 housing units, planners reported a newfound appreciation for the complexities of planning for post-disaster recovery, their role in developing such plans, and the inherent problems resulting from the failure to have plans in place prior to an event.[14] A growing number of planning scholars have embraced this topic, including those who describe how the tools that planners use can be applied to recovery.[15]

BRINGING PROFESSIONAL PLANNING INTO THE DISASTER RECOVERY ASSISTANCE FRAMEWORK

The planning profession has been described as a vehicle to transfer knowledge to action,[16] identify and expand policy alternatives,[17] involve and empower citizens,[18] spur collective action and social change,[19] foster sustainable development,[20] and confront power imbalances.[21]

Planning, which also emphasizes a distinct spatial orientation, has been founded on principles that embrace the health and safety of communities.[22] It also draws on the use of collaborative approaches, including such ADR techniques as policy dialogue, negotiated rule making, facilitation, and mediation, and empowerment strategies, such as public participation, education, outreach, training, and coalition building. In essence, plan making and the use of ADR techniques are mutually reinforcing actions. For almost forty years, the planning profession has applied ADR techniques to resource management, intergovernmental development conflicts, and other land use dilemmas.[23] But the same principles and techniques, while directly applicable to the challenges associated with disaster recovery, are noticeably absent from widespread practice before or after an event.[24]

Although scholars continue to debate the purpose of plans,[25] plans are central to understanding the practice of planning; and as this book contends, a central purpose of planning is to foster collaborative problem solving. Accordingly, plan making, guided not only by planning principles but also by ADR techniques, is seen here as essential to transforming how the recovery assistance framework operates. This is because the use of ADR techniques can contribute to a greater understanding of local needs and the delivery of programs that more accurately reflect the variable nature of assistance networks (i.e., their different capabilities, access to resources, and levels of interorganizational coordination). After Hurricane Floyd, for example, officials created twenty-two state programs targeting unmet needs (see the sidebar in Chapter 2 on North Carolina's disaster recovery assistance programs after Hurricane Floyd) and used negotiation tactics to modify post-disaster congressional appropriations so as to better address identified local conditions (see the sidebar in this chapter on pages 297–298). Similarly, after Hurricane Katrina, the Broadmoor community in New Orleans used mediation and facilitation techniques to develop agreed-upon neighborhood-level recovery strategies that served to integrate organizations horizontally and vertically across the assistance network (see Chapter 3). The resulting strategies were grounded in local needs and tied to resources drawn from inside and outside the community.

Finally, planning can improve the timing of pre- and post-disaster assistance by identifying available resources in advance and developing a strategy to coordinate their delivery. The previous sidebar on page 269, which describes the pre-event identification of homes eligible for relocation out of the floodplain in Charlotte, North Carolina, pending the availability of funding, shows how such planning can speed recovery assistance. Formulation of the relocation strategy, adoption of more stringent floodplain mapping standards, and identification of other complementary objectives, such as reducing non-point-source pollution and developing a greenway adjacent to the flood-prone creek, all evolved from lengthy discussions among stakeholders who had previously viewed each other as adversaries. The time spent involved in what some initially viewed as overly protracted dialogue and debate paid off when state and federal resources became available unexpectedly, thereby allowing for the implementation of the plan.

PLAN QUALITY AND ALTERNATIVE DISPUTE RESOLUTION PRINCIPLES

Plans are rarely evaluated according to recognized metrics.[26] Plan evaluation principles grew out of the elements of content and process, both of which are essential to a good plan as defined by accepted standards of practice.[27] Although the techniques used to evaluate plan quality have been used to assess a range of plans, including those that focus on natural hazards,[28] the principles that underlie quality plans are just beginning to be applied to disaster recovery planning and collaborative planning. A study by Gavin Smith and Victor Flatt, for example, focuses on the application of plan quality principles to a small sample of state disaster recovery plans as part of an effort to create an evaluation tool that can be used in the development of planning standards associated with the emerging NDRF.[29] And Richard Norton has developed a set of "communicative action criteria" in which plans are described as a "communicative policy act" and concepts of accuracy, comprehensibility/legibility, legitimacy, and sincerity are added to the analysis.[30]

Plan quality is strongly influenced by input from those who are affected by the plan and its policies, and from those whose knowledge of local conditions is best obtained through participatory planning. Professional planners are trained in many of the requisite process-oriented skills needed by effective mediators, including the use of ADR techniques.[31] Planning and ADR scholars Lawrence Susskind and Connie Ozawa effectively describe these overlapping skills in their description of the planner as mediator:

The art of persuasion and the creative accommodation of competing interests, coupled with the technical skills of design—the identification of options, the generation of alternative plans or policies, and the assessment of various alternatives—as well as a concern for the implementation of agreements or recommendations are common to the mediator and the planner.[32]

David Godschalk further delineates the connectivity between the two activities by describing complementary "planning process tasks" and "conflict resolution steps" (Exhibit 8–1).

This chapter applies established internal and external plan quality principles to the defining characteristics of the disaster recovery assistance framework and also suggests new principles drawn from the ADR literature. The intent is to expand the breadth of plan quality analysis and help to define a broader suite of practical actions that are pertinent to the creation of recovery plans (Exhibit 8–2). The delineation of plan quality principles is not an academic exercise. Rather, these principles provide a useful set of elements for planners to follow as they craft plans that are grounded in rigorous scholarship and tangible measures of quality.

Internal Plan Quality Principles

Internal principles of planning are issue identification (i.e., establishing a clear vision and an associated set of goals and objectives); the formulation of policies that drive specific actions; a fact base on which to ground voluntary and regulatory policy choices; implementation; monitoring and evaluation strategies; and internal consistency across a plan's vision, goals, and policies.[33] Taken together, they provide a plan's guiding framework for action.

Issue Identification

Developing an actionable disaster recovery plan includes identifying a vision and a set of goals and policies to accomplish it. The vision statement, which describes the broad

---

Exhibit 8–1. Integrating Planning Tasks with Conflict Resolution Steps

Planning Process Tasks	Conflict Resolution Steps
Inventory and Trend Analysis	Issue Identification and Packaging
Goal Setting	Consensus Building
Alternative Plan Generation Process	Dispute Resolution (Negotiations)
Plan Adoption, Implementation, and Updating/Revision	Consensus Maintenance, Monitoring of Agreements

Source: David Godschalk, "Volusia County Conflict Resolution Program," in The Planner as Dispute Resolver, ed. A. Bruce Dotson, David Godschalk, and Jerome Kaufman (Washington, D.C.: National Institute for Dispute Resolution, 1989). Reprinted with permission of the author.

purpose of the plan, may emphasize such themes as achieving a sustainable disaster recovery or creating a more disaster-resilient community (see Figure 8–2 on page 278). It should

---

Exhibit 8–2. Plan Quality and Alternative Dispute Resolution Principles

Plan Quality Principles

Internal Plan Quality Principles

Issue Identification

- Vision
- Goals

Policies

- Voluntary and Regulatory
- Post-Disaster Projects
- Spatial Orientation

Fact Base

- Demographic, Economic, and Land Use Data
- Vulnerability Assessment and Post-Disaster Damage Assessment
- Capability Assessment and Stakeholder Analysis

Implementation

- Time Lines
- Organizational Accountability
- Funding/Resources

Monitoring and Evaluation

- Routine Assessment of Goals
- Timetable for Plan Updates (periodic, following disasters)
- Identify Evaluative Measures

Internal Consistency

External Plan Quality Principles

Organizational Clarity

- Organizing Structure
- Cross-Referencing
- Supporting Documentation
- Visual Aids

Interorganizational Coordination

- Vertical Integration
- Horizontal Integration

Compliance

- Plan Mandates and Voluntary Agreements
- Existing Plans, Policies, and Programs

Alternative Dispute Resolution Principles

Repeated Interaction and Reciprocal Dialogue

Creation of Incentives to Participate and Share Information

Demonstration of the Benefits of ADR

Clarification of the Fact Base

Identification of New Perspectives and the Creation of Multiple Options

High Stakeholder Involvement

Redress of Existing Power Imbalances

Source: The internal and external plan quality principles are modified from Philip R. Berke et al., *Urban Land Use Planning*, 5th ed. (Urbana: Illinois University Press, 2006), 70–74, copyright 2006 by the Board of Trustees of the University of Illinois. Used with permission of the University of Illinois Press, and from Philip Berke and David Godschalk, "Searching for the Good Plan: A Meta-Analysis of Plan Quality Studies," *Journal of Planning Literature* 23, no. 3 (2009): 227–240. Reprinted with permission of the publisher. The alternative dispute resolution section represents an additional facet of plan quality principles and is modified from Gavin Smith, "The Transformation of Environmental Conflict: A Game Theoretic Approach" (PhD diss., Texas A&M University, 1995).

Figure 8–2. The creation of vision statements was an integral part of the New Hartford, Iowa, disaster recovery planning process.

Courtesy of FEMA.

be accompanied by a set of goals through which it can be achieved. Goals are positive, future-oriented statements that are used to frame policies. They also reflect public values derived through stakeholder involvement (see Figure 8–3). For example, three possible disaster recovery plan goals may be (1) to improve the connectivity between disaster recovery programs and local needs; (2) to improve the timing of assistance; and (3) to improve the level of coordination (i.e., horizontal and vertical integration) across the disaster recovery assistance network.

Policies

One of the major problems with the current disaster recovery assistance framework is the failure to tie recovery policies, defined as action-oriented statements, to a unified set of goals that underlie a purpose or vision. This is certainly evident in the NRF, and any attempt to address this organizational artifact through the NDRF must support the development of internally consistent policies that span the larger assistance network. (A discussion of internal consistency is found at the end of this section.) Understood in the context of planning, disaster recovery policies should be developed in consultation with other members of the assistance network in order to avert problems noted in the NRF and in the state and local plans described in Chapter 2.

Figure 8–3. A public meeting in Palo, Iowa, focused on the linkage between the community's vision statement and the creation of disaster recovery goals.

Courtesy of FEMA.

Plans, which often include a range of regulatory and voluntary policies, are strengthened by an emphasis on mandatory policies that have legal standing as defined by legislative or administrative authority. Regulatory policies may include the adoption of stronger building codes and higher land use standards to better account for existing hazard vulnerabilities. More specifically, this may involve the adoption of a cumulative substantial damage ordinance that requires the owner of a structure that has sustained disaster-caused damages exceeding 50 percent of its value to rebuild in accordance with the most recent building codes and standards; depending on the nature of the policy, damage thresholds can be met following one event or a series of events over time. Policies can also be developed and adopted through voluntary agreements, as discussed later in this chapter. Voluntary policies may include the establishment of financial incentives to encourage pre-event recovery planning and the adoption of hazard mitigation measures.

Another example of a policy may involve the adoption of a temporary post-disaster building moratorium. This allows local officials to assess post-disaster conditions and determine whether to strengthen pre-event building codes and standards or amend other policies before issuing construction and repair permits. It also provides additional time to engage the public and the larger assistance network in a multitude of policy choices that must be addressed during recovery (which can be overwhelming, particularly if the community does not have a recovery plan in place prior to a disaster). Additional policies may include the formation of a disaster recovery committee (and the delineation of its associated powers and duties); the creation of a local disaster recovery fund to finance post-disaster operations; the establishment of additional coordinative processes, including communication, education, training, exercise, and mutual aid policies, with members of the assistance network; the treatment of historic buildings after a disaster, including their repair or demolition; the creation of post-disaster permitting processes; and the restoration of damaged environmental systems such as wetlands.

Specific disaster recovery projects are often identified in the post-disaster environment and reflect actions tied to policies associated with the restoration, repair, and reconstruction of damaged infrastructure, critical facilities, and housing. Examples of such projects may be the restoration of public services, including water, sewer, and power systems; the removal of debris generated by both the event and the demolition of damaged structures and infrastructure; the retrofitting of existing buildings to better withstand the impacts of future events; the construction of a temporary housing site; the relocation of a flood-prone neighborhood to higher ground; and the repair or reconstruction of affordable housing units (see Figure 8–4 on page 281).

The Plan-Making Hierarchy in the Los Angeles Recovery and Reconstruction Plan

Vision: Planning and action before a disaster can significantly reduce recovery and reconstruction costs, hasten return to normalcy, and create an improved city afterwards. The vision embodied in this concept is that of a city with the foresight to recover rapidly from any disaster and rebuild wisely as a better place.

Themes: The vision contains four themes.
- Planning: A basic premise for this plan is that planning undertaken in advance of a disaster can accelerate a post-disaster return to normalcy.
- Hazard mitigation: Pre-event mitigation of structural and natural hazards reduces damages and post-event resource expenditures to respond, recover, and reconstruct.
- Short-term recovery: The key objectives of short-term recovery are to restore homes, jobs, services, and facilities quickly and efficiently.
- Long-term reconstruction: The plan aims to rebuild safely and wisely, reducing future hazards and optimizing community improvements.

Policies: The themes are carried out through a series of policies organized around nine functional areas.

- Residential, commercial, and industrial rehabilitation
- Public sector services
- Economic recovery
- Land use/reuse
- Organization and authority
- Psychological rehabilitation
- Vital records
- Interjurisdictional relationships
- Traffic mitigation.

Action (implementation) programs: For each policy a series of actions are listed, including those responsible for policy implementation. Actions are divided into three categories:

- Pre-event
- Post-event short term
- Post-event long term.

Source: Adapted from City of Los Angeles, Emergency Operations Organization, *Recovery and Reconstruction Plan* (1994), 7–11.

An outline of the Los Angeles, California, Recovery and Reconstruction Plan, shown in the accompanying sidebar, provides an example of how key planning elements discussed up to this point come together.

Fact Base

The recovery plan contains three principle fact bases: (1) demographic, economic, and land use data; (2) a vulnerability assessment and post-disaster damage assessment; and (3) a capability assessment and stakeholder analysis. Each background study should include an evaluation of current and projected future conditions in the study area. Because the fact base and its associated data support the plan's vision, goals, policies, and projects, the data should be obtained and analyzed using accepted standards of practice, their sources clearly cited, and their accuracy closely evaluated and monitored over time.

The effective use of data is important in recovery planning for a number of reasons. For instance, the plan should be able to assess current and projected development patterns (before and after disasters), particularly

Figure 8–4. The timing of disaster recovery planning, including the use of post-disaster design workshops, may be a necessary means of implementing aspects of a plan developed after a disaster or of refining a plan that was created before an event. This post-disaster community design workshop in Oakville, Iowa, reflects part of a post-disaster recovery planning process that was not established before the 2008 Iowa floods.

Courtesy of FEMA.

those that infringe on known hazard areas. Decisions regarding the reconstruction of public facilities, infrastructure, and housing are interconnected, affecting settlement patterns, future growth, and vulnerability. To address these and other often complex issues, information should be displayed in maps, tables, and figures so that it is easy to understand. Geographic information systems (GIS) enable planners to visually layer the data, which facilitates the spatial assessment of various conditions and scenarios that span the three principal fact bases (see the sidebar on page 282). Planners increasingly use GIS to analyze a number of data-intensive issues that can be displayed geospatially—including, for example, how different land use choices affect post-disaster reconstruction options.

Demographic, Economic, and Land Use Data

Demographic information typically includes total population, their spatial distribution and density, average age, income, and annual growth rate. Additional demographic data that should be collected include sex, race, ethnicity, and migration patterns across population groups. The spatial distribution of demographic data is an important part of gauging an area's vulnerability to hazards. For example, what are the population densities in mapped hazard areas? Who is living in these locations? Are known hazard areas overrepresented by individuals with lower median incomes? Does the community include those who do not speak English? Are there people living in areas prone to natural hazards who have moved from a locale that is not prone to that type of hazard?

The Use of Geographic Information Systems in Recovery Planning

A geographic information system (GIS) is computer-based software that allows for the storage, retrieval, management, analysis, and display of spatial data. The power of GIS is tied to the ability of the operator to generate multiple geospatial datasets, or layers, and conduct analyses based on the relationships found across geographically referenced information.

GIS software is routinely used to support the creation and maintenance of land use plans, hazard mitigation plans, growth management plans, and a number of other planning documents. It is also used on a widespread basis following disasters. For example, officials collect geospatially referenced information about the level of damage sustained by different properties and infrastructure as part of an initial damage assessment and potential disaster declaration request, an evaluation of evacuation routes relative to the extent of the hazard's impact, and an assessment of the geographic distribution of debris. States and communities may use GIS to document the performance of pre-event hazard mitigation measures after a disaster, including the retrofit of existing public buildings, the relocation of flood-prone homes, and the enactment of an enhanced building code. In addition, GIS can serve as a powerful tool for officials seeking to request or amend post-disaster policy, as suggested by the sidebars on pages 38–39 in Chapter 2 and on pages 297–298 of this chapter. It is important, however, to ensure that the collection, analysis, and interpretation of such data involve more than technical experts, as

shown in the first sidebar in this chapter and in the one on pages 297–298.

The ability to collect, store, and manage pre-event geospatial data is equally vital to recovery planning. Key datasets that might be incorporated into a GIS include demographics (age, median income, education, race, sex, primary language spoken); housing (year built, type of construction, owner-occupied versus rental, square footage); land use (residential, commercial, industrial, mixed, open space/parks); infrastructure (roads, public facilities [schools, government buildings], and critical facilities [police and fire stations, hospitals, emergency operation centers]); geographically defined hazards (floodplain, storm surge inundation areas, landslide-prone areas, earthquake zones, wildland urban interface); other relevant environmental factors (hydric soils, land elevation, slope, and tree cover); and past disaster conditions (extent and severity of damages by structural type and location).

Post-disaster data can be entered into a GIS and displayed geospatially, assuming that the data points (structures, transportation networks, and debris fields) are georeferenced—a process that is typically performed using a global positioning system (GPS). For instance, if the damages are associated with a flood or hurricane-driven storm surge and the community has a digital flood insurance rate map (DFIRM), the damage assessment data can be layered on top of the map. This allows local officials to compare the extent of damages against the location of key structures on the DFIRM

Economic data may include the number and type of businesses in a given area and the number of people employed across different job sector classifications. Those tasked with developing the recovery plan may seek to find out whether the timing of a disaster disproportionately affects some businesses more than others. How is the economic makeup of the community tied to seasonal (e.g., tourism) or external (e.g., regional or international trade) markets? What is the projected exposure among local businesses and their suppliers to identified hazards and different disaster scenarios?

and posit questions that can inform future policy decisions, such as whether the damages are what could have been expected given existing risk assessment information; how many structures located outside the mapped flood hazard area experienced flood-related damages; and what kind of damages were sustained relative to the age of each structure and the building codes in place at the time of its construction.

Metadata (descriptive information that characterizes the primary data) associated with individual structures can be used to conduct higher-level analyses. For example, how many of the affected structures were covered by flood insurance? Were damages predominantly associated with structures built before the community joined the National Flood Insurance Program? How much water did individual structures receive? Were low-income residents disproportionately affected? With the information they obtain, policy makers might conclude that stronger building code and flood ordinance standards need to be adopted. Additional policies may include developing an outreach program targeting those who did not have flood insurance prior to the event or working with local lending institutions to provide low-interest loans to individuals seeking to incorporate risk reduction measures into the repair of their homes. Analysis may also point to pre-event hazard mitigation policies that reduced potential losses, and the results may be used to build support for an expansion of similar strategies in the recovery plan.

To what extent might this level of exposure affect the speed of reopening as well as the larger issues associated with economic loss and recovery? Have business owners developed continuity plans that account for these realities and integrated the business owners' needs into the recovery plans of their communities?

Good plans, including those associated with disaster recovery, possess a distinct spatial orientation; that is, they address the type, density, and location of human settlements. For instance, most local governments comprehensively categorize land uses as residential, commercial, industrial, agricultural, recreational, and mixed. Those involved in disaster recovery need to know how current and future (or proposed) land uses are spatially aligned relative to likely hazards. To what degree are land use choices shaped by hazard vulnerability and the effects of past disasters? For instance, are environmentally sensitive areas that are also prone to natural hazards (e.g., wetlands, steep sloped areas, the wildland-urban interface, and barrier islands) identified, and are limits placed on intensive development in these locations? Have possible modifications to the pattern of existing and future land use been addressed in the recovery plan should a disaster occur (see the Hillsborough County, Florida, sidebar in Chapter 2)? Does the recovery plan consider the issues surrounding the relocation and possible resettlement of severely damaged properties, including neighborhoods and critical facilities? Given the controversies associated with decisions about development and the lessons drawn from successfully mediated land use disputes, these discussions should involve stakeholders early in the process (before a disaster occurs, if possible), and those guiding the process should solicit the input of stakeholders on the formulation of proposed recovery goals and policies,[34] including those linked to hazard vulnerability.

Vulnerability Assessment and Post-Disaster Damage Assessment

Another important fact base in the recovery plan is the vulnerability assessment and the closely associated post-disaster damage assessment. The vulnerability assessment includes an evaluation of hazards found in the area; a determination of the likelihood of their occurrence; and projected levels of physical, social, economic, and environmental impacts (typically measured as expected monetary damages) across various scenarios. (Social and environmental damages are more difficult to monetize than physical and economic damages, so their costs are less frequently included in the vulnerability assessment.) It identifies the hazards that may occur in the study area and describes their physical characteristics; in the case of hurricanes, for instance, this description would include high winds, heavy rainfall, storm surge, coastal erosion, and tornado activity. It also contains a hazards history of the study area—information (often derived from newspaper and other media accounts and studies of past events) that provides local context and that supplements the hazards identification section.

Next, the destructive characteristics of those hazards (i.e., their intensity, scale, duration, and speed of onset) that have a reasonable likelihood of occurrence in the study area are linked to different disaster scenarios. For example, as part of its risk assessment, a California community would likely assess its vulnerability to earthquakes by estimating the type and extent of likely damages, injuries, and loss of life associated with different earthquake intensities (magnitude), locations (including depth underground, position of the epicenter, and proximity to human settlements), times of occurrence (e.g., during the day when people are at work and children are at school, during rush hour when large numbers of people are in transit, or at night when most people are at home), and durations. One factor that makes earthquakes particularly dangerous is their tendency to strike quickly with little or no advanced warning. This is one reason why pre-event earthquake preparedness is so important (see the sidebars in Chapter 3 on two approaches to regional disaster recovery planning and on the Great California Shakeout). All these factors and various combinations thereof affect the type and extent of damages to property and the potential loss of life. It is the intersection of the hazard with the built and natural environment on which people depend that causes the human construct referred to as "a disaster."[35]

While commonly developed as part of a hazard mitigation plan, a vulnerability assessment also enables planners to assess where and how structures and supporting infrastructure should be built after a disaster. It helps communities decide whether it is prudent to rebuild in known hazard areas, strengthen existing building codes and ordinances, modify public investment strategies, or adopt new policies based on expected future losses. The pre-event analysis of expected losses from various disaster scenarios can be monetized, allowing decision makers to measure the projected financial costs and benefits of different policy options, such as relocating flood-prone homes to higher ground, strengthening buildings to better withstand ground motion associated with earthquakes, or constructing a public tornado shelter to protect individuals from high winds and flying debris.

With each new disaster, planners and other members of the assistance network have the opportunity to test the effectiveness of their policies and the accuracy of their risk assessments. Post-disaster findings and observations associated with damage assessments and studies should be used to modify policies that did not work as intended or to enact new policies. While scenario-based planning cannot predict all occurrences and needs, it does allow communities to engage in pre-event exercises and training sessions that can be used to test roles and resource distribution processes. Involving members of the assistance network in planning (including the development of the vulnerability assessment and the crafting and implementation of training scenarios) helps to provide a better understanding of local conditions while gaining support for proposed policies (as evidenced in the Tulsa sidebar in Chapter 4 and the Charlotte–Mecklenburg County sidebar in this chapter).

Capability Assessment and Stakeholder Analysis

The capability assessment, a third component of the fact base, is a review of the fiscal, technical, and administrative abilities of a nation, region, state, community, or organization to recover from the damaging effects of hazards and disasters. It also includes an analysis of stakeholders in the study area (i.e., the disaster recovery assistance network) that are affected by and that help to shape and implement various policies as part of a planning process or through more informal means (see again the sidebar on page 84).

The capability assessment is accomplished through an evaluation of existing policies, programs, and plans—for example, the comprehensive land use plan, the comprehensive emergency management plan, and the hazard mitigation plan—and their associated impacts on disaster recovery. (These plans and their role in improving the disaster recovery assistance framework are discussed more fully in Chapter 9.) This evaluation may lead to the formulation of new policies that address identified short-falls or to the elimination of programs that run counter to the goals and policies of the recovery plan. Similarly, the recovery plan may be amended to reflect policies that are already being achieved through other plans and can thus be cited by reference.

David Godschalk suggests that one way to address the disconnect between plans and actions is to conduct what he refers to as "safe growth audits."[36] The pre-event analysis of policies, ordinances, and plans is intended to evaluate the effects that these documents will have on the community's current and future hazard vulnerability. While the practice is described in the context of hazard mitigation planning, it represents an important tool for educating citizens and elected officials about how planning and development activities affect public safety. With a better understanding of this interconnectivity, a community can make the necessary changes to plans and policies.

Although the capability to implement programs and policies varies significantly across stakeholders and over time, the failure to develop strategies that are based on the capability that does exist is often a major shortcoming of hazards planning.[37] For instance, the routine failure to consider indigenous resources or include community residents shortchanges the collective resource base, including locally based and often emergent knowledge that is key to creating policy that reflects local needs (see the sidebar on page 137).

Public sector recovery plans often focus on the identification of government programs and, to a lesser extent, nonprofit resources rather than undertake a systematic review of the larger assistance network. This limits horizontal and vertical integration as well as the creation of policies that reflect a more holistic vision.[38] As was seen in Chapters 2 through 7, many policies are developed without the adequate involvement of others in the assistance network, including those that are most directly affected by the policy choices that are ultimately adopted or those that possess critically important resources. In the current system, narrowly defined federal programs, principally those delivered after an event, drive the actions of other members of the network. This, in turn, results in reactionary post-disaster planning strategies. Thus, the policy framework limits the degree to which flexible and innovative programs created by others are coupled with better financed, albeit more bureaucratic programs, and implemented in a manner that reflects local needs while being appropriately timed to address existing and unanticipated conditions.

Administrative capabilities are closely associated not only with existing policies, programs, and plans, but also with the abilities of various stakeholders that shape policy-making processes. An analysis of the stakeholders involved in recovery requires the inclusion of those that develop and implement recovery policies as well as those affected by these decisions who may have been left out of the process. Important aspects of this analysis include (1) a list of relevant stakeholders, (2) their interests, (3) the resources and their base of power, and (4) their influence on and interaction with others in the network.[39]

Implementation

A plan should identify the means for implementing proposed policies and projects, the party (or parties) responsible for their implementation, and a time line with established deadlines, which helps to make the plan actionable and holds parties accountable. Tying actions to specific human, financial, and technical resources is essential to ensuring proper and timely implementation over time. Implementation schedules should also account for unanticipated needs, propose modified time lines should the need arise, and identify new members of the network, including those that might emerge unexpectedly both before and after disasters.

It is important to recognize that the adoption of new policies in the post-disaster environment often sets in motion a number of associated actions; these actions should be captured in the plan and their implementation tracked. For instance, a policy that requires the reconstruction of a given percentage of affordable housing units necessitates identifying appropriate sites, hiring design and construction firms willing to take on the project, procuring adequate financing, and possibly contracting with a local community development corporation to manage the project. Given that the previous example represents one policy (and its associated actions), it becomes clear just how complex planning for disaster recovery can be across the larger assistance network.

Monitoring and Evaluation

Plans should be monitored and evaluated regularly to ensure that the multitude of policies are being implemented and that goals reflect changing conditions. The period following a disaster is a good time to reassess the efficacy of selected policy recommendations and adopt new measures based on post-event findings. Plans should also be reevaluated periodically as demographics, development patterns, and available resources (funding, policies, and technical assistance) change over time.

The post-disaster evaluation of a recovery plan may include the degree to which it helped to identify and address local needs, adequately coordinated the timing of assistance, and facilitated horizontal and vertical integration. Other important evaluative issues include (1) the equitable distribution of resources and the closely associated topic of social vulnerability, and (2) the appropriate balancing of the speed of recovery with a strong public participation element, including active deliberation among members of the assistance network. In each case, the evaluation should identify organizations within the network that will take the lead in the routine assessment of whether actions are being taken and goals are being met in accordance with established implementation time lines.

Another measure worthy of evaluation is the degree to which the plan furthers hazard mitigation. This can be assessed in the aftermath of a disaster by determining the amount by which losses were reduced because of the pre-event adoption of hazard mitigation policies and projects. It is also important to assess the degree to which new mitigation initiatives were adopted in the aftermath of a disaster when communities and individuals may be more receptive to embrace risk reduction efforts, particularly if such measures are tied to a defensible fact base created by technical experts, the public, and other members of the assistance network.

Internal Consistency

A plan's vision, goals, policies, and projects should be internally consistent. If the recovery planning vision addresses the concept of sustainable development, for instance, then the goals, policies, and projects associated with post-disaster recovery should reflect this approach. (The ability of a community to weather the impacts of natural hazards is an important, but often underemphasized aspect of sustainable development and resilience.)[40] Moreover, the failure to establish a higher-order vision in a plan can undercut the remaining document. The lack of internal consistency in the NRF, for example, is reflected in its contradictory policies and programs. The tendency to repair damaged infrastructure to its pre-event condition in high-hazard areas following disasters rather than make use of the 406 Public Assistance program or the Hazard Mitigation Grant Program (see Chapter 2) is an example of how inconsistency manifests itself in disaster recovery policy.

External Plan Quality Principles

The measures of a plan's external quality are organizational clarity, interorganizational coordination, and compliance with other plans, policies, and programs.[41] External plan quality principles serve to convey and connect the plan and its associated policies with those responsible for their implementation as well as with plans and policies that lie outside of the assistance network. Strong external plan quality also helps to give the plan standing and influence.

Organizational Clarity

For a plan to serve as an effective decision-making tool, it should outline its goals in a manner that stakeholders can easily understand. The plan should translate what amounts to often complex, technical information in a way that is comprehensible and concise. This is particularly important to laypeople who may not have "technical expertise" per se but who do have the local knowledge that is equally important to the plan's design. The cross-referencing of planning elements (vision, goals, policies, and projects) documents the integrative aspects of internal consistency and shows the reader how the plan is designed in a logical manner, each part connected to the other under a common purpose. The presentation of this information benefits from the use of visual aids—maps, charts, tables, pictures, and diagrams (see Figure 8–5). Taken together, these elements reduce the intimidation factor that can limit public participation.

Figure 8–5. In this Iowa City post-disaster recovery workshop, note the documentation of the process using flipcharts and video.

Courtesy of FEMA.

If properly communicated and easily understood, a plan can show those stakeholders that have not traditionally engaged in disaster recovery planning that they too may have a role to play in this effort. Understood relative to the conditions described in preceding chapters, this outcome can prove extremely important as many stakeholders have not fully recognized how their capabilities might have value in pre- or post disaster recovery planning.

Interorganizational Coordination

Good plans are designed to improve vertical and horizontal integration. The connection between natural hazards and the need to adapt to the localized impacts of climate change—as evidenced by rising sea levels; the potential intensification of hurricanes and other tropical storms; greater flooding; and rising temperatures and associated heat waves, wildfires, and drought—represents an example of global conditions that could spur greater attention to the importance of vertically integrated plans.

A number of plans cited in previous chapters and noted in Exhibit 8–3 have been done at various jurisdictional levels. The creation of policies that span jurisdictional boundaries is difficult to achieve, however, particularly when plans are developed in isolation. While the plan quality literature explicitly emphasizes the importance of horizontal and vertical integration, the degree to which such integration has actually occurred in disaster recovery assistance networks has been inadequate. The ability of the NDRF to address this issue will play a big role in its ultimate success.

A plan should foster horizontal integration across organizations on the level at which it has been constructed. For instance, some experts say that local plans focus too much on future development and not enough on established communities and their existing locally based organizational networks.[42] The growth of neighborhood plans has been a direct response to this concern, involving residents—those who most likely best understand local needs—in decision making.[43] The creation of small-area plans can be particularly useful in locales prone to natural hazards as they allow citizens to actively engage in the planning process.[44] As neighborhoods identify local needs, the municipal government or members of the community can step in with appropriate resources (which exemplifies strong horizontal integration). For the same reason, some experts recommend that hazard mitigation plans also target the needs of a small area, engaging the public in actions that directly affect them. The nationwide trend toward county-level and multicounty regional hazard mitigation plans represents the opposite approach and should be further studied as to the effect such plans have on

Exhibit 8–3. Disaster Recovery Planning Hierarchy

International (Hyogo Framework)

National (National Response Framework, National Disaster Recovery Framework)

State (Governor's Commission on Recovery, Rebuilding and Renewal; Florida Post-Disaster Redevelopment Planning Program)

Regional (Red River Valley Flood Recovery Action Plan; Association of Bay Area Governments Disaster Recovery Initiative)

Local (Hillsborough County, Florida; Charlotte–Mecklenburg County, North Carolina)

Area or Neighborhood (Broadmoor community, New Orleans)

Individual and Household (Gulf Coast Community Design Studio, Biloxi, Mississippi)

neighborhood-level planning and participation and, hence, on horizontal integration (see the sidebar in Chapter 3 on page 82).

Smaller-scale plans may also be more appropriate in locations that have just experienced a disaster and are faced with the complexities of recovery. As evidenced by the Broadmoor community after Hurricane Katrina, this approach can give residents a greater voice in what is happening, empowering them to play a meaningful role in the future of their neighborhoods. In the case of the Gulf Coast Design Studio (see Chapter 3), the recovery planning process has included actions at the neighborhood, site-specific, and individual property owner levels. Some hazards scholars contend that through this method, citizens may learn to appreciate the value of planning and be more willing to participate in larger municipal and regional planning efforts.[45] But this is not always the case, and care should be taken to ensure that local plans are based on clear standards of accountability[46] and are sufficiently integrated vertically, thereby linking local conditions and needs to the array of resources provided by others located outside the community.

State plans can play an important role in guiding or influencing the form, location, and speed of development at the local level,[47] including in known hazard areas.[48] One technique used to achieve this goal is the management of "areas of critical concern," unzoned land outside municipal jurisdictions, developments that create positive and negative regional impacts, and large-scale public investments.[49] However, the degree to which federal and state recovery policies disproportionately shape local decision making merits greater attention in disaster recovery plans.

To achieve this end, an assessment of existing public sector capabilities can help members of the assistance network identify which state and federal policies and programs are complementary to and which may conflict with policies and programs at the local level. Working collaboratively to address policy mismatches can be institutionalized through the use of formal or informal agreements. In some cases, agreements may emerge after a precipitating event such as a disaster or the passage of legislative mandates. For instance, plans created by the states of Mississippi and North Carolina after Hurricanes Katrina and Floyd, respectively, strengthened vertical integration as state recovery policies were constructed following an initial review of existing federal programs and the documentation of their shortfalls.

A good example of horizontal integration achieved through planning is the purposeful connection between a local government's comprehensive land use plan and the disaster recovery plan. Comprehensive plans, which are intended to guide the current and future growth of a community, rely on a number of tools to achieve this aim—including planning tools, which should play an important role in the formulation of a recovery plan.[50] One option for local governments to consider is to incorporate recovery strategies into the local comprehensive plan as an annex. Doing so gives credence to recovery strategies because the comprehensive plan, which has a recognized history, a sense of legitimacy, and legal standing, typically strives to address horizontal integration. Because planners are involved in the development of the comprehensive plan, this approach provides a means to involve them in recovery as well.

Compliance

Plans should have in place specific means to ensure compliance with stated goals and policies contained within them. They should also include the means, guided by the findings of the capability assessment, to ensure commpliance with other plans in the study area. Where a plan does not have adequate measures in place, it may have limited influence over the issues it purports to address and may inadvertently contradict goals found in other plans.

Compliance can be achieved through plan mandates, voluntary agreements, or a combination thereof. Plan mandates, which are discussed further in Chapter 9, require identified parties to engage in a planning process in order to achieve an identified purpose, and may use incentives or sanctions to achieve this goal. Voluntary agreements, which may use informal or formal procedures to achieve desired ends, can also prove effective. Both types of compliance measures, including mandates and voluntary agreements, have used ADR techniques to successfully address these and other issues that require the support of multiple stakeholders.

Alternative Dispute Resolution Principles

The disaster recovery process continues to rely on outdated and discredited methods of information dissemination, resource distribution, and decision making. For instance, the public is often invited to briefings on recovery programs and their associated eligibility requirements following a disaster. Programs are discussed by different agencies and organizations, each with its own agenda, terminology, rules, and timing of assistance. Discussions center on the technical nature of programs (including their narrow, confusing, and sometimes contradictory rules) rather than on the identification of local needs. It is much less common for members of the assistance network to engage in pre-event, open discussions about the myriad programs and how they can be most effectively coordinated when a disaster happens.

This is unfortunate as pre-event planning allows community officials and individual citizens to take the time needed to compile information on the resources available, assess local conditions, and identify projected needs. If this is not done, local officials, community leaders, and recipients of assistance are forced to assimilate large amounts of information about programs in the immediate aftermath of a disaster. Given the overwhelming set of tasks before them, local officials and others are thrust into unfamiliar roles, particularly in areas that have not identified clear responsibilities across the assistance network. In addition, individuals may be unwilling or unable to engage in larger participatory activities following disasters because of traumatic stress, grief, and the need to identify basic services for themselves and their families.[51] Thus, developing collaborative problem-solving approaches that can be applied in the pre- and post-disaster setting is critically important.

ADR principles (as defined here) involve repeated interaction and the use of reciprocal dialogue, the creation of incentives to participate and share information, a demonstration of the tangible benefits of ADR, a clarification of the fact base, the identification of new perspectives and the creation of multiple options, high levels of stakeholder involvement, and the redress of existing power imbalances.[52] While planners regularly apply ADR techniques to settle land use disputes, address natural resource allocation strategies, and involve the public in decisions affecting their communities, there has been surprisingly little discussion of their application to disaster recovery and risk management,[53] although this has changed somewhat since Hurricane Katrina.[54] Nor have ADR principles been sufficiently included in the plan quality literature or incorporated into the development of plan quality evaluation protocols.

The concept of collaborative planning, which represents an evolution in thinking about how to achieve public goals, is closely aligned with the principles of ADR.[55] Participatory planning also emphasizes the use of tools that foster the active involvement of stakeholder groups in planning their future, including those groups that may have been excluded from past decision-making processes. According to Judith Innes and David Booher, "Consensus building processes are not only about producing agreements and plans but also about experimentation, learning, change, and building shared meaning."[56]

ADR techniques differ from policy-making and public sector resource allocation methods—for example, public hearings; the passage of legislation, including "logrolling" or the exchange of votes; referendums; the use of the courts; and administrative procedures—in several important ways (Exhibit 8–4 on page 294). ADR practitioners seek a mutually satisfactory resolution of conflict through reciprocal dialogue, the open exchange of information, and the construction of enduring agreements. Traditional legal and administrative procedures used to resolve policy disputes often rely on highly structured proceedings and debate protocols that distort effective communication, result in adversarial stakeholder interactions, and produce "winners" and "losers." The

Exhibit 8–4. Drawbacks of Traditional Dispute Resolution Institutions

Legislative	Bureaucracy	Courts
Expensive: Effective lobbying requires large expenditures for staff, campaign contributions, etc.	Expensive: Effective administrative lobbying requires funds for large staff and ongoing research capability.	Expensive: Prolonged court battles and appeals involve high costs.
Limited Access: Not all groups have the funds and staff for effective lobbying.	Limited Access: Not all groups have the resources and staff for effective lobbying.	Limited Access: Not all affected parties can afford the high cost of litigation.
Delay: Legislative process prone to delay and deadlock on difficult and controversial issues.	Delay: Participation (e.g., public hearings, comment periods, etc.) often more symbolic than real.	Delay: Postponements, appeals, overcrowded courts cause frequent delays.
Legislators may understand little about local site-specific disputes.	Adversarial atmosphere produces win-lose decisions that rarely resolve conflicts.	Judges lack expertise on technical issues.
Legislation tends to be vague. Basic conflicts are not resolved and tend to reemerge in implementation phase.	Unilateral, top-down decisions lack political legitimacy. Decisions frequently challenged in court.	Adversarial, win-lose approach fails to resolve controversies and encourages losing party to continue conflict.

Source: Adapted with minor modifications from Douglas J. Amy, *The Politics of Environmental Mediation* (New York: Columbia University Press, 1987), 27. Reprinted with permission of the publisher.

losers in these policy debates tend to be disproportionately represented by the poor and disenfranchised, who, when assessed relative to disaster recovery, often have a high degree of social vulnerability.[57] Public hearings, which are frequently used in policy debates, including the post-disaster allocation of resources, appear to represent an opportunity to voice one's opinion and engage in an open dialogue, but in reality they are sometimes used to limit public opposition and can heighten the mistrust of government officials.[58]

According to Melvin Rubin, dispute resolution professionals have an important role to play in the disaster recovery process, and many of his recommended points of intervention address key themes of the disaster recovery assistance framework—specifically, "facilitating decision-making among insureds and insurance carriers, mediating between various governmental agencies at different levels, creating new ADR models to fit the nature of the disaster, and assisting in the utilization of available resources at different times both pre and post disaster."[59] Indeed, there is growing evidence that ADR is being applied to post-disaster recovery, but this is being done on an ad hoc basis. Specific examples include the resolution of insurance settlement claims following the string of 2004 hurricanes in Florida; the disbursement of the Victim Compensation Fund, which was established after the 9/11 terrorist attack in New York City; the Mississippi Mediation Project, which sought to provide community-based training in mediation following Hurricane Katrina; a joint project between AmeriCorps and Community Mediation Services in New Orleans to improve interorganizational collaboration; and the Florida Conflict Resolution Consortium, which worked with a governor's appointed commission to help develop recommended changes to the statewide building code after Hurricane Andrew.[60]

The contentious nature of post-disaster resource allocation necessitates taking a new look at how these issues may be addressed through the use of ADR techniques and other collaborative approaches, and at how these techniques and approaches may be more systematically and effectively integrated into the actions of disaster recovery assistance networks. Collaborative problem solving can take multiple forms and can be led by various members of the assistance network, including professional mediators.

Mediation, which can involve the use of facilitation, negotiation, and fact-finding techniques (although each can be used irrespective of whether a mediator is involved), relies on the use of a neutral third party. The mediator often takes on many of the time-consuming tasks (e.g., assembling information, investigating the nature of the dispute, identifying appropriate procedural forums, and leading meetings), thereby allowing disputants to focus on reaching an agreement. More important, however, the mediator performs several vital process-oriented functions, including analyzing the underlying preconditions of the dispute, helping disputants identify each other's interests and articulate their stated positions, inventing options for mutual gain, insisting on the use of objective criteria in determining appropriate approaches, and working with disputants to design a mutually acceptable agreement.[61] If a mediator feels that the process or potential outcome is inequitable or fails to address existing power imbalances, he or she may either try to address these issues or discontinue the process and refer it to more traditional dispute resolution approaches, such as the courts or administrative proceedings.[62]

The act of facilitation creates the conditions that are favorable to fostering learning, the exchange of information, and joint problem solving. This may involve the use of a trained facilitator, who helps to define agreed-upon ground rules, elicit open dialogue, and document and assimilate information discussed among participants. Unlike the mediator, the facilitator does not play an active role in the settlement of disputes.

Negotiated rule making is a deliberative process in which stakeholders comment on the content of proposed rules and participate in the writing of policy language.[63] In the post-disaster environment, negotiation among members of the assistance network occurs on a regular basis, yet the skills of those involved in these debates vary widely,[64] which can affect the distribution of resources and therefore the speed and degree to which different communities and individuals recover. Knowing how to apply negotiation tactics to obtain desired resources from federal agencies, state legislators, and other members of the assistance network is one of the most important skills to possess following a disaster[65] (see accompanying sidebar).

While this sidebar highlights the effective use of negotiation techniques by one party, it also points out the inconsistent responses received by other parties affected by the disaster. The resulting agreement developed by FEMA and the State of North Carolina produced clear winners and losers. This example also underscores the importance of developing pre-event plans that include robust training and capacity-building initiatives focused on the use of negotiation skills and a more widespread application of ADR techniques across disaster recovery assistance networks.

Applying the Principles of ADR to Disaster Recovery

The success of ADR is grounded in applied techniques proven in practice.[66] Underlying these techniques is a set of process-oriented principles. It is suggested that these principles be incorporated into the plan quality literature and new recovery planning protocols and used to guide procedural elements of disaster recovery plans.

Repeated Interaction and Reciprocal Dialogue

The power of ADR is linked to several procedural benefits, among the most important of which is repeated interaction among stakeholders over time.[67] The use of a reciprocal dialogue among parties to a dispute helps those with seemingly inflexible positions better understand the positions of others; identify areas of agreement and complementary interests; challenge existing procedures, policies, and plans; and craft agreed-upon solutions that benefit those all involved. Although interaction among members of disaster recovery assistance networks varies in amount and quality, it can benefit from the creation of formal and informal mechanisms to stimulate frequent interactions before and after a disaster strikes. Planning provides a means to achieve these ends, and the durability of the resultant plans and their acceptance by the larger assistance network can be significantly affected by the duration and intensity of these interactions. In perhaps the largest post-disaster event of its type ever attempted in the United States, the charrette process employed in Mississippi following Hurricane Katrina had mixed success. While the intensive process did play a key role in highlighting the importance of planning, important procedural elements were missing,

The Role of Negotiation in Post-Disaster Resource Allocation Disputes

In the post-disaster setting, policy formulation and implementation are strongly influenced by the use of negotiation techniques. In the competition for scarce resources, those states, communities, and other entities that can effectively apply negotiation tactics stand to benefit, while those that are not skilled in negotiation are less likely to procure needed resources.[1] The ability to effectively negotiate is tied to the strength of one's bargaining position relative to others involved in the process, and the strength of one's position is closely associated with and bolstered by the work done before negotiations begin: gathering information, identifying options, and garnering support.[2]

In 1999, Hurricane Floyd struck North Carolina, causing major flooding that resulted in estimated losses of $6 billion.[3] Along with North Carolina, nine other states—Connecticut, Delaware, Florida, Maryland, New Jersey, New York, Pennsylvania, South Carolina, and Virginia—were declared federal disaster areas. Given the size of the event, it was clear that Congress would pass emergency appropriations to supplement the federal assistance available under the Stafford Act.

After the disaster, a GIS-based analysis undertaken by the North Carolina Division of Emergency Management showed that up to 10,000 homes might be eligible for hazard mitigation assistance. From its experience following Hurricane Fran in 1996, the state recognized that because local government officials were overwhelmed (many were still dealing with Hazard Mitigation Grant Program [HMGP] projects associated with Fran), it could take a year or more to complete and submit projects to the Federal Emergency Management Agency (FEMA) for approval. Among the most time-consuming tasks was collecting the information necessary to conduct individual benefit-cost analyses.

State officials argued that the HMGP was inappropriately designed to be used effectively after a major disaster given its high degree of complexity and slow administration. At the same time, noting the limited number of federal grants designed to address large-scale housing needs, local officials and leaders in state government viewed the HMGP as both a recovery and a mitigation program. For instance, the governor was very clear that he expected the state to figure out new ways to speed assistance to those affected by Floyd, including the large number of low- and moderate-income residents in eastern North Carolina whose agriculturally based economy had already been in decline before the flood.[4] Thus, the supplemental appropriation became an integral part of a larger state-led housing recovery program, assisting over 4,000 families to relocate outside the floodplain[5] (see the sidebar in Chapter 2 on North Carolina's disaster recovery assistance programs).

The supplemental appropriation language reads: "Up to $215,000,000 may be used by the Director of FEMA for the buyout of homeowners (or relocation of structures) for principal residences that have been made *uninhabitable* by flooding caused by Hurricane Floyd and *surrounding events* and located in the 100-year floodplain."[6] The resulting policy language was strongly influenced by the active involvement of North Carolina officials who, working closely with members of the Congressional Appropriations Committee, sought to define the buyout parameters.

Once the broader eligibility criteria were established, the State of North Carolina entered into negotiations with FEMA officials to establish an agreed-upon method for determining cost-effectiveness that did not involve the use of traditional benefit-cost analysis models. Following several weeks of discussions and debate, FEMA decided that proxies for cost-effectiveness could be used for the state's top priority—the purchase and demolition of flood-damaged homes. Homes located in the 100-year floodplain were deemed eligible if they met one of

continued on page 298

continued from page 297

the following criteria: (1) they were permanent structures other than manufactured homes that received five feet or more of water inside the structure (excluding basements); (2) they were manufactured homes (mobile homes) that were inundated by one or more feet of water above the first habitable floor and were deemed substantially damaged by an authorized local official; (3) they were structures determined to be substantially damaged (i.e., they sustained damages exceeding 50 percent of their pre-disaster value); (4) they were deemed uninhabitable because of environmental contamination; or (5) they had been previously demolished because of environmental contamination as a result of the flood.[7] The agreement represented a major accomplishment as it meant that FEMA would alter long-standing interpretations of program eligibility rules. FEMA agreed to proceed even though the policy met with resistance from the agency's Office of the Inspector General (IG) and some members of Congress.

FEMA, like other federal agencies, has an IG office assigned to monitor the use of federal funds. IG officials questioned why benefit-cost analyses were not performed in North Carolina after Hurricane Floyd and whether structures deemed eligible had, in fact, met a substantial damage threshold used in previous disasters.[8]

Even though the IG opposed the approach, the State of North Carolina successfully used negotiation tactics with FEMA, including the use of verifiable data, to obtain desired policy aims from the federal agency. For instance, having determined how many homes were eligible for assistance helped speed the approval of large sums of money and provided significant leverage to negotiate an array of policy decisions tied to program implementation. Other states in the declared disaster area were denied similar requests or were required to wait months to receive an answer to specific policy interpretations that had been resolved in North Carolina.

Several factors played a role in the differential treatment of North Carolina compared to other states. Of the ten states, North Carolina was the most heavily affected and drew the most significant attention from the media and members of Congress. Recognizing that the scale of the potential federal assistance would draw substantial scrutiny, the state developed a defensible method to estimate losses and showed that current eligibility determination techniques would take too long to implement. It also aggressively pursued a negotiated settlement with FEMA, whereas other states were less assertive—in part because of their weaker bargaining positions. Finally, the disaster spanned two FEMA regions, each with different levels of experience in the large-scale buyout of flood-prone properties. North Carolina was fortunate to be part of FEMA Region IV, whose experienced mitigation staff had developed a close working relationship with state and local officials as a result of being stationed in the area since Hurricane Fran.

1   Gavin Smith, "Holistic Disaster Recovery: Creating a More Sustainable Future" (course developed for the Emergency Management Institute Higher Education Project, Federal Emergency Management Agency, 2004), available online at training.fema.gov/EMIWeb/edu/sdr.asp, session XIII, 7, session XIV, 30–31.

2   Roger Fisher, "Beyond Yes," *Negotiation Journal* 1, no. 1 (1983): 67–70; Connie P. Ozawa and Lawrence Susskind, "Mediating Science-Intensive Policy Disputes," *Journal of Policy Analysis and Management* 5, no. 1 (1985): 23–39.

3   Jay Barnes, *North Carolina's Hurricane History* (Chapel Hill: University of North Carolina Press, 2001); John R. Maiolo, "An Overview of the Perfect Flood," in *Facing Our Future: Hurricane Floyd and Recovery in the Coastal Plain*, eds. John R. Maiolo et al., 1–16 (Greenville, N.C.: Coastal Carolina Press, 2001).

4   Author's personal communication with Governor James B. Hunt, 1999.

5   North Carolina Emergency Management Division, *Hazard Mitigation in North Carolina: Measuring Success* (Raleigh, 2000), www.p2pays.org/ref/14/13619/13619.pdf.

6   Office of the Inspector General, *Buyouts: Hurricane Floyd and Other Issues Relating to FEMA's Hazard Mitigation Grant Program*, Report to the Chairperson, Subcommittee on VA, HUD, and Independent Agencies, Committee on Appropriations, U.S. Senate, Report No. I-02-01 (Washington, D.C.: FEMA, February 2001), 12.

7   Ibid., 12–13.

8   Ibid.

including the ability to engage in sustained, broad-based dialogue over time and the creation of clear incentives to participate in the process.

Creation of Incentives to Participate and Share Information

The efficacy of pre-event activities intended to stimulate cooperation can be hindered by apathy or a low level of political salience when compared to competing agendas. This holds true for all members of the assistance network, not just the public sector. In their discussion of the importance of process-oriented dialogue, debate, and negotiation following disasters, John Forester and Reshmi Theckethil suggest that multistakeholder negotiation should strive toward "networked practical intelligence," whereby participants create "informed, contextually sensitive, insightful working agreements uniquely fitting responses to demanding situations."[68]

The willingness of organizations and individuals to participate in planning activities is often influenced by past experiences. Power imbalances, exclusionary policy-making tactics, and the inequitable distribution of resources lead to mistrust, causing parties to question the value of participating in a process that appears controlling rather than empowering. This became evident in New Orleans and significantly hindered efforts to create a post-disaster recovery plan.[69] A lack of trust can lead to the withholding of information and the development of tough positions. The reciprocation of similarly uninformed positions by others (often called "tit for tat") can lead to a breakdown in productive dialogue, resulting in an impasse.[70]

To overcome these barriers, efforts to create incentives to participate must be made and sustained. This approach should include showing conflicting parties examples of disputes that were successfully resolved by information sharing and collective problem solving. This tactic, described in Chapter 2 as part of proposed changes to the Emergency Management Assistance Compact (EMAC), may include the use of best practices drawn from stakeholders in other assistance networks (e.g., public sector, private sector, quasi-governmental, nonprofit) whose contextual factors (e.g., past experience with disasters and disaster recovery planning, level of power within existing networks, history of collective problem solving) are similar to those of the parties involved in the process. Further, the delivery of this information is often most effective when part of a peer exchange program as exemplified in the Chapter 3 sidebar, Professional Associations in Recovery following Hurricane Katrina on page 104.

In addition to a discussion of hypothetical benefits, participants engaged in this effort should be provided with a targeted and well-conceived resource package (funding, policies, and technical assistance) that supports their efforts over time. Financial support may include the funds necessary to convene information gathering and sharing venues; to hire a mediator; and to pay for the travel of those willing to share testimonials, best practices, and lessons. Supportive policies may include the expansion of existing state dispute resolution programs to address disaster recovery-related conflicts, the modification of EMAC rules to include peer-to-peer exchanges in the pre- and post-disaster environments, and the amendment of the NDRF to establish a cadre of ADR specialists that work in tandem with FEMA's Long-Term Community Recovery (ESF-14) staff, both before and after disasters to help foster improved collaboration across disaster recovery assistance networks.

Specific technical assistance initiatives may include training members of the assistance network on the use of ADR techniques, hosting regular pre-event workshops focused on the development of disaster recovery plans (and including discussions about the role of ADR in plan making, monitoring and evaluation, and implementation), conducting national conferences to share information and techniques, and creating an ongoing education and outreach campaign targeting those who are skeptical of traditional problem-solving techniques or are unaware of their potential role in disaster recovery. While not explicitly tied to disaster recovery, the Great California Shakeout described in Chapter 3 (see pages 92–93) dramatically illustrates the power of a well-coordinated outreach campaign that drew on the combined expertise of federal and state agencies, university research centers, nonprofit organizations, the insurance industry, and the media as part of an effort to increase disaster preparedness. The initial event, which involved more than 5.47 million people, was intended to serve as a platform for ongoing training and exercise programs. Among its most powerful lessons is the demonstrative value of a collaboratively derived technical assistance strategy.

Demonstration of the Benefits of ADR

The development of trust among parties is one of the central preconditions for the creation of institutional arrangements capable of addressing conflict.[71] Establishing an ongoing conversation that leads to positive outcomes can help to engender trust, even among previously competing or contentious parties. This has shown to be true after a number of disputes, including the U.S. civil rights movement, controlled social science experiments, common-pooled natural resource dilemmas, and land use planning debates.[72] As positive results accrue, parties become more willing to address larger issues that involve greater levels of commitment. For instance, the formulation of strategies to address the limitations of the disaster recovery assistance framework may start with smaller procedural efforts, such as members of the assistance network sharing information about the programs they manage and describing the unmet needs they observed following disasters. Through continuing dialogue, an improved assistance distribution strategy may emerge at the neighborhood level (as evidenced in the Broadmoor community) that allows resource providers to assess which organizations are best suited to distribute various types of assistance and when it should be given.

The strategy may also result in the reformulation of state and federal eligibility criteria (see the following sidebar on page 302), or the crafting of new or amended policies and programs based on local needs and the legitimate input of those who have traditionally been viewed one-dimensionally as recipients of assistance and described as "disaster victims" (see the sidebar in Chapter 3 on the Gulf Coast Community Design Studio). Understood in the context of the disaster recovery assistance framework, the application of ADR techniques, including policy dialogue and negotiation, is a critically important but currently underused method for directly confronting identified weaknesses. Clearly demonstrating the value of these techniques is timely as the NDRF takes shape.

Clarification of the Fact Base

An ongoing exchange of information is closely tied to the clarification of the fact base underlying planning decisions. Careful attention is required when addressing distributional conflict so that scientific information does not obscure broader resource allocation issues[73] or exclude the less powerful during the planning process. The public sector, insurance companies, and professional associations that use technical terms as part of their regular lexicon should take care to define these terms for those who are not familiar with them. Explanations of the underlying principles of hazard vulnerability, for example, can be confusing. Concepts such as the 100-year flood or a 1,000-year return period (used to describe an earthquake) seem abstract and lack meaning to many members of the assistance network. Similarly, the findings of a vulnerability assessment or a loss estimation model that can be used to drive the adoption of more stringent building codes or land use ordinances can appear arbitrary, particularly when these tools have been developed without meaningful public involvement and debate.

The National Earthquake Hazard Reduction Program (see sidebar on pages 92–93), for instance, represents an organization committed to tackling the all-important task of translating complex, scientifically generated information to a broad audience, including that associated with disaster recovery and hazard mitigation. Among the methods used to accomplish this aim is the creation of risk assessment tools for use by practitioners and the development of communication strategies for describing hazard vulnerability (see the sidebar on page 302).

Assessing, Understanding, and Mitigating Vulnerability in the Post-Disaster Environment: The Role of the Planner as Mediator

Addressing disputes arising from highly technical and "science-intensive" issues, such as the assessment and mitigation of natural hazard vulnerability, requires balancing facts and values, identifying appropriate representation, and soliciting willing participants.[1] In practice, the contextual underpinnings of such debates are often dominated by a technical expert, who develops a risk assessment based on computer models or other analytical techniques, displays the findings, and seeks "public input." This approach is widely practiced as part of hazard mitigation plans and the testing of the models' accuracy; in the post-disaster environment, it is often used to provide the rationale for enhanced standards and policy regulations. Not surprisingly, this approach routinely leads to heated debates between public officials and citizens.[2]

A number of hazard scholars suggest that the purposeful involvement of community residents in efforts to define and assess their vulnerability and to develop actionable strategies on that basis is more important that a strict reliance on analytical tools.[3] Thus, the challenge lies in balancing what initially appears to be competing approaches—namely, the development of assessments that are based on a sound fact base and the incorporation of input from those whose lives and livelihoods will be directly affected by implemented policies and future events (see accompanying figure). Connie Ozawa and Lawrence Susskind describe three approaches germane to mediation that are particularly relevant to this situation: information sharing, joint fact finding, and collaborative model building.[4]

Pre- and post-disaster decisions can be tied to the results of a vulnerability assessment and a post-event damage assessment, thereby arming local officials with information that can be used to frame policy options. The formulation of "collaboratively derived models" that incorporates different but mutually accepted assumptions derived from joint fact-finding exercises and the sharing of information can increase the likelihood of developing an approach that has widespread support. While rationales for post-disaster

policy decisions should be discussed with the public in advance of a disaster and adopted as part of a local recovery plan, post-disaster findings and input from across the assistance network may reframe the policy debate in unexpected and often fruitful ways, as evidenced in Charlotte–Mecklenburg County, North Carolina.

It is impossible to predict all the needs that will surface after disaster strikes. Thus, the disaster recovery plan should include explicit policies that address local needs that may not have been anticipated as well as procedural methods that foster consensus. A temporary building moratorium, for example, may be needed to provide time for public officials, the public, and other members of the assistance network to assess post-disaster conditions prior to initiating reconstruction efforts and employing dispute resolution principles to address the myriad policy dilemmas that often follow.

The local capacity-building effort led by MDC, a Chapel Hill, North Carolina-based nonprofit, and the University of North Carolina at Chapel Hill, targets low-income communities along the eastern seaboard and Gulf Coast. The intent of the project is to assist communities assess their vulnerability to hazards and develop locally grounded strategies based on their understanding of pre- and post-disaster conditions. The initiative, titled the Community Demonstration Project is funded by FEMA.
Courtesy of MDC.

In those cases where public safety and proprietary information are not compromised, local inspectors may seek the input of individual homeowners and share the information gathered with them.

Increased transparency can lead to greater trust and an improved understanding of the connection between the damages sustained to households, the strength of existing building codes and standards, and a community's overall vulnerability to the effects of natural hazards. Efforts to seek consensus, however, must recognize the nature of the post-disaster environment, which includes often angst-ridden individuals under great stress. While this reality underscores the importance of engaging in this process before a disaster strikes, a sincere commitment to involve the public in post-disaster decision making (in a manner that recognizes the sensitivity of the situation) can help uncover perspectives and options that were heretofore unrecognized.

1   Connie P. Ozawa and Lawrence Susskind, "Mediating Science-Intensive Policy Disputes," *Journal of Policy Analysis and Management* 5, no. 1 (1985): 23–39.

2   Gavin Smith, "Planning for Sustainable and Disaster Resilient Communities," in *Natural Hazards Analysis: Reducing the Impact of Disasters*, ed. John Pine, 221–247 (Washington, D.C.: Taylor Francis, 2009).

3   Andrew Maskrey, "Disaster Mitigation as a Crisis Paradigm: Reconstruction after the Alto Mayo Earthquake, Peru," in *Disasters, Development and Environment*, ed. Ann Varley, 109–123 (New York: John Wiley & Sons, 1994); Philip R. Berke and Timothy Beatley, *After the Hurricane: Linking Recovery to Sustainable Development in the Caribbean* (Baltimore: Johns Hopkins University Press, 1997); N. Emel Ganapati and Sukumar Ganapati, "Enabling Participatory Planning after Disasters: A Case Study of the World Bank's Housing Reconstruction in Turkey," *Journal of the American Planning Association* 75, no. 1 (2009): 41–59.

4   Ozawa and Susskind, "Mediating Science-Intensive Policy Disputes," 32–34.

Identification of New Perspectives and the Creation of Multiple Options

Involving stakeholders in the planning process helps to establish a richer understanding of the complexities associated with pre- and post disaster assistance, identify new perspectives, and generate options that benefit multiple parties. The concept of "inventing options for mutual gain" is widely accepted in the ADR literature and is routinely used in practice by dispute resolution specialists.[74] Involving individuals, organizations, and agencies in the decision-making process as early as possible enables those entities to gain a greater appreciation of the facts underlying the positions held by other parties, which is a prerequisite in the search for mutually agreeable decisions. The process of creating multiple policy options helps to uncover perspectives that may not have been identified using more adversarial methods or involving fewer parties. This approach was used very effectively, for instance, in the Broadmoor community after Hurricane Katrina. In Charlotte–Mecklenburg County, multiple options were uncovered following a lengthy fact-finding process that included both technical (running several development "build-out" scenarios) and procedural (coming to the realization that builders did not want to be associated with the construction of flood-prone housing) elements. This led to unforeseen solutions that were acceptable to parties who initially viewed one another as adversaries.

Considering the importance of dialogue and debate as precursors to effective negotiations and mediated settlements, it should not be surprising that attempts to develop post-disaster recovery plans have achieved varied levels of success. The process of planning for recovery takes time. The time needed to engage in dialogue, debate, and the crafting of settlements can interfere with the desires of community officials and other members of the assistance network who tend to equate successful recovery outcomes almost exclusively with speed rather than quality. Seeking a quick resolution to the issues confronting those tasked with recovery often leaves a number of important options on the table, some of which may be left out because certain stakeholders were excluded.

High Stakeholder Involvement

The involvement of all relevant parties can increase the length of time required to address more complex multiparty disputes. In post-disaster recovery, this may elicit opposition given the desire to return to a sense of normalcy as quickly as possible. In the long run, however, the creation of enduring settlements (often framed as agreements, policies, and plans) that more comprehensively address the problematic dimensions of the disaster recovery assistance framework can outweigh the associated "cost" of deliberation. Settlements can serve as the basis for new or improved policy as advocated by those who are party to the agreement. This was evident in Charlotte–Mecklenburg County, where the developers (and others) became convinced that the more stringent floodplain management standards, derived through a series of meetings and the display of multiple development scenarios, were in the best interests of the community. The direct involvement of developers in this process made them powerful advocates for the remapping effort and resulting policy changes. Similarly, the city of Tulsa has adopted some of the most rigorous floodplain management standards in the country, owing in large part to its ability to garner support from a wide range of stakeholders.

High stakeholder involvement is also crucial to the ability to sustain support for recovery policies, given the changing makeup of those involved in the disaster assistance network over time. For instance, federal, state, and local elected or appointed officials change positions with new administrations or election cycles. (See the sidebars on the city of Tulsa in Chapter 4 and on Project Impact in Chapter 5 for a discussion of the importance of building a broad-based coalition capable of sustaining a program after its initial leader leaves.) Disaster assistance employees, members of EMAC, professional associations, university researchers, and private sector consultants work in disaster-stricken areas for limited periods of time. Job turnover is high among local officials, particularly after major disasters. The media's attention span can be short lived and is often focused on the dramatic images of search and rescue, damaged properties, and individual suffering. Much less focus is placed on telling the story of recovery over time. The recognized value of adopting significant changes to disaster recovery policy is often short-lived, and those changes may face powerful opposition from those who stand to benefit financially from existing policy.[75]

Moreover, the shifting nature of assistance networks can result in an uncoordinated approach to disaster recovery. Establishing cooperative procedures embedded in plans that have widespread endorsement across the network and are supported by policies that have legal and regulatory standing can provide a greater degree of continuity and therefore help to ensure an ongoing decision-making process that reflects a diversity of interests rather than one dominated by a few powerful stakeholder groups.

High stakeholder involvement in U.S. assistance networks must also accept a new, broader definition of what it means to be a member of a global network. This means anticipating the need to accept assistance from overseas, which was dramatically evident after Hurricane Katrina brought to light the paucity of pre-event agreements between the United States and other nations. The failure of the U.S. government to proactively plan for this eventuality and use approaches already in existence to deliver foreign aid to other countries resulted in a number of missed opportunities. Concepts of absorptive capacity, conditionality, and disaster diplomacy, which were addressed in Chapter 6, need to be revisited, particularly in the face of climate change and its effect on natural hazards. Important lessons can be drawn from the international community, including those in developing countries, as well as from international relief organizations based in the United States (see sidebars on pages 206–207, 215–216, and 223).

Redress of Existing Power Imbalances

Among the biggest barriers to cooperation, and planning for that matter, are the existing power imbalances across the disaster recovery assistance network. Power is closely associated with control over the allocation of scarce resources, including money, information, and influence over policy decisions. Forester and Theckethil suggest that we should rethink risk management policies and how the public currently participates in these decision-making activities.[76] They posit that through the adoption of ADR techniques (namely, facilitation and mediation), stakeholders are given a more active voice, able to engage not only in discussions but also in active learning, problem solving, and the codification of agreements designed to tackle disputes.

According to the authors, the modes of interaction during the process of participation are dialogue, debate, and negotiation, and are often interwoven and sequential in nature. Dialogue is described as a conversation among parties, often conducted in the early stages of the process during which stakeholders attempt to gain a greater understanding of one another and their positions. For instance, following a disaster a town manager may call together stakeholders to discuss the degree to which available programs meet local needs, the timing of assistance, and the existing level of coordination among parties. The process of dialogue provides a critical policy subtext. Inclusive dialogue represents an important means to create a more robust fact base, built on a foundation of collective knowledge. This requires the active participation of all stakeholders, including those affected by the policies created and those assigned to implement them. Problems ensue when decisions are made by individual stakeholders acting alone, which is common in the disaster assistance network.

Debate is characterized as a series of arguments between parties, each of whom attempts to demonstrate the strength of its case and expose the weakness of the other's. The authors note that while dialogue may result in much discussion without resolution, an emphasis on debate-based approaches may lead to a resolution, but one that damages the relationships among stakeholders.[77] Described in the context of disaster recovery, debate may focus on the "best" means to address identified problems in the assistance framework but may not give voice to participants in a manner that incorporates their concerns into action. Sherry Arnstein, in her seminal article on public participation, describes the former condition as "tokenism" and the latter as "citizen power."[78]

Debate, like dialogue, provides procedural context for possible negotiations. In the context of multiparty disputes, including those surrounding the struggle for scarce resources during recovery, a concerted attempt to apply principles of negotiation to seek an equitable, just, efficient, and inclusive solution is rarely made. In fact, members of the assistance network are infrequently brought together to debate recovery-related issues; rather, decisions are often made unilaterally by program administrators. Not surprisingly, when parties do come together, they often fail to make it past the debate stage. This can lead to ill-informed policy decisions and a further breakdown in cooperation.

The poor institutional design of the disaster recovery assistance framework, including the lack of procedural forums needed to address conflicts as they emerge, is partly to blame for this condition. Currently, there is no widely accepted means for stakeholders to engage in effective and inclusive negotiations. Nor is there an organization tasked with fostering negotiated settlements based on accepted guidelines or principles. Rather, anecdotal evidence (as described in a number of sidebars) suggests that while experienced members of the assistance network are likely to embrace the use of negotiation tactics, newer members are often unaware that policy-related disputes are settled in this manner since such techniques are not always in evidence in pre-event planning dialogues or incorporated into well-designed training programs (see the previous sidebar on pages 302–303). The lack of communication has resulted in the overreliance on narrowly defined federal grant programs rather than on the pursuit of their modification or the more effective coordination of resources held by others.

Parties that are less experienced in disaster recovery, however, should not necessarily be confused with those that may be skeptical of what they perceive to be another bureaucratic procedure that has excluded them in the past or served as a tool of institutionalized racism. Because dialogue among stakeholders is limited before a disaster occurs, issues remain unresolved only to resurface in heated and often unfruitful debate during the throes of recovery. Such unresolved issues, including long-held mistrust between certain members of the network, reduce the likelihood of these stakeholders participating in a forum that is designed to be more inclusive and has the potential to give them a voice. As a result, segments of a community—including socially vulnerable populations and the organizations that have historically served them—may limit their interaction with other members of the network. These same individuals may rely more heavily on emergent groups, nonprofit organizations, and foundations for assistance, while the groups that provide this type of support may limit their interaction with the wider network, focusing their energy on marginalized populations, even though, if collaborative arrangements and inclusive plans were created, all parties could benefit more than when they act alone.

True participatory venues must work to avoid these pitfalls. They must incentivize collective action—in some cases through the mandated use of ADR (as discussed in the next chapter)—while ensuring that the less powerful and those that have been previously excluded become active decision makers. A key principle of negotiation used to redress power imbalances is the identification of the party's best alternative to a negotiated agreement, or BATNA.[79] The BATNA represents the conditions of an agreement that can be achieved using means other than negotiation. If negotiations do not advance the interests of a party beyond its BATNA, the party should walk away from the bargaining table and use more traditional means to resolve the dispute, such as those discussed in Exhibit 8–4 (e.g., legislation, the court system, and administrative proceedings). The point is to incentivize participation in a well-constructed, inclusive forum that has the potential to craft an acceptable solution rather than limiting settlements to bureaucratic procedures or deal making among powerful groups.[80]

COLLABORATIVE PLANNING IN RECOVERY

Collaborative planning techniques are currently underused in disaster recovery planning,[81] which is disconcerting as their application is directly relevant to the challenges facing disaster recovery assistance networks. The narrowly construed suggestion that the involvement, or lack thereof, of planners (or of any one individual or stakeholder) in recovery can account for the entire variance in a network's ability or willingness to plan for recovery fails to recognize the largely ineffectual nature of the disaster recovery assistance framework. In reality, various members of assistance networks play leadership roles in collaboratively driven recovery planning efforts, and it is incumbent on the public sector to create the incentives that foster such collaboration, recognizing the emergence of leaders and recovery planning advocates.

At the local and state levels, the Broadmoor case study (on pages 116–122) and the sidebars on pages 269–271, 297–298, and 302–303 demonstrate that adopting the principles of mediation and negotiation can produce significant benefits. However, these examples also highlight actions taken *after* a disaster struck. One way to view the operationalization of a plan, including participatory techniques used to achieve it, is through the lens of a negotiated settlement. If one assumes this view, participatory planning processes become more tangible when ADR techniques are applied, as John Forester suggests.[82] ADR scholars Deborah Shmueli, Sanda Kaufman, and Connie Ozawa similarly argue that "negotiation lies at the heart of joint decision processes such as planning, and that the collaborative planning model comes closest to acknowledging it."[83]

The emphasis on increasing the speed of recovery and returning to a sense of normalcy following a disaster can undermine the use of participatory principles.[84] Research further suggests that even communities with a history of public involvement in planning do not always apply participatory principles to recovery and reconstruction activities after an event.[85] Conversely, analysis of hazard mitigation plans has found that communities can learn to adopt increasingly rigorous legal reforms, risk reduction initiatives, and increased citizen participation in decision making.[86] In their study of recovery planning in New Orleans after Hurricane Katrina, Robert Olshansky and colleagues found that post-disaster planning can inform decisions made after an event,[87] while Peter May and colleagues discovered that the use of citizen advisory groups elicited an increased level of interest among stakeholders to address natural hazard threats.[88] These findings coincide with the ADR literature, which shows that the use of collaborative problem-solving approaches can change the nature of past interorganizational relationships among stakeholders and is an important alternative to what is commonly termed the rational planning model (a largely top-down approach driven by "technical experts" who collect, analyze, and display data in support of policies developed in isolation), which limits inclusive decision making.[89]

Change, achieved through mutual learning, can occur under varied circumstances. Innes and Booher, for instance, have found that through what they term "double loop mutual learning," where stakeholders gain a mutual understanding of problems and ways to address them, consensus is more likely.[90] They also contend that more formal time- and resource-intensive methods increase the chance of success. While other planning scholars have shown that less formal processes can engender positive planning outcomes, they too note that some form of dual learning occurred.[91]

In those cases where pre- and post-disaster planning has been found to elicit positive outcomes, most were predicated on the application of participatory techniques.[92] In some ways, these findings echo those of this book, and in others they do not. For instance, many of the communities that developed effective recovery plans did not do so before an event, and many did not involve a professional planner. They did, however, use collaborative techniques that have been embraced by the planning community.

Sidebars and case studies also highlighted successes among a subcluster of stakeholders that did not necessarily include the larger assistance networks in which they operate. The reasons for this, which vary across organizations and the associated networks of which they are a part, include different levels of awareness about other stakeholders and the resources they possess, the mistrust of others, and the use of targeted assistance strategies in response to perceived and real failings of the network to deliver appropriate resources in a timely manner. In each case, the reasons noted are common in complex, multiparty decision-making processes. This has important implications for planners and others who strive to better harness the abilities of assistance networks through changes in the disaster recovery assistance framework.

It has been argued that it is up to the public sector to create the conditions in which collaborative planning can be used to confront the limitations in the disaster recovery assistance framework through expanded partnerships that span disaster recovery assistance networks, recognizing and accounting for the multitude of different players and their interrelationships. A proposed national policy focused on achieving this aim is presented in Chapter 9.

CONCLUSION AND RECOMMENDATIONS

This chapter emphasizes the value of pre-event planning for post-disaster recovery as a means to address the weaknesses in the disaster recovery assistance framework. Key elements of planning include the act of plan making and procedural techniques that improve collaborative problem solving. The literature on plan quality breaks down the principles of planning into discrete parts that help to define what makes a good plan. Plan quality principles also help to demystify planning. The inventory of planning elements provides useful information for practitioners, including policy makers and the collection of stakeholders typically involved in large, multiparty decision-making processes such as disaster recovery.

The widespread failure to adequately engage in pre-event planning for post-disaster recovery requires developing a message that can be used to inform and encourage, or—as discussed in Chapter 9—to mandate the development and adoption of disaster recovery plans. There is no doubt that serious obstacles must be overcome for this approach to work. For instance, applying plan quality principles to the NRF shows that the NRF does not contain important defining elements of a plan. Significant weaknesses include the lack of an overall vision, poor internal consistency across federal recovery policies, the failure to develop an underlying fact base, poor horizontal and vertical integration, and insufficient monitoring and evaluation procedures.

The congressionally mandated development of a national recovery strategy, cast as the NDRF, is timely as it provides a chance to use plan quality principles to guide the creation, monitoring, evaluation, and implementation of federal, state, and local disaster recovery plans. Simply mandating the creation of a new strategy is not enough. To effect change, any national approach must comprehensively address the underlying problems described in the disaster recovery assistance framework and build the capacity of varied networks to effectively engage in pre-event planning and post-disaster actions in a coordinated manner. Part of the capacity-building process includes educating the assistance network about the merits of engaging in pre-event planning activities and the value of following an approach driven by proven standards of practice. The subsequent recommendations provide the beginnings of a planning-based strategy that is further discussed in Chapters 9 and 10.

1. Develop a Recovery Planning Approach Rooted in Collaboration and Learning

Disaster recovery is contentious as the current assistance framework does little to discourage competition among stakeholders to obtain what amounts to a finite set of resources rather than to actively pursue the optimization of those resources (see Exhibit 1–6). As currently framed, the U.S. approach benefits those who possess the requisite knowledge, technical abilities to navigate the confounding reality of existing programs, and the power to influence access to desired resources. Of course, not all stakeholders are as fortunate as those described in the largely positive sidebars and case studies. For instance, the current system also has the unintended effect of increasing vulnerability, which can lead to even greater recovery challenges when the next disaster strikes. This approach has also created powerful disincentives to plan or undertake other collaborative acts that expand policy options and the resources available to implement them. Framing the process as one in which collaboration leads to an expanded resource base, as suggested in Chapter 1, provides part of the larger solution.

One way to encourage this outcome is to show that cooperative behavior works and can lead to greater gains than one would be able to obtain by acting alone. A small but potentially important way to begin to address this issue is to compile a compendium of planning lessons. Examples should include instructional information about the technical aspects of plan making that touch on all of the plan quality and ADR principles noted in Exhibit 8–2. For instance, what makes for a good vision, and how was this vision connected to goals and policies? How did strong levels of vertical and horizontal integration lead to positive recovery outcomes? How were plans implemented and monitored to make sure that post-disaster realities were accounted for and necessary adjustments were made on the basis of new information? How are new perspectives and multiple options uncovered when addressing disaster recovery resource distribution disputes? How can the clarification of the fact base, undertaken in a more participatory manner, lead to better policies and plans?

In addition to documenting lessons in writing, stakeholders that have been involved in the development of pre- and post-disaster disaster recovery plans on different levels (international, national, regional, state, community, and neighborhood) should be invited to provide honest testimonials about the process and how it affected recovery. Dissemination of this information, however, requires more than posting it on a website or placing it in a guidebook. Rather, best practices should be incorporated into ongoing, pre-event education and training seminars that bring together members of disaster assistance networks. This enables members of those networks to discuss needs, identify resource gaps and limitations, and incorporate lessons into their recovery plans.

In many cases, members of assistance networks are unaware that they will be involved in the disaster recovery process until after an event occurs and thus are uncertain what recovery actually entails. Those who have experienced disaster recovery plan making and implementation first-hand recognize the naïveté with which members of the assistance network sometimes approach the recovery process, and they are well positioned to offer advice on what to expect. Conducting educational campaigns targeting the general public, planners, and elected officials about hazard vulnerability and the measures that can be employed to reduce the impact of hazards have been shown to increase resilience.[93] Such lessons should be applied to pre-event planning for post-disaster recovery, assuming an adequate amount of attention is paid to the principles of collaborative planning and lesson drawing across recovery assistance networks.

FEMA is in the process of identifying a cadre of disaster recovery specialists to serve as part of an expanded ESF-14 team, including members who will be assembling best practices. This team should be deployed before and after disasters and should include members of the public sector, private sector, nonprofits, quasi-governmental organizations, international organizations and representatives from other nations, and local residents. University faculty, including hazard scholars in multiple fields (e.g., the social and physical sciences, planning, engineering, data management, and hazards modeling) should also participate. Emphasis should be placed on an honest identification and evaluation of individual, group, and network-based experiences, including those characterized as "success stories" as well as those that highlight areas in need of improvement. This information should serve as part of a larger effort to help communities develop disaster recovery plans.

The emerging field of plan quality studies is gaining wider recognition in academic circles and shows promise as a way of providing information that is of direct use to practitioners. Because a national recovery strategy is currently being developed, there is yet an opportunity to include recognized plan quality principles in its development, study their effectiveness over time, and create an approach that can inform the actions not only of the federal government but also of states, communities, and the larger assistance network. The value of experiential learning and scholarship should not be underestimated. Rather, it should be used as part of a larger strategy to help build the capacity of the network to plan for recovery.

2. Build Federal, State, and Local Government Recovery Planning Capacity

The success of a national recovery planning initiative is closely associated with the capacity of federal, state, and local governments to assist the larger network. The federal government's capacity to plan for recovery is weak but improving. Federal initiatives such as ESF-14, the White House–led multiagency assessment of recovery planning, and the development of a national recovery strategy are promising, but they remain underfunded, understaffed, and understudied, and they are still less salient in the emergency management community than issues associated with disaster response. Most state recovery plans are focused on the administration of federal recovery programs. Local governments often have applicable land use planning tools and expertise at their disposal but place little importance on pre-event planning for post-disaster recovery.

Central to the successful implementation of a national recovery strategy is the need to enhance the capacity of the assistance network to plan for recovery. Past history shows no federal commitment to pre-event capacity-building initiatives tied to disaster recovery planning. Building the capacity to plan across a network means recognizing that the diversity of skills, knowledge, beliefs, values, and resources held by stakeholders represents a unique strength. The ability to effectively harness this strength through planning benefits from the more systematic involvement of the professional planning community.

3. Actively Engage the Professional Planning Community in Disaster Recovery

The planning community has failed to realize its professional obligation to engage in pre-event planning for post-disaster recovery. Moreover, local governments have not been proactive in using their existing legal and administrative authority, which gives planners wide latitude to protect the public's health, safety, and welfare, to aggressively address disaster recovery goals. Even though planners possess a unique combination of relevant skills, they are often unprepared to engage in the process of recovery[94] and do not have a clear understanding of their roles in the aftermath of a disaster.[95] This reality is evident in the opening paragraph of *Rebuilding after Earthquakes: Lessons from Planners*:

> *After an earthquake strikes, as planners, you will be thrust into a world of instant life-and-death decisions, mounds of building permit applications, daily dealings with a new bureaucracy with incredible paperwork requirements, and an unremitting pressure to get things back to normal. Everyone will want a plan, but few will want to take the time to plan. You will be expected to have answers to problems you have not even thought of before. You will be dealing with new experts—geologists, structural engineers and seismologists with information you will need to understand. If damage is severe, you may be saying, "Let's relocate the entire community." Inadequacies in existing plans and regulations will be glaringly apparent. Nothing in your planning education has adequately prepared you to deal with the problems and responsibilities now on your desk.[96]*

The fact that professionally trained planners and ADR specialists are often absent from post-disaster recovery efforts and pre-event planning activities is just a small part of the larger problem facing the assistance network: available resources are not effectively identified, coordinated, and applied to problems inherent in disaster recovery. For instance, FEMA maintains a cadre of ADR staff that has trained federal officials in dispute resolution techniques. That cadre has been deployed to areas affected by disasters and used to resolve personnel disputes among federal employees in the field, establish arbitration hearings under the National Flood Insurance Act to address different interpretations of what constitutes an appropriate insurance settlement, and played a role in the resolution of claims following the Los Alamos, New Mexico, fires in 2000.[97] But these ADR-trained personnel have not been incorporated more systematically into the practice of pre- and post-disaster recovery planning. They remain underused, their services largely unrecognized by the larger assistance network.

The professional planning community is fundamentally important to the success of disaster recovery planning efforts and the proposed Disaster Recovery Act described in the next chapter. The involvement of the American Planning Association (APA) (and the professional planning community more generally) in broader policy debates about the importance of pre-event disaster recovery planning is improving but remains insufficient. The APA has led the writing of several documents tied to natural hazards, including what remains the most widely recognized text for practitioners in recovery planning: *Planning for Post-Disaster Recovery and Reconstruction*.[98] More recently, it has created the Hazards Planning Research Center, through which it continues to produce documents linking hazards management and planning, including a monograph focused on the integration of hazard mitigation into local comprehensive plans.[99] The center also conducts multidisciplinary research, engages in outreach and educational efforts, and produces policy recommendations through the writing of documents advancing the idea of hazard resilience (www.planning.org/nationalcenters/hazards/index.htm 2010).

However, the APA has not effectively developed a means to train the professional planning community on how to develop and implement disaster recovery plans. The recent growth in disaster recovery planning-related research offers promise, provided the research can be more effectively incorporated into education and training efforts and used to help inform the current policy debate surrounding the NDRF. *Planning for Post-Disaster Recovery and Reconstruction*, which is scheduled to be updated in 2011 as a result of an increased emphasis on disaster recovery and the completion of the draft NDRF, offers one way to start this important dialogue. In addition, the proposed APA Natural Hazards Planning Division has continued to gain support and now functions as a recognized interest group within the professional planning organization. Its proposed charter initially discussed efforts to develop training programs, which would provide another important venue to further this important capacity-building initiative.

The notion of taking action to build the collective capacity needed to plan for recovery and implement identified measures before and after a disaster strikes remains foreign to most stakeholders. It is time for the public sector (namely, the federal government), professional emergency management associations, and the professional planning community (regional planning organizations, professional associations, local planners, the dispute resolution community, etc.) to join forces and address this problem. It is not so much a question of who is in charge of recovery, but rather, who should take the lead in developing the conditions in which collaborative planning can thrive?

Endnotes

1   Russell R. Dynes, *Organized Behavior in Disaster* (Lexington, Mass.: Heath Lexington Books, 1970).

2   Robert A. Stallings, "Conflict in Natural Disasters: A Codification of Consensus and Conflict Theories," *Social Science Quarterly* 69 (1988): 569–586; Anthony Oliver-Smith, "Post-Disaster Housing Reconstruction and Social Inequality: A Challenge to Policy and Practice," *Disasters* 14, no. 1 (1990): 7–19.

3   Claire Rubin and Roy Popkin, *Disaster Recovery after Hurricane Hugo in South Carolina* (Boulder: Institute of Behavioral Science, University of Colorado, 1990); Gavin Smith and Dennis Wenger, "Sustainable Disaster Recovery: Operationalizing an Existing Agenda," in *Handbook of Disaster Research,* ed. Havidan Rodriguez, Enrico L. Quarantelli, and Russell Dynes, 234–257 (New York: Springer, 2006); Marla Nelson, Renia Ehrenfeucht, and Shirley Laska, "Planning, Plans, and People: Professional Expertise, Local Knowledge, and Governmental Action in Post-Hurricane Katrina New Orleans," *Cityscape: A Journal of Policy Development and Research* 9, no. 3 (2007): 23–52; Gavin Smith, "Planning for Sustainable and Disaster Resilient Communities," in *Natural Hazards Analysis: Reducing the Impact of Disasters,* ed. John Pine, 221–247 (Washington, D.C.: Taylor Francis, 2009).

4   Raymond J. Burby, Arthur C. Nelson, and Thomas W. Sanchez, "The Problems of Containment and the Promise of Planning," in *Rebuilding Urban Places after Disasters: Lessons from Hurricane Katrina,* ed. Eugenie L. Birch and Susan M. Wachter, 47–65 (Philadelphia: University of Pennsylvania Press, 2006); Smith and Wenger, "Sustainable Disaster Recovery."

5   Claire B. Rubin and Irmak R. Tanali, *Disaster Timeline* (Arlington, Va.: Claire Rubin and Associates, 2001), at www.disastertimeline.com.

6   Thomas A. Birkland, *Lessons of Disaster: Policy Change after Catastrophic Events* (Washington, D.C.: Georgetown University Press, 2006).

7   Gavin Smith, "Lessons from the United States: Planning for Post-Disaster Recovery and Reconstruction," *Australasian Journal of Disaster and Trauma Studies* 2010–1 (2010), www.massey.ac.nz/~trauma/issues/2010-1/smith.htm (accessed February 4, 2011).

8   Wesley G. Skogan, *Police and Community in Chicago: A Tale of Three Cities* (Oxford: Oxford University Press, 2006).

9   David Ronfeldt and Cathryn L. Thorup, *North America in the Era of Citizen Networks: State, Society and Security* (Santa Monica, Calif.: RAND Corporation, 1995).

10   Dennis Mileti, *Disasters by Design: A Reassessment of Natural Hazards in the United States* (Washington, D.C.: Joseph Henry Press, 1999), 278–279.

11   U.S. Government Accountability Office (GAO), *Hurricane Katrina: Comprehensive Policies and Procedures Are Needed to Ensure Appropriate Use of and Accountability for International Assistance,* GAO-06-460 (Washington, D.C., April 6, 2006), www.gao.gov/new.items/d06460.pdf; GAO, *Hurricanes Katrina and Rita: Coordination between FEMA and the Red Cross Should Be Improved for the 2006 Hurricane Season,* GAO 06-712 (Washington, D.C., June 2006), www.gao.gov/new.items/d06712.pdf; GAO, *Various Mitigation Efforts Exist, but Federal Efforts Do Not Provide a Comprehensive Strategic Framework,* GAO-07-403 (Washington, D.C., August 2007), www.gao.gov/new.items/d07403.pdf; GAO, *National Disaster Response: FEMA Should Take Action to Improve Capacity and Coordination between Government and Voluntary Sectors,* GAO-08-369 (Washington, D.C., February 2008), www.gao.gov/new.items/d08369.pdf; GAO, *Disaster Recovery: Past Experiences Offer Insights for Recovering from Hurricanes Ike and Gustav and Other Recent Natural Disasters,* Report to the Senate Committee on Homeland Security and Governmental Affairs, GAO-08-1120 (Washington, D.C., September 2008), www.gao.gov/new.items/d081120.pdf; GAO, *Disaster Recovery: FEMA's Long-term Assistance Was Helpful to State and Local Governments but Had Some Limitations,* GAO-10-404 (Washington D.C., March 2010), www.gao.gov/new.items/d10404.pdf; U.S. Senate, Committee on Homeland Security and Governmental Affairs, Subcommittee on Federal Financial Management, Government Information, and International Security, *Hurricane Katrina: Planning for and Management of Federal Disaster Recovery Contracts,* GAO-06-622T (Washington, D.C.: U.S. Government Accountability Office, April 10, 2006), www.gao.gov/new.items/d06622t.pdf.

12 Smith and Wenger, "Sustainable Disaster Recovery."

13 Mark G. Welsh and Ann-Margaret Esnard, "Closing Gaps in Local Housing Recovery Planning for Disadvantaged Displaced Households," *Cityscape: A Journal of Policy Development and Research* 11, no. 3 (2009): 195–212; Smith, "Lessons from the United States."

14 Kenneth C. Topping, "Wildfire Case Study: Oakland, California," in *Planning for Post-Disaster Recovery and Reconstruction,* Planning Advisory Service (PAS) Report 483/484, by Jim Schwab et al., 261–280 (Chicago: American Planning Association, 1998).

15 William Spangle and Assoc., *Rebuilding after Earthquakes: Lessons from Planners* (Portola Valley, Calif.: William Spangle and Assoc., 1990); Jim Schwab et al., *Planning for Post-Disaster Recovery and Reconstruction* (see note 14); Robert B. Olshansky and Stephanie Chang, "Planning for Disaster Recovery: Emerging Research Needs and Challenges," in special issue, *Progress in Planning* 72, no. 4 (2009): 200–209; Smith and Wenger, "Sustainable Disaster Recovery"; Robert B. Olshansky and Laurie A. Johnson, *Clear as Mud: Planning for the Rebuilding of New Orleans* (Chicago: American Planning Association, 2010).

16 John Friedmann, *Planning in the Public Domain: From Knowledge to Action* (Princeton, N.J.: Princeton University Press, 1987).

17 Harvey S. Perloff, *Planning the Post-Industrial City* (Washington, D.C.: American Planning Association Planner's Press, 1980).

18 Sherry Arnstein, "Ladder of Citizen Participation," *Journal of American Institute of Planners* 35, no. 4 (1969): 216–224; Michael Neuman, "Images as Institution Builders: Metropolitan Planning in Madrid," *European Planning Studies* 4, no. 3 (1996): 293–312; Paul Davidoff, "Advocacy and Pluralism in Planning," *Journal of the American Institute of Planners* 31, no. 4 (1965): 331–338.

19 Manuel Castells, *The City and the Grassroots: A Cross Cultural Theory of Urban Social Movements* (London: Edward Arnold, 1983).

20 Philip R. Berke et al., *Urban Land Use Planning,* 5th ed. (Urbana: Illinois University Press, 2006).

21 John Forester, "Planning in the Face of Power," *Journal of the American Planning Association* 48, no. 1 (1982): 67–80.

22 T. J. Kent Jr., *The Urban General Plan,* 2nd ed. (San Francisco: Chandler, 1991).

23 Lawrence Susskind, "The Future of the Planning Profession," in *Planning for America: Learning from Turbulence,* ed. David Godschalk (Washington, D.C.: American Institute of Planners, 1974); Connie P. Ozawa and Lawrence Susskind, "Mediating Science-Intensive Policy Disputes," *Journal of Policy Analysis and Management* 5, no. 1 (1985): 23–39; Lawrence Susskind and Alan Weinstein, "Toward a Theory of Environmental Dispute Resolution," *Boston College Environmental Affairs Law Review* 9, no. 2 (1981): 311–357; John Forester, "Planning in the Face of Conflict: Negotiation and Mediation Strategies in Local Land Use Regulation," *Journal of the American Planning Association* 53, no. 3 (1987): 303–314; John Forester, "Envisioning the Politics of Public Sector Dispute Resolution," in *Studies in Law, Politics and Society,* vol. 12, ed. Susan S. Sibley and Austin Sarat, 247–286 (Greenwich, Conn.: Jai Press, 1992); David R. Godschalk, "Negotiating Intergovernmental Development Policy Conflicts: Practice-Based Guidelines," *Journal of the American Planning Association* 58, no. 3 (1992): 368–378.

24 Smith and Wenger, "Sustainable Disaster Recovery."

25 Lewis D. Hopkins, *Urban Development: The Logic of Making Plans* (Washington, D.C.: Island Press, 2001).

26 Philip Berke and David Godschalk, "Searching for the Good Plan: A Meta-Analysis of Plan Quality Studies," *Journal of Planning Literature* 23, no. 3 (2009): 227–240.

27 Ibid.; William C. Baer, "General Plan Evaluation Criteria: An Approach to Making Better Plans," *Journal of the American Planning Association* 63, no. 3 (1997): 329–345.

28 Raymond J. Burby and Peter J. May, *Making Governments Plan: Some Experiments in Managing Land Use* (Baltimore: Johns Hopkins University Press, 1997); Philip R. Berke, Jennifer Dixon, and Neil Ericksen, "Coercive and Cooperative Intergovernmental Mandates: A Comparative Analysis of Florida

and New Zealand Environmental Plans," *Environment and Planning B: Planning and Design* 24, no. 3 (1997): 451–468; Robert E. Deyle and Richard A. Smith, "Local Government Compliance with State Plan Mandates: The Effects of State Implementation in Florida," *Journal of the American Planning Association* 64, no. 4 (1998): 457–469; Arthur C. Nelson and Steven P. French, "Plan Quality and Mitigating Damage from Natural Disasters: A Case Study of the Northridge Earthquake with Planning Policy Considerations," *Journal of the American Planning Association* 68, no. 2 (2002): 194–207; Raymond J. Burby, "Making Plans That Matter: Citizen Involvement and Government Action," *Journal of the American Planning Association* 69, no. 1 (2003): 33–39; Philip Berke and Gavin Smith, "Hazard Mitigation, Planning, and Disaster Resiliency: Challenges and Strategic Choices for the 21st Century," in *Building Safer Communities: Risk Governance, Spatial Planning and Responses to Natural Hazards,* ed. Urbano Fra Paleo, 1–20 (Amsterdam: IOS Press, 2009).

29 Gavin Smith and Victor Flatt, *Assessing the Disaster Recovery Planning Capacity of the State of North Carolina,* Policy Brief (Durham, N.C.: Institute for Homeland Security Solutions, January 2011). www.ihssnc.org/portals/0/Documents/VIMSDocuments/IHSS_Research_Brief_Smith.pdf.

30 Richard K. Norton, "Using Content Analysis to Evaluate Local Master Plans and Zoning Codes," *Land Use Policy* 25, no. 3 (2008): 432–454.

31 Forester, "Planning in the Face of Conflict"; John Forester, *Planning in the Face of Power* (Berkeley and Los Angeles: University of California Press, 1989); Susan Carpenter and W. J. D. Kennedy, *Managing Public Disputes: A Practical Guide for Professionals in Government, Business and Citizen's Groups* (San Francisco: Jossey-Bass, 1988); Bruce A. Dotson, David R. Godschalk, and Jerome L. Kaufman, eds., *The Planner as Dispute Resolver* (Washington, D.C.: National Institute of Dispute Resolution, 1989); David Godschalk, "Volusia County Conflict Resolution Program," in Dotson, Godschalk, and Kaufman, *The Planner as Dispute Resolver;* Sanda Kaufman and Janet Smith, "Framing and Reframing in Land Use Conflicts," *Journal of Architectural and Planning Research* 16, no. 2 (1999): 164–180; Deborah F. Shmueli, Sanda Kaufman, and Connie Ozawa, "Mining Negotiation Theory for Planning Insights," *Journal of Planning Education and Research* 27, no. 3 (2008): 359–364.

32 Lawrence Susskind and Connie Ozawa, "Mediated Negotiation in the Public Sector: The Planner as Mediator," *Journal of Planning Education and Research* 4, no. 1 (1984): 5.

33 Baer, "General Plan Evaluation Criteria"; Berke et al., *Urban Land Use Planning,* 70–72; Berke and Godschalk, "Searching for the Good Plan."

34 Godschalk, "Negotiating Intergovernmental Development Policy Conflicts"; Kaufman and Smith, "Framing and Reframing in Land Use Conflicts."

35 Gilbert F. White, "Human Adjustment to Floods," Research Paper no. 29 (PhD diss., University of Chicago, 1945).

36 David R. Godschalk, "Safe Growth Audits," *Zoning Practice* 26, no. 10 (2009): 1–7.

37 Oliver-Smith, "Post-Disaster Housing Reconstruction and Social Inequality"; Philip R. Berke and Timothy Beatley, *Planning for Earthquakes: Risk, Politics, and Policy* (Baltimore: Johns Hopkins University Press, 1992); N. Emel Ganapati and Sukumar Ganapati, "Enabling Participatory Planning after Disasters: A Case Study of the World Bank's Housing Reconstruction in Turkey," *Journal of the American Planning Association* 75, no. 1 (2009): 41–59.

38 Gavin Smith, "Holistic Disaster Recovery: Creating a More Sustainable Future" (course developed for the Emergency Management Institute Higher Education Project, Federal Emergency Management Agency, 2004), available online at training.fema.gov/EMIWeb/edu/sdr.asp.

39 Berke et al., *Urban Land Use Planning,* 275–276.

40 Timothy Beatley, "The Vision of Sustainable Communities," in *Cooperating with Nature: Confronting Natural Hazards with Land-Use Planning for Sustainable Communities,* ed. Raymond J. Burby, 233–262 (Washington, D.C.: Joseph Henry Press, 1998); David R. Godschalk et al., *Natural Hazard Mitigation: Recasting Disaster Policy and Planning* (Washington, D.C.: Island Press, 1999); David R. Godschalk, "Urban Hazard Mitigation: Creating Resilient Cities," *Natural Hazards Review* 4, no. 3 (2003): 136–142; Smith and Wenger, "Sustainable Disaster Recovery"; Timothy Beatley, *Planning*

for *Coastal Resilience: Best Practices for Calamitous Times* (Washington, D.C.: Island Press, 2009); Smith, "Lessons from the United States"; Gavin Smith, "Disaster-Resilient Communities: A New Hazards Risk Management Framework," in *Natural Hazards Analysis: Reducing the Impact of Disasters,* ed. John Pine, 249–267 (Washington, D.C.: Taylor Francis, 2009).

41   Baer, "General Plan Evaluation Criteria"; Berke et al., *Urban Land Use Planning,* 72–74; Berke and Godschalk, "Searching for the Good Plan."

42   F. Stuart Chapin and Edward J. Kaiser, *Urban Land Use Planning,* 4th ed. (Urbana and Chicago: University of Illinois Press, 1985), 368.

43   Berke et al., *Urban Land Use Planning,* 422–424.

44   David R. Godschalk, Samuel Brody, and Raymond Burby, "Public Participation in Natural Hazard Mitigation Policy Formulation: Challenges for Comprehensive Planning," *Journal of Environmental Planning and Management* 46, no. 5 (2003): 733–754.

45   Ibid.

46   Archon Fung, *Empowered Participation: Reinventing Urban Democracy* (Princeton, N.J.: Princeton University Press, 2004).

47   John M. DeGrove, *Land, Growth and Politics* (Chicago: Planners Press, 1984).

48   Raymond J. Burby and Linda C. Dalton, "Plans Can Matter! The Role of Land Use and State Planning Mandates on Limiting Development in Hazardous Areas," *Public Administration Review* 54, no. 3, (1994): 229–238.

49   Robert G. Healy and John S. Rosenberg, *Land Use and the States,* 2nd ed. (Baltimore: Johns Hopkins University Press, 1979).

50   Schwab et al., *Planning for Post-Disaster Recovery and Reconstruction;* William et al., ed., *Pre-Earthquake Planning for Post-Earthquake Rebuilding (PEPPER)* (Los Angeles: Southern California Earthquake Preparedness Project, 1987); George G. Mader and Martha Blair Tyler, *Rebuilding after Earthquakes: Lessons from Planners* (Portola, Calif.: William Spangle and Associates, 1991); Martha Blair Tyler, Katherine O'Prey, and Karen Kristiansson, *Redevelopment after Earthquakes* (Portola Valley, Calif.: Spangle Associates, 2002).

51   Florian Steinberg, "Housing Reconstruction and Rehabilitation in Aceh and Nias, Indonesia—Rebuilding Lives," *Habitat International* 31, no. 1 (2007): 150–166.

52   Gavin Smith, "The Transformation of Environmental Conflict: A Game Theoretic Approach" (PhD diss., Texas A & M University, 1995).

53   Smith and Wenger, "Sustainable Disaster Recovery," 240; Smith, "Planning for Sustainable and Disaster Resilient Communities," 240; John Forester and Reshmi Krishnan Theckethil, "Rethinking Risk Management Policies: From "Participation" to Processes of Dialogue, Debate, and Negotiation," in Paleo, *Building Safer Communities.*

54   "Symposium—ADR in the Aftermath: Post-Disaster Strategies," *Cardozo Journal of Conflict Resolution* 9 (Spring 2008): 283–396.

55   Scott Bollens, "Restructuring Land Use Governance," *Journal of Planning Literature* 7, no. 3 (1993): 211–226; Judith Innes, "Planning through Consensus Building: A New View of the Comprehensive Planning Ideal," *Journal of the American Planning Association* 62, no. 4 (1996): 460–472; Lawrence Susskind, Sarah McKearnan, and Jennifer Thomas-Larmer, *The Consensus Building Handbook* (Thousand Oaks, Calif.: Sage, 1999); Judith Innes and David Booher, "Consensus Building and Complex Adaptive Systems: A Framework for Evaluating Collaborative Planning," *Journal of the American Planning Association* 65, no. 4 (1999): 412–423; Judith Innes and David Booher, "Reframing Public Participation: Strategies for the 21st Century," *Planning Theory and Practice* 5, no. 4 (2004): 419–436; Godschalk, Brody, and Burby, "Public Participation in Natural Hazard Mitigation Policy Formulation."

56   Innes and Booher, "Consensus Building and Complex Adaptive Systems," 412.

57   Walter Gillis Peacock, Betty Hearn Morrow, and Hugh Gladwin, eds., *Hurricane Andrew: Ethnicity, Gender and the Sociology of Disasters* (Miami, Fla.: International Hurricane Center Laboratory for

Social and Behavioral Research, 2000); Oliver-Smith, "Post-Disaster Housing Reconstruction and Social Inequality."

58 Douglas Amy, "Mediation versus Traditional Political Institutions," in *The Politics of Environmental Mediation,* (New York: Columbia University Press, 1987); Ray Kemp, "Planning, Public Hearings, and the Politics of Discourse," in *Critical Theory and Public Life,* ed. John Forester, 177–201 (Cambridge: MIT Press, 1985); Innes and Booher, "Reframing Public Participation"; Arnstein, "Ladder of Citizen Participation."

59 Mel Rubin, "Disaster Mediation: Lessons in Conflict Coordination and Collaboration," *Cardozo Journal of Conflict Resolution* 9 (2007): 351.

60 Linda Baron, "Disaster Basics: The Life Cycle of a Disaster and the Role of Conflict Resolution Professionals." *Cardozo Journal of Conflict Resolution* 9 (2007): 301–315.

61 Roger Fisher and William Ury, *Getting to Yes: Negotiating Agreements without Giving In* (New York: Penguin Books, 1981); Lawrence Susskind and Jeffrey Cruikshank, *Breaking the Impasse: Consensual Approaches to Resolving Public Disputes* (New York: Basic Books, 1987); Forester, "Envisioning the Politics."

62 Fisher and Ury, *Getting to Yes;* Amy, "Mediation versus Traditional Political Institutions."

63 Daniel Fiorino, "Regulatory Negotiation as a Policy Process," *Public Administration Review* 48 (July/August 1988): 764–772; Henry W. Fischer III, *Response to Disaster: Fact versus Fiction and Its Perpetuation: The Sociology of Disaster* (New York: University Press of America, 1998).

64 Smith, "Holistic Disaster Recovery"; Smith and Wenger, "Sustainable Disaster Recovery."

65 Smith. "Holistic Disaster Recovery."

66 Godschalk, "Negotiating Intergovernmental Development Policy Conflicts"; Fisher and Ury, *Getting to Yes;* Lawrence Susskind, "Mediating Public Disputes: A Response to the Skeptics," *Negotiation Journal* (April 1985): 117–120; Susskind and Cruikshank, *Breaking the Impasse;* Lawrence Susskind and Sarah McKearnan, "The Evolution of Public Policy Dispute Resolution," *Journal of Architectural and Planning Research* 16 (Summer 1999): 96–115; Deborah M. Kolb and Judith Williams, *Everyday Negotiation: Navigating the Hidden Agendas in Bargaining* (San Francisco: Jossey-Bass, 2003).

67 Susskind and Weinstein, "Toward a Theory of Environmental Dispute Resolution."

68 Forester and Theckethil, "Rethinking Risk Management Policies," 35.

69 Nelson, Ehrenfeucht, and Laska, "Planning, Plans, and People."

70 Susskind and Cruikshank, *Breaking the Impasse,* 188–189.

71 Robert H. Bates, "Contra Contractarianism: Some Reflections on the New Institutionalism," *Politics and Society* 16, no. 2 (1988): 387–401.

72 Dennis Chong, *Collective Action and the Civil Rights Movement* (Chicago: University of Chicago Press, 1991); Elinor Ostrom, *Governing the Commons: The Evolution of Institutions for Collective Action* (Cambridge: Cambridge University Press, 1990); Forester, "Envisioning the Politics"; Robert Axelrod, "The Emergence of Cooperation among Egoists," *American Political Science Review* 75, no. 2 (1981): 306–318; Robert Axelrod, *The Evolution of Cooperation* (New York: Basic Books, 1984).

73 Ozawa and Susskind, "Mediating Science-Intensive Policy Disputes."

74 Susskind and Cruikshank, *Breaking the Impasse,* 117.

75 William R. Freudenberg et al., *Catastrophe in the Making: The Engineering of Katrina and the Disasters of Tomorrow* (Washington, D.C.: Island Press, 2009).

76 Forester and Theckethil, "Rethinking Risk Management Policies."

77 Ibid., 40.

78 Arnstein, "Ladder of Citizen Participation."

79 Fisher and Ury, *Getting to Yes,* 101–111.

80 John Forester, *Dealing with Differences: Dramas of Mediating Public Disputes* (Oxford: Oxford University Press, 2009); Forester, "Planning in the Face of Power"; Forester and Theckethil, "Rethinking Risk Management Policies."

81 Smith and Wenger, "Sustainable Disaster Recovery."

82 Forester, *Dealing with Differences.*

83 Shmueli, Kaufman, and Ozawa, "Mining Negotiation Theory for Planning Insights," 360.

84 Robert Geipel, *Disaster and Reconstruction: The Friuli (Italy) Earthquakes of 1976* (London: Allen and Unwin, 1982); Olshansky and Chang, "Planning for Disaster Recovery."

85 Smith and Wenger, "Sustainable Disaster Recovery."

86 Samuel D. Brody, "Are We Learning to Make Better Plans? A Longitudinal Analysis of Plan Quality Associated with Natural Hazards," *Journal of Planning and Education Research* 23, no. 2 (2003): 191–201.

87 Robert B. Olshansky et al., "Planning for the Rebuilding of New Orleans," *Journal of the American Planning Association* 74, no. 3 (2008): 273–287.

88 Peter May et al., *Environmental Management and Governance: Intergovernmental Approaches to Hazards and Sustainability* (London: Routledge, 1996).

89 Shmueli, Kaufman, and Ozawa, "Mining Negotiation Theory for Planning Insights."

90 Innes and Booher, "Consensus Building and Complex Adaptive Systems."

91 Judith Innes, "Planning Theory's Emerging Paradigm: Communicative Action and Interactive Practice," *Journal of Planning Education and Research* 14, no. 3 (1995): 183–189; Lynn A. Mandarano, "Evaluating Collaborative Environmental Planning Outputs and Outcomes: Restoring and Protecting Habitat and the New York–New Jersey Harbor Estuary Program," *Journal of Planning Education and Research* 27, no. 4 (2008): 456–468; Burby, "Making Plans That Matter."

92 Geipel, *Disaster and Reconstruction;* Oliver-Smith, "Post-Disaster Housing Reconstruction and Social Inequality"; Burby, "Making Plans That Matter"; Berke and Beatley, *After the Hurricane;* Schwab et al., *Planning for Post-Disaster Recovery and Reconstruction;* May et al., *Environmental Management and Governance.*

93 Godschalk, Brody, and Burby, "Public Participation in Natural Hazard Mitigation Policy Formulation."

94 Smith and Wenger, "Sustainable Disaster Recovery," 240, 244, 250.

95 Spangle and Assoc., *Rebuilding after Earthquakes.*

96 Spangle and Assoc., *Rebuilding after Earthquakes,* 1.

97 Baron, "Disaster Basics."

98 Schwab et al., *Planning for Post-Disaster Recovery and Reconstruction.*

99 James Schwab, ed. *Hazard Mitigation: Integrating Best Practices into Planning,* Planning Advisory Service (PAS) Report 560 (Chicago: American Planning Association, 2010).

Chapter 9

Addressing the Challenges of the Disaster Recovery Assistance Framework: Creating the Disaster Recovery Act

New Orleans public library suffered major damage from Hurricane Katrina.

Photo by Donn Young.

T HE U.S. DISASTER RECOVERY ASSISTANCE framework is in need of significant repair, and a confluence of several factors suggests that now is the time
to address the problems. Hurricane Katrina exposed the lack of a coordinated
system and its effects to a national audience, prompting an expanded study of disaster
recovery as well as increased attention among federal lawmakers and other members
of the disaster recovery assistance network. Evidence of this growing focus includes
the passage of the Post-Katrina Emergency Management Reform Act of 2006, the writing of the draft National Disaster Recovery Framework (NDRF), and the creation of the
White House Long-Term Disaster Recovery Working Group. These events build on

the ever more routine deployment of the Federal Emergency Management Agency's (FEMA) Emergency Support Function 14 (ESF-14), Long-Term Community Recovery, after federally declared disasters; the small but mounting number of states that are developing pre-disaster recovery planning initiatives; and the growing number of experts who support the passage of federal policy that addresses limitations in the delivery of pre- and post-disaster recovery assistance.[1]

Any attempt to alter the current assistance framework must recognize that the existing policy milieu provides powerful disincentives to plan for post-disaster recovery. Some evidence of this can be seen in the limited number of pre-event recovery plans found in the United States. Efforts to find good plans that were developed prior to a disaster and effectively used in its aftermath have proven difficult. While such plans may exist, the fact that they are not readily identifiable is indicative of the challenges ahead for those who would seek to change the assistance framework and those who should actively participate in the development, monitoring, and implementation of pre-event recovery plans. It also appears to confirm the widely accepted notion among federal officials and others in the assistance network that recovery planning is largely a post-disaster exercise.

According to a 2010 Government Accountability Office (GAO) report that assessed the post-disaster delivery of recovery planning assistance after several major disasters, FEMA's ESF-14, while providing helpful guidance and support, faces several challenges. Among the most significant of those challenges are the marginalization of ESF-14 staff by federal coordination officers (FCOs), unclear roles among federal and state agencies involved in recovery, insufficient authority among ESF-14 officials to effectively resolve multiparty disputes, and the failure to appropriately time the delivery of assistance.[2] In several cases, state and local officials cited the timing of information requests by ESF-14 as being too early in the process as they were overwhelmed by other tasks at the time and unable to respond. Others noted that ESF-14 staff should have stayed on site longer than they did, particularly during critically important long-term recovery operations and the implementation of plans.[3]

Another unfortunate outcome of existing post-disaster recovery planning assistance has been the formulation of plans that set unrealistic expectations: in some cases, local officials discovered that projects identified in the post-disaster plans did not meet the eligibility requirements of existing grant programs and were therefore unfunded.[4] Such discoveries can undermine the perceived value of planning and the standing of ESF-14 staff in the eyes of state and local officials and FCOs—a serious problem, as ESF-14 staff are supposed to be responsible for coordinating stakeholders and resolving multiparty conflicts. To remedy these problems, the GAO recommends that FEMA "(1) more effectively align the timing and level of long-term recovery assistance to match the capacity and needs of affected states and localities and (2) evaluate the level of authority needed to effectively coordinate federal agencies involved in disaster recovery."[5]

The problems noted in FEMA's existing post-disaster recovery planning assistance strategy are indicative of a much larger set of institutional issues that span the assistance network. Key weaknesses in the disaster recovery assistance framework should be addressed as part of a coordinated, national planning-based strategy that allows disaster assistance networks across the United States to identify existing and needed resources (funding, policies, and technical assistance), strengthen interorganizational relationships and trust (horizontally and vertically), coordinate the timing of assistance (before and after disasters), codify specific roles and responsibilities through agreements and program modifications, and craft policies that reflect local conditions.

This chapter outlines specific elements of a proposed Disaster Recovery Act (DRA). Mandated planning activities and alternative dispute resolution (ADR) techniques would play a central role in the implementation of this act, creating the conditions that foster sustained cooperation, improving the way that resource distribution conflicts are addressed, and building a coalition that embraces a culture of pre-event planning for post-disaster recovery. These goals would be achieved through a multitiered approach that calls for the following actions:

- Conduct a national audit of state and local disaster recovery plans
- Mandate state and local recovery planning
- Mandate the use of ADR techniques to address pre- and post-disaster recovery-based conflicts
- Establish collaborative leadership initiatives
- Develop an education, training, and outreach agenda
- Establish a national recovery coalition through improved planning practices
- Assess and modify emergency management programs and the scope of plans
- Enhance local self-reliance and accountability: Create a culture of planning for recovery.

CONDUCT A NATIONAL AUDIT OF STATE AND LOCAL DISASTER RECOVERY PLANS

The success of the proposed DRA hinges on the adoption of a robust pre-disaster recovery planning policy. To create good policy that is predicated on the importance of recovery plans, our collective understanding of recovery planning—including that derived from the community of hazard scholars and practitioners—needs to be improved. While a number of studies acknowledge the importance of recovery planning, their emphasis has been on the use of anecdotal case studies rather than on a quantitative analysis of existing plans.[6] Apart from a limited understanding of plans, it is not even clear how many actually exist and what they entail. Nor has the literature on measuring recovery outcomes[7] taken into account the effect of a plan's quality on those outcomes.

The planning literature has shown that plans do matter, including those that address natural hazards.[8] To test the applicability of these findings to recovery plans, FEMA, working closely with hazards planning researchers, professional associations, and others in the assistance network, should conduct an audit of state and local plans in accordance with the plan quality and ADR principles discussed in Chapter 8. Such an audit should seek to assess the relationship between plan quality and recovery outcomes across interdependent social, economic, environmental, physical, and institutional dimensions. Traditional measures of recovery include debris clearance; restoration of infrastructure; repair and reconstruction of housing, public facilities, and businesses; reconstitution of social networks; revitalization of the economy; and restoration of the natural environment. An audit of recovery should also determine the degree to which important policy and planning changes were institutionalized following disasters. Such changes would include the adoption of new or modified institutional arrangements across the network that improve the distribution of resources. Finally, studies should focus on geographically dispersed states and communities across the United States that have adopted pre- and/or post-disaster plans. Research designs should control for pre-event community-level factors, the characteristics of the disaster agent, and facilitators and impediments to disaster recovery[9] (Exhibit 9–1).

Studies of this nature should be part of an ongoing analytical process that informs possible policy changes over time. For instance, a longitudinal assessment of the factors underlying the proposed DRA should consider the effect of pre- and post-disaster technical assistance and capacity-building strategies on plan quality, the degree to which plan-making processes help to foster collaborative leadership and enduring coalitions that support recovery planning efforts, the manner in which plans are implemented following disasters, and the extent to which plans improve a community's level of self-reliance. A comprehensive, ongoing study process would also allow for the evaluation of recovery plans across communities with different hazard types, vulnerabilities, and capabilities. FEMA and others charged with implementing the DRA could use this information to develop plan quality metrics to evaluate plans, suggest improvements, and help to focus training and capacity-building efforts over time. The proposed

Exhibit 9–1. Suggested Elements for a Theory of Sustainable Community Recovery

Pre-Disaster, Community-Level Contextual Variables

Local capacity (including population size, social and economic status, economic viability)

Previous disaster experience

Leadership and advocacy

Nature and extent of horizontal ties

Nature and extent of vertical ties

Level of local government viability and effectiveness

Level of local public participation in collective action

Condition of critical infrastructure and housing

Level of local disaster vulnerability (including social vulnerability)

Characteristics of the Disaster Agent

Intensity of the impact

Scope of the impact

Speed of onset of the disaster

Level and adequacy of warnings

Duration of impact

Facilitators of Sustainable Disaster Recovery

Leveraging resources

Self-reliance and self-determination

Commitment to disaster resilience

State and federal capability and commitment to sustainable disaster recovery

Capacity-building approaches

Multiparty recovery committees

Pre- and post-disaster recovery planning

Use of dispute resolution techniques

Identification of local needs

Program flexibility

Impediments to Sustainable Disaster Recovery

Perception of disaster recovery programs as entitlements

Overreliance on disaster programs that result in more vulnerable communities

Narrowly defined recovery programs

Low capability and commitment

Lack of federal, state, and local recovery planning

Source: Gavin Smith and Dennis Wenger, "Sustainable Disaster Recovery: Operationalizing an Existing Agenda," in *Handbook of Disaster Research*, ed. Havidan Rodriguez, Enrico L. Quarantelli, and Russell Dynes (New York: Springer, 2006), 247. Used with permission of Springer.

Resesiliency and Vulnerability Observation Network (RAVON), described in Chapter 3, is representative of the type of organization that should play a role in such an effort.

Framed in the context of the underlying challenges posed in this book, the audit should consider the following questions:

- To what extent do recovery plans improve access to funding and technical assistance?
- To what extent do plans contribute to the modification or creation of policies that help a community meet local needs before and after disasters?
- To what extent do plans improve the speed and coordinated timing of assistance?

- To what extent do plans enhance horizontal and vertical integration?
- To what extent does the use of collaborative planning and ADR techniques affect recovery outcomes?

Answers to these questions and others can help inform future planning efforts undertaken by members of the assistance network. They can also guide the development of enabling rules and policies associated with an integrated policy framework and a national planning mandate.

MANDATE STATE AND LOCAL RECOVERY PLANNING

This book posits that improvements to the disaster recovery assistance framework are unlikely unless federal legislation mandates that state and local governments develop pre-event recovery plans. However, studies of existing planning mandates report mixed results in terms of their ability to elicit plans that guide informed actions.[10] For instance, an assessment of county- and municipal-level coastal management plans in North Carolina, which are required under the Coastal Zone Management Act, found that plans are weak both analytically and substantively.[11] In a national assessment of state hazard mitigation plans, Philip Berke, Gavin Smith, and Ward Lyles found that plans generally obtain moderate to low quality scores in key areas, such as the identification of clear goals, the development of integrated policies, and the adoption of rigorous participatory procedures.[12] An evaluation of an affordable housing planning mandate in Illinois showed that because local officials were resistant to developing plans, the plans that emerged meet minimal requirements but do not address long-standing exclusionary policies or offer recommended solutions.[13]

Yet the research also shows that states that mandate hazard management plans have ended up with higher-quality plans than states that adopt a voluntary approach.[14] In other cases, a hybrid approach that combines the strengths of voluntary and mandated compliance is recommended.[15] The proposed DRA suggests that for a planning mandate to be successful, it requires the collaborative development of standards and the adequate provision of resources (funding, technical assistance, and policies) necessary to build both capacity and commitment to an ongoing process of pre-event planning for post-disaster recovery. How this can be accomplished is discussed further on in this chapter.

Numerous attempts by the federal government to mandate state and local planning have been stymied by an inadequate level of attention placed on building the technical, fiscal, institutional, and political capacities needed to develop, implement, and maintain plans over time. The first step in building these capabilities involves learning what those organizations and associated networks that are ultimately responsible for implementing planning initiatives are already capable of and then undertaking targeted strategies to address the identified limitations. This information, as well as the appropriate strategies to address identified needs, is best collected through an interactive process. Unfortunately, the approach widely used by federal officials and derisively referred to as the "unfunded mandate" does little to address these concerns. And since states and local governments are not actively involved in the formulation of enabling rules and regulations associated with these mandates, they are unable to express their concerns, suggest potential improvements, identify possible efficiencies achieved through cooperation, and define the resources they may need to meet the aims of the mandate.

Planning mandates that overlook the value of investing the time necessary to encourage meaningful participation in an inherently process-oriented activity or to secure the resources needed to implement program goals have a negative effect on plan quality. For instance, a common approach used in plan making is to outsource work to a consultant, quasi-governmental planning agency, or other third party. But unless robust participatory standards are in place or the entity responsible for the development of the plan has bought into the process, there is no incentive for public officials and the contractor to engage in the time-consuming activity of soliciting input from the larger network.

The literature on mandates suggests that good plans should combine strong procedural elements with clear programmatic and technical requirements. For example, California requires that every local government incorporate a seismic safety element in its comprehensive plan. Arthur Nelson and Steven French note that this mandate has proven to be an effective way to limit earthquake-induced damages, particularly when plans include a strong fact base that informs goals, regulatory policies, and public education programs.[16] It also highlights the importance of linking hazards management strategies to existing, recognized plans that have legal and administrative standing, given that mandates are strengthened when plans serve as routinely used decision-making tools. Nelson and French further conclude that the effectiveness of state-level mandates varies depending on the nature of the state's implementation procedures.[17] Linda Dalton and Raymond Burby have found that high-quality plans indirectly influence the adoption of hazard mitigation practices because they help to garner the political support needed to overcome local opposition to planning.[18] Comparative studies of the United States and New Zealand show that planning mandates benefit from the combination of state, regional, and local capacity-building efforts; ample information to guide state and local efforts; the ongoing solicitation of political support; and funding to implement stated goals.[19]

Any attempt to mandate recovery planning as part of a national policy must address the reluctance of federal agencies to seek input from stakeholders who are directly affected by policy decisions. Evidence suggests that mandating citizen participation can encourage greater and more meaningful involvement in planning decisions, particularly when effective administrative venues are created.[20] Additional tasks that support collaborative decision making and planning include identifying stakeholders and their preferences, deciding when it is appropriate to solicit public involvement, determining what type of information dissemination will occur, and selecting the types of participatory actions to use.[21] Understood relative to disaster recovery and the inherent weaknesses in the disaster recovery assistance framework, mandating state and local recovery planning also means assessing and modifying existing plans, policies, and programs in a way that supports the intent of the mandate, including the ability to effectively address pre- and post-disaster recovery conflicts.

MANDATE THE USE OF ALTERNATIVE DISPUTE RESOLUTION TECHNIQUES TO ADDRESS PRE- AND POST-DISASTER RECOVERY-BASED CONFLICTS

Disaster recovery networks are diffuse by nature, vary from one community to the next, and are subject to change over time. Moreover, their members may have little experience with or knowledge of the planning process. The traditional top-down delivery of information from the public sector limits the opportunity not only for reciprocal learning but also for the crafting of recovery strategies that meet local needs, are appropriately timed, and foster horizontal and vertical integration. Similarly, the widespread reliance on traditional legal and administrative procedures in recovery reduces meaningful discourse. These limitations of the current disaster recovery assistance framework strongly indicate the need for a collaborative planning approach. And the proposed DRA recommends the mandated use of ADR techniques as a way of directly addressing these limitations and translating the tenets of collaborative planning into action.

Several legal and planning scholars have debated whether the use of ADR techniques should be mandated.[22] Much of the debate centers on the apparent contradiction between voluntary participation, which is seen as a defining characteristic of ADR, and the required involvement of disputants.[23] Opponents argue that mandating the mediation process weakens an underlying premise that participants should want or choose to participate rather than being required to do so.[24] In response, David Winston contends that mandatory mediation can still be viewed as voluntary as long as a settlement is agreed to voluntarily.[25] If the mandated mediation process does not produce an amicable agreement among parties, participants can walk away from the process and pursue more traditional administrative and legal procedures, as described in Chapter 8's discussion of the best alternative to a negotiated agreement (BATNA).

In practice, the voluntary nature of ADR can have the unintended effect of excluding those who should participate in collective decision-making procedures. This is evident in the disaster recovery process and is most acute among socially vulnerable populations. As a consequence of the prescriptive nature of the rules governing disaster assistance at the federal level, those who are least able to recover without some form of external assistance are often excluded from the policy-making process, unable to express their needs or provide insights that can be helpful in the development of appropriate policies. In many cases, socially vulnerable populations have had negative experiences, including overt discrimination, when dealing with an unresponsive government bureaucracy. Thus, it is not surprising that some groups choose not to participate in a process that they may view as hostile or from which they have historically derived little benefit.

The growth and maturation of the ADR field offers promise as a procedural technique to confront the problems endemic to the disaster recovery assistance framework. Several factors are worth noting. First, disputants have become increasingly willing to engage in dispute resolution approaches, as evidenced by the rising demand for these services; the increase in negotiated policy settlements; the creation of federal and state dispute resolution offices, a recognized professional association, and a robust private and nonprofit sector specializing in the provision of ADR-related services; and a strong demand for professional training.[26] Second, over time, the ADR community has accumulated an impressive list of successfully mediated settlements. Third, a growing number of federal and state laws encourage public agencies to use ADR techniques. For instance, both the Negotiated Rulemaking Act and the ADR Act, passed in 1990 and 1996, respectively, encourage federal agencies to address governmental disputes using mediation, facilitation, and other consensus-building techniques. The degree to which this has been done varies significantly among federal agencies, depending in large part on the commitment of agency leadership and the allocation of funds needed to support such activities.[27]

Any attempt to address the conflict-laden disaster recovery assistance process requires a greater commitment of resources to train mediators and facilitators capable of assisting in pre- and post-disaster disputes (see Figure 9–1 on page 330). A number of institutional venues currently exist to draw upon. For instance, in addition to the aforementioned federal and state dispute resolution offices, numerous nonprofits and private sector firms specialize in the delivery of ADR services, including training, while university professors in planning, law, and business schools teach courses in dispute resolution and often practice it outside the classroom. Members of the Society of Professionals in Dispute Resolution and the Association of Conflict Resolution have established standards of practice and conduct training as part of their associations' certification programs. Trained mediators, many of whom are members of these associations, may be willing to provide pro bono disaster services and assist in the development of a disaster recovery mediation program.

Several factors should be considered when designing such a program, including the direct involvement of members of the disaster recovery assistance network, the ability to rapidly assess the needs of those affected by a disaster, the use of a neutral administrator to manage the program, the development of procedures to help ensure confidentiality among disputants, the hiring and training of locally based mediators whenever possible, and the provision of adequate security where mediation takes place.[28] A post-disaster assessment conducted in tandem with planners allows mediators to ascertain the existing level of cooperation and the resources available across the network, information they can then use to prioritize actions and select from various ADR techniques. The proper use of these techniques is also shaped by an understanding of the degree to which programs are meeting the needs of those who seek assistance.

Figure 9–1. The Dispute Settlement Center, located in Orange County, North Carolina, is representative of a growing number of nonprofit organizations dedicated to the resolution of multiparty disputes. Specific services include mediation and facilitation training as well as the provision of technical assistance to help individuals and organizations resolve disputes.

Courtesy of the Orange County Dispute Settlement Center.

Neutrality in the administration of mediated disputes is crucial. The impression of neutrality gives the administrator greater standing among members of the assistance network and engenders trust among those whose behavior may have been influenced by contentious interactions in the past. It is also important that administrators gain the trust of those who manage recovery programs, and this will be one of the greatest challenges to the success of the ADR program. Many public sector entities, for example, maintain rigid rules and may be reluctant to alter programs or relinquish their power base, which is partially defined by their ability to dictate the nature of the rules governing post-disaster resource distribution. On the other hand, nonprofits and emergent groups, which have more program flexibility, may balk at a process that could be seen as unnecessarily constraining their ability to provide assistance as they see fit.

Maintaining confidentiality among potential disputants represents another challenge as discretion must be balanced with an open, inclusive decision-making process that provides a degree of distributional continuity across groups facing similar needs. It is also critically important to ensure that as policy precedence is established in agreements, it is applied in future disputes. One way to address this issue is by applying confidentiality tenets to the process used to achieve agreed-upon solutions rather than to the content of the agreements. Mediated settlements can, however, uncover important issues through their fact-finding processes. Such discoveries should be raised to policy makers, who could then change existing program rules, regulations, and statutes.

Collaborative resource distribution strategies—particularly those accounting for the allocation of public resources—may be codified as policy memos, multiparty agreements, rule-making procedures, or law. Once a new or modified policy is suggested, the stakeholders involved in the process should be willing to speak on its behalf. A clear advocate or "champion" who is recognized by all parties to the dispute, as well as by those in charge of traditional policy-making bodies, is important; such an advocate should be able to elucidate benefits that have not been realized using past techniques.

Not only should stakeholders play the role of policy advocate, but those most directly affected by procedural agreements and settlements should play a leadership role in policy formulation and implementation. This leads to another central tenet of the revised framework: that different leaders will emerge according to the nature and composition of the network. Public sector experts can provide technical information associated with recovery planning, but other members of the network can provide local context and experiential knowledge. In many cases, unexpected leaders emerge to play important roles in shepherding the recovery process. It is therefore important to make sure that all members of the network are able to actively engage in the planning process by ensuring access to ADR resources. This requires a concerted effort to create a national cadre of ADR professionals who can train members of assistance networks over time. Professional association members, existing nonprofit mediation centers, private sector mediation firms, and FEMA ADR specialists provide ample resources from which to draw talented, experienced professionals who can help mediate disaster recovery disputes and train others to do so as well.

Planners, who are often trained in negotiation, mediation, and facilitation, can help the parties identify a common vision and shared goals as well as navigate the process of policy agreements and plan implementation. This approach, while ideal for pre-event recovery planning, also lends itself to post-disaster conditions that require an adaptive decision-making process.[29] For instance, ADR, used appropriately, must recognize the temporal nature of recovery, allowing time for individuals, institutions, and the network of stakeholders to come to terms with the initial and sometimes enduring psychosocial impacts associated with a disaster before they can take control of the situation.[30] Post-disaster recovery plans, particularly those that employ ADR and other collaborative planning techniques, can provide a mechanism capable of pro-actively guiding the multitude of interrelated actions in a timely and adaptive manner. These challenges, as exemplified in sidebars on the New Urbanism (Chapter 3), the city of Tulsa (Chapter 4), and Charlotte–Mecklenburg County (Chapter 8), highlight the importance of technical, political, and collaborative leadership.

ESTABLISH COLLABORATIVE LEADERSHIP INITIATIVES

Hazard scholars have found that leadership is a key variable when assessing the effectiveness of recovery assistance providers.[31] For the purposes of this discussion, leadership is discussed across three dimensions: technical/administrative, political, and collaborative.

Technical and administrative leadership skills—for example, plan making, grant writing and implementation, and disaster assistance program administration—are vital to the development and implementation of collaboratively derived policy choices across multiorganizational networks.[32] Yet such interrelated skills are often underap-preciated until a disaster strikes. The failure to anticipate the need for such skills and to train staff accordingly represents poor technical leadership. Conversely, those who have developed and are able to maintain a robust cadre of planners, grants adminis-trators, and program managers (drawn from within their jurisdiction, through pre-event contracts, or through mutual aid agreements with others) dramatically increase their post-disaster recovery capabilities.

Political leadership is important if policy choices are to be enduring. Taking action in the pre- and post-disaster environments often means mustering the political will to act on behalf of the public good even in the face of opposition. For instance, restricting the reconstruction of damaged public infrastructure or housing in a known hazard area after a disaster, or adopting a temporary building moratorium to assess the merits of this idea, can prove unpopular even when it is based on sound technical informa-tion or appears to be in the long-term best interests of the community. Under normal conditions, the use of traditional participatory techniques such as public meetings can effectively exclude the active participation of certain stakeholders,[33] such as those who have experienced discriminatory decision-making tactics used by those in power and are reluctant to attend similar events; those who are uncomfortable expressing their views in large public gatherings; and those whose work schedules, child care duties, or other commitments make it difficult for them to attend scheduled meetings. Avoiding this situation may require the involvement of political actors such as elected officials, agency representatives, and community activists. After a disaster, additional consideration must be given to issues of physical displacement, disrupted transportation systems, and limited or broken information dissemination channels, all of which can hinder efforts to undertake collaborative planning.

Collaborative leadership blends technical and administrative capacity with political realities. Those who are adept at building coalitions recognize that both skills are necessary to sustain collective action across complex multistakeholder policy networks. In the disaster recovery realm, this type of leadership means creating the conditions in which collaborative problem solving can thrive in the pre- and post-disaster environments and empowering stakeholders to act on shared information. This approach has proven effective, even among perceived adversaries, as illustrated in the Charlotte–Mecklenburg County and city of Tulsa sidebars.

Several hazard researchers have drawn important linkages between recovery outcomes and the ability of leaders to foster collaborative planning efforts that harness the power of existing social capital. Yuko Nakagawa and Rajib Shaw, for instance, found in their study of the Kobe, Japan, earthquake (1995) and the Guajarat, India, earthquake (2001) that social capital—defined as a "function of trust, social norms, participation, and network" that "affect social and economic activities"—and leadership are the most important drivers of collective action in disaster recovery.[34] Communities with high levels of social capital, which effective community leaders were able to channel through collaborative planning processes, noted the highest levels of satisfaction with new planning initiatives. Similarly, in his study of the 1922 Kanto earthquake in Japan, Daniel Aldrich found that—when compared to other, more widely recognized variables such as pre-event living conditions, the economic well-being of businesses in the area, the level of damage sustained, and socioeconomic conditions—the strength of social networks is the most significant factor driving the speed of recovery.[35]

Collaborative leadership means taking ownership of the responsibility to act in concert with others in an often uncertain environment. In the disaster recovery assistance network, a leader is rarely designated, and interorganizational relationships are fraught with ambiguity. This necessitates taking a new perspective. A growing number of practitioners and scholars have begun to question who is actually "in charge" of recovery. The most recent example is the White House Long-Term Disaster Recovery Working Group, which is tasked with clarifying federal roles and deciding whether FEMA or the Department of Housing and Urban Development should assume the lead responsibility. Asking this question in some ways presupposes a continued reliance on a top-down approach to recovery. Although federal officials describe the existing process as a "bottom-up" approach, existing policies and the manner in which they shape network behavior foster local dependence rather than empowerment and collective action. Given the uncertainties of pre- and post-disaster recovery, it becomes more pertinent to ask how the responsibility for recovery will be shared across the network and how federal agencies can encourage this type of collaboration.

Central to improving the disaster recovery assistance framework is collaborative leadership that can build local capacity and self-reliance.[36] The ability to foster and sustain local capacity, however, is constrained by increasingly prescriptive federal policies and programs, which perpetuate the perverse relationship between post-disaster assistance and declining levels of self-reliance.[37] The current assistance framework is driven by a focus on post-disaster monetary assistance and devoid of the opportunity for input or feedback from assistance recipients. Existing federal policies do little to build the capacity of stakeholders in the public sector (federal, state, and local) to address community-level hazard vulnerability, pre-event planning, or the development and implementation of complementary recovery strategies. Federal expenditures on pre-event capacity building are minuscule, particularly when compared to the amount spent on post-event recovery programs and reconstruction projects.[38] Courses and other educational programs on how to plan for recovery are rare, although an increasing number of state government agencies, professional associations, nonprofits, and universities are developing training programs aimed at improving the capacity of communities to plan for recovery. The efforts of the Oregon Natural Hazards Workgroup (see the accompanying sidebar) provide one example of a disaster recovery planning process that is focused on pre-event capacity building at the local level.

DEVELOP AN EDUCATION, TRAINING, AND OUTREACH AGENDA

Any attempt to mandate recovery planning without a concomitant national effort focused on building federal, state, and local recovery planning capacity is likely to fail. And any attempt to build the capacity of disaster recovery assistance networks to engage in planning on an ongoing basis requires a robust education, training, and outreach agenda.[39] A successful agenda would include teaching technical and procedural elements, such as planning strategies and ADR techniques, to stakeholders. It would also demonstrate the need for and benefits of a new approach—one focused on pre-event planning for post-disaster recovery.

The Oregon Natural Hazards Workgroup Pre-Disaster Planning for Post-Disaster Disaster Recovery: The Cannon Beach Pilot Program

The Cascadia Subduction Zone, an area where two tectonic plates in the Earth's crust collide, makes communities along the Pacific Coast particularly vulnerable to earthquakes and tsunami. The Oregon Natural Hazards Workgroup (ONHW; now called the Partnership for Disaster Resilience), at the University of Oregon's Community Service Center (CSC), has been working to build the capacity of communities to address long-term recovery issues through the development of pre-disaster recovery plans. After the 2004 Sumatra earthquake, which spawned a devastating tsunami, as well as Hurricane Katrina in 2005, which caused widespread coastal damages in the Gulf of Mexico, the ONHW initiated a pre-disaster recovery planning program targeting coastal communities.[1]

The ONHW began by working with Cannon Beach, a community on the Oregon coast. Together they convened a disaster recovery forum composed of representatives of the Cascadia Region Earthquake Workgroup (CREW), the U.S. Geological Survey (USGS), Oregon Emergency Management, and the city of Cannon Beach to identify the actions necessary to prepare for the challenges associated with long-term recovery should a major earthquake or tsunami occur. The ONHW discussed expected impacts relative to earthquake scenarios developed by CREW. The forum then created a series of actions categorized across several areas of concern, including population, economy, land and development, and critical facilities and infrastructure.

Building on the work done with the city of Cannon Beach, the ONHW has expanded this initiative to the larger Cascadia region, using a capacity-building model similar to the one it developed to help communities develop hazard mitigation plans. That project—the Partners for Disaster Resilience Pre-Disaster Mitigation Planning Initiative—focuses on developing collaborative strategies across multiple stakeholder groups through ongoing training and capacity-building efforts. Both initiatives use the service learning model developed at the CSC, an interdisciplinary organization that emphasizes the education of

The Cannon Beach project represents one in a series of community-level recovery plan-making efforts sponsored by the Oregon Natural Hazards Workgroup in partnership with the U.S. Geologic Survey, Oregon Emergency Management, and Cascadia Region Earthquake Workgroup.
Photo by Andre Le Duc.

students, the professional development of local officials, the provision of technical assistance, and the application of coalition-building strategies.

Source: For more information on the work of the CSC and the Partnership for Disaster Resilience, see csc.uoregon.edu/opdr/.

1 Andre Le Duc, "Pre-Disaster Planning for Catastrophic Disaster Recovery" (proceedings of Coastal Zone 07, Portland Ore., 2007).

The use of outreach techniques furthers the educational agenda. Routinely reaching out to stakeholders and recruiting new members who bring with them fresh perspectives, pertinent information and experiences, and different problem-solving tools and techniques is a necessary part of effective recovery planning. An underlying rationale for modifying existing emergency management programs and plans is the value of working with organizations that have a history of collaboration. Research conducted by education, communication, and planning scholars shows a clear link between a reciprocal processing of information among parties and mutual learning that can be transformative.[40] Individuals who have lived through disasters and understand how assistance programs work—including the degree to which such programs are ill-timed or fail to address local needs—have valuable insights that can be used to educate those responsible for formulating disaster recovery policies and plans.

Along with a willingness on the part of federal agencies to listen to a critical evaluation of program delivery by recipients of assistance and to better recognize indigenous, community-level resources, changing the disaster recovery assistance framework requires better educating federal agency officials about the impact of existing programs and the value of planning. According to the National Response Framework (NRF), ESF-14 is tasked with assessing local needs, coordinating recovery resources, and providing technical support—all key limitations in the current assistance framework. Yet it has been given limited guidance on how to confront these vexing issues in a comprehensive manner. The role of ESF-14 varies widely after disasters and in many cases remains marginalized (see Figure 9–2). Until the NDRF further clarifies ESF-14's mission and provides program administrators with the resources and political support necessary to strategically target identified weaknesses in the assistance framework, the emergency support function will remain relegated to post-disaster assistance and its potential unfulfilled.

Specific efforts toward strengthening the capabilities of ESF-14, as well as enhancing its standing within FEMA and across the larger assistance network, should emphasize building the capacity of its staff and contractors, thereby improving their ability to deliver quality assistance and boosting ESF-14's reputation through demonstrated proficiency. To play a more meaningful role in planning for post-disaster recovery, personnel in leadership positions should have relevant training and experience. Assuming that ESF-14 staff participate in the formulation of long-term recovery policy, it behooves officials to staff more permanent and disaster assistance employee positions with people who can articulate and implement a recovery strategy grounded in pre- and post-disaster planning concepts and the principles described in Chapter 8.

Figure 9–2. ESF-14 staff lead a meeting in rural Greensburg, Kansas, after a tornado nearly destroyed the community in 2007. The resulting recovery plan emphasizes a number of sustainability themes, including public safety, energy efficiency, livability, economic vitality, and green development practices (see the *Long-term Community Recovery Plan: Greensburg and Kiowa County, Kansas* (August 2007) at greensburgks.org/recovery-planning/long-term-community-recovery-plan/GB_LTCR_PLAN_Final_HiRes.070815.pdf). While the Greensburg plan has helped the community manage the recovery process, it is indicative of the approach currently used by FEMA, which emphasizes the post-disaster delivery of planning assistance rather than playing a dual role that includes pre-event capacity-building initiatives.

Source: FEMA.

Most recovery training programs provided by federal and state agencies focus on assisting other government officials with post-disaster grant programs rather than on building the capacity of the larger assistance network to collectively address identified challenges through pre-event planning. In addition to increasing the number of organizations that receive training, programs should be expanded to ensure that the knowledge gained by individual citizens, nonprofits, emergent groups, and others is transferred to the broader network. Improved training regimes should ensure that a reciprocal learning approach across multiple parties replaces the unidirectional approach that is traditionally practiced.

Disaster recovery assistance strike teams, working in tandem with ESF-14, can help build the capacity of the assistance network to plan for recovery and implement strategies before and after a disaster (see the sidebar in Chapter 3 on professional associations in recovery after Katrina). Long-term recovery groups should employ the modified strike team concept initially developed by response-oriented teams, which are made up of individuals with different skills and expertise. Recovery strike teams should include government elected officials and staff; representatives of nonprofit relief organizations; members of professional associations, colleges, and universities; and leaders of private sector organizations that serve disaster-related planning and recovery functions. Linking recovery strike teams to ESF-14 will provide a combination of grounded expertise within an existing program for delivering targeted training and technical assistance. If appropriately deployed, strike teams could match up with existing assistance networks to provide both one-on-one peer training, such as city manager to city manager or nonprofit representative to nonprofit representative, as well as training by the larger team working with local recovery committees or other collective decision-making bodies (Figure 9–3).

For disaster recovery assistance strike teams, ESF-14, and other emergency management programs to provide a coordinated national training platform will require the commitment of federal resources. Funding is necessary to pay for training, and existing programs and policies will need to be modified to emphasize pre-event planning as a way to address the limitations in the assistance framework. In addition, an adequate level of political capital must be maintained to create and sustain a national recovery coalition capable of supporting investments in pre-event activities, which are not as salient to policy makers as post-disaster assistance.

ESTABLISH A NATIONAL RECOVERY COALITION THROUGH IMPROVED PLANNING PRACTICES

The success of planning as a decision-making tool depends on building a commitment to achieve the stated goals and policies in the plan while ensuring that the plan is updated regularly as conditions warrant. Beyond being based on agreed-upon principles and background information, a durable plan is able to adapt to changing conditions—for example, demographic shifts, growth pressures, the adoption of sustainable development principles, new government mandates, the impact of a major disaster, and the election of officials with different political agendas. The involvement of the public and the disaster recovery assistance network in creating, implementing, and amending the plan over time can provide continuity and establish a broad coalition of support for the process, particularly when the benefits of planning are evident.

The ability to build a national coalition of support is an important but often neglected component of the overall recovery planning process.[41] Planning can and

Figure 9–3. After Hurricane Ike, FEMA's Long-Term Community Recovery Program began providing technical assistance through a process they refer to as community mentoring. Using videoconferencing, ESF-14 staff brought together local officials from Colorado, Florida, Iowa, and Mississippi who were involved in long-term recovery efforts. The purpose of the videoconference was to foster the sharing of information and lessons with officials in hard-hit coastal communities in Texas. Topics discussed included beginning the planning process, identifying reconstruction projects and associated funding, coordinating local planning efforts within a region, building a strong working relationship between cities and counties, and collaborating with the state as it faced challenges associated with the administration of disaster funding.

Courtesy of FEMA.

should provide an important basis around which a coalition of technical, public, and political actors can coalesce.[42] Several factors help to explain the connection between planning and coalition building. First, plans are supported by a fact base, which is intended to help shape policy options. Second, involving a broader range of stakeholders—including those that are not traditionally involved in this part of the planning and policy-making process—improves the contextual grounding of the information in a way that technical experts are unable to do on their own. And third, if stakeholders become vested in the process up front, it can help to reframe the policy dialogue and debates that follow.

Policies are ultimately adopted by political actors, be they members of the public sector, private sector, or nonprofit organizations. To be effective and enduring, however, the policies that are adopted should be supported by a larger community, including those who will ultimately be affected. Collaborative planning principles emphasize the value and critical importance of an inclusive, iterative exchange of information. The widespread use of ADR techniques in the development of pre-disaster recovery plans provides tested methods for achieving these aims, including the resolution of seemingly intractable conflicts over resource allocation, while also helping to build strong coalitions.

Good plans enhance horizontal and vertical integration across a network of stakeholders, including those charged with formulating and implementing policy. Strong horizontal ties, while important, represent just part of the equation; a national coalition, or any coalition for that matter, benefits from strong vertical ties as well. Building on what Patsy Healey calls a "collaborative governance culture" means committing to an ongoing process guided by the reciprocal flow of information, inclusion across a range participants, and participant accountability.[43] Federal planners should spend time soliciting information to gain a deeper understanding of how proposed policies will affect individuals, groups, and organizations at the state and community levels. Integrating these findings into policies can help to develop trust and support.

Creating a strong recovery coalition also benefits from an understanding of how public policy is developed and subject to change over time. Because coalitions are reluctant to give up their "core" beliefs, small alterations in secondary aspects of a belief system—what might be called advocacy coalitions—are likely. The Advocacy Coalition Framework (ACF) describes the public policy development process in the context of competing "advocacy coalitions," each seeking its own desired aims within a set of shared beliefs or policy objectives.[44] Composed of various actors from the public and private sectors, advocacy coalitions may be influenced by external factors such as socioeconomic conditions and other policy subsystems.[45] Change often results when clear problems in the current system are identified, policy makers reach an apparent impasse, or experts attack their own policy subsystems in the media, which can sometimes lead to the formation of a new subsystem.

In their study of earthquake mitigation policy in Oakland, California, Richard Olson, Robert Olson, and Vincent Gawronski applied the ACF to the debates over the incorporation of new and enhanced earthquake policy after the 1989 Loma Prieta earthquake.[46] They found that conflict did not hinge on geotechnical or engineering issues per se, but rather on the costs associated with incorporating mitigation techniques into reconstruction and new development, and on questions of who would bear these costs. Their conclusion—that decisions are principally an issue of political economy (i.e., the effect of political actors on growth and economic development)—highlights the critical nature of not only garnering technical evidence and support but also including those who will influence or be affected by new policies in any coalition advocating change. ADR scholars Connie Ozawa and Lawrence Susskind note the importance of "appropriate representation" in policy disputes—representation that includes those who possess important technical knowledge as well as those who have the power to block the creation of proposed solutions.[47] While the literature on the political economy of development is mixed, research has shown that political regimes play an important role in shaping the delivery and use of pre- and post-disaster assistance.[48] Some argue that a small coalition of pro-growth interests control community decision making: John Logan and Harvey Molotch coined the term "growth machine" to describe this.[49] According to William Freudenberg and colleagues, the New Orleans growth machine played a major role in creating the pre-event conditions that led to the Hurricane Katrina disaster.[50] In this case, a relatively small group of development interests, focused on short-term profits, drained swampy lowlands, built faulty levees (managed by politically selected boards with little technical expertise), constructed a poorly designed canal system, and relied on an outdated pumping system that provided a false sense of security for a growing metropolis. Others believe that a more pluralistic political power structure exists in the United States,[51] one that includes those coalitions that emerge as a counterpoint to the growth machine.[52] Regardless of political power structure, engaging diverse interests, including developers and other members of the growth machine, can alter long-standing development practices, as the sidebar on Charlotte–Mecklenburg County in Chapter 8 suggests.

Paul Sabatier and Hank Jenkins-Smith describe the "conditions conducive to policy-oriented learning across belief systems of different coalitions"[53] and, thus, the means to change the nature of a policy subsystem: "The task ... is to identify the conditions under which a productive analytical debate between members of *different* advocacy coalitions is likely to occur."[54] This concept in many ways parallels the idea expressed in Chapter 8 regarding the importance of creating conditions in which collaboration can thrive through pre-event planning for post-disaster recovery. According to Sabatier and Jenkins-Smith, three conditions shape the nature of the debate: (1) level of conflict, (2) the analytical tractability of the issue, and (3) the presence of a professional forum.[55]

Conflict tends to make subsystems gather necessary resources to protect or "defend" their core beliefs, or what the dispute resolution literature refers to as "interests." As the level of conflict escalates, information that threatens core beliefs is more likely to be discounted. This limits learning across policy subsystems and can lead to an impasse. Sabatier and Jenkins-Smith contend that an intermediate level of "informed conflict" between belief systems is more likely to result in policy-oriented learning.[56]

In terms of the disaster recovery policy milieu and the principles of ADR and collaborative planning, this premise makes sense. Disaster recovery, and particularly the competition for scarce resources, is highly contentious. In the immediate aftermath of a disaster, when needs are most acute and the desire to return to normal is strongest, attempts to alter pre-disaster conditions, through either planning or policy making, can heighten conflict, leading to a further defense of core beliefs. After Katrina, for instance, conversations surrounding the notion of abandoning large parts of the predominantly black lower Ninth Ward were, not surprisingly, met with heated opposition by members of these communities, who viewed this as the city's latest effort to abandon them and their needs. Because the pre-event environment does not carry the stressors that accompany post-disaster conditions, undertaking such highly contentious issues before disaster strikes allows affected parties the time to assemble and exchange information with others, including those with different belief systems. But, as noted earlier, pre-event planning for post-disaster recovery is less prominent than other pressing issues, so a commitment to educating the network must be made part of any coalition-building effort.

The second variable affecting policy learning is analytical tractability, or the ability of different advocacy coalitions to agree on claims of facts and values as valid representations of reality.[57] The use of agreed-upon techniques, sources of data, and concepts can improve learning.[58] Within the context of the disaster recovery assistance network, policy formulation without the meaningful participation of state and local officials, nonprofits, and individuals has led to the creation of state and local policies that are strongly influenced by federal rules that do not always meet local needs. This sets the stage for uninformed debate following a disaster rather than a more focused attempt to engage in pre-event collaborative problem solving.

Regarding the third variable, Sabatier and Jenkins-Smith suggest that the nature of the analytical forum—described as open versus formal—plays a role in policy learning.[59] An open forum allows for all mobilized members of the subsystem to participate in the debate, whereas a professional forum limits the discussion to those whose invitation to the table is based on their technical knowledge as defined by professional norms and values. Accordingly, a professional forum can limit the breadth of the debate and the number of competing perspectives, analytical techniques, and core values addressed. This approach can speed the apparent resolution of issues in the short run, but it can also lead to greater conflict, particularly in the aftermath of a disaster. While the authors note that little research has been done comparing the two approaches in terms of their efficacy in resolving policy debates,[60] the ADR literature provides a rich source of evidence supporting the value of an open forum to address a wide range of policy conflicts.[61]

Nevertheless, professional forums are often used in the post-disaster setting, emphasizing the need to return to a sense of normalcy as quickly as possible or citing the disaster as an opportunity to effect positive change. Not surprisingly, this technique has done much to shape the current recovery assistance framework and its inherent problems. At the national and state levels, such forums include congressionally appointed panels of experts, agency-led working groups, state disaster recovery committees, and others who generate policy recommendations or "lessons learned" focused on how the event was "mismanaged." According to Thomas Birkland, narrowly defined professional forums often fail to make substantial changes in the policy subsystem or learn from mistakes made in the past.[62] By way of contrast, the National Earthquake Hazard Reduction Program (NEHRP), an organization that routinely uses a professional forum to address policy questions, has produced a number of positive results linking scientific findings to improved policy making, including that associated with disaster recovery (see the sidebar in Chapter 3). A further analysis of NEHRP is warranted in order to better understand how this professional forum has led to the creation of enduring hazards management policies.

Once a disaster strikes, it is difficult to create a robust competing policy subsystem or to substantially modify the current one in time to address the issues germane to the situation at hand. As described in Chapter 3, the Congress for the New Urbanism and the Gulf Coast Community Design Studio (GCCDS) approached this challenge in two very different ways. Shortly after Hurricane Katrina, the New Urbanists engaged in an intensive, weeklong charrette process in which they sought to instill concepts and practices that they believed were in the best interests of the small coastal towns in Mississippi. This was followed by a series of meetings, workshops, and individual consultations with community leaders and local residents. The GCCDS took a more organic approach, establishing design studios in the three most heavily damaged counties, assessing the needs of communities, and working directly with affected neighborhoods and individuals. During the reconstruction process, GCCDS staff walked current and prospective homeowners through the process of design, construction, and case management. Both approaches yield important lessons that should be used to inform future collaborative planning processes to ensure that they are appropriately timed, address local needs, and foster strong horizontal and vertical integration across the assistance network.

The proposed DRA suggests that the collaborative planning process and the use of ADR principles provide an approach that is not focused on the triumph of one policy subsystem over another. Instead, they establish a practical way to reframe the debate so as to focus on the search for complementary interests, creating an opportunity to craft agreements that benefit all parties—in essence, the foundation of a national coalition—as well as the procedural conditions that enable learning across the network over time. According to Judith Innes and David Booher, collaborative planning "can be understood as part of the societal response to changing conditions in increasingly networked societies, where power and information are widely distributed (Castells 1996, 1997), where differences in knowledge and values among individuals and communities are growing, and where accomplishing anything significant or innovative requires creating flexible linkages among many players."[63]

True change requires constructing and maintaining institutional frameworks capable of creating and carrying out agreements over time.[64] This necessitates a long-term commitment to a broad and focused analysis whose findings can be transferred to all members of the assistance network through pre-event education, training, and capacity-building initiatives, as well as to modified policies, programs, and plans to implement agreed-upon solutions.

Forums that are likely to foster policy learning across subsystems are those that effectively encourage and draw from mobilized participants across multiple coalitions (or subsystems) and are guided by shared norms.[65] In the case of the disaster recovery assistance network, a greater inclusion of open forums is needed to help tackle a series of fundamental problems. Examples of valuable insights span the network and include lessons from the private sector (resource distribution techniques), quasi-governmental organizations (regional planning), nonprofits (organizational adaptation), the international community (sustainable development and capacity building), and emergent groups (improvisation).

The next section describes a range of collaborative venues, most of which were created by the emergency management community and reflect a distinct response orientation. This orientation underscores a serious, albeit not insurmountable, flaw in the current disaster recovery assistance framework: understood in the context of the ACF, the emergency management policy subsystem does not adequately recognize the players involved in long-term recovery (and hazard mitigation for that matter). Changing this reality requires incorporating disaster recovery into existing emergency management accreditation criteria, mutual aid agreements, plans, and other accepted interorganizational resource-sharing programs.

ASSESS AND MODIFY EMERGENCY MANAGEMENT PROGRAMS AND THE SCOPE OF PLANS

A key goal of the proposed DRA is to modify a number of emergency management–related programs and plans to more comprehensively address the problems identified in the disaster recovery assistance framework. The idea of using existing institutional capacities to address large multistakeholder policy dilemmas in a way that stimulates collective action has broad support in the political science[66] and planning literature.[67] More and more, those who study disaster recovery are applying such capacities to the post-disaster delivery of assistance,[68] while those tasked with national disaster recovery policy formulation, oversight, and counsel are discussing the need to better use existing groups and institutions to carry out emerging policy directives aimed at meeting local needs.[69]

Each of the operations described below and outlined in Exhibit 9–2 varies in terms of its current application to disaster recovery and the degree to which it includes members of the assistance network. Most reflect a capacity to engage in disaster response activities, which could be viewed as a more mature approach than that which currently exists in recovery. Traditional response-oriented emergency management programs can and should be modified, however, and recognized state and local planning efforts should be added to the larger policy framework in order to improve recovery outcomes. While not indicative of a quick fix, this approach can lead to what is best characterized as a more expansive *hazards management* policy subsystem that includes disaster recovery as a central element.

Exhibit 9–2. Collaborative Operations in Hazards Management

National Response Framework/ National Disaster Recovery Framework

ESF-14, Long-Term Community Recovery

State and Local Plans

- Disaster Recovery Plan
- Comprehensive Plan
- Comprehensive Emergency Management Plan
- Hazard Mitigation Plan

Emergency Management Assistance Compact

College and University Programs

National Voluntary Organizations Active in Disasters

Accreditation Programs

- National Emergency Management Capability Assessment Program
- Capability Assessment for Readiness
- Emergency Management Accreditation Program

Project Impact and Business Continuity Planning

International Relief Organizations and Nations

Community Emergency Response Teams

National Response Framework/National Disaster Recovery Framework

Although soon to be replaced by the NDRF, the NRF is the principal federal coordinating vehicle for disaster recovery operations. It is discussed in this section for three reasons: (1) it provides an important historical reference that reveals the underemphasis on federal recovery policy, (2) it is still the approach used by the federal government to coordinate recovery assistance, and (3) it contains elements that should be preserved and integrated into the NDRF.

Several of the overriding inadequacies of the disaster recovery assistance network are evident in the NRF—notably, the failures to reflect an understanding of local needs, to address the timely distribution of assistance, and to foster horizontal and vertical integration. An assessment using the plan quality principles discussed in Chapter 8 makes it apparent that the NRF is not actually a plan, a document that translates collectively derived knowledge into action through a unifying set of policies. Instead, it is essentially a list of the programs managed by the federal government and some nonprofit organizations after a disaster. For the NRF to serve a useful purpose in planning for recovery, it should be amended. Stylistically, it should adhere to the internal and external principles found in the plan quality literature. In addition, its scope should be expanded to address the transition from response to recovery operations after a disaster and to include goals that link existing response programs to resources held by members of the network.

A purported guiding objective of the NRF is to drive action to the lowest level of government. The ability to achieve this requires that adequate pre-event levels of local capacity be sustained to respond to and recover from events as they occur. The NRF includes what is referred to as the "capability building cycle," in which plans are developed, exercised, evaluated, and improved over time (Exhibit 9–3). However, this process is used to evaluate and improve local, state, and federal *response* plans. A similar approach has not been applied to recovery planning. Currently, there is no widely recognized recovery planning standard, pre-event training regimen, or exercising of plans once they are created.

Meaningful change in the federal government's role in recovery requires a shift from a focus on response to a more balanced approach that includes pre-event disaster recovery planning. Modifying the NRF to reflect this shift can have several benefits. First, the NRF is an existing institutional vehicle that is recognized by government officials and the emergency management community. Second, planners understand the importance of developing forward-looking documents (although their active involvement in recovery planning remains an ongoing challenge). Third, the NRF advocates the use of pre-event training, exercising, and capacity building, currently an

Exhibit 9–3. The National Response Framework Capability Building Cycle

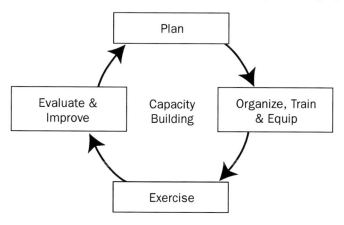

Source: Federal Emergency Management Agency (FEMA), *National Response Framework* (January 2008), 27.

underdeveloped aspect of preparing for long-term recovery. As the government transitions from the NRF to the NDRF to guide federal recovery policy, emphasis should be placed on developing an integrative strategy so that the response and recovery communities do not become further estranged.

ESF-14, Long-Term Community Recovery

The role of ESF-14 is currently dictated by the activities stipulated in the NRF, although the draft NDRF aims to clarify that role. This situation can be viewed as either a significant hindrance or an opportunity to enact change. While the actions adopted by participating ESF members must adhere to what is stated in the document, the guidance is broad and provides for varied interpretations.

Because ESF-14 is the only support function in the NRF that is widely ignored in state plans, federal employees—including those from FEMA and other agencies as well as FEMA contractors—often work directly with local officials and individuals without a state counterpart. This situation effectively breaks the vertical integration of public sector officials, thereby hindering their ability to collectively address local needs after a disaster.

At FEMA headquarters in Washington, D.C., ESF-14 is composed of five full-time staff, of whom three are permanent and two are hired on two-year recurring contract cycles.[70] When a disaster strikes and ESF-14 personnel are deployed, four staff members are typically sent to assist in the management of field operations, leaving one member to address organizational and policy issues. One FEMA regional office, which serves the Midwest, has a permanent staff person assigned to long-term recovery. In all other regions, FEMA personnel who are tasked to assist with ESF-14 operations do so as part of a special assignment and are not part of ESF-14 staff.

For ESF-14 to take a leadership role in pre- and post-disaster recovery—particularly given proposed recommendations in the draft NDRF and the DRA—more staff must be hired in order to assume a growing number of responsibilities and expectations. Such staff should reflect a wide range of skills and experience, such as practice in planning both at multiple levels of government and as part of quasi-governmental organizations, nonprofits, and other planning organizations across the assistance network. ESF-14 employees should also include individuals with expertise in ADR and, in particular, an understanding of how to apply ADR techniques to the resource-based conflicts that arise during recovery. This type of supplemental assistance can be drawn from ESF-14's contractor cadre, FEMA's ADR office, conflict resolution nonprofits, private sector firms, relevant professional associations, and university faculty who teach ADR courses.

Like many other federal government agencies, ESF-14 relies on private sector contractors who are not necessarily invested in the long-term success of the program. But an overreliance on such contractors reduces federal capacity and limits the institutional knowledge that can be gained only through direct involvement in the recovery process. And since these contractors are not stationed in a community over the long term, their ability to build the horizontal and vertical relationships necessary to plan for recovery is limited. Thus, beyond improving the overall administration of the program, an increase in federal staff also allows for the creation of planning policies that reflect a better understanding of the recovery process, and it provides the basis for the enhanced capability required to lead pre-event recovery planning capacity-building initiatives.

Permanent staff should also be able to articulate the value of planning to other members of the assistance network, many of whom remain skeptical. Such staff should include those who have worked in states and local governments that have strong planning mandates as well as in those with weak or nonexistent planning requirements, as understanding the planning culture in a given area is critical to the formulation of pre- or post-disaster plans that reflect local conditions.

A more effective ESF-14 program also means garnering greater support from state officials. To accomplish this, FEMA should provide states with the funding to hire a full-time state recovery planning coordinator. Such an individual would be responsible for creating a pre-disaster state recovery plan; forming a state long-term recovery committee; training state agency officials, local governments, and other members of the assistance network on how to develop local recovery plans; and coordinating with FEMA's ESF-14 staff before and after disasters. The proposed duties are similar in many ways to those assigned to the state hazard mitigation officer, a FEMA-funded position that is responsible for coordinating state-level hazard mitigation initiatives, including federal grant administration and hazard mitigation planning. The funding of a state position focused on pre-event planning, the coordination of programs, and the building of local capacity will go a long way toward proving that FEMA is serious about dealing with this important but underserved part of emergency management.

To improve the delivery of long-term recovery assistance, ESF-14 staff have begun an internal review process, seeking feedback from federal, state, and local officials involved in long-term recovery as well as from researchers who have studied the process. One of the early findings of this assessment is a need to invest greater resources in pre-event planning for post-disaster recovery. Recommendations include the development of pre-event training programs and an expanded disaster recovery planning cadre.

State and Local Plans

An important step in the formulation of the proposed DRA is the evaluation of existing state and local plans, including the degree to which their goals, policies, and other elements complement or contradict those contained in the state's or local government's disaster recovery plan. Good plans are inclusive by design, rich sources of information, and action oriented, identifying policies and those who are responsible for their implementation over time. The comprehensive plan, hazard mitigation plan, and comprehensive emergency management plan (CEMP) are three documents that should be closely linked to the disaster recovery plan. Exhibit 9–4 (page 350) identifies key elements of these plans so that their use in support of recovery planning and improving the disaster recovery assistance framework can be assessed.

Equally important as the evaluation of existing plans is the identification of the authority and/or requirements associated with planning. Understanding the regulatory authorities granted or mandated allows for those tasked with developing the proposed DRA to strategically identify those legal and programmatic conditions that can help strengthen recovery goals, improve coordination across assistance networks, and maximize the effective distribution of finite resources before and after disasters. Exhibit 9–5 (page 351) identifies the federal, state, and local authorities associated with the disaster recovery plan, comprehensive plan, CEMP, and hazard mitigation plan.

Disaster Recovery Plan

The number and quality of state and local recovery plans are unknown.[71] Anecdotal evidence suggests that state recovery plans mirror the NRF and many of its limitations. That is, most plans simply emphasize the legal and programmatic processes that states have in place to access and implement federal recovery programs following a disaster. This has led to a narrow interpretation of recovery rather than to a more holistic view

Exhibit 9-4. Key Planning Elements Found in Comprehensive Plans, Comprehensive Emergency Management Plans, and Hazard Mitigation Plans

Comprehensive Plan
- Is a recognized plan with local standing (legal and political)
- Emphasizes participation
- Is a repository of social, economic, environmental, and land use data
- Emphasizes land use
- Is future oriented
- Is tied to public investments and development goals
- Is composed of relevant policies affecting reconstruction options
- Has strong involvement of planning professionals

Comprehensive Emergency Management Plan
- Is recognized by the federal, state, and local emergency management community
- Has fostered relationships between public and nonprofit sectors, including the formation of interorganizational agreements and resource-sharing protocols (e.g., mutual aid)
- Contains the procedures for conducting a post-disaster damage assessment
- Describes the disaster declaration process
- Institutionalizes the vertical integration of federal, state, and local emergency management officials
- Coordinates emergency management preparedness and response activities, putting less emphasis on hazard mitigation or recovery
- Contains limited or nonexistent involvement of planners

Hazard Mitigation Plan
- Requires state and local plans under the Disaster Mitigation Act of 2000 in order to receive some types of post-disaster federal assistance
- Comprises important fact bases (vulnerability assessment and capability assessment) that should shape the type of recovery and reconstruction policies and projects adopted
- Includes a series of risk reduction policies and projects that can be implemented before and after a disaster
- Links compliance to pre- and post-disaster funding
- State and local plans often led by emergency managers rather than planners
- State and local plans often have weak land use planning goals and policies

that targets state and local needs before and after an event.[72] Moreover, clear regulatory and collaborative policy frameworks have not been sufficiently developed to address the unique aspects of recovery.

In a study of four state recovery plans, several common themes emerged: most states rely on multiple documents rather than on a unified plan to guide recovery actions, most states do not possess a clear vision of recovery, and most plans do not delineate state-level goals and associated policies.[73] State recovery plans and associated implementation strategies provide an important way to link federal programs

Exhibit 9–5. Planning Authorities

	Federal	State	Local
Disaster Recovery Plan	National Response Framework (NRF), National Disaster Recovery Framework (NDRF), Disaster Recovery Act (DRA)?	NRF, NDRF, DRA?	NRF, NDRF, DRA?
Comprehensive Plan		State enabling legislation	Local legislative body
Comprehensive Emergency Management Plan	NRF	State enabling legislation	Local legislative body
Hazard Mitigation Plan	Disaster Mitigation Act (DMA)	DMA	DMA

and local needs, but what they offer remains underused and narrow in scope. State recovery plans tend to focus on the actions of state agencies, including the allocation of grants and the administration of programs. State agencies also provide training and educational initiatives for local governments on how to access state and federal resources. Much less emphasis is placed on pre-event training, although Florida and Oregon represent notable exceptions. Thus, mandated state recovery plans should assess how state policies and programs support or hinder achievement of the goals and objectives at the local level. If state policies are counterproductive, efforts should be made to modify them.

Local recovery plans (if they exist) often reflect similar shortcomings, owing in part to an overreliance on the NRF and local recovery annexes in the jurisdiction's CEMP. Local planners, who are uniquely qualified to assist in pre-event planning for post-disaster recovery, are often not included in this process.[74] As a result, established planning processes and techniques—for example, important land use measures, local economic development, growth management, and urban renewal strategies prevalent in comprehensive plans—may not be incorporated into community-level decision making and reconstruction practices after a disaster.

Comprehensive Plan

A local comprehensive plan provides an effective, albeit underused, means of addressing many of the central recovery issues facing a community before and after a disaster. For instance, it addresses the type, location, density, financing, and timing of development, which makes it a highly relevant document for those assessing the policy choices surrounding how and where post-disaster reconstruction may occur. It also shows how routines or accepted practices, when framed within a larger purpose (rather than simply serving as a means to an end), can be used as part of successful institutional actions following disasters.[75] The ability to rely on familiar and tested institutional arrangements, programs, and policies jibes with the notion of using or modifying accepted planning principles and existing emergency management programs to address recovery challenges.

Some communities, for instance, have chosen to include a recovery and reconstruction ordinance in their local comprehensive plans[76] or to develop and include a recovery planning annex. This approach links recovery issues to a planning document that has legal and administrative standing. It also helps to ensure that recovery planning is grounded in the community's development goals, values, and existing capabilities, as evidenced in the sidebar on Hillsboro County in Chapter 2. In many cases, tasks associated with recovery are often placed as an afterthought into state and local CEMPs, whose principal focus remains geared toward response activities.

Comprehensive Emergency Management Plan

CEMPs are common at the state and local levels and are widely recognized by members of the emergency management community. But while they have proven relatively effective at fostering strong vertical connectivity across federal, state, and local stakeholders, these plans tend to focus principally on response and, to a lesser extent, on preparedness activities. In many ways CEMPs are the institutional manifestation of the NRF; at the state level, this entails the delineation of ESF roles and responsibilities (although, as noted earlier, most states still do not have a comparable ESF-14 in their CEMPs). States may also include a number of specialized annexes in their plans, including one addressing disaster recovery. Recovery annexes tend to focus on lists of federal recovery programs and voluntary organizations active in disasters, not on pre-event planning for post-disaster recovery or on the various roles of other state agencies, nonprofits, quasi-governmental organizations, members of the private sector, emergent groups, and individuals affected by disaster.

At the local level, CEMPs are even more focused on response activities as local governments do not tend to identify those responsible for long-term recovery. Nor do they establish intergovernmental mutual aid agreements with adjacent communities to share recovery-related resources should the need arise; such agreements, like those at the state level, emphasize response. The use of such agreements to assist with recovery remains uncommon but can prove highly effective, as sidebars in Chapters 3 and 8 illustrate. However, the notion of pre-event planning for post-disaster recovery is largely limited to a handful of states that have developed programs to help local governments develop recovery plans (see the sidebars on Florida's Post-Disaster Redevelopment Planning Initiative in Chapter 2 and on the Oregon Natural Hazards Workgroup [ONHW] earlier in this chapter). The resulting disconnect between a national recovery coalition (described in the previous section) as the emergency management–led disaster response network and the current disaster recovery assistance network can be addressed by taking advantage of preexisting relationships and associated resources, assuming that these two groups can be more effectively engaged in the pursuit of common goals through mandated planning.

Hazard Mitigation Plan

A hazard mitigation plan provides another means of addressing issues germane to disaster recovery. Reflecting the recognized value of pre-event planning, a hazard mitigation plan includes a fact base (i.e., a risk assessment and capability assessment) to guide the selection of risk reduction policies, and it preidentifies mitigation projects that will be implemented before and after a disaster (Exhibit 9–6). Indeed, Kenneth Topping suggests that the Stafford Act should be amended to require that state and local hazard mitigation plans include pre-event recovery activities.[77] While the pre-event identification of potential mitigation projects speeds the implementation of risk reduction measures following disasters, as illustrated in the sidebar on Kinston, North Carolina, in Chapter 2, this book is not proposing that the disaster recovery plan be subsumed into the hazard mitigation plan. Rather, it suggests that the disaster recovery

Exhibit 9–6. The Hazard Mitigation Planning Process

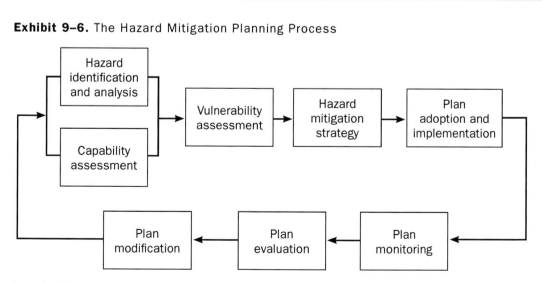

Source: Gavin Smith, "Planning for Sustainable and Disaster Resilient Communities," in *Natural Hazards Analysis: Reducing the Impact of Disasters,* ed. John Pine (Washington, D.C.: Taylor Francis. 2008), 234. Used with permission of Taylor & Francis Group LLC.

planning process is different enough from hazard mitigation planning and of sufficient importance to merit the development of a stand-alone plan or the incorporation of the disaster recovery plan into local comprehensive plans. Regardless, key pieces of information found in the hazard mitigation plan should be used to bolster the recovery plan (and the comprehensive plan for that matter).

Important lessons can be drawn from the development of state and local hazard mitigation plans as well as from the creation and implementation of the Disaster Mitigation Act of 2000. These lessons should be used to support the creation of a more effective disaster recovery strategy that is operationalized through the proposed DRA, the draft NDRF, and state and local disaster recovery plans that adhere to accepted plan quality principles. For instance, the application of planning policies and techniques intended to reduce a community's vulnerability to natural hazards is among the most effective ways to proactively address this growing problem.[78] Yet state and local hazard mitigation plans do not do a good job of clearly linking the findings from vulnerability assessments to the selection of policies and projects intended to systematically reduce identified vulnerabilities.[79] Nor are land use techniques (an important basis of comprehensive plans) widely used to reduce risk, particularly when compared to the many hazard mitigation projects that tend to address mistakes made in the past (e.g., past land use choices that place property in areas that are subject to natural hazards or construction standards that do not reflect the risk facing a community, state, or region).

Assuming that the fact base in the mitigation plan and the plan's associated risk reduction strategies are closely aligned through improved hazard mitigation standards, they should also be aligned with the goals and policies found in the recovery plan. For instance, post-disaster recovery plans should address the question of whether more stringent risk reduction policies should be adopted in the aftermath of future disasters that expose existing hazard vulnerabilities. Once adopted, these policies should be incorporated into the hazard mitigation and comprehensive plans in order to document their use, assign responsibilities for monitoring and implementation, and better institutionalize compliance.

According to the Disaster Mitigation Act's enabling rules, states have the option to develop an enhanced or standard hazard mitigation plan. The enhanced plan designation entitles states to more Hazard Mitigation Grant Program (HMGP) funds after a federally declared disaster. To qualify for enhanced planning status, state plans must demonstrate how they will help local governments develop and implement local plans, and they must take on a greater role in the management of HMGP funds.

Establishing a similar enhanced plan designation for state recovery plans developed under the proposed DRA (e.g., a demonstrated ability to manage pre- and post-disaster recovery activities, including the oversight of local planning programs and the coordination of disaster recovery resources) should result in access to a more flexible combination of resources (funding, supporting policy initiatives, and technical assistance) that are based on local needs. Over time, these resources, documented in recovery plans, should be monitored and used to update resource-sharing agreements across the assistance network. Moreover, states that meet enhanced plan criteria should be required to mentor other states and agree to advise federal agencies and other members of the assistance network. One way to accomplish this is with a modified Emergency Management Assistance Compact (EMAC).

Emergency Management Assistance Compact

Mutual aid agreements such as the EMAC have been used to address state and local needs, the timing of assistance, and horizontal and vertical integration across the disaster *response* network. The success of EMAC is tied to the compact's ability to draw on state and local officials from beyond the immediate disaster area. Most EMAC participants are experienced professionals who understand the unique needs of state and local governments in the immediate aftermath of a disaster. But state and local governments have not routinely used EMAC to address long-term *recovery* issues because they have not thought through specific long-term recovery needs and coupled them to appropriately designed resource typing schemes and interorganizational agreements.

Building inspectors, state hazard mitigation officers, and floodplain administrators have been deployed after disasters, but their involvement has been limited and not tied to specific objectives or larger goals (including those explicitly stated in state and local recovery plans). The EMAC cadre should be expanded to include planners and ADR professionals, assistant city managers, public works officials, professionals in nonprofit organizations, hazards researchers, and other members of the disaster recovery assistance network. In fact, the work of Florida recovery strike teams and professional associations after Hurricane Katrina (see the sidebar in Chapter 3 on page 104) could provide a basis for determining how the use of such associations could be expanded nationwide.

It is not enough to have EMAC personnel on hand; there must be a way to match specific areas of expertise and experience to local needs. Specific tasks tied to a series of predefined needs identified in disaster recovery plans and EMAC protocols should be established, performed during recovery, and modified over time according to feedback from EMAC participants and those who receive assistance. In addition, the use of consensus-building techniques should be codified through EMAC and other organizational agreements in order to assist in both the development of inclusive pre-event disaster recovery plans and the inevitable post-disaster resource allocation debates.

EMAC procedures should also be somewhat flexible, able to draw on the lessons of groups that emerge during recovery to address needs that are not being met by established programs and organizations. EMAC protocols should recognize that some assignments may be exploratory and driven by the identification of unmet needs. The resolution of these issues requires creative thinking and novel solutions. The experiences of strike teams, as described earlier in this chapter, in Chapter 3, and in the sidebar in Chapter 8 on negotiation in post-disaster resource allocation disputes, exemplify the types of issues that EMAC-supported teams might address.

EMAC should also serve as part of a larger pre-event training, education, and outreach program involving members of the assistance network. FEMA currently reimburses states and local governments for the use of shared equipment and personnel during their deployment after a federally declared disaster. While expanding the role of EMAC would require additional funding, changes in administrative rules, and a larger cadre of individuals, it stands to produce significant benefits. Because EMAC provides a tested framework that is well respected by the emergency management community, an EMAC team comprising those skilled in disaster recovery planning can help to break down barriers between planners and local emergency managers. The linkage of EMAC to ESF-14 could enhance the federal government's ability to work collaboratively with state and local government officials and other members of the assistance network to develop and implement well-conceived recovery plans that are grounded in local conditions and knowledge, plan quality principles, and lessons from the recovery literature.

College and University Programs

Hazard scholars and students are involved in a number of pre- and post-disaster activities, including the study of recovery, the training of government officials, and the education of the next generation of researchers and practitioners. Yet the integration of these specialists into the disaster recovery assistance network remains largely reactive. For instance, the appropriate institutional support mechanisms that would enable multidisciplinary research teams to conduct in-depth recovery research over a long period of time are lacking. The Resiliency and Vulnerability Observation Network, or RAVON, which would allow for the longitudinal study of recovery, does not currently exist.

The proposed national audit of federal, state, and local disaster recovery plans, which represents the type of project that would benefit from an organization such as

RAVON, could help to establish a baseline of data, advance our knowledge of recovery planning, and provide information that practitioners, researchers, and students could use and mine over time. Such an audit, conducted every few years, could also be used to create informed disaster recovery planning standards subject to modification over time according to its findings. Longitudinal data sets could be used to track recovery in select disaster-stricken communities; these findings could then be reported to members of the assistance network to enhance their understanding of the complexities of the recovery process.

Practitioners sometimes underestimate the role that hazard scholars play in disaster recovery planning. The better integration of researchers into the disaster recovery assistance network will require improving existing relationships between practitioners and researchers and, in some cases, creating new ones. An improved ability to demonstrate the responsiveness of hazard scholars to questions posed by practitioners and to highlight examples of practitioners acting on the findings of researchers would go a long way toward addressing what amounts to a dysfunctional divide. While examples do exist where the university community has played an important role in recovery-related actions (see the sidebar above on the ONHW as well as those in Chapter 3 on regional planning and hazards management, the National Earthquake Hazard Reduction Program, the Great Southern California Shakeout, and the GCCDS), more needs to be done to develop a systemic partnership that routinely brings together practitioners and researchers to craft policy and address long-standing problems in recovery. Conferences and workshops attended by practitioners and researchers— the venues where the members of the assistance network traditionally discuss these issues—are not adequate. The successful translation of research into practice requires developing more effective procedures and institutions that foster ongoing, repeated dialogue, or modifying existing ones such as EMAC that enable the network to draw on a cadre of university faculty, staff, and students in pre- and post-disaster situations.

An important point of entry into the assistance network is through the teaching of others. Most hazard scholars are also educators, trained to teach students as part of their day-to-day responsibilities. However, their talents as educators remain underused, particularly in the area of disaster recovery. Not only are there a limited number of college courses in recovery, but textbooks on this topic are sparse. Members of the assistance network should reach out to hazard scholars to assist in the teaching of planning for disaster recovery, including the creation of relevant university curricula and textbooks. Courses should target college students as well as practitioners and use a mix of traditional classroom lectures, distance learning, certificate programs, and on-site post-disaster immersion. As the public sector and other members of the assistance network strive to develop an enhanced education and outreach strategy under the proposed DRA, university hazard scholars should play an active role in curriculum development and deployment that reflects the latest in recovery practice, research, and teaching methods.

Hazard centers and university degree programs provide institutional venues intended to bridge research, practice, and education. Many of these programs have formal and informal mechanisms, such as newsletters, seminars, training sessions, working papers, and community engagement, to transfer the knowledge gained through research to practice. Research centers often maintain relationships with federal and state agencies that provide funding to conduct research and disseminate the findings to practice-oriented constituents. Degree programs focused on hazards and disasters serve as training grounds for future researchers and practitioners. Many graduates take with them the theoretical knowledge gained in the classroom and apply it on the job.

The formation of multi-institutional networks across colleges and universities, such as RAVON and the Extension Disaster Education Network (EDEN), provide an additional means of transferring knowledge. As previously discussed, RAVON would create geographically dispersed "data repositories" to collect, analyze, and archive information, thereby providing the institutional architecture needed for the analysis of such complex issues as long-term recovery. It would enable process-oriented questions associated with recovery to be studied in depth, leading to a richer and broader understanding of issues, many of which benefit from a sustained focus. EDEN, which uses the pre-existing network of extension agents to disseminate information through a cadre of individuals who understand local conditions and needs and are trained in community engagement, serves as a model that can be used to synthesize and transfer information. Once established or expanded in scope, these networks should advocate for the specific policy changes indicated by their findings and the feedback they obtain during the field-based transfer of knowledge to practice. University and college faculty can work with other members of the assistance network in this regard to elevate the importance of pre-event planning for post-disaster recovery.

There is a recent precedent for such work in the larger field of hazard management: the university community was instrumental in raising the political awareness of hazard mitigation planning, which led to the passage of the Disaster Mitigation Act of 2000.[80] The lessons from this activity should be captured and shared with the larger network as part of an effort to build a coalition capable of supporting needed changes to the assistance framework. Success hinges on reaching out to organizations focused on recovery as well as those with a response orientation, whose stature in the emergency management community lends credibility and whose established presence provides a preexisting organizational platform from which to expand operations.

National Voluntary Organizations Active in Disasters

The National Voluntary Organizations Active in Disasters (NVOAD), a coalition best known for its delivery of immediate relief following disasters and for its participation in the NRF, has the potential to better integrate volunteer organizations into recovery assistance networks. This is important: the long-term recovery assistance provided by nonprofits is not always well coordinated with that provided by other members of the disaster assistance network, a situation that can result in the ill-timed delivery of recovery assistance, the provision of aid that runs counter to the aims of other parties (including those seeking assistance), and the duplication of effort that may have been more appropriately provided by others. At the same time, nonprofits have demonstrated an important boundary-spanning function in response and hazard mitigation-related efforts as well as in recovery activities, as evident in a number of sidebars in Chapter 4.

The flexibility of nonprofits, including their ability to quickly deliver post-disaster recovery assistance, must be recognized. Organizational flexibility and adaptive rules governing assistance are strengths that should be maximized through enhanced interorganizational coordination across the recovery assistance network. For instance, convergence can overwhelm local officials who fail to plan for it, and the inability to coordinate recovery assistance with local government officials can result in the repair of structures to their pre-event condition before there has been an opportunity to adopt higher construction standards and procure federal grants, insurance proceeds, or personal loans to offset the additional cost of compliance.

It can be difficult to coordinate agencies and organizations that pride themselves on their adaptive and independent nature, including those that see their role as providing an alternative to bureaucratic organizations in the public sector. Thus, the role of NVOAD in recovery should be more clearly determined prior to a disaster, when members of the assistance network have ample time to discuss complex interorganizational relationships, clarify roles, and develop a mutually agreeable set of resource distribution strategies linked to NVOAD's *Long-Term Recovery Manual*,[81] a modified NRF, and the NDRF. The expansion of NVOAD to include the coordination of nonprofit involvement in long-term recovery activities—housing reconstruction, economic development, and case management, for instance—offers promise but requires gaining a greater appreciation for the role of others, such as the private sector, quasi-governmental organizations, and the public sector in recovery. Like other interinstitutional arrangements, such coordination would benefit from the creation of a negotiated agreement that is linked to goals stated in recovery plans that have been collaboratively developed, implemented, and monitored by members of NVOAD and the assistance network. One way to achieve this without unnecessarily constraining the characteristics that make these voluntary organizations such a valuable member of the network is to expand NVOAD's role via modified emergency management accreditation programs.

Accreditation Programs

While national accreditation programs provide an important means of creating standards of practice in recovery, their involvement in such activities as pre-disaster recovery planning, the coordinated distribution of post-event resources, and the development of enduring interorganizational working relationships remains virtually nonexistent. Like other emergency management programs discussed up to this point, this requires an expansion of scope to include the development of new and improved disaster recovery accreditation standards that are integrated with those in the National Emergency Management Capability Assessment Program (NEMBCA).

National Emergency Management Capability Assessment Program and Capability Assessment for Readiness

The NEMBCA, which represents a modified version of the Capability Assessment for Readiness (CAR), was developed by FEMA and the National Emergency Management Association (NEMA) to provide a way to assess the operational capabilities of state emergency management programs. The International Association of Emergency Managers (IAEM) has developed a local CAR with similar objectives. State and local governments that agree to participate are evaluated across thirteen core elements:

- Laws and authorities
- Hazard identification and risk assessment
- Hazard mitigation
- Resource management
- Planning
- Direction, control, and coordination
- Communication and warning
- Operations and procedures
- Logistics and facilities

- Training
- Exercises, evaluations, and corrective actions
- Crisis communications, public education, and information
- Finance and administration.

The CAR process was intended to provide tangible benchmarks for state and local agencies, ultimately leading to accreditation. An important part of this self-assessment is to identify areas in need of improvement so that training and other resources can be targeted to priority needs.

Neither the CAR nor the NEMBCA clearly articulates the roles and responsibilities of organizations in recovery or assesses the readiness of the larger disaster assistance network. There is an evaluation of hazard management planning documents, but no assessment of state or local disaster recovery plans—a failure that undermines the credibility of the assessments and provides a false sense of security to elected officials and the general public. The fact that recovery planning standards do not exist is further evidence of the marginalization of recovery and the failure of those organizations in the emergency management policy subsystem to take ownership of this important responsibility.

To account for these limitations, the NEMBCA should be strengthened in two ways. First, it should call for greater accountability for long-term recovery. To this end, it should require that state and local recovery plans be assessed against the planning principles described in the previous chapter. Second, it should provide tangible benefits to communities and states that take recommended actions to address identified limitations, and it should sanction those that do not. Having a recovery plan that meets acceptable standards should be a requirement for state and local accreditation, while the failure to meet accreditation standards should result in the reduction of federal recovery assistance following a disaster.

Before this strategy is implemented, the NRF and the draft NDRF should be amended to meet rigorous standards of practice while providing an improved platform to deliver pre-event planning guidance to states, local governments, and other members of the disaster recovery assistance network. Building the capacity of federal agencies, states, and local governments to develop robust plans should be a primary concern—part of an ongoing, iterative process whereby the rigor of standards is increased over time as capacity grows.

Exhibit 9–7. Emergency Management Accreditation Standards

- Program management
- Administration and finance
- Laws and authorities
- Hazard identification, risk assessment, and consequence analysis
- Hazard mitigation
- Prevention and security
- Planning
- Incident management
- Resource management and logistics
- Mutual aid
- Communications and warning
- Operations and procedures
- Facilities
- Training
- Exercises, evaluations, and corrective action
- Crisis communications, public education, and information

Source: Emergency Management Accreditation Program, "Emergency Management Standard" (September 2010), www.emaponline.org.

Emergency Management Accreditation Program

The Emergency Management Accreditation Program (EMAP) is an independent, nonprofit organization focused on the development of emergency management accreditation standards. The accreditation process is voluntary and open to state, local, and tribal government emergency management programs. The first step in the process is a self-assessment, which includes documentation of compliance with the National Fire Protection Association (NFPA) 1600, Standard on Disaster/Emergency Management and Business Continuity Programs (2007 ed.), and the sixteen EMAP standards (Exhibit 9–7). This is followed by an evaluation conducted by a team of independent EMAP officials. The final accreditation process is overseen by the EMAP commission, whose nine members are appointed by FEMA, IAEM, and NEMA.

The EMAP process emphasizes the evaluation of disaster preparedness, response, and hazard mitigation capabilities in emergency management organizations. There is little emphasis on evaluating long-term recovery capabilities, and none is placed on recovery planning. Where recovery capabilities are assessed, performance criteria focus on the administration of FEMA recovery programs. The process generally ignores the role of the larger disaster assistance network, including the private sector, quasi-governmental organizations, nonprofits, emergent groups, and individuals. Granted, evaluation of the assistance network is more difficult as players include those who do not consider themselves part of the emergency management community, those who emerge following disasters, and those who are drawn into the process unexpectedly. One way to ensure some continuity across different assistance networks is to focus on the strength of the recovery plan during such an assessment.

The assessment and accreditation of federal, state, and local recovery plans can be achieved by developing a set of plan quality principles. These principles should be clearly linked to national standards as a way to assess capabilities, identify areas in need of improvement, and provide more targeted resources. Their use also enables compliance with standards to be tracked over time. Using standards and tracking progress are both components of the current EMAP review process and could be expanded to include recovery operations and plans. A baseline assessment of plans, their review over time, and the archiving of plans and their associated findings are part of the proposed national audit and a suggested role for RAVON. Hazard researchers, who have played an important role in the development of plan quality evaluation protocols, are a logical choice to participate in the expanded accreditation process.

The American Planning Association (APA) is another organization that should be involved in developing disaster recovery planning certification standards and tracking compliance. APA's American Institute of Certified Planners (AICP) certification program provides a direct line to the planning profession and is recognized by those who hire planners. The AICP has recently established advanced specialty certifications in transportation and environmental planning, and it has plans to create an additional certification in urban design. Perhaps, with the support of the proposed APA Natural Hazards Planning Division, an advanced specialty certification could be developed in natural hazards planning to include focus areas in hazard mitigation and disaster recovery planning.

Project Impact and Business Continuity Planning

A model for improving the linkage between the private sector, communities, and other members of the disaster recovery assistance network could be a modified version of FEMA's Project Impact. Although Congress has documented the importance of clarifying and improving the role of the private sector in preparedness and response activities,[82] the same level of attention has not been applied to the role of the private sector in recovery. Rather, attention in the media, among congressional committees, and among some researchers has focused on those organizations that take advantage of a disaster situation to heighten profits and engage in unethical business practices. As noted in Chapter 5, the private sector has a key role to play in recovery, yet its positive contributions remain largely disconnected from the disaster recovery planning process.

Project Impact, which placed a strong emphasis on preparedness as well as on pre-event hazard mitigation, did not focus on disaster recovery-related activities either. In a larger sense, however, it did provide important lessons about how a similar initiative could be reconstituted, expanded in scope, and maintained. The strengths of the program included its emphasis on raising community awareness through the building of partnerships, the marketing of local achievements, and a close association with the media. While some complained about its high profile compared to other FEMA programs, Project Impact was successful in developing locally championed initiatives tied to disaster preparedness and hazard mitigation activities that citizens, government, and the private sector could adopt in advance of an event. It also gave communities the latitude to develop programs that reflected local needs and the unique skills of involved stakeholders.

Critics also claimed that the nature of the program made it difficult to measure success. Many of Project Impact's initiatives involved outreach and training activities (a key missing link in the disaster recovery assistance framework) rather than "brick-and-mortar" mitigation projects that could be evaluated more easily using traditional cost-benefit analysis techniques. That said, the Multihazard Mitigation Council, a congressionally appointed panel of hazard scholars, found that Project Impact was, in fact, representative of a cost-effective risk reduction program. In reality, an important underlying reason for its discontinuation was its highly politicized nature and the failure of FEMA staff to include key constituents in program development and implementation.

Project Impact was never codified under the Stafford Act, and it was ultimately "replaced" by the Pre-Disaster Mitigation Program, a largely projects-driven funding source tied to the Disaster Mitigation Act. A resurrected program will need to build on Project Impact's technical strengths while assessing its political shortcomings. There should be a greater emphasis on building support among federal agencies (including FEMA and the GAO), Congress (including members of influential appropriation committees), state agency officials (including emergency management directors), and local government officials and other community leaders. Previous relationships developed among those active in the preparedness and hazard mitigation policy arena should be reestablished and expanded to include more members of the disaster recovery assistance network.

One of the groups with which Project Impact developed strong partnerships was business continuity planners. However, business continuity plans are rarely linked to community recovery plans. Most communities, states, and regions have little or no knowledge of the level of recovery readiness among businesses in their jurisdictions unless they have engaged in joint pre-event planning initiatives or other collaborative activities like Project Impact. Therefore, business continuity plans should do a better job of ensuring their connections to the larger assistance network. This means that, beyond conducting a cursory review of existing federal assistance programs that may be available after a disaster, businesses should participate in disaster recovery exercises and the disaster recovery plan-making process. Similarly, local, state, and federal recovery planning efforts should make a concerted effort to include local, state, and national business organizations.

Lessons should be derived from Project Impact communities that embraced the linkage between pre-event hazards planning and business continuity planning as well as the broader aims of actively involving small businesses, mid-sized companies, and corporations in the larger national effort. Clear successes have emerged. For instance, Tulsa, Oklahoma, effectively incorporated business continuity planning into a sustained public-private partnership that continues as a nonprofit organization even though the federal program has been discontinued (see the sidebar in Chapter 4).

International Relief Organizations and Nations

In the United States, the acceptance of pre- and post-disaster assistance from other nations is hindered by the lack of a system that can link international resources, including funding, policy counsel, and technical assistance, to the needs of states, regions, and communities. The U.S. government, including such organizations as the U.S. Agency for International Development (USAID) and its Office of Foreign Disaster Assistance (OFDA), and the State Department need to rethink the largely one-way flow of assistance while embracing the lessons from the developing world that emphasize the connection between disasters, sustainable development, and pre-event capacity-building initiatives.

For instance, the U.S. hazard and disaster research community should undertake a closer analysis of international disaster recovery research and transfer the lessons to a broader domestic audience of practitioners and policy makers. One possibility for improving the knowledge of disaster recovery is the expansion of what is currently a piecemeal exchange of information across nations. The exchange of information and of lessons derived after international disasters should become more prevalent and be used to help inform U.S. disaster recovery policy and practice. There are examples of good international exchange programs between the United States and other nations, such as the Dutch Dialogues described in the sidebar in Chapter 6, but their use remains insufficient to effectively transfer the breadth of information and other types of resources held by various nations and international organizations.

Given the challenges associated with international agreements, there need to be better protocols developed well in advance of a disaster. For instance, USAID and OFDA should modify their delivery systems to identify a clear means for accepting assistance and strategically delivering it to areas in the United States. The UN, acting in its role as an international coordinative body and working with existing relief organizations under its purview, could ensure that appropriate mutual aid agreements are in place with other nations. Similar agreements should address international aid provided by the International Monetary Fund and the World Bank.

The devastating earthquake, tsunami, and nuclear disaster in Japan (2011) provide a striking example of an event that merits close attention. This highly developed nation—one that prides itself on high levels of disaster preparedness and is widely recognized for its speed of recovery and reconstruction activities following the Kobe earthquake—is seeking assistance from other countries. What can U.S. hazard scholars, relief agencies, and diplomats learn that will improve the domestic receipt of foreign assistance after our next major disaster?

Community Emergency Response Teams

The Community Emergency Response Team (CERT) concept was developed by the Los Angeles Fire Department in 1985. It has since been recognized by the Emergency Management Institute and the National Fire Academy and expanded to address all hazards. More recently, the CERT concept has been incorporated into Citizen Corps, a national effort focused on encouraging individuals to volunteer their time to help enhance local preparedness and response capabilities. Additional Citizen Corps programs include Neighborhood Watch, Volunteers in Police Service, and the Medical Reserve Corps.[83]

CERTs are designed to empower individuals at the community level to help one another in the immediate aftermath of a disaster. Specific activities include checking on neighbors, performing basic first aid, notifying emergency crews if assistance is needed, and turning off gas and electrical systems in the event of an emergency or disaster so as to avoid fires. CERTs also emphasize preparedness by encouraging participants to conduct pre-event drills and training exercises and to store adequate caches of food and other supplies in safe and readily accessible places in case people cannot return to their homes for an extended period of time.

The Broadmoor case study in Chapter 3 highlights the value of community-based organizations taking the lead in recovery efforts, supported by other members of the assistance network. If the CERT concept were to be expanded to include pre-event planning for post-disaster recovery, it could address many of the inherent problems in the recovery assistance framework. One way to accomplish this on a nationwide scale is through the formation of community emergency response and recovery teams (CERRTs). Team members would be responsible for generating individual and neighborhood-level interest and participating in the development and implementation of local recovery plans. Because of their strong neighborhood emphasis, CERRTs could also be instrumental in identifying local needs and relaying that information to members of the assistance network. This would provide a local voice to the overall planning process and help guide the type and timing of assistance provided by others.

Once members of the new CERRTs are trained, they could be involved in reaching out to their peers and educating them about their role in pre-event planning for post-disaster recovery, including efforts to enhance local self-reliance and accountability and to help create a culture of planning.

ENHANCE LOCAL SELF-RELIANCE AND ACCOUNTABILITY: CREATE A CULTURE OF PLANNING FOR RECOVERY

The disaster recovery assistance framework suffers from a lack of accountability, the means necessary to build institutional capacity, and the sustained commitment needed to effectively plan for recovery.[84] From what is known about recovery and the largely ineffective approach used to date, it is apparent that a new path must be taken that is more focused on creating a culture of planning grounded in collaborative problem solving. The ability to sustain this effort over time also requires holding assistance networks accountable through the creation of robust standards coupled with a focus on pre-event capacity building and the long-term goal of increased local self-reliance. As with ADR, an important goal of planning is for participants to take ownership of the process.

Federal disaster recovery legislation should explicitly strive to foster the development of a planning culture that embraces the creation, monitoring, and implementation of recovery plans. One of the tangible benefits of participatory planning (including the use of ADR techniques) is that the plans that emerge from the process can increase organizational, individual, and community-level accountability.[85] At the federal level, this means amending the draft NDRF to incorporate disaster recovery plan making into the capacity-building process. More specifically, it means developing training programs and exercises based on the recovery plan that is created, evaluating the plan at key pre-event and post-event periods, and updating it as conditions warrant (Exhibit 9–8 on pages 368–369). Planning criteria, which serve as a key accountability measure, should be developed in a collaborative manner, emphasizing that this is a first step in a larger effort focused on creating an enduring coalition that spans the assistance network.[86]

The creation of ESF-14 and the more recent draft NDRF, as well as a few nascent state-level recovery planning efforts, offer some hope that recovery planning is gaining a toehold in terms of much needed institutional support. The public sector is not, however, capable of providing in-depth training and capacity building without significant assistance from members of the larger recovery assistance network, including nonprofits, quasi-governmental organizations, hazard scholars, the private sector, and professional associations.

An important question has confounded practitioners and hazards scholars: how can planning for events that occur with limited frequency be reconciled with the costs and effort that such planning requires? Certainly part of the blame for the current shortcomings in the assistance framework can be placed on the federal government, which has developed policies that engender dependence of state and local governments following disasters without a similar commitment to building local and state capacity beforehand.[87] Compounding this problem is the reluctance of states and local governments to invest their own time and resources to effectively plan for recovery. Other members of the assistance network are similarly guilty of reactionary strategies. Insurance companies that fail to incentivize communities to adopt pre- and post-disaster recovery plans through reduced insurance premiums; nonprofits organizations and private sector firms that assist in the repair and reconstruction of neighborhoods to their pre-event level of vulnerability; media organizations that spread disaster recovery myths and misinformation; and professional associations that do not adequately train their members to play a greater role in pre-event planning for post-disaster recovery are all indicative of the lack of a strong planning culture.

Planning will become an effective tool for improving recovery outcomes only if it is embraced by members of assistance networks. This requires changing the organizational culture of those networks from one that has been dominated by a response orientation to one that clearly understands the tangible benefits of collaborative pre-event

Exhibit 9–8. ESF-14 Conceptual Diagram

ESF #14 LONG-TERM COMMUNITY RECOVERY (LTCR) PROCESS DIAGRAM

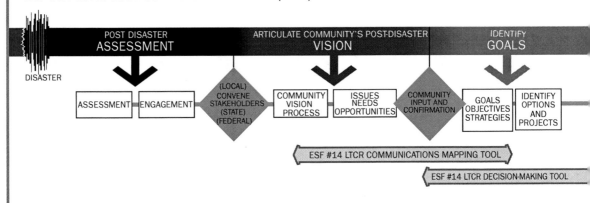

© 2009 FEMA Region VII – ESF #14 Long-Term Community Recovery (LTCR)
Source: Rebuild Iowa Office, Community Recovery Toolbox,

recovery planning. Creating a new culture of recovery preparedness, as reflected in the aggressive development of pre-event recovery plans and the modification of existing emergency management programs and the scope of plans, will take time. But as the ADR literature suggests, ongoing dialogue can foster greater cooperation, particularly when tangible benefits emerge from the process.

Clearly articulating the benefits of planning is necessary for long-term success, but it is not sufficient to establish a lasting recovery planning culture. Also required is an expansion of the recognized definition of the disaster recovery assistance network, a strengthening of ties across organizations, and the establishment of more meaningful roles for those who are left out of decision-making processes. Adhering to the current emergency management–dominated policy framework has led to an overreliance on federal disaster assistance programs that unduly stifle pre-event recovery planning among states, local governments, and other members of the network. Programs also tend to ignore the importance of the network as a collaborative resource, emphasizing and reinforcing instead individual actors and select institutions. A strong planning culture is inclusive and characterized by a diversity of opinions, knowledge, and experience, all operating within a larger, interconnected system.

The emergence of leaders in recovery varies greatly depending on circumstances and reflects the diversity of recovery assistance networks. Also highly variable is the degree to which planning has been embraced by communities, regions, and states

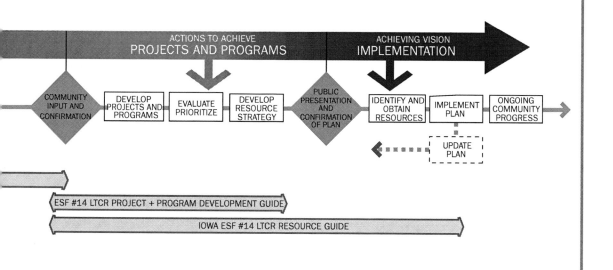

http://www.rio.iowa.gov/community_recovery/tools/1_TOOLBOX%20INTRODUCTION/LTCR_PROCESS_DIAGRAM.pdf

before a disaster occurs. For instance, countering the lack of a strong planning culture like that found in coastal Mississippi before Katrina requires a sustained approach that reflects local needs and capabilities—similar to that adopted by the GCCDS—and not one that seeks to impose a broad predetermined vision. Early attempts to engage in post-disaster planning in New Orleans began by designating areas subject to relocation. For many residents, this was their first exposure to the idea of planning, and it rekindled memories of past government actions that had marginalized poor, largely African-American communities, thereby further perpetuating the idea that planning is a technocratic process dictated by experts. While this is an outdated notion that has been widely discredited by planning scholars and practicing professionals, changing this perspective takes time. The development of a recovery planning culture is a long-term process that should be empowering, not repressive. This is one of many reasons that, if at all possible, the planning process should begin well in advance of a disaster and must reflect local social, economic, environmental, and political realities as well as the other contextual variables described throughout this book.

Creating a culture of planning for recovery must be understood in a historical context as a process whereby different assistance networks strive for greater collective self-reliance and accountability. Their ability to function as interconnected systems rather than as a diffuse set of stakeholders acting independently of one another would represent an institutional paradigm in recovery that does not yet exist in the United States. To be effective, the people responsible for making this a reality must confront an entrenched policy subsystem defined by widespread organizational dependence and strive to create and nurture a system defined by collaboration.

CONCLUSION

The growing reliance of communities on the federal government following disasters represents part of the historical evolution of disaster assistance in America.[88] In the past, communities were largely left to fend for themselves with the assistance of a few nonprofit organizations. Over time, the federal government, insurance companies, consultants, nonprofits, and quasi-governmental organizations began to play increasingly important, albeit uncoordinated roles in recovery. The politicization of the disaster declaration process, as noted in the first sidebar in Chapter 2, and decreasing levels of self-reliance in high-hazard communities, as described in the sidebar in Chapter 3, are but a few examples of how the current policy milieu does little to foster pre-event planning for post-disaster recovery. Taken together, these examples all represent the nature of pre-event conditions and the failings of the U.S. approach to post-disaster assistance that must be directly addressed through the adoption of a new recovery framework.

Transforming the nature of the modern disaster recovery assistance framework will not be easy. It will require a wholesale change in the way disaster assistance is provided, including the modification of existing programs that have shifted disaster recovery from what was once largely a humanitarian effort to a series of what are increasingly viewed as entitlement programs, with little or no demands placed on communities to improve their disaster recovery preparedness in anticipation of the next event. In an improved system, resources will be shared, or at least coordinated, rather than distributed independently of one another. They will be invested up front and will focus on building the collective capacity of the network, not delivered principally through funding programs post-disaster. Resource distribution strategies will also respect local knowledge, conditions, and needs.

Investing in pre- and post-disaster resources needed to build strong plans and a robust planning culture requires holding people and organizations more accountable. Perhaps the greatest challenge will be to develop appropriate incentives and penalties that resonate with different members of the assistance network. For instance, should post-disaster assistance be withheld from individuals living in communities that fail to develop pre-disaster recovery plans that meet accepted plan quality standards? Are there other incentive-based strategies that may prove more effective in encouraging the development of strong recovery plans, including the use of ADR techniques? An assessment of disaster recovery policies and programs across the network shows that many stakeholders are disproportionately affected by public sector grant programs that have effectively discouraged pre-event planning. Thus, it behooves those responsible for the administration of the NDRF and the proposed DRA to actively solicit the involvement of members of the assistance network. Key participants should include those who understand this dilemma, can provide real-world examples of where their pre-event planning and post-event actions have successfully addressed disaster recovery challenges, and are willing to advocate for changes to the current disaster recovery assistance framework.

Endnotes

1   Gavin Smith and Dennis Wenger, "Sustainable Disaster Recovery: Operationalizing an Existing Agenda," in *Handbook of Disaster Research*, ed. Havidan Rodriguez, Enrico L. Quarantelli, and Russell Dynes, 234–257 (New York: Springer, 2006); Kenneth C. Topping, "Toward a National Disaster Recovery Act of 2009," Natural Hazards Observer 33, no. 3 (January 2009): 1–9.

2   U.S. Government Accountability Office (GAO), *Disaster Recovery: FEMA's Long-term Assistance Was Helpful to State and Local Governments but Had Some Limitations*, GAO-10-404 (Washington, D.C.: GAO, March 2010), www.gao.gov/new.items/d10404.pdf.

3   Ibid.

4   Ibid., 24–26.

5   GAO, "Highlights," *Disaster Recovery*, unnumbered page.

6   Smith and Dennis Wenger, "Sustainable Disaster Recovery," 242, 255.

7   Stephanie E. Chang, "Modeling How Cities Recover from Disasters" (paper presented at the First International Conference on Urban Disaster Reduction, Kobe, Japan, January 2005); Stephanie E. Chang, "Urban Disaster Recovery: A Measurement Framework and Its Application to the 1995 Kobe Earthquake," *Disasters* 34, no. 2 (2009): 303–327; Laurie Johnson, "Toward a Comprehensive Theory of Disaster Recovery: Comparing Post-Disaster Financing in Los Angeles and Kobe and the Long-Term Effects on Land Use and Local Finance" (paper presented at the First International Conference on Urban Disaster Reduction, Kobe, Japan, 2005); Stephanie E. Chang and Scott B. Miles, "Resilient Community Recovery: Improving Recovery through Comprehensive Modeling, MCEER Research Progress and Accomplishments: 2001–2003," *MCEER_03_SP01* (May 2003): 139–148, mceer.buffalo.edu/publications/resaccom/03-sp01/10chang.pdf; Stephanie E. Chang and Scott B. Miles, "The Dynamics of Recovery: A Framework," in *Modeling Spatial and Economic Impacts of Disasters,* ed. Yasuhide Okuyama and Stephanie E. Chang, 181–204 (Berlin: Springer-Verlag, 2004).

8   Raymond Burby and Peter May, *Making Governments Plan: Some Experiments in Managing Land Use* (Baltimore: Johns Hopkins University Press, 1997); Philip R. Berke, Jennifer Dixon, and Neil Ericksen, "Coercive and Cooperative Intergovernmental Mandates: A Comparative Analysis of Florida and New Zealand Environmental Plans," *Environment and Planning B: Planning and Design* 24, no. 3 (1997): 451–468; Robert E. Deyle and Richard A. Smith, "Local Government Compliance with State Plan Mandates: The Effects of State Implementation in Florida," *Journal of the Americn Planning Association* 64, no. 4 (1998): 457–469; Arthur C. Nelson and Steven P. French, "Plan Quality and Mitigating Damage from Natural Disasters: A Case Study of the Northridge Earthquake with Planning Policy Considerations," *Journal of the American Planning Association* 68, no. 2 (2002): 194–207; Raymond J. Burby, "Making Plans That Matter: Citizen Involvement and Government Action," *Journal of the American Planning Association* 69, no. 1 (2003): 33–39.

9   Smith and Dennis Wenger, "Sustainable Disaster Recovery," 247.

10 Philip R. Berke and Timothy Beatley, *After the Hurricane: Linking Recovery to Sustainable Development in the Caribbean* (Baltimore: Johns Hopkins University Press, 1997); Kathleen Tierney, Michael K. Lindell, and Ronald W. Perry, *Facing the Unexpected: Disaster Preparedness and Response in the United States* (Washington, D.C.: Joseph Henry Press, 2001); Raymond J. Burby, "Have State Comprehensive Planning Mandates Insured Losses from Natural Disasters?" *Natural Hazards Review* 6, no. 2 (2005): 67–81; Raymond J. Burby and Linda C. Dalton, "Plans Can Matter! The Role of Land Use and State Planning Mandates on Limiting Development in Hazardous Areas," *Public Administration Review* 54, no. 3, (1994): 229–238.

11 Richard K. Norton, "More and Better Local Planning: State-Mandated Local Planning in Coastal North Carolina," *Journal of the American Planning Association* 71, no. 1 (2005): 55–71.

12 Philip Berke, Gavin Smith, and Ward Lyles, "Planning for Resiliency: An Evaluation of Coastal State Hazard Mitigation Plans," *Natural Hazards Review* (forthcoming, 2011).

13 Charles Hoch, "How Plan Mandates Work: Affordable Housing in Illinois," *Journal of the American Planning Association* 73, no. 1 (2007): 86–99.

14 Philip R. Berke, "Enhancing Plan Quality: Evaluating the Role of State Planning Mandates for Natural Hazard Mitigation," *Journal of Environmental Planning and Management* 39, no. (1996): 79–96; Burby and May, *Making Governments Plan.*

15 Raymond J. Burby and Peter J. May, "Command or Cooperate? Rethinking Traditional Central Governments' Hazard Mitigation Policies," in *Building Safer Communities: Risk Governance, Spatial Planning and Responses to Natural Hazards,* ed. Urbano Fra Paleo, 21–33 (Amsterdam: IOS Press, 2009); Burby and Dalton, "Plans Can Matter!"

16 Nelson and French, "Plan Quality and Mitigating Damage."

17 Ibid.

18 Linda C. Dalton and Raymond J. Burby, "Mandates, Plans, and Planners: Building Local Commitment to Development Management," *Journal of the American Planning Association* 60, no. 4 (1994): 151–168.

19 Philip R. Berke et al., "Do Cooperative Planning Mandates Produce Good Plans? Empirical Results from the New Zealand Experience," *Environment and Planning B: Planning and Design* 26, no. 5 (1999): 643–664; Berke, Dixon, and Ericksen, "Coercive and Cooperative Intergovernmental Mandates."

20 Samuel D. Brody, David R. Godschalk, and Raymond J. Burby, "Mandating Citizen Participation in Planning: Six Strategic Planning Choices," *Journal of the American Planning Association* 69, no. 3 (2003): 245–264.

21 Brody, Godschalk, and Burby, "Mandating Citizen Participation in Planning."

22 Jonathan Brock and Gerald Cormick, "Can Negotiation Be Institutionalized or Mandated? Lessons from Public Policy and Regulatory Conflicts," in *Mediation Research,* ed. Kenneth Kressel, 138–167 (San Francisco: Jossey-Bass, 1989); Jack D. Kartez, *Planning for Cooperation: Local Government Choices* (Pullman: Washington State University, 1990); Richard Ingleby, "Court-Sponsored Mediation: The Case against Mandatory Participation, *Modern Law Review* 56, no. 3 (1993): 441–451; David S. Winston, "Participation Standards in Mandatory Mediation Statutes: 'You Can Lead a Horse to Water…,'" *Ohio State Journal on Dispute Resolution* 11, no. 1 (1996): 187–206; Gary Smith, "Unwilling Actors: Why Voluntary Mediation Works, Why Mandatory Mediation Might Not," *Osgoode Hall Law Journal* 36, no. 4 (1998): 847–885; Edward F. Sherman, "'Good Faith' Participation in Mediation: Aspirational, Not Mandatory," *Dispute Resolution Magazine* (Winter 1997): 14–16; Elizabeth Ellen Gordon, "Why Attorneys Support Mandatory Mediation," *Judicature* 82, no. 5 (1999): 224–231.

23 Winston, "Participation Standards in Mandatory Mediation Statutes."

24 Ingleby, "Court-Sponsored Mediation"; Sherman, "'Good Faith' Participation in Mediation."

25 Winston, "Participation Standards in Mandatory Mediation Statutes," 189.

26 Lawrence Susskind and Sarah McKearnan, "The Evolution of Public Policy Dispute Resolution," *Journal of Architectural and Planning Research* 16 (Summer 1999): 96–115.

27 Ibid., 111.

28 Mel Rubin, "Disaster Mediation: Lessons in Conflict Coordination and Collaboration," *Cardozo Journal of Conflict Resolution* 9 (2007): 351–370.

29 Judith E. Innes and David E. Booher, "Consensus Building and Complex Adaptive Systems: A Framework for Evaluating Collaborative Planning," *APA Journal* 65, no. 4 (1999): 412–423.

30 Michael Tsur, "ADR–Appropriate Disaster Recovery," *Cardozo Journal of Conflict Resolution* 9 (2007): 371–379.

31 Norman Uphoff, "Understanding Social Capital: Learning from the Analysis and Experience of Participation," in *Social Capital: A Multi-Faceted Perspective,* ed. Partha Dasgupta and Ismail Serageldin (Washington, D.C.: The World Bank, 2000); Yuko Nakagawa and Rajib Shaw, "Social Capital: A Missing Link to Disaster Recovery," *International Journal of Mass Emergencies and Disasters* 22, no. 1 (2004): 5–34.

32 Deborah F. Shmueli, Sanda Kaufman, and Connie Ozawa, "Mining Negotiation Theory for Planning Insights," *Journal of Planning Education and Research* 27, no. 3 (2008): 359–364.

33 Sherry Arnstein, "Ladder of Citizen Participation," *Journal of American Institute of Planners* 35, no. 4 (1969): 216–224; Douglas Amy, "Mediation versus Traditional Political Institutions," in *The Politics of Environmental Mediation* (New York: Columbia University Press, 1987).

34 Nakagawa and Shaw, "Social Capital," 5, 7.

35 Daniel P. Aldrich, "The Crucial Role of Civil Society in Disaster Recovery and Japan's Preparedness for Emergencies," *Japan aktuell* 3 (March 2008): 81–96.

36 Smith and Wenger, "Sustainable Disaster Recovery."

37 Benigno E. Aguirre, "Can Sustainable Development Sustain Us?" *International Journal of Mass Emergencies and Disasters* 20, no. 2 (2002): 111–125.

38 Smith and Wenger, "Sustainable Disaster Recovery," 242, 250.

39   Ibid., 249–250.

40   Jurgen Habermas, *The Theory of Communicative Action* (Boston: Beacon Press, 1984); Judith Innes, "Planning Theory's Emerging Paradigm: Communicative Action and Interactive Practice," *Journal of Planning Education and Research* 14, no. 3 (1995): 183–189; Judith Innes, "Planning through Consensus Building: A New View of the Comprehensive Planning Ideal," *Journal of the American Planning Association* 62, no. 4 (1996): 460–472; John Forester, *The Deliberative Practitioner: Encouraging Participatory Planning Processes* (Cambridge: MIT Press, 1999).

41   Smith and Wenger, "Sustainable Disaster Recovery," 251–254.

42   Jack D. Kartez, "Rational Arguments and Irrational Audiences: Psychology, Planning, and Public Judgment," *Journal of the American Planning Association* (Autumn 1989): 445–456.

43   Patsy Healey, *Collaborative Planning: Shaping Places in Fragmented Societies* (New York: Palgrave Macmillan, 2006).

44   Paul A. Sabatier and Hank C. Jenkins-Smith, eds., *Policy Change and Learning: An Advocacy Coalition Approach* (Boulder, Colo.: Westview Press, 1993), 41.

45   Ibid., 5.

46   Richard Stuart Olson, Robert A. Olson, and Vincent T. Gawronski, *Some Buildings Just Can't Dance: Politics, Life Safety, and Disaster* (Stamford, Conn.: JAI Press, 1999), 161.

47   Connie P. Ozawa and Lawrence Susskind, "Mediating Science-Intensive Policy Disputes," *Journal of Policy Analysis and Management* 5, no. 1 (1985): 37.

48   Steven D. Stehr, "The Political Economy of Urban Disaster Assistance," *Urban Affairs Review* 41, no. 4 (2006): 492–500.

49   John R. Logan and Harvey L. Molotch, *Urban Fortunes: The Political Economy of Place* (Berkeley: University of California Press, 1987).

50   William R. Freudenberg et al., *Catastrophe in the Making: The Engineering of Katrina and the Disasters of Tomorrow* (Washington, D.C.: Island Press, 2009).

51   Robert A. Dahl, *Who Governs?* (New Haven, Conn.: Yale University Press, 1961); Paul E. Peterson, ed., *The New Urban Reality* (Washington, D.C.: Brookings Institution Press, 1985).

52   Deborah A. Stone, "Causal Stories and the Formation of Policy Agendas," *Political Science Quarterly* 104, no. 2 (1989): 281–300.

53   Sabatier and Jenkins-Smith, *Policy Change and Learning,* 48–55.

54   Ibid., 48.

55   Ibid., 48.

56   Ibid., 50.

57   Ibid.

58   Ibid., 51.

59   Ibid., 53–55.

60   Ibid., 54.

61   David R. Godschalk, "Negotiating Intergovernmental Development Policy Conflicts: Practice-Based Guidelines," *Journal of the American Planning Association* 58, no. 3 (1992): 368–378; Ozawa and Susskind, "Mediating Science-Intensive Policy Disputes."

62   Thomas A. Birkland, *Lessons of Disaster: Policy Change after Catastrophic Events* (Washington, D.C.: Georgetown University Press, 2006).

63   Innes and Booher, "Consensus Building and Complex Adaptive Systems," 412; citations are to Manuel Castells, *The Information Age: Economy, Society and Culture,* vol. 1, *The Rise of the Network Society* (Cambridge, Mass: Blackwell, 1996), and vol. 2, *The Power of Identity* (Malden, Mass: Blackwell, 1997).

64   Kartez, *Planning for Cooperation.*

65   Sabatier and Jenkins-Smith, *Policy Change and Learning,* 53–54.

66 William Blomquist and Elinor Ostrom, "Institutional Capacity and the Resolution of a Commons Dilemma," *Policy Studies Review* 5, no. 2 (1985): 383–393; Elinor Ostrom, *Governing the Commons: The Evolution of Institutions for Collective Action* (Cambridge: Cambridge University Press, 1990); Dennis Chong, *Collective Action and the Civil Rights Movement* (Chicago: University of Chicago Press, 1991).

67 Philip R. Berke et al., *Urban Land Use Planning,* 5th ed. (Urbana: Illinois University Press, 2006); Innes and Booher, "Consensus Building and Complex Adaptive Systems."

68 Richard Sylves, *Disaster Policy and Politics: Emergency Management and Homeland Security* (Washington, D.C.: CQ Press, 2008).

69 GAO, *Hurricane Katrina: Comprehensive Policies and Procedures Are Needed to Ensure Appropriate Use of and Accountability for International Assistance,* GAO-06-460 (Washington, D.C., April 6, 2006), www.gao.gov/new.items/d06460.pdf; GAO, *National Disaster Response: FEMA Should Take Action to Improve Capacity and Coordination between Government and Voluntary Sectors,* GAO-08-369 (Washington, D.C., February 2008), www.gao.gov/new.items/d08369.pdf; U.S. Senate, Committee on Homeland Security and Governmental Affairs, Ad Hoc Subcommittee on State, Local, and Private Sector Preparednness and Integration, *The Next Big Disaster: Is the Private Sector Prepared?,* 111th Cong., 2nd sess., testimony of Stephen Flynn, "Building a More Resilient Nation by Strengthening Private-Public Partnerships," March, 4, 2010), www.centerfornationalpolicy.org/ht/display/ContentDetails/i/17679; National Research Council, *Private-Public Sector Collaboration to Enhance Community Disaster Resilience: A Workshop Report* (Washington, D.C.: National Academies Press, 2010); Federal Emergency Management Agency (FEMA), *National Disaster Recovery Framework,* draft (February 5, 2010), disasterrecoveryworkinggroup.gov/ndrf.pdf; U.S. Senate, Committee on Homeland Security and Governmental Affairs, letter to Homeland Security Secretary Janet Napolitano, 111th Cong., 2nd sess., February 26, 2010.

70 Author's personal communication with Matt Campbell, branch chief, Regional Planning and Long Term Community Recovery, Recovery Directorate, FEMA, 2009.

71 Smith and Wenger, "Sustainable Disaster Recovery," 240, 242.

72 Gavin Smith, "The 21st Century Emergency Manager" (Emmitsburg, Md.: Emergency Management Institute Higher Education Project, FEMA, 2002).

73 Gavin Smith, Victor Flatt, Dylan Sandler, and Daniel Peterson, *Assessing the Quality of State Disaster Recovery Plans, Project Report* (Durham, N.C.: Institute of Homeland Security Solutions, 2011).

74 Smith and Wenger, "Sustainable Disaster Recovery," 244.

75 Aseem Inam, *Planning for the Unplanned: Recovering from Crises in Megacities* (New York: Routledge, 2005).

76 See Kenneth C. Topping, "A Model Recovery and Reconstruction Ordinance," in *Planning for Post-Disaster Recovery and Reconstruction,* Planning Advisory Service (PAS) Report 483/484, ed. Jim Schwab et al., 149–167 (Chicago: American Planning Association, 1998).

77 Topping, "Toward a National Disaster Recovery Act of 2009."

78 Burby, *Cooperating with Nature.*

79 Philip Berke and Gavin Smith, "Hazard Mitigation, Planning, and Disaster Resiliency: Challenges and Strategic Choices for the 21st Century," in Paleo, *Building Safer Communities* (see note 15).

80 Smith and Wenger, "Sustainable Disaster Recovery," 254.

81 NVOAD, *Long-Term Recovery Manual,* rev ed. (Arlington, Va.: NVOAD, January 2004), www.disasterrecoveryresources.net/VOAD-LTRecoveryManual.pdf.

82 Keith Bea, *Emergency Management Preparedness Standards: Overview and Options for Congress,* CRS RL32520 (Washington, D.C.: Congressional Research Service, August 12, 2004), www.fas.org/sgp/crs/homesec/RL32520.pdf.

83 Citizen Corps, *Citizen Corps: A Guide for Local Officials* (Washington, D.C.: The White House, 2002), www.pimahealth.org/cc/guide_local_officials.pdf.

84 Smith and Wenger, "Sustainable Disaster Recovery."

85 Archon Fung, *Empowered Participation: Reinventing Urban Democracy* (Princeton, N.J.: Princeton University Press, 2004); Alnoor Ebrahim and Edward Weisband, eds., *Global Accountabilities: Participation, Pluralism and Public Ethics* (Cambridge: Cambridge University Press, 2007); Sirianni, "Neighborhood Planning as Collaborative Democratic Design."

86 Smith and Wenger, "Sustainable Disaster Recovery," 240, 249–255.

87 Raymond J. Burby and Steven P. French, "Coping with Floods: The Land Use Management Paradox," *Journal of the American Planning Association* 47, no. 3 (July 1981): 289–300; Rutherford Platt, *Disasters and Democracy: The Politics of Extreme Natural Events* (Washington, D.C.: Island Press, 1999); Smith and Wenger, "Sustainable Disaster Recovery," 243, 247, 249–250.

88 Claire B. Rubin, ed., *Emergency Management: The American Experience, 1900–2005* (Fairfax, Va.: Public Entity Risk Institute, 2007).

Chapter 10

The National Disaster Recovery Framework: A New Vision for Recovery?

The sun rises over the Ninth Ward in New Orleans after Hurricane Katrina.

Photo by Donn Young.

T HE PRIMARY AIMS OF THIS book were to describe and critically evaluate disaster recovery as practiced in the United States, identify areas in need of improvement, and suggest policy recommendations to address these problems. Serious challenges must be confronted: a poor connection between local needs and available resources, programs that are ill timed, and the failure to incentivize strong horizontal and vertical integration across disaster recovery assistance networks. Central to these problems is the failure to plan for the actions of multiple parties and to proactively address the resource allocation conflicts that result.

The need to engage in pre-event planning for post-disaster recovery has never been greater. Disaster losses continue to climb, and the U.S. government, as well as other members of the assistance network, continues to spend more money dealing with their costs. Post-disaster funding is tied to the repair and reconstruction of infrastructure, public facilities, businesses, neighborhoods, and homes with virtually no commitment of resources to such pre-event capacity-building activities as planning. Communities, states, developers, and individuals continue to invest in known hazardous areas with little regard for the consequences. The advent of climate change and its concomitant effects on natural hazards—including rising sea levels and increasingly severe droughts, floods, wildfires, winter storms, and heat waves, coupled with shifting weather patterns in areas whose human settlements and way of life are predicated on past conditions—make it a national imperative to invest in a new national policy framework.

The proposed Disaster Recovery Act (DRA) suggests that the type and timing of assistance should shift from a unidimensional focus on the administration of grant programs after a disaster to a more systematic, yet flexible effort that draws on the capacity of assistance networks, recognizing their diversity and unrealized potential. Throughout this book, sidebars have been used to illustrate how different groups within these networks can and do perform a number of important roles in recovery, such as building supportive coalitions, resolving resource-based conflicts, exchanging information, translating research into practice, identifying local needs and supportive state policies, improving the coordination and timing of assistance, creating resource-sharing agreements, establishing participatory decision-making forums, integrating hazard mitigation into recovery, altering narrowly defined program rules, and planning for post-disaster recovery.

THE EVOLUTION OF THE NATIONAL DISASTER RECOVERY FRAMEWORK

Until recently, planning, which employs a number of techniques that are directly applicable to disaster recovery, has been noticeably absent from federal dialogue or, at best, ineffectively integrated into existing policy. The Stafford Act of 1988, as noted in Chapter 2, has created powerful disincentives to plan, enhanced state and local dependency, and often exacerbated the conditions that presage future disasters. Implementation of the act has also created an organizational culture that is focused on the administration of grant programs, not planning. While the Disaster Mitigation Act of 2000 does address pre-event hazard mitigation planning, it does not alter existing and, in many cases, contradictory policies in the Stafford Act that limit planning and other capacity-building initiatives. However, there are indications that this may be changing.

After a series of hearings to address the widely publicized failure of existing response and recovery programs after Hurricane Katrina,[1] Congress concluded that a lack of pre-event planning was to blame for many of the problems. Studies conducted by the Government Accountability Office and disaster experts also suggested the need to improve pre-event recovery planning activities,[2] and several professional associations and nonprofit organizations have begun to advocate for the adoption of a national recovery planning policy.[3]

In its initial attempt to address the limitations of the Stafford Act, Congress passed the Post-Katrina Emergency Management Reform Act of 2006 (PKEMRA), requiring the federal government to develop a national recovery strategy. More recently, the White House Long-Term Disaster Recovery Working Group, composed of representatives from more than twenty federal departments, agencies, and offices, has been tasked with developing the National Disaster Recovery Framework (NRDF). Draft recommendations of the group's report[4] (all page references to which will be cited parenthetically in the text), released February 5, 2010, support placing a greater emphasis on pre- and post-disaster recovery planning, enhancing the focus of recovery activities on a vision predicated on resilience and sustainability, clarifying roles and shared responsibilities across the assistance network, improving capacity-building efforts at the local level, creating scalable recovery programs, making federal policies less prescriptive, and better integrating members of the private and nonprofit sectors.[5]

This draft also states that it will rely on existing "programs, authorities, and best practices" (6)—a statement that partially coincides with an argument made in the previous chapter of this book for the modification of existing emergency management programs and plans. During the drafting of the NDRF, federal policy makers also agreed that they would later produce a follow-up document to include a set of recommendations calling for the creation of new federal rules (6). As currently written, however, the NDRF does not address fundamental shortcomings in existing federal recovery legislation; rather, it serves to reemphasize the need for the creation of the DRA. This book contends that a strengthened NDRF—one that specifies how broad concepts will be achieved and identifies the resources needed to achieve them—is needed. It further suggests that the proposed DRA is necessary to provide the legal and regulatory mechanisms that are required to support the overall process and provide the new federal rules alluded to in the draft NDRF.

The NDRF is a work in progress and, once published, will likely be amended over time. This is evident, given that a "predecisional draft" version of the NDRF was completed in October 2010 as a first draft of this book was nearing completion. Ideally, this book would have been an opportunity to comment on the scope of the October draft and on the degree to which it addresses the problems identified herein as well as in the February draft. Unfortunately, the predecisional draft has not been made available to the public and cannot be cited directly.

Nevertheless, the continuing efforts to craft such a document are noteworthy as the federal government has struggled for some time to move beyond the narrow confines of the Stafford Act and the NRF. Further, the draft NDRF is evidence that the federal government is making a meaningful attempt to finally give disaster recovery the focus it deserves. It does not, however, go far enough to operationalize specific policies, resource allocation strategies, and planning activities. Rather, it appears that the still evolving NDRF is in need of further improvements over time and that the recommendations found throughout this book (and reassembled later in this chapter) can provide the basis for continued policy dialogue among policy makers and the larger disaster recovery assistance network, leading to continued improvements—including the passage of legislation authorizing the DRA.

INTENT AND RECOMMENDATIONS OF THE NATIONAL DISASTER RECOVERY FRAMEWORK

The NDRF is intended to provide enhanced recovery guidance. As stated in its introduction, "The National Disaster Recovery Framework (NDRF) defines an approach to preparing for, planning for, and managing disaster recoveries that addresses the complexity of long term recovery with flexibility and adaptability" (5). To accomplish these goals, the NDRF adds new leadership responsibilities, organizational structure, planning guidance, and the means to provide enhanced technical assistance (6).

Organizational changes include the introduction of federal recovery coordinators (FRCs), state disaster recovery coordinators (SRCs), and local disaster recovery managers (DRMs), and the adoption of recovery support functions (RSFs). The stated intent of the FRCs and SRCs is to foster participation across the assistance network in a coordinated manner. An FRC's responsibilities include coordinating federal assistance, managing RSF activities, assisting communities develop recovery "measures," incorporating hazard mitigation into recovery, establishing a coordinated recovery strategy across the network, and promoting stakeholder involvement (32–33).

The clarification of federal and state roles in recovery represents an important improvement to a system that faced heavy criticism following Hurricane Katrina. Yet as has been noted repeatedly throughout this text and within several illustrative sidebars, recovery means more than identifying who is in charge; it also means creating the conditions that foster coordination across a diffuse network of assistance providers. And it remains unclear how FRCs will interact with existing recovery managers—including, for example, the federal coordinating officer (FCO), who is the official responsible for managing federal response and recovery efforts in the field after a presidentially declared disaster. If, in fact, the FRC's authority is granted by the FCO, the FRC's ability to address the complexities of disaster recovery will require that his or her duties be clearly specified and that the position be fully supported by the FCO cadre to ensure that it is not marginalized in the field after a presidentially declared disaster. Thus, improving the NDRF will mean expanding the role of the FRC to include building relationships with members of different disaster recovery assistance networks, identifying unique local needs, and helping states and communities develop pre-disaster recovery plans.

As described in the Stafford Act and National Response Framework (NRF), each state designates a state coordinating officer (SCO) after a federally declared disaster. However, the NDRF suggests that states and communities also create positions for an SRC and a DRM, respectively. Responsibilities for both positions include establishing recovery priorities and communicating them to appropriate stakeholders; organizing recovery planning efforts and developing plans that are actionable, feasible, supported by the general public, and tied to available funding; incorporating hazard mitigation and resilience into the recovery process; establishing a clear vision and set of prioritized actions; coordinating funding sources and identifying unmet needs; and establishing appropriate measures of recovery (33–34). The appointment of an SRC is almost certain to produce role ambiguity between that position and the SCO, which will somehow need to be addressed. As in the case of the FCO and FRC, roles will need to be clarified and the SRC given the support needed to carry out his or her pre- and post-disaster duties.

The appointment of local DRMs will prove difficult to achieve for two reasons: (1) local emergency managers are less engaged in long-term recovery activities than in preparedness and response-related activities, while local planners often fail to recognize their role in planning for recovery; and (2) local governments lack the resources, including the funding needed to staff the position and provide the training prospective that local recovery managers will need to assume assigned tasks. Establishing an effective group of local DRMs will require a sustained investment of resources (funding, training, and supportive policies) that are focused on building the capacity and commitment of local recovery assistance networks.

The NDRF contains six federal RSFs, which report to the FRC when activated (Exhibit 10–1 on page 382). For each RSF, a coordinating agency is named and assigned to manage it. Primary and support agencies are also identified in order to clarify which agency should take the lead and which are capable of supplementing the work of the lead agency. While the same general technique is used in the NRF to manage emergency support functions (ESFs) 1 through 14, a number of new federal government functions are identified. For example, the Environmental Protection Agency, which is

---

Exhibit 10–1. National Disaster Recovery Framework, Recovery Support Functions, and Coordinators

RSF: Community Planning and Capacity Building
Proposed Coordinating Agency: Department of Homeland Security (DHS)/Federal Emergency Management Agency (FEMA) or Department of Housing and Urban Development (HUD)

Primary Agencies: DHS/FEMA, HUD, and Department of Agriculture (USDA)

Supporting Agencies: Department of Health and Human Services (HHS), Environmental Protection Agency (EPA), Small Business Administration (SBA), Department of Labor (DOL), Treasury, Corporation for National and Community Service (CNCS), Department of Commerce (DOC), Department of Justice (DOJ), and Department of Interior (DOI)

RSF: Economic Development
Proposed Coordinating Agency: DOC

Primary Agencies: DOC, DHS, HUD, USDA, DOL, Treasury, and SBA

Supporting Agencies: Department of Energy (DOE), DOI, HHS, and EPA

RSF: Health, Social and Community Services
Proposed Coordinating Agency: HHS

Primary Agencies: USDA, DOC, Department of Education (ED), DHS (FEMA and Office of Infrastructure Protection [IP]), HUD, DOI, DOJ, Department of Labor (DOL), EPA, Department of Veterans Affairs (DVA), and CNCS

Supporting Agencies: Department of Defense (DOD), DOE, Treasury, DOT, SBA, and NVOAD

RSF: Housing
Proposed Coordinating Agency: HUD

Primary Agencies: HUD, USDA, DHS/FEMA, Access Board, and DOJ

Supporting Agencies: DOC, DVA, SBA, NVOAD, EPA, and HHS

RSF: Infrastructure Systems
Proposed Coordinating Agency: To be decided (TBD)

Primary Agencies: U.S. Army Corps of Engineers (USACE), DHS (FEMA AND National Protection Programs Directorate [NPPD]), DOT, and DOE

Supporting Agencies: USDA, DOC, DOD, HUD, HHS, DHS, EPA, DOI, Federal Communications Commission (FCC), Tennessee Valley Authority (TVA), General Services Administration (GSA), Nuclear Regulatory Commission (NRC), Treasury, and ED

RSF: Natural and Cultural Resources
Proposed Coordinating Agency: DOI

Primary Agencies: DOC, DOI, EPA, and USDA

Supporting Agencies: HUD and DHS/FEMA

Source: National Disaster Recovery Assistance Framework, draft (February 2010), 38–40.

described in the NRF as having an important role dealing with hazardous materials, is described in the NDRF as providing technical assistance tied to smart growth and watershed planning (35). This more explicit delineation of skills represents an important step toward recognizing the range of issues in recovery and of organizations needed to deal with them.

The success of federal RSFs necessitates a similar commitment from states to develop complementary RSFs, and states' reluctance to develop an ESF-14 capability can yield important lessons in this regard. Any plan to create new RSFs and to provide the resources (funding, training, and supportive policies) needed to develop a coordinated system of recovery coordinators must be done in close consultation with states. Otherwise, vertical integration, which is so important in recovery, will be even weaker than it has been, creating an increasingly top-heavy approach to recovery—already one of the central problems in the existing disaster recovery assistance framework.

The NDRF does allude to issues associated with horizontal integration, including the importance of improving partnerships beyond those described in the NRF, such as with representatives of the private sector, nonprofits, housing finance, and economic development. However, except for the National Voluntary Organizations Active in Disasters (NVOAD), non–public sector members of the disaster recovery assistance network are not listed as leading or support organizations in the NDRF. This raises concerns as to the ability of the RSFs to effectively collaborate with such organizations since they are not playing a sanctioned leadership or support role. It also suggests that these organizations were not substantially involved in the development of the RSFs. If that is the case, the failure to involve them has direct implications for the roles that non–public sector actors might be willing to play and the degree to which the nature and timing of resources they provide will be coordinated with the public sector following a disaster. The importance of this concern is evident in the creation and eventual dissolution of Project Impact (see the sidebar in Chapter 5), which demonstrate the relevance of creating enduring coalitions that support collaboration across the assistance network.

It is important to note that the NDRF suggests an approach other than the command-and-control structure currently used in the NRF: a more collaborative, flexible, and exploratory method that recognizes the nature of those who participate in recovery and seeks to develop recovery strategies based on identified needs (35). This proposal is described in very general terms and should be explored more fully through extended dialogue across assistance networks and the creation of actionable agreements among these groups. It also highlights the need to reconcile this approach with the command-and-control structure that remains embedded in the organizational culture of the emergency management profession.

The need to change organizational culture is not limited to the emergency management community. It also extends to the planning profession so that planners embrace their role in disaster recovery and emergency management. Cultivating improved levels of cooperation between emergency managers and planners so as to more effectively realize the benefits of pre-event recovery planning will take time as it necessitates the development of new and modified policies and programs that support rather than stifle this all important interaction.

The provision of such pre-event assistance is not adequately discussed in the NDRF, nor does the emerging policy framework describe the involvement of RSFs in pre-event technical assistance and capacity building, including planning for disaster recovery. Stating that pre-event recovery planning is an important facet of recovery is not enough; the mechanisms must also be in place to provide the resources needed to create, monitor, implement, and revise plans over time. Relative to post-disaster assistance, the NDRF alludes to the importance of the sustained involvement of RSFs, which "are likely to remain active for months to provide disaster recovery support" (35). Yet long-term recovery, particularly in the case of federally declared disasters, can takes years, and major events like Katrina require a committed network of organizations providing assistance for a decade or more.

While the NDRF discusses the importance of pre- and post-disaster recovery planning, including suggested roles for members of the assistance network, the framework does not discuss how federal, state, or local plans will be developed or who will foster the coordination of such efforts. (Key elements of pre- and post-disaster recovery planning noted in the document are listed further on in this chapter [see pages 392–393]). The ultimate strength of the NDRF should be measured by the degree to which this evolving policy framework adequately provides the basis for an implementable recovery strategy.

STRENGTHENING AND OPERATIONALIZING THE NATIONAL DISASTER RECOVERY FRAMEWORK

To affect the change that is needed in the disaster recovery assistance framework and serve as a call to action among participants in disaster recovery assistance networks, planning concepts and principles need to be operationalized.[6] The U.S. Senate Committee on Homeland Security and Governmental Affairs explicitly used the same terminology when it noted "difficulties in operationalizing the NDRF."[7] The proposed DRA is intended to serve this purpose by offering a roadmap, guiding needed policy improvements over time that are based on a better procedural understanding of the recovery process and the value of pre-event planning.

On a conceptual level, the draft NDRF discusses many of the weaknesses described in the current assistance framework. Yet it fails to provide a substantive, detailed explanation of what is needed to effectively change existing practices or provide a suitable national policy that supports the process. This observation is echoed by members of the aforementioned Senate committee. In a letter to the secretary of homeland security, Janet Napolitano, the committee noted several weaknesses similarly described in this critique, including ambiguity in leadership, roles, authorities, and responsibilities; limited detail in the actions of RSFs; confusion about the potentially competing roles of the existing FCO and FRC; an inadequate discussion of federal recovery programs; an ineffective discussion of how the NDRF is scalable to catastrophes; and a limited emphasis on the incorporation of hazard mitigation into recovery.[8]

While the NDRF is undergoing a review in efforts to address what amounts to a seriously flawed system, the recommendations that follow are intended to supplement those offered throughout this book.

Establish Clear Plan Guidance

Planning should provide the procedural mechanism for implementing national disaster recovery policy at the federal, state, and local levels. Mandating the creation of pre-event plans requires developing clear, robust guidance that draws on the disaster recovery literature, a national assessment of state and local plans, and best practices drawn from members of disaster recovery assistance networks. While there may be a limited number of high-quality state and local recovery plans, numerous stakeholders have developed strategies that help to meet local needs, deliver timely assistance, and improve horizontal and vertical integration. Much can be learned from these efforts and used to assist in the development of planning support.

As discussed in Chapter 8, plan quality principles should be used to develop planning standards that address many of the weaknesses described in the U.S. disaster recovery assistance framework. However, adherence to these principles without a commitment to recognized capacity-building efforts is insufficient.

As part of the evolving national approach to disaster recovery, the NDRF states that the mission of the community-planning and capacity-building RSF is to "unify capacity-building expertise and support programs from across the federal government to support local and state governments in restoring and improving their ability to provide governmental services and organize, plan, manage and implement long term recovery activities and initiatives" (38). The supporting narrative in the NDRF does not, however, describe the specifics for pre-event training in plan making or the creation of planning standards, both of which are important for building the capacity of the network to function effectively following a disaster. The *Long-Term Community Recovery Planning Process: A Self-Help Guide*, which was developed prior to the passage of the PKEMRA and the ensuing NDRF, remains one of the few federal documents that is intended to assist local governments with post-disaster recovery planning.[9] Other recovery planning materials, including the Federal Emergency Management Agency's (FEMA)-funded update of the American Planning Association's original text, *Planning for Post-Disaster Recovery and Reconstruction*,[10] and the guidance document developed in Florida,[11] provide important resources from which to begin identifying best practices and building a national training platform.

The draft NDRF alludes to additional support through the provision of pre-disaster capacity building, training, and planning assistance. As part of this new assignment, FRCs are expected to work with members of assistance networks to develop partnerships, assist in plan development, and identify best practices that can be shared with those involved in the plan-making process. However, the manner in which this will happen and the roles of those expected to accomplish it still need to be clarified.

Clarify the Roles and the Timing of Assistance (Pre- and Post-Event)

The NDRF identifies a series of stakeholders in the assistance network that heretofore have not been adequately addressed in the NRF, including individuals and families, the private sector, and nonprofits. In each case, roles are discussed in the context of pre- and post-disaster recovery. The implementation of proposed activities and their integration into the assistance network through a pre- and post-disaster plan is also described (42–50). As in much of the document, however, the NDRF does not detail how the concepts and plans will be implemented. Members of the Senate Committee on Homeland Security and Government Affairs have expressed similar concerns:

> *While it is essential that all federal agencies with potentially applicable resources and programs assist with recovery in a much more active manner than has generally occurred in previous disasters, without more specificity as to who is in charge of federal efforts and what specific roles and responsibilities individual agencies have, it is unlikely that the framework will operate effectively.*[12]

The draft NDRF describes the delivery of federal assistance across a recovery continuum, which categorizes activities as being pre-disaster (preparedness), short term, intermediate, and long term (9–11). Whereas the disaster recovery time line as originally described by Eugene Haas, Robert Kates, and Martyn Bowden[13] has been criticized in this book as being overly prescriptive, the recovery continuum in the NDRF is intended to serve as a broad conceptual tool, helping to differentiate the roles and responsibilities of those guided by the NRF and the NDRF and to delineate activities across the network, many of which overlap. What remains ambiguous, however, is the degree to which the NDRF accounts for the complexities of different disaster recovery assistance networks, including those individuals and organizations that assume leadership roles. This becomes increasingly complex and difficult to "manage" in those cases where leaders emerge who are not from the public sector.

The NDRF states that RSFs will serve as key coordination points and will be activated on an as-needed basis. But the ability to activate RSFs and support staff in the all-important pre-event environment is not discussed and should be part of a more systematic effort to address the appropriate timing of assistance. Otherwise, disaster recovery plans will remain largely a post-disaster exercise, limiting their effectiveness. This issue was similarly noted by the Senate Committee: "The draft is also not clear at what stage the RSFs will be activated… . The draft fails to provide sufficient information as to what additional guidance will be produced and when it will be available."[14]

Pre-event activities are identified and encouraged, but it remains unclear how they will be implemented or funded. A continued overemphasis on post-disaster planning hinders the ability to develop enduring relationships based on trust and an in-depth understanding of stakeholder interests. While the intensity of recovery can engender cooperation, it can also foster continued and often intensified conflict that is tied to the competition for scarce resources. The clarification of RSF roles, supplemented with necessary resources and political support for both pre-event planning and post-disaster actions, is needed to help alleviate conflict and provide meaningful, targeted assistance to states, communities, and other members of the assistance network. This clarification, as well as the incorporation of these roles into a mandated state and local planning process that is tied to clear planning principles with the adequate funding and training needed to achieve this aim, represents the next logical step.

Improve the Integration of Hazard Mitigation Processes and Techniques

Among the most disappointing elements of the draft NDRF is the limited discussion of how the framework will facilitate the integration of pre- and post-disaster hazard mitigation into the recovery process. On a more conceptual level, there is not a clear description of how hazard mitigation relates to disaster resilience and sustainability, which together are one of the "core principles" of the NDRF and could be construed as part of a vision statement for disaster recovery. While it is true that hazard mitigation is best performed before an event, a federally declared disaster still presents a unique opportunity to inject hazard mitigation measures into the recovery process. Not only is Hazard Mitigation Grant Program, Public Assistance, and congressionally appropriated funding available to address vulnerable housing and infrastructure, but there also tends to be an increased level of public attention on hazard vulnerability across the assistance network. That there is not a companion ESF for hazard mitigation in the NRF, that the former National Mitigation Strategy (a federal effort developed by FEMA in the mid-1990s to construct a broad-based, multiagency, national hazard mitigation policy) has been eliminated (and no effort was ever made to replace it),[15] and that mitigation has been removed from ESF-14 are all troubling. Members of the Senate Committee noted similar problems:

> We believe that the draft NDRF puts too little emphasis on mitigation and fails to put in place plans and procedures to make the most of these critical mitigation opportunities. We believe more needs to be added to the final NDRF to ensure we maximize mitigation opportunities both before and after disasters.[16]

According to FEMA officials, the not-yet-released predecisional draft NDRF has added language emphasizing the importance of strengthening the procedural integration of hazard mitigation into pre- and post-disaster recovery activities, including the linkage of information derived from state and local hazard mitigation plans, the identification of hazard mitigation opportunities post-disaster, and the connectivity between steps to reduce risk and increased levels of disaster resilience. Further evidence of this improvement is the inclusion of hazard mitigation into the pre- and post-disaster activities of the six RSFs. Once again, however, an increased level of specificity is needed to address how the broad tasks assigned to the proposed positions will be augmented by other members of the assistance network and supported by adequate levels of funding, staff, and complementary policies.

Increasing the clarity of the relationship between hazard mitigation and disaster recovery in the NDRF and ensuing guidance materials is strongly recommended and underscores the importance of using existing programs and policies to augment recovery capabilities. The Disaster Mitigation Act of 2000 provides this all-important linkage as well as significant lessons regarding the nature and effectiveness of enabling program rules, state and local training initiatives, and existing planning requirements. These and other issues are being tackled by hazard researchers, and their findings are providing constructive guidance that can be used in modifying existing policies and developing new ones. For instance, the degree to which the Disaster Mitigation Act describes the process of incorporating mitigation into recovery should be assessed in order to identify possible areas for integrating mitigation in existing and evolving policies. Among the most important goals of this assessment process and the derivation of applied lessons should be to determine a way in which those involved in the development and operationalization of the Disaster Mitigation Act can recognize local needs and available resources.

Improve the Pre- and Post-Event Assessment of Local Needs and Available Resources

Good recovery plans derive strength and staying power from the clear identification of community needs and the network resources necessary to meet them. This means moving beyond the overemphasis on federal agencies as they are often ill-suited to identify local needs even though they tend to possess significant financial resources and play a disproportionately influential role in shaping recovery policy. In an effort to partially address this problem, FEMA developed the National Disaster Recovery Program Database in 2009 to provide communities with a web-based clearinghouse of recovery programs administered by the federal government, nonprofits, and foundations.[17]

The ability to identify a broad array of available resources is especially important given that most disasters do not trigger federal assistance. Adding further complexity to this state of affairs is the growing threat of slow-onset climate-related disasters such as rising sea levels and changing weather patterns in locales that are not suited to deal with their associated impacts. Clear policies designed to address these problems have yet to be identified. Nevertheless, although the NDRF addresses presidentially declared disasters, key concepts such as pre-disaster planning guidance, the framework's eight core principles (12–14), and identified roles and responsibilities are intended to help support non-presidentially declared events (7–8). This represents an important departure from the Stafford Act and the NRF, which are principally focused on post-disaster policy and large-scale disasters. The Disaster Mitigation Act, which emphasizes pre-event planning, also has the potential to address the significant recovery challenges that can be anticipated in the future.

The draft NDRF discusses the importance of addressing unmet needs and the role of disaster recovery planners in doing so after a disaster. Those needs, which may be unique to rural and urban areas, include

- Mental and behavioral health support
- Transportation

- Long-term housing issues (emergency, transitional, and permanent)
- Child care and education
- Underinsured properties
- Affordability of housing repair and reconstruction
- Middle-income families whose needs may not be addressed by existing programs (53).

In its draft form, however, the NDRF does not adequately address the manner in which the larger assistance network—not just federal government agencies, private sector actors, and nonprofits—should assess local needs or coordinate available financial, technical, and policy-based resources. This requires a much more concerted effort to bring together the multitude of stakeholders involved in disaster recovery, including those that assume leadership roles before and after disasters. It also means recognizing that disaster recovery assistance networks vary over time and space and that any effort to solicit their involvement means identifying these temporal and geographic differences.

In an attempt to answer state and local critics who have complained that past federal disaster policy was developed without their input, the Long-Term Disaster Recovery Working Group held sixteen "listening sessions" across the United States to gather feedback from potential stakeholders (Figure 10–1). But listening sessions really do not reflect the deep two-way flow of information that is found in sustained public policy dialogue; rather, they tend to characterize more traditional bureaucratic methods as described by Douglas Amy[18] in Chapter 8, Exhibit 8–4. Alternative dispute resolution (ADR) techniques, designed to foster productive dialogue that more accurately reflects the needs and resources of stakeholder groups,[19] should

Figure 10–1. The White House Long-Term Disaster Recovery Working Group hosted this listening session on the National Disaster Recovery Framework.

Courtesy of FEMA.

be employed as part of a larger commitment to address the existing gap between local needs and available resources.

The draft NDRF has placed a greater emphasis on outreach by targeting members of the assistance network. To address the broad notion of outreach described in this book, actions should be taken to ensure that specific participatory processes (ADR, collaborative planning, and coalition building) are applied to policy formulation, plan development and implementation, and the construction of enduring coalitions composed of those groups with the technical, locally grounded, and procedural knowledge required to support planning while garnering the political backing needed to sustain a comprehensive approach to disaster recovery.

Enhance the Horizontal and Vertical Integration of Those Involved in Disaster Recovery

The NDRF emphasizes the vertical integration of federal, state, and local government agencies and stakeholder groups. This is evident in the proposed creation of federal, state, and local recovery positions and RSFs that focus on federal government agencies and, to a lesser extent, on nonprofits through NVOAD. It alludes, for instance, to the importance of working with states and local governments, nonprofits, and the private sector in the pre- and post-disaster environment to assist with disaster recovery planning and interorganizational coordination, incentivize the incorporation of hazard mitigation measures into recovery, and evaluate program effectiveness (24–27).

It also provides fuller descriptions of the efforts needed to foster strong horizontal integration at the community level or across the larger disaster recovery assistance network. Promoting inclusiveness; facilitating a unified communications strategy; working with affected communities to establish relevant recovery measures; and improving the coordination of federal funding to address gaps in aid, mitigate post-disaster conflict, and eliminate duplicative resource allocation are all discussed and are indicative of worthy pursuits (32–33).

Among the most noteworthy facets of the evolving policy framework is the more extensive discussion of pre- and post-disaster recovery planning. But while the development of recovery plans is seen as a way to achieve greater horizontal and vertical integration, as discussed in Chapters 1 and 8, the manner in which these plans are to be created remains unclear, and the pre-event resources needed to accomplish what amounts to an ongoing process are not identified. The proposed development of pre-disaster memoranda of understanding, the integration of existing planning initiatives, the creation of pre-event partnerships, and the formation of regionally based interagency steering committees are all good ideas for providing the resources needed to accomplish these and other recommendations described throughout this book.

Provide Adequate Resources to Develop and Implement Disaster Recovery Plans

The development of recovery plans requires an enhanced commitment on the part of the federal government to direct adequate funding, create and modify policies as needed, and deliver expanded technical assistance. But again, the means by which this can be accomplished remains unclear in the NDRF. Planning provides a procedural means to assist in the coordination of resources, but plans are only as effective as the support they receive from existing resource providers. Otherwise, members of the network may resort to the familiar tactic of providing assistance in isolation, which results in the creation of suboptimal strategies and undermines the standing and utility of recovery plans.

The designated pre- and post-disaster roles of the RSF for Community Planning and Capacity Building provides insight into what amounts to an expanded approach to planning for disaster recovery. As presented in the NDRF, pre-disaster activities are as follows:

- *Establishing clear leadership, coordination and decision-making structures at the tribal, state, and local levels.*
- *Developing pre-disaster partnerships to ensure engagement of all potential resources through the following methods:*
  - *Identifying and engaging stakeholders, including the general public, community leaders, and private sector.*
  - *Organizing connections to and interface with tribal, state, local, and federal governments.*
  - *Ensuring community participation of populations that have historically been under-served during the recovery process, including individuals with disabilities and others with access and functional needs, children, and the elderly.*
- *Testing and evaluating pre-disaster plans through seminars, workshops and exercises.*
- *Integrating pre-disaster recovery planning with other appropriate community planning, such as land use, hazard mitigation, accessibility for people with disabilities, and capital improvement planning.*
- *Identifying limitations in community recovery capacity and the means to supplement.*
- *Incorporating sustainability and accessibility throughout all phases of recovery into overall planning guidance.*
- *Developing communications tools that address an array of possible scenarios.*

- *Preparing pre-disaster Memoranda of Understanding as a way to establish early partnership, planning, and expectations.*
- *Developing and implementing long-term training and education as a tool for building recovery capacity and making it available to all other stakeholders (42–43).*

Similarly, key post-disaster activities are identified as follows:

- *Organizing recovery priorities and tasks through the use of a planning process by:*
  - *Assessing risk.*
  - *Evaluating the conditions and needs after a disaster.*
  - *Setting goals and objectives.*
  - *Identifying opportunities to build in future resilience through mitigation.*
  - *Identifying specific projects in areas of critical importance to the community's overall recovery.*
- *Using a process that is community-driven and locally-managed, designed to promote local decision-making and ownership of the recovery planning and implementation effort.*
- *Promoting inclusive and accessible outreach, working collaboratively with and through groups of people affiliated by geographic proximity, common interest, or similar situations to address issues affecting the well-being of those people.*
- *Incorporating considerations that include the concept of "growing smarter" as long-term recovery unfolds. This includes compliance with standards for accessible design and construction.*
- *Building partnerships among local agencies, jurisdictions, the state, tribal and federal governments.*
- *Providing well-defined activities and outcomes aimed at achieving recovery with schedule and milestones.*
- *Developing tools and metrics for evaluating progress against set goals, objectives, and milestones (46–47).*

The success of the NDRF depends on the ability of those who make up disaster recovery networks across the United States to support and embrace the federal government's efforts to advance a more proactive approach to disaster recovery. To accomplish the series of pre- and post-disaster activities identified above, an explicit set of capacity-building measures must be implemented. These measures span the three resource categories described in the disaster recovery assistance framework and are listed below.

Funding. The following positions and processes will require adequate levels of funding:

- Federal
  - Expand the National Long-Term Recovery Coordination Office staff needed to oversee expanded pre- and post-disaster roles.
  - Hire a national cadre of FRCs.
  - Provide financial support to sustain RSF teams across federal agencies.
  - Provide financial support needed to engage in pre- and post-disaster capacity-building initiatives, including the development of state and local recovery plans.
- State
  - Finance the hiring of a national cadre of SRCs.
  - Provide financial assistance needed to identify, assemble, and train state RSF cadres.
  - Provide funding needed to help develop state recovery plans, help develop local recovery plans, and manage post-disaster recovery operations.
- Local
  - Provide funding needed to support local DRMs.
  - Provide funding needed to support the development of pre-disaster recovery plans.
  - Provide funding (as required) to support local post-disaster recovery operations.
  - Provide the funding needed to support the development of local disaster recovery strike teams that can provide peer-to-peer assistance to other communities before and after disasters.

Technical Assistance. The following activities are necessary to help build and sustain the capacity of disaster recovery assistance networks:

- Develop a national training program in partnership with the Emergency Management Institute, professional associations, the academic community, and other members of disaster recovery assistance networks.
- Expand the number of university and college programs that offer hazards management degree programs, including courses in disaster recovery.
- Develop national disaster recovery strike teams (composed of members of assistance networks) that deliver pre- and post-disaster recovery assistance and guidance, including that which is focused on the application of planning and ADR techniques.

Policy. The following policy amendments are necessary to address underlying programmatic, legal, and decision-making problems:

- Continue to refine the NDRF in order to improve coordination, address local needs, and effectively distribute resources in a timely manner in accordance with greater input from members of assistance networks.
- Develop policies that support the emergence of leaders across assistance networks.
- Develop supporting state policies and laws that give federal, state, and local governments; quasi-governmental organizations; nonprofits; members of the private sector; international organizations and nations; emergent groups; individuals; and others, as identified, the opportunity, capacity, and authority needed to engage in collaborative pre-disaster recovery planning and the post-disaster distribution of resources.
- Expand existing state dispute resolution statutes to include the application of ADR techniques to pre- and post-disaster conflicts.
- Develop collaboratively derived policies that encourage improved levels of inter-organizational coordination, including international agreements and protocols.
- Modify the Disaster Mitigation Act to improve the connection between capacity-building initiatives (pre-event plans and identified hazard mitigation projects) and the realities and challenges of long-term recovery (implementing risk-reduction measures post-disaster).
- Create the DRA to mandate federal, state, and local disaster recovery planning; modify existing emergency management programs and the scope of plans; expand capacity-building efforts; support the construction of a disaster recovery coalition; and build a culture of disaster recovery.

Enhance the Standing of the National Disaster Recovery Framework

The NRF and the Stafford Act have not provided adequate guidance when it comes to long-term recovery. They have, however, shaped the manner in which the federal government and other members of the assistance network deal with presidentially declared disasters and their aftermath. The nonexistence of a coherent federal recovery policy together with an entrenched approach that is largely focused on the administration of post-disaster grant programs will require changing federal organizational culture as well as the multi-institutional culture of assistance networks. The ability to implement necessary changes, many of which are proposed in the NDRF, means ensuring that the NDRF is given the political and procedural support it needs to succeed.

After a lengthy discussion between FEMA and HUD as to which federal agency would lead long-term disaster recovery, it has been decided that FEMA will assume this role.[20] But while FEMA has been designated lead federal agency for disaster recovery, it is difficult to determine the degree to which FEMA and HUD officials support the expansion of recovery initiatives as they try to determine how to share the federal responsibilities associated with recovery and operationalize the emerging NDRF. The fact that the White House is also involved in the policy dialogue provides some evidence of political backing. However, the concept of political support should not be limited to political party or ideological beliefs; for instance, the liberal bias mistakenly associated with the concept of sustainable disaster recovery or a highly politicized Project Impact program has limited the construction of a broader, more enduring coalition.[21] Nor should the concept of political support be limited to members of the public sector, particularly as the details of the NDRF are drafted and responsibilities are assigned to various stakeholders.

The passage of the PKEMRA implies that Congress has taken note and expects improvements in how disaster recovery operations will be conducted. Working in concert with the PKEMRA, the NDRF should sharpen the argument for and the means for carrying out the broader goals of federal legislation. Like the Disaster Mitigation Act of 2000, which required the creation of state and local hazard mitigation plans, the 2006 PKEMRA amended the Stafford Act, requiring the creation of a disaster recovery strategy. One of the important lessons of the Disaster Mitigation Act that should be used to inform the creation of the proposed DRA is that more time needs to be invested in the early phases of the policy-making process to create a strong and diverse coalition comprising technical, procedural, and political actors who can support an approach that requires changing an entrenched policy subsystem.

For instance, ESF-14 has been understaffed and often dismissed by state emergency management agencies and some personnel within FEMA. The fact that most states have an individual or a team aligned with ESF-1 through ESF-13, but not with ESF-14, is telling. In an apparent recognition of this and other shortfalls, the NDRF states that the new policy framework will provide a more comprehensive approach tied to new recovery-specific "leadership elements, organizational structure, planning guidance and other components needed to coordinate continued recovery support to individuals, businesses and community" (6) (Figure 10–2).

The overreliance on contractors to do what amounts to a critical process-based initiative (e.g., disaster recovery planning) suggests that the federal government needs to revisit and amend this approach. The ability to carry out recommended improvements highlighted in the more recent NDRF will require a much greater commitment to federal, state, and local staffing as well as a duty to build the capacity of disaster recovery networks through training, education, and outreach efforts. The failure to provide the critical resources needed in both the pre- and post-disaster environments to achieve success could further weaken what remains a disjointed system. The most recent attempts to strengthen the disaster recovery assistance framework, as exemplified by the NDRF, also require clearly articulating how broad policy goals will be implemented at the local level through planning. Otherwise, skeptics will continue to try and define the emergency management profession as one largely dominated by a response orientation and the narrow implementation of uncoordinated grant programs during recovery operations.

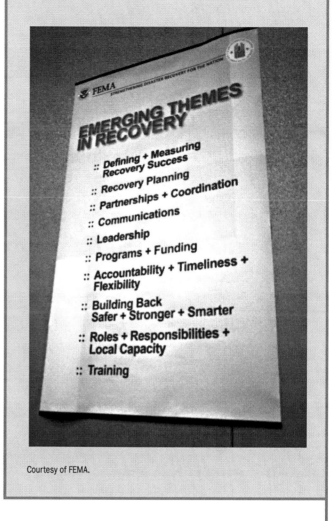

Figure 10–2. This banner highlights the "emerging themes" in the National Disaster Recovery Framework.

Courtesy of FEMA.

FINAL THOUGHTS AND A REVIEW OF RECOMMENDATIONS AIMED AT STRENGTHENING THE U.S. DISASTER RECOVERY ASSISTANCE FRAMEWORK

The suggested improvements to the draft NDRF emphasize the need to operationalize the broad objectives and concepts described. The ability to create specific guidance that enables the assistance network to act in a more coordinated manner is a logical next step and one that the federal government should pursue. To achieve these ends, the proposed DRA has merit because existing authorities spelled out under the Stafford Act and the proposed NDRF are not sufficient to address fundamental problems. Creating clear guidance and standards that can be evaluated and linked to accreditation procedures accepted by the emergency management and broader hazards management community represents a start in building the supportive coalition needed to sustain what amounts to a change in the way the United States confronts long-term recovery.

The formulation of enabling rules and legislation under the proposed DRA provides a unique opportunity to employ planning and ADR techniques early in the process to further refine guidance that is grounded in research, practice, and the experiences of different stakeholders, including those traditionally left out of the decision-making process. Accomplishing these ends requires reaching out to all members of the assistance network to engage in a meaningful, sustained dialogue. It also calls for attention to the lessons from hazards management policy and program venues, including the NRF, Project Impact, the Disaster Mitigation Act, the Emergency Management Assistance Compact, and the Emergency Management Accreditation Program.

The proposed DRA is intended to give members of disaster recovery assistance networks greater standing while providing the tools needed to create enabling rules—not in the narrow sense, but rather as a set of more clearly defined operational principles that are developed collaboratively and enacted as law. The policy formulation process should include (1) an assessment of the number and quality of existing recovery plans in the nation today; (2) the application of a mandated recovery planning program; (3) the creation and maintenance of leadership initiatives; (4) the modification and expansion of existing emergency management programs and the scope of plans; (5) the establishment of an enduring national recovery coalition; and (6) the development of greater local self-reliance and accountability of disaster recovery assistance networks.

The "who's in charge" rhetoric that often follows an event does not capture the essence of the issues surrounding disaster recovery, including the diffuse nature of assistance networks. Most of the stakeholders in disaster recovery—the private sector, nonprofits, quasi-governmental organizations, other nations, individuals, and emergent groups—do not report to government agencies. In fact, many see themselves as an alternative to perceived public sector incompetence.

Instead of building local self-reliance and collective strength, federal disaster recovery policy has created a sense of dependency among state and local governments and a system in which others in the network are reacting to the limitations of public sector policy rather than playing an active role in shaping the formulation of a strategy that maximizes the pre- and post-disaster delivery of resources. This reality speaks to the critically important idea that policy should focus on the pre-event development and nurturing of collaborative leadership. Federal agencies, including those recognized in the NDRF, must be given the resources needed to undertake what amounts to a significantly modified set of responsibilities.

Solutions to the criticisms of the disaster recovery assistance framework can be addressed through the use of collaborative planning techniques, including ADR. The federal government should expand its role to include the functions of mediator and facilitator in both the pre- and post-disaster environments. This should be among the most pressing priorities of federal agencies involved in recovery and should be integrated into their daily operations. The application of ADR techniques should also span the assistance networks; they should be used as part of larger pre-event capacity-building efforts discussed throughout this book and tied to existing collaborative operations described in Chapter 9 in order to help address the inherently conflict-laden post-disaster distribution and management of resources.

Both pre- and post-disaster teams of public and private sector representatives, nonprofits, community organizations, and others have taken on the role of coordinator on a piecemeal and adaptive basis, as the sidebars throughout this book have shown. In each case, collaboration proved critical to achieving a successful recovery. Success stories described in this book were also largely achieved after a disaster had occurred. The fact remains that it proved difficult to identify many examples of good pre-event recovery planning. Therefore, any attempt to expand a predominantly reactive enterprise, including nurturing a nationwide culture of pre-event planning for post-disaster recovery, requires (1) providing the tools necessary to succeed, (2) developing a supportive, yet flexible policy framework that reflects the diversity and dynamism of different disaster assistance networks over time and space, (3) documenting successes and conveying the benefits of these examples to a broad audience as part of an ongoing educational endeavor, and (4) modifying the framework in accordance with feedback from those in the network.

The recommendations listed in Exhibit 10–2 (on page 400), reassembled from earlier chapters, include those that target specific members of the disaster recovery assistance network, those that address planning-related issues, and those that help to define the nature of the DRA. Their reassembly here is intended to help the reader assimilate the findings of the assessment while providing further information worthy of a more focused policy dialogue that includes all members of the disaster recovery assistance network. While the recommendations represent a scathing critique and a daunting challenge, necessary improvements can be accomplished and these recommendations can play a role in this transformation.

From a review of these recommendations, several important proposals emerge:

Exhibit 10–2. Summary of Recommendations

Chapter 2: Public Sector
- Alter the culture of state and local dependence
- Increase the commitment of the public sector to engage in pre-event planning for post-disaster recovery
- Enhance local capacity, self-reliance, and accountability

Chapter 3: Quasi-Governmental and Nongovernmental Organizations
- Apply the capabilities of quasi-governmental organizations to pre-event planning
- Maximize the contributions of nongovernmental organizations through existing and proposed organizational venues

Chapter 4: Nonprofit Relief Organizations
- Create an intergovernmental culture that capitalizes on the strengths of nonprofit organizations in the disaster recovery assistance framework
- Apply the principles of the Council on Foundations to the disaster recovery assistance framework
- Improve the horizontal and vertical integration of US-based nonprofits into the disaster recovery assistance network through planning

Chapter 5: Private Sector
- Include developers, design professionals, consultants, and other private sector stakeholders in recovery planning
- Expand the role of media representatives and organizations
- Enhance public-private partnerships focused on disaster recovery

Chapter 6: International Community
- Incorporate lessons from the international community
- Institutionalize international assistance through recognized agreements and treaties
- Modify U.S. domestic and international relief policies and programs to facilitate the receipt of foreign assistance before and after disasters
- Institutionalize lessons through cross-cultural study and policy analysis

- Establish a clear nexus between planning and international assistance

Chapter 7: Individuals and Emergent Groups
- Incorporate individual and family preparedness activities into disaster recovery operations
- Develop pre-disaster plans that integrate individuals and emergent groups into disaster recovery operations

Chapter 8: Planning for Recovery
- Develop a recovery planning approach rooted in collaboration and learning
- Build federal, state, and local government recovery planning capacity
- Actively engage the professional planning community in disaster recovery

Chapter 9: The Disaster Recovery Act
- Conduct a national audit of state and local disaster recovery plans
- Mandate recovery planning and the use of dispute resolution techniques
- Establish collaborative leadership initiatives
- Develop an education, training, and outreach agenda
- Establish a national recovery coalition
- Modify existing emergency management programs and the scope of plans
- Enhance local self-reliance and accountability: create a culture of planning for recovery

Chapter 10: National Disaster Recovery Framework
- Establish clear plan guidance
- Clarify the roles and the timing of assistance (pre and post-event)
- Improve the integration of hazard mitigation processes and techniques
- Improve the pre- and post-event assessment of local needs and available resources
- Enhance the horizontal and vertical integration of those involved in disaster recovery
- Provide adequate resources to develop and implement disaster recovery plans
- Enhance the standing of the National Disaster Recovery Framework

1. Foster an inclusionary process during the formulation of national policy, throughout the disaster recovery planning process, and the during the distribution of pre- and post-disaster resources.
2. Develop pre-event "collaborative conditions" that allow for different members of disaster recovery assistance networks to play varied, yet coordinated roles in disaster recovery.
3. Develop recovery plans based on sound information derived from across the network.
4. Recognize network diversity and reflect it in pre-event planning and post-event actions.
5. Build the capacity of networks to engage in pre-event planning, consensus building, and the formation of enduring coalitions.

This book has sought to describe and critique disaster recovery as practiced in the United States and to offer a series of recommendations that address identified weaknesses. The dimensions of the disaster recovery assistance framework—the existing disconnectedness between local needs and available resources, the timing of assistance, and low levels of horizontal and vertical integration—can benefit from the development of pre-event plans and informed post-event actions. The emergence of the NDRF and its promising evolution provide hope that the federal government is finally addressing what is still a broken system. The proposed DRA, with its emphasis on planning for recovery, the application of ADR techniques, and the modification of existing programs, will provide the means to operationalize the NDRF and give members of disaster recovery assistance networks the resources they need to undertake this difficult, but critically important process.

EPILOGUE

As this book was going to press, I had a conversation with Craig Fugate, the FEMA administrator, who stated his belief that the NDRF would be ready for final publication in the summer of 2011. Rather than wait for that final version to be published, we decided to go to press with this book. From informal conversations with Administrator Fugate and FEMA staff, it appears that some of the larger concerns I noted in this book and some of the specific details associated with the draft NDRF have been addressed in the final version. Of course, the devil is in the details, and the ability to clearly operationalize and coordinate the many tasks that span members of disaster recovery assistance networks remain to be seen. But by all accounts, the NRDF is a significant improvement over the largely disjointed and dysfunctional system that currently exists.

As a result of her constituents' experiences after Hurricane Katrina, Senator Mary Landrieu of Louisiana, a member of the U.S. Senate Committee on Homeland Security and Government Affairs and the chair of the Disaster Recovery Subcommittee, has strongly advocated for amendments to the Robert T. Stafford Disaster Relief and Emergency Assistance Act. A draft version of a bill tentatively titled "The Disaster Recovery Act" includes many of the issues raised in this book and represents further evidence that support for a national recovery policy is gaining traction. The monitoring of the bill's progress through Congress, its potential passage, and the creation of a strong implementation component will provide an important barometer of the degree to which the federal government is serious about the endemic problems identified in the disaster recovery assistance framework. Thus the question remains, can the federal government create effective policies and support them with the resources and pre-event capacity-building initiatives necessary to create the conditions that allow leaders to emerge and collaborative partnerships to thrive?

Endnotes

1   U.S. Senate, Committee on Homeland Security and Governmental Affairs, Ad Hoc Subcommittee on State, Local, and Private Sector Preparedness and Integration, *The Next Big Disaster: Is the Private Sector Prepared?*, 111th Cong., 2nd sess., testimony of Stephen Flynn, "Building a More Resilient Nation by Strengthening Private-Public Partnerships," March, 4, 2010), www.centerfornationalpolicy.org/ht/display/ContentDetails/i/17679; U.S. Senate, Committee on Homeland Security and Governmental Affairs, letter to Homeland Security Secretary Janet Napolitano, 111th Cong., 2nd sess., February 26, 2010.

2   U.S. Government Accountability Office (GAO), *Disaster Recovery: FEMA's Long-term Assistance Was Helpful to State and Local Governments but Had Some Limitations*, GAO-10-404 (Washington, D.C., March 2010); Robert B. Olshansky, "Planning after Hurricane Katrina," *Journal of the American Planning Association* 72, no. 2 (2006): 147–153; Robert B. Olshansky et al., "Planning for the Rebuilding of New Orleans," *Journal of the American Planning Association* 74, no. 3 (2008): 273–287; Gavin Smith and Dennis Wenger, "Sustainable Disaster Recovery: Operationalizing an Existing Agenda," in *Handbook of Disaster Research*, ed. Havidan Rodriguez, Enrico L. Quarantelli, and Russell Dynes, 234–257 (New York: Springer, 2006); Bruce C. Glavovic, "Sustainable Coastal Communities in the Age of Costal Storms: Reconceptualising Coastal Planning as 'New' Naval Architecture," *Journal of Coastal Conservation* 12, no. 3 (2008): 125–134; Mark G. Welsh and Ann-Margaret Esnard, "Closing Gaps in Local Housing Recovery Planning for Disadvantaged Displaced Households," *Cityscape: A Journal of Policy Development and Research* 11, no. 3 (2009): 195–212.

3   Fernando Costa et al., *Charting the Course for Rebuilding a Great American City: An Assessment of the Planning Function in Post-Katrina New Orleans* (Chicago: American Planning Association, 2005); Monteic A. Sizer, "Voices: Stimulus Dollars Should go to Recovery Preparedness," Institute for Southern Studies guest blogger, February 18, 2009, www.southernstudies.org/2009/02/voices-louisiana-should-focus-on-recovery-preparedness-when-spending-stimulus-dollars.html; Richard P. Nathan and Marc Landy, *Disaster Recovery. Who's in Charge? Who Should Be? The Role of Federal Government in Megadisasters: Based on Lessons from Hurricane Katrina* (Albany, N.Y.: Nelson A. Rockefeller Institute of Government, June 2, 2009), www.rockinst.org.

4   Long-Term Disaster Recovery Working Group, National Disaster Recovery Framework (draft, February 5, 2010), www.fema.gov/pdf/recoveryframework/omb_ndrf.pdf.

5   Carlos Monje, presentation given at the National Leadership Exercise on Disaster Recovery, White House Domestic Policy Council, Washington, D.C., April 7, 2010.

6   Smith and Wenger, "Sustainable Disaster Recovery."

7   U.S. Senate, Committee on Homeland Security and Governmental Affairs, letter to Homeland Security Secretary Janet Napolitano, 111th Cong., 2nd sess., February 26, 2010, available at hsgac.senate.gov/public/index.cfm?FuseAction=Press.MajorityNews&ContentRecord_id= 1badde58-5056-8059-7655-3bddd99e5015.

8   Ibid.

9   Federal Emergency Management Agency (FEMA), *Long-Term Community Recovery Planning Process: A Self-Help Guide* (December 2005), www.fema.gov/library/viewRecord.do?id=2151.

10 Jim Schwab et al., *Planning for Post-Disaster Recovery and Reconstruction,* Planning Advisory Service (PAS) Report 483/484 (Chicago: American Planning Association, 1998); FEMA update, March 2009.

11 Florida Department of Community Affairs, Florida Division of Emergency Management, *Post-Disaster Redevelopment Planning: A Guide for Florida Communities* (2010), www.dca.state.fl.us/fdcp/dcp/ PDRP/Files/PDRPGuide.pdf.

12 Senate Committee on Homeland Security and Government Affairs, letter to Janet Napolitano.

13 Eugene Haas, Robert W. Kates, and Martyn J. Bowden, *Reconstruction following Disaster* (Cambridge: MIT Press, 1977).

14 Senate Committee on Homeland Security and Government Affairs, letter to Janet Napolitano.

15 Gavin Smith, "Disaster-Resilient Communities: A New Hazards Risk Management Framework," in *Natural Hazards Analysis: Reducing the Impact of Disasters,* ed. John Pine, 249–267 (Washington, D.C.: Taylor Francis, 2009), 256.

16 Senate Committee on Homeland Security and Government Affairs, letter to Janet Napolitano.

17 FEMA, National Disaster Recovery Program Database, asd.fema.gov/inter/ndhpd/public/home.htm.

18 Douglas Amy, "Mediation versus Traditional Political Institutions," in *The Politics of Environmental Mediation* (New York: Columbia University Press, 1987), 27.

19 Ibid.; Ray Kemp, "Planning, Public Hearings, and the Politics of Discourse," in *Critical Theory and Public Life,* ed. John Forester, 177–201 (Cambridge: MIT Press, 1985); Judith Innes and David Booher, "Reframing Public Participation: Strategies for the 21st Century," *Planning Theory and Practice* 5, no. 4 (2004): 419–436.

20 Author's conversation with Craig Fugate, FEMA administrator, March 31, 2011.

21 Smith and Wenger, "Sustainable Disaster Recovery," 252, 254.

Postscript

The demolition of Bayshore Elementary, the school I attended as a youth. The school, which was severely damaged by Hurricane Ike, has been relocated several miles inland.

Source: FEMA.

Interior image of my childhood home following Hurricane Ike.

Photo by Gavin Smith.

During the writing of this book, Hurricane Ike struck my hometown of Shoreacres, Texas. Witnessing the destruction of this small coastal town was particularly troubling as many of the homes in my old neighborhood have since been demolished. Three years after the storm, vacant lots dot the area where homes once stood. Many homeowners remain uncertain of their future. This represents an all too common post-disaster condition that merits serious attention. It is hoped that the information in the preceding pages can play a small part in reducing what has become a routine occurrence, while serving as a personal and professional request to tackle identified weaknesses in our current approach to disaster recovery so that in the future our nation is better prepared to address the challenges described in this book.

Index

Note: An "e" following a page number indicates an exhibit and "f" indicates a figure.

Absorptive capacity, 198–199

Accountability, 291

Accreditation programs, 360–363, 362e, 397

Additionality, 227

Adirondack Park Agency, 82

Administrative capabilities, 286–287

ADR techniques. *See* Alternative dispute resolution (ADR) techniques

Advocacy Coalition Framework (ACF), 340

After Katrina: Building Back Better Than Ever, 183

Agriculture, 41e

Alaska Earthquake (1964), 92

Albala-Bertrand, J.M., 208

Aldrich, Daniel, 333

Alternative dispute resolution (ADR) professionals, 294

  "appropriate representation" in, 341

  National Disaster Recovery Framework and, 390–391

Alternative dispute resolution (ADR) techniques, 6, 28, 90, 265–266, 276e, 292, 399

  applying to disaster recovery, 296–307

  benefits of, 300–301

  confidentiality and, 331

  facilitation, 295

  fact base clarification, 301

  incentives to participate/share information, 299–300

  mandating use of, 328–332

  mediation, 295, 302–303

  negotiated rule making, 295–296

  negotiation, 297–298

  principles of, 293

  repeated interaction/reciprocal dialogue, 296, 299–300

  traditional dispute resolution drawbacks, 294e

Alternative Housing Research Guide, 97–98

American Institute of Architects, 85

American Institute of Certified Planners (AICP), 363

American Planning Association (APA), 85, 207

  American Institute of Certified Planners, 363

  Natural Hazards Division, 113, 114e

  Natural Hazards Planning Division, 314, 363

  North Carolina chapter, 132

The American Red Cross, 130, 131, 138, 142

American Society of Civil Engineers, 85

AmeriCorps, 295

Amy, Douglas, 390

Analytical tractability, 342

Anderson, Mary B., 52, 218

Appalachian Trail, 82

Applied research, 110

Arnstein, Sherry, 306

Asian Disaster Preparedness Center (ADPC), 210–211

Assessment of Research on Natural Hazards, 91

Assistance distribution strategy, 300–301

Association of Bay Area Governments Disaster Recovery Initiative, 84

Association of State Floodplain Managers, 85, 103

> "No Adverse Impact" campaign, 109

Bam, Iran earthquake (2003), 196

Bangladesh, 197

Barbour, Haley, 2*f*

Barksdale, James, 182

Bartholomew, Harlan, 82

Barton, Clara, 131

Bates, Frederick, 12

BATNA (best alternative to a negotiated agreement), 307

Beatley, Timothy, 16

Berke, Philip, 16, 22–23, 25, 199*f*

Bernstein, Abram, 134

Best alternative to a negotiated agreement (BATNA), 307

Birkland, Thomas, 106, 186, 343

Blanco, Kathleen, 39, 135

Bolin, Robert, 69, 202, 241

Bolton, Patricia, 202, 241

Bonds, 81

Booher, David, 293, 308, 344

Bowden, Martyn, 60, 387

Broadmoor Improvement Association, 260*f*, 291, 303

Broadmoor Project, 23, 308

> community development plan, 120*e*

> community model, 121, 122

"Partner Network," 117*e*

> planning process, 116–121

Building moratoriums, 279

Burby, Ray, 106

Bush, George H. W., 39

Bush, George W., 38, 39, 200, 203

Bush-Clinton Katrina Fund, 135

Business continuity planning, 363–365

California earthquake program, 92

Call Kinston Home, 65

Cannon Beach (Oregon) Pilot Program, 335

Capability assessment, 285–287

Capability Assessment for Readiness (CAR), 360–361

Carter, Jimmy, 38

Case study: Broadmoor Project, 116–122

Catastrophic planning scenarios, 231

Charlotte-Mecklenburg County (North Carolina), 303

> Floodplain Mapping Program, 188, 269–271, 275

> Stormwater Services, 269–270

Charrettes, 87, 90, 296

Chilean earthquake (2010), 196, 198*f*

Ciborowski, Adolf, 4

Citizen Corps, 366

Citizen power, 306

Clean Water Act of 1977, 80

Climate change, 199, 224, 225, 378

> adaptation plans, 230–231

Clinton, Bill, 39, 84

Cluster development, 80

Coalition building, 338–344

Coastal adaptation strategies, 231

"Coastal element" in Florida planning, 53

Coastal erosion, 200*f*

Codes. *See* Regulations and codes

Collaborative governance culture, 340

Collaborative leadership initiatives, 332–334, 333, 334

Collaborative planning principles, 340

Collaborative planning techniques, 307–309, 399

Colleges and universities, 91, 96, 99–100

    Disaster Recovery Act proposal for, 356–359

    horizontal and vertical integration, 109–111

    land-grant, 110

    timing of assistance, 107

    understanding local needs, 104–106

Common-interest communities, 79–80

Communications, 41e, 301

Communities

    greenbelt, 82

    long-term community recovery, 43e

    reactive approach to recovery and, 3–5

    transformation of self-reliance in high-hazard, 103

Community Development Block Grants, 83

Community development corporations, 78–79, 111, 148

    pre-event planning capabilities, 112

    timing of assistance, 106

    understanding local needs, 101

Community Development Financial Institution Fund, 79

Community emergency response and recovery teams (CERRTs), 366

Community emergency response teams (CERTs), 101, 366–367

Community needs

    Gulf Coast Community Design Studio and, 94–98

    identification of, 389

Community organizations, 134, 137–138

Community Planning and Capacity Building, 382e, 392

Community Rating System, 149

Comprehensive emergency management plan (CEMP), 53, 349, 350e, 352–353

Comprehensive plans, 349, 350e, 351–352

Conditionality, 227

Congress for the New Urbanism, 343

Contractors, 396–397

Convergence, 49–50

Coolidge, Calvin, 39

Cooperative extension services, 110

Cooperative State Research, Education, and Extension Service, 110

Coordinated assistance delivery, 141

Council on Foundations and principles of disaster management, 136, 137, 151

Cross-cultural research, 229–230, 232

Cuba, 201–202

Cultural resources, 382e

Cumulative substantial damage ordinance, 279

Delta Urbanism, 207

Department of Homeland Security (DHS), 199

Dependable Affordable Sustainable Homes, 104

Detention areas, 80

Developing countries. See also International community

    assistance for, 240–241

    disaster recovery lessons, 197

    international relief organizations, 196

    pre-event capacity building, 219

    timing of assistance/government improvisation, 197

Dewey, John, 95

Deyle, Robert, 51

Disaster assistance distribution strategy, 300–301

Disaster assistance employees, 46

Disaster diplomacy, 201–202, 219

Disaster Mitigation Act (2000), 40, 82, 149, 189, 230–231, 258, 268, 272–273, 354, 358, 364, 378, 388–389
    Pre-Disaster Mitigation Program, 184
    programs under, 64
    relief programs under, 64, 66–67
    state/local assistance, 68–69
    supplemental emergency funding, 66–67

Disaster myths, 247

Disaster recovery. *See also* Planning
    auditing state/local plans for, 323–326, 325*d*
    collaborative leadership initiatives, 332–334
    conflict and cooperation, 266–268
    defined, 6, 12
    earthquakes and, 92–93
    failure to plan for, 1–2
    lack of integrative policy framework, 268, 272–274
    mandating ADR to address conflict, 328–332
    mandating state/local planning, 326–328
    negative cycle of, 23
    social/political change and, 12–13
    value of pre-event planning in, 272
    vision statement, 276–277, 278*f*

Disaster Recovery Act proposals, 314
    accreditation programs, 360–363, 362*e*
    alternative dispute resolution, 328–332
    assess/modify emergency management programs, 345–367
    audit state/local recovery plans, 323–326
    collaborative leadership initiatives, 332–334
    collaborative planning process in, 344
    college and university programs, 356–359
    Community Emergency Response Team (CERT), 366–367
    comprehensive emergency management plan (CEMP), 349, 350*e*, 352–353
    comprehensive plans, 349, 350*e*, 351–352
    education/training/outreach agenda, 334–338
    Emergency Management Assistance Compact, 355–356
    enhance local self-reliance/accountability, 367–370
    establish national recovery coalition, 338–344
    hazard mitigation plans, 349, 350*e*, 353–355, 353*e*
    international relief organizations and nations, 365–366
    mandate state/local planning, 326–328
    National Voluntary Organizations Active in Disasters, 359–360
    NDRF and, 379
    planning authorities, 351*e*
    recommendations summary, 400*e*
    state and local plans, 349–355

Disaster recovery assistance framework. *See also* Disaster Mitigation Act (2000)
    accountability and, 367–370
    addressing challenges of, 321–323
    creation of, 2

horizontal and vertical integration, 23–26, 25*e,* 69–70

individuals and emergent groups within, 244–255

new urbanism and, 87–90

principal dimensions of, 266

timing of assistance, 16–23, 17*e,* 20*e,* 60–69

transforming, 26–30, 27*e*

understanding local needs, 13–16, 14*e,* 55–60, 100–106

Disaster recovery assistance strike teams, 337–338

Disaster recovery committee, 52, 52*e,* 279

Disaster recovery plans, 349–351, 392–395

Disaster Reduction and Recovery Program, 210

Disaster relief-recovery gap, 217

Disaster Research Center typology of organized responses, 253

Disaster Resistant Business Council, 148–149

Disaster-Resistant Universities, 110

Discrimination, 333

Dispute resolution techniques, 227

Double loop mutual learning, 308

Drabek, Thomas, 243, 254

Drucker, Peter, 132

Dutch Dialogues, 206–207, 233, 365

Dyer, Christopher, 60

Earthquakes, 83. *See also* specific location of

importance of pre-event preparedness, 284

National Earthquake Hazard Reduction Program, 92

zoning and, 92

East Biloxi. *See* Gulf Coast Community Design Studio

Economic development, 382*e*

Economic Development Administration assistance, 60

EDEN (Extension Disaster Education Network), 111

Education

developing agenda for, 334

emergency management degrees, 99

pre-event seminars, 311

Emergence concept, 254

Emergency and restoration phase, 51

Emergency assistance, 41*e*

Emergency housing. *See* Housing, emergency

Emergency management, 41*e*

accreditation standards, 362*e*

proposed Disaster Recovery Act and, 345–367

regional approach to, 81–82

Emergency Management Accreditation Program (EMAP), 362–363

Emergency Management Assistance Compact (EMAC), 47–48, 89, 104, 115, 222, 233, 299, 355–356

Emergency Management Institute Higher Education Project, 99

Emergency Management Performance Grant, 103

Emergency Management Reform Act, 90

Emergency Response Division (ERD), 210

Emergency Support Function 14, Long-Term Community Recovery, 84, 89, 229, 272

long-term community recovery process diagram, 368*e*

Emergency support functions (ESFs), 40, 41*e*

Emergent groups, 139

dimensions of disaster recovery assistance framework, 245–255 within disaster recovery assistance framework, 244–245

gaps in assistance addressed by, 242–244

horizontal and vertical integration, 251–255

integrating with individuals, 259

recommendations summary, 400e

timing of assistance, 248–252

understanding local needs, 246–248

The Enabling Project, 106

Energy, 43e

Enterprise Community Partners, 79

Environmental damage assessment, 284

Environmental degradation, 227

Environmental Diplomacy: Negotiating More Effective Global Agreements (Susskind), 227

Environmental groups, 128, 132–133

Environmentally sensitive areas, 283

Environmental racism, 133

Erosion, 200f

ESF-14. See Emergency Support Function 14, Long-Term Community Recovery

Esnard, Ann-Margaret, 152

Exclusion, 138

Expanding organizations, 253

Experience and Nature (Dewey), 95

Extending organizations, 253

Extension Disaster Education Network (EDEN), 111, 358

External affairs, 43e

Facilitation, 295

Faith-based relief groups, 131–132, 139, 253

Fannie Mae, 104

Fargo-Moorhead Area Foundation, 135

Faupel, Charles, 52

Federal Action Plan for Recovery, 84

Federal coordination officers (FCOs), 322, 381

Federal disaster declarations

damages and per capita thresholds, 215–216

local needs and prescriptive nature of, 12

Red River flooding, 84

Federal disaster recovery policy, 398

Federal Emergency Management Agency (FEMA)

allocation dispute following Hurricane Floyd, 297–298

Disaster-Resistant Universities, 110

earthquakes and, 92

emergency housing and, 87

ESF-14, 89, 115, 272, 311–312, 336, 337, 347–349, 368

Hazard Mitigation Grant Program, 57, 61, 63–64, 64f, 83, 184, 270, 288, 354

Inspector General office, 298

Long-Term Community Recovery Program, 339f

long-term disaster recovery and, 396

National Disaster Recovery Program Database, 389

on-call recovery contracts, 164

personnel, 46–47

Project Impact, 110, 148, 181, 184–185, 363–365, 383

Red Cross and, after Katrina, 142

state recovery planning coordinators, 348

team members and findings, 115

understanding local needs, 138

Federal government agencies, 37–42. See also specific agency

current disaster policy, 37–40

isolationism and, 37

Federal home mortgage insurance, 80

Federal Housing Authority (FHA), 80

Federal recovery coordinators (FRCs), 380

Federal roles in recovery, 380

FEMA. *See* Federal Emergency Management Agency (FEMA)

Financial assistance/funding, 12

    avoiding over-dependence on, 214

    federal, 38, 40

    foundations and, 135–136, 151–152

    for hazards research, 91

    local assistance, 69–70

    National Disaster Recovery Framework and, 393–394

    of pre-event capacity building programs, 229

    providers of, 15

    regional planning organizations and grants, 83

    state agencies, 45–46, 68–69

    supplemental emergency, 66–67

Financial institutions, 166–167, 211–212

Financial Management Support Annex, 220

Firefighting, 41*e*

Flatt, Victor, 275

Flood-hazard reduction programs, 147

Flooding

    in Charlotte, North Carolina, 269

    compact urban form design and, 90

    detention areas and, 80

    following Hurricane Floyd, 56–57, 132

    Midwestern, early 1990s, 135

    in Tulsa, Oklahoma, 146–149

Flood insurance, 103, 149

Flood insurance rate maps (FIRMs), 87, 269

Flood Mitigation Assistance Program, 64

Florida

    experimental recovery planning program, 273

    Hillsborough County Post-Disaster Redevelopment Plan, 53–54

    Post-Disaster Redevelopment Plan, 44, 47, 353

    recovery strike teams, 104

Florida Conflict Resolution Consortium, 295

Fondo Hondureño de Inversión Social, 197

Fordham, Maureen, 196

Fore, Henrietta H., 230

Foreign assistance

    absorptive capacity, 198–199

    conditionality, 200

    convergence, 202–203

    database for tracking, 221

    disaster diplomacy, 201–202

    mismatched assistance, 203–204

    need for information sharing, 204, 219

Forester, John, 299, 308

For-profit organizations. *See* Private sector organizations

Foundations, 135–136, 140, 141

406 Public Assistance program, 62, 288

Freudenberg, William, 341

Fritz, Charles, 106

Fruili, Italy earthquake (1976), 196

Fugate, Craig, 401

Funding. *See* Financial assistance/funding

Gated communities, 102, 103

Gawronski, Vincent, 340

Geipel, Robert, 196

Geographic information system (GIS), 281, 282

Global issues. *See* International community

Godschalk, David, 276, 286

Government organizations. *See also* Quasi-governmental organizations
    federal, 37–42
    local, 49–55, 52*e*
    politics of disaster, 38
    state, 46–49
Governor's Commission on Recovery, Rebuilding and Renewal (Mississippi), 181, 182–183
Grants, 63
    regional planning organizations and, 83
    timing of, 141
Grassroots nonprofits, 134
Great California Shakeout, 92–93, 284, 300
Greenbelt communities, 82
Greenhouse gas emissions, 225–227
Greensburg, Kansas recovery plan, 337
"Growth machine," 86
Gujarat, India earthquake (2001), 195–196
Gulf Coast Community Design Studio, 94–98, 145, 145*f*, 291, 343
    Alternative Housing Research Guide, 97–98
    information dissemination, 95–97
    Main Street Neighborhood Study, 97
    mission of, 94–95
    Renaissance Builder and Developer Guild, 98

Haas, Eugene, 60, 387
Haiti earthquake (2010), 196
Hazard areas
    "H Transect" designation, 90
    New Urbanists and, 89–90
    socially constructed vulnerability, 240
Hazard mitigation, 148, 149, 258

capacity building and, in Vietnam, 197
    improving processes of, 387–389
    initiatives, 102
    partnerships, 143
    plan, 349, 350*e*, 353–355, 353*e*
    political awareness of, 358
Hazard Mitigation Assistance (HMA) program, 64–65
Hazard Mitigation Grant Program, 57, 61, 63–64, 64*f*, 83, 184, 270, 288, 354
Hazard Mitigation Technical Assistance Program, 189
Hazardous materials response, 41*e*
Hazard Reduction and Recovery Center, 99*f*
Hazards management
    collaborative operations in, 345*e*
    colleges/universities and, 91
    history of, 82
Hazards Planning Research Center, 314
Healey, Patsy, 340
Health, social, and community services, 382*e*
Higher education. *See* Colleges and universities
Higher Education Project, 99
Higher Ground: A Report on Voluntary Property Buyouts in the Nation's Floodplains (NWF), 132
Hillsborough County (Florida) Post-Disaster Redevelopment Plan, 53–54, 188
Hoffman, Susanna, 241
Homeowners associations, 79–80
    horizontal and vertical integration, 108
    pre-event planning capabilities, 112
    timing of assistance, 106
    understanding local needs, 101–102
Honduras hurricanes, 197

Hoover, Herbert, 39

Horizontal integration, 23–24

Housing
emergency, 87, 90, 217*f,* 382*e*
post-disaster construction, 143*f*

Housing and Employment Leading People to Success (HELPS), 65

Housing and human services, 41*e*

Housing and Urban Development (HUD), 79

"H Transect," 90

Hughes, Karen, 200

Hurricane Andrew, 39
assistance from Economic Development Administration, 60
follow-up study, 5

Hurricane Danny, 269

Hurricane Floyd
North Carolina's disaster recovery assistance programs, 56–58
post-disaster resource allocation disputes, 297–298

Hurricane Fran, 65

Hurricane Gilbert, 144

Hurricane Hugo, 144, 223

Hurricane Ike, 405

Hurricane Katrina
Biloxi memorial, 21*f*
conditionality and, 200
Dutch Dialogues, 206–207
failed disaster diplomacy, 201
failed response and recovery programs, 379
ineffective leadership following, 39
Louisiana Disaster Recovery Foundation and, 135
mediation training following, 295
Memorial in Biloxi, Mississippi, 21*f*
mismatched assistance, 203

Mississippi Governor's Commission, 24

Mississippi Renewal Forum, 87–89, 183

post-disaster housing, 87–88

professional associations in recovery following, 104

recovery breakdown, 5

successful assistance delivery, 204

unresponsiveness of federal government following, 39

U.S. disaster recovery assistance framework and, 229

Hurricane Katrina Task Force, 220–221, 222

Hurricane Mitch, 197

Hurricanes. *See also* specific hurricane
climate change and, 225

Hyogo Framework for Action, 226

Incident annexes, 40

Incident Command System, 104

India earthquake (2001, Gujarat), 195–196, 333

Indian Ocean tsunami of 2004, 196

Individual Assistance program, 61

Individuals and assistance
conclusions/recommendations, 255–261, 400*e*
within disaster recovery assistance framework, 244–245
gaps in assistance addressed by, 242–244
horizontal and vertical integration, 251–255
integrating with emergent groups, 259
multiorganizational networks, 256
redefining individuals, 240–242
timing of assistance, 248–251

understanding local needs, 246–248

Information dissemination, 181, 299–300

Infrastructure restoration, 279, 382e

Innes, Judith, 293, 308, 344

Institutional racism, 307

Institutional recovery, 242

Insurance, 80, 167–169, 168f

International Assistance System Concept of Operations (IAS CONOPS), 220

International Association of Emergency Managers, 90, 360

International Bank for Reconstruction and Development, 211

International City/County Management Association, 104

International community, 195–233

    assistance and sustainable development, 205, 208–213, 219

    conclusions and recommendations, 224–233, 400e

    cooperation approaches, 206–207

    disaster recovery in developing countries, 197

    financial institutions, 211–212

    foreign assistance and the U.S., 198–205

    horizontal and vertical integration, 219–224

    incorporating lessons from, 224

    negotiated agreements and treaties, 225–226

    nonprofit relief organizations, 210–211

    timing of assistance, 217–219

    understanding local needs, 204, 213–217

    United Nations, 208–210

    U.S. agencies in international relief, 212–213

    U.S. international/domestic assistance programs compared, 215–216

International Coordination Support Annex, 220

International Decade for Disaster Reduction, 222

International Decade of Hazard Reduction, 134

International Development Association, 211

International Monetary Fund (IMF), 211, 212, 365

International mutual aid agreements, 222

International Panel on Climate Change (IPCC), 225

International Red Cross Code of Conduct, 214, 222

International relief organizations, 365–366

International Strategy for Disaster Risk Reduction, 205

Iowa City post-disaster recovery workshop, 289f

Iran

    disaster diplomacy, 202

    earthquake (2003, Bam), 196

Japan earthquake and tsunami disaster (2011), 366

Jenkins-Smith, Hank, 341, 342

Kaboom!, 129f, 144f

Kanto, Japan earthquake (1922), 333

Kartez, Jack, 22–23, 25, 52

Kates, Robert, 13, 19, 60, 387

Katrina Cottage, 87, 90

Kaufman, Sanda, 308

Kelman, Ilan, 201

Kiesling, Ernst, 148

Kinship recovery, 242

Kinston, North Carolina pre-event planning, 65

Kunreuther, Howard, 186

Lake Tahoe Regional Planning Authority, 82

Land-grant universities, 110–111

Landrieu, Mary, 402

Land Trust Alliance, 132

Land use policies, 50, 354

Lending institutions, 166–167

Lessons of Disaster: Policy Change after Catastrophic Events, 186

Lindell, Michael, 186

Local disaster recovery managers (DRMs), 380

Local government, 49–55
>   disaster recovery committee, 52*e*
>   land use policies and planning tools, 50–52
>   resource management, 49–50

Local Initiatives Support Corporation, 79

Local needs, 13–16, 14*e*

Local recovery plans, 351, 366

Logan, John, 86, 341

Long Beach, Mississippi, 104

Long-term community recovery, 43*e*, 347–349

Long-term Community Recovery Plan: Greensburg and Kiowa County, Kansas, 337

Long-Term Community Recovery Planning Process: A Self-Help Guide, 386

Long-Term Disaster Recovery Working Group, 90, 334, 379, 390*f*

Long-Term Recovery Manual (NVOAD), 128, 152, 359

Los Angeles Fire Department, 366

Los Angeles Recovery and Reconstruction Plan, 280

Los Angeles Regional Planning Commission, 82

Louisiana Coastal Protection and Restoration Project, 207

Louisiana Disaster Recovery Foundation, 135

Louisiana Recovery Authority, 181

MacKaye, Benton, 82

The Main Street Neighborhood Study, 97

Manpower Development Corporation, 245*f*

Marsh, George Perkins, 81

Mass care, 41*e*

May, Peter, 69, 308

McClellan, Scott, 201

McEntire, David, 243

McHarg, Ian, 82

McReady program, 148

Medair, 211*f*

Media, 170–173
>   attention, 251–252
>   information dissemination, 181, 186
>   pre-event planning and, 189
>   sustaining recovery reports, 303

Mediation, 295, 302–303

Medical Reserve Corps, 366

Memoranda of Understanding, 393

Memorandum of agreement, pre-event, 206–207

Mileti, Dennis, 268

Mississippi
>   Governor's Commission on Recovery, Rebuilding and Renewal, 181, 182–183
>   Gulf Coast Community Design Studio, 94–98
>   Hurricane Katrina Memorial, Biloxi, 21*f*
>   New Urbanists, 87–90
>   professional associations in recovery, 104
>   river floods of 1927, 39

state recovery planning approach, 181

Mississippi Alternative Housing Program, 88

Mississippi Governor's Expo, 4f

Mississippi Governor's Office of Recovery and Renewal, 2, 24, 272f

Mississippi Mediation Project, 295

Mississippi Renewal Forum, 87–89, 113, 183, 188

    deconstructing, 88–89

    lessons and observations, 89–90

Mississippi State University Gulf Coast Community Design Studio, 94–99

Mitchell, James, 134

Molotch, Harvey, 86, 341

Monserrat and Hurricane Hugo, 223

Moore Community House Women in Construction Program, 145

Morrill Acts of 1862 and 1890, 110

Morrow, Betty Hearn, 5

Multihazard Mitigation Council, 184, 364

Multiorganizational networks, 254, 256–257

Mutual aid agreements

    international, 222, 365

    state and local, 355

Nakagawa, Yuko, 333

Napolitano, Janet, 385

National Academy of Sciences (NAS), 93

National accreditation programs, 360–363

National Disaster Housing Strategy, 90

National Disaster Recovery Framework (NDRF), 221, 231–232, 268, 377–402

    clarifying roles/timing of assistance, 386–387

    developing/implementing disaster recovery plans, 392–395

    emerging themes, 397f

    enhancing horizontal/vertical integration, 391–392

    enhancing standing of, 395–397

    epilogue, 401

    evolution of, 378–380

    funding and, 393–394

    hazard mitigation processes, 387–389

    horizontal integration and, 383

    intent and recommendations of, 380–384

    planning guidance, 385–386

    policy, 395

    pre-event assistance and, 384

    pre-/post-event assessment of local needs/resources, 389–391

    proposed Disaster Recovery Act and, 346–347

    recommendations review, 397–401, 400e

    recovery support functions/coordinators, 382e

    strengthening/operationalizing, 384–397

    technical assistance, 394

National Disaster Recovery Program Database, 389

National Earthquake Hazard Reduction Program, 92, 301, 343

National Emergency Management Association (NEMA), 85, 90, 115, 360

National Emergency Management Capability Assessment Program (NEMBCA), 360–361

National Fire Protection Association (NFPA), 362

National Flood Insurance Program, 103

National Fund for Social Investment, 197

National Institute for Standards and Technology (NIST), 92

National Mitigation Strategy, 388

National Oceanic and Atmospheric Administration, 225

National planning scenarios, 40

National recovery coalition, 338–344

National recovery strategy, 310

National Response Framework (NRF), 40–42, 138, 220, 232, 268, 278, 346–347

    capability building cycle, 347e

    emergency support functions/coordinators, 41e, 42f, 43e

    policies, 278

National Science Foundation

    mentoring program, 115–116

    rapid response research grants, 107

National sovereignty, 219, 228

National Voluntary Organizations Active in Disasters (NVOAD), 128, 138, 383

    Disaster Recovery Act proposal for, 359–360

    horizontal and vertical integration, 144

    Long Term Recovery Manual, 152

National Wildlife Federation (NWF), 132

Natural Hazards Informer, 110

Natural Hazards Observer, 110

Natural Hazards Project (OAS), 210

Natural Hazards Research and Applications Information Center (NHRAIC), 93

    horizontal and vertical integration, 110

    rapid response research grants, 107

Natural resources, 41e, 43e, 382e

Negotiated rule making, 295–296

Neighborhood Survival Network (NSN), 251

Neighborhood Watch, 366

NeighborWorks, 78–79, 104

New Deal, 82

New Jersey Pinelands Commission, 82

New Madrid fault, 83

New Orleans, Louisiana. *See also* Broadmoor Improvement Association; Broadmoor Project; Hurricane Katrina

    growth and pre-event conditions, 341

New Urbanism, 188

    Mississippi Renewal Forum, 87–89

    "Smartcode," 89, 90

New Urbanist communities, 4

Next Generation of Hazard Scholars, 116

NGOs in Disaster Relief, 214, 222

No Adverse Impact campaign, 103–104, 109

Nongovernmental organizations (NGOs), 85–100, 213

    colleges and universities, 91, 96, 99–100, 109–111

    conclusions and recommendations, 111–112, 400e

    dimensions of disaster assistance framework, 100–111

    horizontal and vertical integration, 78, 109–111

    maximizing contributions of, 113–116

    professional associations, 85–86, 86e, 91, 102–104

    timing of assistance, 106–108

    understanding local needs, 100–106

Nonprofit relief organizations, 127–153, 210–211

    The American Red Cross, 131

    capitalizing on strengths of, 150–151

    community organizations, 134, 137–138

    conclusions and recommendations, 150–153, 400e

    environmental groups, 128, 132–133

    faith-based groups, 131–132, 139

foundations, 135–136, 140

horizontal and vertical integration, 142–145

influence of, 129

national organizations, 130–133, 138

post-disaster hazard mitigation plans and, 144

social justice groups, 128, 133

timing of assistance, 17e, 18, 140–142

understanding local needs, 136–140

volunteerism and, 129

North Carolina

Charlotte/Mecklenburg County, 269–271

Hurricane Floyd flooding, 24, 56–58, 132

Kinston pre-event planning, 65

resource allocation disputes, 297–298

North Carolina Emergency Management Division 56-58, 64

North Carolina Redevelopment Center, 58

North-South conflict, 227

Norton, Richard, 275

NVOAD. See National Voluntary Organizations Active in Disasters (NVOAD)

Oakland Hills, California wildfires, 273

Obama, Barack, 39

Office for the Coordination of Humanitarian Affairs (OCHA), 209

Office of Food for Peace, 212

Office of Foreign Disaster Assistance (OFDA), 212–213, 215, 221, 365

Oil and hazardous materials response, 41e

Olasky, Marvin, 131

Oliver-Smith, Anthony, 16, 196, 245

Olmsted, Frederick Law, 82

Olshansky, Robert, 308

Olson, Richard, 340

Olson, Robert, 340

Open space principles, 80

Oregon Natural Hazards Workgroup, 273, 334, 335, 353

Organisation for Economic Co-operation and Development (OECD), 216

Organizational culture, 384

Organization of American States (OAS), 210

Organized responses, typology of, 253

Our Common Future, 228

Outreach agenda development, 336–338

Overseas Development Institute, 213, 216

Ozawa, Connie, 275, 302, 308, 341

Pacific Disaster Center, 210

Pan American Health Organization, 210

Partners for Disaster Resilience Pre-Disaster Mitigation Planning Initiative, 335

Partnership for Disaster Resilience, 335

Pascagoula, Mississippi, 104

Pass Christian, Mississippi, 104

Paterson, Robert, 143

Patton, Ann, 146

Peacock, Walter, 5, 7, 12, 249

Perkes, David, 94–96

Perry, Ronald, 186

Personnel

Emergency Management Assistance Compact and, 47, 48

FEMA, 46–47

state agencies, 46–49

Pijawka, David, 19

Planning, 265. See also Regional planning organizations

alternative dispute resolution principles, 276*e*, 277*e*, 292

assistance timing and, 51

building government capacity for, 312–313

capability assessment/stakeholder analysis, 285–287

central purpose for, 274–275

collaboration and learning in, 310–12

collaborative techniques of, 293, 307–309

compliance, 292

conclusion and recommendations, 309–314, 400*e*

connection to coalition building, 338–344

demographic data in, 281–282

economic data in, 282

enhancing local capacity, self-reliance, and accountability, 72

establishing clear plan guidance, 385–386

external plan quality principles, 288–292

fact base, 280–287

geographic information systems in, 282

hierarchy, 290*e*

horizontal integration through, 291–292

implementation, 287

importance of, 6–7, 12–13

internal consistency, 288

internal plan quality principles, 276–288

interorganizational coordination, 290–292

involving stakeholders in process of, 303–305

issue identification, 276–278

land use data in, 283

local government and, 50–52

monitoring/evaluation, 287–288

national planning scenarios, 40

organizational clarity, 289

plan mandates, 292

policies, 278–280

power imbalances, redressing, 305–307

pre-event, 272

pre-event planning for disaster recovery, 399

professional planning community engagement, 313–314

quality of, 275–292, 277*e*, 371

recovery planning culture development, 367–370

response planning, 51

timing of, 281

vulnerability and damage assessment, 284–285

Planning for Post-Disaster Recovery and Reconstruction, 314, 386

Playbooks, 40

Policy disputes, interorganizational, 152

Policy-oriented learning, 342–343

Popkin, Roy, 20

Post-Katrina Emergency Management Reform Act, 272, 379

Pre-disaster activities (NDRF), 392–393

Pre-Disaster Mitigation, 64, 83

Preparedness exercises, 92–93

Presidential Disaster Declaration. *See* Federal disaster declarations

Press, Frank, 205

Private sector organizations, 157–191

businesses and corporations, 169–170

conclusions and recommendations, 187–191, 400*e*

contracting, 159, 165–166

corporate responsibility/profits, 174, 175

enhancing public-private partnerships, 190–191

financial and lending institutions, 166–167

horizontal and vertical integration, 181, 186–187

information sharing/education, 176–177

insurance, 167–169

media, 170–173

stakeholders and recovery planning, 187–188

timing of assistance, 178–180

understanding local needs, 174–177

Private sector stakeholders, 267

Professional associations, 85–86, 86e, 91

with disaster-related programs/responsibilties, 86e

horizontal and vertical integration, 109

in recovery following Hurricane Katrina, 104

timing of assistance, 107

understanding local needs, 102–104

Professional emergency management associations, 90

Professional forums, 343

Project Impact, 110, 181, 184–185, 383

business continuity planning, 363–365

Psychological stress, 241

Public Assistance program, 61–62

Public health and medical services, 41e

Public safety and security, 43e

Public sector. See also Federal government agencies; Local government; State government agencies

altering culture of state/local dependence, 71

enhancing local capacity/self-reliance/accountability, 72

pre-event planning and, 71–72

recommendations summary, 70–72, 400e

Public works and engineering, 41e

Quarantelli, Enrico L., 260

Quasi-governmental organizations, 77–85

common-interest communities and homeowners associations, 79–80, 101–102, 108

community development corporations, 78–79, 101

conclusions and recommendations, 111–113, 400e

dimensions of disaster assistance framework, 100–111

horizontal and vertical integration, 78, 108–111

pre-event planning, 112–113

regional planning organizations, 81–85, 101

special districts, 81

timing of assistance, 106–108

understanding local needs, 100–106

Racism, 138

environmental, 133

institutional, 307

Ragsdale, Kathleen, 7, 249

RAND Corporation, 140

Rapid response research grants, 107

RAVON (Resiliency and Vulnerability Observation Network), 105, 115

Rebuilding after Earthquakes: Lessons from Planners, 313

Rebuild Iowa, 56f

Reciprocal dialogue, 296, 299–300

Recovery
> reactive approach to, 3–5
> responsibility for, 334

Recovery strategy, congressionally mandated, 310

Recovery strike teams, 104, 337

Recovery support functions, 380

Red Crescent Movement, 214, 222

Red Cross, 130, 131

Red River Valley Flood Recovery Action Plan, 84

Regional Planning Association of America, 82

Regional planning organizations, 81–85, 111
> grants management and, 83
> history of, 82
> multijurisdictional aspects of, 83
> pre-event planning capabilities, 112
> recovery approaches, 84
> timing of assistance, 106
> understanding local needs, 101

Regulations and codes, resistance to, 86, 91

Relocation and resettlement, 283

Renaissance Builder and Developer Guild, 98

Renaissance Corporation, 183

Research
> applied research, 110
> blending research and practice, 5
> cross-cultural, 229–230, 232
> higher education, 91–100, 104–106
> timing of, 107

Research grants, 141

Resiliency and Vulnerability Observation Network (RAVON), 105, 115, 356–357, 358

Resource management

allocation disputes, 297–298
> (*See also* Alternative dispute resolution (ADR) techniques)

distribution trajectories, 17*e*, 19

improving pre- and post-event needs/resources assessment, 389–391

local, 49–50

pre-event distribution of resources, 17*e*, 18

Resource support, 41*e*

Risk reduction strategies, 354

Robert T. Stafford Act. *See* Stafford Act (1988)

Rocky Mountain Model of Disaster Recovery, 20, 22*e*

Rubin, Claire, 20

Rubin, Melvin, 294

Sabatier, Paul, 341, 342

"Safe Room" project, 148

Saint Louis Home Builders Association, 86, 91

Saint Louis Regional Response System, 83

Salvation Army, 130, 132, 138

San Diego Regional Disaster Fund, 135

San Fernando Earthquake (1971), 92

San Francisco Bay Area Governments, 84

San Francisco Bay Conservation and Development Commission, 82

Sea-grant universities, 110–111

Search and rescue, 41*e*

Seismic Safety Commission, 92

Self-reliance, enhancing, 367

Senate Committee on Homeland Security and Government Affairs, 386

Severe Repetitive Loss Program, 64

Shaw, Rajib, 333

Shishmaref, Alaska, 200*f*

Shmueli, Deborah, 308

Shoreacres, Texas, 405

"Smartcode" (New Urbanist), 89, 90

Smith, Gavin, 2f, 275

Smith, Richard, 51

Smith-Lever Act, 110

Social capital, 333

Social damage assessment, 284

Social justice groups, 128, 133

Social vulnerability, 209f, 240

Space-grant universities, 110

S.S. Hurricane Camille, 1

Stafford Act (1988), 184, 221, 229, 353, 378–379

    disaster relief programs under, 61–64

    key programs, 61

    proposed amendments to, 402

Stakeholder groups, 11–12, 14–15

    multiple, and non-profits, 143

    "zone of uncertainty," 14e, 15

Stallworth, Bill, 96

Standard on Disaster/Emergency Management, 362

Stanford, Lois, 69

State capability assessments, 233

State coordinating officer, 381

State disaster recovery coordinators (SRCs), 380

State emergency management, 273

State government agencies, 43–49

    disaster assistance cadres, 47, 48

    disaster-related funding, 45–46

    personnel, 46–49

    pre-event mutual aid agreements and, 48

    quality of recovery plans, 70

State roles in recovery, 380

State sovereignty, 228

Storm-water management, 147, 149

Storm-water runoff, 80

Strike teams, 104, 337–338

Substantial damage ordinance, 279

"Supplemental myth," 38

Support annexes, 40

Surface Water Improvement and Management Panel (Mecklenburg County), 270–271

Susskind, Lawrence, 227, 275, 302, 341

Sustainability, 81

Sustainable development, 101, 205, 208–213, 232

Sustainable Redevelopment Working Group, 58

Sylves, Richard, 113

Technical assistance, 13, 394

Terrorism, 199

Terrorist attacks of 9/11, 295

Theckethil, Reshmi, 299

Timing of assistance, coordination of, 17e, 18

Tokenism, 306

Topping, Kenneth, 353

Trainer, Patricia, 241

Transportation, 41e

Tropical Storm Jerry, 269

Tsunami (Indian Ocean 2004), 196

Tulsa Partners, 146–149, 153

Typhoon Ondoy, 209f

United Nations, 208–210

    Development Programme (UNDP), 209, 210

    International Decade for Natural Disaster Reduction, 205

United Nations Children's Fund (UNICEF), 209

United States acceptance of foreign assistance, 198–205, 214–216, 305

    facilitating receipt of, 228–229

    need for protocols, 218

Universities. *See* Colleges and universities

University of Colorado Natural Hazards Research and Applications Information Center (NHRAIC), 93, 107, 110

"Up with Trees," 149

U.S. Agency for International Development (USAID), 212–213, 215, 220, 221, 229, 365

U.S. Geological Survey (USGS) "Shakeout Scenario" drill, 92–93

U.S. Government Accountability Office (GAO), 142

U.S. Treasury Department, 79

US Army Corps of Engineers Memorandum of Agreement, 207

Vertical integration, 24

Victim Compensation Fund, 295

Vietnam hazard mitigation, 197

Vision statement, 276–277, 278f

Volunteerism, nonprofit relief organizations and, 129–130

Volunteers in Police Service, 366

Vulnerability assessment, 284–285

Waggonner, David, 207, 233

Welsh, Mark, 152

Wenger, Dennis, 6, 22–23, 25, 106

We Will Build committee, 252

White House Long-Term Disaster Recovery Working Group, 90, 334, 379, 390f

Wildfires, 273

Witt, James Lee, 184, 185

Women Will Rebuild, 252

Woodrow, Peter J., 52, 218

World Bank, 211, 216, 365

World Food Programme (WFP), 209, 210

World Health Organization (WHO), 209–210

"Zone of uncertainty," 14e, 15

Zoning, 80, 92

About the Author

Dr. Gavin Smith is an Associate Research Professor in the Department of City and Regional Planning at the University of North Carolina at Chapel Hill. Areas of interest include disaster recovery, hazard mitigation, the translation of research to practice, and educating the next generation of hazards researchers and practitioners. Dr. Smith is currently serving as co-editor of the book, *Adapting to Climate Change: Lessons from Natural Hazards Planning* (forthcoming, 2012).

Dr. Smith is also the Executive Director of the Center for the Study of Natural Hazards and Disasters (UNC Hazards Center) and the Department of Homeland Security's Center of Excellence – Coastal Hazard Center. The Coastal Hazard Center research focus areas include hazard modeling, engineering, human behavior, and land use planning. Dr. Smith is currently engaged in planning-related research and translation within the center, focusing on a national evaluation of state and local hazard mitigation plans while assisting the State of North Carolina update their disaster recovery plan.

Prior to accepting the position of Executive Director at the University of North Carolina at Chapel Hill, Dr. Smith served as a Principal in the private sector firm PBS&J. As one of 10 individuals designated a Principal within a 4,000 person firm, specific duties included assisting states and local governments develop hazard mitigation plans and the provision of policy counsel to governors, federal agencies, corporations, universities, and nations regarding disaster recovery and hazard mitigation practice.

Following Hurricane Katrina, Dr. Smith worked in the Mississippi Office of the Governor, serving as the Director of the Office of Recovery and Renewal. In this role, he and his staff focused on four primary tasks – the identification of federal, corporate, non-profit, and foundation-related financial assistance; the delivery of education, outreach, and training to local governments, state agencies, and nonprofits; the provision of policy counsel to the Governor, his staff, and state agency officials regarding disaster recovery policy issues; and the implementation of the Governor's Commission Report: After Katrina: Building Back Better than Ever. In this role he testified before Congress twice, providing recommended policy changes to improve the distribution of post-disaster recovery assistance. He also helped develop the concept and wrote policy guidance associated with the 400 million dollar Alternative Housing Pilot

Program, an initiative intended to test the construction and deployment of improved emergency housing alternatives following Hurricane Katrina.

Dr. Smith was employed with the North Carolina Division of Emergency Management from 1996 to 2002. During this time, Dr. Smith held positions including National Flood Insurance Program planner, Hazard Mitigation Grants Management Coordinator, and State Hazard Mitigation Officer. During the last three years at the Division, Dr. Smith served as the Assistant Director for Hazard Mitigation. In this capacity, Dr. Smith was responsible for the management of five branches: Grants Management, Risk Assessment and Training, Hazard Mitigation Planning, Floodplain Management, and the Real Estate/Legal Team. Specific programs within the following branches include the Hazard Mitigation Grant Program, Flood Mitigation Assistance Program, North Carolina Hazard Mitigation Planning Initiative, National Flood Insurance Program, and the Earthquake Program. During his tenure with the Division, the Mitigation Section administered mitigation and disaster recovery grant funds in excess of 800 million dollars associated with 10 Presidential disaster declarations and created the North Carolina Hazard Mitigation Planning Initiative, a state-wide hazard mitigation planning effort that pre-dated the Disaster Mitigation Act.

Following Hurricane Floyd, Dr. Smith served as an advisor to Governor Hunt on policies and programs associated with long-term recovery in North Carolina. Among his duties included assisting in the formulation of 22 state recovery programs intended to compliment federal assistance, such as the development of the North Carolina Floodplain Mapping Initiative, a nationally recognized effort to remap and update the states Flood Insurance Rate Maps. In addition, Dr. Smith led one of the nation's largest single-state post-disaster hazard mitigation programs, leading to the relocation of over 5,000 homes and elevating another 800.

Prior to working at the North Carolina Division of Emergency Management, Dr. Smith was a Research Associate at the Hazard Reduction and Recovery Center at Texas A&M University. Work centered on several research projects including a nationwide review of search and rescue activities and a national analysis of the level of coordination between local emergency managers and land-use planners. During his four years at the Hazard Reduction and Recovery Center, Dr. Smith completed his Ph.D. in Urban and Regional Planning, specializing in environmental planning and policy, environmental dispute resolution, and hazard mitigation. Dr. Smith also received B.S. and M.S. degrees in Sociology from Texas A&M University. Areas of emphasis included organizational management, urban sociology, the politics of urban development, and demography.